CODE OF FEDERAL REGULATIONS

Title 24
Housing and Urban Development

Parts 500 to 699

Revised as of April 1, 2025

Containing a codification of documents of general applicability and future effect

As of April 1, 2025

Table of Contents

Cite this Code: CFR

To cite the regulations in this volume use title, part and section number. Thus, 24 CFR 500.1 *refers to title 24, part 500, section 1.*

Explanation

The Code of Federal Regulations is a codification of the general and permanent rules published in the Federal Register by the Executive departments and agencies of the Federal Government. The Code is divided into 50 titles which represent broad areas subject to Federal regulation. Each title is divided into chapters which usually bear the name of the issuing agency. Each chapter is further subdivided into parts covering specific regulatory areas.

Each volume of the Code is revised at least once each calendar year and issued on a quarterly basis approximately as follows:

Title 1 through Title 16	as of January 1
Title 17 through Title 27	as of April 1
Title 28 through Title 41	as of July 1
Title 42 through Title 50	as of October 1

The appropriate revision date is printed on the cover of each volume.

LEGAL STATUS

The contents of the Federal Register are required to be judicially noticed (44 U.S.C. 1507). The Code of Federal Regulations is prima facie evidence of the text of the original documents (44 U.S.C. 1510).

HOW TO USE THE CODE OF FEDERAL REGULATIONS

The Code of Federal Regulations is kept up to date by the individual issues of the Federal Register. These two publications must be used together to determine the latest version of any given rule.

To determine whether a Code volume has been amended since its revision date (in this case, April 1, 2025), consult the "List of CFR Sections Affected (LSA)," which is issued monthly, and the "Cumulative List of Parts Affected," which appears in the Reader Aids section of the daily Federal Register. These two lists will identify the Federal Register page number of the latest amendment of any given rule.

EFFECTIVE AND EXPIRATION DATES

Each volume of the Code contains amendments published in the Federal Register since the last revision of that volume of the Code. Source citations for the regulations are referred to by volume number and page number of the Federal Register and date of publication. Publication dates and effective dates are usually not the same and care must be exercised by the user in determining the actual effective date. In instances where the effective date is beyond the cutoff date for the Code a note has been inserted to reflect the future effective date. In those instances where a regulation published in the Federal Register states a date certain for expiration, an appropriate note will be inserted following the text.

OMB CONTROL NUMBERS

The Paperwork Reduction Act of 1980 (Pub. L. 96–511) requires Federal agencies to display an OMB control number with their information collection request.

Many agencies have begun publishing numerous OMB control numbers as amendments to existing regulations in the CFR. These OMB numbers are placed as close as possible to the applicable recordkeeping or reporting requirements.

PAST PROVISIONS OF THE CODE

Provisions of the Code that are no longer in force and effect as of the revision date stated on the cover of each volume are not carried. Code users may find the text of provisions in effect on any given date in the past by using the appropriate List of CFR Sections Affected (LSA). For the convenience of the reader, a "List of CFR Sections Affected" is published at the end of each CFR volume. For changes to the Code prior to the LSA listings at the end of the volume, consult previous annual editions of the LSA. For changes to the Code prior to 2001, consult the List of CFR Sections Affected compilations, published for 1949-1963, 1964-1972, 1973-1985, and 1986-2000.

"[RESERVED]" TERMINOLOGY

The term "[Reserved]" is used as a place holder within the Code of Federal Regulations. An agency may add regulatory information at a "[Reserved]" location at any time. Occasionally "[Reserved]" is used editorially to indicate that a portion of the CFR was left vacant and not dropped in error.

INCORPORATION BY REFERENCE

What is incorporation by reference? Incorporation by reference was established by statute and allows Federal agencies to meet the requirement to publish regulations in the Federal Register by referring to materials already published elsewhere. For an incorporation to be valid, the Director of the Federal Register must approve it. The legal effect of incorporation by reference is that the material is treated as if it were published in full in the Federal Register (5 U.S.C. 552(a)). This material, like any other properly issued regulation, has the force of law.

What is a proper incorporation by reference? The Director of the Federal Register will approve an incorporation by reference only when the requirements of 1 CFR part 51 are met. Some of the elements on which approval is based are:

(a) The incorporation will substantially reduce the volume of material published in the Federal Register.

(b) The matter incorporated is adequately summarized in the preamble of the final rule and is available to the extent necessary to afford fairness and uniformity in the administrative process.

(c) The incorporating document is drafted and submitted for publication in accordance with 1 CFR part 51.

What if the material incorporated by reference cannot be found? If you have any problem locating or obtaining a copy of material listed as an approved incorporation by reference, please contact the agency that issued the regulation containing that incorporation. If, after contacting the agency, you find the material is not available, please notify the Director of the Federal Register, National Archives and Records Administration, 8601 Adelphi Road, College Park, MD 20740-6001, or email fr.inspection@nara.gov.

CFR INDEXES AND TABULAR GUIDES

A subject index to the Code of Federal Regulations is contained in a separate volume, revised annually as of January 1, entitled CFR INDEX AND FINDING AIDS. This volume contains the Parallel Table of Authorities and Rules. A list of CFR titles, chapters, subchapters, and parts and an alphabetical list of agencies publishing in the CFR are also included in this volume.

An index to the text of "Title 3—The President" is carried within that volume.

The Federal Register Index is issued monthly in cumulative form. This index is based on a consolidation of the "Contents" entries in the daily Federal Register.

A List of CFR Sections Affected (LSA) is published monthly, keyed to the revision dates of the 50 CFR titles.

REPUBLICATION OF MATERIAL

There are no restrictions on the republication of material appearing in the Code of Federal Regulations.

INQUIRIES

For a legal interpretation or explanation of any regulation in this volume, contact the issuing agency. The issuing agency's name appears at the top of odd-numbered pages.

For inquiries concerning CFR reference assistance, call 202–741–6000 or write to the Director, Office of the Federal Register, National Archives and Records Administration, 8601 Adelphi Road, College Park, MD 20740-6001 or e-mail *fedreg.info@nara.gov.*

THIS TITLE

Title 24—HOUSING AND URBAN DEVELOPMENT is composed of five volumes. The first four volumes containing parts 0–199, parts 200–499, parts 500–699, parts 700–1699, represent the regulations of the Department of Housing and Urban Development. The fifth volume, containing part 1700 to end, continues with regulations of the Department of Housing and Urban Development and also includes regulations of the Neighborhood Reinvestment Corporation. The contents of these volumes represent all current regulations codified under this title of the CFR as of April 1, 2025.

For this volume, Michele Bugenhagen was Chief Editor. The Code of Federal Regulations publication program is under the direction of John Hyrum Martinez, assisted by Stephen J. Frattini.

Title 24—Housing and Urban Development

(This book contains parts 500 to 699)

SUBTITLE B—REGULATIONS RELATING TO HOUSING AND URBAN DEVELOPMENT (CONTINUED)

Subtitle B—Regulations Relating to Housing and Urban Development (Continued)

CHAPTER V—OFFICE OF ASSISTANT SECRETARY FOR COMMUNITY PLANNING AND DEVELOPMENT, DEPARTMENT OF HOUSING AND URBAN DEVELOPMENT

SUBCHAPTER A—GENERAL

PART 500—EXPIRING PROGRAMS—SAVINGS CLAUSE

AUTHORITY: 42 U.S.C. 3535(d).

SOURCE: 79 FR 58195, Sept. 2, 2014, unless otherwise noted.

§ 500.1 Expiring programs—Savings clause.

No new grants or grant agreements are being made under the programs listed in this section. Existing grants or grant agreements making designation under these programs continue to be governed by the regulations in effect as they existed immediately before October 2, 2014 (see 24 CFR parts 500 to 699, revised as of April 1, 2014):

24 CFR Part 511 Rental Rehabilitation Grant Program (42 U.S.C. 1437o)

24 CFR Part 572 HOPE for Homeownership of Single Family Homes (HOPE 3) (42 U.S.C. 12891)

24 CFR Part 585 Youthbuild (42 U.S.C. 8011)

24 CFR Part 590 Urban homesteading (12 U.S.C. 1706e)

24 CFR Part 597 Urban empowerment zones and enterprise communities (Round one designations) (26 U.S.C. 1391)

24 CFR Part 598 Urban empowerment zones; Round two and three designations (26 U.S.C. 1391)

SUBCHAPTER B—SLUM CLEARANCE AND URBAN RENEWAL

PART 510—SECTION 312 REHABILITATION LOAN PROGRAM

AUTHORITY: 42 U.S.C. 1452b and 3535(d).

SOURCE: 79 FR 51895, Sept. 2, 2014, unless otherwise noted. Redesignated at 79 FR 51895, Sept. 2, 2014.

§ 510.1 Multi-family property loans.

(a) In cases in which a corporation is a borrower on a section 312 loan, the Assistant Secretary for CPD or his designee may require an officer of the corporation or a principal stockholder to personally guarantee the section 312 loan or to cosign the loan note as a borrower, where necessary to make the finding of acceptable risk required for assumption of the loan.

(b) All partners of any partnership which is a borrower on a section 312 loan shall be personally liable for repayment of the section 312 loan. Limited partners shall assume personal liability by co-signing the loan note as a borrower or by personally guaranteeing the loan.

(c) Any personal guarantee or endorsement shall not relieve the partnership or corporate borrower from securing the section 312 loan by a mortgage or deed of trust on the property to be rehabilitated.

[44 FR 21751, Apr. 11, 1979, as amended at 44 FR 47513, Aug. 13, 1979; 44 FR 55562, Sept. 27, 1979. Redesignated and amended at 61 FR 7061, Feb. 23, 1996]

SUBCHAPTER C—COMMUNITY FACILITIES

PART 570—COMMUNITY DEVELOPMENT BLOCK GRANTS

Subpart A—General Provisions

Subpart B [Reserved]

Subpart C—Eligible Activities

Subpart D—Entitlement Grants

Subpart E—Special Purpose Grants

Subpart F—Small Cities, Non-Entitlement CDBG Grants in Hawaii and Insular Areas Programs

Subpart G—Urban Development Action Grants

Subpart H [Reserved]

Subpart I—State Community Development Block Grant Program

AUTHORITY: 12 U.S.C. 1701x, 1701 x–1; 42 U.S.C. 3535(d) and 5301–5320.

SOURCE: 40 FR 24693, June 9, 1975, unless otherwise noted.

Subpart A—General Provisions

SOURCE: 53 FR 34437, Sept. 6, 1988, unless otherwise noted.

§ 570.1 Purpose and primary objective.

(a) This part describes policies and procedures applicable to the following programs authorized under title I of the Housing and Community Development Act of 1974, as amended:

(1) Entitlement grants program (subpart D);

(2) Nonentitlement Funds: HUD-administered Small Cities and Insular Area programs (subpart F);

(3) State program: State-administered CDBG nonentitlement funds (subpart I);

(4) Special Purpose Grants (subpart E);

(5) Urban Development Action Grant program (subpart G); and

(6) Loan Guarantees (subpart M).

(b) Subparts A, C, J, K, and O apply to all programs in paragraph (a) except as modified or limited under the provisions of these subparts or the applicable program regulations. In the application of the subparts to Special Purpose Grants or the Urban Development Action Grant program, the reference to funds in the form of grants in the term "*CDBG funds*", as defined in §570.3, shall mean the grant funds under those programs. The subparts do not apply to the State program (subpart I) except to the extent expressly referred to.

(c) The primary objective of the programs authorized under title I of the Housing and Community Development Act of 1974, as amended, is described in section 101(c) of the Act (42 U.S.C. 5301(c)).

[53 FR 34437, Sept. 6, 1988, as amended at 56 FR 56126, Oct. 31, 1991; 61 FR 11475, Mar. 20, 1996; 69 FR 32778, June 10, 2004]

§570.3 Definitions.

The terms Affirmatively Furthering Fair Housing, HUD, and Secretary are defined in 24 CFR part 5. All of the following definitions in this section that rely on data from the United States Bureau of the Census shall rely upon the data available from the latest decennial census or the American Community Survey.

Act means title I of the Housing and Community Development Act of 1974 as amended (42 U.S.C. 5301 *et seq.*).

Age of housing means the number of year-round housing units, as further defined in section 102(a)(11) of the Act.

Applicant means a State or unit of general local government that makes application pursuant to the provisions of subpart E, F, G or M.

Buildings for the general conduct of government shall have the meaning provided in section 102(a)(21) of the Act.

CDBG funds means Community Development Block Grant funds, including funds received in the form of grants under subpart D, F, or §570.405 of this part, funds awarded under section 108(q) of the Housing and Community Development Act of 1974, loans guaranteed under subpart M of this part, urban renewal surplus grant funds, and program income as defined in §570.500(a).

Chief executive officer of a State or unit of general local government means the elected official or the legally designated official, who has the primary responsibility for the conduct of that entity's governmental affairs. Examples of the "chief executive officer" of a unit of general local government are: the elected mayor of a municipality; the elected county executive of a county; the chairperson of a county commission or board in a county that has no elected county executive; and the official designated pursuant to law by the governing body of a unit of general local government.

City means the following:

(1) For purposes of Entitlement Community Development Block Grant and Urban Development Action Grant eligibility:

(i) Any unit of general local government that is classified as a municipality by the United States Bureau of the Census, or

(ii) Any other unit of general local government that is a town or township and that, in the determination of the Secretary:

(A) Possesses powers and performs functions comparable to those associated with municipalities;

(B) Is closely settled (except that the Secretary may reduce or waive this requirement on a case by case basis for the purposes of the Action Grant program); and

(C) Contains within its boundaries no incorporated places as defined by the United States Bureau of the Census that have not entered into cooperation agreements with the town or township for a period covering at least 3 years to undertake or assist in the undertaking of essential community development and housing assistance activities. The determination of eligibility of a town or township to qualify as a city will be based on information available from the United States Bureau of the Census and information provided by the town or township and its included units of general local government.

(2) For purposes of Urban Development Action Grant eligibility only, Guam, the Virgin Islands, American Samoa, the Commonwealth of the Northern Mariana Islands, the counties of Kauai, Maui, and Hawaii in the State of Hawaii, and Indian tribes that are eligible recipients under the State and Local Government Fiscal Assistance Act of 1972 and located on reservations in Oklahoma as determined by the Secretary of the Interior or in Alaskan Native Villages.

Community Development Financial Institution has the same meaning as used in the Community Development Banking and Financial Institutions Act of 1994 (12 U.S.C. 4701 note).

Consolidated plan. The plan prepared in accordance with 24 CFR part 91, which describes needs, resources, priorities and proposed activities to be undertaken with respect to HUD programs, including the CDBG program. An approved consolidated plan means a consolidated plan that has been approved by HUD in accordance with 24 CFR part 91.

Discretionary grant means a grant made from the various Special Purpose Grants in accordance with subpart E of this part.

Entitlement amount means the amount of funds which a metropolitan city or urban county is entitled to receive under the Entitlement grant program, as determined by formula set forth in section 106 of the Act

Extent of growth lag shall have the meaning provided in section 102(a)(12) of the Act.

Extent of housing overcrowding shall have the meaning provided in section 102(a)(10) of the Act.

Extent of poverty means the number of persons whose incomes are below the poverty level based on data compiled and published by the United States Bureau of the Census available from the latest census referable to the same point or period in time and the latest reports from the Office of Management and Budget. For purposes of this part, the Secretary has determined that it is neither feasible nor appropriate to make adjustments at this time in the computations of "extent of poverty" for regional or area variations in income and cost of living.

Family refers to the definition of "family" in 24 CFR 5.403.

Household means all persons occupying a housing unit. The occupants may be a family, as defined in 24 CFR 5.403; two or more families living together; or any other group of related or unrelated persons who share living arrangements, regardless of actual or perceived, sexual orientation, gender identity, or marital status.

Income. For the purpose of determining whether a family or household is low- and moderate-income under subpart C of this part, grantees may select any of the three definitions listed below for each activity, except that integrally related activities of the same type and qualifying under the same paragraph of §570.208(a) shall use the same definition of income. The option to choose a definition does not apply to activities that qualify under §570.208(a)(1) (Area benefit activities), except when the recipient carries out a survey under §570.208(a)(1)(vi). Activities qualifying under §570.208(a)(1) generally must use the area income data supplied to recipients by HUD. The three definitions are as follows:

(1)(i) "Annual income" as defined under the Section 8 Housing Assistance Payments program at 24 CFR 5.609 (except that if the CDBG assistance being provided is homeowner rehabilitation under §570.202, the value of the homeowner's primary residence may be excluded from any calculation of Net Family Assets); or

(ii) Annual income as reported under the Census long-form for the most recent available decennial Census. This definition includes:

(A) Wages, salaries, tips, commissions, etc.;

(B) Self-employment income from own nonfarm business, including proprietorships and partnerships;

(C) Farm self-employment income;

(D) Interest, dividends, net rental income, or income from estates or trusts;

(E) Social Security or railroad retirement;

(F) Supplemental Security Income, Aid to Families with Dependent Children, or other public assistance or public welfare programs;

(G) Retirement, survivor, or disability pensions; and

(H) Any other sources of income received regularly, including Veterans' (VA) payments, unemployment compensation, and alimony; or

(iii) Adjusted gross income as defined for purposes of reporting under Internal Revenue Service (IRS) Form 1040 for individual Federal annual income tax purposes.

(2) Estimate the annual income of a family or household by projecting the prevailing rate of income of each person at the time assistance is provided for the individual, family, or household (as applicable). Estimated annual income shall include income from all family or household members, as applicable. Income or asset enhancement derived from the CDBG-assisted activity shall not be considered in calculating estimated annual income.

Insular area shall have the meaning provided in section 102(a)(24) of the Act.

Low- and moderate-income household means a household having an income equal to or less than the Section 8 low-income limit established by HUD.

Low- and moderate-income person means a member of a family having an income equal to or less than the Section 8 low-income limit established by HUD. Unrelated individuals will be considered as one-person families for this purpose.

Low-income household means a household having an income equal to or less than the Section 8 very low-income limit established by HUD.

Low-income person means a member of a family that has an income equal to or less than the Section 8 very low-income limit established by HUD. Unrelated individuals shall be considered as one-person families for this purpose.

Metropolitan area shall have the meaning provided in section 102(a)(3) of the Act.

Metropolitan city shall have the meaning provided in section 102(a)(4) of the Act except that the term "central city" is replaced by "principal city."

Microenterprise shall have the meaning provided in section 102(a)(22) of the Act.

Moderate-income household means a household having an income equal to or less than the Section 8 low-income limit and greater than the Section 8 very low-income limit, established by HUD.

Moderate-income person means a member of a family that has an income equal to or less than the Section 8 low-income limit and greater than the Section 8 very low-income limit, established by HUD. Unrelated individuals shall be considered as one-person families for this purpose.

Nonentitlement amount means the amount of funds which is allocated for use in a State's nonentitlement areas as determined by formula set forth in section 106 of the Act.

Nonentitlement area shall have the meaning provided in section 102(a)(7) of the Act.

Origin year means the specific Federal fiscal year during which the annual grant funds were appropriated.

Population means the total resident population based on data compiled and published by the United States Bureau of the Census available from the latest census or which has been upgraded by the Bureau to reflect the changes resulting from the Boundary and Annexation Survey, new incorporations and consolidations of governments pursuant to §570.4, and which reflects, where applicable, changes resulting from the Bureau's latest population determination through its estimating technique using natural changes (birth and death) and net migration, and is referable to the same point or period in time.

Small business means a business that meets the criteria set forth in section 3(a) of the Small Business Act (15 U.S.C. 631, 636, 637).

State shall have the meaning provided in section 102(a)(2) of the Act.

Unit of general local government shall have the meaning provided in section 102(a)(1) of the Act.

Urban county shall have the meaning provided in section 102(a)(6) of the Act. For the purposes of this definition, HUD will determine whether the county's combined population contains the required percentage of low- and moderate-income persons by identifying the number of persons that resided in applicable areas and units of general local government based on data from the most recent decennial census, and using income limits that would have applied for the year in which that census was taken.

Urban Development Action Grant (UDAG) means a grant made by the Secretary pursuant to section 119 of the Act and subpart G of this part.

[53 FR 34437, Sept. 6, 1988; 53 FR 41330, Oct. 21, 1988, as amended at 56 FR 56126, Oct. 31, 1991; 60 FR 1915, 1943, Jan. 5, 1995; 60 FR 56909, Nov. 9, 1995; 61 FR 5209, Feb. 9, 1996; 61 FR 11475, Mar. 20, 1996; 61 FR 18674, Apr. 29, 1996; 68 FR 69582, Dec. 12, 2003; 69 FR 32778, June 10, 2004; 77 FR 5675, Feb. 3, 2012; 80 FR 42366, July 16, 2015; 80 FR 69870, Nov. 12, 2015; 85 FR 47910, Aug. 7, 2020; 88 FR 9665, Feb. 14, 2023]

§ 570.4 Allocation of funds.

(a) The determination of eligibility of units of general local government to receive entitlement grants, the entitlement amounts, the allocation of appropriated funds to States for use in nonentitlement areas, the reallocation of funds, the allocation of appropriated funds to insular areas, and the allocation of appropriated funds for discretionary grants under the Secretary's Fund shall be governed by the policies and procedures described in sections 106 and 107 of the Act, as appropriate.

(b) The definitions in § 570.3 shall govern in applying the policies and procedures described in sections 106 and 107 of the Act.

(c) In determining eligibility for entitlement and in allocating funds under section 106 of the Act for any federal fiscal year, HUD will recognize corporate status and geographical boundaries and the status of metropolitan areas and principal cities effective as of July 1 preceding such federal fiscal year, subject to the following limitations:

(1) With respect to corporate status as certified by the applicable State and available for processing by the Census Bureau as of such date;

(2) With respect to boundary changes or annexations, as are used by the Census Bureau in preparing population estimates for all general purpose governmental units and are available for processing by the Census Bureau as of such date, except that any such boundary changes or annexations which result in the population of a unit of general local government reaching or exceeding 50,000 shall be recognized for this purpose whether or not such changes are used by the Census Bureau in preparing such population estimates; and

(3) With respect to the status of Metropolitan Statistical Areas and principal cities, as officially designated by the Office of Management and Budget as of such date.

(d) In determining whether a county qualifies as an urban county, and in computing entitlement amounts for urban counties, the demographic values of population, poverty, housing overcrowding, and age of housing of any Indian tribes located within the county shall be excluded. In allocating amounts to States for use in nonentitlement areas, the demographic values of population, poverty, housing overcrowding and age of housing of all Indian tribes located in all nonentitled areas shall be excluded. It is recognized that all such data on Indian tribes are not generally available from the United States Bureau of the Census and that missing portions of data will have to be estimated. In accomplishing any such estimates the Secretary may use such other related information available from reputable sources as may seem appropriate, regardless of the data's point or period of time and shall use the best judgement possible in adjusting such data to reflect the same point or period of time as the overall data from which the Indian tribes are being deducted, so that such deduction shall not create an imbalance with those overall data.

(e) Amounts remaining after closeout of a grant which are required to be returned to HUD under the provisions of § 570.509, Grant closeout procedures, shall be considered as funds available for reallocation unless the appropriation under which the funds were provided to the Department has lapsed.

[53 FR 34437, Sept. 6, 1988, as amended at 68 FR 69582, Dec. 12, 2003; 69 FR 32778, June 10, 2004]

§570.5 Waivers.

HUD's authority for the waiver of regulations and for the suspension of requirements to address damage in a Presidentially declared disaster area is described in 24 CFR part 5 and in section 122 of the Act, respectively.

[61 FR 11476, Mar. 20, 1996]

Subpart B [Reserved]

Subpart C—Eligible Activities

SOURCE: 53 FR 34439, Sept. 6, 1988, unless otherwise noted.

§570.200 General policies.

(a) *Determination of eligibility.* An activity may be assisted in whole or in part with CDBG funds only if all of the following requirements are met:

(1) *Compliance with section 105 of the Act.* Each activity must meet the eligibility requirements of section 105 of the Act as further defined in this subpart.

(2) *Compliance with national objectives.* Grant recipients under the Entitlement and HUD-administered Small Cities programs and recipients of insular area funds under section 106 of the Act must certify that their projected use of funds has been developed so as to give maximum feasible priority to activities which will carry out one of the national objectives of benefit to low- and moderate-income families or aid in the prevention or elimination of slums or blight. The projected use of funds may also include activities that the recipient certifies are designed to meet other community development needs having a particular urgency because existing conditions pose a serious and immediate threat to the health or welfare of the community where other financial resources are not available to meet such needs. Consistent with the foregoing, each recipient under the Entitlement or HUD-administered Small Cities programs, and each recipient of insular area funds under section 106 of the Act must ensure and maintain evidence that each of its activities assisted with CDBG funds meets one of the three national objectives as contained in its certification. Criteria for determining whether an activity addresses one or more of these objectives are found in §570.208.

(3) *Compliance with the primary objective.* The primary objective of the Act is described in section 101(c) of the Act. Consistent with this objective, entitlement recipients, non-entitlement CDBG grantees in Hawaii, and recipients of insular area funds under section 106 of the Act must ensure that, over a period of time specified in their certification not to exceed three years, not less than 70 percent of the aggregate of CDBG fund expenditures shall be for activities meeting the criteria under §570.208(a) or under §570.208(d)(5) or (6) for benefiting low- and moderate-income persons. For grants under section 107 of the Act, insular area recipients must meet this requirement for each separate grant. See §570.420(d)(3) for additional discussion of the primary objective requirement for insular areas funded under section 106 of the Act. The requirements for the HUD-administered Small Cities program in New York are at §570.420(d)(2). In determining the percentage of funds expended for such activities:

(i) Cost of administration and planning eligible under §570.205 and §570.206 will be assumed to benefit low and moderate income persons in the same proportion as the remainder of the CDBG funds and, accordingly shall be excluded from the calculation;

(ii) Funds deducted by HUD for repayment of urban renewal temporary loans pursuant to §570.802(b) shall be excluded;

(iii) Funds expended for the repayment of loans guaranteed under the provisions of subpart M of this part (including repayment of the portion of a loan used to pay any issuance, servicing, underwriting, or other costs as may be incurred under §570.705(g)) shall also be excluded;

(iv) Funds expended for the acquisition, new construction or rehabilitation of property for housing that qualifies under §570.208(a)(3) shall be counted for this purpose but shall be limited to an amount determined by multiplying the total cost (including CDBG and non-CDBG costs) of the acquisition, construction or rehabilitation by the percent of units in such housing to be occupied by low and moderate income persons.

(v) Funds expended for any other activities qualifying under § 570.208(a) shall be counted for this purpose in their entirety.

(4) *Compliance with environmental review procedures.* The environmental review procedures set forth at 24 CFR part 58 must be completed for each activity (or project as defined in 24 CFR part 58), as applicable.

(5) *Cost principles.* Costs incurred, whether charged on a direct or an indirect basis, must be in conformance with 2 CFR part 200, subpart E. All items of cost listed in 2 CFR part 200, subpart E, that require prior Federal agency approval are allowable without prior approval of HUD to the extent they comply with the general policies and principles stated in 2 CFR part 200, subpart E and are otherwise eligible under this subpart C, except for the following:

(i) Depreciation methods for fixed assets shall not be changed without the approval of the Federal cognizant agency.

(ii) Fines penalties, damages, and other settlements are unallowable costs to the CDBG program.

(iii) Costs of housing (*e.g.*, depreciation, maintenance, utilities, furnishings, rent), housing allowances and personal living expenses (goods or services for personal use) regardless of whether reported as taxable income to the employees (2 CFR 200.445);

(iv) Organization costs (2 CFR 200.455); and

(v) Pre-award costs are limited to those authorized under paragraph (h) of this section.

(b) *Special policies governing facilities.* The following special policies apply to:

(1) *Facilities containing both eligible and ineligible uses.* A public facility otherwise eligible for assistance under the CDBG program may be provided with CDBG funds even if it is part of a multiple use building containing ineligible uses, if:

(i) The facility which is otherwise eligible and proposed for assistance will occupy a designated and discrete area within the larger facility; and

(ii) The recipient can determine the costs attributable to the facility proposed for assistance as separate and distinct from the overall costs of the multiple-use building and/or facility.

Allowable costs are limited to those attributable to the eligible portion of the building or facility.

(2) *Fees for use of facilities.* Reasonable fees may be charged for the use of the facilities assisted with CDBG funds, but charges such as excessive membership fees, which will have the effect of precluding low and moderate income persons from using the facilities, are not permitted.

(c) *Special assessments under the CDBG program.* The following policies relate to special assessments under the CDBG program:

(1) *Definition of special assessment.* The term "special assessment" means the recovery of the capital costs of a public improvement, such as streets, water or sewer lines, curbs, and gutters, through a fee or charge levied or filed as a lien against a parcel of real estate as a direct result of benefit derived from the installation of a public improvement, or a one-time charge made as a condition of access to a public improvement. This term does not relate to taxes, or the establishment of the value of real estate for the purpose of levying real estate, property, or ad valorem taxes, and does not include periodic charges based on the use of a public improvement, such as water or sewer user charges, even if such charges include the recovery of all or some portion of the capital costs of the public improvement.

(2) *Special assessments to recover capital costs.* Where CDBG funds are used to pay all or part of the cost of a public improvement, special assessments may be imposed as follows:

(i) Special assessments to recover the CDBG funds may be made only against properties owned and occupied by persons not of low and moderate income. Such assessments constitute program income.

(ii) Special assessments to recover the non-CDBG portion may be made provided that CDBG funds are used to pay the special assessment in behalf of all properties owned and occupied by low and moderate income persons; except that CDBG funds need not be used to pay the special assessments in behalf of properties owned and occupied by moderate income persons if the grant recipient certifies that it does not have sufficient CDBG funds to pay the assessments in behalf of all of the low and moderate income owner-occupant persons. Funds collected through such special assessments are not program income.

(3) *Public improvements not initially assisted with CDBG funds.* The payment of special assessments with CDBG funds constitutes CDBG assistance to the public improvement. Therefore, CDBG funds may be used to pay special assessments provided:

(i) The installation of the public improvements was carried out in compliance with requirements applicable to activities assisted under this part including environmental, citizen participation and Davis-Bacon requirements;

(ii) The installation of the public improvement meets a criterion for national objectives in §570.208(a)(1), (b), or (c); and

(iii) The requirements of §570.200(c)(2)(ii) are met.

(d) *Consultant activities.* Consulting services are eligible for assistance under this part for professional assistance in program planning, development of community development objectives, and other general professional guidance relating to program execution. The use of consultants is governed by the following:

(1) *Employer-employee type of relationship.* No person providing consultant services in an employer-employee type of relationship shall receive more than a reasonable rate of compensation for personal services paid with CDBG funds. In no event, however, shall such compensation exceed the equivalent of the daily rate paid for Level IV of the Executive Schedule. Such services shall be evidenced by written agreements between the parties which detail the responsibilities, standards, and compensation.

(2) *Independent contractor relationship.* Consultant services provided under an independent contractor relationship are governed by the procurement requirements in 2 CFR part 200, subpart D, and are not subject to the compensation limitation of Level IV of the Executive Schedule.

(e) *Recipient determinations required as a condition of eligibility.* In several instances under this subpart, the eligibility of an activity depends on a special local determination. Recipients shall maintain documentation of all such determinations. A written determination is required for any activity carried out under the authority of §§570.201(f), 570.201(i)(2), 570.201(p), 570.201(q), 570.202(b)(3), 570.206(f), 570.209, 570.210, and 570.309.

(f) *Means of carrying out eligible activities.* (1) Activities eligible under this subpart, other than those authorized under §570.204(a), may be undertaken, subject to local law:

(i) By the recipient through:

(A) Its employees, or

(B) Procurement contracts governed by the requirements of 2 CFR part 200, subpart D; or

(ii) Through loans or grants under agreements with subrecipients, as defined at §570.500(c); or

(iii) By one or more public agencies, including existing local public agencies, that are designated by the chief executive officer of the recipient.

(2) Activities made eligible under §570.204(a) may only be undertaken by entities specified in that section.

(g) *Limitation on planning and administrative costs*—(1) *Origin year grant expenditure test.* For origin year 2015 grants and subsequent grants, no more than 20 percent of any origin year grant shall be expended for planning and program administrative costs, as defined in §§570.205 and 570.206, respectively. Expenditures of program income for planning and program administrative costs are excluded from this calculation.

(2) *Program year obligation test.* For all grants and recipients subject to subpart D, the amount of CDBG funds obligated during each program year for planning plus administrative costs, as defined in §§570.205 and 570.206, respectively, shall be limited to an amount no greater than 20 percent of the sum of the grant made for that program year (if any) plus the program income received by the recipient and its subrecipients (if any) during that program year. For origin year 2015 grants and

subsequent grants, recipients must apply this test consistent with paragraph (g)(1) of this section.

(3) Funds from a grant of any origin year may be used to pay planning and program administrative costs associated with any grant of any origin year.

(h) *Reimbursement for pre-award costs.* The effective date of the grant agreement is the program year start date or the date that the consolidated plan is received by HUD, whichever is later. For a Section 108 loan guarantee, the effective date of the grant agreement is the date of HUD execution of the grant agreement amendment for the particular loan guarantee commitment.

(1) Prior to the effective date of the grant agreement, a recipient may incur costs or may authorize a subrecipient to incur costs, and then after the effective date of the grant agreement pay for those costs using its CDBG funds, provided that:

(i) The activity for which the costs are being incurred is included, prior to the costs being incurred, in a consolidated plan action plan, an amended consolidated plan action plan, or an application under subpart M of this part, except that a new entitlement grantee preparing to receive its first allocation of CDBG funds may incur costs necessary to develop its consolidated plan and undertake other administrative actions necessary to receive its first grant, prior to the costs being included in its consolidated plan;

(ii) Citizens are advised of the extent to which these pre-award costs will affect future grants;

(iii) The costs and activities funded are in compliance with the requirements of this part and with the Environmental Review Procedures stated in 24 CFR part 58;

(iv) The activity for which payment is being made complies with the statutory and regulatory provisions in effect at the time the costs are paid for with CDBG funds;

(v) CDBG payment will be made during a time no longer than the next two program years following the effective date of the grant agreement or amendment in which the activity is first included; and

(vi) The total amount of pre-award costs to be paid during any program year pursuant to this provision is no more than the greater of 25 percent of the amount of the grant made for that year or $300,000.

(2) Upon the written request of the recipient, HUD may authorize payment of pre-award costs for activities that do not meet the criteria at paragraph (h)(1)(v) or (h)(1)(vi) of this section, if HUD determines, in writing, that there is good cause for granting an exception upon consideration of the following factors, as applicable:

(i) Whether granting the authority would result in a significant contribution to the goals and purposes of the CDBG program;

(ii) Whether failure to grant the authority would result in undue hardship to the recipient or beneficiaries of the activity;

(iii) Whether granting the authority would not result in a violation of a statutory provision or any other regulatory provision;

(iv) Whether circumstances are clearly beyond the recipient's control; or

(v) Any other relevant considerations.

(i) *Urban Development Action Grant.* Grant assistance may be provided with Urban Development Action Grant funds, subject to the provisions of subpart G, for:

(1) Activities eligible for assistance under this subpart; and

(2) Notwithstanding the provisions of § 570.207, such other activities as the Secretary may determine to be consistent with the purposes of the Urban Development Action Grant program.

(j) *Equal participation of faith-based organizations.* The HUD program requirements in § 5.109 of this title apply to the CDBG program, including the requirements regarding disposition and change in use of real property by a faith-based organization.

(k) Any unexpended CDBG origin year grant funds in the United States Treasury account on September 30 of the fifth Federal fiscal year after the end of the origin year grant's period of availability for obligation by HUD will be canceled. HUD may require an earlier expenditure and draw down deadline under a grant agreement.

[53 FR 34439, Sept. 6, 1988, as amended at 54 FR 47031, Nov. 8, 1989; 57 FR 27119, June 17, 1992; 60 FR 1943, Jan. 5, 1995; 60 FR 17445, Apr. 6, 1995; 60 FR 56910, Nov. 9, 1995; 61 FR 11476, Mar. 20, 1996; 61 FR 18674, Apr. 29, 1996; 65 FR 70215, Nov. 21, 2000; 68 FR 56404, Sept. 30, 2003; 69 FR 32778, June 10, 2004; 70 FR 76369, Dec. 23, 2005; 72 FR 46370, Aug. 17, 2007; 80 FR 67633, Nov. 3, 2015; 80 FR 69870, Nov. 12, 2015; 80 FR 75936, Dec. 7, 2015; 81 FR 19418, Apr. 4, 2016]

EFFECTIVE DATE NOTE: At 90 FR 894, Jan. 6, 2025, §570.200 was amended and further amended at 90 FR 8780, Feb. 3, 2025, effective Apr. 20, 2025.

§570.201 Basic eligible activities.

CDBG funds may be used for the following activities:

(a) *Acquisition*. Acquisition in whole or in part by the recipient, or other public or private nonprofit entity, by purchase, long-term lease, donation, or otherwise, of real property (including air rights, water rights, rights-of-way, easements, and other interests therein) for any public purpose, subject to the limitations of §570.207.

(b) *Disposition*. Disposition, through sale, lease, donation, or otherwise, of any real property acquired with CDBG funds or its retention for public purposes, including reasonable costs of temporarily managing such property or property acquired under urban renewal, provided that the proceeds from any such disposition shall be program income subject to the requirements set forth in §570.504.

(c) *Public facilities and improvements*. Acquisition, construction, reconstruction, rehabilitation or installation of public facilities and improvements, except as provided in §570.207(a), carried out by the recipient or other public or private nonprofit entities. (However, activities under this paragraph may be directed to the removal of material and architectural barriers that restrict the mobility and accessibility of elderly or severely disabled persons to public facilities and improvements, including those provided for in §570.207(a)(1).) In undertaking such activities, design features and improvements which promote energy efficiency may be included. Such activities may also include the execution of architectural design features, and similar treatments intended to enhance the aesthetic quality of facilities and improvements receiving CDBG assistance, such as decorative pavements, railings, sculptures, pools of water and fountains, and other works of art. Facilities designed for use in providing shelter for persons having special needs are considered public facilities and not subject to the prohibition of new housing construction described in §570.207(b)(3). Such facilities include shelters for the homeless; convalescent homes; hospitals, nursing homes; battered spouse shelters; halfway houses for run-away children, drug offenders or parolees; group homes for mentally retarded persons and temporary housing for disaster victims. In certain cases, nonprofit entities and subrecipients including those specified in §570.204 may acquire title to public facilities. When such facilities are owned by nonprofit entities or subrecipients, they shall be operated so as to be open for use by the general public during all normal hours of operation. Public facilities and improvements eligible for assistance under this paragraph are subject to the policies in §570.200(b).

(d) *Clearance and remediation activities*. Clearance, demolition, and removal of buildings and improvements, including movement of structures to other sites and remediation of known or suspected environmental contamination. Demolition of HUD-assisted or HUD-owned housing units may be undertaken only with the prior approval of HUD. Remediation may include project-specific environmental assessment costs not otherwise eligible under §570.205.

(e) *Public services*. Provision of public services (including labor, supplies, and materials) including but not limited to those concerned with employment, crime prevention, child care, health, drug abuse, education, fair housing counseling, energy conservation, welfare (but excluding the provision of income payments identified under §570.207(b)(4)), homebuyer downpayment assistance, or recreational needs. If housing counseling, as defined in 24 CFR 5.100, is provided, it must be carried out in accordance with 24 CFR

5.111. To be eligible for CDBG assistance, a public service must be either a new service or a quantifiable increase in the level of an existing service above that which has been provided by or on behalf of the unit of general local government (through funds raised by the unit or received by the unit from the State in which it is located) in the 12 calendar months before the submission of the action plan. (An exception to this requirement may be made if HUD determines that any decrease in the level of a service was the result of events not within the control of the unit of general local government.) The amount of CDBG funds used for public services shall not exceed paragraphs (e) (1) or (2) of this section, as applicable:

(1) The amount of CDBG funds used for public services shall not exceed 15 percent of each grant, except that for entitlement grants made under subpart D of this part, nonentitlement CDBG grants in Hawaii, and for recipients of insular area funds under section 106 of the Act, the amount shall not exceed 15 percent of the grant plus 15 percent of program income, as defined in § 570.500(a). For entitlement grants under subpart D of this part, nonentitlement CDBG grants in Hawaii, and for recipients of insular area funds under section 106 of the Act, compliance is based on limiting the amount of CDBG funds obligated for public service activities in each program year to an amount no greater than 15 percent of the entitlement grant made for that program year plus 15 percent of the program income received during the grantee's immediately preceding program year.

(2) A recipient which obligated more CDBG funds for public services than 15 percent of its grant funded from origin year 1982 or 1983 appropriations (excluding program income and any assistance received under Public Law 98–8), may obligate more CDBG funds than allowable under paragraph (e)(1) of this section, so long as the total amount obligated in any program year does not exceed:

(i) For an entitlement grantee, 15% of the program income it received during the preceding program year; plus

(ii) A portion of the grant received for the program year which is the highest of the following amounts:

(A) The amount determined by applying the percentage of the grant it obligated for public services in the 1982 program year against the grant for its current program year;

(B) The amount determined by applying the percentage of the grant it obligated for public services in the 1983 program year against the grant for its current program year;

(C) The amount of funds it obligated for public services in the 1982 program year; or,

(D) The amount of funds it obligated for public services in the 1983 program year.

(f) *Interim assistance.* (1) The following activities may be undertaken on an interim basis in areas exhibiting objectively determinable signs of physical deterioration where the recipient has determined that immediate action is necessary to arrest the deterioration and that permanent improvements will be carried out as soon as practicable:

(i) The repairing of streets, sidewalks, parks, playgrounds, publicly owned utilities, and public buildings; and

(ii) The execution of special garbage, trash, and debris removal, including neighborhood cleanup campaigns, but not the regular curbside collection of garbage or trash in an area.

(2) In order to alleviate emergency conditions threatening the public health and safety in areas where the chief executive officer of the recipient determines that such an emergency condition exists and requires immediate resolution, CDBG funds may be used for:

(i) The activities specified in paragraph (f)(1) of this section, except for the repair of parks and playgrounds;

(ii) The clearance of streets, including snow removal and similar activities, and

(iii) The improvement of private properties.

(3) All activities authorized under paragraph (f)(2) of this section are limited to the extent necessary to alleviate emergency conditions.

(g) *Payment of non-Federal share.* Payment of the non-Federal share required in connection with a Federal grant-in-aid program undertaken as part of CDBG activities, provided, that such payment shall be limited to activities otherwise eligible and in compliance with applicable requirements under this subpart.

(h) *Urban renewal completion.* Payment of the cost of completing an urban renewal project funded under title I of the Housing Act of 1949 as amended. Further information regarding the eligibility of such costs is set forth in § 570.801.

(i) *Relocation.* Relocation payments and other assistance for permanently and temporarily relocated individuals families, businesses, nonprofit organizations, and farm operations where the assistance is (1) required under the provisions of § 570.606 (b) or (c); or (2) determined by the grantee to be appropriate under the provisions of § 570.606(d).

(j) *Loss of rental income.* Payments to housing owners for losses of rental income incurred in holding, for temporary periods, housing units to be used for the relocation of individuals and families displaced by program activities assisted under this part.

(k) *Housing services.* Housing services, as provided in section 105(a)(21) of the Act (42 U.S.C. 5305(a)(21)). If housing counseling, as defined in 24 CFR 5.100, is provided, it must be carried out in accordance with 24 CFR 5.111.

(l) *Privately owned utilities.* CDBG funds may be used to acquire, construct, reconstruct, rehabilitate, or install the distribution lines and facilities of privately owned utilities, including the placing underground of new or existing distribution facilities and lines.

(m) *Construction of housing.* CDBG funds may be used for the construction of housing assisted under section 17 of the United States Housing Act of 1937.

(n) *Homeownership assistance.* CDBG funds may be used to provide direct homeownership assistance to low- or moderate-income households in accordance with section 105(a) of the Act.

(o)(1) The provision of assistance either through the recipient directly or through public and private organizations, agencies, and other subrecipients (including nonprofit and for-profit subrecipients) to facilitate economic development by:

(i) Providing credit, including, but not limited to, grants, loans, loan guarantees, and other forms of financial support, for the establishment, stabilization, and expansion of microenterprises;

(ii) Providing technical assistance, advice, and business support services to owners of microenterprises and persons developing microenterprises; and

(iii) Providing general support, including, but not limited to, peer support programs, counseling, child care, transportation, and other similar services, to owners of microenterprises and persons developing microenterprises.

(2) Services provided this paragraph (o) shall not be subject to the restrictions on public services contained in paragraph (e) of this section.

(3) For purposes of this paragraph (o), "persons developing microenterprises" means such persons who have expressed interest and who are, or after an initial screening process are expected to be, actively working toward developing businesses, each of which is expected to be a microenterprise at the time it is formed.

(4) Assistance under this paragraph (o) may also include training, technical assistance, or other support services to increase the capacity of the recipient or subrecipient to carry out the activities under this paragraph (o).

(p) *Technical assistance.* Provision of technical assistance to public or nonprofit entities to increase the capacity of such entities to carry out eligible neighborhood revitalization or economic development activities. (The recipient must determine, prior to the provision of the assistance, that the activity for which it is attempting to build capacity would be eligible for assistance under this subpart C, and that the national objective claimed by the grantee for this assistance can reasonably be expected to be met once the entity has received the technical assistance and undertakes the activity.) Capacity building for private or public entities (including grantees) for other purposes may be eligible under § 570.205.

(q) *Assistance to institutions of higher education.* Provision of assistance by the recipient to institutions of higher education when the grantee determines that such an institution has demonstrated a capacity to carry out eligible activities under this subpart C.

[53 FR 34439, Sept. 6, 1988, as amended at 53 FR 31239, Aug. 17, 1988; 55 FR 29308, July 18, 1990; 57 FR 27119, June 17, 1992; 60 FR 1943, Jan. 5, 1995; 60 FR 56911, Nov. 9, 1995; 61 FR 18674, Apr. 29, 1996; 65 FR 70215, Nov. 21, 2000; 67 FR 47213, July 17, 2002; 71 FR 30034, May 24, 2006; 80 FR 69870, Nov. 12, 2015; 81 FR 90659, Dec. 14, 2016]

§ 570.202 Eligible rehabilitation and preservation activities.

(a) *Types of buildings and improvements eligible for rehabilitation assistance.* CDBG funds may be used to finance the rehabilitation of:

(1) Privately owned buildings and improvements for residential purposes; improvements to a single-family residential property which is also used as a place of business, which are required in order to operate the business, need not be considered to be rehabilitation of a commercial or industrial building, if the improvements also provide general benefit to the residential occupants of the building;

(2) Low-income public housing and other publicly owned residential buildings and improvements;

(3) Publicly or privately owned commercial or industrial buildings, except that the rehabilitation of such buildings owned by a private for-profit business is limited to improvement to the exterior of the building, abatement of asbestos hazards, lead-based paint hazard evaluation and reduction, and the correction of code violations;

(4) Nonprofit-owned nonresidential buildings and improvements not eligible under § 570.201(c); and

(5) Manufactured housing when such housing constitutes part of the community's permanent housing stock.

(b) *Types of assistance.* CDBG funds may be used to finance the following types of rehabilitation activities, and related costs, either singly, or in combination, through the use of grants, loans, loan guarantees, interest supplements, or other means for buildings and improvements described in paragraph (a) of this section, except that rehabilitation of commercial or industrial buildings is limited as described in paragraph (a)(3) of this section.

(1) Assistance to private individuals and entities, including profit making and nonprofit organizations, to acquire for the purpose of rehabilitation, and to rehabilitate properties, for use or resale for residential purposes;

(2) Labor, materials, and other costs of rehabilitation of properties, including repair directed toward an accumulation of deferred maintenance, replacement of principal fixtures and components of existing structures, installation of security devices, including smoke detectors and dead bolt locks, and renovation through alterations, additions to, or enhancement of existing structures and improvements, abatement of asbestos hazards (and other contaminants) in buildings and improvements that may be undertaken singly, or in combination;

(3) Loans for refinancing existing indebtedness secured by a property being rehabilitated with CDBG funds if such financing is determined by the recipient to be necessary or appropriate to achieve the locality's community development objectives;

(4) Improvements to increase the efficient use of energy in structures through such means as installation of storm windows and doors, siding, wall and attic insulation, and conversion, modification, or replacement of heating and cooling equipment, including the use of solar energy equipment;

(5) Improvements to increase the efficient use of water through such means as water savings faucets and shower heads and repair of water leaks;

(6) Connection of residential structures to water distribution lines or local sewer collection lines;

(7) For rehabilitation carried out with CDBG funds, costs of:

(i) Initial homeowner warranty premiums;

(ii) Hazard insurance premiums, except where assistance is provided in the form of a grant; and

(iii) Flood insurance premiums for properties covered by the Flood Disaster Protection Act of 1973, pursuant to § 570.605.

(8) Costs of acquiring tools to be lent to owners, tenants, and others who will use such tools to carry out rehabilitation;

(9) Rehabilitation services, such as rehabilitation counseling, energy auditing, preparation of work specifications, loan processing, inspections, and other services related to assisting owners, tenants, contractors, and other entities, participating or seeking to participate in rehabilitation activities authorized under this section, under section 312 of the Housing Act of 1964, as amended, under section 810 of the Act, or under section 17 of the United States Housing Act of 1937;

(10) Assistance for the rehabilitation of housing under section 17 of the United States Housing Act of 1937; and

(11) Improvements designed to remove material and architectural barriers that restrict the mobility and accessibility of elderly or severely disabled persons to buildings and improvements eligible for assistance under paragraph (a) of this section.

(c) *Code enforcement.* Costs incurred for inspection for code violations and enforcement of codes (e.g., salaries and related expenses of code enforcement inspectors and legal proceedings, but not including the cost of correcting the violations) in deteriorating or deteriorated areas when such enforcement together with public or private improvements, rehabilitation, or services to be provided may be expected to arrest the decline of the area.

(d) *Historic preservation.* CDBG funds may be used for the rehabilitation, preservation or restoration of historic properties, whether publicly or privately owned. Historic properties are those sites or structures that are either listed in or eligible to be listed in the National Register of Historic Places, listed in a State or local inventory of historic places, or designated as a State or local landmark or historic district by appropriate law or ordinance. Historic preservation, however, is not authorized for buildings for the general conduct of government.

(e) *Renovation of closed buildings.* CDBG funds may be used to renovate closed buildings, such as closed school buildings, for use as an eligible public facility or to rehabilitate such buildings for housing.

(f) *Lead-based paint activities.* Lead-based paint activities pursuant to § 570.608.

(g) *Broadband infrastructure.* Any substantial rehabilitation, as substantial rehabilitation is defined by 24 CFR 5.100, of a building with more than 4 rental units, for which CDBG funds are first obligated by the recipient on or after April 19, 2017, must include installation of broadband infrastructure, as this term is also defined in 24 CFR 5.100, except where the recipient determines and, in accordance with § 570.506, documents the determination that:

(1) The location of the substantial rehabilitation makes installation of broadband infrastructure infeasible;

(2) The cost of installing broadband infrastructure would result in a fundamental alteration in the nature of its program or activity or in an undue financial burden; or

(3) The structure of the housing to be substantially rehabilitated makes installation of broadband infrastructure infeasible.

[53 FR 34439, Sept. 6, 1988; 53 FR 41330, Oct. 21, 1988, as amended at 60 FR 1944, Jan. 5, 1995; 60 FR 56911, Nov. 9, 1995; 64 FR 50225, Sept. 15, 1999; 71 FR 30035, May 24, 2006; 82 FR 92636, Dec. 20, 2016]

§ 570.203 Special economic development activities.

A recipient may use CDBG funds for special economic development activities in addition to other activities authorized in this subpart that may be carried out as part of an economic development project. Guidelines for selecting activities to assist under this paragraph are provided at § 570.209. The recipient must ensure that the appropriate level of public benefit will be derived pursuant to those guidelines before obligating funds under this authority. Special activities authorized under this section do not include assistance for the construction of new housing. Activities eligible under this section may include costs associated with project-specific assessment or remediation of known or suspected environmental contamination. Special economic development activities include:

(a) The acquisition, construction, reconstruction, rehabilitation or installation of commercial or industrial buildings, structures, and other real property equipment and improvements, including railroad spurs or similar extensions. Such activities may be carried out by the recipient or public or private nonprofit subrecipients.

(b) The provision of assistance to a private for-profit business, including, but not limited to, grants, loans, loan guarantees, interest supplements, technical assistance, and other forms of support, for any activity where the assistance is appropriate to carry out an economic development project, excluding those described as ineligible in § 570.207(a). In selecting businesses to assist under this authority, the recipient shall minimize, to the extent practicable, displacement of existing businesses and jobs in neighborhoods.

(c) Economic development services in connection with activities eligible under this section, including, but not limited to, outreach efforts to market available forms of assistance; screening of applicants; reviewing and underwriting applications for assistance; preparation of all necessary agreements; management of assisted activities; and the screening, referral, and placement of applicants for employment opportunities generated by CDBG-eligible economic development activities, including the costs of providing necessary training for persons filling those positions.

[53 FR 34439, Sept. 6, 1988, as amended at 60 FR 1944, Jan. 5, 1995; 71 FR 30035, May 24, 2006]

§ 570.204 Special activities by Community-Based Development Organizations (CBDOs).

(a) *Eligible activities.* The recipient may provide CDBG funds as grants or loans to any CBDO qualified under this section to carry out a neighborhood revitalization, community economic development, or energy conservation project. The funded project activities may include those listed as eligible under this subpart, and, except as described in paragraph (b) of this section, activities not otherwise listed as eligible under this subpart. For purposes of qualifying as a project under paragraphs (a)(1), (a)(2), and (a)(3) of this section, the funded activity or activities may be considered either alone or in concert with other project activities either being carried out or for which funding has been committed. For purposes of this section:

(1) Neighborhood revitalization project includes activities of sufficient size and scope to have an impact on the decline of a geographic location within the jurisdiction of a unit of general local government (but not the entire jurisdiction) designated in comprehensive plans, ordinances, or other local documents as a neighborhood, village, or similar geographical designation; or the entire jurisdiction of a unit of general local government which is under 25,000 population;

(2) Community economic development project includes activities that increase economic opportunity, principally for persons of low- and moderate-income, or that stimulate or retain businesses or permanent jobs, including projects that include one or more such activities that are clearly needed to address a lack of affordable housing accessible to existing or planned jobs and those activities specified at 24 CFR 91.1(a)(1)(iii); activities under this paragraph may include costs associated with project-specific assessment or remediation of known or suspected environmental contamination;

(3) Energy conservation project includes activities that address energy conservation, principally for the benefit of the residents of the recipient's jurisdiction; and

(4) To carry out a project means that the CBDO undertakes the funded activities directly or through contract with an entity other than the grantee, or through the provision of financial assistance for activities in which it retains a direct and controlling involvement and responsibilities.

(5) Any new construction or substantial rehabilitation, as substantial rehabilitation is defined by 24 CFR 5.100, of a building with more than 4 rental units, for which CDBG funds are first obligated by the recipient on or after April 19, 2017, must include installation of broadband infrastructure, as this term is also defined in 24 CFR 5.100, except where the recipient determines and, in accordance with § 570.506, documents the determination that:

(i) The location of the new construction or substantial rehabilitation makes installation of broadband infrastructure infeasible;

(ii) The cost of installing broadband infrastructure would result in a fundamental alteration in the nature of its program or activity or in an undue financial burden; or

(iii) The structure of the housing to be substantially rehabilitated makes installation of broadband infrastructure infeasible.

(b) *Ineligible activities.* Notwithstanding that CBDOs may carry out activities that are not otherwise eligible under this subpart, this section does not authorize:

(1) Carrying out an activity described as ineligible in §570.207(a);

(2) Carrying out public services that do not meet the requirements of §570.201(e), except that:

(i) Services carried out under this section that are specifically designed to increase economic opportunities through job training and placement and other employment support services, including, but not limited to, peer support programs, counseling, child care, transportation, and other similar services; and

(ii) Services of any type carried out under this section pursuant to a strategy approved by HUD under the provisions of 24 CFR 91.215(e) shall not be subject to the limitations in §570.201(e)(1) or (2), as applicable;

(3) Providing assistance to activities that would otherwise be eligible under §570.203 that do not meet the requirements of §570.209; or

(4) Carrying out an activity that would otherwise be eligible under §570.205 or §570.206, but that would result in the recipient's exceeding the spending limitation in §570.200(g).

(c) *Eligible CBDOs.* (1) A CBDO qualifying under this section is an organization which has the following characteristics:

(i) Is an association or corporation organized under State or local law to engage in community development activities (which may include housing and economic development activities) primarily within an identified geographic area of operation within the jurisdiction of the recipient, or in the case of an urban county, the jurisdiction of the county; and

(ii) Has as its primary purpose the improvement of the physical, economic or social environment of its geographic area of operation by addressing one or more critical problems of the area, with particular attention to the needs of persons of low and moderate income; and

(iii) May be either non-profit or for-profit, provided any monetary profits to its shareholders or members must be only incidental to its operations; and

(iv) Maintains at least 51 percent of its governing body's membership for low- and moderate-income residents of its geographic area of operation, owners or senior officers of private establishments and other institutions located in and serving its geographic area of operation, or representatives of low- and moderate-income neighborhood organizations located in its geographic area of operation; and

(v) Is not an agency or instrumentality of the recipient and does not permit more than one-third of the membership of its governing body to be appointed by, or to consist of, elected or other public officials or employees or officials of an ineligible entity (even though such persons may be otherwise qualified under paragraph (c)(1)(iv) of this section); and

(vi) Except as otherwise authorized in paragraph (c)(1)(v) of this section, requires the members of its governing body to be nominated and approved by the general membership of the organization, or by its permanent governing body; and

(vii) Is not subject to requirements under which its assets revert to the recipient upon dissolution; and

(viii) Is free to contract for goods and services from vendors of its own choosing.

(2) A CBDO that does not meet the criteria in paragraph (c)(1) of this section may also qualify as an eligible entity under this section if it meets one of the following requirements:

(i) Is an entity organized pursuant to section 301(d) of the Small Business Investment Act of 1958 (15 U.S.C. 681(d)), including those which are profit making; or

(ii) Is an SBA approved Section 501 State Development Company or Section 502 Local Development Company, or an SBA Certified Section 503 Company under the Small Business Investment Act of 1958, as amended; or

(iii) Is a Community Housing Development Organization (CHDO) under 24 CFR 92.2, designated as a CHDO by the HOME Investment Partnerships program participating jurisdiction, with a geographic area of operation of no more than one neighborhood, and has received HOME funds under 24 CFR 92.300 or is expected to receive HOME funds as described in and documented in accordance with 24 CFR 92.300(e).

(3) A CBDO that does not qualify under paragraph (c)(1) or (2) of this section may also be determined to qualify as an eligible entity under this section if the recipient demonstrates to the satisfaction of HUD, through the provision of information regarding the organization's charter and by-laws, that the organization is sufficiently similar in purpose, function, and scope to those entities qualifying under paragraph (c)(1) or (2) of this section.

[60 FR 1944, Jan. 5, 1995, as amended at 71 FR 30035, May 24, 2006; 81 FR 92636, Dec. 20, 2016]

§ 570.205 Eligible planning, urban environmental design and policy-planning-management-capacity building activities.

(a) Planning activities which consist of all costs of data gathering, studies, analysis, and preparation of plans and the identification of actions that will implement such plans, including, but not limited to:

(1) Comprehensive plans;

(2) Community development plans;

(3) Functional plans, in areas such as:

(i) Housing, including the development of a consolidated plan;

(ii) Land use and urban environmental design;

(iii) Economic development;

(iv) Open space and recreation;

(v) Energy use and conservation;

(vi) Floodplain and wetlands management in accordance with the requirements of Executive Orders 11988 and 11990;

(vii) Transportation;

(viii) Utilities; and

(ix) Historic preservation.

(4) Other plans and studies such as:

(i) Small area and neighborhood plans;

(ii) Capital improvements programs;

(iii) Individual project plans (but excluding engineering and design costs related to a specific activity which are eligible as part of the cost of such activity under §§ 570.201–570.204);

(iv) The reasonable costs of general environmental, urban environmental design and historic preservation studies; and general environmental assessment- and remediation-oriented planning related to properties with known or suspected environmental contamination. However, costs necessary to comply with 24 CFR part 58, including project specific environmental assessments and clearances for activities eligible for assistance under this part, are eligible as part of the cost of such activities under §§ 570.201–570.204. Costs for such specific assessments and clearances may also be incurred under this paragraph but would then be considered planning costs for the purposes of § 570.200(g);

(v) Strategies and action programs to implement plans, including the development of codes, ordinances and regulations;

(vi) Support of clearinghouse functions, such as those specified in Executive Order 12372; and

(vii) Developing an inventory of properties with known or suspected environmental contamination.

(5) [Reserved]

(6) Policy—planning—management—capacity building activities which will enable the recipient to:

(1) Determine its needs;

(2) Set long-term goals and short-term objectives, including those related to urban environmental design;

(3) Devise programs and activities to meet these goals and objectives;

(4) Evaluate the progress of such programs and activities in accomplishing these goals and objectives; and

(5) Carry out management, coordination and monitoring of activities necessary for effective planning implementation, but excluding the costs necessary to implement such plans.

[53 FR 34439, Sept. 6, 1988, as amended at 56 FR 56127, Oct. 31, 1991; 60 FR 1915, Jan. 5, 1995; 71 FR 30035, May 24, 2006; 80 FR 42366, July 16, 2015; 85 FR 47910, Aug. 7, 2020]

§ 570.206 Program administrative costs.

Payment of reasonable program administrative costs and carrying charges related to the planning and execution of community development activities assisted in whole or in part with funds provided under this part and, where applicable, housing activities (described in paragraph (g) of this section) covered in the recipient's housing assistance plan. This does not include staff and overhead costs directly related to carrying out activities eligible under § 570.201 through § 570.204, since those costs are eligible as part of such activities.

(a) *General management, oversight and coordination.* Reasonable costs of overall program management, coordination, monitoring, and evaluation. Such costs include, but are not necessarily limited to, necessary expenditures for the following:

(1) Salaries, wages, and related costs of the recipient's staff, the staff of local public agencies, or other staff engaged in program administration. In charging costs to this category the recipient may either include the entire salary, wages, and related costs allocable to the program of each person whose *primary* responsibilities with regard to the program involve program administration assignments, or the pro rata share of the salary, wages, and related costs of each person whose job includes *any* program administration assignments. The recipient may use only one of these methods during the program year. Program administration includes the following types of assignments:

(i) Providing local officials and citizens with information about the program;

(ii) Preparing program budgets and schedules, and amendments thereto;

(iii) Developing systems for assuring compliance with program requirements;

(iv) Developing interagency agreements and agreements with subrecipients and contractors to carry out program activities;

(v) Monitoring program activities for progress and compliance with program requirements;

(vi) Preparing reports and other documents related to the program for submission to HUD;

(vii) Coordinating the resolution of audit and monitoring findings;

(viii) Evaluating program results against stated objectives; and

(ix) Managing or supervising persons whose primary responsibilities with regard to the program include such assignments as those described in paragraph (a)(1)(i) through (viii) of this section.

(2) Travel costs incurred for official business in carrying out the program;

(3) Administrative services performed under third party contracts or agreements, including such services as general legal services, accounting services, and audit services; and

(4) Other costs for goods and services required for administration of the program, including such goods and services as rental or purchase of equipment, insurance, utilities, office supplies, and rental and maintenance (but not purchase) of office space.

(b) *Public information.* The provisions of information and other resources to residents and citizen organizations participating in the planning, implementation, or assessment of activities being assisted with CDBG funds.

(c) *Fair housing activities.* Provision of fair housing services designed to further the fair housing objectives of the Fair Housing Act (42 U.S.C. 3601–20) by making all persons, without regard to race, color, religion, sex, national origin, familial status or handicap, aware of the range of housing opportunities available to them; other fair housing enforcement, education, and outreach activities; and other activities designed to further the housing objective of avoiding undue concentrations of assisted persons in areas containing a high proportion of low and moderate income persons.

(d) [Reserved]

(e) *Indirect costs.* Indirect costs may be charged to the CDBG program under a cost allocation plan prepared in accordance with 2 CFR part 200, subpart E.

(f) *Submission of applications for federal programs.* Preparation of documents required for submission to HUD to receive funds under the CDBG and

UDAG programs. In addition, CDBG funds may be used to prepare applications for other Federal programs where the recipient determines that such activities are necessary or appropriate to achieve its community development objectives.

(g) *Administrative expenses to facilitate housing.* CDBG funds may be used for necessary administrative expenses in planning or obtaining financing for housing as follows: for entitlement recipients, assistance authorized by this paragraph is limited to units which are identified in the recipient's HUD approved housing assistance plan; for HUD-administered small cities recipients, assistance authorized by the paragraph is limited to facilitating the purchase or occupancy of existing units which are to be occupied by low and moderate income households, or the construction of rental or owner units where at least 20 percent of the units in each project will be occupied at affordable rents/costs by low and moderate income persons. Examples of eligible actions are as follows:

(1) The cost of conducting preliminary surveys and analysis of market needs;

(2) Site and utility plans, narrative descriptions of the proposed construction, preliminary cost estimates, urban design documentation, and "sketch drawings," but excluding architectural, engineering, and other details ordinarily required for construction purposes, such as structural, electrical, plumbing, and mechanical details;

(3) Reasonable costs associated with development of applications for mortgage and insured loan commitments, including commitment fees, and of applications and proposals under the Section 8 Housing Assistance Payments Program pursuant to 24 CFR parts 880–883;

(4) Fees associated with processing of applications for mortgage or insured loan commitments under programs including those administered by HUD, Farmers Home Administration (FmHA), Federal National Mortgage Association (FNMA), and the Government National Mortgage Association (GNMA);

(5) The cost of issuance and administration of mortgage revenue bonds used to finance the acquisition, rehabilitation or construction of housing, but excluding costs associated with the payment or guarantee of the principal or interest on such bonds; and

(6) Special outreach activities which result in greater landlord participation in Section 8 Housing Assistance Payments Program-Existing Housing or similar programs for low and moderate income persons.

(h) *Section 17 of the United States Housing Act of 1937.* Reasonable costs equivalent to those described in paragraphs (a), (b), (e) and (f) of this section for overall program management of the Rental Rehabilitation and Housing Development programs authorized under section 17 of the United States Housing Act of 1937, whether or not such activities are otherwise assisted with funds provided under this part.

(i) Whether or not such activities are otherwise assisted by funds provided under this part, reasonable costs equivalent to those described in paragraphs (a), (b), (e), and (f) of this section for overall program management of:

(1) A Federally designated Empowerment Zone or Enterprise Community; and

(2) The HOME program under title II of the Cranston-Gonzalez National Affordable Housing Act (42 U.S.C. 12701 note).

[53 FR 34439, Sept. 6, 1988; 53 FR 41330, Oct. 21, 1988, as amended at 54 FR 37411, Sept. 8, 1989; 60 FR 56912, Nov. 9, 1995; 69 FR 32778, June 10, 2004; 80 FR 69870, Nov. 12, 2015; 80 FR 75937, Dec. 7, 2015]

§ 570.207 Ineligible activities.

The general rule is that any activity that is not authorized under the provisions of §§ 570.201–570.206 is ineligible to be assisted with CDBG funds. This section identifies specific activities that are ineligible and provides guidance in determining the eligibility of other activities frequently associated with housing and community development.

(a) The following activities may not be assisted with CDBG funds:

(1) *Buildings or portions thereof, used for the general conduct of government* as defined at § 570.3(d) cannot be assisted

with CDBG funds. This does not include, however, the removal of architectural barriers under §570.201(c) involving any such building. Also, where acquisition of real property includes an existing improvement which is to be used in the provision of a building for the general conduct of government, the portion of the acquisition cost attributable to the land is eligible, provided such acquisition meets a national objective described in §570.208.

(2) *General government expenses.* Except as otherwise specifically authorized in this subpart or under 2 CFR part 200, subpart E, expenses required to carry out the regular responsibilities of the unit of general local government are not eligible for assistance under this part.

(3) *Political activities.* CDBG funds shall not be used to finance the use of facilities or equipment for political purposes or to engage in other partisan political activities, such as candidate forums, voter transportation, or voter registration. However, a facility originally assisted with CDBG funds may be used on an incidental basis to hold political meetings, candidate forums, or voter registration campaigns, provided that all parties and organizations have access to the facility on an equal basis, and are assessed equal rent or use charges, if any.

(b) The following activities may not be assisted with CDBG funds unless authorized under provisions of §570.203 or as otherwise specifically noted herein or when carried out by an entity under the provisions of §570.204.

(1) *Purchase of equipment.* The purchase of equipment with CDBG funds is generally ineligible.

(i) *Construction equipment.* The purchase of construction equipment is ineligible, but compensation for the use of such equipment through leasing or depreciation pursuant to 2 CFR part 200, subpart E, as applicable for an otherwise eligible activity is an eligible use of CDBG funds. However, the purchase of construction equipment for use as part of a solid waste disposal facility is eligible under §570.201(c).

(ii) *Fire protection equipment.* Fire protection equipment is considered for this purpose to be an integral part of a public facility and thus, purchase of such equipment would be eligible under §570.201(c).

(iii) *Furnishings and personal property.* The purchase of equipment, fixtures, motor vehicles, furnishings, or other personal property not an integral structural fixture is generally ineligible. CDBG funds may be used, however, to purchase or to pay depreciation in accordance with 2 CFR part 200, subpart E, for such items when necessary for use by a recipient or its subrecipients in the administration of activities assisted with CDBG funds, or when eligible as fire fighting equipment, or when such items constitute all or part of a public service pursuant to §570.201(e).

(2) *Operating and maintenance expenses.* The general rule is that any expense associated with repairing, operating or maintaining public facilities, improvements and services is ineligible. Specific exceptions to this general rule are operating and maintenance expenses associated with public service activities, interim assistance, and office space for program staff employed in carrying out the CDBG program. For example, the use of CDBG funds to pay the allocable costs of operating and maintaining a facility used in providing a public service would be eligible under §570.201(e), even if no other costs of providing such a service are assisted with such funds. Examples of ineligible operating and maintenance expenses are:

(i) Maintenance and repair of publicly owned streets, parks, playgrounds, water and sewer facilities, neighborhood facilities, senior centers, centers for persons with a disabilities, parking and other public facilities and improvements. Examples of maintenance and repair activities for which CDBG funds may not be used include the filling of pot holes in streets, repairing of cracks in sidewalks, the mowing of recreational areas, and the replacement of expended street light bulbs; and

(ii) Payment of salaries for staff, utility costs and similar expenses necessary for the operation of public works and facilities.

(3) *New housing construction.* For the purpose of this paragraph, activities in support of the development of low or

moderate income housing including clearance, site assemblage, provision of site improvements and provision of public improvements and certain housing pre-construction costs set forth in § 570.206(g), are not considered as activities to subsidize or assist new residential construction. CDBG funds may not be used for the construction of new permanent residential structures or for any program to subsidize or assist such new construction, except:

(i) As provided under the last resort housing provisions set forth in 24 CFR part 42;

(ii) As authorized under § 570.201(m) or (n);

(iii) When carried out by an entity pursuant to § 570.204(a);

(4) *Income payments.* The general rule is that CDBG funds may not be used for income payments. For purposes of the CDBG program, "income payments" means a series of subsistence-type grant payments made to an individual or family for items such as food, clothing, housing (rent or mortgage), or utilities, but excludes emergency grant payments made over a period of up to three consecutive months to the provider of such items or services on behalf of an individual or family.

[53 FR 34439, Sept. 6, 1988; 53 FR 41330, Oct. 21, 1988, as amended at 60 FR 1945, Jan. 5, 1995; 60 FR 56912, Nov. 9, 1995; 65 FR 70215, Nov. 21, 2000; 80 FR 75937, Dec. 7, 2015]

§ 570.208 Criteria for national objectives.

The following criteria shall be used to determine whether a CDBG-assisted activity complies with one or more of the national objectives as required under § 570.200(a)(2):

(a) *Activities benefiting low- and moderate-income persons.* Activities meeting the criteria in paragraph (a) (1), (2), (3), or (4) of this section as applicable, will be considered to benefit low and moderate income persons unless there is substantial evidence to the contrary. In assessing any such evidence, the full range of direct effects of the assisted activity will be considered. (The recipient shall appropriately ensure that activities that meet these criteria do not benefit moderate income persons to the exclusion of low income persons.)

(1) *Area benefit activities.* (i) An activity, the benefits of which are available to all the residents in a particular area, where at least 51 percent of the residents are low and moderate income persons. Such an area need not be coterminous with census tracts or other officially recognized boundaries but must be the entire area served by the activity. An activity that serves an area that is not primarily residential in character shall not qualify under this criterion.

(ii) For metropolitan cities and urban counties, an activity that would otherwise qualify under § 570.208(a)(1)(i), except that the area served contains less than 51 percent low- and moderate-income residents, will also be considered to meet the objective of benefiting low- and moderate-income persons where the proportion of such persons in the area is within the highest quartile of all areas in the recipient's jurisdiction in terms of the degree of concentration of such persons. This exception is inapplicable to non-entitlement CDBG grants in Hawaii. In applying this exception, HUD will determine the lowest proportion a recipient may use to qualify an area for this purpose, as follows:

(A) All census block groups in the recipient's jurisdiction shall be rank ordered from the block group of highest proportion of low and moderate income persons to the block group with the lowest. For urban counties, the rank ordering shall cover the entire area constituting the urban county and shall not be done separately for each participating unit of general local government.

(B) In any case where the total number of a recipient's block groups does not divide evenly by four, the block group which would be fractionally divided between the highest and second quartiles shall be considered to be part of the highest quartile.

(C) The proportion of low and moderate income persons in the last census block group in the highest quartile shall be identified. Any service area located within the recipient's jurisdiction and having a proportion of low and moderate income persons at or above this level shall be considered to be within the highest quartile.

(D) If block group data are not available for the entire jurisdiction, other data acceptable to the Secretary may be used in the above calculations.

(iii) An activity to develop, establish, and operate for up to two years after the establishment of, a uniform emergency telephone number system serving an area having less than the percentage of low- and moderate-income residents required under paragraph (a)(1)(i) of this section or (as applicable) paragraph (a)(1)(ii) of this section, provided the recipient obtains prior HUD approval. To obtain such approval, the recipient must:

(A) Demonstrate that the system will contribute significantly to the safety of the residents of the area. The request for approval must include a list of the emergency services that will participate in the emergency telephone number system;

(B) Submit information that serves as a basis for HUD to determine whether at least 51 percent of the use of the system will be by low- and moderate-income persons. As available, the recipient must provide information that identifies the total number of calls actually received over the preceding 12-month period for each of the emergency services to be covered by the emergency telephone number system and relates those calls to the geographic segment (expressed as nearly as possible in terms of census tracts, block numbering areas, block groups, or combinations thereof that are contained within the segment) of the service area from which the calls were generated. In analyzing this data to meet the requirements of this section, HUD will assume that the distribution of income among the callers generally reflects the income characteristics of the general population residing in the same geographic area where the callers reside. If HUD can conclude that the users have primarily consisted of low- and moderate-income persons, no further submission is needed by the recipient. If a recipient plans to make other submissions for this purpose, it may request that HUD review its planned methodology before expending the effort to acquire the information it expects to use to make its case;

(C) Demonstrate that other Federal funds received by the recipient are insufficient or unavailable for a uniform emergency telephone number system. For this purpose, the recipient must submit a statement explaining whether the lack of funds is due to the insufficiency of the amount of the available funds, restrictions on the use of such funds, or the prior commitment of funds by the recipient for other purposes; and

(D) Demonstrate that the percentage of the total costs of the system paid for by CDBG funds does not exceed the percentage of low- and moderate-income persons in the service area of the system. For this purpose, the recipient must include a description of the boundaries of the service area of the emergency telephone number system, the census divisions that fall within the boundaries of the service area (census tracts or block numbering areas), the total number of persons and the total number of low- and moderate-income persons within each census division, the percentage of low- and moderate-income persons within the service area, and the total cost of the system.

(iv) An activity for which the assistance to a public improvement that provides benefits to all the residents of an area is limited to paying special assessments (as defined in § 570.200(c)) levied against residential properties owned and occupied by persons of low and moderate income.

(v) For purposes of determining qualification under this criterion, activities of the same type that serve different areas will be considered separately on the basis of their individual service area.

(vi) In determining whether there is a sufficiently large percentage of low- and moderate-income persons residing in the area served by an activity to qualify under paragraph (a)(1) (i), (ii), or (vii) of this section, the most recently available decennial census information must be used to the fullest extent feasible, together with the section 8 income limits that would have applied at the time the income information was collected by the Census Bureau. Recipients that believe that the census data does not reflect current relative income levels in an area, or where census boundaries do not coincide sufficiently well with the service area of an activity, may conduct (or have conducted) a current survey of the residents of the area to determine the percent of such persons that are low and moderate income. HUD will accept information obtained through such surveys, to be used in lieu of the decennial census data, where it determines that the survey was conducted in such a manner that the results meet standards of statistical reliability that are comparable to that of the decennial census data for areas of similar size. Where there is substantial evidence that provides a clear basis to believe that the use of the decennial census data would substantially overstate the proportion of persons residing there that are low and moderate income, HUD may require that the recipient rebut such evidence in order to demonstrate compliance with section 105(c)(2) of the Act.

(vii) Activities meeting the requirements of paragraph (d)(5)(i) of this section may be considered to qualify under this paragraph, provided that the area covered by the strategy is either a Federally-designated Empowerment Zone or Enterprise Community or primarily residential and contains a percentage of low- and moderate-income residents that is no less than the percentage computed by HUD pursuant to paragraph (a)(1)(ii) of this section or 70 percent, whichever is less, but in no event less than 51 percent. Activities meeting the requirements of paragraph (d)(6)(i) of this section may also be considered to qualify under paragraph (a)(1) of this section.

(2) *Limited clientele activities.* (i) An activity which benefits a limited clientele, at least 51 percent of whom are low- or moderate-income persons. (The following kinds of activities may not qualify under paragraph (a)(2) of this section: activities, the benefits of which are available to all the residents of an area; activities involving the acquisition, construction or rehabilitation of property for housing; or activities where the benefit to low- and moderate-income persons to be considered is the creation or retention of jobs, except as provided in paragraph (a)(2)(iv) of this section.) To qualify under paragraph (a)(2) of this section, the activity must meet one of the following tests:

(A) Benefit a clientele who are generally presumed to be principally low and moderate income persons. Activities that exclusively serve a group of persons in any one or a combination of the following categories may be presumed to benefit persons, 51 percent of whom are low- and moderate-income: abused children, battered spouses, elderly persons, adults meeting the Bureau of the Census' Current Population Reports definition of "severely disabled," homeless persons, illiterate adults, persons living with AIDS, and migrant farm workers; or

(B) Require information on family size and income so that it is evident that at least 51 percent of the clientele are persons whose family income does not exceed the low and moderate income limit; or

(C) Have income eligibility requirements which limit the activity exclusively to low and moderate income persons; or

(D) Be of such nature and be in such location that it may be concluded that the activity's clientele will primarily be low and moderate income persons.

(ii) An activity that serves to remove material or architectural barriers to the mobility or accessibility of elderly persons or of adults meeting the Bureau of the Census' Current Population Reports definition of "severely disabled" will be presumed to qualify under this criterion if it is restricted, to the extent practicable, to the removal of such barriers by assisting:

(A) The reconstruction of a public facility or improvement, or portion thereof, that does not qualify under paragraph (a)(1) of this section;

(B) The rehabilitation of a privately owned nonresidential building or improvement that does not qualify under paragraph (a)(1) or (4) of this section; or

(C) The rehabilitation of the common areas of a residential structure that contains more than one dwelling unit and that does not qualify under paragraph (a)(3) of this section.

(iii) A microenterprise assistance activity carried out in accordance with the provisions of § 570.201(o) with respect to those owners of microenterprises and persons developing microenterprises assisted under the activity during each program year who are low- and moderate-income persons. For purposes of this paragraph, persons determined to be low and moderate income may be presumed to continue to qualify as such for up to a three-year period.

(iv) An activity designed to provide job training and placement and/or other employment support services, including, but not limited to, peer support programs, counseling, child care, transportation, and other similar services, in which the percentage of low- and moderate-income persons assisted is less than 51 percent may qualify under this paragraph in the following limited circumstance:

(A) In such cases where such training or provision of supportive services assists business(es), the only use of CDBG assistance for the project is to provide the job training and/or supportive services; and

(B) The proportion of the total cost of the project borne by CDBG funds is no greater than the proportion of the total number of persons assisted who are low or moderate income.

(3) *Housing activities.* An eligible activity carried out for the purpose of providing or improving permanent residential structures which, upon completion, will be occupied by low- and moderate-income households. This would include, but not necessarily be limited to, the acquisition or rehabilitation of property by the recipient, a subrecipient, a developer, an individual homebuyer, or an individual homeowner; conversion of nonresidential structures; and new housing construction. If the structure contains two dwelling units, at least one must be so occupied, and if the structure contains more than two dwelling units, at least 51 percent of the units must be so occupied. Where two or more rental buildings being assisted are or will be located on the same or contiguous properties, and the buildings will be under common ownership and management, the grouped buildings may be considered for this purpose as a single structure. Where housing activities being assisted meet the requirements of paragraph § 570.208 (d)(5)(ii) or (d)(6)(ii) of this section, all such housing may also be considered for this purpose as a single structure. For rental housing, occupancy by low and moderate income households must be at affordable rents to qualify under this criterion. The recipient shall adopt and make public its standards for determining "affordable rents" for this purpose. The following shall also qualify under this criterion:

(i) When less than 51 percent of the units in a structure will be occupied by low and moderate income households, CDBG assistance may be provided in the following limited circumstances:

(A) The assistance is for an eligible activity to reduce the development cost of the new construction of a multifamily, non-elderly rental housing project;

(B) Not less than 20 percent of the units will be occupied by low and moderate income households at affordable rents; and

(C) The proportion of the total cost of developing the project to be borne by CDBG funds is no greater than the proportion of units in the project that will be occupied by low and moderate income households.

(ii) When CDBG funds are used to assist rehabilitation eligible under § 570.202(b)(9) or (10) in direct support of the recipient's Rental Rehabilitation program authorized under 24 CFR part 511, such funds shall be considered to benefit low and moderate income persons where not less than 51 percent of the units assisted, or to be assisted, by the recipient's Rental Rehabilitation program overall are for low and moderate income persons.

(iii) When CDBG funds are used for housing services eligible under § 570.201(k), such funds shall be considered to benefit low- and moderate-income persons if the housing units for which the services are provided are HOME-assisted and the requirements at 24 CFR 92.252 or 92.254 are met.

(4) *Job creation or retention activities.* An activity designed to create or retain permanent jobs where at least 51 percent of the jobs, computed on a full time equivalent basis, involve the employment of low- and moderate-income

persons. To qualify under this paragraph, the activity must meet the following criteria:

(i) For an activity that creates jobs, the recipient must document that at least 51 percent of the jobs will be held by, or will be available to, low- and moderate-income persons.

(ii) For an activity that retains jobs, the recipient must document that the jobs would actually be lost without the CDBG assistance and that either or both of the following conditions apply with respect to at least 51 percent of the jobs at the time the CDBG assistance is provided:

(A) The job is known to be held by a low- or moderate-income person; or

(B) The job can reasonably be expected to turn over within the following two years and that steps will be taken to ensure that it will be filled by, or made available to, a low- or moderate-income person upon turnover.

(iii) Jobs that are not held or filled by a low- or moderate-income person may be considered to be available to low- and moderate-income persons for these purposes only if:

(A) Special skills that can only be acquired with substantial training or work experience or education beyond high school are not a prerequisite to fill such jobs, or the business agrees to hire unqualified persons and provide training; and

(B) The recipient and the assisted business take actions to ensure that low- and moderate-income persons receive first consideration for filling such jobs.

(iv) For purposes of determining whether a job is held by or made available to a low- or moderate-income person, the person may be presumed to be a low- or moderate-income person if:

(A) He/she resides within a census tract (or block numbering area) that either:

(*1*) Meets the requirements of paragraph (a)(4)(v) of this section; or

(*2*) Has at least 70 percent of its residents who are low- and moderate-income persons; or

(B) The assisted business is located within a census tract (or block numbering area) that meets the requirements of paragraph (a)(4)(v) of this section and the job under consideration is to be located within that census tract.

(v) A census tract (or block numbering area) qualifies for the presumptions permitted under paragraphs (a)(4)(iv)(A)(*1*) and (B) of this section if it is either part of a Federally-designated Empowerment Zone or Enterprise Community or meets the following criteria:

(A) It has a poverty rate of at least 20 percent as determined by the most recently available decennial census information;

(B) It does not include any portion of a central business district, as this term is used in the most recent Census of Retail Trade, unless the tract has a poverty rate of at least 30 percent as determined by the most recently available decennial census information; and

(C) It evidences pervasive poverty and general distress by meeting at least one of the following standards:

(*1*) All block groups in the census tract have poverty rates of at least 20 percent;

(*2*) The specific activity being undertaken is located in a block group that has a poverty rate of at least 20 percent; or

(*3*) Upon the written request of the recipient, HUD determines that the census tract exhibits other objectively determinable signs of general distress such as high incidence of crime, narcotics use, homelessness, abandoned housing, and deteriorated infrastructure or substantial population decline.

(vi) As a general rule, each assisted business shall be considered to be a separate activity for purposes of determining whether the activity qualifies under this paragraph, except:

(A) In certain cases such as where CDBG funds are used to acquire, develop or improve a real property (e.g., a business incubator or an industrial park) the requirement may be met by measuring jobs in the aggregate for all the businesses which locate on the property, provided such businesses are not otherwise assisted by CDBG funds.

(B) Where CDBG funds are used to pay for the staff and overhead costs of an entity making loans to businesses exclusively from non-CDBG funds, this requirement may be met by aggregating the jobs created by all of the businesses receiving loans during each program year.

(C) Where CDBG funds are used by a recipient or subrecipient to provide technical assistance to businesses, this requirement may be met by aggregating the jobs created or retained by all of the businesses receiving technical assistance during each program year.

(D) Where CDBG funds are used for activities meeting the criteria listed at §570.209(b)(2)(v), this requirement may be met by aggregating the jobs created or retained by all businesses for which CDBG assistance is obligated for such activities during the program year, except as provided at paragraph (d)(7) of this section.

(E) Where CDBG funds are used by a Community Development Financial Institution to carry out activities for the purpose of creating or retaining jobs, this requirement may be met by aggregating the jobs created or retained by all businesses for which CDBG assistance is obligated for such activities during the program year, except as provided at paragraph (d)(7) of this section.

(F) Where CDBG funds are used for public facilities or improvements which will result in the creation or retention of jobs by more than one business, this requirement may be met by aggregating the jobs created or retained by all such businesses as a result of the public facility or improvement.

(*1*) Where the public facility or improvement is undertaken principally for the benefit of one or more particular businesses, but where other businesses might also benefit from the assisted activity, the requirement may be met by aggregating only the jobs created or retained by those businesses for which the facility/improvement is principally undertaken, provided that the cost (in CDBG funds) for the facility/improvement is less than $10,000 per permanent full-time equivalent job to be created or retained by those businesses.

(*2*) In any case where the cost per job to be created or retained (as determined under paragraph (a)(4)(vi)(F)(*1*) of this section) is $10,000 or more, the requirement must be met by aggregating the jobs created or retained as a result of the public facility or improvement by all businesses in the service area of the facility/improvement. This aggregation must include businesses which, as a result of the public facility/improvement, locate or expand in the service area of the facility/improvement between the date the recipient identifies the activity in its action plan under part 91 of this title and the date one year after the physical completion of the facility/improvement. In addition, the assisted activity must comply with the public benefit standards at §570.209(b).

(b) *Activities which aid in the prevention or elimination of slums or blight.* Activities meeting one or more of the following criteria, in the absence of substantial evidence to the contrary, will be considered to aid in the prevention or elimination of slums or blight:

(1) *Activities to address slums or blight on an area basis.* An activity will be considered to address prevention or elimination of slums or blight in an area if:

(i) The area, delineated by the recipient, meets a definition of a slum, blighted, deteriorated or deteriorating area under State or local law;

(ii) The area also meets the conditions in either paragraph (A) or (B):

(A) At least 25 percent of properties throughout the area experience one or more of the following conditions:

(*1*) Physical deterioration of buildings or improvements;

(*2*) Abandonment of properties;

(*3*) Chronic high occupancy turnover rates or chronic high vacancy rates in commercial or industrial buildings;

(*4*) Significant declines in property values or abnormally low property values relative to other areas in the community; or

(*5*) Known or suspected environmental contamination.

(B) The public improvements throughout the area are in a general state of deterioration.

(iii) Documentation is to be maintained by the recipient on the boundaries of the area and the conditions and standards used that qualified the area at the time of its designation. The recipient shall establish definitions of the conditions listed at

§ 570.208(b)(1)(ii)(A), and maintain records to substantiate how the area met the slums or blighted criteria. The designation of an area as slum or blighted under this section is required to be redetermined every 10 years for continued qualification. Documentation must be retained pursuant to the recordkeeping requirements contained at § 570.506 (b)(8)(ii).

(iv) The assisted activity addresses one or more of the conditions which contributed to the deterioration of the area. Rehabilitation of residential buildings carried out in an area meeting the above requirements will be considered to address the area's deterioration only where each building rehabilitated is considered substandard under local definition before rehabilitation, and all deficiencies making a building substandard have been eliminated. At a minimum, the local definition for this purpose must be such that buildings that it would render substandard would also fail to meet the standards for the condition of HUD housing at 24 CFR 5.703.

(2) *Activities to address slums or blight on a spot basis.* The following activities may be undertaken on a spot basis to eliminate specific conditions of blight, physical decay, or environmental contamination that are not located in a slum or blighted area: acquisition; clearance; relocation; historic preservation; remediation of environmentally contaminated properties; or rehabilitation of buildings or improvements. However, rehabilitation must be limited to eliminating those conditions that are detrimental to public health and safety. If acquisition or relocation is undertaken, it must be a precursor to another eligible activity (funded with CDBG or other resources) that directly eliminates the specific conditions of blight or physical decay, or environmental contamination.

(3) *Activities to address slums or blight in an urban renewal area.* An activity will be considered to address prevention or elimination of slums or blight in an urban renewal area if the activity is:

(i) Located within an urban renewal project area or Neighborhood Development Program (NDP) action area; i.e., an area in which funded activities were authorized under an urban renewal Loan and Grant Agreement or an annual NDP Funding Agreement, pursuant to title I of the Housing Act of 1949; and

(ii) Necessary to complete the urban renewal plan, as then in effect, including *initial* land redevelopment permitted by the plan.

NOTE: Despite the restrictions in (b) (1) and (2) of this section, any rehabilitation activity which benefits low and moderate income persons pursuant to paragraph (a)(3) of this section can be undertaken without regard to the area in which it is located or the extent or nature of rehabilitation assisted.

(c) *Activities designed to meet community development needs having a particular urgency.* In the absence of substantial evidence to the contrary, an activity will be considered to address this objective if the recipient certifies that the activity is designed to alleviate existing conditions which pose a serious and immediate threat to the health or welfare of the community which are of recent origin or which recently became urgent, that the recipient is unable to finance the activity on its own, and that other sources of funding are not available. A condition will generally be considered to be of recent origin if it developed or became critical within 18 months preceding the certification by the recipient.

(d) *Additional criteria.* (1) Where the assisted activity is acquisition of real property, a preliminary determination of whether the activity addresses a national objective may be based on the planned use of the property after acquisition. A final determination shall be based on the actual use of the property, excluding any short-term, temporary use. Where the acquisition is for the purpose of clearance which will eliminate specific conditions of blight or physical decay, the clearance activity shall be considered the actual use of the property. However, any subsequent use or disposition of the cleared property shall be treated as a "change of use" under § 570.505.

(2) Where the assisted activity is relocation assistance that the recipient is required to provide, such relocation assistance shall be considered to address the same national objective as is addressed by the displacing activity.

Where the relocation assistance is voluntary on the part of the grantee the recipient may qualify the assistance either on the basis of the national objective addressed by the displacing activity or on the basis that the recipients of the relocation assistance are low and moderate income persons.

(3) In any case where the activity undertaken for the purpose of creating or retaining jobs is a public improvement and the area served is primarily residential, the activity must meet the requirements of paragraph (a)(1) of this section as well as those of paragraph (a)(4) of this section in order to qualify as benefiting low and moderate income persons.

(4) CDBG funds expended for planning and administrative costs under §570.205 and §570.206 will be considered to address the national objectives.

(5) Where the grantee has elected to prepare an area revitalization strategy pursuant to the authority of §91.215(e) of this title and HUD has approved the strategy, the grantee may also elect the following options:

(i) Activities undertaken pursuant to the strategy for the purpose of creating or retaining jobs may, at the option of the grantee, be considered to meet the requirements of this paragraph under the criteria at paragraph (a)(1)(vii) of this section in lieu of the criteria at paragraph (a)(4) of this section; and

(ii) All housing activities in the area for which, pursuant to the strategy, CDBG assistance is obligated during the program year may be considered to be a single structure for purposes of applying the criteria at paragraph (a)(3) of this section.

(6) Where CDBG-assisted activities are carried out by a Community Development Financial Institution whose charter limits its investment area to a primarily residential area consisting of at least 51 percent low- and moderate-income persons, the grantee may also elect the following options:

(i) Activities carried out by the Community Development Financial Institution for the purpose of creating or retaining jobs may, at the option of the grantee, be considered to meet the requirements of this paragraph under the criteria at paragraph (a)(1)(vii) of this section in lieu of the criteria at paragraph (a)(4) of this section; and

(ii) All housing activities for which the Community Development Financial Institution obligates CDBG assistance during the program year may be considered to be a single structure for purposes of applying the criteria at paragraph (a)(3) of this section.

(7) Where an activity meeting the criteria at §570.209(b)(2)(v) may also meet the requirements of either paragraph (d)(5)(i) or (d)(6)(i) of this section, the grantee may elect to qualify the activity under either the area benefit criteria at paragraph (a)(1)(vii) of this section or the job aggregation criteria at paragraph (a)(4)(vi)(D) of this section, but not both. Where an activity may meet the job aggregation criteria at both paragraphs (a)(4)(vi)(D) and (E) of this section, the grantee may elect to qualify the activity under either criterion, but not both.

[53 FR 34439, Sept. 6, 1988; 53 FR 41330, Oct. 21, 1988, as amended at 60 FR 1945, Jan. 5, 1995; 60 FR 17445, Apr. 6, 1995; 60 FR 56912, Nov. 9, 1995; 61 FR 18674, Apr. 29, 1996; 71 FR 30035, May 24, 2006; 72 FR 46370, Aug. 17, 2007; 88 FR 30498, May 11, 2023]

§570.209 Guidelines for evaluating and selecting economic development projects.

The following guidelines are provided to assist the recipient to evaluate and select activities to be carried out for economic development purposes. Specifically, these guidelines are applicable to activities that are eligible for CDBG assistance under §570.203. These guidelines also apply to activities carried out under the authority of §570.204 that would otherwise be eligible under §570.203, were it not for the involvement of a Community-Based Development Organization (CBDO). (This would include activities where a CBDO makes loans to for-profit businesses.) These guidelines are composed of two components: guidelines for evaluating project costs and financial requirements; and standards for evaluating public benefit. The standards for evaluating public benefit are *mandatory*, but the guidelines for evaluating projects costs and financial requirements are not.

(a) *Guidelines and objectives for evaluating project costs and financial requirements.* HUD has developed guidelines that are designed to provide the recipient with a framework for financially underwriting and selecting CDBG-assisted economic development projects which are financially viable and will make the most effective use of the CDBG funds. These guidelines, also referred to as the underwriting guidelines, are published as appendix A to this part. The use of the underwriting guidelines published by HUD is not mandatory. However, grantees electing not to use these guidelines would be expected to conduct basic financial underwriting prior to the provision of CDBG financial assistance to a for-profit business. Where appropriate, HUD's underwriting guidelines recognize that different levels of review are appropriate to take into account differences in the size and scope of a proposed project, and in the case of a microenterprise or other small business to take into account the differences in the capacity and level of sophistication among businesses of differing sizes. Recipients are encouraged, when they develop their own programs and underwriting criteria, to also take these factors into account. The objectives of the underwriting guidelines are to ensure:

(1) That project costs are reasonable;

(2) That all sources of project financing are committed;

(3) That to the extent practicable, CDBG funds are not substituted for non-Federal financial support;

(4) That the project is financially feasible;

(5) That to the extent practicable, the return on the owner's equity investment will not be unreasonably high; and

(6) That to the extent practicable, CDBG funds are disbursed on a pro rata basis with other finances provided to the project.

(b) *Standards for evaluating public benefit.* The grantee is responsible for making sure that at least a minimum level of public benefit is obtained from the expenditure of CDBG funds under the categories of eligibility governed by these guidelines. The standards set forth below identify the types of public benefit that will be recognized for this purpose and the minimum level of each that must be obtained for the amount of CDBG funds used. Unlike the guidelines for project costs and financial requirements covered under paragraph (a) of this section, the use of the standards for public benefit is mandatory. Certain public facilities and improvements eligible under § 570.201(c) of the regulations, which are undertaken for economic development purposes, are also subject to these standards, as specified in § 570.208(a)(4)(vi)(F)(*2*).

(1) *Standards for activities in the aggregate.* Activities covered by these guidelines must, in the aggregate, either:

(i) Create or retain at least one full-time equivalent, permanent job per $35,000 of CDBG funds used; or

(ii) Provide goods or services to residents of an area, such that the number of low- and moderate-income persons residing in the areas served by the assisted businesses amounts to at least one low- and moderate-income person per $350 of CDBG funds used.

(2) *Applying the aggregate standards.* (i) A metropolitan city, an urban county, a non-entitlement CDBG grantee in Hawaii, or an Insular Area shall apply the aggregate standards under paragraph (b)(1) of this section to all applicable activities for which CDBG funds are first obligated within each single CDBG program year, without regard to the source year of the funds used for the activities. For Insular Areas, the preceding sentence applies to grants received in program years after Fiscal Year 2004. A grantee under the HUD-administered Small Cities Program, or Insular Areas CDBG grants prior to Fiscal Year 2005, shall apply the aggregate standards under paragraph (b)(1) of this section to all funds obligated for applicable activities from a given grant; program income obligated for applicable activities will, for these purposes, be aggregated with the most recent open grant. For any time period in which a community has no open HUD-administered or Insular Areas grants, the aggregate standards shall be applied to all applicable activities for which program income is obligated during that period.

(ii) The grantee shall apply the aggregate standards to the number of jobs to be created/retained, or to the number of persons residing in the area served (as applicable), as determined at the time funds are obligated to activities.

(iii) Where an activity is expected both to create or retain jobs and to provide goods or services to residents of an area, the grantee may elect to count the activity under either the jobs standard or the area residents standard, but not both.

(iv) Where CDBG assistance for an activity is limited to job training and placement and/or other employment support services, the jobs assisted with CDBG funds shall be considered to be created or retained jobs for the purposes of applying the aggregate standards.

(v) Any activity subject to these guidelines which meets one or more of the following criteria may, at the grantee's option, be excluded from the aggregate standards described in paragraph (b)(1) of this section:

(A) Provides jobs exclusively for unemployed persons or participants in one or more of the following programs:

(*1*) Jobs Training Partnership Act (JTPA);

(*2*) Jobs Opportunities for Basic Skills (JOBS); or

(*3*) Aid to Families with Dependent Children (AFDC);

(B) Provides jobs predominantly for residents of Public and Indian Housing units;

(C) Provides jobs predominantly for homeless persons;

(D) Provides jobs predominantly for low-skilled, low- and moderate-income persons, where the business agrees to provide clear opportunities for promotion and economic advancement, such as through the provision of training;

(E) Provides jobs predominantly for persons residing within a census tract (or block numbering area) that has at least 20 percent of its residents who are in poverty;

(F) Provides assistance to business(es) that operate(s) within a census tract (or block numbering area) that has at least 20 percent of its residents who are in poverty;

(G) Stabilizes or revitalizes a neighborhood that has at least 70 percent of its residents who are low- and moderate-income;

(H) Provides assistance to a Community Development Financial Institution that serve an area that is predominantly low- and moderate-income persons;

(I) Provides assistance to a Community-Based Development Organization serving a neighborhood that has at least 70 percent of its residents who are low- and moderate-income;

(J) Provides employment opportunities that are an integral component of a project designed to promote spatial deconcentration of low- and moderate-income and minority persons;

(K) With prior HUD approval, provides substantial benefit to low-income persons through other innovative approaches;

(L) Provides services to the residents of an area pursuant to a strategy approved by HUD under the provisions of §91.215(e) of this title;

(M) Creates or retains jobs through businesses assisted in an area pursuant to a strategy approved by HUD under the provisions of §91.215(e) of this title.

(N) Directly involves the economic development or redevelopment of environmentally contaminated properties.

(3) *Standards for individual activities.* Any activity subject to these guidelines which falls into one or more of the following categories will be considered by HUD to provide insufficient public benefit, and therefore may under no circumstances be assisted with CDBG funds:

(i) The amount of CDBG assistance exceeds either of the following, as applicable:

(A) $50,000 per full-time equivalent, permanent job created or retained; or

(B) $1,000 per low- and moderate-income person to which goods or services are provided by the activity.

(ii) The activity consists of or includes any of the following:

(A) General promotion of the community as a whole (as opposed to the promotion of specific areas and programs);

(B) Assistance to professional sports teams;

(C) Assistance to privately-owned recreational facilities that serve a predominantly higher-income clientele, where the recreational benefit to users or members clearly outweighs employment or other benefits to low- and moderate-income persons;

(D) Acquisition of land for which the specific proposed use has not yet been identified; and

(E) Assistance to a for-profit business while that business or any other business owned by the same person(s) or entity(ies) is the subject of unresolved findings of noncompliance relating to previous CDBG assistance provided by the recipient.

(4) *Applying the individual activity standards.* (i) Where an activity is expected both to create or retain jobs and to provide goods or services to residents of an area, it will be disqualified only if the amount of CDBG assistance exceeds both of the amounts in paragraph (b)(3)(i) of this section.

(ii) The individual activity standards in paragraph (b)(3)(i) of this section shall be applied to the number of jobs to be created or retained, or to the number of persons residing in the area served (as applicable), as determined at the time funds are obligated to activities.

(iii) Where CDBG assistance for an activity is limited to job training and placement and/or other employment support services, the jobs assisted with CDBG funds shall be considered to be created or retained jobs for the purposes of applying the individual activity standards in paragraph (b)(3)(i) of this section.

(c) *Amendments to economic development projects after review determinations.* If, after the grantee enters into a contract to provide assistance to a project, the scope or financial elements of the project change to the extent that a significant contract amendment is appropriate, the project should be reevaluated under these and the recipient's guidelines. (This would include, for example, situations where the business requests a change in the amount or terms of assistance being provided, or an extension to the loan payment period required in the contract.) If a reevaluation of the project indicates that the financial elements and public benefit to be derived have also substantially changed, then the recipient should make appropriate adjustments in the amount, type, terms or conditions of CDBG assistance which has been offered, to reflect the impact of the substantial change. (For example, if a change in the project elements results in a substantial reduction of the total project costs, it may be appropriate for the recipient to reduce the amount of total CDBG assistance.) If the amount of CDBG assistance provided to the project is increased, the amended project must still comply with the public benefit standards under paragraph (b) of this section.

(d) *Documentation.* The grantee must maintain sufficient records to demonstrate the level of public benefit, based on the above standards, that is actually achieved upon completion of the CDBG-assisted economic development activity(ies) and how that compares to the level of such benefit anticipated when the CDBG assistance was obligated. If the grantee's actual results show a pattern of substantial variation from anticipated results, the grantee is expected to take all actions reasonably within its control to improve the accuracy of its projections. If the actual results demonstrate that the recipient has failed the public benefit standards, HUD may require the recipient to meet more stringent standards in future years as appropriate.

[60 FR 1947, Jan. 5, 1995, as amended at 60 FR 17445, Apr. 6, 1995; 71 FR 30035, May 24, 2006; 72 FR 12535, Mar. 15, 2007; 72 FR 46370, Aug. 17, 2007]

§ 570.210 Prohibition on use of assistance for employment relocation activities.

(a) *Prohibition.* CDBG funds may not be used to directly assist a business, including a business expansion, in the relocation of a plant, facility, or operation from one LMA to another LMA if the relocation is likely to result in a significant loss of jobs in the LMA from which the relocation occurs.

(b) *Definitions.* The following definitions apply to this section:

(1) *Directly assist.* Directly assist means the provision of CDBG funds for activities pursuant to:

(i) § 570.203(b); or

(ii) §§ 570.201(a)–(d), 570.201(l), 570.203(a), or § 570.204 when the grantee, subrecipient, or, in the case of an activity carried out pursuant to §570.204, a Community Based Development Organization (CDBO) enters into an agreement with a business to undertake one or more of these activities as a condition of the business relocating a facility, plant, or operation to the grantee's LMA. Provision of public facilities and indirect assistance that will provide benefit to multiple businesses does not fall under the definition of "directly assist," unless it includes the provision of infrastructure to aid a specific business that is the subject of an agreement with the specific assisted business.

(2) *Labor market area (LMA)*. For metropolitan areas, an LMA is an area defined as such by the BLS. An LMA is an economically integrated geographic area within which individuals can live and find employment within a reasonable distance or can readily change employment without changing their place of residence. In addition, LMAs are nonoverlapping and geographically exhaustive. For metropolitan areas, grantees must use employment data, as defined by the BLS, for the LMA in which the affected business is currently located and from which current jobs may be lost. For non-metropolitan areas, an LMA is either an area defined by the BLS as an LMA, or a state may choose to combine non-metropolitan LMAs. States are required to define or reaffirm prior definitions of their LMAs on an annual basis and retain records to substantiate such areas prior to any business relocation that would be impacted by this rule. Metropolitan LMAs cannot be combined, nor can a non-metropolitan LMA be combined with a metropolitan LMA. For the HUD-administered Small Cities Program, each of the three participating counties in Hawaii will be considered to be its own LMA. Recipients of Fiscal Year 1999 Small Cities Program funding in New York will follow the requirements for State CDBG recipients.

(3) *Operation*. A business operation includes, but is not limited to, any equipment, employment opportunity, production capacity or product line of the business.

(4) *Significant loss of jobs*. (i) A loss of jobs is significant if: The number of jobs to be lost in the LMA in which the affected business is currently located is equal to or greater than one-tenth of one percent of the total number of persons in the labor force of that LMA; or in all cases, a loss of 500 or more jobs. Notwithstanding the aforementioned, a loss of 25 jobs or fewer does not constitute a significant loss of jobs.

(ii) A job is considered to be lost due to the provision of CDBG assistance if the job is relocated within three years of the provision of assistance to the business; or the time period within which jobs are to be created as specified by the agreement between the business and the recipient if it is longer than three years.

(c) *Written agreement*. Before directly assisting a business with CDBG funds, the recipient, subrecipient, or a CDBO (in the case of an activity carried out pursuant to §570.204) shall sign a written agreement with the assisted business. The written agreement shall include:

(1) *Statement*. A statement from the assisted business as to whether the assisted activity will result in the relocation of any industrial or commercial plant, facility, or operation from one LMA to another, and, if so, the number of jobs that will be relocated from each LMA;

(2) *Required information*. If the assistance will not result in a relocation covered by this section, a certification from the assisted business that neither it, nor any of its subsidiaries, has plans to relocate jobs at the time the agreement is signed that would result in a significant job loss as defined in this rule; and

(3) *Reimbursement of assistance*. The agreement shall provide for reimbursement of any assistance provided to, or expended on behalf of, the business in the event that assistance results in a relocation prohibited under this section.

(d) *Assistance not covered by this section*. This section does not apply to:

(1) *Relocation assistance*. Relocation assistance required by the Uniform Assistance and Real Property Acquisition Policies Act of 1970, (URA) (42 U.S.C. 4601–4655);

(2) *Microenterprises.* Assistance to microenterprises as defined by Section 102(a)(22) of the Housing and Community Development Act of 1974; and

(3) *Arms-length transactions.* Assistance to a business that purchases business equipment, inventory, or other physical assets in an arms-length transaction, including the assets of an existing business, provided that the purchase does not result in the relocation of the sellers' business operation (including customer base or list, goodwill, product lines, or trade names) from one LMA to another LMA and does not produce a significant loss of jobs in the LMA from which the relocation occurs.

[70 FR 76369, Dec. 23, 2005]

Subpart D—Entitlement Grants

SOURCE: 53 FR 34449, Sept. 6, 1988, unless otherwise noted.

§ 570.300 General.

This subpart describes the policies and procedures governing the making of community development block grants to entitlement communities and to non-entitlement counties in the State of Hawaii. The policies and procedures set forth in subparts A, C, J, K, and O of this part also apply to entitlement grantees and to non-entitlement grantees in the State of Hawaii. Sections 570.307 and 570.308 of this subpart do not apply to the Hawaii non-entitlement grantees.

[72 FR 46370, Aug. 17, 2007]

§ 570.301 Activity locations and float-funding.

The consolidated plan, action plan, and amendment submission requirements referred to in this section are those in 24 CFR part 91.

(a) For activities for which the grantee has not yet decided on a specific location, such as when the grantee is allocating an amount of funds to be used for making loans or grants to businesses or for residential rehabilitation, the description in the action plan or any amendment shall identify who may apply for the assistance, the process by which the grantee expects to select who will receive the assistance (including selection criteria), and how much and under what terms the assistance will be provided, or in the case of a planned public facility or improvement, how it expects to determine its location.

(b) *Float-funded activities and guarantees.* A recipient may use undisbursed funds in the line of credit and its CDBG program account that are budgeted in statements or action plans for one or more other activities that do not need the funds immediately, subject to the limitations described below. Such funds shall be referred to as the "float" for purposes of this section and the action plan. Each activity carried out using the float must meet all of the same requirements that apply to CDBG-assisted activities generally, and must be expected to produce program income in an amount at least equal to the amount of the float so used. Whenever the recipient proposes to fund an activity with the float, it must include the activity in its action plan or amend the action plan for the current program year. For purposes of this section, an activity that uses such funds will be called a "float-funded activity."

(1) Each float-funded activity must be individually listed and described as such in the action plan.

(2)(i) The expected time period between obligation of assistance for a float-funded activity and receipt of program income in an amount at least equal to the full amount drawn from the float to fund the activity may not exceed 2.5 years. An activity from which program income sufficient to recover the full amount of the float assistance is expected to be generated more than 2.5 years after obligation may not be funded from the float, but may be included in an action plan if it is funded from CDBG funds other than the float (e.g., grant funds or proceeds from an approved Section 108 loan guarantee).

(ii) Any extension of the repayment period for a float-funded activity shall be considered to be a new float-funded activity for these purposes and may be implemented by the grantee only if the extension is made subject to the same limitations and requirements as apply to a new float-funded activity.

(3) Unlike other projected program income, the full amount of income expected to be generated by a float-funded activity must be shown as a source of program income in the action plan containing the activity, whether or not some or all of the income is expected to be received in a future program year (in accordance with 24 CFR 91.220(g)(1)(ii)(D)).

(4) The recipient must also clearly declare in the action plan that identifies the float-funded activity the recipient's commitment to undertake one of the following options:

(i) Amend or delete activities in an amount equal to any default or failure to produce sufficient income in a timely manner. If the recipient makes this choice, it must include a description of the process it will use to select the activities to be amended or deleted and how it will involve citizens in that process; and it must amend the applicable statement(s) or action plan(s) showing those amendments or deletions promptly upon determining that the float-funded activity will not generate sufficient or timely program income;

(ii) Obtain an irrevocable line of credit from a commercial lender for the full amount of the float-funded activity and describe the lender and terms of such line of credit in the action plan that identifies the float-funded activity. To qualify for this purpose, such line of credit must be unconditionally available to the recipient in the amount of any shortfall within 30 days of the date that the float-funded activity fails to generate the projected amount of program income on schedule;

(iii) Transfer general local government funds in the full amount of any default or shortfall to the CDBG line of credit within 30 days of the float-funded activity's failure to generate the projected amount of the program income on schedule; or

(iv) A method approved in writing by HUD for securing timely return of the amount of the float funding. Such method must ensure that funds are available to meet any default or shortfall within 30 days of the float-funded activity's failure to generate the projected amount of the program income on schedule.

(5) When preparing an action plan for a year in which program income is expected to be received from a float-funded activity, and such program income has been shown in a prior statement or action plan, the current action plan shall identify the expected income and explain that the planned use of the income has already been described in prior statements or action plans, and shall identify the statements or action plans in which such descriptions may be found.

[60 FR 56913, Nov. 9, 1995]

§570.302 Submission requirements.

In order to receive its annual CDBG entitlement grant, a grantee must submit a consolidated plan in accordance with 24 CFR part 91. That part includes requirements for the content of the consolidated plan, for the process of developing the consolidated plan, including citizen participation provisions, for the submission date, for HUD approval, and for the amendment process.

(Approved by the Office of Management and Budget under control number 2506–0117)

[60 FR 1915, Jan. 5, 1995]

§570.303 Certifications.

The jurisdiction must make the certifications that are set forth in 24 CFR part 91 as part of the consolidated plan.

(Approved by the Office of Management and Budget under control number 2506–0117)

[60 FR 1915, Jan. 5, 1995]

§570.304 Making of grants.

(a) *Approval of grant.* HUD will approve a grant if the jurisdiction's submissions have been made and approved in accordance with 24 CFR part 91, and the certifications required therein are satisfactory to the Secretary. The certifications will be satisfactory to the Secretary for this purpose unless the Secretary has determined pursuant to subpart O of this part that the grantee has not complied with the requirements of this part, has failed to carry out its consolidated plan as provided under §570.903, or has determined that there is evidence, not directly involving the grantee's past performance under this program, that tends to challenge in a substantial manner the grantee's certification of future performance. If the Secretary makes any such determination, however, further assurances may be required to be submitted by the grantee as the Secretary may deem warranted or necessary to find the grantee's certification satisfactory.

(b) *Grant agreement.* The grant will be made by means of a grant agreement executed by both HUD and the grantee.

(c) *Grant amount.* The Secretary will make a grant in the full entitlement amount, generally within the last 30 days of the grantee's current program year, unless:

(1) Either the consolidated plan is not received by August 16 of the federal fiscal year for which funds are appropriated or the consolidated plan is not approved under 24 CFR part 91, subpart F—in which case, the grantee will forfeit the entire entitlement amount; or

(2) The grantee's performance does not meet the performance requirements or criteria prescribed in subpart O and the grant amount is reduced.

[53 FR 34449, Sept. 6, 1988, as amended at 60 FR 1915, Jan. 5, 1995; 60 FR 16379, Mar. 30, 1995; 60 FR 56913, Nov. 9, 1995]

§ 570.307 Urban counties.

(a) *Determination of qualification.* The Secretary will determine the qualifications of counties to receive entitlements as urban counties upon receipt of qualification documentation from counties at such time, and in such manner and form as prescribed by HUD. The Secretary shall determine eligibility and applicable portions of each eligible county for purposes of fund allocation under section 106 of the Act on the basis of information available from the U.S. Bureau of the Census with respect to population and other pertinent demographic characteristics, and based on information provided by the county and its included units of general local government.

(b) *Qualification as an urban county.* (1) A county will qualify as an urban county if such county meets the definition at § 570.3(3). As necessitated by this definition, the Secretary shall determine which counties have authority to carry out essential community development and housing assistance activities in their included units of general local government without the consent of the local governing body and which counties must execute cooperation agreements with such units to include them in the urban county for qualification and grant calculation purposes.

(2) At the time of urban county qualification, HUD may refuse to recognize the cooperation agreement of a unit of general local government in an urban county where, based on past performance and other available information, there is substantial evidence that such unit does not cooperate in the implementation of the essential community development or housing assistance activities or where legal impediments to such implementation exist, or where participation by a unit of general local government in noncompliance with the applicable law in subpart K would constitute noncompliance by the urban county. In such a case, the unit of general local government will not be permitted to participate in the urban county, and its population or other needs characteristics will not be considered in the determination of whether the county qualifies as an urban county or in determining the amount of funds to which the urban county may be entitled. HUD will not take this action unless the unit of general local government and the county have been given an opportunity to challenge HUD's determination and to informally consult with HUD concerning the proposed action.

(c) *Essential activities.* For purposes of this section, the term "essential community development and housing assistance activities" means community renewal and lower income housing activities, specifically urban renewal and publicly assisted housing. In determining whether a county has the required powers, the Secretary will consider both its authority and, where applicable, the authority of its designated agency or agencies.

(d) *Period of qualification.* (1) The qualification by HUD of an urban county shall remain effective for three successive Federal fiscal years regardless of changes in its population during that period, except as provided under paragraph (f) of this section and except as provided under §570.3(3) where the period of qualification shall be two successive Federal fiscal years.

(2) During the period of qualification, no included unit of general local government may withdraw from nor be removed from the urban county for HUD's grant computation purposes.

(3) If some portion of an urban county's unincorporated area becomes incorporated during the urban county qualification period, the newly incorporated unit of general local government shall not be excluded from the urban county nor shall it be eligible for a separate grant under subpart D, F, or I until the end of the urban county's current qualification period, unless the urban county fails to receive a grant for any year during that qualification period.

(e) *Grant ineligibility of included units of general local government.* (1) An included unit of general local government cannot become eligible for an entitlement grant as a metropolitan city during the period of qualification of the urban county (even if it becomes a principal city of a metropolitan area or its population surpasses 50,000 during that period). Rather, such a unit of general local government shall continue to be included as part of the urban county for the remainder of the urban county's qualification period, and no separate grant amount shall be calculated for the included unit.

(2) An included unit of general local government which is part of an urban county shall be ineligible to apply for grants under subpart F, or to be a recipient of assistance under subpart I, during the entire period of urban county qualification.

(f) *Failure of an urban county to receive a grant.* Failure of an urban county to receive a grant during any year shall terminate the existing qualification of that urban county, and that county shall requalify as an urban county before receiving an entitlement grant in any successive Federal fiscal year. Such termination shall release units of general local government included in the urban county, in subsequent years, from the prohibition to receive grants under paragraphs (d)(3), (e)(1) and (e)(2) of this section. For this purpose an urban county shall be deemed to have received a grant upon having satisfied the requirements of sections 104 (a), (b), (c), and (d) of the Act, without regard to adjustments which may be made to this grant amount under section 104(e) or 111 of the Act.

(g) *Notifications of the opportunity to be excluded.* Any county seeking to qualify for an entitlement grant as an urban county for any Federal fiscal year shall notify each unit of general local government which is located, in whole or in part, within the county and which would otherwise be included in the urban county, but which is eligible to elect to have its population excluded from that of the urban county, that it has the opportunity to make such an election, and that such an election, or the failure to make such an election, shall be effective for the period for which the county qualifies as an urban county. These notifications shall be made by a date specified by HUD. A unit of general local government which elects to be excluded from participation as a part of the urban county shall notify the county and HUD in writing by a date specified by HUD. Such a unit of government may subsequently elect to participate in the urban county for the remaining one or two year period by notifying HUD and the county, in writing, of such election by a date specified by HUD.

[53 FR 34449, Sept. 6, 1988, as amended at 56 FR 56127, Oct. 31, 1991; 68 FR 69582, Dec. 12, 2003]

§570.308 Joint requests.

(a) *Joint requests and cooperation agreements.* (1) Any urban county and any metropolitan city located, in whole or in part, within that county may submit a joint request to HUD to approve the inclusion of the metropolitan city as a part of the urban county for purposes of planning and implementing a joint community development and housing program. Such a joint request shall only be considered if submitted at the time the county is seeking a three year qualification or requalification as an urban county. Such a joint request shall, upon approval by HUD, remain effective for the period for which the county is qualified as an urban county. An urban county may be joined by more than one metropolitan city, but a metropolitan city located in more than one urban county may only be included in one urban county for any program year. A joint request shall be deemed approved by HUD unless HUD notifies the city and the county of its disapproval and the reasons therefore within 30 days of receipt of the request by HUD.

(2) Each metropolitan city and urban county submitting a joint request shall submit an executed cooperation agreement to undertake or to assist in the undertaking of essential community development and housing assistance activities, as defined in § 570.307(c).

(b) *Joint grant amount.* The grant amount for a joint recipient shall be the sum of the amounts authorized for the individual entitlement grantees, as described in section 106 of the Act. The urban county shall be the grant recipient.

(c) *Effect of inclusion.* Upon urban county qualification and HUD approval of the joint request and cooperation agreement, the metropolitan city shall be considered a part of the urban county for purposes of program planning and implementation for the period of the urban county qualification, and shall be treated the same as any other unit of general local government which is part of the urban county.

(d) *Submission requirements.* In requesting a grant under this part, the urban county shall make a single submission which meets the submission requirements of 24 CFR part 91 and covers all members of the joint recipient.

[53 FR 34449, Sept. 6, 1988, as amended at 60 FR 1915, Jan. 5, 1995]

§ 570.309 Restriction on location of activities.

CDBG funds may assist an activity outside the jurisdiction of the grantee only if the grantee determines that such an activity is necessary to further the purposes of the Act and the recipient's community development objectives, and that reasonable benefits from the activity will accrue to residents within the jurisdiction of the grantee. The grantee shall document the basis for such determination prior to providing CDBG funds for the activity.

[60 FR 56914, Nov. 9, 1995]

Subpart E—Special Purpose Grants

§ 570.400 General.

(a) *Applicability.* The policies and procedures set forth in subparts A, C, J, K, and O of this part shall apply to this subpart, except to the extent that they are specifically modified or augmented by the contents of this subpart, including specified exemptions described herein. The HUD Environmental Review Procedures contained in 24 CFR part 58 also apply to this subpart, unless otherwise specifically provided herein.

(b) *Data.* Wherever data are used in this subpart for selecting applicants for assistance or for determining grant amounts, the source of such data shall be the most recent information available from the U.S. Bureau of the Census which is referable to the same point or period of time.

(c) *Review of applications for discretionary assistance*—(1) *Review components.* An application for assistance under this subpart shall be reviewed by HUD to ensure that:

(i) The application is postmarked or received on or before any final date established by HUD;

(ii) The application is complete;

(iii) Required certifications have been included in the application; and

(iv) The application meets the specific program requirements listed in the FEDERAL REGISTER Notice published in connection with a competition for funding, and any other specific requirements listed under this subpart for each of the programs.

(2) *Timing and review.* HUD is not required by the Act to review and approve an application for assistance or a contract proposal within any specified time period. However, HUD will attempt to complete its review of any application/proposal within 75 days.

(3) *Notification to applicant/proposer.* HUD will notify the applicant/proposer in writing that the applicant/proposal has been approved, partially approved,

or disapproved. If an application/proposal is partially approved or disapproved, the applicant/proposer will be informed of the basis for HUD's decision. HUD may make conditional approvals under §570.304(d).

(d) *Program amendments.* (1) Recipients shall request prior written HUD approval for all program amendments involving changes in the scope or the location of approved activities.

(2) Any program amendments, whether or not they require HUD approval, must be fully documented in the recipient's records.

(e) *Performance reports.* Any performance report required of a discretionary assistance recipient shall be submitted in the form specified in this subpart, in the award document, or (if the report relates to a specific competition for an assistance award) in a form specified in a Notice published in the FEDERAL REGISTER.

(f) *Performance reviews and findings.* HUD may review the recipient's performance in carrying out the activities for which assistance is provided in a timely manner and in accordance with its approved application, all applicable requirements of this part and the terms of the assistance agreement. Findings of performance deficiencies may be cause for appropriate corrective and remedial actions under §570.910.

(g) *Funding sanctions.* Following notice and opportunity for informal consultation, HUD may withhold, reduce or terminate the assistance where any corrective or remedial actions taken under §570.910 fail to remedy a recipient's performance deficiencies, and the deficiencies are sufficiently substantial, in the judgment of HUD, to warrant sanctions.

(h) *Publication of availability of funds.* HUD will publish by Notice in the FEDERAL REGISTER each year the amount of funds available for the special purpose grants authorized by each section under this subpart.

[50 FR 37525, Sept. 16, 1985, as amended at 56 FR 18968, Apr. 24, 1991]

§570.401 Community adjustment and economic diversification planning assistance.

(a) *General*—(1) *Purpose.* The purpose of this program is to assist units of general local government in nonentitlement areas to undertake the planning of community adjustments and economic diversification activities, in response to physical, social, economic or governmental impacts on the communities generated by the actions of the Department of Defense (DoD) defined in paragraph (a)(2) of this section.

(2) *Impacts.* Funding under this section is available only to communities affected by one or more of the following DoD-related impacts:

(i) The proposed or actual establishment, realignment, or closure of a military installation;

(ii) The cancellation or termination of a DoD contract or the failure to proceed with an approved major weapon system program;

(iii) A publicly announced planned major reduction in DoD spending that would directly and adversely affect a unit of general local government and result in the loss of 1,000 or more full-time DoD and contractor employee positions over a five-year period in the unit of general local government and the surrounding area; or

(iv) The Secretary of HUD (in consultation with the Secretary of DoD) determines that an action described in paragraphs (a)(2)(i)–(iii) of this section is likely to have a direct and significant adverse consequence on the unit of general local government.

(3) *Form of awards.* Planning assistance will be awarded in the form of grants.

(4) *Program administration.* HUD will publish in the FEDERAL REGISTER early in each fiscal year the amount of funds to be available for that fiscal year for awards under this section. HUD will accept applications throughout the fiscal year, and will review and consider for funding each application according to the threshold and qualifying factors in paragraphs (f) and (g) of this section.

(b) *Definitions.* In addition to the definitions in §570.3 of this part, the following definitions apply to this section:

(1) *Adjustment planning.* Generally, developing plans and proposals in direct response to contraction or expansion of the local economy, or changes in the physical development or the social conditions of the community, resulting from a DoD-generated impact. Typically, this planning includes one or more of the following tasks: Collecting, updating, and analyzing data; identifying problems; formulating solutions; proposing long- and short-term policies; recommending public- and private-sector actions to implement community adjustments and economic diversification activities; securing citizen involvement; and coordinating with Federal, State, and local entities with respect to the DoD-related impacts.

(2) *Community adjustment.* Any proposed action to change the physical, economic, or social infrastructure within the jurisdiction or surrounding area, directly and appropriately in response to the DoD-generated impact.

(3) *Contract.* (i) Any defense contract in an amount not less than $5 million (without regard to the date on which the contract was awarded); and

(ii) Any subcontract that is entered into in connection with a contract (without regard to the effective date of the subcontract) and involves not less than $500,000.

(4) *Defense facility.* Any private facility producing goods or services pursuant to a defense contract.

(5) *DoD.* The Department of Defense.

(6) *Economic diversification activities.* Any public or private sector actions to change the local mix of industrial, commercial, and service sectors, or the mix of business ventures within a sector, that are intended to mitigate decline in the local economy resulting from DoD-generated impacts or, in the case of expansion of a military installation or a defense facility, that are intended to respond to new economic growth spawned by that expansion.

(7) *Military installation.* Any camp, post, station, base, yard, or other jurisdiction of a military department that is located within any of the several States, the District of Columbia, the Commonwealth of Puerto Rico, or Guam.

(8) *Realignment.* Any action that both reduces and relocates functions and civilian personnel positions, but does not include a reduction in force resulting from workload adjustments, reduced personnel or funding levels, or skill imbalances.

(9) *Section 107* means section 107 of the Housing and Community Development Act of 1974, 42 U.S.C. 5307. Section 107(b)(6) was added by section 801 of the Housing and Community Development Act of 1992 (Pub. L. 102–550, approved October 28, 1992).

(10) *Section 2391(b).* The Department of Defense adjustment planning program as set out in 10 U.S.C. 2391(b).

(11) *Small Cities CDBG Program.* The Community Development Block Grant program for nonentitlement areas in which the States have elected not to administer available program funds. The regulations governing this program are set out in subpart F of this part.

(12) *Surrounding area.* The labor market area as defined by the Bureau of Labor Statistics that:

(i) Includes all or part of the applicant's jurisdictions; and

(ii) Includes additional areas outside the jurisdiction.

(c) *Eligible applicants.* Any unit of general local government, excluding units of general government that are entitlement cities or are included in an urban county, and which does not include Indian Tribes.

(d) *Eligible activities.* Activities eligible for adjustment planning assistance include, generally:

(1) Initial assessments and quick studies of physical, social, economic, and fiscal impacts on the community;

(2) Preliminary identification of potential public and private sector actions needed for the community to initiate its response;

(3) If timely, modification of the applicant's current comprehensive plan or any functional plan, such as for housing, including shelter for the homeless, or for transportation or other physical infrastructure;

(4) If timely, modification of the applicant's current economic plans and programs, such as for business development, job training, or industrial or commercial development;

(5) Preparation for and conduct of initial community outreach activities to begin involving local citizens and the private sector in planning for adjustment and diversification;

(6) Environmental reviews related to DoD-related impacts;

(7) Initial identification of and coordination with Federal, State and local entities that may be expected to assist in the community's adjustment and economic development; and with State-designated enterprise zones, and Federal empowerment zones and enterprise communities when selected and announced.

(8) Any other planning activity that may enable the community to organize itself, establish a start-up capacity to plan, propose specific plans and programs, coordinate with appropriate public or private entities, or qualify more quickly for the more substantial planning assistance available from DoD.

(e) *Ineligible activities.* Activities ineligible for adjustment planning assistance are:

(1) Base re-use planning.

(2) Site planning, architectural and engineering studies, feasibility and cost analyses and similar planning for specific projects to implement community adjustment or economic diversification, unless as last resort funding for those applicants which are unable to obtain planning assistance from other sources.

(3) Planning by communities which are encroaching on military installations.

(4) Demonstration planning activities intended to evolve new planning techniques for impacted communities.

(5) Any planning activity proposed to supplement or replace planning that has been or is being assisted by the DoD Sec. 2391(b) adjustment planning program.

(6) Any other planning activity the purpose of which is not demonstrably in direct response to a DOD-related impact triggered by one or more of the four criteria specified in paragraph (a)(2) of this section.

(f) *Threshold requirements.* No application will qualify for funding unless it meets the following requirements:

(1) Verification by HUD that the applicant is a unit of general government in a nonentitlement area.

(2) Verification by HUD and DoD that a triggering event described in paragraph (a)(2) of this section has occurred or will occur.

(3) With respect to communities affected by the 49 base closings and 28 realignments listed by the 1991 Base Closure and Realignment Commission, verification by DoD that it has provided no prior funding and that the applicant may benefit from start-up planning assistance from HUD.

(4) Determination by HUD that the proposed planning activities are eligible.

(5) Determination by HUD that the submission requirements in paragraph (h) of this section have been satisfied.

(g) *Qualifying factors.* HUD will make funding decisions on qualified applications on the basis of the factors listed below, in the order of such applications received, while program funds remain available. HUD will also request and consider advise from DoD's Office of Economic Assistance concerning the relative merits of each application.

(1) The adequacy of the applicant's initial assessment of actual or probable impacts on the community and the surrounding area;

(2) The adequacy and appropriateness of the start-up planning envisioned by the applicant in response to the impacts;

(3) The type, extent, and adequacy of coordination that the applicant has achieved, or plans to achieve, in order to undertake planning for community adjustment and economic diversification.

(4) The cost-effectiveness of the proposed budget to carry out the planning work envisioned by the applicant;

(5) The capability of the organization the applicant proposes to do the planning;

(6) The credentials and experience of the key staff the applicant proposes to do the planning;

(7) The presence of significant private sector impact, as measured by the extent to which the DoD-generated impact is projected to decrease or increase the employment base by 10% or more;

(8) The presence of significant public sector impact, as measured by the extent to which the DoD-generated impact is projected to decrease or increase the applicant's capital and operating budgets for the next fiscal year by 10% or more;

(9) The degree of urgency, to the extent that a suddenly announced action, e.g. a plant closing, is officially scheduled to occur within a year of the date of application.

(h) *Submission requirements.* Applicants may submit applications at any time to: Director, Office of Technical Assistance, room 7214, 451 Seventh Street, SW., Washington, DC 20410. Each application (an original and three copies) shall include the following:

(1) The Standard Form SF–424 as a face sheet, signed and dated by a person authorized to represent and contractually or otherwise commit the applicant;

(2) A concise title and brief abstract of the proposed planning work, including the total cost;

(3) A narrative that:

(i) Documents one or more of the triggering events described in paragraph (a)(2) of this section that qualifies the applicant to apply for planning assistance for community adjustments and economic diversification;

(ii) Provides an initial assessment of actual or probable impacts on the applicant community and the surrounding area;

(iii) Provides an initial assessment of the type and extent of start-up planning envisioned by the applicant in response to the DoD-generated impact; and

(iv) Describes the measures by which the applicant has already coordinated, or plans to coordinate, with the DoD Office of Economic Assistance, the Economic Development Administration of the Department of Commerce, the Department of Labor, any military department, or any other appropriate Federal agency; appropriate State agencies, specifically including the agency administering the Small Cities CDBG Program; appropriate State-designated enterprise zones; appropriate Federal empowerment zones and enterprise communities, when selected and announced; appropriate other units of general local government in the nonentitlement area; appropriate businesses, corporations, and defense facilities concerned with impacts on the applicant community; and homeless nonprofit organizations, with respect to title V of the Stewart B. McKinney Act (42 U.S.C. 11411–11412), requiring the Federal property be considered for use in assisting the homeless.

(4) A Statement of Work describing the specific project tasks proposed to be undertaken in order to plan for community adjustment and economic diversification activities;

(5) A proposed budget showing the estimated costs and person-days of effort for each task, by cost categories, with supporting documentation of costs and a justification of the person-days of effort;

(6) A description of the qualifications of the proposed technical staff, including their names and resumes;

(7) A work plan that describes the schedule for accomplishing the tasks described in the Statement of Work, the time needed to do each task, and the elapsed time needed for all the tasks; and

(8) Other materials, as prescribed in the application kit; these materials will include required certifications dealing with: Drug-Free Workplace Requirements; Disclosure Regarding Payments to Influence Certain Federal Transactions; and Prohibition Regarding Excessive Force.

(i) *Approval procedures*—(1) *Acceptance.* HUD's acceptance of an application meeting the threshold requirements of paragraph (f) does not assure a commitment to provide funding or to provide the full amount requested. HUD may elect to negotiate both proposed tasks and budgets in order to promote more cost-effective planning.

(2) *Notification.* HUD will provide notification about whether a project will be funded, rejected, or held for further consideration by HUD and DoD.

(3) *Form of award.* HUD will award funds in the form of grants.

(4) *Administration.* Project administration will be governed by the terms of individual awards and by the following provisions of this part:

(i) Subpart A, § 570.5;

(ii) Subpart E, §§570.400(d), (e), (f), and (g);

(iii) Subpart J, §§570.500(c), 570.501, 570.502, 570.503, and 570.509;

(iv) Subpart K, §§570.601, 570.602, 570.609, 570.610, and 570.611.

The environmental review requirements of 24 CFR part 58 do not apply.

(Approved by the Office of Management and Budget under control number 2535–0084)

[59 FR 15016, Mar. 30, 1994]

§570.402 Technical assistance awards.

(a) *General.* (1) The purpose of the Community Development Technical Assistance Program is to increase the effectiveness with which States, units of general local government, and Indian tribes plan, develop, and administer assistance under title I and section 810 of the Act. Title I programs are the Entitlement Program (24 CFR part 570, subpart D); the section 108 Loan Guarantee Program (24 CFR part 570, subpart M); the Urban Development Action Grant Program (24 CFR part 570, subpart G); the HUD-administered Small Cities Program (24 CFR part 570, subpart F); the State-administered Program for Non-Entitlement Communities (24 CFR part 570, subpart I); the grants for Indian Tribes program (24 CFR part 571); and the Special Purpose Grants for Insular Areas, Community Development Work Study and Historically Black Colleges and Universities (24 CFR part 570, subpart E).

(2) Funding under this section is awarded for the provision of technical expertise in planning, managing or carrying out such programs including the activities being or to be assisted thereunder and other actions being or to be undertaken for the purpose of the program, such as increasing the effectiveness of public service and other activities in addressing identified needs, meeting applicable program requirements (e.g., citizen participation, nondiscrimination, 2 CFR part 200, increasing program management or capacity building skills, attracting business or industry to CDBG assisted economic development sites or projects, assisting eligible CDBG subrecipients such as neighborhood nonprofits or small cities in how to obtain CDBG funding from cities and States. The provision of technical expertise in other areas which may have some tangential benefit or effect on a program is insufficient to qualify for funding.

(3) Awards may be made pursuant to HUD solicitations for assistance applications or procurement contract proposals issued in the form of a publicly available document which invites the submission of applications or proposals within a prescribed period of time. HUD may also enter into agreements with other Federal agencies for awarding the technical assistance funds:

(i) Where the Secretary determines that such funding procedures will achieve a particular technical assistance objective more effectively and the criteria for making the awards will be consistent with this section, or

(ii) The transfer of funds to the other Federal agency for use under the terms of the agreement is specifically authorized by law. The Department will not accept or fund unsolicited proposals.

(b) *Definitions.* (1) *Areawide planning organization* (APO) means an organization authorized by law or local agreement to undertake planning and other activities for a metropolitan or nonmetropolitan area.

(2) *Technical assistance* means the facilitating of skills and knowledge in planning, developing and administering activities under title I and section 810 of the Act in entities that may need but do not possess such skills and knowledge, and includes assessing programs and activities under title I.

(c) *Eligible applicants.* Eligible applicants for award of technical assistance funding are:

(1) States, units of general local government, APOs, and Indian Tribes; and

(2) Public and private non-profit or for-profit groups, including educational institutions, qualified to provide technical assistance to assist such governmental units to carry out the title I or Urban Homesteading programs. An applicant group must be designated as a technical assistance provider to a unit of government's title I program or Urban Homesteading program by the chief executive officer of each unit to be assisted, unless the assistance is limited to conferences/workshops attended by more than one unit of government.

(d) *Eligible activities.* Activities eligible for technical assistance funding include:

(1) The provision of technical or advisory services;

(2) The design and operation of training projects, such as workshops, seminars, or conferences;

(3) The development and distribution of technical materials and information; and

(4) Other methods of demonstrating and making available skills, information and knowledge to assist States, units of general local government, or Indian Tribes in planning, developing, administering or assessing assistance under title I and Urban Homesteading programs in which they are participating or seeking to participate.

(e) *Ineligible activities.* Activities for which costs are ineligible under this section include:

(1) In the case of technical assistance for States, the cost of carrying out the administration of the State CDBG program for non-entitlement communities;

(2) The cost of carrying out the activities authorized under the title I and Urban Homesteading programs, such as the provision of public services, construction, rehabilitation, planning and administration, for which the technical assistance is to be provided;

(3) The cost of acquiring or developing the specialized skills or knowledge to be provided by a group funded under this section;

(4) Research activities;

(5) The cost of identifying units of governments needing assistance (except that the cost of selecting recipients of technical assistance under the provisions of paragraph (k) is eligible); or

(6) Activities designed primarily to benefit HUD, or to assist HUD in carrying out the Department's responsibilities; such as research, policy analysis of proposed legislation, training or travel of HUD staff, or development and review of reports to the Congress.

(f) *Criteria for competitive selection.* In determining whether to fund competitive applications or proposals under this section, the Department will use the following criteria:

(1) *For solicited assistance applications.* The Department will use two types of criteria for reviewing and selecting competitive assistance applications solicited by HUD:

(i) Evaluation criteria: These criteria will be used to rank applications according to weights which may vary with each competition:

(A) Probable effectiveness of the application in meeting needs of localities and accomplishing project objectives;

(B) Soundness and cost-effectiveness of the proposed approach;

(C) Capacity of the applicant to carry out the proposed activities in a timely and effective fashion;

(D) The extent to which the results may be transferable or applicable to other title I or Urban Homesteading program participants.

(ii) Program policy criteria: These factors may be used by the selecting official to select a range of projects that would best serve program objectives for a particular competition:

(A) Geographic distribution;

(B) Diversity of types and sizes of applicant entities; and

(C) Diversity of methods, approaches, or kinds of projects.

The Department will publish a Notice of Fund Availability (NOFA) in the FEDERAL REGISTER for each competition indicating the objective of the technical assistance, the amount of funding available, the application procedures, including the eligible applicants and activities to be funded, any special conditions applicable to the solicitation, including any requirements for a matching share or for commitments for CDBG or other title I funding to carry out eligible activities for which the technical assistance is to be provided, the maximum points to be awarded each evaluation criterion for the purpose of ranking applications, and any special factors to be considered in assigning the points to each evaluation criterion. The Notice will also indicate which program policy factors will be used, the impact of those factors on the selection process, the justification for their use and, if appropriate, the relative priority of each program policy factor.

(2) *For competitive procurement contract bids/proposals.* The Department's

criteria for review and selection of solicited bids/proposals for procurement contracts will be described in its public announcement of the availability of an Invitation for Bids (IFB) or a Request for Proposals (RFP). The public notice, solicitation and award of procurement contracts, when used to acquire technical assistance, shall be procured in accordance with the Federal Acquisition Regulation (48 CFR chapter 1) and the HUD Acquisition Regulation (48 CFR chapter 24).

(g) *Submission procedures.* Solicited assistance applications shall be submitted in accordance with the time and place and content requirements described in the Department's NOFA. Solicited bids/proposals for procurement contracts shall be submitted in accordance with the requirements in the IFB or RFP.

(h) *Approval procedures*—(1) *Acceptance.* HUD's acceptance of an application or proposal for review does not imply a commitment to provide funding.

(2) *Notification.* HUD will provide notification of whether a project will be funded or rejected.

(3) *Form of award.* (i) HUD will award technical assistance funds as a grant, cooperative agreement or procurement contract, consistent with this section, the Federal Grant and Cooperative Agreement Act of 1977, 31 U.S.C. 6301–6308, the HUD Acquisition Regulation, and the Federal Acquisition Regulation.

(ii) When HUD's primary purpose is the transfer of technical assistance to assist the recipients in support of the title I or Section 810 programs, an assistance instrument (grant or cooperative agreement) will be used. A grant instrument will be used when substantial Federal involvement is not anticipated. A cooperative agreement will be used when substantial Federal involvement is anticipated. When a cooperative agreement is selected, the agreement will specify the nature of HUD's anticipated involvement in the project.

(iii) A contract will be used when HUD's primary purpose is to obtain a provider of technical assistance to act on the Department's behalf. In such cases the Department will define the specific tasks to be performed. However, nothing in this section shall preclude the Department from awarding a procurement contract in any other case when it is determined to be in the Department's best interests.

(4) *Administration.* Project administration will be governed by the terms of individual awards and relevant regulations. As a general rule, proposals will be funded to operate for one to two years, and periodic and final reports will be required.

(i) *Environmental and intergovernmental review.* The requirements for Environmental Reviews and Intergovernmental Reviews do not apply to technical assistance awards.

(j) *Selection of recipients of technical assistance.* Where under the terms of the funding award the recipient of the funding is to select the recipients of the technical assistance to be provided, the funding recipient shall publish, and publicly make available to potential technical assistance recipients, the availability of such assistance and the specific criteria to be used for the selection of the recipients to be assisted. Selected recipients must be entities participating or planning to participate in the title I or Urban Homesteading programs or activities for which the technical assistance is to be provided.

(Approved by the Office of Management and Budget under control numbers 2535–0085 and 2535–0084)

[56 FR 41938, Aug. 26, 1991, as amended at 80 FR 75937, Dec. 7, 2015]

§570.403 New Communities.

The regulations for New Communities grants in this section, that were effective immediately before April 19, 1996, will continue to govern the rights and obligations of recipients and HUD with respect to grants under the New Communities program.

[61 FR 11476, Mar. 20, 1996]

§570.404 Historically Black colleges and universities program.

(a) *General.* Grants under this section will be awarded to historically Black colleges and universities to expand their role and effectiveness in addressing community development needs, including neighborhood revitalization, housing and economic development in their localities, consistent with the purposes of title I of the Housing and Community Development Act of 1974.

(b) *Eligible applicants.* Only historically Black colleges and universities (as determined by the Department of Education in accordance with that Department's responsibilities under Executive Order 12677, dated April 28, 1989) are eligible to submit applications.

(c) *Eligible activities.* Activities that may be funded under this section are those eligible under §§ 570.201 through 570.207, provided that any activity which is required by State or local law to be carried out by a governmental entity may not be funded under this section. Notwithstanding the provisions of §§ 570.200(g), grants under this section are not subject to the 20 percent limitation on planning and program administration costs, as defined in §§ 570.205 and 570.206, respectively.

(d) *Applications.* Applications will only be accepted from eligible applicants in response to a Request for Applications (RFA) which will be issued either concurrently with or after the publication of a Notice of Funding Availability (NOFA) published in the FEDERAL REGISTER. The NOFA will describe any special objectives sought to be achieved by the funding to be provided, including any limitations on the type of activities to be funded to achieve the objectives, points to be awarded to each of the selection criteria listed in paragraph (e) of this section, and any special factors to be evaluated in assigning points under the selection factors to achieve the stated objectives. The NOFA will also state the deadline for the submission of applications, the total funding available for the competition, and the maximum amount of individual grants. The NOFA will include further information and instructions for the submission of acceptable applications to HUD.

(e) *Selection criteria.* Each application submitted under this section will be evaluated by HUD using the following criteria:

(1) The extent to which the applicant addresses the objectives published in the NOFA and the RFA.

(2) The extent to which the applicant demonstrates to HUD that the proposed activities will have a substantial impact in achieving the stated objectives.

(3) The special needs of the applicant or locality to be met in carrying out the proposed activities, particularly with respect to benefiting low- and moderate-income persons.

(4) The feasibility of the proposed activities, *i.e.*, their technical and financial feasibility, for achieving the stated objectives, including local support for activities proposed to be carried out in the locality and any matching funds proposed to be provided from other sources.

(5) The capability of the applicant to carry out satisfactorily the proposed activities in a timely fashion, including satisfactory performance in carrying out any previous HUD-assisted projects or activities.

(6) In the case of proposals/projects of approximately equal merit, HUD retains the right to exercise discretion in selecting projects in a manner that would best serve the program objectives, with consideration given to the needs of localities, types of activities proposed, an equitable geographical distribution, and program balance.

(f) *Certifications.* (1) Certifications required to be submitted by applicants shall be as prescribed in the RFA packages.

(2) In the absence of independent evidence which tends to challenge in a substantial manner the certifications made by the applicant, the required certifications will be accepted by HUD. If independent evidence is available to HUD, however, HUD may require further information or assurances to be submitted in order to determine whether the applicant's certifications are satisfactory.

(g) *Multiyear funding commitments.* (1) HUD may make funding commitments of up to five years, subject to the availability of appropriations. In determining the number of years for which a commitment will be made, HUD will consider the nature of the activities proposed, the capability of the recipient to carry out the proposed activities, and year-by-year funding requirements.

(2) Awards will be made on the basis of a 12-month period of performance.

Once a recipient has been selected for a multi-year award, that recipient would not be required to compete in a competition for the subsequent funding years covered by the multi-year funding commitment. Recipients performing satisfactorily will be invited to submit applications for subsequent funding years in accordance with requirements outlined in the Notice of Funding Availability and Request for Grant Application. Subject to the availability of appropriations, subsequent-year funding will be determined by the following:

(i) The recipient has submitted all reports required for the previous year or years in a timely, complete and satisfactory manner in accordance with the terms and conditions of the grant.

(ii) The recipient has submitted sufficient evidence to demonstrate successful completion of the tasks and deliverables of the grant. A determination of satisfactory performance will be made by HUD based upon evidence of task completions provided by the recipient, along with data from client feedback and site evaluations.

(iii) The recipient has submitted the next annual application.

(iv) The subsequent year's application is consistent with that described in the original application.

(3) Recipients participating in multiyear funding projects are not eligible to apply for additional grants for the same project or activity subject area for which they are receiving funds. Recipients are, however, eligible to compete for grants for other project or activity areas.

(h) *Selection and notification.* The HUD decision to approve, disapprove or conditionally approve an application shall be communicated in writing to the applicant.

(i) *Environmental and intergovernmental review.* The requirements for Intergovernmental Reviews do not apply to HBCU awards. HUD will conduct an environmental review in accordance with 24 CFR part 50 before giving its approval to a proposal.

[56 FR 18968, Apr. 24, 1991]

§570.405 The insular areas.

(a) *Eligible applicants.* Eligible applicants are Guam, the Virgin Islands, American Samoa, the Trust Territory of the Pacific Islands, and the Commonwealth of the Northern Mariana Islands.

(b) *Threshold requirements.* HUD shall review each grantee's progress on outstanding grants made under this section based on the grantee's performance report, the timeliness of closeouts and compliance with fund management requirements and pertinent regulations, taking into consideration the size of the grant and the degree and complexity of the program. If HUD determines upon such review that the applicant does not have the capacity effectively to administer a new grant, or a portion of a new grant, in addition to grants currently under administration, the applicant shall not be invited to submit an application for the current year's funding.

(c) *Previous audit findings and outstanding monetary obligations.* HUD shall not accept for review an application from an applicant that has either an outstanding audit finding for any HUD program, or an outstanding monetary obligation to HUD that is in arrears, or for which a repayment schedule has not been established and agreed to. The Field Office manager may waive this restriction if he or she finds that the applicant has made a good faith effort to clear the audit. In no instance, however, shall a waiver be provided when funds are due HUD, unless a satisfactory arrangement for repayment of the debt has been made and payments are current.

(d) *Criteria for funding.* The Secretary shall establish, for each fiscal year, an amount for which eligible applicants may apply. Grant amounts will be based on population of the applicant and its performance in previous years. In determining performance, HUD will consider program achievements and the applicant's effectiveness in using program funds. Effectiveness in using program funds shall be measured by reviewing audit, monitoring and performance reports.

(e) *Application and performance reporting.* Application and performance reporting requirements are as follows:

(1) Applicants must submit applications within 90 days of the notification of the grant amount from HUD.

(2) Applicants shall prepare and publish or post a proposed application in accordance with the citizen participation requirements of paragraph (h) of this section.

(3) Applicants shall submit to HUD a final application containing its community development objectives and activities. This application shall be submitted to the appropriate HUD office, together with the required certifications, in a form prescribed by HUD.

(4) Grant recipients must submit to HUD an annual performance report on progress achieved on previously funded grants. Grant recipients must submit the report at a time and in a format determined by HUD. The report should be made available to citizens in accordance with the requirements of paragraph (h)(1)(iv) of this section.

(f) *Costs incurred by the applicant.* (1) Notwithstanding any other provision of this part, HUD will not reimburse or recognize any costs incurred by an applicant before submission of the application to HUD.

(2) Normally, HUD will not reimburse or recognize costs incurred before HUD approval of the application for funding. However, under unusual circumstances, the Field office manager may consider and conditionally approve written requests to recognize and reimburse costs that will be incurred after submission of the application but before it is approved where failure to do so would impose undue or unreasonable hardship on the applicant. Conditional approvals will be made only before the costs are incurred and where the conditions for release of funds have been met in accordance with 24 CFR 58.22, and with the understanding that HUD has no obligation whatsoever to approve the application or to reimburse the applicant should the application be disapproved.

(g) *Criteria for conditional approval.* HUD may approve a grant subject to specified conditions. In any such case, the obligation and utilization of funds may be restricted. The reasons for the conditional approval and the actions necessary to remove the conditions shall be specified. Failure of the applicant to satisfy the conditions may result in a termination of the grant. A conditional approval may be granted under any of the following circumstances:

(1) When local environmental reviews under 24 CFR part 58 have not yet been completed;

(2) To ensure that actual provision of other resources required to complete the proposed activities will be available within a reasonable period of time;

(3) To ensure that a project can be completed within its estimated costs;

(4) Where the grantee is required to satisfy an outstanding debt due to HUD under a payment plan executed between the grantee and the Department;

(5) Pending resolution of problems related to specific projects or the capability of the grantee to obtain resources needed to carry out, operate or maintain the project; or

(6) Pending approval of site and neighborhood standards for proposed housing projects.

(h) *Citizen participation.* (1) The applicant shall provide for appropriate citizen participation in the application and amendment process. The applicant must, at least, do each of the following:

(i) Furnish citizens with information concerning the amount of funds available for community development and housing activities and the range of activities that may be undertaken, including the estimated amount proposed to be used for activities that will benefit persons of low and moderate income, and the plans of the grantee for minimizing displacement of persons as a result of activities assisted with such funds and to assist persons actually displaced;

(ii) Hold one or more public hearings (scheduled at convenient times and places) to obtain the views of citizens on community development and housing needs;

(iii) Develop and publish or post the community development statement in such a manner as to afford affected citizens an opportunity to examine its contents and to submit comments;

(iv) Afford citizens an opportunity to review and comment on the applicant's performance under any community development block grant.

(2) Before submitting the application to HUD, the applicant shall certify that it has:

(i) Met the requirements of paragraph (h)(1) of this section;

(ii) Considered any comments and views expressed by citizens; and

(iii) If appropriate, modified the application accordingly and made the modified application available to citizens.

[50 FR 37526, Sept. 16, 1985, as amended at 60 FR 56914, Nov. 9, 1995; 61 FR 32269, June 21, 1996]

EFFECTIVE DATE NOTE: At 61 FR 32269, June 21, 1996, §570.405(e)(4) was revised. This paragraph contains information collection and recordkeeping requirements and will not become effective until approval has been given by the Office of Management and Budget.

§570.406 Formula miscalculation grants.

(a) *General.* Grants under this section will be made to States and units of general local government determined by the Secretary to have received insufficient amounts under section 106 of the Act as a result of a miscalculation of its share of funds under such section.

(b) *Application.* Since the grant is to correct a technical error in the formula amount which should have been awarded under section 106, no application is required.

(c) *Use of funds.* The use of funds shall be subject to the requirements, certifications and Final Statement otherwise applicable to the grantee's section 106 grant funds provided for the fiscal year in which the grant under this section is made.

(d) *Unavailability of funds.* If sufficient funds are not available to make the grant in the fiscal year in which the Secretary makes the determination required in paragraph (a) of this section, the grant will be made, subject to the availability of appropriations for this subpart, in the next fiscal year.

[56 FR 41940, Aug. 26, 1991]

§570.410 Special Projects Program.

(a) *Program objectives.* The Community Development Special Projects Program enables HUD to award grants to States and units of general local government, subject to availability of funds, for special projects that address community development activities or techniques consistent with the purposes of title I of the Housing and Community Development Act of 1974, as amended.

(b) *Eligible applicants.* Only States and units of general local government (as defined in §570.3) are eligible to submit proposals or applications for Special Projects grants. Proposals or applications may be submitted by eligible applicants on behalf of themselves, on behalf of other eligible applicants, or jointly by more than one eligible applicant.

(c) *Eligible activities.* (1) Project activities that may be funded under this section are those eligible under 24 CFR part 570—Community Development Block Grants, subpart C—Eligible Activities. No more than twenty (20) percent of the funds awarded under this section may be used for overall program administration or planning activities eligible under §§570.205 and 570.206.

(2) The amount of funds awarded to a unit of general local government under this section that may be used for public service activities is limited. The applicant may use whichever of the following methods of calculation yields the highest amount:

(i) Fifteen percent of the special projects grant;

(ii) An amount equal to 15 percent of the sum of special project grant funds plus grant funds received for the same origin year under the Entitlement or State program, less the amount of the Entitlement or State program grant funds which will be used for other public service activities; or

(iii) In the case of an applicant that is an Entitlement grantee subject to the exception in §570.201(e)(2), an amount equal to the amount of the Entitlement grant funds received for the same origin year that may be used for public service activities, less the amount of the Entitlement grant funds which will be used for other public service activities.

(d) *Proposals.* Eligible applicants may submit unsolicited proposals. HUD may ask proposers to submit additional information if necessary for evaluation. There is no HUD commitment to fund any unsolicited proposal regardless of its merit. If HUD elects to fund a proposal, it will request that the proposer submit a formal application.

(1) Three (3) copies of a proposal must be sent to the address stated in (3), below. Each proposal submitted pursuant to this section shall be evaluated by HUD using the following criteria:

(i) The extent to which the proposal satisfies purposes of this title and addresses a special community development need.

(ii) The eligibility of proposed activities.

(iii) The feasibility of the project; i.e., its technical and financial feasibility for achieving the goals stated in the proposal.

(iv) The capacity of the proposer to carry out satisfactorily the proposed project activities.

(2) If the proposal is submitted jointly by, or on behalf of, more than one eligible applicant, the proposal must:

(i) Contain a cooperation agreement signed by the Chief Executive Officer of each participating jurisdiction which specifies concurrence with the purpose and intent of the proposal and intent to comply with grant requirements;

(ii) Address problems faced by all jurisdictions listed in the proposal; and,

(iii) Be submitted by the lead jurisdiction. The lead jurisdiction shall be responsible for overall coordination and administration of the project.

(3) Unsolicited proposals may be submitted any time during the year. However, if there are no funds available for such proposals, they will be returned without review. Proposals shall contain a Standard Form 424 signed by the Chief Executive Officer of the State or unit of general local government. They shall be sent to: Department of Housing and Urban Development, Office of Community Planning and Development, 451 Seventh Street, SW., Washington, DC 20410, Attention: Director, Office of Program Policy Development, CPP.

(e) *Applications.* Applications are accepted only from eligible applicants in response to letters of solicitations, or to competition announcements published in Notices in the FEDERAL REGISTER. Submission requirements and criteria to be used by HUD to evaluate solicited applications and instructions regarding their submission shall be stated in each Notice or letter.

(f) *Certifications.* Applications shall contain the certifications required by 24 CFR 570.303, except that regarding citizen participation: The applicant must certify that citizens likely to be affected by the project, particularly low- and moderate-income persons, have been provided an opportunity to comment on the proposal or application. If the application is submitted jointly, or on behalf of more than one jurisdiction, each jurisdiction shall submit the required certifications.

(g) *Selection and notification.* The HUD decision to approve, disapprove or conditionally approve a proposal or application shall be communicated in writing to the applicant.

[47 FR 30054, July 12, 1982, as amended at 54 FR 31672, Aug. 1, 1989; 55 FR 29309, July 18, 1990; 56 FR 56127, Oct. 31, 1991; 80 FR 69870, Nov. 12, 2015]

§ 570.411 Joint Community Development Program.

(a) *General.* Grants under this section will be awarded to institutions of higher education or to States and local governments applying jointly with institutions of higher education. Institutions of higher education must demonstrate the capacity to carry out activities under title I of the Housing and Community Development Act of 1974. For ease of reference, this program may be called the Joint CD Program.

(b) *Definitions.*

Demonstrated capacity to carry out eligible activities under title I means recent satisfactory activity by the institution of higher education's staff designated to work on the program, including subcontractors and consultants firmly committed to work on the proposed activities, in title I programs or similar programs without the need for oversight by a State or unit of general local government.

Institution of higher education means a college or university granting 4-year degrees and accredited by a national or regional accrediting agency recognized by the U.S. Department of Education.

(c) *Eligible applicants.* Institutions of higher education or States and units of general local government jointly with institutions of higher education may apply. Institutions of higher education with demonstrated capacity to carry out eligible activities under title I may apply on their own, without the joint participation of a State or unit of general local government. States or unit of general local governments must file jointly with an institution of higher education. For these approved joint applications, the grant will be made to the State or unit of general local government and the institution of higher education jointly. If an eligible applicant is an institution of higher education, it will not be funded more than once for the same kinds of activities. These grantees may not receive funding under a subsequent NOFA if it has the same program objectives as the one under which the grantee previously received funding. However, a State or unit of general local government is eligible to apply if it files jointly with a different institution of higher education in each NOFA cycle. HUD may further limit the type of eligible applicant to be funded. Any such limitations will be contained in the Notice of Funding Availability described below in paragraph (h) of this section.

(d) *Role of participants in joint applications.* An institution of higher education and a State or unit of general local government may carry out eligible activities approved in joint applications. Where there are joint applicants, the grant will be made to both and both will be responsible for oversight, compliance, and performance. The application will have to clearly delineate the role of each applicant in the joint application. Any funding sanctions or other remedial actions by HUD for noncompliance or nonperformance, whether by the State or unit of general local government or by the institution of higher education, shall be taken against both grantees.

(e) *Eligible activities.* Activities that may be funded under this section are those eligible under 24 CFR part 570—Community Development Block Grants, subpart C—Eligible Activities. These activities may be designed to assist residents of colonias, as defined in section 916(d) of the Cranston-Gonzalez National Affordable Housing Act (42 U.S.C. 5306 note), to improve living conditions and standards within colonias. HUD may limit the activities to be funded. Any such limitations will be contained in the Notice of Funding Availability described in paragraph (h) of this section.

(f) *Applications.* Applications will only be accepted from eligible applicants in response to a publication of a Notice of Funding Availability (NOFA) published by HUD in the FEDERAL REGISTER.

(g) *Local approval.* (1) Where an institution of higher education is the applicant, each unit of general local government that is an entitlement jurisdiction where an activity is to take place must approve the activity and certify that the activity is consistent with its Consolidated Plan.

(2) Where a State is the joint applicant and it proposes to carry out an activity within the jurisdiction of one or more units of general local government, then each such unit must approve the activity and state that the activity is consistent with its Consolidated Plan.

(3) These approvals and findings must accompany each application and may take the form of a letter by the chief executive officer of each unit of general local government affected or a resolution of the legislative body of each such unit of general local government.

(h) *NOFA contents.* The NOFA will describe any special objectives sought to be achieved by the funding to be provided, including any limitations on the type of activities to be funded to achieve the objectives, any limitations on the type of eligible applicants, and points to be awarded to each of the selection criteria and any special factors to be evaluated in assigning points under the selection criteria to achieve the stated objectives. The NOFA will also state the deadline for the submission of applications, the total funding available for the competition, the period of performance and the maximum and minimum amount of individual grants. The NOFA will also state which of the various possible levels of competition HUD will use: national and/or regional or entitlement areas vs. nonentitlement areas; and States or units of general local government vs. institutions of higher education vs. institutions of higher education with a demonstrated capacity. The NOFA will include further information and instructions for the submission of acceptable applications to HUD.

(i) *Selection criteria.* Each application submitted under this section will be evaluated by HUD using the following criteria:

(1) The extent to which the applicant addresses the objectives published in the NOFA and demonstrates how the proposed activities will have a substantial impact in achieving the objectives.

(2) The extent of the needs to be addressed by the proposed activities, particularly with respect to benefiting low- and moderate-income persons and residents of colonias, where applicable.

(3) The feasibility of the proposed activities, i.e., their technical and financial feasibility, for achieving the stated objectives.

(4) The capability of the applicant to carry out satisfactorily the proposed activities in a timely fashion, including satisfactory performance in carrying out any previous HUD-assisted projects or activities.

(5) The extent of commitment to fair housing and equal opportunity, as indicated by such factors as previous HUD monitoring/compliance activity, actions to promote minority- and women-owned business enterprise, affirmatively furthering fair housing issues, and nondiscriminatory delivery of services.

(j) *Selection discretion.* HUD retains the right to exercise discretion in selecting projects in a manner that would best serve the program objectives, with consideration given to the needs of States and units of general local government and institutions of higher education, types of activities proposed, an equitable geographical distribution, and program balance. The NOFA will state whether HUD will use this discretion in any specific competition.

(k) *Certifications.* (1) Certifications, including those indicating that applicants have adhered to all civil rights requirements under subpart K of this part and the Americans with Disabilities Act of 1990, required to be submitted by applicants shall be as prescribed in the NOFA.

(2) In the absence of independent evidence which tends to challenge in a substantial manner the certifications made by the applicant, the required certifications will be accepted by HUD. However, if independent evidence is available, HUD may require further information or assurances to be submitted in order to determine whether the applicant's certifications are satisfactory.

(l) *Consolidated plan.* An applicant that proposes any housing activities as part of its application will be required to submit a certification that these activities are consistent with the Consolidated Plan of the jurisdiction to be served.

(m) *Citizen participation.* The citizen participation requirements of §§ 570.301, 570.431, 570.485(c) and 570.486(a) are modified to require the following: The applicant must certify that citizens likely to be affected by the project regardless of race, color, creed, sex, national origin, familial status, or handicap, particularly low- and moderate-income persons, have been provided an opportunity to comment on the proposal or application.

(n) *Environmental and Intergovernmental Review.* The requirements for Intergovernmental Reviews do not apply to these awards. When required, an environmental review in accordance with 24 CFR part 58 must be carried out by the State or unit of general local government when it is the applicant. HUD will conduct any required environmental review when an institution of higher education is the applicant.

(Approved by the Office of Management and Budget under control number 2535–0084)

[60 FR 15837, Mar. 27, 1995]

§ 570.415 Community Development Work Study Program.

(a) *Applicability and objectives.* HUD makes grants under CDWSP to institutions of higher education, either directly or through areawide planning organizations or States, for the purpose of providing assistance to economically disadvantaged and minority students who participate in a work study program while enrolled in full-time graduate programs in community and economic development, community planning, and community management. The primary objectives of the program are to attract economically disadvantaged and minority students to careers in community and economic development, community planning, and community management, and to provide a cadre of well-qualified professionals to plan, implement and administer local community development programs.

(b) *Definitions.* The following definitions apply to CDWSP:

Applicant means an institution of higher education, a State, or an areawide planning organization that submits an application for assistance under CDWSP.

Areawide planning organization (APO) means an organization authorized by law or by interlocal agreement to undertake planning and other activities for a metropolitan or nonmetropolitan area. For an organization operating in a nonmetropolitan area to be considered an APO, its jurisdiction must cover at least one county.

CDWSP means the Community Development Work Study Program.

Community building means community and economic development, community planning, community management, land use and housing activities.

Community building academic program or academic program means a graduate degree program whose purpose and focus is to educate students in community building. "Community building academic program" or "academic program" includes but is not limited to graduate degree programs in community and economic development, community planning, community management, public administration, public policy, urban economics, urban management, and urban planning. "Community building academic program" or "academic program" excludes social and humanistic fields such as law, economics (except for urban economics), education and history. "Community building academic program" or "academic program" excludes joint degree programs except where both joint degree fields have the purpose and focus of educating students in community building.

Economically disadvantaged and minority students means students who satisfy all applicable guidelines established at the participating institution of higher education to measure financial need for academic scholarship or loan assistance, including, but not limited to, students who are Black, American Indian/Alaskan Native, Hispanic, or Asian/Pacific Island, and including students with disabilities.

Institution of higher education means a public or private educational institution that offers a community building academic program and that is accredited by an accrediting agency or association recognized by the Secretary of Education under 34 CFR part 602.

Recipient means an approved applicant that executes a grant agreement with HUD.

Student means a student enrolled in an eligible full-time academic program. He/she must be a first-year student in a two-year graduate program. Students enrolled in Ph.D. programs are ineligible.

Student with disabilities means a student who meets the definition of "person with disabilities" in the Americans with Disabilities Act of 1990.

(c) *Assistance provided*—(1) *Types of assistance available.* HUD provides funding in the form of grants to recipients who make assistance available to eligible students. Grants are provided to cover the costs of student assistance and for an administrative allowance.

(i) *Student assistance.* Grants are made to recipients to cover the costs of assistance provided to eligible students in the form of student stipends, tuition support, and additional support.

(A) *Student stipend.* The amount of the student stipend is based upon the prevailing hourly rate for initial entry positions in community building and the number of hours worked by the student at the work placement assignment, except that the hourly rate used should be sufficiently high to allow a student to earn the full stipend without working over 20 hours per week during the school year and 40 hours per week during the summer. The amount of the stipend the student receives may not exceed the actual amount earned, up to $9,000 per year.

(B) *Tuition support and additional support.* The amount of support for tuition, fees, books, and travel related to the academic program, workplace assignment or conferences may not exceed actual costs incurred or $5,000 per year, whichever is higher. The conferences are limited to those dealing with community building, sponsored by professional organizations.

(ii) *Administrative allowance.* HUD provides an allowance to recipients to cover the administrative costs of the program. The administrative allowance is $1,000 per year for each student participating in the program.

(2) *Number of students assisted.* The minimum number of students that may be assisted is three students per participating institution of higher education. If an APO or State receives assistance for a program that is conducted by two or more institutions of higher education, each participating institution must have a minimum of three students in the program. The maximum number of students that may be assisted under CDWSP is five students per participating institution of higher education.

(d) *Recipient eligibility and responsibilities*—(1) *Recipient eligibility.* (i) The following organizations are eligible to apply for assistance under the program:

(A) *Institutions of higher education.* Institutions of higher education offering a community building academic program are eligible for assistance under CDWSP.

(B) *Areawide planning organizations and States.* An APO or a State may apply for assistance for a program to be conducted by two or more institutions of higher education. Institutions participating in an APO program must be located within the particular area that is served by the APO and is identified by the State law or interlocal agreement creating the APO. Institutions of higher education participating in a State program must be located within the State.

(ii) To be eligible in future funding competitions for CDWSP, recipients are required to maintain a 50-percent rate of graduation from a CDWSP-funded academic program.

(iii) If an institution of higher education that submits an individual application is also included in the application of an APO or State, then the separate individual application of the institution of higher education will be disregarded. Additionally, if an institution of higher education is included in the application of both an APO and a State, then the references to the institution in the application of the State will be stricken. The State's application will then be ineligible if fewer than two institutions of higher education remain as participants in the State's application.

(2) *Recipient responsibilities.* (i) The recipient is responsible for the administration of the program, for compliance with all program requirements, and for the coordination of program activities carried out by the work placement agencies and (if the recipient is an APO or State), by the participating institutions of higher education. The recipient must:

(A) Recruit and select students for participation in CDWSP. The recipient shall establish recruitment procedures that identify economically disadvantaged and minority students pursuing careers in community building, and make such students aware of the availability of assistance opportunities. Students must be selected before the beginning of the semester for which funding has been provided.

(B) Recruit and select work placement agencies, and negotiate and execute agreements covering each work placement assignment.

(C) Refer participating students to work placement agencies and assist students in the selection of work placement assignments.

(D) Assign sufficient staff to administer and supervise the program on a day-to-day basis, and, where the recipient is an APO or State, to monitor the activities of the work study coordinating committee.

(E) Encourage participating students to obtain employment for a minimum of two years after graduation with a unit of State or local government, Indian tribe or nonprofit organization engaged in community building.

(F) Maintain records by racial and ethnic categories for each economically disadvantaged student enrolled in the CDWSP.

(G) Keep records and make such reports as HUD may require.

(H) Comply with all other applicable Federal requirements.

(ii) If the recipient is an APO or State, the recipient must also:

(A) Establish a committee to coordinate activities between program participants, to advise the recipient on policy matters, to assist the recipient in ranking and selection of participating students, and to review disputes concerning compliance with program agreements and performance. The committee shall be chaired by a representative of the recipient, and shall include representatives of the participating institutions of higher education, work placement agencies, students, and HUD.

(B) Allocate the assistance awarded under the program to the participating institutions of higher education. APOs and States may not make fractional awards to institutions. (E.g., awards to institutions must assist a fixed number of students and not, for example, 6.5 students.)

(e) *Institutions of higher education.* Institutions of higher education participating in a program are responsible for providing its educational component. Where the recipient is an APO or State, the institution of higher education shall assist the APO or State in the administration and operation of the program. Responsibilities include assisting the recipient in the selection of students by determining the eligibility of students for the academic program, and by making the analysis of students under the financial need guidelines established by the institution. All institutions of higher education must comply with other applicable Federal requirements.

(f) *Work placement agencies eligibility and responsibilities*—(1) *Eligibility.* To be eligible to participate in the CDWSP, the work placement agencies must be involved in community building and must be an agency of a State or unit of local government, an APO, an Indian tribe, or a nonprofit organization.

(2) *Responsibilities.* Work placement agencies must:

(i) Provide practical experience and training in community building.

(ii) Consult with the institution of higher education (and the APO or State, where an APO or State is the recipient) to ensure that the student's work placement assignment provides the requisite experience and training to meet the required number of work hours specified in the student work placement agreement.

(iii) Provide a sufficient number of work placement assignments to provide participating students with a wide choice of work experience.

(iv) Require each student to devote 12–20 hours per week during the regular school year, or 35–40 hours a week during the summer, to the work placement assignment. Work placement agencies may provide flexibility in the work period, if such a schedule is consistent with the requirements of the student's academic program. However, a participating student may receive stipend payment only during the period that the student is placed with the work placement agency.

(v) Comply with all other applicable Federal requirements.

(vi) Maintain such records as HUD may require.

(g) *Student eligibility and responsibilities.* Students apply directly to recipients receiving grants under CDWSP. Students shall be selected in accordance with the following eligibility requirements and selection procedures.

(1) *Eligibility.* To be eligible for CDWSP, the student:

(i) Must satisfy all applicable guidelines established at the participating institution of higher education to measure financial need for academic scholarship or loan assistance.

(ii) Must be a full-time student enrolled in the first year of graduate study in a community building academic program at the participating institution of higher education. Individuals enrolled in doctoral programs are ineligible.

(iii) Must demonstrate an ability to maintain a satisfactory level of performance in the community building academic program and in work placement assignments, and to comply with the professional standards set by the recipient and the work placement agencies.

(iv) May not have previously participated in CDWSP.

(v) Must provide appropriate written evidence that he or she is lawfully admitted for permanent residence in the United States, if the individual is not a citizen.

(2) *Selection.* In selecting among eligible students, the recipient must consider the extent to which each student has demonstrated:

(i) Financial need under the applicable financial need guidelines established at the institution of higher education;

(ii) An interest in, and commitment to, a professional career in community building;

(iii) The ability satisfactorily to complete academic and work placement responsibilities under CDWSP.

(3) *Student responsibilities.* Participating students must:

(i) Enroll in a two-year program. A student's academic and work placement responsibilities include: Full-time enrollment in an approved academic program; maintenance of a satisfactory level of performance in the community building academic program and in work placement assignments; and compliance with the professional conduct standards set by the recipient and the work placement agency. A satisfactory level of academic performance consists of maintaining a B average. A student's participation in CDWSP shall be terminated for failure to meet these responsibilities and standards. If a student's participation is terminated, the student is ineligible for further CDWSP assistance.

(ii) Agree to make a good-faith effort to obtain employment in community building with a unit of State or local government, an Indian tribe, or a non-profit organization. The term of employment should be for at least two consecutive years following graduation from the academic program. If the student does not obtain such employment, the student is not required to repay the assistance received.

(h) *Notice of fund availability.* HUD will solicit grant applications from institutions of higher education, APO's and States by publishing a notice of fund availability in the FEDERAL REGISTER. The notice will:

(1) Explain how application packages (requests for grant applications) providing specific application requirements and guidance may be obtained;

(2) Specify the place for filing completed applications, and the date by which the applications must be physically received at that location;

(3) State the amount of funding available under the notice;

(4) Provide other appropriate program information and guidance.

(i) *Recipient selection process.* The selection process for applications under CDWSP consists of a threshold review, ranking of eligible applications and final selection.

(1) *Threshold.* To be eligible for ranking, applicants must meet each of the following threshold requirements:

(i) The application must be filed in the application form prescribed by HUD, and within the required time periods;

(ii) The applicant must demonstrate that it is eligible to participate;

(iii) The applicant must demonstrate that each institution of higher education participating in the program as a recipient has the required academic programs and faculty to carry out its activities under CDWSP. Each work placement agency must have the required staff and community building work study program to carry out its activities under CDWSP.

(2) *Rating.* All applications that meet the threshold requirements for applicant eligibility will be rated based on the following selection criteria:

(i) *Quality of academic program.* The quality of the academic program offered by the institution of higher education, including without limitation the:

(A) Quality of course offerings;

(B) Appropriateness of course offerings for preparing students for careers in community building; and

(C) Qualifications of faculty and percentage of their time devoted to teaching and research in community building.

(ii) *Rates of graduation.* The rates of graduation of students previously enrolled in a community building academic program at the institution of higher education, specifically including (where applicable) graduation rates from any previously funded CDWSP academic programs or similar programs.

(iii) *Extent of financial commitment.* The commitment and ability of the institution of higher education to assure that CDWSP students will receive sufficient financial assistance (including loans, where necessary) above and beyond the CDWSP funding to complete their academic program in a timely manner and without working in excess of 20 hours per week during the school year.

(iv) *Quality of work placement assignments.* The extent to which the participating students will receive a sufficient number and variety of work placement assignments, the assignments will provide practical and useful experience to students participating in the program, and the assignments will further the participating students' preparation for professional careers in community building.

(v) *Likelihood of fostering students' permanent employment in community building.* The extent to which the proposed program will lead participating students directly and immediately to permanent employment in community building, as indicated by, without limitation:

(A) The past success of the institution of higher education in placing its graduates (particularly CDWSP-funded and similar program graduates where applicable) in permanent employment in community building; and

(B) The amount of faculty and staff time and institutional resources devoted to assisting students (particularly students in CDWSP-funded and similar programs where applicable) in finding permanent employment in community building.

(vi) *Effectiveness of program administration.* The degree to which an applicant will be able effectively to coordinate and administer the program. HUD will allocate the maximum points available under this criterion equally among the following considerations set forth in paragraphs (i)(2)(vi) (A), (B), and (C) of this section, except that the maximum points available under this criterion will be allocated equally between the considerations set forth in paragraphs (i)(2)(vi) (A) and (B) of this section only where the applicant has not previously administered a CDWSP-funded program.

(A) The strength and clarity of the applicant's plan for placing CDWSP students on rotating work placement assignments and monitoring CDWSP students' progress both academically and in their work placement assignments;

(B) The degree to which the individual who will coordinate and administer the program has clear responsibility, ample available time, and sufficient authority to do so; and

(C) The effectiveness of the applicant's prior coordination and administration of a CDWSP-funded program, where applicable (including the timeliness and completeness of the applicant's compliance with CDWSP reporting requirements).

(vii) *Commitment to meeting economically disadvantaged and minority students' needs.* The applicant's commitment to meeting the needs of economically disadvantaged and minority students as demonstrated by policies and plans regarding, and past effort and success in, recruiting, enrolling and financially assisting economically disadvantaged and minority students. If the applicant is an APO or State, then HUD will consider the demonstrated commitment of each institution of higher education on whose behalf the APO or State is applying; HUD will then also consider the demonstrated commitment of the APO or State to recruit and hire economically disadvantaged and minority students.

(3) *Final selection.* Eligible applications will be considered for selection in their rank order. HUD may make awards out of rank order to achieve geographic diversity, and may provide assistance to support a number of students that is less than the number requested under applications in order to provide assistance to as many highly ranked applications as possible.

(j) *Agreements*—(1) *Grant agreement.* The responsibilities of the recipient under CDWSP will be incorporated in a grant agreement executed by HUD and the recipient.

(2) *Student agreement.* The recipient and each participating student must execute a written agreement incorporating their mutual responsibilities under CDWSP. The agreement must be executed before the student can be enrolled in the program. A student's participation in CDWSP shall be terminated for failure to meet the responsibilities and standards in the agreement.

(3) *Work placement assignment agreement.* The institution of higher education, the APO or state (if an APO or State is the grant recipient), the participating student, and the work placement agency must execute a written agreement covering each work placement assignment. The agreement must address the responsibilities of each of the parties, the educational objectives, the nature of supervision, the standards of evaluation, and the student's time commitments under the work placement assignment.

(4) *APO (or state) and institution of higher education.* Where the recipient is an APO (or a State), the recipient and each participating institution of higher education must execute a written agreement incorporating their mutual responsibilities under CDWSP.

(k) *Grant administration*—(1) *Initial obligation of funds.* When HUD selects an application for funding, and notifies the recipient, HUD will obligate funds to cover the amount of the approved grant. The initial obligation of funds will provide for student grants for two years.

(2) *Disbursement.* Recipients will receive grant payments by direct deposit on a reimbursement basis. If that is not possible, grant payments will be made by U.S. Treasury checks.

(3) *Deobligation and recipient repayment.* (i) HUD may deobligate amounts for grants if proposed activities are not begun or completed within a reasonable time after selection.

(ii) If a student's participation in CDWSP is terminated before the completion of the two-year term of the student's program, the recipient may substitute another student to complete the two-year term of a student whose participation has terminated. The substituted student must have a sufficient number of academic credits to complete the degree program within the remaining portion of the terminated student's two-year term. With respect to any CDWSP grant, there is no requirement, regardless of the date of grant award, for students who are terminated from the CDWSP to repay tuition and additional assistance or for the grant recipient to repay such funds to HUD. Funds must still be otherwise expended consistent with CDWSP regulations and the grant agreement, or repayment may be required under paragraph (k)(3)(iii) of this section.

(iii) Consistent with 2 CFR part 200, HUD, in the grant agreement, will set forth in detail other circumstances under which funds may be deobligated, recipients may be liable for repayment, or other sanctions may be imposed.

(l) *Other Federal requirements*—(1) *Handicap provision.* Recipients must provide a statement certifying that no otherwise qualified handicapped person shall, solely by reason of handicap, be excluded from participation in, be denied the benefits of, or otherwise be subjected to discrimination under the CDWSP.

(2) *Nondiscrimination.* The recipient must adhere to the following nondiscrimination provisions: The requirements of title VIII of the Civil Rights Act of 1968, 42 U.S.C. 3600–20 (Fair Housing Act) and implementing regulations issued at subchapter A of title 24 of the Code of Federal Regulations; title VI of the Civil Rights Act of 1964 (42 U.S.C. 2000d–4) (Nondiscrimination in Federally Assisted Programs) and implementing regulations issued at 24 CFR part 1; section 504 of the Rehabilitation Act of 1973 (29 U.S.C. 794) and implementing regulations at 24 CFR part 8; Executive Order 11063 and implementing regulations at 24 CFR part 107; and the Age Discrimination Act of 1975 and implementing regulations at 24 CFR part 146.

[54 FR 27131, June 27, 1989, as amended at 61 FR 36458, July 10, 1996; 63 FR 31869, June 10, 1998; 80 FR 75937, Dec. 7, 2015]

§570.416 Hispanic-serving institutions work study program.

(a) *Applicability and objectives.* HUD makes grants under the Hispanic-serving Institutions Work Study Program (HSI-WSP) to public and private nonprofit Hispanic-serving Institutions (HSI's) of higher education for the purpose of providing assistance to economically disadvantaged and minority students who participate in a work study program while enrolled in full-time community college programs in community building, and to provide entry to pre-professional careers in these fields.

(b) *Definitions.* The following definitions apply to HSI-WSP:

Applicant means a public or private non-profit Hispanic-serving institution of higher education that offers only two-year degree programs, including at least one community building academic degree program, and that applies for funding under HSI-WSP.

Community building means community and economic development, community planning, community management, public policy, urban economics, urban management, urban planning, land use planning, housing, and related fields. Related fields include, but are not limited to, administration of justice, child development, and human services.

Community building academic program or *academic program* means an undergraduate associate degree program whose purpose and focus is to educate students in community building. The terms "community building academic program" or "academic program" refer to the types of academic programs encompassed in the statutory phrase "community or economic development, community planning or community management." For purposes of HSI-WSP, such programs include, but are not limited to, associate degree programs in community and economic development, community planning, community management, public administration, public policy, urban economics, urban management, urban planning, land use planning, housing, and related fields of study. Related fields of study that promote community building, such as administration of justice, child development, and human services are eligible, while fields such as natural sciences, computer sciences, mathematics, accounting, electronics, engineering, and the humanities (such as English or history) would not be eligible. A transfer program (i.e., one that leads to transfer to a four-year institution of higher education for the student's junior year) in a community building academic discipline is eligible only if the student is required to declare his/her major in this discipline while at the community college.

Community building field means any of the fields of study eligible under a community building academic program.

Economically disadvantaged and minority students means students who satisfy all the applicable guidelines established at the participating institution of higher education to measure financial need for academic scholarship or loan assistance, including, but not limited to, students with disabilities and students who are Black, American Indian/Alaska Native, Hispanic, Asian/Pacific Islanders, where such students satisfy the financial needs guidelines defined above.

Hispanic-serving institution is an institution of higher education that certifies to the satisfaction of the Secretary that it meets the criteria set out at 20 U.S.C. 1059c(b)(1), including the following: An institution that has an enrollment of undergraduate full-time students that is at least 25 percent Hispanic; in which not less than 50 percent of the Hispanic students are low-income individuals (i.e., their families' taxable income for the preceding year did not exceed 150 percent of the poverty level) who are first generation college students; and in which another 25 percent are either low-income individuals or first generation college students.

HSI-WSP or *HSI-WSP program* means the Hispanic-serving Institutions Work Study program.

Institution of higher education means a public or private educational institution that offers two-year associate degrees in a community building academic program and that is accredited by an accrediting agency or association recognized by the Secretary of Education. Institutions offering BOTH four-year and two-year degrees are not eligible for HSI-WSP.

Recipient means an approved applicant that executes a grant agreement with HUD.

Student means a person attending the institution of higher education on a full-time basis, as defined by that institution and pursuing an eligible community building degree. Students must have attained no more than half of the credits required for their degree at the time they first receive assistance under HSI-WSP.

Student with disabilities means a student who meets the definition of a "person with disabilities" in the Americans with Disabilities Act of 1990.

(c) *Assistance provided*—(1) *Types of assistance available.* HUD provides funding in the form of grants to recipients who make assistance available to eligible students. Grants are provided to cover the costs of student assistance and for an administrative allowance.

(2) *Maximum amount of assistance.* The maximum amount that can be provided to a student is $13,200 a year, including $1,000 for an administrative allowance, subject to the 20% limitation described at 570.416(c)(4) below. HUD will not set maximums on how much should be spent to each eligible expenditure, other than for administrative costs. The institution must be able to document that the amounts paid are customary for that institution and that it has actually paid that amount to the students. If a student is receiving a Pell grant, he/she may not receive funding for the same educational support through HSI-WSP. However, HSI-WSP can substitute for all or part of the Pell grant.

(3) *Student assistance.* Grants are provided in the form of student stipends, tuition support, and additional support.

(i) *Student stipend.* The amount of the student stipend should be based on the hourly rate for initial entry positions in the community building field and the number of hours worked by the student at the work placement assignment. The stipend should be sufficiently high to allow the student to earn the full stipend, as determined by the recipient, without working over 20 hours per week during the school year and 40 hours per week during the summer.

(ii) *Tuition support.* The amount of tuition support may not exceed the tuition and required fees charged at the participating institution of higher education.

(iii) *Additional support.* The recipient may provide additional support for books, tutoring, and travel related to the academic program or work placement assignment. Costs associated with reasonable accommodations for students with disabilities including, but not limited to, interpreters for the deaf/hard of hearing, special equipment, and braille materials are eligible under this category.

(4) *Administrative allowance.* HUD provides an allowance to recipients to cover the administrative costs of the program. The administrative allowance is $1,000 per year for each student participating in the program; however, no more than 20 percent of the grant may be used for planning and program administrative costs.

(5) *Number of students assisted.* The minimum number of students that may be assisted is three students per participating institution of higher education. The maximum number of students that may be assisted is ten students per participating institution of higher education; however, a lower maximum or higher minimum may be established for a particular funding round by the NOFA announcing the availability of the funds.

(d) *Recipient eligibility and responsibilities*—(1) *Recipient eligibility.* Public or private Hispanic-serving institutions of higher education offering only undergraduate two-year degrees, including degrees in at least one community building academic program, are eligible for assistance under HSI-WSP. HSIs that offer BOTH two-year and four-year degrees are not eligible for HSI-WSP assistance.

(2) *Recipient responsibilities.* The recipient is responsible for administering the program, for compliance with all program requirements, and for coordination of program activities carried out by the work placement agencies. The recipient must:

(i) Recruit students for participation in HSI-WSP. The recipient shall establish recruitment procedures that identify eligible economically disadvantaged and minority students pursuing careers in community building, and make them aware of the availability of assistance opportunities. While the program is restricted to HSIs, the recipient may neither restrict the program to any particular minority group or groups, nor provide any preferential treatment in the selection process based on race or ethnicity. Only economically disadvantaged students, as defined herein, may be assisted.

(ii) Select students for participation in HSI-WSP. In selecting among the eligible students, the recipient must consider the extent to which each student has demonstrated financial need under the applicable guidelines established at the institution of higher education; an interest in, and commitment to, a career in community building; and the ability to satisfactorily complete the academic and work placement responsibilities under HSI-WSP. Students must be selected before the beginning of the semester for which funding is being provided. If a student's participation terminates, the student may not be replaced; the grant will be reduced by the amount of unused funds allotted for that student.

(iii) Provide the educational component for participating students.

(iv) Recruit and select work placement agencies, and negotiate and execute an agreement covering each work placement assignment.

(v) Refer participating students to work placement agencies and assist students in the selection of work placement assignments.

(vi) Assign sufficient staff to administer and supervise the program on a day-to-day basis.

(vii) Encourage participating students to either: obtain post-graduation employment with a unit of State or local government, an areawide planning organization (APO), Indian tribe or nonprofit organization engaged in community building; or transfer to a four-year institution of higher education to obtain a bachelor's degree in a community building academic discipline.

(viii) Maintain records by racial and ethnic categories for each economically disadvantaged and minority student participating in HSI-WSP.

(ix) Keep records and make such reports as HUD may require.

(x) Comply with all other applicable Federal requirements.

(e) *Work placement agencies eligibility and responsibilities*—(1) *Eligibility.* To be eligible to participate in HSI-WSP, the work placement agency must be an agency of a State or local government, an APO, an Indian tribe, or a private nonprofit organization involved in community building activities. A work placement site that is part of the institution of higher education (e.g., a child care center) can only be an eligible site if the services provided by that site are offered to people in the broader community outside the institution.

(2) *Responsibilities.* Work placement agencies must:

(i) Provide practical experience and training in the community building field to participating students through work placement assignments.

(ii) Consult with the institution of higher education to ensure that the student's work placement assignment provides the requisite experience and training to meet the required number of work hours specified in the student work placement agreement.

(iii) Provide a sufficient number and variety of work assignments to provide participating students with a wide choice of work experience.

(iv) Require each student to devote 12–20 hours per week during the regular school year, and 35–40 hours a week during the summer, to the work placement assignment. Work placement agencies may provide flexibility in the work period, if such a schedule is consistent with the requirements of the student's academic program. However, a participating student may receive a stipend payment only during the period when the student is placed with the work placement agency.

(v) Comply with all other applicable Federal requirements.

(vi) Maintain such records as HUD may require.

(f) *Student eligibility and responsibilities.* Students apply directly to recipients receiving grants under HSI-WSP.

(1) *Eligibility.* To be eligible for HSI-WSP, the student:

(i) Must satisfy all applicable guidelines established at the participating institution of higher education to measure financial need for academic scholarship or loan assistance.

(ii) Must be a full-time student enrolled in a community building associate degree program at the participating institution of higher education. The student must have attained no more than 50 percent of the credits required for his/her degree at the time the student first receives assistance under this program.

(iii) Must demonstrate an ability to maintain a satisfactory level of performance in community building academic program (i.e., maintain a B average, as defined by the institution) and in work placement assignments, and comply with the professional standards set by the recipient and the work placement agencies.

(iv) May not have previously participated in HSI-WSP.

(2) *Student responsibilities.* Participating students must:

(i) Enroll or be enrolled in a two-year community building associate degree program. A student's academic and work placement responsibilities include: Full-time enrollment in an approved academic program; maintenance of a satisfactory level of performance in the community building academic program and in work placement assignments; and compliance with the professional conduct standards set by the recipient and by the work placement agency. A satisfactory level of academic performance consists of maintaining a B average, as defined by the institution. A student's participation in HSI-WSP shall be terminated for failure to meet these responsibilities and standards. If the student's participation is terminated, the student is ineligible for further HSI-WSP assistance.

(ii) Devote 12–20 hours per week during the regular school year, and 35–40 hours a week during the summer, to the work placement assignment. Work placement agencies may provide flexibility in the work period, if such a schedule is consistent with the requirements of the student's academic program. However, a participating student may receive a stipend payment only during the period when the student is placed with the work placement agency.

(iii) Agree to make a good-faith effort to either: obtain employment in community building with a unit of State or local government, an APO, an Indian tribe, or a non-profit organization; or to transfer to a four-year institution of higher education to obtain a bachelor's degree in a community building academic discipline. However, if the student does not obtain such employment or transfer to a four-year institution, the student is not required to repay the assistance received.

(g) *Notice of funding availability.* HUD will solicit grant applications from eligible institutions of higher education by publishing a notice of funding availability in the FEDERAL REGISTER. The notice will:

(1) Explain how application kits providing specific application requirements and guidance may be obtained;

(2) Specify the place for filing completed applications, and the date by which applications must be physically received at that location;

(3) State the amount of funding available under the notice, which may include funds recaptured from previously awarded grants;

(4) Provide other appropriate program information and guidance.

(h) *Agreements*—(1) *Grant agreement.* The responsibilities of the recipient under HSI-WSP will be incorporated in a grant agreement executed by HUD and the recipient.

(2) *Student agreement.* The recipient and each participating student must execute a written agreement incorporating their mutual responsibilities under HSI-WSP. The agreement must be executed before the student can be enrolled in the program. The Recipient shall terminate a student's participation in HSI-WSP for failure to meet the responsibilities and standards in the agreement.

(3) *Work placement assignment agreement.* The recipient, the student, and the work placement agency must execute a written agreement covering each work placement assignment. The

agreement must address the responsibilities of each of the parties, the educational objectives, the nature of the supervision, the standards of evaluation, and the student's time commitments under the work placement assignment.

(i) *Grant administration*—(1) *Initial obligation of funds.* When HUD selects an application for funding, HUD will obligate funds to cover the amount of the approved grant. The term of the award will be for two calendar years, unless subsequently altered by HUD at its discretion for good cause.

(2) *Disbursement.* Recipients will receive grant payments by direct deposit on a reimbursement basis. If that is not possible, grant payments will be made by U.S. Treasury checks.

(3) *Deobligation.* HUD may deobligate amounts for grants if proposed activities are not begun or completed within a reasonable period of time after selection.

(j) *Other Federal requirements*—(1) *Applicability of part 570.* HSI-WSP shall be subject to the policies and procedures set forth in subparts A, K, and O of 24 CFR part 570, as applicable, except as modified or limited under the provisions of this Notice. The provisions of subparts C and J of part 570 shall not apply to HSI-WSP.

(2) *Uniform administrative requirements.* Recipients under HSI–WSP shall comply with the requirements and standards of 2 CFR part 200, "Uniform Administrative Requirements, Cost Principles, and Audit Requirements for Federal Awards." Audits in accordance with 2 CFR part 200, subpart F, shall be conducted annually.

[62 FR 17493, Apr. 9, 1997, as amended at 63 FR 9683, Feb. 25, 1998; 80 FR 75937, Dec. 7, 2015]

Subpart F—Small Cities, Non-Entitlement CDBG Grants in Hawaii and Insular Areas Programs

SOURCE: 62 FR 62914, Nov. 25, 1997, unless otherwise noted.

§570.420 General.

(a) *Administration of Non-entitlement CDBG funds in New York by HUD or Insular Areas*—(1) *Small cities.* The Act permits each state to elect to administer all aspects of the CDBG program annual fund allocation for the non-entitlement areas within its jurisdiction. All states except Hawaii have elected to administer the CDBG program for non-entitlement areas within their jurisdiction. This section is applicable only to active HUD-administered small cities grants in New York. The requirements for the non-entitlement CDBG grants in Hawaii are set forth in §570.429 of this subpart. States that elected to administer the program after the close of Fiscal Year 1984 cannot return administration of the program to HUD. A decision by a state to discontinue administration of the program would result in the loss of CDBG funds for non-entitlement areas in that state and the reallocation of those funds to all states in the succeeding fiscal year.

(2) *Insular areas.* Title V of Public Law 108–186 amended the Act to move the insular areas funding authorization from sections 107(a) and (b) to section 106(a). This revision identified a specific portion of the CDBG allocation for insular areas that is separate from the distribution for special purpose grants, as well as from the Entitlement and State formula distribution. The insular areas of Guam, the Northern Mariana Islands, the Virgin Islands, and American Samoa are permitted to administer all aspects of their Community Development Block Grant (CDBG) program under section 106 of the Act in accordance with their final statement as further described at §570.440.

(b) *Scope and applicability.* (1) This subpart describes the policies and procedures of the Small Cities program that apply to non-entitlement areas in states where HUD administers the CDBG program. HUD currently administers the Small Cities program in only two states—New York (for grants prior to FY 2000) and Hawaii (for non-entitlement CDBG grants in Hawaii). The Small Cities portion of this subpart addresses the requirements for New York Small Cities grants in §§570.421, 570.426, 570.427, and 570.431. Section 570.429 identifies special procedures applicable to Hawaii.

(2) This subpart also describes the policies and procedures governing community development block grants to insular areas under section 106 of the Act. Sections 570.440 and 570.441 identify procedures applicable to the Insular Areas program under section 106 of the Act. Fund reservations for insular areas under section 107 of the Act shall remain governed by the policies and procedures described in section 107(a)(1)(A) of the Act and §§ 570.400 and 570.405 of this part.

(3) The policies and procedures set forth in the following identified subparts of this part apply to the HUD-administered Small Cities and Insular Areas programs, except as modified or limited under the provisions thereof or this subpart:

(i) Subpart A—General Provisions;

(ii) Subpart C—Eligible Activities;

(iii) Subpart J—Grant Administration;

(iv) Subpart K—Other Program Requirements;

(v) Subpart M—Loan Guarantees; and

(vi) Subpart O—Performance Reviews.

(c) *Abbreviated consolidated plan.* Applications for the HUD-administered Small Cities Program and the Insular Areas program under section 106 of the Act that contain housing activities must include a certification that the proposed housing activities are consistent with the applicant's consolidated plan as described at 24 CFR part 91.

(d) *National and primary objectives.* (1) Each activity funded through the Small Cities program and the Insular Areas program under section 106 of the Act must meet one of the following national objectives as defined under the criteria in § 570.208:

(i) Benefit low- and moderate-income families;

(ii) Aid in the prevention or elimination of slums or blight; or

(iii) Be an activity that the grantee certifies is designed to meet other community development needs having a particular urgency because existing conditions pose a serious and immediate threat to the health or welfare of the community and other financial resources are not available to meet such needs.

(2) In addition to the objectives described in paragraph (e)(1) of this section, with respect to grants made through the Small Cities program, not less than 70 percent of the total of grant funds from each grant and Section 108 loan guarantee funds received under subpart M of this part within a fiscal year must be expended for activities which benefit low- and moderate-income persons under the criteria of § 570.208(a) or of § 570.208(d)(5) or (6). In the case of multiyear plans in New York State approved in response to NOFAs published prior to calendar year 1997, not less than 70 percent of the total funding for grants approved pursuant to a multiyear plan for a time period of up to three years must be expended for activities which benefit low- and moderate-income persons. Thus, 70 percent of the grant for year 1 of a multiyear plan approved in response to NOFAs published prior to calendar year 1997 must meet the 70 percent requirement, 70 percent of the combined grants from years 1 and 2 must meet the requirement, and 70 percent of the combined grants from years 1, 2, and 3 must meet the requirement. In determining the percentage of funds expended for such activity, the provisions of § 570.200(a)(3)(i), (iii), (iv), and (v) shall apply.

(3) In addition to the objectives described in paragraph (e)(1) of this section, grants made through the Insular Areas program shall also comply with the primary objective of 70 percent benefit to low- and moderate-income persons. Insular area recipients must meet this requirement for each separate grant under section 107 of the Act. For grants made under section 106 of the Act, insular area recipients must ensure that over a period of time specified in their certifications not to exceed three years, not less than 70 percent of the aggregate of CDBG fund expenditures shall be for low- and moderate-income activities meeting the criteria under § 570.208(a) or under § 570.208(d)(5) or (6). See also § 570.200(a)(3) for further discussion of the primary objective.

(e) *Allocation of funds*—The allocation of appropriated funds for insular areas under section 106 of the Act shall be governed by the policies and procedures described in section 106(a)(2) of the Act and §§570.440, 570.441, and 570.442 of this subpart. The annual appropriations described in this section shall be distributed to insular areas on the basis of the ratio of the population of each insular area to the population of all insular areas.

[69 FR 32779, June 10, 2004, as amended at 72 FR 46370, Aug. 17, 2007]

§570.421 New York Small Cities Program design.

(a) *Selection system*—(1) *Competitive applications.* Each competitive application will be rated and scored against at least the following factors:

(i) Need-absolute number of persons in poverty as further explained in the NOFA;

(ii) Need-percent of persons in poverty as further explained in the NOFA;

(iii) Program Impact; and

(iv) Fair Housing and Equal Opportunity, which may include the applicant's Section 3 plan and implementation efforts with respect to actions to affirmatively further fair housing. The NOFA described in paragraph (b) of this section will contain a more detailed description of these factors, and the relative weight that each factor will be given.

(2) In addition HUD reserves the right to establish minimal thresholds for selection factors and otherwise select grants in accordance with §570.425 and the applicable NOFA.

(3) *Imminent threats to public health and safety.* The criteria for these grants are described in §570.424.

(4) *Repayment of Section 108 loans.* The criteria for these grants are described in §570.432.

(5) *Economic development grants.* HUD intends to use the Section 108 loan guarantee program to the maximum extent feasible to fund economic development projects in the nonentitlement areas of New York. In the event that there are not enough Section 108 loan guarantee funds available to fund viable economic development projects, if a project needs a grant in addition to a loan guarantee to make it viable, or if the project does not meet the requirements of the Section 108 program but is eligible for a grant under this subpart, HUD may fund Economic Development applications as they are determined to be fundable in a specific amount by HUD up to the sum set aside for economic development projects in a notice of funding availability, notwithstanding paragraph (g) of this section. HUD also has the option in a NOFA of funding economic development activities on a competitive basis, as a competitive application as described in paragraph (a)(1) of this section. In order for an applicant to receive Small Cities grant funds on a noncompetitive basis, the field office must determine that the economic development project will have a substantial impact on the needs identified by the applicant.

(b) *Notice of funding availability.* HUD will issue one or more Notice(s) of Funding Availability (NOFA) each fiscal year which will indicate the amount of funds available, the annual grant limits per grantee, type of grants available, the application requirements, and the rating factors that will be used for those grants which are competitive. A NOFA may set forth, subject to the requirements of this subpart, additional selection criteria for all grants.

(c) *Eligible applicants.* (1) Eligible applicants in New York are units of general local government, excluding: Metropolitan cities, urban counties, units of general local government which are participating in urban counties or metropolitan cities, even if only part of the participating unit of government is located in the urban county or metropolitan city. Indian tribes are also ineligible for assistance under this subpart. An application may be submitted individually or jointly by eligible applicants.

(2) Counties, cities, towns, and villages may apply and receive funding for separate projects to be done in the same jurisdiction. Only one grant will be made under each funding round for the same type of project to be located within the jurisdiction of a unit of general local government (e.g., both the county and village cannot receive funding for a sewer system to be located in the same village, but the county can receive funding for a sewer system that is located in the same village as a rehabilitation project for which the village

receives funding). The NOFA will contain additional information on applicant eligibility.

(3) Counties may apply on behalf of units of general local government located within their jurisdiction when the unit of general local government has authorized the county to apply. At the time that the county submits its application for funding, it must submit a resolution by the governing body of the unit of local government that authorizes the county to submit an application on behalf of the unit of general local government. The county will be considered the grantee and will be responsible for executing all grant documents. The county is responsible for ensuring compliance with all laws, regulations, and Executive Orders applicable to the CDBG Program. HUD will deal exclusively with the county with respect to issues of program administration and performance, including remedial actions. The unit of general local government will be considered the grantee for the purpose of determining grant limits. The unit of general local government's statistics will be used for purposes of the selection factors referred to in § 570.421(a).

(d) *Public service activities cap.* Public service activities may be funded up to a maximum of fifteen (15) percent of a State's nonentitlement allocation for any fiscal year. HUD may award a grant to a unit of general local government for public service activities with up to 100 percent of the funds intended for public service activities. HUD will apply the 15 percent statewide cap to public service activities by funding public service activities in the highest rated applications in each NOFA until the cap is reached.

(e) *Activities outside an applicant's boundaries.* An applicant may conduct eligible CDBG activities outside its boundaries. These activities must be demonstrated to be appropriate to meeting the applicant's needs and objectives, and must be consistent with State and local law. This provision includes using funds provided under this subpart in a metropolitan city or an urban county.

(f) *Multiyear plans.* HUD will not make any new multiyear commitments for NOFAs published in calendar year 1997 or later. HUD will continue to honor the terms of the multiyear plans that were approved under the provisions of NOFAs published prior to calendar year 1997.

(g) *Maximum grant amount.* The maximum grant amount that will be awarded to a single unit of general local government in response to the annual Small Cities NOFA published in calendar year 1997 or later is $400,000, except that counties may apply for up to $600,000 in HUD-administered Small Cities funds. HUD may specify lower grant limits in the NOFA, which may include different limits for different types of grants available or different types of applicants. This paragraph (g) does not apply to multiyear plans that were approved under the provisions of NOFAs published prior to calendar year 1997, nor does it apply to grants awarded in connection with paragraphs (a)(3) through (a)(5) of this section. The maximum limits in this paragraph (g) apply to grants for economic development projects awarded under NOFAs in which there is no set-aside of funds for such projects.

§§ 570.422–425 [Reserved]

§ 570.426 Program income.

(a) The provisions of § 570.504(b) apply to all program income generated by a specific grant and received prior to grant closeout.

(b) If the unit of general local government has another ongoing CDBG grant at the time of closeout, the program income will be considered to be program income of the ongoing grant. The grantee can choose which grant to credit the program income to if it has multiple open CDBG grants.

(c) If the unit of general local government has no open ongoing CDBG grant at the time of closeout, program income of the unit of general local government or its subrecipients which amounts to less than $25,000 per year will not be considered to be program income unless needed to repay a Section 108 guaranteed loan. When more than $25,000 of program income is generated from one or more closed out grants in a year after closeout, the entire amount of the program income is subject to the requirements of this part. This will be a subject of the close-out agreement described in §570.509(c).

§570.427 Program amendments.

(a) *HUD approval of certain program amendments.* Grantees shall request prior HUD approval for all program amendments involving new activities or alteration of existing activities that will significantly change the scope, location, or objectives of the approved activities or beneficiaries. Approval is subject to the amended activities meeting the requirements of this part and being able to be completed promptly.

(b) *Documentation of program amendments.* Any program amendments that do not require HUD approval must be fully documented in the grantee's records.

(c) *Citizen participation requirements.* Whenever an amendment requires HUD approval, the requirements for citizen participation in §570.431 must be met.

[62 FR 62914, Nov. 25, 1997, as amended at 72 FR 46370, Aug. 17, 2007]

§570.428 [Reserved]

§570.429 Hawaii general and grant requirements.

(a) *General.* This section applies to non-entitlement CDBG grants in Hawaii. The non-entitlement counties in the State of Hawaii will be treated as entitlement grantees except for the calculation of allocations, and the source of their funding, which will be from section 106(d) of the Act.

(b) *Scope and applicability.* Except as modified or limited under the provisions thereof or this subpart, the policies and procedures outlined in subparts A, C, D, J, K, and O of this part apply to non-entitlement CDBG grants in Hawaii.

(c) *Grant amounts.* (1) For each eligible unit of general local government, a formula grant amount will be determined which bears the same ratio to the total amount available for the non-entitlement area of the State as the weighted average of the ratios between:

(i) The population of that eligible unit of general local government and the population of all eligible units of general local government in the non-entitlement areas of the State;

(ii) The extent of poverty in that eligible unit of general local government and the extent of poverty in all the eligible units of general local government in the nonentitlement areas of the State; and

(iii) The extent of housing overcrowding in that eligible unit of general local government and the extent of housing overcrowding in all the eligible units of general local government in the nonentitlement areas of the State.

(2) In determining the average of the ratios under this paragraph (c), the ratio involving the extent of poverty shall be counted twice and each of the other ratios shall be counted once. (0.25 + 0.50 + 0.25 = 1.00).

(d) *Reallocation.* (1) Any amounts that become available as a result of any reductions under subpart O of this part shall be reallocated in the same or future fiscal year to any remaining eligible applicants on a pro rata basis.

(2) Any formula grant amounts reserved for an applicant that chooses not to submit an application shall be reallocated to any remaining eligible applicants on a pro rata basis.

(3) No amounts shall be reallocated under paragraph (d) of this section in any fiscal year to any applicant whose grant amount was reduced under subpart O of this part.

(Approved by the Office of Management and Budget under control number 2506–0060)

[62 FR 62914, Nov. 25, 1997, as amended at 72 FR 46371, Aug. 17, 2007]

§570.431 Citizen participation.

(a) *General.* An applicant that is located in a nonentitlement area of a State that has not elected to distribute funds shall comply with the citizen participation requirements described in this section, including requirements for the preparation of the proposed application and the final application. The requirements for citizen participation do not restrict the responsibility or authority of the applicant for the development and execution of its community development program.

(b) *Citizen participation plan.* The applicant must develop and follow a detailed citizen participation plan and must make the plan public. The plan must be completed and available before the application for assistance is submitted to HUD, and the applicant must certify that it is following the plan. The plan must set forth the applicant's policies and procedures for:

(1) Giving citizens timely notice of local meetings and reasonable and timely access to local meetings, information, and records relating to the grantee's proposed and actual use of CDBG funds including, but not limited to:

(i) The amount of CDBG funds expected to be made available for the coming year, including the grant and anticipated program income;

(ii) The range of activities that may be undertaken with those funds;

(iii) The estimated amount of those funds proposed to be used for activities that will benefit low- and moderate-income persons;

(iv) The proposed CDBG activities likely to result in displacement and the applicant's plans, consistent with the policies developed under § 570.606(b), for minimizing displacement of persons as a result of its proposed activities; and

(v) The types and levels of assistance the applicant plans to make available (or to require others to make available) to persons displaced by CDBG-funded activities, even if the applicant expects no displacement to occur;

(2) Providing technical assistance to groups representative of persons of low- and moderate-income that request assistance in developing proposals. The level and type of assistance to be provided is at the discretion of the applicant. The assistance need not include the provision of funds to the groups;

(3) Holding a minimum of two public hearings, for the purpose of obtaining citizens' views and formulating or responding to proposals and questions. Each public hearing must be conducted at a different stage of the CDBG program. Together, the hearings must address community development and housing needs, development of proposed activities and review of program performance. There must be reasonable notice of the hearings and the hearings must be held at times and accessible locations convenient to potential or actual beneficiaries, with reasonable accommodations including material in accessible formats for persons with disabilities. The applicant must specify in its plan how it will meet the requirement for hearings at times and locations convenient to potential or actual beneficiaries;

(4) Meeting the needs of non-English speaking residents in the case of public hearings where a significant number of non-English speaking residents can reasonably be expected to participate;

(5) Responding to citizen complaints and grievances, including the procedures that citizens must follow when submitting complaints and grievances. The applicant's policies and procedures must provide for timely written answers to written complaints and grievances within 15 working days of the receipt of the complaint, where practicable; and

(6) Encouraging citizen participation, particularly by low- and moderate-income persons who reside in slum or blighted areas, and in other areas in which CDBG funds are proposed to be used.

(c) *Publication of proposed application.* (1) The applicant shall publish a proposed application consisting of the proposed community development activities and community development objectives in order to afford affected citizens an opportunity to:

(i) Examine the application's contents to determine the degree to which they may be affected;

(ii) Submit comments on the proposed application; and

(iii) Submit comments on the performance of the applicant.

(2) The requirement for publishing in paragraph (c)(1) of this section may be met by publishing a summary of the proposed application in one or more newspapers of general circulation, and by making copies of the proposed application available at libraries, government offices, and public places. The summary must describe the contents and purpose of the proposed application, and must include a list of the locations where copies of the entire proposed application may be examined.

(d) *Preparation of a final application.* An applicant must prepare a final application. In the preparation of the final application, the applicant shall consider comments and views received related to the proposed application and may, if appropriate, modify the final application. The final application shall be made available to the public and shall include the community development objectives and projected use of funds, and the community development activities.

(e) *New York grantee amendments.* To assure citizen participation on program amendments to final applications that require HUD approval under §570.427, the grantee shall:

(1) Furnish citizens information concerning the amendment;

(2) Hold one or more public hearings to obtain the views of citizens on the proposed amendment;

(3) Develop and publish the proposed amendment in such a manner as to afford affected citizens an opportunity to examine the contents, and to submit comments on the proposed amendment;

(4) Consider any comments and views expressed by citizens on the proposed amendment and, if the grantee finds it appropriate, modify the final amendment accordingly; and

(5) Make the final amendment to the community development program available to the public before its submission to HUD.

§570.440 Application requirements for insular area grants funded under section 106.

(a) *Applicability.* The requirements of this section apply to insular grants funded under section 106 of the Act. An insular area jurisdiction may choose to prepare program statements following either:

(1) The abbreviated consolidated plan procedures described in this subpart and in 24 CFR 91.235; or

(2) The complete consolidated plan procedures applicable to local governments, discussed at 24 CFR 91.200 through 91.230.

(b) *Proposed statement.* An insular area jurisdiction shall prepare and publish a proposed statement and comply with the citizen participation requirements described in §570.441, if it submits an abbreviated consolidated plan under 24 CFR 91.235. The jurisdiction shall follow the citizen participation requirements of 24 CFR 91.105 and 91.100 (with the exception of §91.100(a)(4)), if it submits a complete consolidated plan.

(c) *Final statement.* The insular area jurisdiction shall submit to HUD a final statement describing its community development objectives and activities. The statement also must include a priority nonhousing community development plan in accordance with 24 CFR 91.235. This final statement shall be submitted, together with the required certifications, to the appropriate field office in a form prescribed by HUD.

(d) *Submission requirement.* Each insular area jurisdiction shall submit its final statement to HUD no later than 45 days before the start of its program year. Each jurisdiction may choose the start date for the annual period of its program year that most closely fits its own needs. HUD may grant an extension of the submission deadline for good cause.

(e) *Certifications.* The insular area jurisdiction's final statement must be accompanied by appropriate certifications as further described under 24 CFR 91.225. The jurisdiction should submit all general certifications, as well as all program certifications for each program from which it receives funding, if it submits a complete consolidated plan. For insular area jurisdictions receiving CDBG funds under an abbreviated consolidated plan, these certifications shall include at a minimum:

(1) The following general certifications described at §91.225(a) of this title: Affirmatively furthering fair housing; anti-displacement and relocation plan; drug-free workplace; anti-lobbying; authority of jurisdiction; consistency with plan; acquisition and relocation; and Section 3.

(2) The following CDBG certifications described at §91.225(b) of this title: Citizen participation; community development plan; following a plan; use of funds; excessive force; compliance with anti-discrimination laws; compliance with lead-based paint procedures; and compliance with laws.

(f) *HUD action on final statement.* Following the review of the statement, HUD will promptly notify each jurisdiction of the action taken with regard to its statement. HUD will approve a grant if the jurisdiction's submissions have been made and approved in accordance with 24 CFR part 91, and if the certifications required in such submissions are satisfactory to HUD. The certifications will be satisfactory to HUD for this purpose, unless HUD determines pursuant to subpart O of this part that the jurisdiction has not complied with the requirements of this part, has failed to carry out its consolidated plan (or abbreviated consolidated plan) as provided under § 570.903, or has determined that there is evidence, not directly involving the jurisdiction's past performance under this program, that tends to challenge in a substantial manner the jurisdiction's certification of future performance. If HUD makes any such determination, however, further assurances may be required to be submitted by the jurisdiction as HUD may deem warranted or necessary to find the jurisdiction's certification satisfactory.

(g) *Reimbursement for pre-award costs.* Insular area jurisdictions may request reimbursement for pre-award costs in accordance with § 570.200(h).

(h) *Float funding.* An insular area jurisdiction may use undisbursed funds in the line of credit and its CDBG program account that are budgeted in final statements or action plans for one or more activities that do not need the funds immediately, subject to the limitations described in § 570.301(b).

(i) *Program amendments.* (1) The insular area jurisdiction's citizen participation plan (*see* § 570.441) must specify the criteria the jurisdiction will use for determining what changes in the jurisdiction's planned or actual activities will constitute a substantial amendment to its final statement. It must include changes in the use of CDBG funds from one eligible activity to another among the changes that qualify as a substantial amendment.

(2) The citizen participation plan must provide citizens with reasonable notice and an opportunity to comment on substantial amendments. The citizen participation plan must state how reasonable notice and an opportunity to comment will be given, as well as provide a period of not less than 30 days to receive comments on the substantial amendment before the amendment is implemented.

(3) The citizen participation plan shall require the jurisdiction to consider comments or views of citizens received in writing, or orally at public hearings, if any, in preparing the substantial amendment of its statement. A summary of comments or views not accepted and the reasons for non-acceptance shall be attached to the substantial amendment.

(4) Any program amendment, regardless of whether it is considered to be substantial, must be fully documented in the jurisdiction's records.

(j) *Performance reports.* Each insular area jurisdiction must submit annual performance reports in accordance with 24 CFR 91.520.

[69 FR 32780, June 10, 2004]

§ 570.441 Citizen participation—insular areas.

(a) *General.* An insular area jurisdiction submitting an abbreviated consolidated plan under 24 CFR 91.235 shall comply with the citizen participation requirements described in this section. An insular area jurisdiction submitting a complete consolidated plan in accordance with 24 CFR 91.200 through 91.230 shall follow the citizen participation requirements of § 91.100 and § 91.105, except for § 91.100(a)(4). For funding under section 106 of the Act, these requirements are applicable to all aspects of the Insular Areas program, including the preparation of the proposed statement and final statements as described in § 570.440. The requirements for citizen participation do not restrict the responsibility or authority of the jurisdiction for the development and execution of its community development program.

(b) *Citizen participation plan.* The insular area jurisdiction must develop and follow a detailed citizen participation plan and must make the plan public. The plan must be completed and available before the statement for assistance is submitted to HUD, and the jurisdiction must certify that it is following the plan. The plan must set forth the jurisdiction's policies and procedures for:

(1) Giving citizens timely notice of local meetings and reasonable and

timely access to local meetings consistent with accessibility and reasonable accommodation requirements in accordance with section 504 of the Rehabilitation Act of 1973 and the regulations at 24 CFR part 8, and the Americans with Disabilities Act and the regulations at 28 CFR parts 35 and 36, as applicable, as well as information and records relating to the grantee's proposed and actual use of CDBG funds including, but not limited to:

(i) The amount of CDBG funds expected to be made available for the coming year, including the grant and anticipated program income;

(ii) The range of activities that may be undertaken with those funds;

(iii) The estimated amount of those funds proposed to be used for activities that will benefit low- and moderate-income persons;

(iv) The proposed CDBG activities likely to result in displacement and the jurisdiction's plans, consistent with the policies developed under §570.606(b), for minimizing displacement of persons as a result of its proposed activities; and

(v) The types and levels of assistance the jurisdiction plans to make available (or to require others to make available) to persons displaced by CDBG-funded activities, even if the jurisdiction expects no displacement to occur;

(2) Providing technical assistance to groups that are representative of persons of low- and moderate-income that request assistance in developing proposals. The level and type of assistance to be provided is at the discretion of the jurisdiction. The assistance need not include the provision of funds to the groups;

(3) Holding a minimum of two public hearings for the purpose of obtaining residents' views and formulating or responding to proposals and questions. Each public hearing must be conducted at a different stage of the CDBG program year. Together, the hearings must address, community development and housing needs, development of proposed activities, and a review of program performance. There must be reasonable notice of the hearings, and the hearings must be held at times and accessible locations convenient to potential or actual beneficiaries, with reasonable accommodations, including materials in accessible formats, for persons with disabilities. The jurisdiction must specify in its citizen participation plan how it will meet the requirement for hearings at times and accessible locations convenient to potential or actual beneficiaries;

(4) Assessing its language needs, identifying any need for translation of notices and other vital documents and, in the case of public hearings, meeting the needs of non-English speaking residents where a significant number of non-English speaking residents can reasonably be expected to participate. At a minimum, the citizen participation plan shall require the jurisdiction to make reasonable efforts to provide language assistance to ensure meaningful access to participation by non-English speaking persons;

(5) Responding to citizen complaints and grievances, including the procedures that citizens must follow when submitting complaints and grievances. The jurisdiction's policies and procedures must provide for timely written answers to written complaints and grievances within 15 working days after the receipt of the complaint, where practicable; and

(6) Encouraging citizen participation, particularly by low- and moderate-income persons who reside in areas in which CDBG funds are proposed to be used.

(c) *Publication of proposed statement.* (1) The insular area jurisdiction shall publish a proposed statement consisting of the proposed community development activities and community development objectives (as applicable) in order to afford affected residents an opportunity to:

(i) Examine the document's contents to determine the degree to which they may be affected;

(ii) Submit comments on the proposed document; and

(iii) Submit comments on the performance of the jurisdiction.

(2) The requirement for publishing in paragraph (c)(1) of this section may be met by publishing a summary of the proposed document in one or more newspapers of general circulation and

by making copies of the proposed document available on the Internet, on the grantee's official government Web site, and as well at libraries, government offices, and public places. The summary must describe the contents and purpose of the proposed document and must include a list of the locations where copies of the entire proposed document may be examined.

(d) *Preparation of the final statement.* An insular area jurisdiction must prepare a final statement. In the preparation of the final statement, the jurisdiction shall consider comments and views received relating to the proposed document and may, if appropriate, modify the final document. The final statement shall be made available to the public. The final statement shall include the community development objectives, projected use of funds, and the community development activities.

(e) *Program amendments.* To assure citizen participation on program amendments to final statements, the insular area grantee shall:

(1) Furnish its residents with information concerning the amendment to the consolidated plan;

(2) Hold one or more public hearings to obtain the views of residents on the proposed amendment to the consolidated plan;

(3) Develop and publish the proposed amendment to the consolidated plan in such a manner as to afford affected residents an opportunity to examine the contents, and to submit comments on the proposed amendment to the consolidated plan;

(4) Consider any comments and views expressed by residents on the proposed amendment to the consolidated plan, and, if the grantee finds it appropriate, make modifications accordingly; and

(5) Make the final amendment to the community development program available to the public before its submission to HUD.

(f) *Performance reports.* (1) The citizen participation plan must provide citizens with reasonable notice and an opportunity to comment on performance reports. The citizen participation plan must state how reasonable notice and an opportunity to comment will be given. The citizen participation plan must provide a period of not less than 15 days to receive comments on the performance report before it is to be submitted to HUD.

(2) The citizen participation plan shall require the jurisdiction to consider comments or views of citizens received in writing or orally at public hearings in preparing the performance report. A summary of these comments or views shall be attached to the performance report.

(g) *Application for loan guarantees.* Insular area jurisdictions intending to apply for the Section 108 Loan Guarantee program must ensure that they follow the applicable presubmission and citizen participation requirements of § 570.704.

[69 FR 32780, June 10, 2004, as amended at 80 FR 42366, July 16, 2015; 85 FR 47910, Aug. 7, 2020]

§ 570.442 Reallocations-Insular Areas.

(a) Any Insular Area funds that become available as a result of reductions under subpart O of this part, shall be reallocated in the same or future fiscal year to any remaining eligible Insular Area grantees pro rata according to population.

(b) Any Insular Area grant funds for a fiscal year reserved for an applicant that chooses not to submit a final statement in accordance with § 570.440 to receive such funds, shall be reallocated in the same or future fiscal year to any remaining eligible Insular Area grantees pro rata according to population.

(c) No amounts shall be reallocated under this section in any fiscal year to any applicant whose grant amount in such fiscal year was reduced under subpart O of this part or who did not submit a final statement in accordance with § 570.440 for that fiscal year.

(d) Insular Area grantees receiving additional funds under this section will be evaluated for timeliness under § 570.902 based upon the original grant amount plus the additional funds received. Accordingly, references in § 570.902 to an Insular Area's grant amount for its current program year include such additional funds, and references to unexpended or undisbursed funds include such additional funds.

[72 FR 12536, Mar. 15, 2007]

Subpart G—Urban Development Action Grants

SOURCE: 47 FR 7983, Feb. 23, 1982, unless otherwise noted.

§ 570.450 Purpose.

The purpose of urban development action grants is to assist cities and urban counties that are experiencing severe economic distress to help stimulate economic development activity needed to aid in economic recovery. This subpart G contains those regulations that are essential for the continued operation of this grant program.

[61 FR 11476, Mar. 20, 1996]

§ 570.456 Ineligible activities and limitations on eligible activities.

(a) Large cities and urban counties may not use assistance under this subpart for planning the project or developing the application. However, they may use entitlement community development block grant funds for this purpose, provided that the UDAG project meets the eligibility test of this part. Any small city which submits a project application which is selected for preliminary approval and for which legally binding grant agreement and for which a release of funds pursuant to 24 CFR part 58 has been issued may devote up to three (3) percent of the approved amount of its action grant to defray its actual costs in planning the project and preparing its application.

(b) Assistance under this subpart may not be used for public services as described in § 570.201(e).

(c)(1) No assistance may be provided under this subpart for speculative projects intended to facilitate the relocation of industrial or commercial plants or facilities from one area to another. The provisions of this paragraph (c)(1) shall not apply to a relocation of any such plant or facility within a metropolitan area.

(i) HUD will presume that a proposed project which includes speculative commercial or industrial space is intended to facilitate the relocation of a plant or facility from one area to another, if it is demonstrated to HUD's satisfaction that:

(A) The proposed project is reasonably proximate (i.e., within 50 miles) to an area from which there has been a significant current pattern of movement, to areas reasonably proximate, of jobs of the category for which such space is appropriate; and

(B) There is a likelihood of continuation of the pattern, based on measurable comparisons between the area from which the movement has been occurring and the area of the proposed project in terms of tax rates, energy costs, and similar relevant factors.

(ii) The restrictions established in this paragraph (c)(1) shall not apply if the Secretary determines that the relocation does not significantly and adversely affect the employment or economic base of the area from which the industrial or commercial plant or facility is to be relocated. However, the Secretary will not be required to make a determination whether there is a significant and adverse effect. If such a determination is undertaken, the Secretary will presume that there is a significant and adverse effect where the significant pattern of job movement and the likelihood of continuation of such a pattern has been from a distressed community.

(iii) The presumptions established in accordance with this paragraph (c)(1) are rebuttable by the applicant. However, the burden of overcoming the presumptions will be on the applicant.

(iv) The presumptions established in this paragraph (c)(1) will not apply if the speculative space contained in a commercial or industrial plant or facility included in a project constitutes a lesser percentage of the total space contained in that plant or facility than the threshold amounts specified below:

Size of plant or facility	Amount of speculative space
0 to 50,000 sq. ft. ...	10 percent.
50,001 to 250,000 sq. ft.	5,000 sq. ft. or 8 percent, whichever is greater.
250,001 to 1,000,000 sq. ft.	20,000 sq. ft. or 5 percent, whichever is greater.
1,000,001 or more sq. ft.	50,000 sq. ft. or 3 percent, whichever is greater.

(2) *Projects with identified intended occupants.* No assistance may be provided or utilized under this subpart for any project with identified intended occupants that is likely to facilitate:

(i) A relocation of any operation of an industrial or commercial plant or facility or other business establishment from any UDAG eligible jurisdiction; or

(ii) An expansion of any operation of an industrial or commercial plant or facility or other business establishment that results in a substantial reduction of any such operation in any UDAG eligible jurisdiction. The provisions of this paragraph (c)(2) shall not apply to a relocation of an operation or to an expansion of an operation within a metropolitan area. The provisions of this paragraph (c)(2) shall apply only to projects that do not have speculative space, or to projects that include both identified intended occupant space and speculative space.

(iii) *Significant and adverse effect.* The restrictions established in this paragraph (c)(2) shall not apply if the Secretary determines that the relocation or expansion does not significantly and adversely affect the employment or economic base of the UDAG eligible jurisdiction from which the relocation or expansion occurs. However, the Secretary will not be required to make a determination whether there is a significant and adverse effect. If such a determination is undertaken, among the factors which the Secretary will consider are:

(A) Whether it is reasonable to anticipate that there will be a significant net loss of jobs in the plant or facility being abandoned; and

(B) Whether an equivalent productive use will be made of the plant or facility being abandoned by the relocating or expanding operation, thus creating no deterioration of economic base.

(3) Within 90 days following notice of intent to withhold, deny or cancel assistance under paragraph (c) (1) or (2) of this section, the applicant may appeal in writing to the Secretary the withholding, denial or cancellation of assistance. The applicant will be notified and given an opportunity within a prescribed time for an informal consultation regarding the action.

(4) *Assistance for individuals adversely affected by prohibited relocations.* (i) Any amount withdrawn by, recaptured by, or paid to the Secretary because of a violation (or a settlement of an alleged violation) of this section (or any regulation issued or contractual provision entered into to carry out this section) by a project with identified intended occupants will be made available by the Secretary as a grant to the UDAG eligible jurisdiction from which the operation of an industrial or commercial plant or facility or other business establishment was relocated, or in which the operation was reduced.

(ii)(A) Any amount made available under this paragraph shall be used by the grantee to assist individuals who were employed by the operation involved before the relocation or reduction and whose employment or terms of employment were adversely affected by the relocation or reduction. The assistance shall include job training, job retraining, and job placement.

(B) If any amount made available to a grantee under this paragraph (c)(4) is more than is required to provide the assistance described in paragraph (c)(4)(ii)(A) of this section, the grantee shall use the excess amount to carry out community development activities eligible under section 105(a) of the Housing and Community Development Act of 1974.

(iii)(A) The provisions of this paragraph (c)(4) shall be applicable to any amount withdrawn by, recaptured by, or paid to the Secretary under this section, including any amount withdrawn, recaptured, or paid before the effective date of this paragraph.

(B) Grants may be made under this paragraph (c)(4) only to the extent of amounts provided in appropriation Acts.

(5) For purposes of this section, the following definitions apply:

(i) "Operation" means any plant, equipment, facility, substantial number of positions, substantial employment opportunities, production capacity, or product line.

(ii) "Metropolitan area" means a metropolitan area as defined in § 570.3 and which consists of either a free-standing metropolitan area or a primary metropolitan statistical area where both primary and consolidated areas exist.

(iii) "Likely" means probably or reasonably to be expected, as determined by firm evidence such as resolutions of a corporation to close a plant or facility, notifications of closure to collective bargaining units, correspondence and notifications of corporate officials relative to a closure, and supportive evidence, such as newspaper articles and notices to employees regarding closure of a plant or facility. Consultant studies and marketing studies may be submitted as supportive evidence, but by themselves are not firm evidence.

(iv) "UDAG eligible jurisdiction" means a distressed community, a Pocket of Poverty, a Pocket of Poverty community, or an identifiable community described in section 119(p) of the Housing and Community Development Act of 1974.

(6) Notwithstanding any other provision of this subpart, nothing in this subpart may be construed to permit an inference or conclusion that the policy of the urban development action grant program is to facilitate the relocation of businesses from one area to another.

[47 FR 7983, Feb. 23, 1982, as amended at 53 FR 33028, Aug. 29, 1988; 54 FR 21169, May 16, 1989; 56 FR 56128, Oct. 31, 1991]

§570.457 Displacement, relocation, acquisition, and replacement of housing.

The displacement, relocation, acquisition, and replacement of housing requirements of §570.606 apply to applicants under this subpart G.

[55 FR 29309, July 18, 1990]

§570.461 Post-preliminary approval requirements; lead-based paint.

The recipient may receive preliminary approval prior to the accomplishment of lead-based paint activities conducted pursuant to part 35, subparts A, B, J, K, and R of this title, but no funds will be released until such actions are complete and evidence of compliance is submitted to HUD.

[64 FR 50225, Sept. 15, 1999]

§570.463 Project amendments and revisions.

(a) *Pre-approval revisions to the application.* Applicants must submit to the HUD Area Office and to Central Office all revisions to the application. A revision is considered significant if it alters the scope, location, or scale of the project or changes the beneficiaries' population.

The applicant must hold at least one public hearing prior to making a significant revision to the application.

(b) *Post preliminary approval amendments.* Applicants receiving preliminary approval must submit to the HUD Central Office, a request for approval of any significant amendment. A copy of the request must also be submitted to the Area Office. A significant amendment involves new activities or alterations thereof which will change the scope, location, scale, or beneficiaries of such activities or which, as a result of a number of smaller changes, add up to an amount that exceeds ten percent of the grant. HUD approval of amendments may be granted to those requests which meet all of the following criteria:

(1) New or significantly altered activities must meet the criteria for selection applicable at the time of receipt of the program amendment.

(2) The recipient must have complied with all requirements of this subpart.

(3) The recipient may make amendments other than those requiring prior HUD approval as defined in paragraph (b) of this section but each recipient must notify both the Area and Central Offices of such changes.

[47 FR 7983, Feb. 23, 1982, as amended at 61 FR 11476, Mar. 20, 1996]

§570.464 Project closeout.

HUD will advise the recipient to initiate closeout procedures when HUD determines, in consultation with the recipient, that there are not impediments to closeout. Closeout shall be carried out in accordance with §570.509 and applicable HUD guidelines.

[53 FR 8058, Mar. 11, 1988]

§570.465 Applicability of rules and regulations.

The provisions of subparts A, B, C, J, K, and O of this part 570 shall apply to this subpart except to the extent that they are modified or augmented by this subpart.

§ 570.466 Additional application submission requirements for Pockets of Poverty—employment opportunities.

Applicants for Action Grants under the Pockets of Poverty provision must describe the number and, to the extent possible, the types of new jobs (construction and permanent) that will be provided to the low- and moderate-income residents of the Pocket of Poverty as a direct result of the proposed project. If the application calls for job training programs (such as those related to the CETA program) or job recruiting services for the pocket's residents, then such proposed activities must be clearly and fully explained. HUD requires applicants to ensure that at least 75 percent of whatever permanent jobs initially result from the project are provided to low- and moderate-income persons and that at least 51 percent of whatever permanent jobs initially result from the project are provided to low- and moderate-income residents from the pocket. HUD encourages applicants to ensure that at least 20 percent of all permanent jobs are filled by persons from the pocket qualified to participate in the CETA program on a continuous basis. HUD requires all applicants to continuously use best efforts to ensure that at least 75 percent of all permanent jobs resulting from any Action Grant-assisted project are provided to low- and moderate-income persons and that at least 51 percent of all permanent jobs resulting from any Action Grant-assisted project are provided to low- and moderate-income residents from the pocket. The application should clearly describe how the applicant intends to meet initial and continuous job requirements. Private participating parties must meet these employment requirements in the aggregate. To enable the private participants to do so, lease agreements executed by a private participating party shall include:

(a) Provisions requiring lessees to follow hiring practices that the private participating party has determined will enable it to meet these requirements in the aggregate; and

(b) Provisions that will enable the private participating party to declare a default under the lease agreement if the lessees do not follow such practices.

[61 FR 11476, Mar. 20, 1996]

Subpart H [Reserved]

Subpart I—State Community Development Block Grant Program

SOURCE: 57 FR 53397, Nov. 9, 1992, unless otherwise noted.

§ 570.480 General.

(a) This subpart describes policies and procedures applicable to states that have permanently elected to receive Community Development Block Grant (CDBG) funds for distribution to units of general local government in the state's nonentitlement areas under the Housing and Community Development Act of 1974, as amended (the Act). Other subparts of part 570 are not applicable to the State CDBG program, except as expressly provided otherwise. Regulations of part 570 outside of this subpart that apply to the State CDBG program include §§ 570.200(j) and 570.606.

(b) HUD's authority for the waiver of regulations and for the suspension of requirements to address damage in a Presidentially-declared disaster area is described in 24 CFR part 5 and in section 122 of the Act, respectively.

(c) In exercising the Secretary's obligation and responsibility to review a state's performance, the Secretary will give maximum feasible deference to the state's interpretation of the statutory requirements and the requirements of this regulation, provided that these interpretations are not plainly inconsistent with the Act and the Secretary's obligation to enforce compliance with the intent of the Congress as declared in the Act. The Secretary will not determine that a state has failed to carry out its certifications in compliance with requirements of the Act (and this regulation) unless the Secretary finds that procedures and requirements adopted by the state are insufficient to afford reasonable assurance that activities undertaken by units of general local government were not plainly inappropriate to meeting the primary objectives of the Act, this regulation, and the state's community development objectives.

(d) Administrative action taken by the Secretary that is not explicitly and fully part of this regulation shall only apply to a specific case or issue at a specific time, and shall not be generally applicable to the state-administered CDBG program.

(e) Religious organizations are eligible to participate under the State CDBG Program as provided in §570.200(j).

(f) In administering the CDBG program, a state may impose additional or more restrictive provisions on units of general local government participating in the state's program, provided that such provisions are not inconsistent with the Act or other statutory or regulatory provisions that are applicable to the State CDBG program.

(g) States shall make CDBG program grants only to units of general local government. This restriction does not limit a state's authority to make payments to other parties for state administrative expenses and technical assistance activities authorized in section 106(d) of the Act.

(h) Any unexpended CDBG origin year grant funds in the United States Treasury account on September 30 of the fifth Federal fiscal year after the end of the origin year grant's period of availability for obligation by HUD will be canceled. HUD may require an earlier expenditure and draw down deadline under a grant agreement.

[57 FR 53397, Nov. 9, 1992, as amended at 61 FR 11477, Mar. 20, 1996; 61 FR 54921, Oct. 22, 1996; 69 FR 41718, July 9, 2004; 77 FR 24142, Apr. 23, 2012; 80 FR 69870, Nov. 12, 2015]

§570.481 Definitions.

(a) Except for terms defined in applicable statutes or this subpart, the Secretary will defer to a state's definitions, provided that these definitions are explicit, reasonable and not plainly inconsistent with the Act. As used in this subpart, the following terms shall have the meaning indicated:

(1) *Act* means title I of the Housing and Community Development Act of 1974 (42 U.S.C. 5301 *et seq.*).

(2) *CDBG funds* means Community Development Block Grant funds, in the form of grants under this subpart including any reimbursements, program income, and loans guaranteed under section 108 of the Act.

(3) *Origin year* means the specific Federal fiscal year during which the annual grant funds were appropriated.

(b) [Reserved]

[57 FR 53397, Nov. 9, 1992, as amended at 61 FR 5209, Feb. 9, 1996; 74 FR 36389, July 22, 2009; 80 FR 69871, Nov. 12, 2015]

§570.482 Eligible activities.

(a) *General.* The choice of activities on which block grant funds are expended represents the determination by state and local participants, developed in accordance with the state's program design and procedures, as to which approach or approaches will best serve these interests. The eligible activities are listed at section 105(a) of the Act.

(b) *Special assessments under the CDBG program.* The following policies relate to special assessments under the CDBG program:

(1) *Public improvements initially assisted with CDBG funds.* Where CDBG funds are used to pay all or part of the cost of a public improvement, special assessments may be imposed as follows:

(i) Special assessments to recover the *CDBG funds* may be made only against properties owned and occupied by persons *not* of low and moderate income. These assessments constitute program income.

(ii) Special assessments to recover the *non-CDBG* portion may be made, provided that CDBG funds are used to pay the special assessment in behalf of all properties owned and occupied by low and moderate income persons; except that CDBG funds need not be used to pay the special assessments in behalf of properties owned and occupied by moderate income persons if, when permitted by the state, the unit of general local government certifies that it does not have sufficient CDBG funds to pay the assessments in behalf of all of the low and moderate income owner-occupant persons. Funds collected through such special assessments are not program income.

(2) *Public improvements not initially assisted with CDBG funds.* CDBG funds may be used to pay special assessments

levied against property when this form of assessment is used to recover the capital cost of eligible public improvements initially financed solely from sources other than CDBG funds. The payment of special assessments with CDBG funds constitutes CDBG assistance to the public improvement. Therefore, CDBG funds may be used to pay special assessments, provided that:

(i) The installation of the public improvements was carried out in compliance with requirements applicable to activities assisted under this subpart, including labor, environmental and citizen participation requirements;

(ii) The installation of the public improvement meets a criterion for national objectives. (See § 570.483(b)(1), (c), and (d).)

(iii) The requirements of § 570.482(b)(1)(ii) are met.

(c) *Special eligibility provisions.* (1) Microenterprise development activities eligible under section 105(a)(23) of the Housing and Community Development Act of 1974, as amended (42 U.S.C. 5301 *et seq.*) (the Act) may be carried out either through the recipient directly or through public and private organizations, agencies, and other subrecipients (including nonprofit and for-profit subrecipients).

(2) *Provision of public services.* The following activities shall not be subject to the restrictions on public services under section 105(a)(8) of the Act:

(i) Support services provided under section 105(a)(23) of the Act, and paragraph (c) of this section;

(ii) Services carried out under the provisions of section 105(a)(15) of the Act, that are specifically designed to increase economic opportunities through job training and placement and other employment support services, including, but not limited to, peer support programs, counseling, child care, transportation, and other similar services; and

(iii) Services of any type carried out under the provisions of section 105(a)(15) of the Act pursuant to a strategy approved by a state under the provisions of § 91.315(e)(2) of this title.

(3) Environmental cleanup and economic development or redevelopment of contaminated properties. Remediation of known or suspected environmental contamination may be undertaken under the authority of section 205 of Public Law 105–276 and section 105(a)(4) of the Act. Economic development activities carried out under sections 105(a)(14), (a)(15), or (a)(17) of the Act may include costs associated with project-specific assessment or remediation of known or suspected environmental contamination.

(4) Housing counseling, as defined in 24 CFR 5.100, that is funded with or provided in connection with CDBG funds must be carried out in accordance with 24 CFR 5.111.

(5) *Broadband infrastructure in housing.* Any new construction or substantial rehabilitation, as substantial rehabilitation is defined by 24 CFR 5.100, of a building with more than 4 rental units, for which CDBG funds are first obligated by the State's grant recipient on or after July 18, 2017, must include installation of broadband infrastructure, as this term is also defined in 24 CFR 5.100, except where the State or the State's grant recipient determines and documents the determination that:

(i) The location of the new construction or substantial rehabilitation makes installation of broadband infrastructure infeasible;

(ii) The cost of installing broadband infrastructure would result in a fundamental alteration in the nature of its program or activity or in an undue financial burden; or

(iii) The structure of the housing to be substantially rehabilitated makes installation of broadband infrastructure infeasible.

(d) [Reserved]

(e) *Guidelines and objectives for evaluating project costs and financial requirements*—(1) *Applicability.* The following guidelines, also referred to as the underwriting guidelines, are provided to assist the recipient to evaluate and select activities to be carried out for economic development purposes. Specifically, these guidelines are applicable to activities that are eligible for CDBG assistance under section 105(a)(17) of the Act, economic development activities eligible under section 105(a)(14) of the Act, and activities that are part of a community economic development project eligible under section 105(a)(15) of the Act. The use of the underwriting guidelines published by HUD is not mandatory. However, states electing not to use these guidelines would be expected to ensure that the state or units of general local government conduct basic financial underwriting prior to the provision of CDBG financial assistance to a for-profit business.

(2) *Objectives.* The underwriting guidelines are designed to provide the recipient with a framework for financially underwriting and selecting CDBG-assisted economic development projects which are financially viable and will make the most effective use of the CDBG funds. Where appropriate, HUD's underwriting guidelines recognize that different levels of review are appropriate to take into account differences in the size and scope of a proposed project, and in the case of a microenterprise or other small business to take into account the differences in the capacity and level of sophistication among businesses of differing sizes. Recipients are encouraged, when they develop their own programs and underwriting criteria, to also take these factors into account. These underwriting guidelines are published as appendix A to this part. The objectives of the underwriting guidelines are to ensure:

(i) That project costs are reasonable;

(ii) That all sources of project financing are committed;

(iii) That to the extent practicable, CDBG funds are not substituted for non-Federal financial support;

(iv) That the project is financially feasible;

(v) That to the extent practicable, the return on the owner's equity investment will not be unreasonably high; and

(vi) That to the extent practicable, CDBG funds are disbursed on a pro rata basis with other finances provided to the project.

(f) *Standards for evaluating public benefit*—(1) *Purpose and applicability.* The grantee is responsible for making sure that at least a minimum level of public benefit is obtained from the expenditure of CDBG funds under the categories of eligibility governed by these standards. The standards set forth below identify the types of public benefit that will be recognized for this purpose and the minimum level of each that must be obtained for the amount of CDBG funds used. These standards are applicable to activities that are eligible for CDBG assistance under section 105(a)(17) of the Act, economic development activities eligible under section 105(a)(14) of the Act, and activities that are part of a community economic development project eligible under section 105(a)(15) of the Act. Certain public facilities and improvements eligible under section 105(a)(2) of the Act, which are undertaken for economic development purposes, are also subject to these standards, as specified in §570.483(b)(4)(vi)(F)(*2*). Unlike the guidelines for project costs and financial requirements covered under paragraph (a) of this section, the use of the standards for public benefit is mandatory.

(2) *Standards for activities in the aggregate.* Activities covered by these standards must, in the aggregate, either:

(i) Create or retain at least one full-time equivalent, permanent job per $35,000 of CDBG funds used; or

(ii) Provide goods or services to residents of an area, such that the number of low- and moderate-income persons residing in the areas served by the assisted businesses amounts to at least one low- and moderate-income person per $350 of CDBG funds used.

(3) *Applying the aggregate standards.* (i) A state shall apply the aggregate standards under paragraph (e)(2) of this section to all funds distributed for applicable activities from each annual grant. This includes the amount of the annual grant, any funds reallocated by HUD to the state, any program income distributed by the state and any guaranteed loan funds made under the provisions of subpart M of this part covered in the method of distribution in the final statement for a given annual grant year.

(ii) The grantee shall apply the aggregate standards to the number of jobs to be created/retained, or to the number of persons residing in the area served (as applicable), as determined at the time funds are obligated to activities.

(iii) Where an activity is expected both to create or retain jobs and to provide goods or services to residents of an area, the grantee may elect to count the activity under either the jobs standard or the area residents standard, but not both.

(iv) Where CDBG assistance for an activity is limited to job training and placement and/or other employment support services, the jobs assisted with CDBG funds shall be considered to be created or retained jobs for the purposes of applying the aggregate standards.

(v) Any activity subject to these standards which meets one or more of the following criteria may, at the grantee's option, be excluded from the aggregate standards described in paragraph (f)(2) of this section:

(A) Provides jobs exclusively for unemployed persons or participants in one or more of the following programs:

(*1*) Jobs Training Partnership Act (JTPA);

(*2*) Jobs Opportunities for Basic Skills (JOBS); or

(*3*) Aid to Families with Dependent Children (AFDC);

(B) Provides jobs predominantly for residents of Public and Indian Housing units;

(C) Provides jobs predominantly for homeless persons;

(D) Provides jobs predominantly for low-skilled, low- and moderate-income persons, where the business agrees to provide clear opportunities for promotion and economic advancement, such as through the provision of training;

(E) Provides jobs predominantly for persons residing within a census tract (or block numbering area) that has at least 20 percent of its residents who are in poverty;

(F) Provides assistance to business(es) that operate(s) within a census tract (or block numbering area) that has at least 20 percent of its residents who are in poverty;

(G) Stabilizes or revitalizes a neighborhood income that has at least 70 percent of its residents who are low- and moderate-income;

(H) Provides assistance to a Community Development Financial Institution (as defined in the Community Development Banking and Financial Institutions Act of 1994, (12 U.S.C. 4701 note)) serving an area that has at least 70 percent of its residents who are low- and moderate-income;

(I) Provides assistance to an organization eligible to carry out activities under section 105(a)(15) of the Act serving an area that has at least 70 percent of its residents who are low- and moderate-income;

(J) Provides employment opportunities that are an integral component of a project designed to promote spatial deconcentration of low- and moderate-income and minority persons;

(K) With prior HUD approval, provides substantial benefit to low-income persons through other innovative approaches;

(L) Provides services to the residents of an area pursuant to a strategy approved by the State under the provisions of § 91.315(e)(2) of this title;

(M) Creates or retains jobs through businesses assisted in an area pursuant to a strategy approved by the State under the provisions of § 91.315(e)(2) of this title.

(N) Directly involves the economic development or redevelopment of environmentally contaminated properties.

(4) *Standards for individual activities.* Any activity subject to these standards which falls into one or more of the following categories will be considered by HUD to provide insufficient public benefit, and therefore may under no circumstances be assisted with CDBG funds:

(i) The amount of CDBG assistance exceeds either of the following, as applicable:

(A) $50,000 per full-time equivalent, permanent job created or retained; or

(B) $1,000 per low- and moderate-income person to which goods or services are provided by the activity.

(ii) The activity consists of or includes any of the following:

(A) General promotion of the community as a whole (as opposed to the promotion of specific areas and programs);

(B) Assistance to professional sports teams;

(C) Assistance to privately-owned recreational facilities that serve a predominantly higher-income clientele, where the recreational benefit to users or members clearly outweighs employment or other benefits to low- and moderate-income persons;

(D) Acquisition of land for which the specific proposed use has not yet been identified; and

(E) Assistance to a for-profit business while that business or any other business owned by the same person(s) or entity(ies) is the subject of unresolved findings of noncompliance relating to previous CDBG assistance provided by the recipient.

(5) *Applying the individual activity standards.* (i) Where an activity is expected both to create or retain jobs and to provide goods or services to residents of an area, it will be disqualified only if the amount of CDBG assistance exceeds both of the amounts in paragraph (f)(4)(i) of this section.

(ii) The individual activity tests in paragraph (f)(4)(i) of this section shall be applied to the number of jobs to be created or retained, or to the number of persons residing in the area served (as applicable), as determined at the time funds are obligated to activities.

(iii) Where CDBG assistance for an activity is limited to job training and placement and/or other employment support services, the jobs assisted with CDBG funds shall be considered to be created or retained jobs for the purposes of applying the individual activity standards in paragraph (f)(4)(i) of this section.

(6) *Documentation.* The state and its grant recipients must maintain sufficient records to demonstrate the level of public benefit, based on the above standards, that is actually achieved upon completion of the CDBG-assisted economic development activity(ies) and how that compares to the level of such benefit anticipated when the CDBG assistance was obligated. If a state grant recipient's actual results show a pattern of substantial variation from anticipated results, the state and its recipient are expected to take those actions reasonably within their respective control to improve the accuracy of the projections. If the actual results demonstrate that the state has failed the public benefit standards, HUD may require the state to meet more stringent standards in future years as appropriate.

(g) *Amendments to economic development projects after review determinations.* If, after the grantee enters into a contract to provide assistance to a project, the scope or financial elements of the project change to the extent that a significant contract amendment is appropriate, the project should be reevaluated under these and the recipient's guidelines. (This would include, for example, situations where the business requests a change in the amount or terms of assistance being provided, or an extension to the loan payment period required in the contract.) If a reevaluation of the project indicates that the financial elements and public benefit to be derived have also substantially changed, then the recipient should make appropriate adjustments in the amount, type, terms or conditions of CDBG assistance which has been offered, to reflect the impact of the substantial change. (For example, if a change in the project elements results in a substantial reduction of the total project costs, it may be appropriate for the recipient to reduce the amount of total CDBG assistance.) If the amount of CDBG assistance provided to the project is increased, the amended project must still comply with the public benefit standards under paragraph (f) of this section.

(h) *Prohibition on use of assistance for employment relocation activities*—(1) *Prohibition.* CDBG funds may not be used to directly assist a business, including a business expansion, in the relocation of a plant, facility, or operation from one labor market area (LMA) to another LMA if the relocation is likely to result in a significant loss of jobs in the LMA from which the relocation occurs.

(2) *Definitions.* The following definitions apply to the section:

(i) *Directly assist.* Directly assist means the provision of CDBG funds to a business pursuant to section 105(a)(15) or (17) of the Housing and Community Development Act of 1974 (42 U.S.C. 5301 *et seq*). Direct assistance also includes assistance under section 105(a)(1), (2), (4), (7), and (14) of the Housing and Community Development Act of 1974, when the state's grantee, subrecipient, or nonprofit entity eligible under section 105(a)(15) enters into an agreement with a business to undertake one or more of these activities as a condition of the business relocating a facility, plant, or operation to the LMA. Provision of public facilities and indirect assistance that will provide benefit to multiple businesses does not fall under the definition of "directly assist," unless it includes the provision of infrastructure to aid a specific business that is the subject of an agreement with the specific assisted business.

(ii) *Labor market area (LMA).* For metropolitan areas, an LMA is an area defined as such by the U.S. Bureau of Labor Statistics (BLS). An LMA is an economically integrated geographic area within which individuals can live and find employment within a reasonable distance or can readily change employment without changing their place of residence. In addition, LMAs are nonoverlapping and geographically exhaustive. For metropolitan areas, grantees must use employment data, as defined by the BLS, for the LMA in which the affected business is currently located and from which current jobs may be lost. For non-metropolitan areas, grantees must use employment data, as defined by the BLS, for the LMA in which the assisted business is currently located and from which current jobs may be lost. For non-metropolitan areas, a LMA is either an area defined by the BLS as an LMA, or a state may choose to combine non-metropolitan LMAs. States are required to define or reaffirm prior definitions of their LMAs on an annual basis and retain records to substantiate such areas prior to any business relocation that would be impacted by this rule. Metropolitan LMAs cannot be combined, nor can a non-metropolitan LMA be combined with a metropolitan LMA. For the Insular Areas, each jurisdiction will be considered to be an LMA. For the HUD-administered Small Cities Program, each of the three participating counties in Hawaii will be considered to be its own LMA. Recipients of Fiscal Year 1999 Small Cities Program funding in New York will follow the requirements for State CDBG recipients.

(iii) *Operation.* A business operation includes, but is not limited to, any equipment, employment opportunity, production capacity, or product line of the business.

(iv) *Significant loss of jobs.* (A) A loss of jobs is significant if: The number of jobs to be lost in the LMA in which the affected business is currently located is equal to or greater than one-tenth of one percent of the total number of persons in the labor force of that LMA; or in all cases, a loss of 500 or more jobs. Notwithstanding the aforementioned, a loss of 25 jobs or fewer does not constitute a significant loss of jobs.

(B) A job is considered to be lost due to the provision of CDBG assistance if the job is relocated within three years from the date the assistance is provided to the business or the time period within which jobs are to be created as specified by the agreement among the business, the recipient, and the state (as applicable) if it is longer than three years.

(3) *Written agreement.* Before directly assisting a business with CDBG funds, the recipient, subrecipient, or (in the case of any activity carried out pursuant to 105(a)(15)) nonprofit entity shall sign a written agreement with the assisted business. The written agreement shall include:

(i) *Statement.* A statement from the assisted business as to whether the assisted activity will result in the relocation of any industrial or commercial plant, facility, or operation from one LMA to another and, if so, the number of jobs that will be relocated from each LMA;

(ii) *Required certification.* If the assistance will not result in a relocation covered by this section, a certification from the assisted business that neither it, nor any of its subsidiaries, has plans to relocate jobs at the time the agreement is signed that would result in a significant job loss as defined in this rule; and

(iii) *Reimbursement of assistance.* The agreement shall provide for reimbursement to the recipient of any assistance provided to, or expended on behalf of, the business in the event that assistance results in a relocation prohibited under this section.

(4) *Assistance not covered by this paragraph.* This paragraph does not apply to:

(i) *Relocation assistance.* Relocation assistance required by the Uniform Assistance and Real Property Acquisition

Policies Act of 1970 (URA), (42 U.S.C. 4601–4655); optional relocation assistance under section 105(a)(11), as implemented at 570.606(d);

(ii) *Microenterprises.* Assistance to microenterprises as defined by section 102(a)(22) of the Housing and Community Development Act of 1974; and

(iii) *Arms-length transactions.* Assistance to a business that purchases business equipment, inventory, or other physical assets in an arms-length transaction, including the assets of an existing business, provided that the purchase does not result in the relocation of the sellers' business operation (including customer base or list, goodwill, product lines, or trade names) from one LMA to another LMA and does not produce a significant loss of jobs in the LMA from which the relocation occurs.

[57 FR 53397, Nov. 9, 1992, as amended at 60 FR 1949, Jan. 5, 1995; 61 FR 54921, Oct. 22, 1996; 70 FR 76370, Dec. 23, 2005; 71 FR 30035, May 24, 2006; 81 FR 90659, Dec. 14, 2016; 81 FR 92636, Dec. 20, 2016]

§570.483 Criteria for national objectives.

(a) *General.* The following criteria shall be used to determine whether a CDBG assisted activity complies with one or more of the national objectives as required to section 104(b)(3) of the Act. (HUD is willing to consider a waiver of these requirements in accordance with §570.480(b)).

(b) *Activities benefiting low and moderate income persons.* An activity will be considered to address the objective of benefiting low and moderate income persons if it meets one of the criteria in paragraph (b) of this section, unless there is substantial evidence to the contrary. In assessing any such evidence, the full range of direct effects of the assisted activity will be considered. The activities, when taken as a whole, must not benefit moderate income persons to the exclusion of low income persons:

(1) *Area benefit activities.* (i) An activity, the benefits of which are available to all the residents in a particular area, where at least 51 percent of the residents are low and moderate income persons. Such an area need not be coterminous with census tracts or other officially recognized boundaries but must be the entire area served by the activity. Units of general local government may, at the discretion of the state, use either HUD-provided data comparing census data with appropriate low and moderate income levels or survey data that is methodologically sound. An activity that serves an area that is not primarily residential in character shall not qualify under this criterion.

(ii) An activity, where the assistance is to a public improvement that provides benefits to all the residents of an area, that is limited to paying special assessments levied against residential properties owned and occupied by persons of low and moderate income.

(iii)(A) An activity to develop, establish and operate (not to exceed two years after establishment), a uniform emergency telephone number system serving an area having less than 51 percent of low and moderate income residents, when the system has not been made operational before the receipt of CDBG funds, provided a prior written determination is obtained from HUD. HUD's determination will be based upon certifications by the State that:

(*1*) The system will contribute significantly to the safety of the residents of the area. The unit of general local government must provide the state a list of jurisdictions and unincorporated areas to be served by the system and a list of the emergency services that will participate in the emergency telephone number system;

(*2*) At least 51 percent of the use of the system will be by low and moderate income persons. The state's certification may be based upon information which identifies the total number of calls actually received over the preceding twelve-month period for each of the emergency services to be covered by the emergency telephone number system and relates those calls to the geographic segment (expressed as nearly as possible in terms of census tracts, enumeration districts, block groups, or combinations thereof that are contained within the segment) of the service area from which the calls were generated. In analyzing this data to meet the requirements of this section, the state will assume that the distribution of income among callers generally reflects the income characteristics of the general population residing in the same geographic area where the callers reside. Alternatively, the state's certification may be based upon other data, agreed to by HUD and the state, which shows that over the preceding twelve-month period the users of all the services to be included in the emergency telephone number system consisted of at least 51 percent low and moderate income persons.

(*3*) Other federal funds received by the unit of general local government are insufficient or unavailable for a uniform emergency telephone number system. The unit of general local government must submit a statement explaining whether the problem is caused by the insufficiency of the amount of such funds, the restrictions on the use of such funds, or the prior commitment of such funds for other purposes by the unit of general local government.

(*4*) The percentage of the total costs of the system paid for by CDBG funds does not exceed the percentage of low and moderate income persons in the service area of the system. The unit of general local government must include a description of the boundaries of the service area of the system; the census tracts or enumeration districts within the boundaries; the total number of persons and the total number of low and moderate income persons in each census tract or enumeration district, and the percentage of low and moderate income persons in the service area; and the total cost of the system.

(B) The certifications of the state must be submitted along with a brief statement describing the factual basis upon which the certifications were made.

(iv) Activities meeting the requirements of paragraph (e)(4)(i) of this section may be considered to qualify under paragraph (b)(1) of this section.

(v) HUD will consider activities meeting the requirements of paragraph (e)(5)(i) of this section to qualify under paragraph (b)(1) of this section, provided that the area covered by the strategy meets one of the following criteria:

(A) The area is in a Federally-designated Empowerment Zone or Enterprise Community;

(B) The area is primarily residential and contains a percentage of low and moderate income residents that is no less than 70 percent;

(C) All of the census tracts (or block numbering areas) in the area have poverty rates of at least 20 percent, at least 90 percent of the census tracts (or block numbering areas) in the area have poverty rates of at least 25 percent, and the area is primarily residential. (If only part of a census tract or block numbering area is included in a strategy area, the poverty rate shall be computed for those block groups (or any part thereof) which are included in the strategy area.)

(D) Upon request by the State, HUD may grant exceptions to the 70 percent low and moderate income or 25 percent poverty minimum thresholds on a case-by-case basis. In no case, however, may a strategy area have both a percentage of low and moderate income residents less than 51 percent and a poverty rate less than 20 percent.

(2) *Limited clientele activities.* (i) An activity which benefits a limited clientele, at least 51 percent of whom are low and moderate income persons. The following kinds of activities may not qualify under paragraph (b)(2) of this section:

(A) Activities, the benefits of which are available to all the residents of an area;

(B) Activities involving the acquisition, construction or rehabilitation of property for housing; or

(C) Activities where the benefit to low- and moderate-income persons to be considered is the creation or retention of jobs, except as provided in paragraph (b)(2)(v) of this section.

(ii) To qualify under paragraph (b)(2) of this section, the activity must meet one or the following tests:

(A) It must benefit a clientele who are generally presumed to be principally low and moderate income persons. Activities that exclusively serve a group of persons in any one or a combination of the following categories may be presumed to benefit persons, 51 percent of whom are low and moderate income: abused children, battered spouses, elderly persons, adults meeting the Bureau of the Census' Current Population Reports definition of "severely disabled," homeless persons, illiterate adults, persons living with AIDS, and migrant farm workers; or

(B) It must require information on family size and income so that it is evident that at least 51 percent of the clientele are persons whose family income does not exceed the low and moderate income limit; or

(C) It must have income eligibility requirements which limit the activity exclusively to low and moderate income persons; or

(D) It must be of such a nature, and be in such a location, that it may be concluded that the activity's clientele will primarily be low and moderate income persons.

(iii) An activity that serves to remove material or architectural barriers to the mobility or accessibility of elderly persons or of adults meeting the Bureau of the Census' Current Population Reports definition of "severely disabled" will be presumed to qualify under this criterion if it is restricted, to the extent practicable, to the removal of such barriers by assisting:

(A) The reconstruction of a public facility or improvement, or portion thereof, that does not qualify under § 570.483(b)(1);

(B) The rehabilitation of a privately owned nonresidential building or improvement that does not qualify under § 570.483(b) (1) or (4); or

(C) The rehabilitation of the common areas of a residential structure that contains more than one dwelling unit and that does not qualify under § 570.483(b)(3).

(iv) A microenterprise assistance activity (carried out in accordance with the provisions of section 105(a)(23) of the Act or § 570.482(c) and limited to microenterprises) with respect to those owners of microenterprises and persons developing microenterprises assisted under the activity who are low- and moderate-income persons. For purposes of this paragraph, persons determined to be low and moderate income may be presumed to continue to qualify as such for up to a three-year period.

(v) An activity designed to provide job training and placement and/or other employment support services, including, but not limited to, peer support programs, counseling, child care, transportation, and other similar services, in which the percentage of low- and moderate-income persons assisted is less than 51 percent may qualify under this paragraph in the following limited circumstances:

(A) In such cases where such training or provision of supportive services is an integrally-related component of a larger project, the only use of CDBG assistance for the project is to provide the job training and/or supportive services; and

(B) The proportion of the total cost of the project borne by CDBG funds is no greater than the proportion of the total number of persons assisted who are low or moderate income.

(3) *Housing activities.* An eligible activity carried out for the purpose of providing or improving permanent residential structures that, upon completion, will be occupied by low and moderate income households. This would include, but not necessarily be limited to, the acquisition or rehabilitation of property by the unit of general local government, a subrecipient, an entity eligible to receive assistance under section 105(a)(15) of the Act, a developer, an individual homebuyer, or an individual homeowner; conversion of nonresidential structures; and new housing construction. If the structure contains two dwelling units, at least one must be so occupied, and if the structure contains more than two dwelling units, at least 51 percent of the units must be so occupied. If two or more rental buildings being assisted are or will be located on the same or contiguous properties, and the buildings will be under common ownership and management, the grouped buildings may be considered for this purpose as a single structure. If housing activities being assisted meet the requirements of paragraph (e)(4)(ii) or (e)(5)(ii) of this section, all such housing may also be considered for this purpose as a single structure. For rental housing, occupancy by low and moderate income households must be at affordable rents to qualify under this criterion. The unit of general local government shall adopt and make public its standards

for determining "affordable rents" for this purpose. The following shall also qualify under this criterion:

(i) When less than 51 percent of the units in a structure will be occupied by low and moderate income households, CDBG assistance may be provided in the following limited circumstances:

(A) The assistance is for an eligible activity to reduce the development cost of the new construction of a multifamily, non-elderly rental housing project; and

(B) Not less than 20 percent of the units will be occupied by low and moderate income households at affordable rents; and

(C) The proportion of the total cost of developing the project to be borne by CDBG funds is no greater than the proportion of units in the project that will be occupied by low and moderate income households.

(ii) Where CDBG funds are used to assist rehabilitation delivery services or in direct support of the unit of general local government's Rental Rehabilitation Program authorized under 24 CFR part 511, the funds shall be considered to benefit low and moderate income persons where not less than 51 percent of the units assisted, or to be assisted, by the Rental Rehabilitation Program overall are for low and moderate income persons.

(iii) When CDBG funds are used for housing services eligible under section 105(a)(21) of the Act, such funds shall be considered to benefit low and moderate income persons if the housing units for which the services are provided are HOME-assisted and the requirements of § 92.252 or § 92.254 of this title are met.

(4) *Job creation or retention activities.* (i) An activity designed to create permanent jobs where at least 51 percent of the jobs, computed on a full time equivalent basis, involve the employment of low and moderate income persons. For an activity that creates jobs, the unit of general local government must document that at least 51 percent of the jobs will be held by, or will be made available to low and moderate income persons.

(ii) For an activity that retains jobs, the unit of general local government must document that the jobs would actually be lost without the CDBG assistance and that either or both of the following conditions apply with respect to at least 51 percent of the jobs at the time the CDBG assistance is provided: The job is known to be held by a low or moderate income person; or the job can reasonably be expected to turn over within the following two years and that it will be filled by, or that steps will be taken to ensure that it is made available to, a low or moderate income person upon turnover.

(iii) Jobs will be considered to be available to low and moderate income persons for these purposes only if:

(A) Special skills that can only be acquired with substantial training or work experience or education beyond high school are not a prerequisite to fill such jobs, or the business agrees to hire unqualified persons and provide training; and

(B) The unit of general local government and the assisted business take actions to ensure that low and moderate income persons receive first consideration for filling such jobs.

(iv) For purposes of determining whether a job is held by or made available to a low- or moderate-income person, the person may be presumed to be a low- or moderate-income person if:

(A) He/she resides within a census tract (or block numbering area) that either:

(*1*) Meets the requirements of paragraph (b)(4)(v) of this section; or

(*2*) Has at least 70 percent of its residents who are low- and moderate-income persons; or

(B) The assisted business is located within a census tract (or block numbering area) that meets the requirements of paragraph (b)(4)(v) of this section and the job under consideration is to be located within that census tract.

(v) A census tract (or block numbering area) qualifies for the presumptions permitted under paragraphs (b)(4)(iv) (A)(*1*) and (B) of this section if it is either part of a Federally-designated Empowerment Zone or Enterprise Community or meets the following criteria:

(A) It has a poverty rate of at least 20 percent as determined by the most recently available decennial census information;

(B) It does not include any portion of a central business district, as this term is used in the most recent Census of Retail Trade, unless the tract has a poverty rate of at least 30 percent as determined by the most recently available decennial census information; and

(C) It evidences pervasive poverty and general distress by meeting at least one of the following standards:

(*1*) All block groups in the census tract have poverty rates of at least 20 percent;

(*2*) The specific activity being undertaken is located in a block group that has a poverty rate of at least 20 percent; or

(*3*) Upon the written request of the recipient, HUD determines that the census tract exhibits other objectively determinable signs of general distress such as high incidence of crime, narcotics use, homelessness, abandoned housing, and deteriorated infrastructure or substantial population decline.

(vi) As a general rule, each assisted business shall be considered to be a separate activity for purposes of determining whether the activity qualifies under this paragraph, except:

(A) In certain cases such as where CDBG funds are used to acquire, develop or improve a real property (e.g., a business incubator or an industrial park) the requirement may be met by measuring jobs in the aggregate for all the businesses that locate on the property, provided the businesses are not otherwise assisted by CDBG funds.

(B) Where CDBG funds are used to pay for the staff and overhead costs of an entity specified in section 105(a)(15) of the Act making loans to businesses exclusively from non-CDBG funds, this requirement may be met by aggregating the jobs created by all of the businesses receiving loans during any one-year period.

(C) Where CDBG funds are used by a recipient or subrecipient to provide technical assistance to businesses, this requirement may be met by aggregating the jobs created or retained by all of the businesses receiving technical assistance during any one-year period.

(D) Where CDBG funds are used for activities meeting the criteria listed at §570.482(f)(3)(v), this requirement may be met by aggregating the jobs created or retained by all businesses for which CDBG assistance is obligated for such activities during any one-year period, except as provided at paragraph (e)(6) of this section.

(E) Where CDBG funds are used by a Community Development Financial Institution to carry out activities for the purpose of creating or retaining jobs, this requirement may be met by aggregating the jobs created or retained by all businesses for which CDBG assistance is obligated for such activities during any one-year period, except as provided at paragraph (e)(6) of this section.

(F) Where CDBG funds are used for public facilities or improvements which will result in the creation or retention of jobs by more than one business, this requirement may be met by aggregating the jobs created or retained by all such businesses as a result of the public facility or improvement.

(*1*) Where the public facility or improvement is undertaken principally for the benefit of one or more particular businesses, but where other businesses might also benefit from the assisted activity, the requirement may be met by aggregating only the jobs created or retained by those businesses for which the facility/improvement is principally undertaken, provided that the cost (in CDBG funds) for the facility/improvement is less than $10,000 per permanent full-time equivalent job to be created or retained by those businesses.

(*2*) In any case where the cost per job to be created or retained (as determined under paragraph (b)(4)(vi)(F)(*1*) of this section) is $10,000 or more, the requirement must be met by aggregating the jobs created or retained as a result of the public facility or improvement by all businesses in the service area of the facility/improvement. This aggregation must include businesses which, as a result of the public facility/improvement, locate or expand in the service area of the public facility/improvement between the date the state awards the CDBG funds to the recipient and the date one year after the physical completion of the public facility/improvement. In addition, the assisted activity must comply with the public benefit standards at § 570.482(f).

(5) *Planning-only activities.* An activity involving planning (when such activity is the only activity for which the grant to the unit of general local government is given, or if the planning activity is unrelated to any other activity assisted by the grant) if it can be documented that at least 51 percent of the persons who would benefit from implementation of the plan are low and moderate income persons. Any such planning activity for an area or a community composed of persons of whom at least 51 percent are low and moderate income shall be considered to meet this national objective.

(c) *Activities which aid in the prevention or elimination of slums or blight.* Activities meeting one or more of the following criteria, in the absence of substantial evidence to the contrary, will be considered to aid in the prevention or elimination of slums or blight:

(1) *Activities to address slums or blight on an area basis.* An activity will be considered to address prevention or elimination of slums or blight in an area if the state can determine that:

(i) The area, delineated by the unit of general local government, meets a definition of a slum, blighted, deteriorated or deteriorating area under state or local law;

(ii) The area also meets the conditions in either paragraph (c)(1)(ii)(A) or(c)(1)(ii)(B) of this section.

(A) At least 25 percent of properties throughout the area experience one or more of the following conditions:

(*1*) Physical deterioration of buildings or improvements;

(*2*) Abandonment of properties;

(*3*) Chronic high occupancy turnover rates or chronic high vacancy rates in commercial or industrial buildings;

(*4*) Significant declines in property values or abnormally low property values relative to other areas in the community; or

(*5*) Known or suspected environmental contamination.

(B) The public improvements throughout the area are in a general state of deterioration.

(iii) The assisted activity addresses one or more of the conditions which contributed to the deterioration of the area. Rehabilitation of residential buildings carried out in an area meeting the above requirements will be considered to address the area's deterioration only where each such building rehabilitated is considered substandard before rehabilitation, and all deficiencies making a building substandard have been eliminated if less critical work on the building is also undertaken. The State shall ensure that the unit of general local government has developed minimum standards for building quality which may take into account local conditions.

(iv) The state keeps records sufficient to document its findings that a project meets the national objective of prevention or elimination of slums and blight. The state must establish definitions of the conditions listed at § 570.483(c)(1)(ii)(A) and maintain records to substantiate how the area met the slums or blighted criteria. The designation of an area as slum or blighted under this section is required to be redetermined every 10 years for continued qualification. Documentation must be retained pursuant to the recordkeeping requirements contained at § 570.490.

(2) *Activities to address slums or blight on a spot basis.* The following activities can be undertaken on a spot basis to eliminate specific conditions of blight, physical decay, or environmental contamination that are not located in a slum or blighted area: Acquisition; clearance; relocation; historic preservation; remediation of environmentally contaminated properties; or rehabilitation of buildings or improvements. However, rehabilitation must be limited to eliminating those conditions that are detrimental to public health and safety. If acquisition or relocation is undertaken, it must be a precursor to another eligible activity (funded with CDBG or other resources) that directly eliminates the specific conditions of blight or physical decay, or environmental contamination.

(3) *Planning only activities.* An activity involving planning (when the activity is the only activity for which the

grant to the unit of general local government is given, or the planning activity is unrelated to any other activity assisted by the grant) if the plans are for a slum or blighted area, or if all elements of the planning are necessary for and related to an activity which, if funded, would meet one of the other criteria of elimination of slums or blight.

(d) *Activities designed to meet community development needs having a particular urgency.* In the absence of substantial evidence to the contrary, an activity will be considered to address this objective if the unit of general local government certifies, and the state determines, that the activity is designed to alleviate existing conditions which pose a serious and immediate threat to the health or welfare of the community which are of recent origin or which recently became urgent, that the unit of general local government is unable to finance the activity on its own, and that other sources of funding are not available. A condition will generally be considered to be of recent origin if it developed or became urgent within 18 months preceding the certification by the unit of general local government.

(e) *Additional criteria.* (1) In any case where the activity undertaken is a public improvement and the activity is clearly designed to serve a primarily residential area, the activity must meet the requirements of paragraph (b)(1) of this section whether or not the requirements of paragraph (b)(4) of this section are met in order to qualify as benefiting low and moderate income persons.

(2) Where the assisted activity is acquisition of real property, a preliminary determination of whether the activity addresses a national objective may be based on the planned use of the property after acquisition. A final determination shall be based on the actual use of the property, excluding any short-term, temporary use. Where the acquisition is for the purpose of clearance which will eliminate specific conditions of blight or physical decay, the clearance activity shall be considered the actual use of the property. However, any subsequent use or disposition of the cleared property shall be treated as a "change of use" under § 570.489(j).

(3) Where the assisted activity is relocation assistance that the unit of general local government is required to provide, the relocation assistance shall be considered to address the same national objective as is addressed by the displacing activity. Where the relocation assistance is voluntary, the unit of general local government may qualify the assistance either on the basis of the national objective addressed by the displacing activity or, if the relocation assistance is to low and moderate income persons, on the basis of the national objective of benefiting low and moderate income persons.

(4) Where CDBG-assisted activities are carried out by a Community Development Financial Institution whose charter limits its investment area to a primarily residential area consisting of at least 51 percent low- and moderate-income persons, the unit of general local government may also elect the following options:

(i) Activities carried out by the Community Development Financial Institution for the purpose of creating or retaining jobs may, at the option of the unit of general local government, be considered to meet the requirements of this paragraph under the criteria at paragraph (b)(1)(iv) of this section in lieu of the criteria at paragraph (b)(4) of this section; and

(ii) All housing activities for which the Community Development Financial Institution obligates CDBG assistance during any one-year period may be considered to be a single structure for purposes of applying the criteria at paragraph (b)(3) of this section.

(5) If the unit of general local government has elected to prepare a community revitalization strategy pursuant to the authority of § 91.315(e)(2) of this title, and the State has approved the strategy, the unit of general local government may also elect the following options:

(i) Activities undertaken pursuant to the strategy for the purpose of creating or retaining jobs may, at the option of the grantee, be considered to meet the requirements of paragraph (b) of this section under the criteria at

§ 570.483(b)(1)(v) instead of the criteria at § 570.483(b)(4); and

(ii) All housing activities in the area undertaken pursuant to the strategy may be considered to be a single structure for purposes of applying the criteria at paragraph (b)(3) of this section.

(6) If an activity meeting the criteria in § 570.482(f)(3)(v) also meets the requirements of either paragraph (e)(4)(i) or (e)(5)(i) of this section, the unit of general local government may elect to qualify the activity either under the area benefit criteria at paragraph (b)(1)(iv) or (v) of this section or under the job aggregation criteria at paragraph (b)(4)(vi)(D) of this section, but not under both. Where an activity may meet the job aggregation criteria at both paragraphs (b)(4)(vi)(D) and (E) of this section, the unit of general local government may elect to qualify the activity under either criterion, but not both.

(f) *Planning and administrative costs.* CDBG funds expended for eligible planning and administrative costs by units of general local government in conjunction with other CDBG assisted activities will be considered to address the national objectives.

[57 FR 53397, Nov. 9, 1992, as amended at 60 FR 1951, Jan. 5, 1995; 60 FR 17445, Apr. 6, 1995; 61 FR 54921, Oct. 22, 1996; 71 FR 30036, May 24, 2006]

§ 570.484 Overall benefit to low and moderate income persons.

(a) *General.* The State must certify that, in the aggregate, not less than 70 percent of the CDBG funds received by the state during a period specified by the state, not to exceed three years, will be used for activities that benefit persons of low and moderate income. The period selected and certified to by the state shall be designated by fiscal year of annual grants, and shall be for one, two or three consecutive annual grants. The period shall be in effect until all included funds are expended. No CDBG funds may be included in more than one period selected, and all CDBG funds received must be included in a selected period.

(b) *Computation of 70 percent benefit.* Determination that a state has carried out its certification under paragraph (a) of this section requires evidence that not less than 70 percent of the aggregate of the designated annual grant(s), any funds reallocated by HUD to the state, any distributed program income and any guaranteed loan funds under the provisions of subpart M of this part covered in the method of distribution in the final statement or statements for the designated annual grant year or years have been expended for activities meeting criteria as provided in § 570.483(b) for activities benefiting low and moderate income persons. In calculating the percentage of funds expended for such activities:

(1) All CDBG funds included in the period selected and certified to by the state shall be accounted for, except for funds used by the State, or by the units of general local government, for program administration, or for planning activities other than those which must meet a national objective under § 570.483 (b)(5) or (c)(3).

(2) Any funds expended by a state for the purpose of repayment of loans guaranteed under the provisions of subpart M of this part shall be excepted from inclusion in this calculation.

(3) Except as provided in paragraph (b)(4) of this section, CDBG funds expended for an eligible activity meeting the criteria for activities benefiting low and moderate income persons shall count in their entirety towards meeting the 70 percent benefit to persons of low and moderate income requirement.

(4) Funds expended for the acquisition, new construction or rehabilitation of property for housing that qualifies under § 570.483(b)(3) shall be counted for this purpose, but shall be limited to an amount determined by multiplying the total cost (including CDBG and non-CDBG costs) of the acquisition, construction or rehabilitation by the percent of units in such housing to be occupied by low and moderate income persons, except that the amount counted shall not exceed the amount of CDBG funds provided.

§ 570.485 Making of grants.

(a) *Required submissions.* In order to receive its annual CDBG grant under this subpart, a State must submit a consolidated plan in accordance with 24

CFR part 91. That part includes requirements for the content of the consolidated plan, for the process of developing the plan, including citizen participation provisions, for the submission date, for HUD approval, and for the amendment process.

(b) *Failure to make submission.* The state's failure to make the submission required by paragraph (a) of this section within the prescribed deadline constitutes the state's election not to receive and distribute amounts allocated for its nonentitlement areas for the applicable fiscal year. Funds will be either:

(1) Administered by HUD pursuant to subpart F of this part if the state has not administered the program in any previous fiscal year; or

(2) Reallocated to all states in the succeeding fiscal year according to the formula of section 106(d) of the Act, if the state administered the program in any previous year.

(c) *Approval of grant.* HUD will approve a grant if the State's submissions have been made and approved in accordance with 24 CFR part 91, and the certifications required therein are satisfactory to the Secretary. The certifications will be satisfactory to the Secretary for this purpose unless the Secretary has determined pursuant to §570.493 that the State has not complied with the requirements of this subpart, or has determined that there is evidence, not directly involving the State's past performance under this program, that tends to challenge in a substantial manner the State's certification of future performance. If the Secretary makes any such determination, however, the State may be required to submit further assurances as the Secretary may deem warranted or necessary to find the grantee's certification satisfactory.

(d) *Specific conditions.*—HUD may impose additional specific award conditions on States in accordance with 2 CFR 200.207.

[57 FR 53397, Nov. 9, 1992, as amended at 60 FR 1916, Jan. 5, 1995; 61 FR 54922, Oct. 22, 1996; 80 FR 69871, Nov. 12, 2015]

§570.486 Local government requirements.

(a) *Citizen participation requirements of a unit of general local government.* Each unit of general local government shall meet the following requirements as required by the state at §91.115(e) of this title.

(1) Provide for and encourage citizen participation, particularly by low and moderate income persons who reside in slum or blighted areas and areas in which CDBG funds are proposed to be used;

(2) Ensure that residents will be given reasonable and timely access to local meetings, consistent with accessibility and reasonable accommodation requirements in accordance with section 504 of the Rehabilitation Act of 1973 and the regulations at 24 CFR part 8, and the Americans with Disabilities Act and the regulations at 28 CFR parts 35 and 36, as applicable, as well as information and records relating to the unit of local government's proposed and actual use of CDBG funds;

(3) Furnish citizens information, including but not limited to:

(i) The amount of CDBG funds expected to be made available for the current fiscal year (including the grant and anticipated program income);

(ii) The range of activities that may be undertaken with the CDBG funds;

(iii) The estimated amount of the CDBG funds proposed to be used for activities that will meet the national objective of benefit to low and moderate income persons; and

(iv) The proposed CDBG activities likely to result in displacement and the unit of general local government's antidisplacement and relocation plans required under §570.488.

(4) Provide technical assistance to groups that are representative of persons of low- and moderate-income that request assistance in developing proposals (including proposed strategies and actions to affirmatively further fair housing) in accordance with the procedures developed by the State. Such assistance need not include providing funds to such groups;

(5) Provide for a minimum of two public hearings, each at a different stage of the program, for the purpose of

obtaining residents' views and responding to proposals and questions. Together the hearings must cover community development and housing needs (including affirmatively furthering fair housing), development of proposed activities, and a review of program performance. The public hearings to cover community development and housing needs must be held before submission of an application to the State. There must be reasonable notice of the hearings and they must be held at times and accessible locations convenient to potential or actual beneficiaries, with accommodations for persons with disabilities. Public hearings shall be conducted in a manner to meet the needs of non-English speaking residents where a significant number of non-English speaking residents can reasonably be expected to participate;

(6) Provide citizens with reasonable advance notice of, and opportunity to comment on, proposed activities in an application to the state and, for grants already made, activities which are proposed to be added, deleted or substantially changed from the unit of general local government's application to the state. Substantially changed means changes made in terms of purpose, scope, location or beneficiaries as defined by criteria established by the state.

(7) Provide citizens the address, phone number, and times for submitting complaints and grievances, and provide timely written answers to written complaints and grievances, within 15 working days where practicable.

(b) *Activities serving beneficiaries outside the jurisdiction of the unit of general local government.* Any activity carried out by a recipient of State CDBG program funds must significantly benefit residents of the jurisdiction of the grant recipient, and the unit of general local government must determine that the activity is meeting its needs in accordance with section 106(d)(2)(D) of the Act. For an activity to significantly benefit residents of the recipient jurisdiction, the CDBG funds expended by the unit of general local government must not be unreasonably disproportionate to the benefits to its residents.

(c) *Activities located in Entitlement jurisdictions.* Any activity carried out by a recipient of State CDBG program funds in entitlement jurisdictions must significantly benefit residents of the jurisdiction of the grant recipient, and the State CDBG recipient must determine that the activity is meeting its needs in accordance with section 106(d)(2)(D) of the Act. For an activity to significantly benefit residents of the recipient jurisdiction, the CDBG funds expended by the unit of general local government must not be unreasonably disproportionate to the benefits to its residents. In addition, the grant cannot be used to provide a significant benefit to the entitlement jurisdiction unless the entitlement grantee provides a meaningful contribution to the project.

[57 FR 53397, Nov. 9, 1992, as amended at 61 FR 54922, Oct. 22, 1996; 77 FR 24143, Apr. 23, 2012; 80 FR 42367, July 16, 2015]

§ 570.487 Other applicable laws and related program requirements.

(a) *General.* Certain statutes are expressly made applicable to activities assisted under the Act by the Act itself, while other laws not referred to in the Act may be applicable to such activities by their own terms. Certain statutes or executive orders that may be applicable to activities assisted under the Act by their own terms are administered or enforced by governmental officials, departments or agencies other than HUD. Paragraphs (d) and (c) of this section contain two of the requirements expressly made applicable to CDBG activities by the Act itself.

(b) *Affirmatively furthering fair housing.* The Act requires the state to certify to HUD's satisfaction that it will affirmatively further fair housing pursuant to §§ 5.151 and 5.152 of this title. The Act also requires each unit of general local government to certify that it will affirmatively further fair housing.

(c) *Lead-Based Paint Poisoning Prevention Act.* States shall devise, adopt and carry out procedures with respect to CDBG assistance that fulfill the objectives and requirements of the Lead-Based Paint Poisoning Prevention Act (42 U.S.C. 4821–4846), the Residential Lead-Based Paint Hazard Reduction

Act of 1992 (42 U.S.C. 4851–4856), and implementing regulations at part 35, subparts A, B, J, K, and R of this title.

(d) States shall comply with section 3 of the Housing and Urban Development Act of 1968 (12 U.S.C. 1701u) and the implementing regulations in 24 CFR part 75. Section 3 requires that employment and other economic opportunities arising in connection with housing rehabilitation, housing construction, or other public construction projects shall, to the greatest extent feasible, and consistent with existing Federal, State, and local laws and regulations, be given to low- and very low-income persons.

(e) *Architectural Barriers Act and the Americans with Disabilities Act.* The Architectural Barriers Act of 1968 (42 U.S.C. 4151–4157) requires certain Federal and Federally-funded buildings and other facilities to be designed, constructed, or altered in accordance with standards that ensure accessibility to, and use by, physically handicapped people. A building or facility designed, constructed, or altered with funds allocated or reallocated under this subpart after November 21, 1996 and that meets the definition of *residential structure* as defined in 24 CFR 40.2, or the definition of *building* as defined in 41 CFR 101–19.602(a), is subject to the requirements of the Architectural Barriers Act of 1968 and shall comply with the Uniform Federal Accessibility Standards. For general type buildings, these standards are in appendix A to 41 CFR part 101–19.6. For residential structures, these standards are available from the Department of Housing and Urban Development, Office of Fair Housing and Equal Opportunity, Disability Rights Division, Room 5240, 451 Seventh Street, SW, Washington, DC 20410; telephone (202) 708–2333 (voice) or (202) 708–1734 (TTY) (these are not toll-free numbers).

[57 FR 53397, Nov. 9, 1992, as amended at 59 FR 33894, June 30, 1994; 60 FR 1916, Jan. 5, 1995; 61 FR 54922, Oct. 22, 1996; 64 FR 50225, Sept. 15, 1999; 80 FR 42367, July 16, 2015; 85 FR 47911, Aug. 7, 2020; 85 FR 61567, Sept. 29, 2020; 86 FR 30792, June 10, 2021]

EFFECTIVE DATE NOTE: At 90 FR 11024, Mar. 3, 2025, §570.487 was amended, effective Apr. 2, 2025.

§570.488 Displacement, relocation, acquisition, and replacement of housing.

The requirements for States and state recipients with regard to the displacement, relocation, acquisition, and replacement of housing are in §570.606 and 24 CFR part 42.

[61 FR 11477, Mar. 20, 1996]

§570.489 Program administrative requirements.

(a) *Administrative and planning costs.*—(1) *State administrative and technical assistance costs.* (i) The State is responsible for the administration of all CDBG funds. The State may use CDBG funds not to exceed $100,000, plus 50 percent of administrative expenses incurred in excess of $100,000. Amounts of CDBG funds used to pay administrative expenses in excess of $100,000 shall not, subject to paragraph (a)(1)(iii) of this section, exceed the sum of 3 percent of the State's annual grant; 3 percent of program income received by units of general local government during each program year, regardless of the origin year in which the State grant funds that generate the program income were appropriated (whether retained by units of general local government or paid to the State); and 3 percent of funds reallocated by HUD to the State.

(ii) To pay the costs of providing technical assistance to local governments and nonprofit program recipients, a State may, subject to paragraph (a)(1)(iii) of this section, use CDBG funds received on or after January 23, 2004, in an amount not to exceed the sum of 3 percent of its annual grant; 3 percent of program income received by units of general local government during each program year, regardless of the origin year in which the State grant funds that generate the program income were appropriated (whether retained by units of general local government or paid to the State); and 3 percent of funds reallocated by HUD to the State during each program year.

(iii) The amount of CDBG funds used to pay the sum of administrative costs in excess of $100,000 paid pursuant to paragraph (a)(1)(i) of this section and technical assistance costs paid pursuant to paragraph (a)(1)(ii) of this section must not exceed the sum of 3 percent of the State's annual grant; 3 percent of program income received by units of general local government during each program year, regardless of the origin year in which the State grant funds that generate the program income were appropriated (whether retained by the unit of general local government or paid to the State); and 3 percent of funds reallocated by HUD to the State.

(iv) In calculating the amount of CDBG funds that may be used to pay State administrative expenses prior to January 23, 2004, the State may include in the calculation the following elements only to the extent that they are within the following time limitations:

(A) $100,000 per annual grant beginning with FY 1984 allocations;

(B) Two percent of the sum of a State's annual grant and funds reallocated by HUD to the State within a program year, without limitation based on when such amounts were received;

(C) Two percent of program income returned by units of general local government to States after August 21, 1985; and

(D) Two percent of program income received and retained by units of general local government after February 11, 1991.

(v) In regard to its administrative costs, for grants before origin year 2015, the State has the option of selecting its approach for demonstrating compliance with the requirements of paragraph (a)(1) of this section. For grants beginning with origin year 2015 grants and subsequent grants, the State must use the approach in paragraph (a)(1)(v)(A) of this section. Any State whose matching cost contributions toward State administrative expense matching requirements are in arrears must bring matching cost contributions up to the level of CDBG funds expended for such costs. A State grant may not be closed out if the State's matching cost contribution is not at least equal to the amount of CDBG funds in excess of $100,000 expended for administration. The two approaches for demonstrating compliance with this paragraph (a)(1) are:

(A) *Year-to-year tracking and limitation on drawdown of funds.* The State will calculate the maximum allowable amount of CDBG funds that may be used for State administrative expenses from the sum of each origin year grant, program income received during that associated program year and reallocations by HUD to the State during that associated program year. The State will draw down amounts of those funds only upon its own expenditure of an equal or greater amount of matching funds from its own resources after the expenditure of the initial $100,000 for State administrative expenses. The State will be considered to be in compliance with the applicable requirements if the actual amount of CDBG funds spent on State administrative expenses does not exceed the maximum allowable amount, and if the amount of matching funds that the State has expended for that grant year is equal to or greater than the amount of CDBG funds in excess of $100,000 spent during that same grant year. Under this approach, the State must demonstrate that it has paid from its own funds at least 50 percent of its administrative expenses in excess of $100,000 by the closeout of each grant.

(B) *Cumulative accounting of administrative costs incurred by the State since its assumption of the CDBG program for grants before origin year 2015.* Under this approach, the State will identify, for each grant it has received, the CDBG funds eligible to be used for State administrative expenses, as well as the minimum amount of matching funds that the State is required to contribute. The amounts will then be aggregated for all grants received. The State must keep records demonstrating the actual amount of CDBG funds from each grant received that was used for State administrative expenses, as well as matching amounts that were contributed by the State. The State will be considered to be in compliance with the applicable requirements if the aggregate of the actual amounts of CDBG funds spent on State administrative expenses does not exceed the aggregate maximum allowable amount and if the aggregate amount of matching funds that the State has expended is equal to or greater than the aggregate amount of CDBG funds in excess of $100,000 (for each annual grant within the subject period) spent on administrative expenses during its 3- to 5-year Consolidated Planning period. If the State grant for any grant year within the 3- to 5-year period has been closed out, the aggregate amount of CDBG funds spent on State administrative expenses, the aggregate maximum allowable amount, the aggregate matching funds expended, and the aggregate amount of CDBG funds in excess of $100,000 (for each annual grant within the subject period) will be reduced by amounts attributable to the grant year for which the State grant has been closed out.

(2) The State may not charge fees of any entity for processing or considering any application for CDBG funds, or for carrying out its responsibilities under this subpart.

(3)(i) Administrative costs are those described at §570.489(a)(1) for States and, for units of general local government, are those described at sections 105(a)(12) and (a)(13) of the Act.

(ii) The combined expenditures by the State and its funded units of general local government for planning, management, and administrative costs shall not exceed 20 percent of the aggregate amount of the origin year grant, any origin year grant funds reallocated by HUD to the State, and the amount of any program income received during the program year.

(iii) For origin year 2015 grants and subsequent grants, no more than 20 percent of any annual grant (excluding program income) shall be expended by the State and its funded units of general local government for planning, management, and administrative costs. In addition, the combined expenditures by the States and its unit of general local government for planning, management, and administrative costs shall not exceed 20 percent of any origin year grant funds reallocated by HUD to the State.

(iv) Funds from a grant of any origin year may be used to pay planning and program administrative costs associated with any grant of any origin year.

(b) *Reimbursement of pre-agreement costs.* The State may permit, in accordance with such procedures as the State may establish, a unit of general local government to incur costs for CDBG activities before the establishment of a formal grant relationship between the State and the unit of general local government and to charge these pre-agreement costs to the grant, provided that the activities are eligible and undertaken in accordance with the requirements of this part and 24 CFR part 58. A State may incur costs prior to entering into a grant agreement with HUD and charge those pre-agreement costs to the grant, provided that the activities are eligible and are undertaken in accordance with the requirements of this part, part 58 of this title, and the citizen participation requirements of part 91 of this title.

(c) *Federal grant payments.* The State's requests for payment, and the Federal Government's payments upon such requests, must comply with 31 CFR part 205. The State must use procedures to minimize the time elapsing between the transfer of grant funds and disbursement of funds by the State to units of general local government. States must also have procedures in place, and units of general local government must use these procedures to minimize the time elapsing between the transfer of funds by the State and disbursement for CDBG activities.

(d) *Fiscal controls and accounting procedures.* (1) A State shall have fiscal and administrative requirements for expending and accounting for all funds received under this subpart. These requirements must be available for Federal inspection and must:

(i) Be sufficiently specific to ensure that funds received under this subpart are used in compliance with all applicable statutory and regulatory provisions and the terms and conditions of the award:

(ii) Ensure that funds received under this subpart are only spent for reasonable and necessary costs of operating programs under this subpart; and

(iii) Ensure that funds received under this subpart are not used for general expenses required to carry out other responsibilities of State and local governments.

(2) A State may satisfy this requirement by:

(i) Using fiscal and administrative requirements applicable to the use of its own funds;

(ii) Adopting new fiscal and administrative requirements; or

(iii) Applying the provisions in 2 CFR part 200.

(A) A State that opts to satisfy this requirement for fiscal controls and administrative procedures by applying the provisions of 2 CFR part 200 must comply with the requirements therein.

(B) A State that opts to satisfy this requirement for fiscal controls and administrative procedures by applying the provisions of 2 CFR part 200 must also ensure that recipients of the State's CDBG funds comply with 2 CFR part 200.

(e) *Program income.* (1) For the purposes of this subpart, "program income" is defined as gross income received by a State, a unit of general local government, or a subgrantee of the unit of general local government that was generated from the use of CDBG funds, regardless of when the CDBG funds were appropriated and whether the activity has been closed out, except as provided in paragraph (e)(2) of this section. When income is generated by an activity that is only partially assisted with CDBG funds, the income must be prorated to reflect the percentage of CDBG funds used (e.g., a single loan supported by CDBG funds and other funds; or a single parcel of land purchased with CDBG funds and other funds). Program income includes, but is not limited to, the following:

(i) Proceeds from the disposition by sale or long-term lease of real property purchased or improved with CDBG funds, except as provided in paragraph (e)(2)(v) of this section;

(ii) Proceeds from the disposition of equipment purchased with CDBG funds;

(iii) Gross income from the use or rental of real or personal property acquired by the unit of general local government or subgrantee of the unit of general local government with CDBG funds, less the costs incidental to the generation of the income;

(iv) Gross income from the use or rental of real property, owned by the unit of general local government or other entity carrying out a CDBG activity that was constructed or improved with CDBG funds, less the costs incidental to the generation of the income;

(v) Payments of principal and interest on loans made using CDBG funds, except as provided in paragraph (e)(2)(iii) of this section;

(vi) Proceeds from the sale of loans made with CDBG funds, less reasonable legal and other costs incurred in the course of such sale that are not otherwise eligible costs under sections 105(a)(13) or 106(d)(3)(A) of the Act;

(vii) Proceeds from the sale of obligations secured by loans made with CDBG funds, less reasonable legal and other costs incurred in the course of such sale that are not otherwise eligible costs under sections 105(a)(13) or 106(d)(3)(A) of the Act;

(viii) Interest earned on funds held in a revolving fund account;

(ix) Interest earned on program income pending disposition of the income;

(x) Funds collected through special assessments made against nonresidential properties and properties owned and occupied by households not of low and moderate income, if the special assessments are used to recover all or part of the CDBG portion of a public improvement; and

(xi) Gross income paid to a unit of general local government or subgrantee of the unit of general local government from the ownership interest in a for-profit entity acquired in return for the provision of CDBG assistance.

(2) "Program income" does not include the following:

(i) The total amount of funds, which does not exceed $35,000 received in a single year from activities, other than revolving loan funds that is retained by a unit of general local government and its subgrantees (all funds received from revolving loan funds are considered program income, regardless of amount);

(ii) Amounts generated by activities eligible under section 105(a)(15) of the Act and carried out by an entity under the authority of section 105(a)(15) of the Act;

(iii) Payments of principal and interest made by a subgrantee carrying out a CDBG activity for a unit of general local government, toward a loan from the local government to the subgrantee, to the extent that program income received by the subgrantee is used for such payments;

(iv) The following classes of interest, which must be remitted to HUD for transmittal to the Department of the Treasury, and will not be reallocated under section 106(c) or (d) of the Act:

(A) Interest income from loans or other forms of assistance provided with CDBG funds that are used for activities determined by HUD to be not eligible under § 570.482 or section 105(a) of the Act, to fail to meet a national objective in accordance with the requirements of § 570.483, or to fail substantially to meet any other requirement of this subpart or the Act;

(B) Interest income from deposits of amounts reimbursed to a State's CDBG program account prior to the state's disbursement of the reimbursed funds for eligible purposes; and

(C) Interest income received by units of general local government on deposits of grant funds before disbursement of the funds for activities, except that the unit of general local government may keep interest payments of up to $100 per year for administrative expenses otherwise permitted to be paid with CDBG funds.

(v) Proceeds from the sale of real property purchased or improved with CDBG funds, if the proceeds are received more than 5 years after expiration of the grant agreement between the State and the unit of general local government.

(3) The State may permit the unit of general local government which receives or will receive program income to retain it, subject to the requirements of paragraph (e)(3)(ii) of this section, or may require the unit of general local government to pay the program income to the State. The State, however, must permit the unit of general local government to retain the program income if it will be used to continue the activity from which it was derived. The State will determine when an activity is being continued.

(i) *Program income paid to the State.* Except as described in paragraph (e)(3)(ii)(A) of this section, the State may require the unit of general local government that receives or will receive program income to return the program income to the State. Program income that is paid to the State is treated as additional CDBG funds subject to the requirements of this subpart. Except for program income retained and used by the State for administrative costs or technical assistance under paragraph (a) of this section, program income paid to the State must be distributed to units of general local government in accordance with the method of distribution in the action plan under 24 CFR 91.320(k)(1)(i) that is in effect at the time the program income is distributed. To the maximum extent feasible, the State must distribute program income before it makes additional withdrawals from the United States Treasury, except as provided in paragraph (f) of this section.

(ii) *Program income retained by a unit of general local government.* A State may permit a unit of general local government that receives or will receive program income to retain it. Alternatively, a State may require that the unit of general local government pay any such income to the State unless the exception in paragraph (e)(3)(ii)(A) of this section applies.

(A) A State must permit the unit of general local government to retain the program income if the program income will be used to continue the activity from which it was derived. A State will determine when an activity is being continued. In making such a determination, a State may consider whether the unit of general local government is or will be unable to comply with the requirements of paragraph (e)(3)(ii)(B) of this section or other requirements of this part, and the extent to which the program income is unlikely to be applied to continue the activity within the reasonably near future. When a State determines that the program income will be applied to continue the activity from which it was derived, but the amount of program income held by the unit of general local government exceeds projected cash needs for the reasonably near future, the State may require the local government to return all or part of the program income to the State until such time as it is needed by the unit of general local government. When a State determines that a unit of local government is not likely to apply any significant amount of program income to continue the activity within a reasonable amount of time, or that it is not likely to apply the program income in accordance with applicable requirements, the State may require the unit of general local government to return all of the program income to the State for disbursement to other units of local government. A State that intends to require units of general local government to return program income in accordance with this paragraph must describe its approach in the State's action plan required under 24 CFR 91.320 of this title or in a substantial amendment if the State intends to implement this option after the action plan is submitted to and approved by HUD.

(B) Program income that is received and retained by the unit of general local government is treated as additional CDBG funds and is subject to all applicable requirements of this subpart, regardless of whether the activity that generated the program income has been closed out. If the grant between the State and the unit of general local government that generated the program income is still open when it is generated, program income permitted to be retained will be considered part of the unit of general local government's grant that generated the program income. If the grant between the State and the unit of general local government is closed out, program income permitted to be retained will be considered to be part of the unit of general local government's most recently awarded open grant. If the unit of general local government has no open grants with the State, the program income retained by the unit of general local government will be counted as part of the State's program year in which the program income was received. A State must employ one or more of the following methods to ensure that units of general local government comply with applicable program income requirements:

(*1*) Maintaining contractual relationships with units of general local government for the duration of the existence of the program income;

(*2*) Closing out the underlying activity, but requiring as a condition of closeout that the unit of general local government obtain advance State approval of either a unit of general local government's plan for the use of program income or of each use of program income by grant recipients via regularly occurring reports and requests for approval;

(*3*) Closing out the underlying activity, but requiring as a condition of closeout that the unit of general local government report to the State when new program income is received; or

(*4*) With prior HUD approval, other approaches that demonstrate that the State will ensure compliance with the requirements of this subpart by units of general local government.

(iii) *Transfer of program income to Entitlement program.* A unit of general local government that becomes eligible to be an Entitlement grantee may request the State's approval to transfer State CDBG grant-generated program income to the unit of general local government's Entitlement program. A State may approve the transfer, provided that the unit of general local government:

(A) Has officially elected to participate in the Entitlement grant program;

(B) Agrees to use such program income in accordance with Entitlement program requirements; and

(C) Has set up Integrated Disbursement Information System (IDIS) access and agrees to enter receipt of program income into IDIS.

(iv) *Transfer of program income of grantees losing Entitlement status.* Upon entry into the State CDBG program, a unit of general local government that has lost or relinquished its Entitlement status must, with respect to program income that a unit of general local government would otherwise be permitted to retain, either:

(A) Retain program income generated under Entitlement grants and continue to comply with Entitlement program requirements for program income; or

(B) Retain the program income and transfer it to the State CDBG program, in which case the unit of general local government must comply with the State's rules for program income and the requirements of this paragraph (e).

(4) The State must report on the receipt and use of all program income (whether retained by units of general local government or paid to the State) in its annual performance and evaluation report.

(f) *Revolving funds.* (1) The State may permit units of general local government to establish revolving funds to carry out specific, identified activities. A revolving fund, for this purpose, is a separate fund (with a set of accounts that are independent of other program accounts) established to carry out specific activities which, in turn, generate payments to the fund for use in carrying out such activities. These payments to the revolving fund are program income and must be substantially disbursed from the revolving fund before additional grant funds are drawn from the Treasury for revolving fund activities. Such program income is not required to be disbursed for non-revolving fund activities.

(2) The State may establish one or more State revolving funds to distribute grants to units of general local government throughout a State or a region of the State to carry out specific, identified activities. A revolving fund, for this purpose, is a separate fund (with a set of accounts that are independent of other program accounts) established to fund grants to units of general local government to carry out specific activities which, in turn, generate payments to the fund for additional grants to units of general local government to carry out such activities. Program income in the revolving fund must be disbursed from the fund before additional grant funds are drawn from the Treasury for payments to units of general local government which could be funded from the revolving fund.

(3) A revolving fund established by either the State or unit of general local government shall not be directly funded or capitalized with grant funds.

(g) *Procurement.* When procuring property or services to be paid for in whole or in part with CDBG funds, the State shall follow its procurement policies and procedures. The State shall establish requirements for procurement policies and procedures for units of general local government, based on full and open competition. Methods of procurement (e.g., small purchase, sealed bids/formal advertising, competitive proposals, and noncompetitive proposals) and their applicability shall be specified by the State. Cost plus a percentage of cost and percentage of construction costs methods of contracting shall not be used. The policies and procedures shall also include standards of conduct governing employees engaged in the award or administration of contracts. (Other conflicts of interest are covered by §570.489(h).) The State shall ensure that all purchase orders and contracts include any clauses required by Federal statutes, Executive orders, and implementing regulations. The State shall make subrecipient and contractor determinations in accordance with the standards in 2 CFR 200.330.

(h) *Conflict of interest*—(1) *Applicability.* (i) In the procurement of supplies, equipment, construction, and services by the States, units of local general governments, and subrecipients, the conflict of interest provisions in paragraph (g) of this section shall apply.

(ii) In all cases not governed by paragraph (g) of this section, this paragraph (h) shall apply. Such cases include the acquisition and disposition of real property and the provision of assistance with CDBG funds by the unit of general local government or its subrecipients, to individuals, businesses and other private entities.

(2) *Conflicts prohibited.* Except for eligible administrative or personnel costs, the general rule is that no persons described in paragraph (h)(3) of this section who exercise or have exercised any functions or responsibilities with respect to CDBG activities assisted under this subpart or who are in a position to participate in a decision-making process or gain inside information with regard to such activities, may obtain a financial interest or benefit from the activity, or have an interest or benefit from the activity, or

have an interest in any contract, subcontract or agreement with respect thereto, or the proceeds thereunder, either for themselves or those with whom they have family or business ties, during their tenure or for one year thereafter.

(3) *Persons covered.* The conflict of interest provisions for paragraph (h)(2) of this section apply to any person who is an employee, agent, consultant, officer, or elected official or appointed official of the State, or of a unit of general local government, or of any designated public agencies, or subrecipients which are receiving CDBG funds.

(4) *Exceptions: Thresholds requirements.* Upon written request by the State, an exception to the provisions of paragraph (h)(2) of this section involving an employee, agent, consultant, officer, or elected official or appointed official of the State may be granted by HUD on a case-by-case basis. In all other cases, the State may grant such an exception upon written request of the unit of general local government provided the State shall fully document its determination in compliance with all requirements of paragraph (h)(4) of this section including the State's position with respect to each factor at paragraph (h)(5) of this section and such documentation shall be available for review by the public and by HUD. An exception may be granted after it is determined that such an exception will serve to further the purpose of the Act and the effective and efficient administration of the program or project of the State or unit of general local government as appropriate. An exception may be considered only after the State or unit of general local government, as appropriate, has provided the following:

(i) A disclosure of the nature of the conflict, accompanied by an assurance that there has been public disclosure of the conflict and a description of how the public disclosure was made; and

(ii) An opinion of the attorney for the State or the unit of general local government, as appropriate, that the interest for which the exception is sought would not violate State or local law.

(5) *Factors to be considered for exceptions.* In determining whether to grant a requested exception after the requirements of paragraph (h)(4) of this section have been satisfactorily met, the cumulative effect of the following factors, where applicable, shall be considered:

(i) Whether the exception would provide a significant cost benefit or an essential degree of expertise to the program or project which would otherwise not be available;

(ii) Whether an opportunity was provided for open competitive bidding or negotiation;

(iii) Whether the person affected is a member of a group or class of low or moderate income persons intended to be the beneficiaries of the assisted activity, and the exception will permit such person to receive generally the same interests or benefits as are being made available or provided to the group or class;

(iv) Whether the affected person has withdrawn from his or her functions or responsibilities, or the decisionmaking process with respect to the specific assisted activity in question;

(v) Whether the interest or benefit was present before the affected person was in a position as described in paragraph (h)(3) of this section;

(vi) Whether undue hardship will result either to the State or the unit of general local government or the person affected when weighed against the public interest served by avoiding the prohibited conflict; and

(vii) Any other relevant considerations.

(i) *Closeout of grants to units of general local government.* The State shall establish requirements for timely closeout of grants to units of general local government and shall take action to ensure the timely closeout of such grants.

(j) *Change of use of real property.* The standards described in this section apply to real property within the unit of general local government's control (including activities undertaken by subrecipients) which was acquired or improved in whole or in part using CDBG funds in excess of the threshold for small purchase procurement (2 CFR 200.88). These standards shall apply from the date CDBG funds are first spent for the property until five years after closeout of the unit of general local government's grant.

(1) A unit of general local governments may not change the use or planned use of any such property (including the beneficiaries of such use) from that for which the acquisition or improvement was made, unless the unit of general local government provides affected citizens with reasonable notice of and opportunity to comment on any proposed change, and either:

(i) The new use of the property qualifies as meeting one of the national objectives and is not a building for the general conduct of government; or

(ii) The requirements in paragraph (j)(2) of this section are met.

(2) If the unit of general local government determines, after consultation with affected citizens, that it is appropriate to change the use of the property to a use which does not qualify under paragraph (j)(1) of this section, it may retain or dispose of the property for the changed use if the unit of general local government's CDBG program is reimbursed or the State's CDBG program is reimbursed, at the discretion of the State. The reimbursement shall be in the amount of the current fair market value of the property, less any portion of the value attributable to expenditures of non-CDBG funds for acquisition of, and improvements to, the property, except that if the change in use occurs after grant closeout but within 5 years of such closeout, the unit of general local government shall make the reimbursement to the State's CDBG program account.

(3) Following the reimbursement of the CDBG program in accordance with paragraph (j)(2) of this section, the property no longer will be subject to any CDBG requirements.

(k) *Accountability for real and personal property*. The State shall establish and implement requirements, consistent with State law and the purposes and requirements of this subpart (including paragraph (j) of this section) governing the use, management, and disposition of real and personal property acquired with CDBG funds.

(l) *Debarment and suspension*. The requirements in 2 CFR part 2424 are applicable. CDBG funds may not be provided to excluded or disqualified persons.

(m) *Subrecipient monitoring and management*. The provisions of 2 CFR 200.330 through 200.332 are applicable.

(n) *Audits*. Notwithstanding any other provision of this title, audits of a State and units of general local government shall be conducted in accordance with 2 CFR part 200, subpart F, which implements the Single Audit Act. States shall develop and administer an audits management system to ensure that audits of units of general local government are conducted in accordance with 2 CFR part 200, subpart F.

(o) *Grant Closeout*.—HUD will close grants to States in accordance with the grant closeout requirements of 2 CFR 200.343.

(p) *Cost principles and prior approval*. A State must ensure that costs incurred by the State and by its recipients are in conformance with 2 CFR part 200, subpart E. All cost items described in 2 CFR part 200, subpart E, that require Federal agency approval are allowable without prior approval of HUD, to the extent that they otherwise comply with the requirements of 2 CFR part 200, subpart E, and are otherwise eligible, except for the following:

(1) Depreciation methods for fixed assets shall not be changed without the express approval of the cognizant Federal agency (2 CFR 200.436).

(2) Fines, penalties, damages, and other settlements are unallowable costs to the CDBG program (2 CFR 200.441).

(3) Costs of housing (*e.g.*, depreciation, maintenance, utilities, furnishings, rent), housing allowances, and personal living expenses (goods or services for personal use) regardless of whether reported as taxable income to the employees (2 CFR 200.445).

(4) Organization costs (2 CFR 200.455).

[57 FR 53397, Nov. 9, 1992, as amended at 60 FR 1952, Jan. 5, 1995; 61 FR 54922, Oct. 22, 1996; 67 FR 15112, Mar. 29, 2002; 72 FR 73496, Dec. 27, 2007; 77 FR 24143, Apr. 23, 2012; 80 FR 69871, Nov. 12, 2015; 80 FR 71936, Nov. 18, 2015; 80 FR 75937, Dec. 7, 2015]

§570.490 Recordkeeping requirements.

(a) *State records*. (1) The State shall establish and maintain such records as may be necessary to facilitate review and audit by HUD of the State's administration of CDBG funds under § 570.493. The content of records maintained by the State shall be as jointly agreed upon by HUD and the States and sufficient to enable HUD to make the determinations described at § 570.493. For fair housing and equal opportunity purposes, whereas such data is already being collected and where applicable, such records shall include data on the racial, ethnic, and gender characteristics of persons who are applicants for, participants in, or beneficiaries of the program. The records shall also permit audit of the States in accordance with 24 CFR part 85.

(2) The state shall keep records to document its funding decisions reached under the method of distribution described in 24 CFR 91.320(j)(1), including all the criteria used to select applications from local governments for funding and the relative importance of the criteria (if applicable), regardless of the organizational level at which final funding decisions are made, so that they can be reviewed by HUD, the Inspector General, the Government Accountability Office, and citizens pursuant to the requirements of § 570.490(c).

(3) *Integrated Disbursement and Information System (IDIS).* The state shall make entries into IDIS in a form prescribed by HUD to accurately capture the state's accomplishment and funding data, including program income, for each program year. It is recommended that the state enter IDIS data on a quarterly basis and it is required to be entered annually.

(b) *Unit of general local government's record.* The State shall establish recordkeeping requirements for units of general local government receiving CDBG funds that are sufficient to facilitate reviews and audits of such units of general local government under §§ 570.492 and 570.493. For fair housing and equal opportunity purposes, whereas such data is already being collected and where applicable, such records shall include data on the racial, ethnic, and gender characteristics of persons who are applicants for, participants in, or beneficiaries of the program.

(c) *Access to records.* (1) Representatives of HUD, the Inspector General, and the General Accounting Office shall have access to all books, accounts, records, reports, files, and other papers, or property pertaining to the administration, receipt and use of CDBG funds and necessary to facilitate such reviews and audits.

(2) The State shall provide citizens with reasonable access to records regarding the past use of CDBG funds and ensure that units of general local government provide citizens with reasonable access to records regarding the past use of CDBG funds consistent with State or local requirements concerning the privacy of personal records.

(d) *Record retention.* Records of the State and units of general local government, including supporting documentation, shall be retained for the greater of three years from closeout of the grant to the state, or the period required by other applicable laws and regulations as described in § 570.487 and § 570.488.

[57 FR 53397, Nov. 9, 1992, as amended at 71 FR 6971, Feb. 9, 2006; 77 FR 24146, Apr. 23, 2012; 80 FR 42367, July 16, 2015; 80 FR 75937, Dec. 7, 2015; 85 FR 47911, Aug. 7, 2020]

EFFECTIVE DATE NOTE: At 90 FR 11024, Mar. 3, 2025, § 570.490 was amended, effective Apr. 2, 2025.

§ 570.491 Performance and evaluation report.

The annual performance and evaluation report shall be submitted in accordance with 24 CFR part 91.

(Approved by the Office of Management and Budget under control number 2506–0117)

[60 FR 1916, Jan. 5, 1995]

§ 570.492 State's reviews and audits.

(a) The state shall make reviews and audits including on-site reviews, of units of general local government as may be necessary or appropriate to meet the requirements of section 104(e)(2) of the Act.

(b) In the case of noncompliance with these requirements, the State shall take such actions as may be appropriate to prevent a continuance of the deficiency, mitigate any adverse effects or consequences and prevent a recurrence. The state shall establish remedies for units of general local government noncompliance.

§ 570.493 HUD's reviews and audits.

(a) *General.* At least on an annual basis, HUD shall make such reviews and audits as may be necessary or appropriate to determine:

(1) Whether the state has distributed CDBG funds to units of general local government in a timely manner in conformance to the method of distribution described in its action plan under part 91 of this title;

(2) Whether the state has carried out its certifications in compliance with the requirements of the Act and this subpart and other applicable laws; and

(3) Whether the state has made reviews and audits of the units of general local government required by § 570.492.

(b) *Information considered.* In conducting performance reviews and audits, HUD will rely primarily on information obtained from the state's performance report, records maintained by the state, findings from on-site monitoring, audit reports, and the status of the state's unexpended grant funds. HUD may also consider relevant information on the state's performance gained from other sources, including litigation, citizens' comments, and other information provided by the state. A State's failure to maintain records in accordance with § 570.490 may result in a finding that the State has failed to meet the applicable requirement to which the record pertains.

[57 FR 53397, Nov. 9, 1992, as amended at 61 FR 54922, Oct. 22, 1996]

§ 570.494 Timely distribution of funds by states.

(a) States are encouraged to adopt and achieve a goal of obligating and announcing 95 percent of funds to units of general local government within 12 months of the state signing its grant agreement with HUD.

(b) HUD will review each state to determine if the state has distributed CDBG funds in a timely manner. The state's distribution of CDBG funds is timely if:

(1) All of the state's annual grant (excluding state administration) has been obligated and announced to units of general local government within 15 months of the state signing its grant agreement with HUD; and

(2) Recaptured funds and program income received by the state are expeditiously obligated and announced to units of general local government.

(c) HUD may collect necessary information from states to determine whether CDBG funds have been distributed in a timely manner.

§ 570.495 Reviews and audits response.

(a) If HUD's review and audit under § 570.493 results in a negative determination, or if HUD otherwise determines that a state or unit of general local government has failed to comply with any requirement of this subpart, the state will be given an opportunity to contest the finding and will be requested to submit a plan for corrective action. If the state is unsuccessful in contesting the validity of the finding to the satisfaction of HUD, or if the state's plan for corrective action is not satisfactory to HUD, HUD may take one or more of the following actions to prevent a continuation of the deficiency; mitigate, to the extent possible, the adverse effects or consequence of the deficiency; or prevent a recurrence of the deficiency:

(1) Issue a letter of warning that advises the State of the deficiency and puts the state on notice that additional action will be taken if the deficiency is not corrected or is repeated;

(2) Advise the state that additional information or assurances will be required before acceptance of one or more of the certifications required for the succeeding year grant;

(3) Advise the state to suspend or terminate disbursement of funds for a deficient activity or grant;

(4) Advise the state to reimburse its grant in any amounts improperly expended;

(5) Change the method of payment to the state from an advance basis to a reimbursement basis;

(6) Based on the state's current failure to comply with a requirement of this subpart which will affect the use of the succeeding year grant, condition the use of the succeeding fiscal years grant funds upon appropriate corrective action by the state. When the use of funds is conditioned, HUD shall

specify the reasons for the conditions and the actions necessary to satisfy the conditions.

(b)(1) Whenever HUD determines that a state or unit of general local government which is a recipient of CDBG funds has failed to comply with section 109 of the Act (nondiscrimination requirements), HUD shall notify the governor of the State or chief executive officer of the unit of general local government of the noncompliance and shall request the governor or the chief executive officer to secure compliance. If within a reasonable time, not to exceed sixty days, the governor or chief executive officer fails or refuses to secure compliance, HUD may take the following action:

(i) Refer the matter to the Attorney General with a recommendation that an appropriate civil action be instituted;

(ii) Exercise the powers and functions provided by title VI of the Civil Rights Act of 1964 (42 U.S.C. 2000d–2000d–7);

(iii) Exercise the powers and functions provided for in §570.496; or

(iv) Take such other action as may be provided by law.

(2) When a matter is referred to the Attorney General pursuant to paragraph (b)(1)(i) of this section, or whenever HUD has reason to believe that a State or unit of general local government is engaged in a pattern or practice in violation of the provisions of section 109 of the Act, the Attorney General may bring a civil action in any appropriate United States district court for such relief as may be appropriate, including injunctive relief.

§570.496 Remedies for noncompliance; opportunity for hearing.

(a) *General.* Action pursuant to this section will be taken only after at least one of the corrective or remedial actions specified in §570.495 has been taken, and only then if the State or unit of general local government has not made an appropriate or timely response.

(b) *Remedies.* (1) If HUD finds after reasonable notice and opportunity for hearing that a State or unit of general local government has failed to comply with any provision of this subpart, until HUD is satisfied that there is no longer failure to comply, HUD shall:

(i) Terminate payments to the state;

(ii) Reduce payments for current or future grants to the state by an amount equal to the amount of CDBG funds distributed or used without compliance with the requirements of this subpart;

(iii) Limit the availability of payments to the state to activities not affected by the failure to comply or to activities designed to overcome the failure to comply;

(iv) Based on the state's failure to comply with a requirement of this subpart (other than the state's current failure to comply which will affect the use of the succeeding year grant), condition the use of the grant funds upon appropriate corrective action by the state specified by HUD; or

(v) With respect to a CDBG grant awarded by the state to a unit of general local government, withhold, reduce, or withdraw the grant, require the state to withhold, reduce, or withdraw the grant, or take other action as appropriate, except that CDBG funds expended on eligible activities shall not be recaptured or deducted from future CDBG grants to such unit of general local government.

(2) HUD may on due notice suspend payments at any time after the issuance of a notice of opportunity for hearing pursuant to paragraph (d) of this section, pending such hearing and a final decision, to the extent HUD determines such action necessary to prevent a continuation of the noncompliance.

(c) In lieu of, or in addition to, the action authorized by paragraph (b) of this section, if HUD has reason to believe that the state or unit of general local government has failed to comply substantially with any provision of this subpart, HUD may:

(1) Refer the matter to the Attorney General of the United States with a recommendation that an appropriate civil action be instituted; and

(2) Upon such a referral, the Attorney General may bring a civil action in any United States district court having venue thereof for such relief as may be appropriate, including an action to recover the amount of the CDBG funds

which was not expended in accordance with this subpart, or for mandatory or injunctive relief.

(d) *Proceedings.* When HUD proposes to take action pursuant to this section, the respondent in the proceedings will be the state. At the option of HUD, a unit of general local government may also be a respondent. These procedures are to be followed before imposition of a sanction described in paragraph (b)(1) of this section:

(1) *Notice of opportunity for hearing.* HUD shall notify the respondent in writing of the proposed action and of the opportunity for a hearing. The notice shall be sent to the respondent by first class mail and shall provide notice:

(i) In a manner which is adequate to allow the respondent to prepare its response, the basis upon which HUD determined that the respondent failed to comply with a provision of this subpart;

(ii) That the hearing procedures are governed by these rules;

(iii) That the respondent has 14 days from receipt of the notice within which to provide a written request for a hearing to the Docket Clerk, Office of Hearings and Appeals, and the address and telephone number of the Docket Clerk;

(iv) Of the action which HUD proposes to take and that the authority for this action is §570.496 of this subpart;

(v) That if the respondent fails to request a hearing within the time specified, HUD's determination that the respondent failed to comply with a provision of this subpart shall be final and HUD may proceed to take the proposed action.

(2) *Initiation of hearing.* The respondent shall be allowed 14 days from receipt of the notice within which to notify HUD in writing of its request for a hearing. If no request is received within the time specified, HUD's determination that the respondent failed to comply with a provision of this subpart shall be final and HUD may proceed to take the proposed action.

(3) *Administrative Law Judge.* Proceedings conducted under these rules shall be presided over by an Administrative Law Judge (ALJ), appointed as provided by section 11 of the Administrative Procedure Act (5 U.S.C. 3105). The case shall be referred to the ALJ by HUD at the time a hearing is requested. The ALJ shall promptly notify the parties of the time and place at which the hearing will be held. The ALJ shall conduct a fair and impartial hearing and take all action necessary to avoid delay in the disposition of proceedings and to maintain order. The ALJ shall have all powers necessary to those ends, including but not limited to the power:

(i) To administer oaths and affirmations;

(ii) To issue subpoenas as authorized by law;

(iii) To rule upon offers of proof and receive relevant evidence;

(iv) To order or limit discovery before the hearing as the interests of justice may require;

(v) To regulate the course of the hearing and the conduct of the parties and their counsel;

(vi) To hold conferences for the settlement or simplification of the issues by consent of the parties;

(vii) To consider and rule upon all procedural and other motions appropriate in adjudicative proceedings; and

(viii) To make and file initial determinations.

(4) *Ex parte communications.* An ex parte communication is any communication with an ALJ, direct or indirect, oral or written, concerning the merits or procedures of any pending proceeding which is made by a party in the absence of any other party. Ex parte communications are prohibited except where the purpose and content of the communication have been disclosed in advance or simultaneously to all parties, or the communication is a request for information concerning the status of the case. Any ALJ who receives an ex parte communication which the ALJ knows or has reason to believe is unauthorized shall promptly place the communication, or its substance, in all files and shall furnish copies to all parties. Unauthorized ex parte communications shall not be taken into consideration in deciding any matter in issue.

(5) *The hearing.* All parties shall have the right to be represented at the hearing by counsel. The ALJ shall conduct

the proceedings in an expeditious manner while allowing the parties to present all oral and written evidence which tends to support their respective positions, but the ALJ shall exclude irrelevant, immaterial or unduly repetitious evidence. HUD has the burden of proof in showing by a preponderance of evidence that the respondent failed to comply with a provision of this subpart. Each party shall be allowed to cross-examine adverse witnesses and to rebut and comment upon evidence presented by the other party. Hearings shall be open to the public. So far as the orderly conduct of the hearing permits, interested persons other than the parties may appear and participate in the hearing.

(6) *Transcripts.* Hearings shall be recorded and transcribed only by a reporter under the supervision of the ALJ. The original transcript shall be a part of the record and shall constitute the sole official transcript. Respondents and the public, at their own expense, shall obtain copies of the transcript.

(7) *The ALJ's decisions.* At the conclusion of the hearing, the ALJ shall give the parties a reasonable opportunity to submit proposed findings and conclusions and supporting reasons therefor. Generally, within 60 days after the conclusion of the hearing, the ALJ shall prepare a written decision which includes a Statement of findings and conclusions, and the reasons or basis therefor, on all the material issues of fact, law or discretion presented on the record and the appropriate sanction or denial thereof. The decision shall be based on consideration of the whole record or those parts thereof cited by a party and supported by and in accordance with the reliable, probative, and substantial evidence. A copy of the decision shall be furnished to the parties immediately by first class mail and shall include a notice that any requests for review by the Secretary must be made in writing to the Secretary within 30 days of the receipt of the decision.

(8) *Record.* The transcript of testimony and exhibits, together with the decision of the ALJ and all papers and requests filed in the proceeding, constitutes the exclusive record for decision and, on payment of its reasonable cost, shall be made available to the parties. After reaching the initial decision, the ALJ shall certify to the complete record and forward the record to the Secretary.

(9) *Review by the Secretary.* The decision by the ALJ shall constitute the final decision of HUD unless, within 30 days after the receipt of the decision, either the respondent or the Assistant Secretary for Community Planning and Development files an exception and request for review by the Secretary. The excepting party must transmit simultaneously to the Secretary and the other party the request for review and the bases of the party's exceptions to the findings of the ALJ. The other party shall be allowed 30 days from receipt of the exception to provide the Secretary and the excepting party with a written reply. The Secretary shall then review the record of the case, including the exceptions and the reply. On the basis of such review, the Secretary shall issue a written determination, including a Statement of the rationale therefor, affirming, modifying or revoking the decision of the ALJ. The Secretary's decision shall be made and transmitted to the parties within 60 days after the decision of the ALJ was furnished to the parties.

(10) *Judicial review.* The respondent may seek judicial review of HUD's decision pursuant to section 111(c) of the Act.

[74 FR 4636, Jan. 26, 2009; 87 FR 8197, Feb. 14, 2022]

§ 570.497 Condition of State election to administer State CDBG Program.

Pursuant to section 106(d)(2)(A)(i) of the Act, a State has the right to elect, in such manner and at such time as the Secretary may prescribe, to administer funds allocated under subpart A of this part for use in nonentitlement areas of the State. After January 26, 1995, any State which elects to administer the allocation of CDBG funds for use in nonentitlement areas of the State in any year must, in addition to all other requirements of this subpart, submit a pledge by the State in accordance with section 108(d)(2) of the Act, and in a form acceptable to HUD, of any future CDBG grants it may receive under subpart A and this subpart. Such pledge shall be for the purpose of assuring repayment of any debt obligations (as defined in §570.701), in accordance with their terms, that HUD may have guaranteed in the respective State on behalf of any nonentitlement public entity (as defined in §570.701) or its designated public agency prior to the State's election.

[59 FR 66604, Dec. 27, 1994]

Subpart J—Grant Administration

SOURCE: 53 FR 8058, Mar. 11, 1988, unless otherwise noted.

§570.500 Definitions.

For the purposes of this subpart, the following terms shall apply:

(a) *Program income* means gross income received by the recipient or a subrecipient directly generated from the use of CDBG funds, except as provided in paragraph (a)(4) of this section.

(1) Program income includes, but is not limited to, the following:

(i) Proceeds from the disposition by sale or long-term lease of real property purchased or improved with CDBG funds;

(ii) Proceeds from the disposition of equipment purchased with CDBG funds;

(iii) Gross income from the use or rental of real or personal property acquired by the recipient or by a subrecipient with CDBG funds, less costs incidental to generation of the income;

(iv) Gross income from the use or rental of real property, owned by the recipient or by a subrecipient, that was constructed or improved with CDBG funds, less costs incidental to generation of the income;

(v) Payments of principal and interest on loans made using CDBG funds, except as provided in paragraph (a)(3) of this section;

(vi) Proceeds from the sale of loans made with CDBG funds;

(vii) Proceeds from sale of obligations secured by loans made with CDBG funds;

(viii) [Reserved]

(ix) Interest earned on program income pending its disposition; and

(x) Funds collected through special assessments made against properties owned and occupied by households *not* of low and moderate income, where the assessments are used to recover all or part of the CDBG portion of a public improvement.

(2) Program income does not include income earned (except for interest described in §570.513) on grant advances from the U.S. Treasury. The following items of income earned on grant advances must be remitted to HUD for transmittal to the U.S. Treasury, and will not be reallocated under section 106(c) or (d) of the Act:

(i) Interest earned from the investment of the initial proceeds of a grant advance by the U.S. Treasury;

(ii) Interest earned on loans or other forms of assistance provided with CDBG funds that are used for activities determined by HUD either to be ineligible or to fail to meet a national objective in accordance with the requirements of subpart C of this part, or that fail substantially to meet any other requirement of this part; and

(iii) Interest earned on the investment of amounts reimbursed to the CDBG program account prior to the use of the reimbursed funds for eligible purposes.

(3) The calculation of the amount of program income for the recipient's CDBG program as a whole (i.e., comprising activities carried out by a grantee and its subrecipients) shall exclude payments made by subrecipients of principal and/or interest on CDBG-funded loans received from grantees if such payments are made using program income received by the subrecipient. (By making such payments, the subrecipient shall be deemed to have transferred program income to the grantee.) The amount of program income derived from this calculation shall be used for reporting purposes, for purposes of applying the requirement under §570.504(b)(2)(iii), and in determining limitations on planning and administration and public services activities to be paid for with CDBG funds.

(4) Program income does not include:

(i) Any income received in a single program year by the recipient and all its subrecipients if the total amount of such income does not exceed $25,000; and

(ii) Amounts generated by activities that are financed by a loan guaranteed under section 108 of the Act and meet one or more of the public benefit criteria specified at § 570.209(b)(2)(v) or are carried out in conjunction with a grant under section 108(q) in an area determined by HUD to meet the eligibility requirements for designation as an Urban Empowerment Zone pursuant to 24 CFR part 597, subpart B. Such exclusion shall not apply if CDBG funds are used to repay the guaranteed loan. When such a guaranteed loan is partially repaid with CDBG funds, the amount generated shall be prorated to reflect the percentage of CDBG funds used. Amounts generated by activities financed with loans guaranteed under section 108 which are not defined as program income shall be treated as miscellaneous revenue and shall not be subject to any of the requirements of this part, except that the use of such funds shall be limited to activities that are located in a revitalization strategy area and implement a HUD approved area revitalization strategy pursuant to § 91.215(e) of this title. However, such treatment shall not affect the right of the Secretary to require the section 108 borrower to pledge such amounts as security for the guaranteed loan. The determination whether such amounts shall constitute program income shall be governed by the provisions of the contract required at § 570.705(b)(1).

(5) Examples of other receipts that are not considered program income are proceeds from fund raising activities carried out by subrecipients receiving CDBG assistance (the costs of fundraising are generally unallowable under the applicable OMB circulars referenced in 24 CFR 84.27), funds collected through special assessments used to recover the non-CDBG portion of a public improvement, and proceeds from the disposition of real property acquired or improved with CDBG funds when the disposition occurs after the applicable time period specified in § 570.503(b)(8) for subrecipient-controlled property, or in § 570.505 for recipient-controlled property.

(b) *Revolving fund* means a separate fund (with a set of accounts that are independent of other program accounts) established for the purpose of carrying out specific activities which, in turn, generate payments to the fund for use in carrying out the same activities. Each revolving loan fund's cash balance must be held in an interest-bearing account, and any interest paid on CDBG funds held in this account shall be considered interest earned on grant advances and must be remitted to HUD for transmittal to the U.S. Treasury no less frequently than annually. (Interest paid by borrowers on eligible loans made from the revolving loan fund shall be program income and treated accordingly.)

(c) *Subrecipient* means a public or private nonprofit agency, authority, or organization, or a for-profit entity authorized under § 570.201(o), receiving CDBG funds from the recipient or another subrecipient to undertake activities eligible for such assistance under subpart C of this part. The term excludes an entity receiving CDBG funds from the recipient under the authority of § 570.204, unless the grantee explicitly designates it as a subrecipient. The term includes a public agency designated by a unit of general local government to receive a loan guarantee under subpart M of this part, but does not include contractors providing supplies, equipment, construction, or services subject to the procurement requirements in 2 CFR part 200, subpart D.

[53 FR 8058, Mar. 11, 1988, as amended at 57 FR 27120, June 17, 1992; 60 FR 1952, Jan. 5, 1995; 60 FR 17445, Apr. 6, 1995; 60 FR 56914, Nov. 9, 1995; 80 FR 75937, Dec. 7, 2015]

§ 570.501 Responsibility for grant administration.

(a) One or more public agencies, including existing local public agencies, may be designated by the chief executive officer of the recipient to undertake activities assisted by this part. A public agency so designated shall be subject to the same requirements as are applicable to subrecipients.

(b) The recipient is responsible for ensuring that CDBG funds are used in accordance with all program requirements. The use of designated public agencies, subrecipients, or contractors does not relieve the recipient of this responsibility. The recipient is also responsible for determining the adequacy of performance under subrecipient agreements and procurement contracts, and for taking appropriate action when performance problems arise, such as the actions described in §570.910. Where a unit of general local government is participating with, or as part of, an urban county, or as part of a metropolitan city, the recipient is responsible for applying to the unit of general local government the same requirements as are applicable to subrecipients, except that the five-year period identified under §570.503(b)(8)(i) shall begin with the date that the unit of general local government is no longer considered by HUD to be a part of the metropolitan city or urban county, as applicable, instead of the date that the subrecipient agreement expires.

[53 FR 8058, Mar. 11, 1988, as amended at 57 FR 27120, June 17, 1992]

§570.502 Applicability of uniform administrative requirements.

(a) Grantees and subrecipients shall comply with 2 CFR part 200, "Uniform Administrative Requirements, Cost Principles, and Audit Requirements for Federal Awards", except that:

(1) Section 200.305 "Payment" is modified for lump sum drawdown for financing of property rehabilitation activities, in accordance with §570.513.

(2) Section 200.306 "Cost sharing or matching" does not apply.

(3) Section 200.307 "Program income" does not apply. Program income is governed by §570.504.

(4) Section 200.308 "Revisions of budget and program plans" does not apply.

(5) Section 200.311 "Real property" does not apply, except as provided in §570.200(j). Real property is governed by §570.505.

(6) Section 200.313 "Equipment" applies, except that when the equipment is sold, the proceeds shall be program income. Equipment not needed by the subrecipient for CDBG activities shall be transferred to the recipient for the CDBG program or shall be retained after compensating the recipient.

(7) Section 200.333 "Retention requirements for records" applies except that:

(i) For recipients:

(A) The period shall be 4 years from the date of execution of the closeout agreement for a grant, as further described in this part;

(B) Records for individual activities subject to the reversion of assets provisions at §570.503(b)(7) or the change of use provisions at §570.505 must be maintained for 3 years after those provisions no longer apply to the activity;

(C) Records for individual activities for which there are outstanding loan balances, other receivables, or contingent liabilities must be retained for 3 years after the receivables or liabilities have been satisfied.

(ii) For subrecipients:

(A) The retention period for individual CDBG activities shall be the longer of 3 years after the expiration or termination of the subrecipient agreement under §570.503, or 3 years after the submission of the annual performance and evaluation report, as prescribed in §91.520 of this title, in which the specific activity is reported on for the final time;

(B) Records for individual activities subject to the reversion of assets provisions at §570.503(b)(7) or change of use provisions at §570.505 must be maintained for as long as those provisions continue to apply to the activity; and

(C) Records for individual activities for which there are outstanding loan balances, other receivables, or contingent liabilities must be retained until such receivables or liabilities have been satisfied.

(8) Section 200.343 "Closeout" applies to closeout of subrecipients.

(b) [Reserved]

[80 FR 75937, Dec. 7, 2015]

§570.503 Agreements with subrecipients.

(a) Before disbursing any CDBG funds to a subrecipient, the recipient shall sign a written agreement with the subrecipient. The agreement shall remain in effect during any period that the subrecipient has control over CDBG funds, including program income.

(b) At a minimum, the written agreement with the subrecipient shall include provisions concerning the following items:

(1) *Statement of work.* The agreement shall include a description of the work

to be performed, a schedule for completing the work, and a budget. These items shall be in sufficient detail to provide a sound basis for the recipient effectively to monitor performance under the agreement.

(2) *Records and reports.* The recipient shall specify in the agreement the particular records the subrecipient must maintain and the particular reports the subrecipient must submit in order to assist the recipient in meeting its recordkeeping and reporting requirements.

(3) *Program income.* The agreement shall include the program income requirements set forth in § 570.504(c). The agreement shall also specify that, at the end of the program year, the grantee may require remittance of all or part of any program income balances (including investments thereof) held by the subrecipient (except those needed for immediate cash needs, cash balances of a revolving loan fund, cash balances from a lump sum drawdown, or cash or investments held for section 108 security needs).

(4) *Uniform requirements.* The agreement shall require the subrecipient to comply with applicable uniform requirements, as described in § 570.502.

(5) *Other program requirements.* The agreement shall require the subrecipient to carry out each activity in compliance with all Federal laws and regulations described in subpart K of these regulations, except that:

(i) The subrecipient does not assume the recipient's environmental responsibilities described at § 570.604; and

(ii) The subrecipient does not assume the recipient's responsibility for initiating the review process under the provisions of 24 CFR part 52.

(6) *Suspension and termination.* The agreement shall set forth remedies for noncompliance and provisions on termination in accordance with 2 CFR part 200, subpart D.

(7) *Reversion of assets.* The agreement shall specify that upon its expiration the subrecipient shall transfer to the recipient any CDBG funds on hand at the time of expiration and any accounts receivable attributable to the use of CDBG funds. It shall also include provisions designed to ensure that any real property under the subrecipient's control that was acquired or improved in whole or in part with CDBG funds (including CDBG funds provided to the subrecipient in the form of a loan) in excess of $25,000 is either:

(i) Used to meet one of the national objectives in § 570.208 (formerly § 570.901) until five years after expiration of the agreement, or for such longer period of time as determined to be appropriate by the recipient; or

(ii) Not used in accordance with paragraph (b)(7)(i) of this section, in which event the subrecipient shall pay to the recipient an amount equal to the current market value of the property less any portion of the value attributable to expenditures of non-CDBG funds for the acquisition of, or improvement to, the property. The payment is program income to the recipient. (No payment is required after the period of time specified in paragraph (b)(7)(i) of this section.)

[53 FR 8058, Mar. 11, 1988, as amended at 53 FR 41331, Oct. 21, 1988; 57 FR 27120, June 17, 1992; 60 FR 56915, Nov. 9, 1995; 68 FR 56405, Sept. 30, 2003; 80 FR 69873, Nov. 12, 2015; 80 FR 75938, Dec. 7, 2015]

§ 570.504 Program income.

(a) *Recording program income.* The receipt and expenditure of program income as defined in § 570.500(a) shall be recorded as part of the financial transactions of the grant program.

(b) *Disposition of program income received by recipients.* (1) Program income received before grant closeout may be retained by the recipient if the income is treated as additional CDBG funds subject to all applicable requirements governing the use of CDBG funds.

(2) If the recipient chooses to retain program income, that program income shall be disposed of as follows:

(i) Program income in the form of repayments to, or interest earned on, a revolving fund as defined in § 570.500(b) shall be substantially disbursed from the fund before additional cash withdrawals are made from the U.S. Treasury for the same activity. (This rule does not prevent a lump sum disbursement to finance the rehabilitation of privately owned properties as provided for in § 570.513.)

(ii) Substantially all other program income shall be disbursed for eligible activities before additional cash withdrawals are made from the U.S. Treasury.

(iii) At the end of each program year, the aggregate amount of program income cash balances and any investment thereof (except those needed for immediate cash needs, cash balances of a revolving loan fund, cash balances from a lump-sum drawdown, or cash or investments held for section 108 loan guarantee security needs) that, as of the last day of the program year, exceeds one-twelfth of the most recent grant made pursuant to §570.304 shall be remitted to HUD as soon as practicable thereafter, to be placed in the recipient's line of credit. This provision applies to program income cash balances and investments thereof held by the grantee and its subrecipients. (This provision shall be applied for the first time at the end of the program year for which Federal Fiscal Year 1996 funds are provided.)

(3) Program income on hand at the time of closeout shall continue to be subject to the eligibility requirements in subpart C and all other applicable provisions of this part until it is expended.

(4) Unless otherwise provided in any grant closeout agreement, and subject to the requirements of paragraph (b)(5) of this section, income received after closeout shall not be governed by the provisions of this part, except that, if at the time of closeout the recipient has another ongoing CDBG grant received directly from HUD, funds received after closeout shall be treated as program income of the ongoing grant program.

(5) If the recipient does not have another ongoing grant received directly from HUD at the time of closeout, income received after closeout from the disposition of real property or from loans outstanding at the time of closeout shall not be governed by the provisions of this part, except that such income shall be used for activities that meet one of the national objectives in §570.901 and the eligibility requirements described in section 105 of the Act.

(c) *Disposition of program income received by subrecipients.* The written agreement between the recipient and the subrecipient, as required by §570.503, shall specify whether program income received is to be returned to the recipient or retained by the subrecipient. Where program income is to be retained by the subrecipient, the agreement shall specify the activities that will be undertaken with the program income and that all provisions of the written agreement shall apply to the specified activities. When the subrecipient retains program income, transfers of grant funds by the recipient to the subrecipient shall be adjusted according to the principles described in paragraphs (b)(2) (i) and (ii) of this section. Any program income on hand when the agreement expires, or received after the agreement's expiration, shall be paid to the recipient as required by §570.503(b)(8).

(d) *Disposition of certain program income received by urban counties.* Program income derived from urban county program activities undertaken by or within the jurisdiction of a unit of general local government which thereafter terminates its participation in the urban county shall continue to be program income of the urban county. The urban county may transfer the program income to the unit of general local government, upon its termination of urban county participation, provided that the unit of general local government has become an entitlement grantee and agrees to use the program income in its own CDBG entitlement program.

(e)(1) *Transfer of program income to Entitlement program.* A unit of general local government that becomes eligible to be an Entitlement grantee may request the state's approval to transfer State CDBG grant-generated program income to the unit of general local government's Entitlement program. A state may approve the transfer, provided that the unit of general local government:

(i) Has officially elected to participate in the Entitlement grant program;

(ii) Agrees to use such program income in accordance with Entitlement program requirements; and

(iii) Has set up Integrated Disbursement and Information System (IDIS) access and agrees to enter receipt of program income into IDIS.

(2) *Transfer of program income of grantees losing Entitlement status.* Upon entry into the State CDBG program, a unit of general local government that has lost or relinquished its Entitlement status must, with respect to program income that a unit of general local government would otherwise be permitted to retain, either:

(i) Retain the program income generated under Entitlement grants and continue to comply with Entitlement program requirements for program income; or

(ii) Retain the program income and transfer it to the State CDBG program, in which case the unit of general local government must comply with the state's rules for program income and the requirements of § 570.489(e).

[53 FR 8058, Mar. 11, 1988, as amended at 60 FR 56915, Nov. 9, 1995; 77 FR 24146, Apr. 23, 2012]

§ 570.505 Use of real property.

The standards described in this section apply to real property within the recipient's control which was acquired or improved in whole or in part using CDBG funds in excess of $25,000. These standards shall apply from the date CDBG funds are first spent for the property until five years after closeout of an entitlement recipient's participation in the entitlement CDBG program or, with respect to other recipients, until five years after the closeout of the grant from which the assistance to the property was provided.

(a) A recipient may not change the use or planned use of any such property (including the beneficiaries of such use) from that for which the acquisition or improvement was made unless the recipient provides affected citizens with reasonable notice of, and opportunity to comment on, any proposed change, and either:

(1) The new use of such property qualifies as meeting one of the national objectives in § 570.208 (formerly § 570.901) and is not a building for the general conduct of government; or

(2) The requirements in paragraph (b) of this section are met.

(b) If the recipient determines, after consultation with affected citizens, that it is appropriate to change the use of the property to a use which does not qualify under paragraph (a)(1) of this section, it may retain or dispose of the property for the changed use if the recipient's CDBG program is reimbursed in the amount of the current fair market value of the property, less any portion of the value attributable to expenditures of non-CDBG funds for acquisition of, and improvements to, the property.

(c) If the change of use occurs after closeout, the provisions governing income from the disposition of the real property in § 570.504(b)(4) or (5), as applicable, shall apply to the use of funds reimbursed.

(d) Following the reimbursement of the CDBG program in accordance with paragraph (b) of this section, the property no longer will be subject to any CDBG requirements.

[53 FR 8058, Mar. 11, 1988, as amended at 53 FR 41331, Oct. 21, 1988]

§ 570.506 Records to be maintained.

Each recipient shall establish and maintain sufficient records to enable the Secretary to determine whether the recipient has met the requirements of this part. At a minimum, the following records are needed:

(a) Records providing a full description of each activity assisted (or being assisted) with CDBG funds, including its location (if the activity has a geographical locus), the amount of CDBG funds budgeted, obligated and expended for the activity, and the provision in subpart C under which it is eligible.

(b) Records demonstrating that each activity undertaken meets one of the criteria set forth in § 570.208. (Where information on income by family size is required, the recipient may substitute evidence establishing that the person assisted qualifies under another program having income qualification criteria at least as restrictive as that used in the definitions of "low and moderate income person" and "low and moderate income household" (as applicable) at § 570.3, such as Job Training Partnership Act (JTPA) and welfare programs; or the recipient may substitute evidence that the assisted person is homeless; or the recipient may substitute a copy of a verifiable certification from the assisted person that his or her family income does not exceed the applicable income limit established in accordance with §570.3; or the recipient may substitute a notice that the assisted person is a referral from a state, county or local employment agency or other entity that agrees to refer individuals it determines to be low and moderate income persons based on HUD's criteria and agrees to maintain documentation supporting these determinations.) Such records shall include the following information:

(1) For each activity determined to benefit low and moderate income persons, the income limits applied and the point in time when the benefit was determined.

(2) For each activity determined to benefit low and moderate income persons based on the area served by the activity:

(i) The boundaries of the service area;

(ii) The income characteristics of families and unrelated individuals in the service area; and

(iii) If the percent of low and moderate income persons in the service area is less than 51 percent, data showing that the area qualifies under the exception criteria set forth at §570.208(a)(1)(ii).

(3) For each activity determined to benefit low and moderate income persons because the activity involves a facility or service designed for use by a limited clientele consisting exclusively or predominantly of low and moderate income persons:

(i) Documentation establishing that the facility or service is designed for the particular needs of or used exclusively by senior citizens, adults meeting the Bureau of the Census' Current Population Reports definition of "severely disabled," persons living with AIDS, battered spouses, abused children, the homeless, illiterate adults, or migrant farm workers, for which the regulations provide a presumption concerning the extent to which low- and moderate-income persons benefit; or

(ii) Documentation describing how the nature and, if applicable, the location of the facility or service establishes that it is used predominantly by low and moderate income persons; or

(iii) Data showing the size and annual income of the family of each person receiving the benefit.

(4) For each activity carried out for the purpose of providing or improving housing which is determined to benefit low and moderate income persons:

(i) A copy of a written agreement with each landlord or developer receiving CDBG assistance indicating the total number of dwelling units in each multifamily structure assisted and the number of those units which will be occupied by low and moderate income households after assistance;

(ii) The total cost of the activity, including both CDBG and non-CDBG funds.

(iii) For each unit occupied by a low and moderate income household, the size and income of the household;

(iv) For rental housing only:

(A) The rent charged (or to be charged) after assistance for each dwelling unit in each structure assisted; and

(B) Such information as necessary to show the affordability of units occupied (or to be occupied) by low and moderate income households pursuant to criteria established and made public by the recipient;

(v) For each property acquired on which there are no structures, evidence of commitments ensuring that the criteria in §570.208(a)(3) will be met when the structures are built;

(vi) Where applicable, records demonstrating that the activity qualifies under the special conditions at §570.208(a)(3)(i);

(vii) For any homebuyer assistance activity qualifying under §570.201(e), 570.201(n), or 570.204, identification of the applicable eligibility paragraph and evidence that the activity meets the eligibility criteria for that provision; for any such activity qualifying under §570.208(a), the size and income of each homebuyer's household; and

(viii) For a §570.201(k) housing services activity, identification of the HOME project(s) or assistance that the housing services activity supports, and evidence that project(s) or assistance meet the HOME program income targeting requirements at 24 CFR 92.252 or 92.254.

(5) For each activity determined to benefit low and moderate income persons based on the creation of jobs, the recipient shall provide the documentation described in either paragraph (b)(5)(i) or (ii) of this section.

(i) Where the recipient chooses to document that at least 51 percent of the jobs will be available to low and moderate income persons, documentation for each assisted business shall include:

(A) A copy of a written agreement containing:

(*1*) A commitment by the business that it will make at least 51 percent of the jobs available to low and moderate income persons and will provide training for any of those jobs requiring special skills or education;

(*2*) A listing by job title of the permanent jobs to be created indicating which jobs will be available to low and moderate income persons, which jobs require special skills or education, and which jobs are part-time, if any; and

(*3*) A description of actions to be taken by the recipient and business to ensure that low and moderate income persons receive first consideration for those jobs; and

(B) A listing by job title of the permanent jobs filled, and which jobs of those were available to low and moderate income persons, and a description of how first consideration was given to such persons for those jobs. The description shall include what hiring process was used; which low and moderate income persons were interviewed for a particular job; and which low and moderate income persons were hired.

(ii) Where the recipient chooses to document that at least 51 percent of the jobs will be held by low and moderate income persons, documentation for each assisted business shall include:

(A) A copy of a written agreement containing:

(*1*) A commitment by the business that at least 51 percent of the jobs, on a full-time equivalent basis, will be held by low and moderate income persons; and

(*2*) A listing by job title of the permanent jobs to be created, identifying which are part-time, if any;

(B) A listing by job title of the permanent jobs filled and which jobs were initially held by low and moderate income persons; and

(C) For each such low and moderate income person hired, the size and annual income of the person's family prior to the person being hired for the job.

(6) For each activity determined to benefit low and moderate income persons based on the retention of jobs:

(i) Evidence that in the absence of CDBG assistance jobs would be lost;

(ii) For each business assisted, a listing by job title of permanent jobs retained, indicating which of those jobs are part-time and (where it is known) which are held by low and moderate income persons at the time the CDBG assistance is provided. Where applicable, identification of any of the retained jobs (other than those known to be held by low and moderate income persons) which are projected to become available to low and moderate income persons through job turnover within two years of the time CDBG assistance is provided. Information upon which the job turnover projections were based shall also be included in the record;

(iii) For each retained job claimed to be held by a low and moderate income person, information on the size and annual income of the person's family;

(iv) For jobs claimed to be available to low and moderate income persons based on job turnover, a description covering the items required for "available to" jobs in paragraph (b)(5) of this section; and

(v) Where jobs were claimed to be available to low and moderate income persons through turnover, a listing of each job which has turned over to date, indicating which of those jobs were either taken by, or available to, low and moderate income persons. For jobs made available, a description of how first consideration was given to such persons for those jobs shall also be included in the record.

(7) For purposes of documenting, pursuant to paragraph (b)(5)(i)(B), (b)(5)(ii)(C), (b)(6)(iii) or (b)(6)(v) of this section, that the person for whom a job was either filled by or made available to a low- or moderate-income person based upon the census tract where the person resides or in which the business is located, the recipient, in lieu of

maintaining records showing the person's family size and income, may substitute records showing either the person's address at the time the determination of income status was made or the address of the business providing the job, as applicable, the census tract in which that address was located, the percent of persons residing in that tract who either are in poverty or who are low- and moderate-income, as applicable, the data source used for determining the percentage, and a description of the pervasive poverty and general distress in the census tract in sufficient detail to demonstrate how the census tract met the criteria in §570.208(a)(4)(v), as applicable.

(8) For each activity determined to aid in the prevention or elimination of slums or blight based on addressing one or more of the conditions which qualified an area as a slum or blighted area:

(i) The boundaries of the area; and

(ii) A description of the conditions which qualified the area at the time of its designation in sufficient detail to demonstrate how the area met the criteria in §570.208(b)(1).

(9) For each residential rehabilitation activity determined to aid in the prevention or elimination of slums or blight in a slum or blighted area:

(i) The local definition of "substandard";

(ii) A pre-rehabilitation inspection report describing the deficiencies in each structure to be rehabilitated; and

(iii) Details and scope of CDBG assisted rehabilitation, by structure.

(10) For each activity determined to aid in the prevention or elimination of slums or blight based on the elimination of specific conditions of blight or physical decay not located in a slum or blighted area:

(i) A description of the specific condition of blight or physical decay treated; and

(ii) For rehabilitation carried out under this category, a description of the specific conditions detrimental to public health and safety which were identified and the details and scope of the CDBG assisted rehabilitation by structure.

(11) For each activity determined to aid in the prevention or elimination of slums or blight based on addressing slums or blight in an urban renewal area, a copy of the Urban Renewal Plan, as in effect at the time the activity is carried out, including maps and supporting documentation.

(12) For each activity determined to meet a community development need having a particular urgency:

(i) Documentation concerning the nature and degree of seriousness of the condition requiring assistance;

(ii) Evidence that the recipient certified that the CDBG activity was designed to address the urgent need;

(iii) Information on the timing of the development of the serious condition; and

(iv) Evidence confirming that other financial resources to alleviate the need were not available.

(c)(1) Records that demonstrate that the recipient has made the determinations required as a condition of eligibility of certain activities, as prescribed in §§570.201(f), 570.201(i)(2), 570.201(p), 570.201(q), 570.202(b)(3), 570.206(f), 570.209, 570.210, and 570.309.

(2) Where applicable, records which either demonstrate compliance with the requirements of §570.202(g) or §570.204(a)(5) or document the State's or State's grant recipient's basis for an exception to the requirements of those paragraphs.

(d) Records which demonstrate compliance with §570.503(b)(7) or §570.505 regarding any change of use of real property acquired or improved with CDBG assistance.

(e) Records that demonstrate compliance with the citizen participation requirements prescribed in 24 CFR part 91, subpart B, for entitlement recipients, or in 24 CFR part 91, subpart C, for HUD-administered small cities recipients.

(f) Records which demonstrate compliance with the requirements in §570.606 regarding acquisition, displacement, relocation, and replacement housing.

(g) Fair housing and equal opportunity records containing:

(1) Documentation of the actions the participating jurisdiction has taken to affirmatively further fair housing pursuant to §§5.151, 5.152, 91.225, 91.325, and 91.425 of this title.

(2) Data on the extent to which each racial and ethnic group and single-headed households (by gender of household head) have applied for, participated in, or benefited from, any program or activity funded in whole or in part with CDBG funds. Such information shall be used only as a basis for further investigation as to compliance with nondiscrimination requirements. No recipient is required to attain or maintain any particular statistical measure by race, ethnicity, or gender in covered programs.

(3) Data on employment in each of the recipient's operating units funded in whole or in part with CDBG funds, with such data maintained in the categories prescribed on the Equal Employment Opportunity Commission's EEO–4 form; and documentation of any actions undertaken to assure equal employment opportunities to all persons regardless of race, color, national origin, sex or handicap in operating units funded in whole or in part under this part.

(4) Data indicating the race and ethnicity of households (and gender of single heads of households) displaced as a result of CDBG funded activities, together with the address and census tract of the housing units to which each displaced household relocated. Such information shall be used only as a basis for further investigation as to compliance with nondiscrimination requirements. No recipient is required to attain or maintain any particular statistical measure by race, ethnicity, or gender in covered programs.

(5) Documentation of actions undertaken to meet the requirements of § 570.607(b) which implements section 3 of the Housing Development Act of 1968, as amended (12 U.S.C. 1701U) relative to the hiring and training of low and moderate income persons and the use of local businesses.

(6) Data indicating the racial/ethnic character of each business entity receiving a contract or subcontract of $25,000 or more paid, or to be paid, with CDBG funds, data indicating which of those entities are women's business enterprises as defined in Executive Order 12138, the amount of the contract or subcontract, and documentation of recipient's affirmative steps to assure that minority business and women's business enterprises have an equal opportunity to obtain or compete for contracts and subcontracts as sources of supplies, equipment, construction and services. Such affirmative steps may include, but are not limited to, technical assistance open to all businesses but designed to enhance opportunities for these enterprises and special outreach efforts to inform them of contract opportunities. Such steps shall not include preferring any business in the award of any contract or subcontract solely or in part on the basis of race or gender.

(7) Documentation of the affirmative action measures the recipient has taken to overcome prior discrimination, where the courts or HUD have found that the recipient has previously discriminated against persons on the ground of race, color, national origin or sex in administering a program or activity funded in whole or in part with CDBG funds.

(h) Financial records, in accordance with the applicable requirements listed in § 570.502, including source documentation for entities not subject to 2 CFR part 200. Grantees shall maintain evidence to support how the CDBG funds provided to such entities are expended. Such documentation must include, to the extent applicable, invoices, schedules containing comparisons of budgeted amounts and actual expenditures, construction progress schedules signed by appropriate parties (e.g., general contractor and/or a project architect), and/or other documentation appropriate to the nature of the activity. Grantee records pertaining to obligations, expenditures, and drawdowns must be able to relate financial transactions to either a specific origin year grant or to program income received during a specific program year.

(i) Agreements and other records related to lump sum disbursements to private financial institutions for financing rehabilitation as prescribed in § 570.513; and

(j) Records required to be maintained in accordance with other applicable laws and regulations set forth in subpart K of this part.

(Approved by the Office of Management and Budget under control number 2506–0077)

[53 FR 34454, Sept. 6, 1988; 53 FR 41330, Oct. 21, 1988, as amended at 60 FR 1916, 1953, Jan. 5, 1995; 60 FR 56915, Nov. 9, 1995; 61 FR 18674, Apr. 29, 1996; 64 FR 38813, July 19, 1999; 70 FR 76370, Dec. 23, 2005; 80 FR 42368, July 16, 2015; 80 FR 69873, Nov. 12, 2015; 81 FR 92637, Dec. 20, 2016; 85 FR 47911, Aug. 7, 2020; 86 FR 30792, June 10, 2021]

EFFECTIVE DATE NOTE: At 90 FR 11024, Mar. 3, 2025, §570.506 was amended, effective Apr. 2, 2025.

§570.507 Reports.

(a) *Performance and evaluation report*—(1) *Entitlement grant recipients and HUD-administered small cities recipients in Hawaii.* The annual performance and evaluation report shall be submitted in accordance with 24 CFR part 91.

(2) *HUD-administered Small Cities recipients in New York, and Hawaii recipients for pre-FY 1995 grants*—(i) *Content.* Each performance and evaluation report must contain completed copies of all forms and narratives prescribed by HUD, including a summary of the citizen comments received on the report.

(ii) *Timing.* The performance and evaluation report on each grant shall be submitted:

(A) No later than October 31 for all grants executed before April 1 of the same calendar year. The first report should cover the period from the execution of the grant until September 30. Reports on grants made after March 31 of a calendar year will be due October 31 of the following calendar year, and the reports will cover the period of time from the execution of the grant until September 30 of the calendar year following grant execution. After the initial submission, the performance and evaluation report will be submitted annually on October 31 until completion of the activities funded under the grant;

(B) Hawaii grantees will submit their small cities performance and evaluation report for each pre-FY 1995 grant no later than 90 days after the completion of their most recent program year. After the initial submission, the performance and evaluation report will be submitted annually until completion of the activities funded under the grant; and

(C) No later than 90 days after the criteria for grant closeout, as described in §570.509(a), have been met.

(iii) *Citizen comments on the report.* Each recipient shall make copies of the performance and evaluation report available to its citizens in sufficient time to permit the citizens to comment on the report before its submission to HUD. Each recipient may determine the specific manner and times the report will be made available to citizens consistent with the preceding sentence.

(b) *Equal employment opportunity reports.* Recipients of entitlement grants or HUD-administered small cities grants shall submit to HUD each year a report (HUD/EEO–4) on recipient employment containing data as of June 30.

(c) *Minority business enterprise reports.* Recipients of entitlement grants, HUD-administered small cities grants or Urban Development Action Grants shall submit to HUD, by April 30, a report on contracts and subcontract activity during the first half of the fiscal year and by October 31 a report on such activity during the second half of the year.

(d) *Other reports.* Recipients may be required to submit such other reports and information as HUD determines are necessary to carry out its responsibilities under the Act or other applicable laws.

(Approved by the Office of Management and Budget under control numbers 2506–0077 for paragraph (a) and 2529–0008 for paragraph (b) and 2506–0066 for paragraph (c))

[53 FR 34456, Sept. 6, 1988, as amended at 60 FR 1916, Jan. 5, 1995; 61 FR 32269, June 21, 1996]

§570.508 Public access to program records.

Notwithstanding 2 CFR 200.337, recipients shall provide citizens with reasonable access to records regarding the past use of CDBG funds, consistent with applicable State and local laws regarding privacy and obligations of confidentiality.

[53 FR 8058, Mar. 11, 1988, as amended at 80 FR 75938, Dec. 7, 2015]

§ 570.509 Grant closeout procedures.

(a) *Criteria for closeout.* HUD may make grant closeout determinations for individual grants or multiple grants simultaneously. A grant will be closed out when HUD determines, in consultation with the recipient, that the following criteria have been met:

(1) All costs to be paid with CDBG funds from a given origin year's grant have been expended and drawn down, with the exception of closeout costs (e.g., audit costs) and costs resulting from contingent liabilities described in the closeout agreement pursuant to paragraph (c) of this section. Contingent liabilities include, but are not limited to, third-party claims against the recipient, as well as related administrative costs.

(2) All activities for which funds were expended from the origin year grant are physically completed, are eligible, have met a national objective under § 570.208, and the grantee has reported on all accomplishments resulting from the activity.

(3) A final performance and expenditure report for completed activities has been submitted to HUD pursuant to 24 CFR 91.520, and HUD has determined the plan is satisfactory.

(4) All program income received by the grantee during the grantee program year associated with the origin year grant has been expended, or identified in a more recent program year's Action Plan, pursuant to 24 CFR 91.220(l).

(5) For origin year 2015 grants and subsequent grants, the grantee has expended no more than 20 percent of the origin year grant for planning and program administrative costs, under § 570.200(g)(1).

(6) Other responsibilities of the recipient under the grant agreement and applicable laws and regulations appear to have been carried out satisfactorily or there is no further Federal interest in keeping the grant agreement open for the purpose of securing performance.

(b) *Closeout actions.*

(1) Based on the information provided in the performance report and other relevant information, HUD, in consultation with the recipient, will prepare a closeout agreement in accordance with paragraph (c) of this section.

(2) HUD will cancel any unused portion of the awarded grant, as shown in the signed grant closeout agreement. Any unused grant funds disbursed from the U.S. Treasury which are in the possession of the recipient shall be refunded to HUD. Any funds which have exceeded the statutory time limit on the use of funds will be recaptured by the U.S. Treasury pursuant to 24 CFR 570.200(k).

(3) Any costs paid with CDBG funds which were not audited previously shall be subject to coverage in the recipient's next single audit performed in accordance with HUD regulations implementing the Single Audit Act requirements at 2 CFR part 200. The recipient may be required to repay HUD any disallowed costs based on the results of the audit, or on additional HUD reviews provided for in the closeout agreement.

(c) *Closeout agreement.* Any obligations remaining as of the date of the closeout shall be covered by the terms of a closeout agreement. The agreement shall be prepared by the HUD field office in consultation with the recipient. The agreement shall identify the grant being closed out, and include provisions with respect to the following:

(1) Identification of any closeout costs or contingent liabilities subject to payment with CDBG funds after the closeout agreement is signed;

(2) Identification of any unused grant funds to be canceled by HUD;

(3) Description of the recipient's responsibility after closeout for:

(i) Compliance with all program requirements, certifications, and assurances in using any remaining CDBG funds available for closeout costs and contingent liabilities;

(ii) Use of real property assisted with CDBG funds in accordance with the principles described in §§ 570.503(b)(7) and 570.505;

(iii) Compliance with requirements governing future program income or receivables generated from activities funded from the origin year grant, as described in § 570.504(b)(4) and (5);

(iv) Ensuring that flood insurance coverage for affected property owners is maintained for the mandatory period; and

(4) Other provisions appropriate to any special circumstances of the grant closeout, in modification of or in addition to the obligations in paragraphs (c)(1) through (4) of this section. The agreement shall authorize monitoring by HUD, and shall provide that findings of noncompliance may be taken into account by HUD, as unsatisfactory performance of the recipient, in the consideration of any future grant award under this part.

(d) *Status of consolidated plan after closeout.* Unless otherwise provided in a closeout agreement, the Consolidated Plan will remain in effect after closeout until the expiration of the program year covered by the last approved consolidated plan.

(e) *Termination of grant for convenience.* Grant assistance provided under this part may be terminated for convenience in whole or in part before the completion of the assisted activities, in accordance with the provisions of 2 CFR 200.339. The recipient shall not incur new obligations for the terminated portions after the effective date, and shall cancel as many outstanding obligations as possible. HUD shall allow full credit to the recipient for those portions of obligations which could not be canceled and which had been properly incurred by the recipient in carrying out the activities before the termination. The closeout policies contained in this section shall apply in such cases, except where the approved grant is terminated in its entirety. Responsibility for the environmental review to be performed under 24 CFR part 50 or 24 CFR part 58, as applicable, shall be determined as part of the closeout process.

(f) *Termination for cause.* In cases in which the Secretary terminates the recipient's grant under the authority of subpart O of this part, or under the terms of the grant agreement, the closeout policies contained in this section shall apply, except where the approved grant is cancelled in its entirety. The provisions in 2 CFR 200.342) on the effects of termination shall also apply. HUD shall determine whether an environmental assessment or finding of inapplicability is required, and if such review is required, HUD shall perform it in accordance with 24 CFR part 50.

[53 FR 8058, Mar. 11, 1988, as amended at 56 FR 56128, Oct. 31, 1991; 60 FR 1916, Jan. 5, 1995; 60 FR 16379, Mar. 30, 1995; 80 FR 69873, Nov. 12, 2015; 80 FR 75938, Dec. 7, 2015]

§ 570.510 Transferring projects from urban counties to metropolitan cities.

Section 106(c)(3) of the Act authorizes the Secretary to transfer unobligated grant funds from an urban county to a new metropolitan city, provided: the city was an included unit of general local government in the urban county immediately before its qualification as a metropolitan city; the funds to be transferred were received by the county before the qualification of the city as a metropolitan city; the funds to be transferred had been programmed by the urban county for use in the city before such qualification; and the city and county agree to transfer responsibility for the administration of the funds being transferred from the county's letter of credit to the city's letter of credit. The following rules apply to the transfer of responsibility for an activity from an urban county to the new metropolitan city.

(a) The urban county and the metropolitan city must execute a legally binding agreement which shall specify:

(1) The amount of funds to be transferred from the urban county's letter of credit to the metropolitan city's letter of credit;

(2) The activities to be carried out by the city with the funds being transferred;

(3) The county's responsibility for all expenditures and unliquidated obligations associated with the activities before the time of transfer, including a statement that responsibility for all audit and monitoring findings associated with those expenditures and obligations shall remain with the county;

(4) The responsibility of the metropolitan city for all other audit and monitoring findings;

(5) How program income (if any) from the activities specified shall be divided between the metropolitan city and the urban county; and

(6) Such other provisions as may be required by HUD.

(b) Upon receipt of a request for the transfer of funds from an urban county to a metropolitan city and a copy of the executed agreement, HUD, in consultation with the Department of the Treasury, shall establish a date upon which the funds shall be transferred from the letter of credit of the urban county to the letter of credit of the metropolitan city, and shall take all necessary actions to effect the requested transfer of funds.

(c) HUD shall notify the metropolitan city and urban county of any special audit and monitoring rules which apply to the transferred funds when the date of the transfer is communicated to the city and the county.

§570.511 Use of escrow accounts for rehabilitation of privately owned residential property.

(a) *Limitations.* A recipient may withdraw funds from its letter of credit for immediate deposit into an escrow account for use in funding loans and grants for the rehabilitation of privately owned residential property under §570.202(a)(1). The following additional limitations apply to the use of escrow accounts for residential rehabilitation loans and grants closed after September 7, 1990:

(1) The use of escrow accounts under this section is limited to loans and grants for the rehabilitation of primarily residential properties containing no more than four dwelling units (and accessory neighborhood-scale non-residential space within the same structure, if any, *e.g.*, a store front below a dwelling unit).

(2) An escrow account shall not be used unless the contract between the property owner and the contractor selected to do the rehabilitation work specifically provides that payment to the contractor shall be made through an escrow account maintained by the recipient, by a subrecipient as defined in §570.500(c), by a public agency designated under §570.501(a), or by an agent under a procurement contact governed by the requirements of 2 CFR part 200, subpart D. No deposit to the escrow account shall be made until after the contract has been executed between the property owner and the rehabilitation contractor.

(3) All funds withdrawn under this section shall be deposited into one interest earning account with a financial institution. Separate bank accounts shall not be established for individual loans and grants.

(4) The amount of funds deposited into an escrow account shall be limited to the amount expected to be disbursed within 10 working days from the date of deposit. If the escrow account, for whatever reason, at any time contains funds exceeding 10 days cash needs, the grantee immediately shall transfer the excess funds to its program account. In the program account, the excess funds shall be treated as funds erroneously drawn in accordance with the requirements of U.S. Treasury Financial Manual, paragraph 6–2075.30.

(5) Funds deposited into an escrow account shall be used only to pay the actual costs of rehabilitation incurred by the owner under the contract with a private contractor. Other eligible costs related to the rehabilitation loan or grant, e.g., the recipient's administrative costs under §570.206 or rehabilitation services costs under §570.202(b)(9), are not permissible uses of escrowed funds. Such other eligible rehabilitation costs shall be paid under normal CDBG payment procedures (e.g., from withdrawals of grant funds under the recipient's letter of credit with the Treasury).

(b) *Interest.* Interest earned on escrow accounts established in accordance with this section, less any service charges for the account, shall be remitted to HUD at least quarterly but not more frequently than monthly. Interest earned on escrow accounts is not required to be remitted to HUD to the extent the interest is attributable to the investment of program income.

(c) *Remedies for noncompliance.* If HUD determines that a recipient has failed to use an escrow account in accordance with this section, HUD may, in addition to imposing any other sanctions provided for under this part, require the recipient to discontinue the use of escrow accounts, in whole or in part.

[55 FR 32369, Aug. 8, 1990, as amended at 80 FR 75938, Dec. 7, 2015]

§570.512 [Reserved]

§570.513 Lump sum drawdown for financing of property rehabilitation activities.

Subject to the conditions prescribed in this section, recipients may draw funds from the letter of credit in a lump sum to establish a rehabilitation fund in one or more private financial institutions for the purpose of financing the rehabilitation of privately owned properties. The fund may be used in conjunction with various rehabilitation financing techniques, including loans, interest subsidies, loan guarantees, loan reserves, or such other uses as may be approved by HUD consistent with the objectives of this section. The fund may also be used for making grants, but only for the purpose of leveraging non-CDBG funds for the rehabilitation of the same property.

(a) *Limitation on drawdown of grant funds.* (1) The funds that a recipient deposits to a rehabilitation fund shall not exceed the grant amount that the recipient reasonably expects will be required, together with anticipated program income from interest and loan repayments, for the rehabilitation activities during the period specified in the agreement to undertake activities, based on either:

(i) Prior level of rehabilitation activity; or

(ii) Rehabilitation staffing and management capacity during the period specified in the agreement to undertake activities.

(2) No grant funds may be deposited under this section solely for the purpose of investment, notwithstanding that the interest or other income is to be used for the rehabilitation activities.

(3) The recipient's rehabilitation program administrative costs and the administrative costs of the financial institution may not be funded through lump sum drawdown. Such costs must be paid from periodic letter of credit withdrawals in accordance with standard procedures or from program income, other than program income generated by the lump sum distribution.

(b) *Standards to be met.* The following standards shall apply to all lump sum drawdowns of CDBG funds for rehabilitation:

(1) *Eligible rehabilitation activities.* The rehabilitation fund shall be used to finance the rehabilitation of privately owned properties eligible under the general policies in §570.200 and the specific provisions of either §570.202, including the acquisition of properties for rehabilitation, or §570.203.

(2) *Requirements for agreement.* The recipient shall execute a written agreement with one or more private financial institutions for the operation of the rehabilitation fund. The agreement shall specify the obligations and responsibilities of the parties, the terms and conditions on which CDBG funds are to be deposited and used or returned, the anticipated level of rehabilitation activities by the financial institution, the rate of interest and other benefits to be provided by the financial institution in return for the lump sum deposit, and such other terms as are necessary for compliance with the provisions of this section. Upon execution of the agreement, a copy must be provided to the HUD field office for its record and use in monitoring. Any modifications made during the term of the agreement must also be provided to HUD.

(3) *Period to undertake activities.* The agreement must provide that the rehabilitation fund may only be used for authorized activities during a period of no more than two years. The lump sum deposit shall be made only after the agreement is fully executed.

(4) *Time limit on use of deposited funds.* Use of the deposited funds for rehabilitation financing assistance must start (e.g., first loan must be made, subsidized or guaranteed) within 45 days of the deposit. In addition, substantial disbursements from the fund must occur within 180 days of the receipt of the deposit. (Where CDBG funds are used as a guarantee, the funds that must be substantially disbursed are the guaranteed funds.) For a recipient with an agreement specifying two years to undertake activities, the disbursement of 25 percent of the fund (deposit plus any interest earned) within 180 days

will be regarded as meeting this requirement. If a recipient with an agreement specifying two years to undertake activities determines that it has had substantial disbursement from the fund within the 180 days although it had not met this 25 percent threshold, the justification for the recipient's determination shall be included in the program file. Should use of deposited funds not start within 45 days, or substantial disbursement from such fund not occur within 180 days, the recipient may be required by HUD to return all or part of the deposited funds to the recipient's letter of credit.

(5) *Program activity.* Recipients shall review the level of program activity on a yearly basis. Where activity is substantially below that anticipated, program funds shall be returned to the recipient's letter of credit.

(6) *Termination of agreement.* In the case of substantial failure by a private financial institution to comply with the terms of a lump sum drawdown agreement, the recipient shall terminate its agreement, provide written justification for the action, withdraw all unobligated deposited funds from the private financial institution, and return the funds to the recipient's letter of credit.

(7) *Return of unused deposits.* At the end of the period specified in the agreement for undertaking activities, all unobligated deposited funds shall be returned to the recipient's letter of credit unless the recipient enters into a new agreement conforming to the requirements of this section. Any program income which will be governed by a new agreement must be identified in the current program year Action Plan, pursuant to 24 CFR 91.220(l). In addition, the recipient shall reserve the right to withdraw any unobligated deposited funds required by HUD in the exercise of corrective or remedial actions authorized under §570.910(b), §570.911, §570.912 or §570.913.

(8) *Rehabilitation loans made with non-CDBG funds.* If the deposited funds or program income derived from deposited funds are used to subsidize or guarantee repayment of rehabilitation loans made with non-CDBG funds, or to provide a supplemental loan or grant to the borrower of the non-CDBG funds, the rehabilitation activities are considered to be CDBG-assisted activities subject to the requirements applicable to such activities, except that repayment of non-CDBG funds shall not be treated as program income.

(9) *Provision of consideration.* In consideration for the lump sum deposit by the recipient in a private financial institution, the deposit must result in appropriate benefits in support of the recipient's local rehabilitation program. Minimum requirements for such benefits are:

(i) Grantees shall require the financial institution to pay interest on the lump sum deposit.

(A) The interest rate paid by the financial institution shall be no more than three points below the rate on one year Treasury obligations at constant maturity.

(B) When an agreement sets a fixed interest rate for the entire term of the agreement, the rate should be based on the rate at the time the agreement is excuted.

(C) The agreement may provide for an interest rate that would fluctuate periodically during the term of the agreement, but at no time shall the rate be established at more than three points below the rate on one year Treasury obligations at constant maturity.

(ii) In addition to the payment of interest, at least one of the following benefits must be provided by the financial institution:

(A) Leverage of the deposited funds so that the financial institution commits private funds for loans in the rehabilitation program in an amount substantially in excess of the amount of the lump sum deposit;

(B) Commitment of private funds by the financial institution for rehabilitation loans at below market interest rates, at higher than normal risk, or with longer than normal repayment periods; or

(C) Provision of administrative services in support of the rehabilitation program by the participating financial institution at no cost or at lower than actual cost.

(c) *Program income.* Interest earned on lump sum deposits and payments on loans made from such deposits are program income and, during the period of the agreement, shall be used for rehabilitation activities under the provisions of this section.

(d) *Outstanding findings.* Notwithstanding any other provision of this section, no recipient shall enter into a new agreement during any period of time in which an audit or monitoring finding on a previous lump sum drawdown agreement remains unresolved.

(e) *Prior notification.* The recipient shall provide the HUD field office with written notification of the amount of funds to be distributed to a private financial institution before distribution under the provisions of this section.

(f) *Recordkeeping requirements.* The recipient shall maintain in its files a copy of the written agreement and related documents establishing conformance with this section and concerning performance by a financial institution in accordance with the agreement.

[53 FR 8058, Mar. 11, 1988, as amended at 80 FR 69873, Nov. 12, 2015]

Subpart K—Other Program Requirements

SOURCE: 53 FR 34456, Sept. 6, 1988, unless otherwise noted.

§570.600 General.

(a) This subpart K enumerates laws that the Secretary will treat as applicable to grants made under section 106 of the Act, other than grants to states made pursuant to section 106(d) of the Act, for purposes of the Secretary's determinations under section 104(e)(1) of the Act, including statutes expressly made applicable by the Act and certain other statutes and Executive Orders for which the Secretary has enforcement responsibility. This subpart K applies to grants made under the Insular Areas Program in §570.405 and §570.440 with the exception of §570.612. The absence of mention herein of any other statute for which the Secretary does not have direct enforcement responsibility is not intended to be taken as an indication that, in the Secretary's opinion, such statute or Executive Order is not applicable to activities assisted under the Act. For laws that the Secretary will treat as applicable to grants made to states under section 106(d) of the Act for purposes of the determination required to be made by the Secretary pursuant to section 104(e)(2) of the Act, see §570.487.

(b) This subpart also sets forth certain additional program requirements which the Secretary has determined to be applicable to grants provided under the Act as a matter of administrative discretion.

(c) In addition to grants made pursuant to section 106(b) and 106(d)(2)(B) of the Act (subparts D and F, respectively), the requirements of this subpart K are applicable to grants made pursuant to sections 107 and 119 of the Act (subparts E and G, respectively), and to loans guaranteed pursuant to subpart M.

[53 FR 34456, Sept. 6, 1988, as amended at 61 FR 11477, Mar. 20, 1996; 72 FR 12536, Mar. 15, 2007]

§570.601 Public Law 88–352 and Public Law 90–284; affirmatively furthering fair housing; Executive Order 11063.

(a) The following requirements apply according to sections 104(b) and 107 of the Act:

(1) Public Law 88–352, which is title VI of the Civil Rights Act of 1964 (42 U.S.C. 2000d *et seq.*), and implementing regulations in 24 CFR part 1.

(2) Public Law 90–284, which is the Fair Housing Act (42 U.S.C. 3601–3620). In accordance with the Fair Housing Act, the Secretary requires that grantees administer all programs and activities related to housing and community development in a manner to affirmatively further the policies of the Fair Housing Act.

(b) Executive Order 11063, as amended by Executive Order 12259 (3 CFR, 1959–1963 Comp., p. 652; 3 CFR, 1980 Comp., p. 307) (Equal Opportunity in Housing), and implementing regulations in 24 CFR part 107, also apply.

[61 FR 11477, Mar. 20, 1996, as amended at 80 FR 42368, July 16, 2015; 85 FR 47911, Aug. 7, 2020; 86 FR 30792, June 10, 2021]

EFFECTIVE DATE NOTE: At 90 FR 11024, Mar. 3, 2025, §570.601 was amended, effective Apr. 2, 2025.

§ 570.602 Section 109 of the Act.

Section 109 of the Act requires that no person in the United States shall on the grounds of race, color, national origin, religion, or sex be excluded from participation in, be denied the benefits of, or be subjected to discrimination under any program or activity receiving Federal financial assistance made available pursuant to the Act. Section 109 also directs that the prohibitions against discrimination on the basis of age under the Age Discrimination Act and the prohibitions against discrimination on the basis of disability under Section 504 shall apply to programs or activities receiving Federal financial assistance under Title I programs. The policies and procedures necessary to ensure enforcement of section 109 are codified in 24 CFR part 6.

[64 FR 3802, Jan. 25, 1999]

§ 570.603 Labor standards.

(a) Section 110(a) of the Act contains labor standards that apply to nonvolunteer labor financed in whole or in part with assistance received under the Act. In accordance with section 110(a) of the Act, the Contract Work Hours and Safety Standards Act (40 U.S.C. 327 *et seq.*) also applies. However, these requirements apply to the rehabilitation of residential property only if such property contains not less than 8 units.

(b) The regulations in 24 CFR part 70 apply to the use of volunteers.

[61 FR 11477, Mar. 20, 1996]

§ 570.604 Environmental standards.

For purposes of section 104(g) of the Act, the regulations in 24 CFR part 58 specify the other provisions of law which further the purposes of the National Environmental Policy Act of 1969, and the procedures by which grantees must fulfill their environmental responsibilities. In certain cases, grantees assume these environmental review, decisionmaking, and action responsibilities by execution of grant agreements with the Secretary.

[61 FR 11477, Mar. 20, 1996]

§ 570.605 National Flood Insurance Program.

Notwithstanding the date of HUD approval of the recipient's application (or, in the case of grants made under subpart D of this part or HUD-administered small cities recipients in Hawaii, the date of submission of the grantee's consolidated plan, in accordance with 24 CFR part 91), section 202(a) of the Flood Disaster Protection Act of 1973 (42 U.S.C. 4106) and the regulations in 44 CFR parts 59 through 79 apply to funds provided under this part 570.

[61 FR 11477, Mar. 20, 1996]

§ 570.606 Displacement, relocation, acquisition, and replacement of housing.

(a) *General policy for minimizing displacement.* Consistent with the other goals and objectives of this part, grantees (or States or state recipients, as applicable) shall assure that they have taken all reasonable steps to minimize the displacement of persons (families, individuals, businesses, nonprofit organizations, and farms) as a result of activities assisted under this part.

(b) *Relocation assistance for displaced persons at URA levels.* (1) A displaced person shall be provided with relocation assistance at the levels described in, and in accordance with the requirements of 49 CFR part 24, which contains the government-wide regulations implementing the Uniform Relocation Assistance and Real Property Acquisition Policies Act of 1970 (URA) (42 U.S.C. 4601–4655).

(2) *Displaced person.* (i) For purposes of paragraph (b) of this section, the term "*displaced person*" means any person (family, individual, business, nonprofit organization, or farm) that moves from real property, or moves his or her personal property from real property, permanently and involuntarily, as a direct result of rehabilitation, demolition, or acquisition for an activity assisted under this part. A permanent, involuntary move for an assisted activity includes a permanent move from real property that is made:

(A) After notice by the grantee (or the state recipient, if applicable) to move permanently from the property, if the move occurs after the initial official submission to HUD (or the State, as applicable) for grant, loan, or loan guarantee funds under this part that are later provided or granted.

(B) After notice by the property owner to move permanently from the property, if the move occurs after the date of the submission of a request for financial assistance by the property owner (or person in control of the site) that is later approved for the requested activity.

(C) Before the date described in paragraph (b)(2)(i)(A) or (B) of this section, if either HUD or the grantee (or State, as applicable) determines that the displacement directly resulted from acquisition, rehabilitation, or demolition for the requested activity.

(D) After the "initiation of negotiations" if the person is the tenant-occupant of a dwelling unit and any one of the following three situations occurs:

(*1*) The tenant has not been provided with a reasonable opportunity to lease and occupy a suitable decent, safe, and sanitary dwelling in the same building/complex upon the completion of the project, including a monthly rent that does not exceed the greater of the tenant's monthly rent and estimated average utility costs before the initiation of negotiations or 30 percent of the household's average monthly gross income; or

(*2*) The tenant is required to relocate temporarily for the activity but the tenant is not offered payment for all reasonable out-of-pocket expenses incurred in connection with the temporary relocation, including the cost of moving to and from the temporary location and any increased housing costs, or other conditions of the temporary relocation are not reasonable; and the tenant does not return to the building/complex; or

(*3*) The tenant is required to move to another unit in the building/complex, but is not offered reimbursement for all reasonable out-of-pocket expenses incurred in connection with the move.

(ii) Notwithstanding the provisions of paragraph (b)(2)(i) of this section, the term "*displaced person-*" does not include:

(A) A person who is evicted for cause based upon serious or repeated violations of material terms of the lease or occupancy agreement. To exclude a person on this basis, the grantee (or State or state recipient, as applicable) must determine that the eviction was not undertaken for the purpose of evading the obligation to provide relocation assistance under this section;

(B) A person who moves into the property after the date of the notice described in paragraph (b)(2)(i)(A) or (B) of this section, but who received a written notice of the expected displacement before occupancy.

(C) A person who is not displaced as described in 49 CFR 24.2(g)(2).

(D) A person who the grantee (or State, as applicable) determines is not displaced as a direct result of the acquisition, rehabilitation, or demolition for an assisted activity. To exclude a person on this basis, HUD must concur in that determination.

(iii) A grantee (or State or state recipient, as applicable) may, at any time, request HUD to determine whether a person is a displaced person under this section.

(3) *Initiation of negotiations.* For purposes of determining the type of replacement housing assistance to be provided under paragraph (b) of this section, if the displacement is the direct result of privately undertaken rehabilitation, demolition, or acquisition of real property, the term "*initiation of negotiations*" means the execution of the grant or loan agreement between the grantee (or State or state recipient, as applicable) and the person owning or controlling the real property.

(c) *Residential antidisplacement and relocation assistance plan.* The grantee shall comply with the requirements of 24 CFR part 42, subpart B.

(d) *Optional relocation assistance.* Under section 105(a)(11) of the Act, the grantee may provide (or the State may permit the state recipient to provide, as applicable) relocation payments and other relocation assistance to persons displaced by activities that are not subject to paragraph (b) or (c) of this section. The grantee may also provide (or the State may also permit the state recipient to provide, as applicable) relocation assistance to persons receiving assistance under paragraphs (b) or (c) of this section at levels in excess of those required by these paragraphs. Unless such assistance is provided under State or local law, the grantee (or state recipient, as applicable) shall provide such assistance only upon the basis of a written determination that the assistance is appropriate (see, e.g., 24 CFR 570.201(i), as applicable). The grantee (or state recipient, as applicable) must adopt a written policy available to the public that describes the relocation assistance that the grantee (or state recipient, as applicable) has elected to provide and that provides for equal relocation assistance within each class of displaced persons.

(e) *Acquisition of real property*. The acquisition of real property for an assisted activity is subject to 49 CFR part 24, subpart B.

(f) *Appeals*. If a person disagrees with the determination of the grantee (or the state recipient, as applicable) concerning the person's eligibility for, or the amount of, a relocation payment under this section, the person may file a written appeal of that determination with the grantee (or state recipient, as applicable). The appeal procedures to be followed are described in 49 CFR 24.10. In addition, a low- or moderate-income household that has been displaced from a dwelling may file a written request for review of the grantee's decision to the HUD Field Office. For purposes of the State CDBG program, a low- or moderate-income household may file a written request for review of the state recipient's decision with the State.

(g) *Responsibility of grantee or State*. (1) The grantee (or State, if applicable) is responsible for ensuring compliance with the requirements of this section, notwithstanding any third party's contractual obligation to the grantee to comply with the provisions of this section. For purposes of the State CDBG program, the State shall require state recipients to certify that they will comply with the requirements of this section.

(2) The cost of assistance required under this section may be paid from local public funds, funds provided under this part, or funds available from other sources.

(3) The grantee (or State and state recipient, as applicable) must maintain records in sufficient detail to demonstrate compliance with the provisions of this section.

(Approved by the Office of Management and Budget under OMB control number 2506–0102)

[61 FR 11477, Mar. 20, 1996, as amended at 61 FR 51760, Oct. 3, 1996]

§ 570.607 Employment and contracting opportunities.

To the extent that they are otherwise applicable, grantees shall comply with:

(a) Executive Order 11246, as amended by Executive Orders 11375, 11478, *12086*, and 12107 (3 CFR 1964–1965 Comp. p. 339; 3 CFR, 1966–1970 Comp., p. 684; 3 CFR, 1966–1970., p. 803; 3 CFR, 1978 Comp., p. 230; 3 CFR, 1978 Comp., p. 264 (Equal Employment Opportunity), and Executive Order 13279 (Equal Protection of the Laws for Faith-Based and Community Organizations), 67 FR 77141, 3 CFR, 2002 Comp., p. 258; and the implementing regulations at 41 CFR chapter 60; and

(b) Section 3 of the Housing and Urban Development Act of 1968 (12 U.S.C. 1701u) and implementing regulations at 24 CFR part 75.

[68 FR 56405, Sept. 30, 2003, as amended at 85 FR 61567, Sept. 29, 2020]

§ 570.608 Lead-based paint.

The Lead-Based Paint Poisoning Prevention Act (42 U.S.C. 4821–4846), the Residential Lead-Based Paint Hazard Reduction Act of 1992 (42 U.S.C. 4851–4856), and implementing regulations at part 35, subparts A, B, J, K, and R of this part apply to activities under this program.

[64 FR 50226, Sept. 15, 1999]

§ 570.609 Use of debarred, suspended or ineligible contractors or subrecipients.

The requirements set forth in 24 CFR part 5 apply to this program.

[61 FR 5209, Feb. 9, 1996]

§ 570.610 Uniform administrative requirements, cost principles, and audit requirements for Federal awards.

The recipient, its agencies or instrumentalities, and subrecipients shall comply with 2 CFR part 200, "Uniform Administrative Requirements, Cost Principles, and Audit Requirements for

Federal Awards'', as set forth at §570.502.

[80 FR 75938, Dec. 7, 2015]

§570.611 Conflict of interest.

(a) *Applicability.* (1) In the procurement of supplies, equipment, construction, and services by recipients and by subrecipients, the conflict of interest provisions in 2 CFR 200.317 and 200.318 shall apply.

(2) In all cases not governed by 2 CFR 200.317 and 200.318, the provisions of this section shall apply. Such cases include the acquisition and disposition of real property and the provision of assistance by the recipient or by its subrecipients to individuals, businesses, and other private entities under eligible activities that authorize such assistance (e.g., rehabilitation, preservation, and other improvements of private properties or facilities pursuant to §570.202; or grants, loans, and other assistance to businesses, individuals, and other private entities pursuant to §570.203, 570.204, 570.455, or 570.703(i)).

(b) *Conflicts prohibited.* The general rule is that no persons described in paragraph (c) of this section who exercise or have exercised any functions or responsibilities with respect to CDBG activities assisted under this part, or who are in a position to participate in a decisionmaking process or gain inside information with regard to such activities, may obtain a financial interest or benefit from a CDBG-assisted activity, or have a financial interest in any contract, subcontract, or agreement with respect to a CDBG-assisted activity, or with respect to the proceeds of the CDBG-assisted activity, either for themselves or those with whom they have business or immediate family ties, during their tenure or for one year thereafter. For the UDAG program, the above restrictions shall apply to all activities that are a part of the UDAG project, and shall cover any such financial interest or benefit during, or at any time after, such person's tenure.

(c) *Persons covered.* The conflict of interest provisions of paragraph (b) of this section apply to any person who is an employee, agent, consultant, officer, or elected official or appointed official of the recipient, or of any designated public agencies, or of subrecipients that are receiving funds under this part.

(d) *Exceptions.* Upon the written request of the recipient, HUD may grant an exception to the provisions of paragraph (b) of this section on a case-by-case basis when it has satisfactorily met the threshold requirements of (d)(1) of this section, taking into account the cumulative effects of paragraph (d)(2) of this section.

(1) *Threshold requirements.* HUD will consider an exception only after the recipient has provided the following documentation:

(i) A disclosure of the nature of the conflict, accompanied by an assurance that there has been public disclosure of the conflict and a description of how the public disclosure was made; and

(ii) An opinion of the recipient's attorney that the interest for which the exception is sought would not violate State or local law.

(2) *Factors to be considered for exceptions.* In determining whether to grant a requested exception after the recipient has satisfactorily met the requirements of paragraph (d)(1) of this section, HUD shall conclude that such an exception will serve to further the purposes of the Act and the effective and efficient administration of the recipient's program or project, taking into account the cumulative effect of the following factors, as applicable:

(i) Whether the exception would provide a significant cost benefit or an essential degree of expertise to the program or project that would otherwise not be available;

(ii) Whether an opportunity was provided for open competitive bidding or negotiation;

(iii) Whether the person affected is a member of a group or class of low- or moderate-income persons intended to be the beneficiaries of the assisted activity, and the exception will permit such person to receive generally the same interests or benefits as are being made available or provided to the group or class;

(iv) Whether the affected person has withdrawn from his or her functions or responsibilities, or the decisionmaking process with respect to the specific assisted activity in question;

(v) Whether the interest or benefit was present before the affected person was in a position as described in paragraph (b) of this section;

(vi) Whether undue hardship will result either to the recipient or the person affected when weighed against the public interest served by avoiding the prohibited conflict; and

(vii) Any other relevant considerations.

[60 FR 56916, Nov. 9, 1995, as amended at 80 FR 75938, Dec. 7, 2015]

§ 570.612 Executive Order 12372.

(a) *General.* Executive Order 12372, Intergovernmental Review of Federal Programs, and the Department's implementing regulations at 24 CFR part 52, allow each State to establish its own process for review and comment on proposed Federal financial assistance programs.

(b) *Applicability.* Executive Order 12372 applies to the CDBG Entitlement program and the UDAG program. The Executive Order applies to all activities proposed to be assisted under UDAG, but it applies to the Entitlement program only where a grantee proposes to use funds for the planning or construction (reconstruction or installation) of water or sewer facilities. Such facilities include storm sewers as well as all sanitary sewers, but do not include water and sewer lines connecting a structure to the lines in the public right-of-way or easement. It is the responsibility of the grantee to initiate the Executive Order review process if it proposes to use its CDBG or UDAG funds for activities subject to review.

§ 570.613 Eligibility restrictions for certain resident aliens.

(a) *Restriction.* Certain newly legalized aliens, as described in 24 CFR part 49, are not eligible to apply for benefits under covered activities funded by the programs listed in paragraph (e) of this section. "Benefits" under this section means financial assistance, public services, jobs and access to new or rehabilitated housing and other facilities made available under covered activities funded by programs listed in paragraph (e) of this section. "Benefits" do not include relocation services and payments to which displacees are entitled by law.

(b) *Covered activities.* "Covered activities" under this section means activities meeting the requirements of § 570.208(a) that either:

(1) Have income eligibility requirements limiting the benefits exclusively to low and moderate income persons; or

(2) Are targeted geographically or otherwise to primarily benefit low and moderate income persons (excluding activities serving the public at large, such as sewers, roads, sidewalks, and parks), and that provide benefits to persons on the basis of an application.

(c) *Limitation on coverage.* The restrictions under this section apply only to applicants for new benefits not being received by covered resident aliens as of the effective date of this section.

(d) *Compliance.* Compliance can be accomplished by obtaining certification as provided in 24 CFR 49.20.

(e) *Programs affected.* (1) The Community Development Block Grant program for small cities, administered under subpart F of part 570 of this title until closeout of the recipient's grant.

(2) The Community Development Block Grant program for entitlement grants, administered under subpart D of part 570 of this title.

(3) The Community Development Block Grant program for States, administered under subpart I of part 570 of this title until closeout of the unit of general local government's grant by the State.

(4) The Urban Development Action Grants program, administered under subpart G of part 570 of this title until closeout of the recipient's grant.

[55 FR 18494, May 2, 1990]

§ 570.614 Architectural Barriers Act and the Americans with Disabilities Act.

(a) The Architectural Barriers Act of 1968 (42 U.S.C. 4151–4157) requires certain Federal and Federally funded buildings and other facilities to be designed, constructed, or altered in accordance with standards that insure accessibility to, and use by, physically handicapped people. A building or facility designed, constructed, or altered with funds allocated or reallocated under this part after December 11, 1995, and that meets the definition of "residential structure" as defined in 24 CFR 40.2 or the definition of "building" as defined in 41 CFR 101–19.602(a) is subject to the requirements of the Architectural Barriers Act of 1968 (42 U.S.C. 4151–4157) and shall comply with the Uniform Federal Accessibility Standards (appendix A to 24 CFR part 40 for residential structures, and appendix A to 41 CFR part 101–19, subpart 101–19.6, for general type buildings).

(b) The Americans with Disabilities Act (42 U.S.C. 12131; 47 U.S.C. 155, 201, 218 and 225) (ADA) provides comprehensive civil rights to individuals with disabilities in the areas of employment, public accommodations, State and local government services, and telecommunications. It further provides that discrimination includes a failure to design and construct facilities for first occupancy no later than January 26, 1993, that are readily accessible to and usable by individuals with disabilities. Further, the ADA requires the removal of architectural barriers and communication barriers that are structural in nature in existing facilities, where such removal is readily achievable—that is, easily accomplishable and able to be carried out without much difficulty or expense.

[60 FR 56917, Nov. 9, 1995]

§ 570.615 Housing counseling.

Housing counseling, as defined in 24 CFR 5.100, that is funded with or provided in connection with CDBG funds must be carried out in accordance with 24 CFR 5.111.

[81 FR 90659, Dec. 14, 2016]

Subpart L [Reserved]

Subpart M—Loan Guarantees

SOURCE: 59 FR 66604, Dec. 27, 1994, unless otherwise noted.

§ 570.700 Purpose.

This subpart contains requirements governing the guarantee under section 108 of the Act of debt obligations as defined in § 570.701.

§ 570.701 Definitions.

Borrower means the public entity or its designated public agency or the State that issues debt obligations under this subpart.

Credit subsidy cost means the estimated long-term cost to the Federal Government of a Section 108 loan guarantee or a modification thereof, calculated on a net present value basis, excluding administrative costs and any incidental effects on governmental receipts or outlays.

Debt obligation means a promissory note or other obligation issued by a public entity or its designated public agency or by a State and guaranteed by HUD under this subpart, or a trust certificate or other obligation offered by HUD or by a trust or other offeror approved for purposes of this subpart by HUD, which is guaranteed by HUD under this subpart and is based on and backed by a trust or pool composed of notes or other obligations issued by public entities or their designated public agencies or by States and guaranteed or eligible for guarantee by HUD under this subpart.

Designated public agency means a public agency designated by a public entity to issue debt obligations as borrower under this subpart.

Entitlement public entity means a metropolitan city or an urban county receiving a grant under subpart D of this part.

Guaranteed loan funds means the proceeds payable to the borrower from the issuance of debt obligations under this subpart and includes funds received by a nonentitlement public entity from a State under § 570.711.

Nonentitlement public entity means any unit of general local government in a nonentitlement area.

Public entity shall have the meaning provided for the term "*Eligible public entity*" in section 108(o) of the Act.

State-assisted public entity means a unit of general local government in a nonentitlement area which is assisted by a State as required in § 570.704(b)(9) and § 570.705(b)(2) or pursuant to § 570.711.

[59 FR 66604, Dec. 27, 1994, as amended at 61 FR 11481, Mar. 20, 1996; 74 FR 36389, July 22, 2009; 80 FR 67633, Nov. 3, 2015]

§ 570.702 Eligible applicants.

The following public entities may apply for loan guarantee assistance under this subpart.

(a) Entitlement public entities.

(b) Nonentitlement public entities that are assisted in the submission of applications by States that administer the CDBG program (under subpart I of this part). Such assistance shall consist, at a minimum, of the certifications required under § 570.704(b)(9) (and actions pursuant thereto).

(c) Nonentitlement public entities eligible to apply for grant assistance under subpart F of this part.

§ 570.703 Eligible activities.

Guaranteed loan funds may be used for the following activities, provided such activities meet the requirements of § 570.200. However, guaranteed loan funds may not be used to reimburse the CDBG program account or line of credit for costs incurred by the public entity or designated public agency and paid with CDBG grant funds or program income.

(a) Acquisition of improved or unimproved real property in fee or by long-term lease, including acquisition for economic development purposes.

(b) Rehabilitation of real property owned or acquired by the public entity or its designated public agency.

(c) Payment of interest on obligations guaranteed under this subpart.

(d) Relocation payments and other relocation assistance for individuals, families, businesses, nonprofit organizations, and farm operations who must relocate permanently or temporarily as a result of an activity financed with guaranteed loan funds, where the assistance is:

(1) Required under the provisions of § 570.606(b) or (c); or

(2) Determined by the public entity to be appropriate under the provisions of § 570.606(d).

(e) Clearance, demolition, and removal, including movement of structures to other sites and remediation of properties with known or suspected environmental contamination, of buildings and improvements on real property acquired or rehabilitated pursuant to paragraphs (a) and (b) of this section. Remediation may include project-specific environmental assessment costs not otherwise eligible under § 570.205.

(f) Site preparation, including construction, reconstruction, installation of public and other site improvements, utilities or facilities (other than buildings), or remediation of properties (remediation can include project-specific environmental assessment costs not otherwise eligible under § 570.205) with known or suspected environmental contamination, which is:

(1) Related to the redevelopment or use of the real property acquired or rehabilitated pursuant to paragraphs (a) and (b) of this section, or

(2) For an economic development purpose.

(g) Payment of issuance, underwriting, servicing, trust administration and other costs associated with private sector financing of debt obligations under this subpart.

(h) Housing rehabilitation eligible under § 570.202.

(i) The following economic development activities:

(1) Activities eligible under § 570.203; and

(2) Community economic development projects eligible under § 570.204.

(j) Construction of housing by nonprofit organizations for homeownership under section 17(d) of the United States Housing Act of 1937 (Housing Development Grants Program, 24 CFR part 850).

(k) A debt service reserve to be used in accordance with requirements specified in the contract entered into pursuant to § 570.705(b)(1).

(l) Acquisition, construction, reconstruction, rehabilitation or historic preservation, or installation of public facilities (except for buildings for the general conduct of government) to the extent eligible under § 570.201(c), including public streets, sidewalks, other site improvements and public utilities, and remediation of known or suspected environmental contamination in conjunction with these activities. Remediation may include project-specific environmental assessment costs not otherwise eligible under § 570.205.

(m) In the case of applications by public entities which are, or which contain, "colonias" as defined in section

916 of the Cranston-Gonzalez National Affordable Housing Act (42 U.S.C. 5306 note), as amended by section 810 of the Housing and Community Development Act of 1992, acquisition, construction, reconstruction, rehabilitation or installation of public works and site or other improvements which serve the colonia.

(n) Payment of fees charged by HUD pursuant to § 570.712.

[59 FR 66604, Dec. 27, 1994, as amended at 61 FR 11481, Mar. 20, 1996; 71 FR 30036, May 24, 2006; 80 FR 67633, Nov. 3, 2015; 81 FR 1121, Jan. 11, 2016]

§ 570.704 Application requirements.

(a) *Presubmission and citizen participation requirements.* (1) Before submission of an application for loan guarantee assistance to HUD, the public entity must:

(i) Develop a proposed application that includes the following items:

(A) The community development objectives the public entity proposes to pursue with the guaranteed loan funds.

(B) The activities the public entity proposes to carry out with the guaranteed loan funds. Each activity must be described in sufficient detail, including the specific provision of § 570.703 under which it is eligible and the national objective to be met, amount of guaranteed loan funds expected to be used, and location, to allow citizens to determine the degree to which they will be affected. The proposed application must indicate which activities are expected to generate program income. The application must also describe where citizens may obtain additional information about proposed activities.

(C) A description of the pledge of grants required under § 570.705(b)(2). In the case of applications by State-assisted public entities, the description shall note that pledges of grants will be made by the State and by the public entity.

(D) A description of any CDBG funds, including guaranteed loan funds and grant funds, that will be used to pay fees required under § 570.705(g). The description must include an estimate of the amount of CBDG funds that will be used for this purpose. If the applicant will use grant funds to pay required fees, it must include this planned use of grant funds in its consolidated plan.

(ii) Fulfill the applicable requirements in its citizen participation plan developed in accordance with § 570.704(a)(2).

(iii) Publish community-wide its proposed application so as to afford affected citizens an opportunity to examine the application's contents and to provide comments on the proposed application.

(iv) Prepare its final application. Once the public entity has held the public hearing and published the proposed application as required by paragraphs (a)(1)(ii) and (iii) of this section, respectively, the public entity must consider any such comments and views received and, if the public entity deems appropriate, modify the proposed application. Upon completion, the public entity must make the final application available to the public. The final application must describe each activity in sufficient detail to permit a clear understanding of the nature of each activity, as well as identify the specific provision of § 570.703 under which it is eligible, the national objective to be met, and the amount of guaranteed loan funds to be used. The final application must also indicate which activities are expected to generate program income.

(v) If an application for loan guarantee assistance is to be submitted by an entitlement or nonentitlement public entity simultaneously with the public entity's submission for its grant, the public entity shall include and identify in its proposed and final consolidated plan the activities to be undertaken with the guaranteed loan funds, the national objective to be met by each of these activities, the amount of any program income expected to be received during the program year, and the amount of guaranteed loan funds to be used. The public entity shall also include in the consolidated plan a description of the pledge of grants, as required under § 570.705(b)(2), and the use of grant funds to pay for any fees required under § 570.705(g). In such cases the proposed and final application requirements of paragraphs (a)(1)(i), (iii), and (iv) of this section will be deemed to have been met.

(2) *Citizen participation plan.* The public entity must develop and follow a detailed citizen participation plan and make the plan public. The plan must be completed and available before the application is submitted to HUD. The plan may be the citizen plan required for the consolidated plan, modified to include guaranteed loan funds. The public entity is not required to hold a separate public hearing for its consolidated plan and for the guaranteed loan funds to obtain citizens' views on community development and housing needs. The plan must set forth the public entity's policies and procedures for:

(i) Giving citizens timely notice of local meetings and reasonable and timely access to local meetings, information, and records relating to the public entity's proposed and actual use of guaranteed loan funds, including, but not limited to:

(A) The amount of guaranteed loan funds expected to be made available for the coming year, including program income anticipated to be generated by the activities carried out with guaranteed loan funds;

(B) The range of activities that may be undertaken with guaranteed loan funds;

(C) The estimated amount of guaranteed loan funds (including program income derived therefrom) proposed to be used for activities that will benefit low and moderate income persons;

(D) The proposed activities likely to result in displacement and the public entity's plans, consistent with the policies developed under § 570.606 for minimizing displacement of persons as a result of its proposed activities.

(ii) Providing technical assistance to groups representative of persons of low and moderate income that request assistance in developing proposals. The level and type of assistance to be provided is at the discretion of the public entity. Such assistance need not include the provision of funds to such groups.

(iii) Holding a minimum of two public hearings, each at a different stage of the public entity's program, for the purpose of obtaining the views of citizens and formulating or responding to proposals and questions. Together the hearings must address community development and housing needs, development of proposed activities and review of program performance. At least one of these hearings must be held before submission of the application to obtain the views of citizens on community development and housing needs. Reasonable notice of the hearing must be provided and the hearing must be held at times and locations convenient to potential or actual beneficiaries, with accommodation for the handicapped. The public entity must specify in its plan how it will meet the requirement for a hearing at times and locations convenient to potential or actual beneficiaries.

(iv) Meeting the needs of non-English speaking residents in the case of public hearings where a significant number of non-English speaking residents can reasonably be expected to participate.

(v) Providing affected citizens with reasonable advance notice of, and opportunity to comment on, proposed activities not previously included in an application and activities which are proposed to be deleted or substantially changed in terms of purpose, scope, location, or beneficiaries. The criteria the public entity will use to determine what constitutes a substantial change for this purpose must be described in the citizen participation plan.

(vi) Responding to citizens' complaints and grievances, including the procedures that citizens must follow when submitting complaints and grievances. The public entity's policies and procedures must provide for timely written answers to written complaints and grievances within 15 working days of the receipt of the complaint, where practicable.

(vii) Encouraging citizen participation, particularly by low and moderate income persons who reside in slum or blighted areas, and other areas in which guaranteed loan funds are proposed to be used.

(b) *Submission requirements.* An application for loan guarantee assistance may be submitted at any time. The application (or consolidated plan) shall be submitted to the appropriate HUD Office and shall be accompanied by the following:

(1) A description of how each of the activities to be carried out with the

guaranteed loan funds meets one of the criteria in § 570.208.

(2) A schedule for repayment of the loan which identifies the sources of repayment, together with a statement identifying the entity that will act as borrower and issue the debt obligations.

(3) A certification providing assurance that the public entity possesses the legal authority to make the pledge of grants required under § 570.705(b)(2).

(4) A certification providing assurance that the public entity has made efforts to obtain financing for activities described in the application without the use of the loan guarantee, the public entity will maintain documentation of such efforts for the term of the loan guarantee, and the public entity cannot complete such financing consistent with the timely execution of the program plans without such guarantee.

(5)–(6) [Reserved]

(7) The anti-lobbying statement required under 24 CFR part 87 (appendix A).

(8) Certifications by the public entity that:

(i) It possesses the legal authority to submit the application for assistance under this subpart and to use the guaranteed loan funds in accordance with the requirements of this subpart.

(ii) Its governing body has duly adopted or passed as an official act a resolution, motion or similar official action:

(A) Authorizing the person identified as the official representative of the public entity to submit the application and amendments thereto and all understandings and assurances contained therein, and directing and authorizing the person identified as the official representative of the public entity to act in connection with the application to provide such additional information as may be required; and

(B) Authorizing such official representative to execute such documents as may be required in order to implement the application and issue debt obligations pursuant thereto (provided that the authorization required by this paragraph (B) may be given by the local governing body after submission of the application but prior to execution of the contract required by § 570.705(b);

(iii) Before submission of its application to HUD, the public entity has:

(A) Furnished citizens with information required by § 570.704(a)(2)(i);

(B) Held at least one public hearing to obtain the views of citizens on community development and housing needs; and

(C) Prepared its application in accordance with § 570.704(a)(1)(iv) and made the application available to the public.

(iv) It is following a detailed citizen participation plan which meets the requirements described in § 570.704(a)(2).

(v) The public entity will affirmatively further fair housing, and the guaranteed loan funds will be administered in compliance with:

(A) Title VI of the Civil Rights Act of 1964 (42 U.S.C. 2000d *et seq.*); and

(B) The Fair Housing Act (42 U.S.C. 3601–3619).

(vi)(A) (For entitlement public entities only.) In the aggregate, at least 70 percent of all CDBG funds, as defined at § 570.3, to be expended during the one, two, or three consecutive years specified by the public entity for its CDBG program will be for activities which benefit low and moderate income persons, as described in criteria at § 570.208(a).

(B) (For nonentitlement public entities eligible under subpart F of this part only.) It will comply with primary and national objectives requirements, as applicable under subpart F of this part.

(vii) It will comply with the requirements governing displacement, relocation, real property acquisition, and the replacement of low and moderate income housing described in § 570.606.

(viii) It will comply with the requirements of § 570.200(c)(2) with regard to the use of special assessments to recover the capital costs of activities assisted with guaranteed loan funds.

(ix) (Where applicable, the public entity may also include the following additional certification.) It lacks sufficient resources from funds provided under this subpart or program income to allow it to comply with the provisions of § 570.200(c)(2), and it must therefore assess properties owned and occupied by moderate income persons, to recover the guaranteed loan funded portion of the capital cost without paying such assessments in their behalf from guaranteed loan funds.

(x) It will comply with the other provisions of the Act and with other applicable laws.

(9) In the case of an application submitted by a State-assisted public entity, certifications by the State that:

(i) It agrees to make the pledge of grants required under § 570.705(b)(2).

(ii) It possesses the legal authority to make such pledge.

(iii) At least 70 percent of the aggregate use of CDBG grant funds received by the State, guaranteed loan funds, and program income during the one, two, or three consecutive years specified by the State for its CDBG program will be for activities that benefit low and moderate income persons.

(iv) It agrees to assume the responsibilities described in § 570.710.

(c) *HUD review and approval of applications.* (1) HUD will normally accept the certifications submitted with the application. HUD may, however, consider relevant information which challenges the certifications and require additional information or assurances from the public entity or State as warranted by such information.

(2) [Reserved]

(3) HUD may disapprove an application, or may approve loan guarantee assistance for an amount less than requested, for any of the following reasons:

(i) HUD determines that the guarantee constitutes an unacceptable financial risk. Factors that will be considered in assessing financial risk shall include, but not be limited to, the following:

(A) The length of the proposed repayment period;

(B) The ratio of expected annual debt service requirements to expected annual grant amount;

(C) The likelihood that the public entity or State will continue to receive grant assistance under this part during the proposed repayment period;

(D) The public entity's or State's ability to furnish adequate security pursuant to § 570.705(b), and

(E) The amount of program income the proposed activities are reasonably estimated to contribute toward repayment of the guaranteed loan.

(ii) The requested loan amount exceeds any of the limitations specified under § 570.705(a).

(iii) Funds are not available in the amount requested.

(iv) The performance of the public entity, its designated public agency or State under this part is unacceptable.

(v) Activities to be undertaken with the guaranteed loan funds are not eligible under § 570.703.

(vi) Activities to be undertaken with the guaranteed loan funds do not meet the criteria in § 570.208 for compliance with one of the national objectives of the Act.

(4) HUD will notify the public entity or State in writing that the loan guarantee request has either been approved, reduced, or disapproved. If the request is reduced or disapproved, the public entity or State shall be informed of the specific reasons for reduction or disapproval. If the request is reduced or disapproved, the public entity shall be informed of the specific reasons for reduction or disapproval. If the request is approved, HUD shall issue an offer of commitment to guarantee debt obligations of the borrower identified in the application subject to compliance with this part, including the requirements under § 570.705(b), (d), (g) and (h) for securing and issuing debt obligations, the conditions for release of funds described in paragraph (d) of this section, and such other conditions as HUD may specify in the commitment documents in a particular case.

(5) *Amendments.* If the public entity or State wishes to carry out or assist in an activity not previously described in its application or to substantially change the purpose, scope, location, or beneficiaries of an activity, the amendment must be approved by HUD. Amendments by State-assisted public entities must also be approved by the State. The public entity shall follow the citizen participation requirements for amendments in § 570.704(a)(2).

(d) *Environmental review.* The public entity shall comply with HUD environmental review procedures (24 CFR part 58) for the release of funds for each project carried out with loan guarantee assistance. These procedures set forth the regulations, policies, responsibilities and procedures governing the carrying out of environmental review responsibilities of public entities. All public entities, including nonentitlement public entities, shall submit the request for release of funds and related certification for each project to be assisted with guaranteed loan funds to the appropriate HUD Field Office.

(e) *Displacement, relocation, acquisition, and replacement of housing.* The public entity (or the designated public agency) shall comply with the displacement, relocation, acquisition, and replacement of low/moderate-income housing requirements in §570.606 in connection with any activity financed in whole or in part with guaranteed loan funds.

[59 FR 66604, Dec. 27, 1994, as amended at 60 FR 1917, Jan. 5, 1995; 61 FR 11481, Mar. 20, 1996; 69 FR 32781, June 10, 2004; 72 FR 73496, Dec. 27, 2008; 74 FR 36389, July 22, 2009; 80 FR 67633, Nov. 3, 2015]

§570.705 Loan requirements.

(a) *Limitations on commitments.* (1) If loan guarantee commitments have been issued in any fiscal year in an aggregate amount equal to 50 percent of the amount approved in an appropriation act for that fiscal year, HUD may limit the amount of commitments any one public entity may receive during such fiscal year as follows (except that HUD will not decrease commitments already issued):

(i) The amount any one entitlement public entity may receive may be limited to $35,000,000.

(ii) The amount any one nonentitlement public entity may receive may be limited to $7,000,000.

(iii) The amount any one public entity may receive may be limited to such amount as is necessary to allow HUD to give priority to applications containing activities to be carried out in areas designated as empowerment zones/enterprise communities by the Federal Government or by any State.

(2) In addition to the limitations specified in paragraph (a)(1) of this section, the following limitations shall apply.

(i) *Entitlement public entities.* No commitment to guarantee shall be made if the total unpaid balance of debt obligations guaranteed under this subpart (excluding any amount defeased under the contract entered into under §570.705(b)(1)) on behalf of the public entity would thereby exceed an amount equal to five times the amount of the most recent grant made pursuant to §570.304 to the public entity.

(ii) *States and State-assisted public entities.* No commitment to guarantee shall be made if the total unpaid balance of debt obligations guaranteed under this subpart (excluding any amount defeased under the contract entered into under §570.705(b)(1)) on behalf of the State and all State-assisted public entities in the State would thereby exceed an amount equal to five times the amount of the most recent grant received by such State under subpart I.

(iii) *Nonentitlement public entities eligible under subpart F of this part.* No commitment to guarantee shall be made with respect to a nonentitlement public entity in an insular area or the State of Hawaii if the total unpaid balance of debt obligations guaranteed under this subpart (excluding any amount defeased under the contract entered into under §570.705(b)(1)) on behalf of the public entity would thereby exceed an amount equal to five times the amount of the most recent grant made pursuant to §570.429 or §570.440 (as applicable) to the public entity.

(A) The most recent grant approved for the public entity pursuant to subpart F of this part,

(B) The average of the most recent three grants approved for the public entity pursuant to subpart F of this part, excluding any grant in the same fiscal year as the commitment, or

(C) The average amount of grants made under subpart F of this part to units of general local government in New York State in the previous fiscal year.

(b) *Security requirements.* To assure the repayment of debt obligations and the charges incurred under paragraph (g) of this section and as a condition for receiving loan guarantee assistance, the public entity (and State and designated public agency, as applicable) shall:

(1) Enter into a contract for loan guarantee assistance with HUD, in a form acceptable to HUD, including provisions for repayment of debt obligations guaranteed hereunder;

(2) Pledge all grants made or for which the public entity or State may become eligible under this part; and

(3) Furnish, at the discretion of HUD, such other security as may be deemed appropriate by HUD in making such guarantees. Other security shall be required for all loans with repayment periods of ten years or longer. Such other security shall be specified in the contract entered into pursuant to § 570.705(b)(1). Examples of other security HUD may require are:

(i) Program income as defined in § 570.500(a);

(ii) Liens on real and personal property;

(iii) Debt service reserves; and

(iv) Increments in local tax receipts generated by activities carried out with the guaranteed loan funds.

(c) *Use of grants for loan repayment, issuance, underwriting, servicing, and other costs.* Notwithstanding any other provision of this part:

(1) Community Development Block Grants allocated pursuant to section 106 of the Act (including program income derived therefrom) may be used for:

(i) Paying principal and interest due (including such issuance, servicing, underwriting, or other costs as may be incurred under paragraph (g) of this section) on the debt obligations guaranteed under this subpart;

(ii) Defeasing such debt obligations; and

(iii) Establishing debt service reserves as additional security pursuant to paragraph (b)(3) of this section.

(2) HUD may apply grants pledged pursuant to paragraph (b)(2) of this section to any amounts due under the debt obligations, the payment of costs incurred under paragraph (g) of this section, or to the purchase or defeasance of such debt obligations, in accordance with the terms of the contract required by paragraph (b)(1) of this section.

(d) *Debt obligations.* Debt obligations guaranteed under this subpart shall be in the form and denominations prescribed by HUD. Such debt obligations may be issued and sold only under such terms and conditions as may be prescribed by HUD. HUD may prescribe the terms and conditions of debt obligations, or of their issuance and sale, by regulation or by contractual arrangements authorized by section 108(r)(4) of the Act and paragraph (h) of this section. Unless specifically provided otherwise in the contract for loan guarantee assistance required under paragraph (b) of this section, debt obligations shall not constitute general obligations of any public entity or State secured by its full faith and credit.

(e) *Taxable obligations.* Interest earned on debt obligations under this subpart shall be subject to Federal taxation as provided in section 108(j) of the Act.

(f) *Loan repayment period.* The term of debt obligations under this subpart shall not exceed twenty years.

(g) *Issuance, underwriting, servicing, and other costs.* (1) Each public entity or its designated public agency and each State issuing debt obligations under this subpart must pay the issuance, underwriting, servicing, trust administration, and other costs associated with the private sector financing of the debt obligations.

(2) Each public entity or its designated public agency and each state issuing debt obligations under this subpart must pay any and all fees charged by HUD pursuant to § 570.712.

(h) *Contracting with respect to issuance and sale of debt obligations; effect of other laws.* No State or local law, and no Federal law, shall preclude or limit HUD's exercise of:

(1) The power to contract with respect to public offerings and other sales of debt obligations under this subpart upon such terms and conditions as HUD deems appropriate;

(2) The right to enforce any such contract by any means deemed appropriate by HUD;

(3) Any ownership rights of HUD, as applicable, in debt obligations under this subpart.

[59 FR 66604, Dec. 27, 1994, as amended at 69 FR 32782, June 10, 2004; 74 FR 36389, July 22, 2009; 80 FR 67633, Nov. 3, 2015]

§570.706 Federal guarantee; subrogation.

Section 108(f) of the Act provides for the incontestability of guarantees by HUD under subpart M of this part in the hands of a holder of such guaranteed obligations. If HUD pays a claim under a guarantee made under section 108 of the Act, HUD shall be fully subrogated for all the rights of the holder of the guaranteed debt obligation with respect to such obligation.

[61 FR 11481, Mar. 20, 1996]

§570.707 Applicability of rules and regulations.

(a) *Entitlement public entities.* The provisions of subparts A, C, J, K and O of this part applicable to entitlement grants shall apply equally to guaranteed loan funds and other CDBG funds, except to the extent they are specifically modified or augmented by the provisions of this subpart.

(b) *State-assisted public entities.* The provisions of subpart I of this part, and the requirements the State imposes on units of general local government receiving Community Development Block Grants or program income to the extent applicable, shall apply equally to guaranteed loan funds and Community Development Block Grants (including program income derived therefrom) administered by the State under the CDBG program, except to the extent they are specifically modified or augmented by the provisions of this subpart.

(c) *Nonentitlement public entities eligible under subpart F of this part.* The provisions of subpart F of this part shall apply equally to guaranteed loan funds and other CDBG funds, except to the extent they are specifically modified or augmented by the provisions of this subpart.

§570.708 Sanctions.

(a) *Non-State assisted public entities.* The performance review procedures described in subpart O of this part apply to all public entities receiving guaranteed loan funds other than State-assisted public entities. Performance deficiencies in the use of guaranteed loan funds made available to such public entities (or program income derived therefrom) or violations of the contract entered into pursuant to §570.705(b)(1) may result in the imposition of a sanction authorized pursuant to §570.900(b)(7) against pledged CDBG grants. In addition, upon a finding by HUD that the public entity has failed to comply substantially with any provision of the Act with respect to either the pledged grants or the guaranteed loan funds or program income, HUD may take action against the pledged grants as provided in §570.913 and/or may take action as provided in the contract for loan guarantee assistance.

(b) *State-assisted public entities.* Performance deficiencies in the use of guaranteed loan funds (or program income derived therefrom) or violations of the contract entered into pursuant to §570.705(b)(1) may result in an action authorized pursuant to §570.495 or §570.496. In addition, upon a finding by HUD that the State or public entity has failed to comply substantially with any provision of the Act with respect to the pledged CDBG nonentitlement funds, the guaranteed loan funds, or program income, HUD may take action against the pledged funds as provided in §570.496 and/or may take action as provided in the contract.

§570.709 Allocation of loan guarantee assistance.

Of the amount approved in any appropriation act for guarantees under this subpart in any fiscal year, 70 percent shall be allocated for entitlement public entities and 30 percent shall be allocated for States and nonentitlement public entities. HUD need not comply with these percentage requirements in any fiscal year to the extent that there is an absence of applications approvable under this subpart from entitlement public entities or from States and nonentitlement public entities.

[74 FR 36389, July 22, 2009]

§570.710 State responsibilities.

The State is responsible for choosing public entities that it will assist under this subpart. States are free to develop procedures and requirements for determining which activities will be assisted, subject to the requirements of this subpart. Upon approval by HUD of an application from a State or a State-assisted public entity, the State will be principally responsible, subject to HUD oversight under subpart I of this part, for ensuring compliance with all applicable requirements governing the use of the guaranteed loan funds. Notwithstanding the State's responsibilities described in this section, HUD may take any action necessary for ensuring compliance with requirements affecting the security interests of HUD with respect to the guaranteed loan.

[59 FR 66604, Dec. 27, 1994, as amended at 74 FR 36389, July 22, 2009]

§ 570.711 State borrowers; additional requirements and application procedures.

This section contains additional requirements and alternative application procedures for guarantees of debt obligations under section 108 of the Act pursuant to the additional authority provided in paragraph (a) of section 222 of the Transportation, Housing and Urban Development, and Related Agencies Appropriations Act, 2009, Public Law 111–8; 123 Stat. 524 at 976 (Division I of the Omnibus Appropriations Act, 2009) ("section 222" and the "2009 Appropriations Act"). If any other federal law or laws are enacted after March 11, 2009, the effect of which with respect to loan guarantee authority provided in an appropriations act is equivalent to the effect of section 222 with respect to the loan guarantee authority provided in the 2009 Appropriations Act, the additional requirements and alternative application procedures in this section shall also apply to guarantees of debt obligations under section 108 of the act, pursuant to the additional authority provided in such other federal law or laws.

(a) *Applications by States.* Notwithstanding § 570.702 and § 570.704, states that administer the CDBG program (under subpart I of this part) may apply for loan guarantee assistance under this subpart, and such application shall consist of the following:

(1) A copy of the State's CDBG method of distribution in the action plan most recently submitted or amended pursuant to 24 CFR part 91. In addition to the requirements of 24 CFR part 91, such method of distribution must note the approximate amount of section 108 guaranteed obligations issued by the State and all nonentitlement public entities that are outstanding at the time of such submission or amendment, identify the maximum amount of guaranteed loan funds for which the State will apply during the period covered by the action plan, describe the pledge of grants required under § 570.705(b)(2), and identify the nonentitlement public entities in the State that may be assisted with such guaranteed loan funds (to satisfy this requirement, the method of distribution may identify one or more specific nonentitlement public entities that may be assisted, or may indicate that all or a specified subset of the nonentitlement public entities in the State may be assisted and describe how applications will be selected for assistance).

(2) Either:

(i) A description of each activity to be carried out with the guaranteed loan funds, including the specific provision of § 570.703 under which the activity is eligible and how the activity meets one of the criteria in § 570.208; or

(ii) An indication of the type or types of activities to be assisted, the provisions of § 570.703 under which such activities are eligible, and the criteria in § 570.208 intended to be met, in which case HUD shall require that the description referred to in paragraph (a)(2)(i) of this section be submitted to and approved by HUD before the State disburses guaranteed loan funds to a public entity for the activity.

(3) A schedule for repayment of the loan which identifies the sources of repayment.

(b) *Distribution to Local Governments.* Proceeds payable to a State from the issuance of debt obligations under this subpart may be used only for:

(1) Loans and grants to the nonentitlement public entities identified in the State's approved application for activities eligible under § 570.703; and

(2) The uses specified in paragraphs (c), (g), and (k) of § 570.703.

(c) *Certification of need.* Prior to approving a nonentitlement public entity's application for assistance, the State shall obtain a certification from such public entity conforming to § 570.704(b)(4).

(d) *Local government citizen participation requirements.* The presubmission and citizen participation requirements in § 570.704(a) and the third sentence of § 570.704(c)(5) shall not apply with respect to nonentitlement public entities' applications to a State for assistance under this section. Nonentitlement public entities shall comply with the provisions of § 570.486(a) with respect to such applications and such assistance.

(e) *Environmental review; displacement, relocation, acquisition, and replacement of housing.* Nonentitlement public entities assisted by a State under this section shall comply with § 570.704(d) and (e).

[74 FR 36389, July 22, 2009]

§ 570.712 Collection of fees; procedure to determine amount of the fee.

This section contains additional procedures for guarantees of debt obligations under section 108 when HUD is required or authorized to collect fees to pay the credit subsidy costs of the loan guarantee program.

(a) *Collection of fees.* HUD may collect fees from borrowers for the purpose of paying the credit subsidy cost of the loan guarantee. Each public entity or its designated public agency and each State issuing debt obligations under this subpart is responsible for the payment of any and all fees charged pursuant to this section. The fees are payable from the grant allocated to the issuer pursuant to the Act (including program income derived therefrom) or from other sources, but are only payable from guaranteed loan funds if the fee is deducted from the disbursement of guaranteed loan funds.

(b) *Amount and determination of fee.* (1) HUD shall calculate the amount of the fee as a percentage of the principal amount of the guaranteed loan as provided by this section, based on a determination that the fees when collected will reduce the credit subsidy cost to the amount established by applicable appropriation acts. The amount of the fee payable by the public entity or State shall be based on the date of the loan guarantee commitment and shall be determined by applying the percentages announced by FEDERAL REGISTER notice to guaranteed loan disbursements as they occur or periodically to outstanding principal balances, or both.

(2) HUD shall publish in the FEDERAL REGISTER the fees required under paragraph (a) of this section, announcing the fee to be applied, the effective date of the fee, and any other necessary information regarding payment of the fee and, if necessary, provide a 30-day public comment period for the purpose of inviting comment on the proposed fee before adopting changes to the assumptions underlying the fee calculation or if the fee structure itself raises new considerations for Borrowers. HUD will publish a second FEDERAL REGISTER notice, if necessary, after consideration of public comments.

[80 FR 67633, Nov. 3, 2015]

Subpart N—Urban Renewal Provisions

SOURCE: 41 FR 20524, May 18, 1976, unless otherwise noted.

§ 570.800 Urban renewal regulations.

The regulations governing urban renewal projects and neighborhood development programs in subpart N of this part, that were effective immediately before April 19, 1996, will continue to govern the rights and obligations of recipients and HUD with respect to such projects and programs.

[61 FR 11481, Mar. 20, 1996]

Subpart O—Performance Reviews

SOURCE: 53 FR 34466, Sept. 6, 1988, unless otherwise noted.

§ 570.900 General.

(a) *Performance review authorities*—(1) *Entitlement, Insular Areas, and HUD-administered Small Cities performance reviews.* Section 104(e)(1) of the Act requires that the Secretary shall, at least on an annual basis, make such reviews and audits as may be necessary or appropriate to determine whether the recipient has carried out its activities in a timely manner, whether the recipient has carried out those activities and its certifications in accordance with the requirements and the primary objectives of the Act and with other applicable laws, and whether the recipient has a continuing capacity to carry out those activities in a timely manner.

(2) *Urban Development Action Grant (UDAG) performance reviews.* Section 119(g) of the Act requires the Secretary, at least on an annual basis, to make such reviews and audits of recipients of Urban Development Action Grants as necessary to determine whether the recipient's progress in carrying out the approved activities is substantially in accordance with the recipient's approved plans and timetables.

(b) *Performance review procedures.* This paragraph describes the review procedures the Department will use in conducting the performance reviews required by sections 104(e) and 119(g) of the Act:

(1) The Department will determine the performance of each entitlement, Insular Areas, and HUD-administered small cities recipient in accordance with section 104(e)(1) of the Act by reviewing for compliance with the requirements described in § 570.901 and by applying the performance criteria described in §§ 570.902 and 570.903 relative to carrying out activities in a timely manner. The review criteria in § 570.904 will be used to assist in determining if the recipient's program is being carried out in compliance with civil rights requirements.

(2) The Department will review UDAG projects and activities to determine whether such projects and activities are being carried out substantially in accordance with the recipient's approved plans and schedules. The Department will also review to determine if the recipient has carried out its UDAG program in accordance with all other requirements of the Grant Agreement and with all applicable requirements of this part.

(3) In conducting performance reviews, HUD will primarily rely on information obtained from the recipient's performance report, records maintained, findings from monitoring, grantee and subrecipient audits, audits and surveys conducted by the HUD Inspector General, and financial data regarding the amount of funds remaining in the line of credit plus program income. HUD may also consider relevant information pertaining to a recipient's performance gained from other sources, including litigation, citizen comments, and other information provided by or concerning the recipient. A recipient's failure to maintain records in the prescribed manner may result in a finding that the recipient has failed to meet the applicable requirement to which the record pertains.

(4) If HUD determines that a recipient has not met a civil rights review criterion in § 570.904, the recipient will be provided an opportunity to demonstrate that it has nonetheless met the applicable civil rights requirement.

(5) If HUD finds that a recipient has failed to comply with a program requirement or has failed to meet a performance criterion in § 570.902 or § 570.903, HUD will give the recipient an opportunity to provide additional information concerning the finding.

(6) If, after considering any additional information submitted by a recipient, HUD determines to uphold the finding, HUD may advise the recipient to undertake appropriate corrective or remedial actions as specified in § 570.910. HUD will consider the recipient's capacity as described in § 570.905 prior to selecting the corrective or remedial actions.

(7) If the recipient fails to undertake appropriate corrective or remedial actions which resolve the deficiency to the satisfaction of the Secretary, the Secretary may impose a sanction pursuant to § 570.911, 570,912, or 570.913, as applicable.

[53 FR 34466, Sept. 6, 1988, as amended at 60 FR 56917, Nov. 9, 1995; 72 FR 12536, Mar. 15, 2007]

§ 570.901 Review for compliance with the primary and national objectives and other program requirements.

HUD will review each entitlement, Insular Areas, and HUD-administered small cities recipient's program to determine if the recipient has carried out its activities and certifications in compliance with:

(a) The requirement described at §570.200(a)(3) that, consistent with the primary objective of the Act, not less than 70 percent of the aggregate amount of CDBG funds received by the recipient shall be used over the period specified in its certification for activities that benefit low and moderate income persons;

(b) The requirement described at §570.200(a)(2) that each CDBG assisted activity meets the criteria for one or more of the national objectives described at §570.208;

(c) All other activity eligibility requirements defined in subpart C of this part;

(d) For entitlement grants and non-entitlement CDBG grants in Hawaii, the submission requirements of 24 CFR part 91 and the displacement policy requirements at §570.606;

(e) For HUD-administered Small Cities grants in New York, the citizen participation requirements at §570.431, the amendment requirements at §570.427, and the displacement policy requirements of §570.606;

(f) For Insular Areas Program grants only, the application and amendment requirements at §570.440, the citizen participation requirements at §570.441, the displacement policy requirements of §570.606, and the lead-based paint requirements of 24 CFR 35.940;

(g) The grant administration requirements described in subpart J;

(h) Other applicable laws and program requirements described in subpart K; and

(i) Where applicable, the requirements pertaining to loan guarantees (subpart M) and urban renewal completions (subpart N).

[53 FR 34466, Sept. 6, 1988, as amended at 60 FR 1917, Jan. 5, 1995; 60 FR 56917, Nov. 9, 1995; 72 FR 12536, Mar. 15, 2007; 72 FR 46371, Aug. 17, 2007]

§570.902 Review to determine if CDBG-funded activities are being carried out in a timely manner.

HUD will review the performance of each entitlement, HUD-administered small cities, and Insular Areas recipient to determine whether each recipient is carrying out its CDBG-assisted activities in a timely manner.

(a) *Entitlement recipients and Non-entitlement CDBG grantees in Hawaii.* (1) Before the funding of the next annual grant and absent contrary evidence satisfactory to HUD, HUD will consider an entitlement recipient or a non-entitlement CDBG grantee in Hawaii to be failing to carry out its CDBG activities in a timely manner if:

(i) Sixty days prior to the end of the grantee's current program year, the amount of entitlement grant funds available to the recipient under grant agreements but undisbursed by the U.S. Treasury is more than 1.5 times the entitlement grant amount for its current program year; and

(ii) The grantee fails to demonstrate to HUD's satisfaction that the lack of timeliness has resulted from factors beyond the grantee's reasonable control.

(2) Notwithstanding that the amount of funds in the line of credit indicates that the recipient is carrying out its activities in a timely manner pursuant to paragraph (a)(1) of this section, HUD may determine that the recipient is not carrying out its activities in a timely manner if:

(i) The amount of CDBG program income the recipient has on hand 60 days prior to the end of its current program year, together with the amount of funds in its CDBG line of credit, exceeds 1.5 times the entitlement grant amount for its current program year; and

(ii) The grantee fails to demonstrate to HUD's satisfaction that the lack of timeliness has resulted from factors beyond the grantee's reasonable control.

(3) In determining the appropriate corrective action to take with respect to a HUD determination that a recipient is not carrying out its activities in a timely manner pursuant to paragraphs (a)(1) or (a)(2) of this section, HUD will consider the likelihood that the recipient will expend a sufficient amount of funds over the next program year to reduce the amount of unexpended funds to a level that will fall within the standard described in paragraph (a)(1) of this section when HUD next measures the grantee's timeliness performance. For these purposes, HUD will take into account the extent to

which funds on hand have been obligated by the recipient and its subrecipients for specific activities at the time the finding is made and other relevant information.

(b) *HUD-administered Small Cities program in New York.* The Department will, absent substantial evidence to the contrary, deem a HUD-administered Small Cities recipient in New York to be carrying out its CDBG-funded activities in a timely manner if the schedule for carrying out its activities, as contained in the approved application (including any subsequent amendment(s)), is being substantially met.

(c) *Insular Areas recipients.* (1) Before the funding of the next annual grant and absent contrary evidence satisfactory to HUD, HUD will consider an Insular Areas recipient to be failing to carry out its CDBG activities in a timely manner if:

(i) Sixty days prior to the end of the grantee's current program year, the amount of Insular Area grant funds available to the recipient under grant agreements but undisbursed by the U.S. Treasury is more than 2.0 times the Insular Area's grant amount for its current program year; and

(ii) The grantee fails to demonstrate to HUD's satisfaction that the lack of timeliness has resulted from factors beyond the grantee's reasonable control.

(2) Notwithstanding that the amount of funds in the line of credit indicates that the Insular Area recipient is carrying out its activities in a timely manner pursuant to paragraph (c)(1) of this section, HUD may determine that the recipient is not carrying out its activities in a timely manner if:

(i) The amount of CDBG program income the recipient has on hand 60 days prior to the end of its current program year, together with the amount of funds in its CDBG line of credit, exceeds 2.0 times the Insular Area's grant amount for its current program year; and

(ii) The grantee fails to demonstrate to HUD's satisfaction that the lack of timeliness has resulted from factors beyond the grantee's reasonable control.

(3) In determining the appropriate corrective action to take with respect to a HUD determination that a recipient is not carrying out its activities in a timely manner pursuant to paragraphs (c)(1) or (c)(2) of this section, HUD will consider the likelihood that the recipient will expend a sufficient amount of funds over the next program year to reduce the amount of unexpended funds to a level that will fall within the standards described in paragraphs (c)(1) and (2) of this section when HUD next measures the grantee's timeliness performance. For these purposes, HUD will take into account the extent to which funds on hand have been obligated by the recipient and its sub-recipients for specific activities at the time the finding is made and other relevant information.

(4) If a recipient is determined to be untimely pursuant to paragraphs (c)(1) or (c)(2) of this section in one year, and the recipient is again determined to be untimely in the following year, HUD may reduce the recipient's next grant by 100 percent of the amount in excess of twice the Insular Area's most recent CDBG grant, unless HUD determines that the untimeliness resulted from factors outside of the grantee's reasonable control.

(5) The first review under paragraphs (c)(1) and (c)(2) of this section will take place 60 days prior to the conclusion of the Fiscal Year 2006 program year.

[53 FR 34466, Sept. 6, 1988, as amended at 60 FR 56917, Nov. 9, 1995; 72 FR 12536, Mar. 15, 2007; 72 FR 46371, Aug. 17, 2007]

§ 570.903 Review to determine if the recipient is meeting its consolidated plan responsibilities.

The consolidated plan, action plan, and amendment submission requirements referred to in this section are in 24 CFR part 91. For the purpose of this section, the term consolidated plan includes an abbreviated consolidated plan that is submitted pursuant to 24 CFR 91.235.

(a) *Review timing and purpose.* HUD will review the consolidated plan performance of each entitlement, Insular Areas, and Hawaii HUD-administered Small Cities grant recipient prior to acceptance of a grant recipient's annual certification under 24 CFR 91.225(b)(3) to determine whether the recipient followed its HUD-approved consolidated plan for the most recently completed program year, and whether activities assisted with CDBG funds during that period were consistent with that consolidated plan, except that grantees are not bound by the consolidated plan with respect to the use or distribution of CDBG funds to meet non-housing community development needs.

(b) *Following a consolidated plan.* The recipient will be considered to be following its consolidated plan if it has taken all of the planned actions described in its action plan. This includes, but is not limited to:

(1) Pursuing all resources that the grantee indicated it would pursue;

(2) Providing certifications of consistency, when requested to do so by applicants for HUD programs for which the grantee indicated that it would support application by other entities, in a fair and impartial manner; and

(3) Not hindering implementation of the consolidated plan by action or willful inaction.

(c) *Disapproval.* If HUD determines that a recipient has not met the criteria outlined in paragraph (b) of this section, HUD will notify the recipient and provide the recipient up to 45 days to demonstrate to the satisfaction of the Secretary that it has followed its consolidated plan. HUD will consider all relevant circumstances and the recipient's actions and lack of actions affecting the provision of assistance covered by the consolidated plan within its jurisdiction. Failure to so demonstrate in a timely manner will be cause for HUD to find that the recipient has failed to meet its certification. A complete and specific response by the recipient shall describe:

(1) Any factors beyond the control of the recipient that prevented it from following its consolidated plan, and any actions the recipient has taken or plans to take to alleviate such factors; and

(2) Actions taken by the recipient, if any, beyond those described in the consolidated plan performance report to facilitate following the consolidated plan, including the effects of such actions.

(d) *New York HUD-administered Small Cities.* New York HUD-administered grantees shall follow the provisions of paragraph (b) of this section for their abbreviated or full consolidated plan to the extent that the provisions of paragraph (b) of this section are applicable. If the grantee does not comply with the requirements of paragraph (b) of this section, and does not provide HUD with an acceptable explanation, HUD may decide, in accordance with the requirements of the notice of fund availability, that the grantee does not meet threshold requirements to apply for a new small cities grant.

[60 FR 56918, Nov. 9, 1995, as amended at 72 FR 12537, Mar. 15, 2007]

§570.904 Equal opportunity and fair housing review criteria.

(a) *General.* (1) Where the criteria in this section are met, the Department will presume that the recipient has carried out its CDBG-funded program in accordance with civil rights certifications and civil rights requirements of the Act relating to equal employment opportunity, equal opportunity in services, benefits and participation, and is affirmatively furthering fair housing unless:

(i) There is evidence which shows, or from which it is reasonable to infer, that the recipient, motivated by considerations of race, color, religion where applicable, sex, national origin, age or handicap, has treated some persons less favorably than others, or

(ii) There is evidence that a policy, practice, standard or method of administration, although neutral on its face, operates to deny or affect adversely in a significantly disparate way the provision of employment or services, benefits or participation to persons of a particular race, color, religion where applicable, sex, national origin, age or handicap, or fair housing to persons of a particular race, color, religion, sex, or national origin, or

(iii) Where the Secretary required a further assurance pursuant to §570.304 in order to accept the recipient's prior civil rights certification, the recipient has failed to meet any such assurance.

(2) In such instances, or where the review criteria in this section are not met, the recipient will be afforded an opportunity to present evidence that it has not failed to carry out the civil

rights certifications and fair housing requirements of the Act. The Secretary's determination of whether there has been compliance with the applicable requirements will be made based on a review of the recipient's performance, evidence submitted by the recipient, and all other available evidence. The Department may also initiate separate compliance reviews under title VI of the Civil Rights Act of 1964 or section 109 of the Act.

(b) *Review for equal opportunity.* Title VI of the Civil Rights Act of 1964 (42 U.S.C. 2000d *et seq.*), and implementing regulations in 24 CFR part 1, together with section 109 of the Act (see § 570.602), prohibit discrimination in any program or activity funded in whole or in part with funds made available under this part.

(1) *Review for equal employment opportunity.* The Department will presume that a recipient's hiring and employment practices have been carried out in compliance with its equal opportunity certifications and requirements of the Act. This presumption may be rebutted where, based on the totality of circumstances, there has been a deprivation of employment, promotion, or training opportunities by a recipient to any person within the meaning of section 109. The extent to which persons of a particular race, gender, or ethnic background are represented in the workforce may in certain circumstances be considered, together with complaints, performance reviews, and other information.

(2) *Review of equal opportunity in services, benefits and participation.* The Department will presume a recipient is carrying out its programs and activities in accordance with the civil rights certifications and requirements of the Act. This presumption may be rebutted where, based on the totality of circumstances, there has been a deprivation of services, benefits, or participation in any program or activity funded in whole or in part with block grant funds by a recipient to any person within the meaning of section 109. The extent to which persons of a particular race, gender, or ethnic background participate in a program or activity may in certain circumstances be considered, together with complaints, performance reviews, and other information.

(c) *Review for fair housing*—(1) *General.* See the requirements in the Fair Housing Act (42 U.S.C. 3601–20), as well as § 570.601(a).

(2) *Affirmatively furthering fair housing.* HUD will review a recipient's performance to determine if it has administered all programs and activities related to housing and urban development in accordance with § 570.601(a)(2), which sets forth the grantee's responsibility to affirmatively further fair housing.

(d) *Actions to use minority and women's business firms.* The Department will review a recipient's performance to determine if it has administered its activities funded with assistance under this part in a manner to encourage use of minority and women's business enterprises described in Executive Orders 11625, 12432 and 12138, and 2 CFR 200.321. In making this review, the Department will determine if the grantee has taken actions required under 2 CFR 200.321, and will review the effectiveness of those actions in accomplishing the objectives of 2 CFR 200.321 and the Executive Orders. No recipient is required by this part to attain or maintain any particular statistical level of participation in its contracting activities by race, ethnicity, or gender of the contractor's owners or managers.

[53 FR 34466, Sept. 6, 1988; 53 FR 41330, Oct. 21, 1988, as amended at 54 FR 37411, Sept. 9, 1989; 60 FR 1917, Jan. 5, 1995; 61 FR 11482, Mar. 20, 1996; 80 FR 42368, July 16, 2015; 80 FR 75938, Dec. 7, 2015]

§ 570.905 Review of continuing capacity to carry out CDBG funded activities in a timely manner.

If HUD determines that the recipient has not carried out its CDBG activities and certifications in accordance with the requirements and criteria described in § 570.901 or 570.902, HUD will undertake a further review to determine whether or not the recipient has the continuing capacity to carry out its activities in a timely manner. In making the determination, the Department will consider the nature and extent of the recipient's performance deficiencies, types of corrective actions the recipient has undertaken and the success or likely success of such actions.

§570.906 Review of urban counties.

In reviewing the performance of an urban county, HUD will hold the county accountable for the actions or failures to act of any of the units of general local government participating in the urban county. Where the Department finds that a participating unit of government has failed to cooperate with the county to undertake or assist in undertaking an essential community development or assisted housing activity and that such failure results, or is likely to result, in a failure of the urban county to meet any requirement of the program or other applicable laws, the Department may prohibit the county's use of funds made available under this part for that unit of government. HUD will also consider any such failure to cooperate in its review of a future cooperation agreement between the county and such included unit of government described at §570.307(b)(2).

§§570.907–570.909 [Reserved]

§570.910 Corrective and remedial actions.

(a) *General.* Consistent with the procedures described in §570.900(b), the Secretary may take one or more of the actions described in paragraph (b) of this section. Such actions shall be designed to prevent a continuation of the performance deficiency; mitigate, to the extent possible, the adverse effects or consequences of the deficiency; and prevent a recurrence of the deficiency.

(b) *Actions authorized.* The following lists the actions that HUD may take in response to a deficiency identified during the review of a recipient's performance:

(1) Issue a letter of warning advising the recipient of the deficiency and putting the recipient on notice that additional action will be taken if the deficiency is not corrected or is repeated;

(2) Recommend, or request the recipient to submit, proposals for corrective actions, including the correction or removal of the causes of the deficiency, through such actions as:

(i) Preparing and following a schedule of actions for carrying out the affected CDBG activities, consisting of schedules, timetables and milestones necessary to implement the affected CDBG activities;

(ii) Establishing and following a management plan which assigns responsibilities for carrying out the actions identified in paragraph (b)(2)(i) of this section;

(iii) For entitlement and Insular Areas recipients, canceling or revising affected activities that are no longer feasible to implement due to the deficiency and re-programming funds from such affected activities to other eligible activities (pursuant to the citizen participation requirements in 24 CFR part 91); or

(iv) Other actions which will serve to prevent a continuation of the deficiency, mitigate (to the extent possible) the adverse effects or consequences of the deficiency, and prevent a recurrence of the deficiency;

(3) Advise the recipient that a certification will no longer be acceptable and that additional assurances will be required;

(4) Advise the recipient to suspend disbursement of funds for the deficient activity;

(5) Advise the recipient to reimburse its program account or letter of credit in any amounts improperly expended and reprogram the use of the funds in accordance with applicable requirements;

(6) Change the method of payment to the recipient from a letter of credit basis to a reimbursement basis;

(7) In the case of claims payable to HUD or the U.S. Treasury, institute collection procedures pursuant to subpart B of 24 CFR part 17; and

(8) In the case of an entitlement or Insular Areas recipient, condition the use of funds from a succeeding fiscal year's allocation upon appropriate corrective action by the recipient. The failure of the recipient to undertake the actions specified in the condition may result in a reduction, pursuant to §570.911, of the entitlement or Insular Areas recipient's annual grant by up to the amount conditionally granted.

[53 FR 34466, Sept. 6, 1988, as amended at 60 FR 1917, Jan. 5, 1995; 72 FR 12537, Mar. 15, 2007]

§ 570.911 Reduction, withdrawal, or adjustment of a grant or other appropriate action.

(a) *Opportunity for an informal consultation.* Prior to a reduction, withdrawal, or adjustment of a grant or other appropriate action, taken pursuant to paragraph (b), (c), or (d) of this section, the recipient shall be notified of such proposed action and given an opportunity within a prescribed time period for an informal consultation.

(b) *Entitlement grants, Non-entitlement CDBG grants in Hawaii, and Insular Areas grants.* Consistent with the procedures described in § 570.900(b), the Secretary may make a reduction in the entitlement, non-entitlement CDBG grants in Hawaii, or Insular Areas grant amount either for the succeeding program year or, if the grant had been conditioned, up to the amount that had been conditioned. The amount of the reduction shall be based on the severity of the deficiency and may be for the entire grant amount.

(c) *HUD-administered small cities grants.* Consistent with the procedures described in § 570.900(b), the Secretary may adjust, reduce or withdraw the grant or take other actions as appropriate, except that funds already expended on eligible approved activities shall not be recaptured or deducted from future grants.

(d) *Urban Development Action Grants.* Consistent with the procedures described in § 570.900(b), the Secretary may adjust, reduce or withdraw the grant or take other actions as appropriate, except that funds already expended on eligible approved activities shall not be recaptured or deducted from future grants made to the recipient.

[61 FR 11481, Mar. 20, 1996, as amended at 72 FR 12537, Mar. 15, 2007; 72 FR 46371, Aug. 17, 2007]

§ 570.912 Nondiscrimination compliance.

(a) Whenever the Secretary determines that a unit of general local government which is a recipient of assistance under this part has failed to comply with § 570.602, the Secretary shall notify the governor of such State or chief executive officer of such unit of general local government of the noncompliance and shall request the governor or the chief executive officer to secure compliance. If within a reasonable period of time, not to exceed sixty days, the governor or chief executive officer fails or refuses to secure compliance, the Secretary is authorized to:

(1) Refer the matter to the Attorney General with a recommendation that an appropriate civil action be instituted;

(2) Exercise the powers and functions provided by title VI of the Civil Rights Act of 1964 (42 U.S.C. 2000d);

(3) Exercise the powers and functions provided for in § 570.913; or

(4) Take such other action as may be provided by law.

(b) When a matter is referred to the Attorney General pursuant to paragraph (a)(1) of this section, or whenever the Secretary has reason to believe that a State or a unit of general local government is engaged in a pattern or practice in violation of the provisions of § 570.602, the Attorney General may bring a civil action in any appropriate United States district court for such relief as may be appropriate, including injunctive relief.

§ 570.913 Other remedies for noncompliance.

(a) *Action to enforce compliance.* When the Secretary acts to enforce the civil rights provisions of Section 109, as described in § 570.602 and 24 CFR part 6, the procedures described in 24 CFR parts 6 and 180 apply. If the Secretary finds, after reasonable notice and opportunity for hearing, that a recipient has failed to comply substantially with any other provisions of this part, the provisions of this section apply. The Secretary, until he/she is satisfied that there is no longer any such failure to comply, shall:

(1) Terminate payments to the recipient;

(2) Reduce payments to the recipient by an amount equal to the amount of such payments which were not expended in accordance with this part; or

(3) Limit the availability of payments to programs or activities not affected by such failure to comply.

Provided, however, that the Secretary may on due notice suspend payments at any time after the issuance of a notice of opportunity for hearing pursuant to paragraph (c)(1) of this section, pending such hearing and a final decision, to the extent the Secretary determines such action necessary to preclude the further expenditure of funds for activities affected by such failure to comply.

(b) In lieu of, or in addition to, any action authorized by paragraph (a) of this section, the Secretary may, if he/she has reason to believe that a recipient has failed to comply substantially with any provision of this part;

(1) Refer the matter to the Attorney General of the United States with a recommendation that an appropriate civil action be instituted; and

(2) Upon such a referral, the Attorney General may bring a civil action in any United States district court having venue thereof for such relief as may be appropriate, including an action to recover the amount of the assistance furnished under this part which was not expended in accordance with it, or for mandatory or injunctive relief;

(c) *Proceedings.* When the Secretary proposes to take action pursuant to this section, the respondent is the unit of general local government or State receiving assistance under this part. These procedures are to be followed prior to imposition of a sanction described in paragraph (a) of this section:

(1) *Notice of opportunity for hearing:* The Secretary shall notify the respondent in writing of the proposed action and of the opportunity for a hearing. The notice shall:

(i) Specify, in a manner which is adequate to allow the respondent to prepare its response, allegations with respect to a failure to comply substantially with a provision of this part;

(ii) State that the hearing procedures are governed by these rules;

(iii) State that a hearing may be requested within 10 days from receipt of the notice and the name, address and telephone number of the person to whom any request for hearing is to be addressed:

(iv) Specify the action which the Secretary proposes to take and that the authority for this action is section 111(a) of the Act;

(v) State that if the respondent fails to request a hearing within the time specified a decision by default will be rendered against the respondent; and

(vi) Be sent to the respondent by certified mail, return receipt requested.

(2) *Initiation of hearing.* The respondent shall be allowed at least 10 days from receipt of the notice within which to notify HUD of its request for a hearing. If no request is received within the time specified, the Secretary may proceed to make a finding on the issue of compliance with this part and to take the proposed action.

(3) *Administrative Law Judge.* Proceedings conducted under these rules shall be presided over by an Administrative Law Judge (ALJ), appointed as provided by section 11 of the Administrative Procedures Act (5 U.S.C. 3105). The case shall be referred to the ALJ by the Secretary at the time a hearing is requested. The ALJ shall promptly notify the parties of the time and place at which the hearing will be held. The ALJ shall conduct a fair and impartial hearing and take all action necessary to avoid delay in the disposition of proceedings and to maintain order. The ALJ shall have all powers necessary to those ends, including but not limited to the power to:

(i) Administer oaths and affirmations;

(ii) Issue subpoenas as authorized by law;

(iii) Rule upon offers of proof and receive relevant evidence;

(iv) Order or limit discovery prior to the hearing as the interests of justice may require;

(v) Regulate the course of the hearing and the conduct of the parties and their counsel;

(vi) Hold conferences for the settlement or simplification of the issues by consent of the parties;

(vii) Consider and rule upon all procedural and other motions appropriate in adjudicative proceedings; and

(viii) Make and file initial determinations.

(4) *Ex parte communications.* An ex parte communication is any communication with an ALJ, direct or indirect, oral or written, concerning the merits or procedures of any pending proceeding which is made by a party in

the absence of any other party. Ex parte communications are prohibited except where the purpose and content of the communication have been disclosed in advance or simultaneously to all parties, or the communication is a request for information concerning the status of the case. Any ALJ who receives an ex parte communication which the ALJ knows or has reason to believe is unauthorized shall promptly place the communication, or its substance, in all files and shall furnish copies to all parties. Unauthorized ex parte communications shall not be taken into consideration in deciding any matter in issue.

(5) *The hearing.* All parties shall have the right to be represented at the hearing by counsel. The ALJ shall conduct the proceedings in an expeditious manner while allowing the parties to present all oral and written evidence which tends to support their respective positions, but the ALJ shall exclude irrelevant, immaterial or unduly repetitious evidence. The Department has the burden of proof in showing by a preponderance of the evidence that the respondent failed to comply substantially with a provision of this part. Each party shall be allowed to cross-examine adverse witnesses and to rebut and comment upon evidence presented by the other party. Hearings shall be open to the public. So far as the orderly conduct of the hearing permits, interested persons other than the parties may appear and participate in the hearing.

(6) *Transcripts.* Hearing shall be recorded and transcribed only by a reporter under the supervision of the ALJ. The orginal transcript shall be a part of the record and shall constitute the sole official transcript. Respondents and the public, at their own expense, may obtain copies of the transcript.

(7) *The ALJ's decision.* At the conclusion of the hearing, the ALJ shall give the parties a reasonable opportunity to submit proposed findings and conclusions and supporting reasons therefor. Within 25 days after the conclusion of the hearing, the ALJ shall prepare a written decision which includes a statement of findings and conclusions, and the reasons or basis therefor, on all the material issues of fact, law or discretion presented on the record and the appropriate sanction or denial thereof. The decision shall be based on consideration of the whole record or those parts thereof cited by a party and supported by and in accordance with the reliable, probative, and substantial evidence. A copy of the decision shall be furnished to the parties immediately by certified mail, return receipt requested, and shall include a notice that any requests for review by the Secretary must be made in writing to the Secretary within 30 days of the receipt of the decision.

(8) *The record.* The transcript of testimony and exhibits, together with the decision of the ALJ and all papers and requests filed in the proceeding, constitutes the exclusive record for decision and, on payment of its reasonable cost, shall be made available to the parties. After reaching his/her initial decision, the ALJ shall certify to the complete record and forward the record to the Secretary.

(9) *Review by the Secretary.* The decision by the ALJ shall constitute the final decision of the Secretary unless, within 30 days after the receipt of the decision, either the respondent or the Assistant Secretary for Community Planning and Development files an exception and request for review by the Secretary. The excepting party must transmit simultaneously to the Secretary and the other party the request for review and the basis of the party's exceptions to the findings of the ALJ. The other party shall be allowed 30 days from receipt of the exception to provide the Secretary and the excepting party with a written reply. The Secretary shall then review the record of the case, including the exceptions and the reply. On the basis of such review, the Secretary shall issue a written determination, including a statement of the reasons or basis therefor, affirming, modifying or revoking the decision of the ALJ. The Secretary's decision shall be made and transmitted to the parties within 80 days after the decision of the ALJ was furnished to the parties.

(10) *Judicial review.* The respondent may seek judicial review of the Secretary's decision pursuant to section 111(c) of the Act.

[53 FR 34466, Sept. 6, 1988, as amended at 64 FR 3802, Jan. 25, 1999]

APPENDIX A TO PART 570—GUIDELINES AND OBJECTIVES FOR EVALUATING PROJECT COSTS AND FINANCIAL REQUIREMENTS

I. *Guidelines and Objectives for Evaluating Project Costs and Financial Requirements.* HUD has developed the following guidelines that are designed to provide the recipient with a framework for financially underwriting and selecting CDBG-assisted economic development projects which are financially viable and will make the most effective use of the CDBG funds. *The use of these underwriting guidelines as published by HUD is not mandatory.* However, grantees electing not to use these underwriting guidelines would be expected to conduct basic financial underwriting prior to the provision of CDBG financial assistance to a for-profit business. States electing not to use these underwriting guidelines would be expected to ensure that the state or units of general local government conduct basic financial underwriting prior to the provision of CDBG financial assistance to a for-profit business.

II. Where appropriate, HUD's underwriting guidelines recognize that different levels of review are appropriate to take into account differences in the size and scope of a proposed project, and in the case of a microenterprise or other small business to take into account the differences in the capacity and level of sophistication among businesses of differing sizes.

III. Recipients are encouraged, when they develop their own programs and underwriting criteria, to also take these factors into account. For example, a recipient administering a program providing only technical assistance to small businesses might choose to apply underwriting guidelines to the technical assistance program as a whole, rather than to each instance of assistance to a business. Given the nature and dollar value of such a program, a recipient might choose to limit its evaluation to factors such as the extent of need for this type of assistance by the target group of businesses and the extent to which this type of assistance is already available.

IV. The objectives of the underwriting guidelines are to ensure:

(1) that project costs are reasonable;

(2) that all sources of project financing are committed;

(3) that to the extent practicable, CDBG funds are not substituted for non-Federal financial support;

(4) that the project is financially feasible;

(5) that to the extent practicable, the return on the owner's equity investment will not be unreasonably high; and

(6) that to the extent practicable, CDBG funds are disbursed on a pro rata basis with other finances provided to the project.

1. Project costs are reasonable. i. Reviewing costs for reasonableness is important. It will help the recipient avoid providing either too much or too little CDBG assistance for the proposed project. Therefore, it is suggested that the grantee obtain a breakdown of all project costs and that each cost element making up the project be reviewed for reasonableness. The amount of time and resources the recipient expends evaluating the reasonableness of a cost element should be commensurate with its cost. For example, it would be appropriate for an experienced reviewer looking at a cost element of less than $10,000 to judge the reasonableness of that cost based upon his or her knowledge and common sense. For a cost element in excess of $10,000, it would be more appropriate for the reviewer to compare the cost element with a third-party, fair-market price quotation for that cost element. Third-party price quotations may also be used by a reviewer to help determine the reasonableness of cost elements below $10,000 when the reviewer evaluates projects infrequently or if the reviewer is less experienced in cost estimations. If a recipient does not use third-party price quotations to verify cost elements, then the recipient would need to conduct its own cost analysis using appropriate cost estimating manuals or services.

ii. The recipient should pay particular attention to any cost element of the project that will be carried out through a non-arms-length transaction. A non-arms-length transaction occurs when the entity implementing the CDBG assisted activity procures goods or services from itself or from another party with whom there is a financial interest or family relationship. If abused, non-arms-length transactions misrepresent the true cost of the project.

2. *Commitment of all project sources of financing.* The recipient should review all projected sources of financing necessary to carry out the economic development project. This is to ensure that time and effort is not wasted on assessing a proposal that is not able to proceed. To the extent practicable, prior to the commitment of CDBG funds to the project, the recipient should verify that: sufficient sources of funds have been identified to finance the project; all participating parties providing those funds have affirmed their intention to make the funds available; and the participating parties have the financial capacity to provide the funds.

3. *Avoid substitution of CDBG funds for non-Federal financial support.* i. The recipient should review the economic development project to ensure that, to the extent practicable, CDBG funds will not be used to substantially reduce the amount of non-Federal financial support for the activity. This will help the recipient to make the most efficient use of its CDBG funds for economic development. To reach this determination, the recipient's reviewer would conduct a financial underwriting analysis of the project, including reviews of appropriate projections of revenues, expenses, debt service and returns on equity investments in the project. The extent of this review should be appropriate for the size and complexity of the project and should use industry standards for similar projects, taking into account the unique factors of the project such as risk and location.

ii. Because of the high cost of underwriting and processing loans, many private financial lenders do not finance commercial projects that are less than $100,000. A recipient should familiarize itself with the lending practices of the financial institutions in its community. If the project's total cost is one that would normally fall within the range that financial institutions participate, then the recipient should normally determine the following:

A. *Private debt financing*—whether or not the participating private, for-profit business (or other entity having an equity interest) has applied for private debt financing from a commercial lending institution and whether that institution has completed all of its financial underwriting and loan approval actions resulting in either a firm commitment of its funds or a decision not to participate in the project; and

B. *Equity participation*—whether or not the degree of equity participation is reasonable given general industry standards for rates of return on equity for similar projects with similar risks and given the financial capacity of the entrepreneur(s) to make additional financial investments.

iii. If the recipient is assisting a microenterprise owned by a low- or moderate-income person(s), in conducting its review under this paragraph, the recipient might only need to determine that non-Federal sources of financing are not available (at terms appropriate for such financing) in the community to serve the low- or moderate-income entrepreneur.

4. *Financial feasibility of the project.* i. The public benefit a grantee expects to derive from the CDBG assisted project (the subject of separate regulatory standards) will not materialize if the project is not financially feasible. To determine if there is a reasonable chance for the project's success, the recipient should evaluate the financial viability of the project. A project would be considered financially viable if all of the assumptions about the project's market share, sales levels, growth potential, projections of revenue, project expenses and debt service (including repayment of the CDBG assistance if appropriate) were determined to be realistic and met the project's break-even point (which is generally the point at which all revenues are equal to all expenses). Generally speaking, an economic development project that does not reach this break-even point over time is not financially feasible. The following should be noted in this regard:

A. some projects make provisions for a negative cash flow in the early years of the project while space is being leased up or sales volume built up, but the project's projections should take these factors into account and provide sources of financing for such negative cash flow; and

B. it is expected that a financially viable project will also project sufficient revenues to provide a reasonable return on equity investment. The recipient should carefully examine any project that is not economically able to provide a reasonable return on equity investment. Under such circumstances, a business may be overstating its real equity investment (actual costs of the project may be overstated as well), or it may be overstating some of the project's operating expenses in the expectation that the difference will be taken out as profits, or the business may be overly pessimistic in its market share and revenue projections and has downplayed its profits.

ii. In addition to the financial underwriting reviews carried out earlier, the recipient should evaluate the experience and capacity of the assisted business owners to manage an assisted business to achieve the projections. Based upon its analysis of these factors, the recipient should identify those elements, if any, that pose the greatest risks contributing to the project's lack of financial feasibility.

5. *Return on equity investment.* To the extent practicable, the CDBG assisted activity should provide not more than a reasonable return on investment to the owner of the assisted activity. This will help ensure that the grantee is able to maximize the use of its CDBG funds for its economic development objectives. However, care should also be taken to avoid the situation where the owner is likely to receive too small a return on his/her investment, so that his/her motivation remains high to pursue the business with vigor. The amount, type and terms of the CDBG assistance should be adjusted to allow the owner a reasonable return on his/her investment given industry rates of return for that investment, local conditions and the risk of the project.

6. *Disbursement of CDBG funds on a pro rata basis.* To the extent practicable, CDBG funds used to finance economic development activities should be disbursed on a pro rata

basis with other funding sources. Recipients should be guided by the principle of not placing CDBG funds at significantly greater risk than non-CDBG funds. This will help avoid the situation where it is learned that a problem has developed that will block the completion of the project, even though all or most of the CDBG funds going in to the project have already been expended. When this happens, a recipient may be put in a position of having to provide additional financing to complete the project or watch the potential loss of its funds if the project is not able to be completed. When the recipient determines that it is not practicable to disburse CDBG funds on a pro rata basis, the recipient should consider taking other steps to safeguard CDBG funds in the event of a default, such as insisting on securitizing assets of the project.

[60 FR 1953, Jan. 5, 1995]

PART 573—LOAN GUARANTEE RECOVERY FUND

AUTHORITY: Pub. L. 104–155, 110 Stat. 1392, 18 U.S.C. 241 note; 42 U.S.C. 3535(d).

SOURCE: 61 FR 47405, Sept. 6, 1996, unless otherwise noted.

§ 573.1 Authority and purpose.

Section 4 of the Church Arson Prevention Act of 1996 (Pub. L. 104–155, approved July 3, 1996) authorizes HUD to guarantee loans made by financial institutions to certain nonprofit organizations to finance activities designed to remedy the damage and destruction to real and personal property caused by acts of arson or terrorism. This part establishes the general procedures and requirements that apply to HUD's guarantee of these loans.

§ 573.2 Definitions.

The following definitions are only applicable to loan guarantees under this part, and are not criminal definitions.

Act means "The Church Arson Prevention Act of 1996" (Pub. L. 104–155, approved July 3, 1996).

Arson means a fire or explosion causing damage to (or destruction of) real or personal property that a Qualified Certification Official determines, or reasonably believes, to be deliberately set.

Borrower means an organization described in section 501(c)(3) of the Internal Revenue Code of 1986, as amended, whose property has been damaged or destroyed as a result of an act of arson or terrorism and that incurs a debt obligation to a financial institution for the purpose of carrying out activities eligible under his part.

Financial Institution means a lender which may be a bank, trust company, savings and loan association, credit union, mortgage company, or other issuer regulated by the Federal Deposit Insurance Corporation, the Office of Thrift Supervision, the Credit Union Administration, or the U.S. Comptroller of the Currency. A Financial Institution may also be a Pension Fund.

Guarantee means an obligation of the United States Government guaranteeing payment of the outstanding principal loan amount, in whole or in part, plus interest thereon, on a debt obligation of the Borrower to a Financial Institution upon failure of the Borrower to repay the debt.

Guaranteed Loan Funds means funds received by the borrower from the Financial Institution to finance eligible activities under this part, the repayment of which is guaranteed by HUD.

Loan Guarantee Agreement means an agreement between a Financial Institution and the Secretary detailing the rights, responsibilities, procedures, terms, and conditions under which a loan provided by a Financial Institution to a Borrower may be guaranteed under section 4 of the Act.

Qualified Certification Official (QCO)—(1) *For the purpose of certifying an act of arson.* A State or local official authorized to investigate possible acts of arson. For the purposes of this definition, such an official is authorized to execute an Official Incident Report or its equivalent and may be an official or employee of such agencies as the local fire department, the local police department, or the State Fire Marshall Office or its equivalent. The term "Qualified Certification Official" also includes HUD, which will consult with the Bureau of Alcohol, Tobacco, and Firearms of the Department of the Treasury in making its determinations.

(2) *For the purpose of certifying an act of terrorism.* The Secretary or his designee, in consultation with the Federal Bureau of Investigation, shall determine whether an act of violence is a terrorist act or is reasonably believed to be a terrorist act.

Section 4 Guaranteed Loan means a HUD guaranteed loan made by a Financial Institution to a Borrower for the purpose of carrying out eligible activities to address damage or destruction caused by acts of arson or terrorism.

Terrorism means an act of violence causing damage to (or destruction of) real or personal property that the Secretary or his designee, in consultation with the Federal Bureau of Investigation, determines to be, or reasonably believes to be, a terrorist act, as defined by applicable Federal law or guidelines.

§ 573.3 Eligible activities.

Guaranteed Loan Funds may be used by a Borrower for the following activities when it is certified in accordance with § 573.6(e) that the activity is necessary to address damage caused by an act or acts of arson or terrorism as certified in accordance with § 573.6(f):

(a) Acquisition of improved or unimproved real property in fee or under long term lease.

(b) Acquisition and installation of personal property.

(c) Rehabilitation of real property owner, acquired, or leased by the Borrower.

(d) Construction, reconstruction, or replacement of real property improvement.

(e) Clearance, demolition, and removal, including movement of structures to other sites, of buildings, fixtures and improvements on real property.

(f) Site preparation, including construction, reconstruction, or installation of site improvements, utilities, or facilities, which is related to the activities described in paragraph (a), (c), or (d) of this section.

(g) Architectural, engineering, and similar services necessary to develop plans in connection with activities financed under paragraph (a), (b), (c), or (d) of this section.

(h) Acquisition, installation and restoration of security systems.

(i) Loans for refinancing existing indebtedness secured by a property which has been or will be acquired, constructed, rehabilitated or reconstructed, if such financing is determined to be appropriate to achieve the objectives of the Act and this part.

(j) Other necessary project costs such as insurance, bonding, legal fees, appraisals, surveys, relocation, closing costs, etc., paid or incurred by the Borrower in connection with the completion of the above activities.

[61 FR 47405, Sept. 6, 1996, as amended at 62 FR 24574, May 6, 1997]

§ 573.4 Loan term.

The term of the loan to be guaranteed by HUD under this part may not exceed 20 years.

§ 573.5 Underwriting standards and availability of loan guarantee assistance.

(a) HUD may, in its discretion, accept the underwriting standards of the Financial Institution making a loan to a Borrower.

(b) HUD will not make the loan guarantee unless it determines that the guaranteed loan is an acceptable financial risk under HUD's generally applicable loan underwriting standards based on the following:

(1) The Borrower's ability to pay debt service; and

(2) The value of the collateral assigned or pledged as security for the repayment of the loan.

(c) The provision of a loan guarantee to a Financial Institution and the amount of the guarantee do not depend in any way on the purpose, function, or identity of the organization to which the Financial Institution has made, or intends to make, a Section 4 Guaranteed Loan.

(d) HUD may disapprove a request for loan guarantee assistance based on the availability of funding.

(e) HUD may decline any Financial Institution's participation if its underwriting criteria are insufficient to make the guarantee an acceptable financial risk, or if the proposed interest rates or fees are unacceptable. HUD expects the proposed interest rates to take into account the value of the Federal guarantee.

(f) HUD may limit the availability of Guaranteed Loan Funds to geographic areas having the greatest need, as determined by a needs analysis of the most current available date conducted by HUD.

(g) Other requirements associated with the underwriting standards and guidelines shall be contained in the Loan Guarantee Agreement.

§573.6 Submission requirements.

A Financial Institution seeking a Section 4 Guaranteed Loan must submit to HUD the following documentation:

(a) A statement that the institution is a Financial Institution as defined at §573.2.

(b) A statement that the Borrower is eligible as defined at §573.2.

(c) A description of each eligible activity for which the loan is requested.

(d) A statement of other available funds to be used to finance the eligible activities (e.g., insurance proceeds).

(e) A certification by the Borrower that the activities to be assisted resulted from an act of arson or terrorism which is the subject of the certification described in paragraph (f) of this section.

(f) A certification by a QCO that the damage or destruction to be remedied by the use of the Guaranteed Loan Funds resulted from an act of arson or terrorism.

(g) The environmental documentation required by §573.8.

(h) A narrative of the institution's underwriting standards used in reviewing the Borrower's loan request.

(i) The interest rate on the loan and fees the lender intends to use in connection with the loan; and

(j) The percentage of the loan for which a guarantee is requested.

§573.7 Loan guarantee agreement.

(a) The rights and responsibilities with respect to the guaranteed loan shall be substantially described in an agreement entered into between the Financial Institution, as the lender, and the Secretary, as the guarantor, which agreement shall provide that:

(1) The lender has submitted or will submit a request for loan guarantee assistance that is accompanied by the Borrower's request for a loan to carry out eligible activities described in §573.3;

(2) The lender will require the Borrower to execute a promissory note promising to repay the guaranteed loan in accordance with the terms thereof;

(3) The lender will require the Borrower to provide collateral security, to an extent and in a form, acceptable to HUD;

(4) HUD reserves the right to limit loan guarantees to loans financing the replacement of damaged property with comparable new property;

(5) The lender will follow certain claim procedures to be specified by HUD in connection with any defaults, including appropriate notification of default as required by HUD;

(6) The lender will follow procedures for payment under the guarantee whereby the lender will be paid (up to the amount of guarantee) the amount owed to the lender less any amount recovered from the underlying collateral security for the loan; and

(7) The lender will act as the fiscal agent for the loan, servicing the guaranteed loan, maintaining loan documents, and receiving the Borrower's payments of principal and interest. The Borrower and the lender may be required to execute a fiscal agency agreement.

(b) In addition, the agreement shall contain other requirements, terms, and conditions required or approved by HUD.

§573.8 Environmental procedures and standards.

The environmental review requirements at 24 CFR part 50 are applicable to this part.

(a) *Environmental procedures.* Before any lender's submission requesting a loan guarantee for the acquisition, rehabilitation, or construction of real property can be selected for a loan guarantee, HUD shall determine whether any environmental thresholds are exceeded in accordance with 24 CFR part 50, which implements the National Environmental Policy Act (NEPA) and the related Federal environmental laws and authorities listed under 24 CFR 50.4. To assist in complying with environmental requirements, Borrowers are encouraged to select sites that are free of environmental hazards and are to provide HUD with environmental data needed to make a determination of compliance. For successful Borrowers, the costs for preparing the environmental data are eligible as project costs.

(1) If HUD determines that one or more of the thresholds are exceeded, HUD shall conduct a compliance review of the issue and, if appropriate, establish mitigating measures that the applicant shall carry out for the property.

(2) The lender's submissions under §573.6 shall provide HUD with:

(i) Documentation for environmental threshold review; and

(ii) Any previously issued environmental reviews prepared by local, State, or other Federal agencies for the proposed property.

(3) In providing the above information, the Borrower is encouraged to contact the local community development agency to obtain any previously issued environmental reviews for the proposed property as well as for other relevant information that can be used in the applicant documentation for the environmental threshold review.

(4) HUD reserves the right to disqualify any request where one or more environmental thresholds are exceeded if HUD determines that the compliance review cannot be satisfactorily completed.

(5) If Guaranteed Loan Funds are requested for acquisition, rehabilitation, or construction, Borrowers and Financial Institutions are prohibited from committing or expending State, local, or other funds to undertake property acquisition, rehabilitation or construction under this part until HUD issues a letter of commitment notifying the lender of HUD approval of the loan guarantee.

(b) *Environmental thresholds.* HUD shall determine whether a NEPA environmental assessment is required. Also, HUD shall determine whether the proposed property triggers thresholds for the applicable Federal environmental laws and authorities listed under 24 CFR 50.4 as follows:

(1) For minor rehabilitation of a building and acquisition of any property, Federal environmental laws and authorities may apply when the property is:

(i) Located within designated coastal barrier resources;

(ii) Contaminated by toxic chemicals or radioactive materials;

(iii) Located within a floodplain;

(iv) A building for which flood insurance protection is required;

(v) Located within a runway clear zone at a civil airport or within a clear zone or accident potential zone at a military airfield; or

(vi) Listed on, or eligible for listing on, the National Register of Historic Places; located within, or adjacent to, an historic district, or is a property whose area of potential effects includes a historic district or property.

(2) For major rehabilitation of a building or for new construction or rebuilding, and environmental assessment under NEPA is required and, in addition to paragraph (b)(1)(i) through (vi) of this section, other Federal environmental laws and authorities may apply when the property:

(i) Affects coastal zone management;

(ii) Is located near hazardous industrial operations handling fuels or chemicals of an explosive or flammable nature;

(iii) Affects a sole source aquifer;

(iv) Affects endangered species;

(v) Is located within a designated wetland; or

(vi) Is located in a high noise area.

(c) *Qualified data sources.* The environmental threshold information provided by applicants mut be from qualified data sources. A qualified data source means any Federal, State, or local agency with expertise or experience in environmental protection (e.g., the local community development agency; the local planning agency; the

State environmental protection agency; or the State Historic Preservation Officer) or any other source qualified to provide reliable information on the particular property.

(d) *Definition.* Minor rehabilitation means proposed fixing and repairs:

(1) Whose estimated cost is less than 75 percent of the estimated cost of replacement after completion;

(2) That does not involve changes in land use from residential to nonresidential, or from nonresidential to residential; and

(3) In the case of residential properties, that does not increase density more than 20 percent.

(e) *Project consultants.* In achieving compliance with these procedures, Borrower's architectural and engineering consultants shall consider these environmental factors and provide information in their plan narratives as to how their construction plans conform with the above environmental factors. To facilitate HUD's compliance with part 50, the Borrower is required to submit the consultant's information and plan narrative discussing the pertinent environmental factors under this section.

§573.9 Other requirements.

(a) *Nondiscrimination and equal opportunity.* The nondiscrimination and equal opportunity requirements described in 24 CFR part 5, subpart A apply to this part.

(b) *2 CFR part 200.* The provisions of 2 CFR part 200 apply to guaranteed loans under this part.

(c) *Lead-based paint.* Housing assisted under this part is subject to the lead-based paint requirements described in part 35, subparts A, B, E, G, and R of this title.

(d) *Labor standards*—(1) *Davis-Bacon.* All laborers and mechanics employed by contractors or subcontractors in the performance of construction work financed in whole or in part with Guaranteed Loan Funds under this part shall be paid wages at rates not less than those prevailing on similar construction in the locality as determined by the Secretary of Labor in accordance with the Davis-Bacon Act, as amended (40 U.S.C. 276a–276a–5). This paragraph shall apply to the rehabilitation of residential property only if such property contains not less than 8 units.

(2) *Volunteers.* The provisions of paragraph (d)(1) of this section shall not apply to volunteers under the conditions set forth in 24 CFR part 70. In applying part 70, loan guarantees under this part shall be treated as a program for which there is a statutory exemption for volunteers.

(3) *Labor standards.* Any contract, subcontract, or building loan agreement executed for a project subject to Davis-Bacon wage rates under paragraph (d)(1) of this section shall comply with all labor standards and provisions of 29 CFR parts 1, 3 and 5 that would be applicable to a loan guarantee program to which Davis-Bacon wage rates are made applicable by statute.

[61 FR 47405, Sept. 6, 1996, as amended at 64 FR 50226, Sept. 15, 1999; 80 FR 75938, Dec. 7, 2015]

§573.10 Fees for guaranteed loans.

(a) No fees will be assessed by HUD for its guaranty of a loan under this part.

(b) The lender may assess the Borrower loan origination fees or other charges provided that such fees and charges are those charged by the lender to its other customers for similar transactions, and are no higher than those charged by the lender for similar transactions.

§573.11 Record access and recordkeeping.

Records pertaining to the loans made by the Financial Institution shall be held for the life of the loan. A lender with a Section 4 Guaranteed Loan shall allow HUD, the Comptroller General of the United States, and their authorized representatives access from time to time to any documents, papers or files which are pertinent to the guaranteed loan, and to inspect and make copies of such records which relate to any Section 4 Loan. Any inspection will be made during the lender's regular business hours or any other mutually convenient time.

PART 574—HOUSING OPPORTUNITIES FOR PERSONS WITH AIDS

AUTHORITY: 12 U.S.C. 1701x, 1701 x–1; 42 U.S.C. 3535(d) and 5301–5320.

SOURCE: 57 FR 61740, Dec. 28, 1992, unless otherwise noted.

Subpart A—General

§ 574.3 Definitions.

The terms *Grantee* and *Secretary* are defined in 24 CFR part 5.

Acquired immunodeficiency syndrome (AIDS) or related diseases means the disease of acquired immunodeficiency syndrome or any conditions arising from the etiologic agent for acquired immunodeficiency syndrome, including infection with the human immunodeficiency virus (HIV).

Administrative costs mean costs for general management, oversight, coordination, evaluation, and reporting on eligible activities. Such costs do not include costs directly related to carrying out eligible activities, since those costs are eligible as part of the activity delivery costs of such activities.

Applicant means a State or city applying for a formula allocation as described under § 574.100 or a State, unit of general local government, or a nonprofit organization applying for a competitive grant as described under § 574.210.

City has the meaning given it in section 102(a) of the Housing and Community Development Act of 1974 (42 U.S.C. 5302).

Eligible Metropolitan Statistical Area (EMSA) means a metropolitan statistical area that has a population of more than 500,000 and has more than 1,500 cumulative cases of AIDS.

Eligible person means a person with acquired immunodeficiency syndrome or related diseases who is a low-income individual, as defined in this section, and the person's family. A person with AIDS or related diseases or a family member regardless of income is eligible to receive housing information services, as described in §574.300(b)(1). Any person living in proximity to a community residence is eligible to participate in that residence's community outreach and educational activities regarding AIDS or related diseases, as provided in §574.300(b)(9).

Eligible State means a State that has:

(1) More than 1,500 cumulative cases of AIDS in those areas of the State outside of eligible metropolitan statistical areas that are eligible to be funded through a qualifying city; and

(2) A consolidated plan prepared, submitted, and approved in accordance with 24 CFR part 91 that covers the assistance to be provided under this part. (A State may carry out activities anywhere in the State, including within an EMSA.)

Family is defined in 24 CFR 5.403 and includes one or more eligible persons living with another person or persons, regardless of actual or perceived sexual orientation, gender identity, or marital status, who are determined to be important to the eligible person or person's care or well-being, and the surviving member or members of any family described in this definition who were living in a unit assisted under the HOPWA program with the person with AIDS at the time of his or her death.

Low-income individual has the meaning given it in section 853(3) of the AIDS Housing Opportunity Act (42 U.S.C. 12902).

Metropolitan statistical area has the meaning given it in section 853(5) of the AIDS Housing Opportunity Act (42.U.S.C. 12902).

Nonprofit organization means any nonprofit organization (including a State or locally chartered, nonprofit organization) that:

(1) Is organized under State or local laws;

(2) Has no part of its net earnings inuring to the benefit of any member, founder, contributor, or individual;

(3) Has a functioning accounting system that is operated in accordance with generally accepted accounting principles, or has designated an entity that will maintain such an accounting system; and

(4) Has among its purposes significant activities related to providing services or housing to persons with acquired immunodeficiency syndrome or related diseases.

Non-substantial rehabilitation means rehabilitation that involves costs that are less than or equal to 75 percent of the value of the building after rehabilitation.

Population means total resident population based on data compiled by the U.S. Census and referable to the same point in time.

Project sponsor means any nonprofit organization or governmental housing agency that receives funds under a contract with the grantee to carry out eligible activities under this part. The selection of project sponsors is not subject to the procurement requirements of 2 CFR part 200, subpart D.

Qualifying city means a city that is the most populous unit of general local government in an eligible metropolitan statistical area (EMSA) and that has a consolidated plan prepared, submitted, and approved in accordance with 24 CFR part 91 that covers the assistance to be provided under this part.

Rehabilitation means the improvement or repair of an existing structure, or an addition to an existing structure that does not increase the floor area by more than 100 percent.

State has the meaning given it in section 853(9) of the AIDS Housing Opportunity Act (42 U.S.C. 12902).

Substantial rehabilitation means rehabilitation that involves costs in excess of 75 percent of the value of the building after rehabilitation.

Unit of general local government means any city, town, township, parish, county, village, or other general purpose political subdivision of a State; Guam, the Northern Mariana Islands, the Virgin Islands, American Samoa, the Federated States of Micronesia and Palau, the Marshall Islands, or a general purpose political subdivision thereof; and any agency or instrumentality thereof that is established pursuant to legislation and designated by the chief executive to act on behalf of the jurisdiction with regard to provisions of the National Affordable Housing Act.

[57 FR 61740, Dec. 28, 1992, as amended at 59 FR 17199, Apr. 11, 1994; 60 FR 1917, Jan. 5, 1995; 61 FR 5209, Feb. 9, 1996; 61 FR 7963, Feb. 29, 1996; 77 FR 5675, Feb. 3, 2012; 80 FR 75938, Dec. 7, 2015]

Subpart B—Formula Entitlements

§ 574.100 Eligible applicants.

(a) Eligible States and qualifying cities, as defined in § 574.3, qualify for formula allocations under HOPWA.

(b) HUD will notify eligible States and qualifying cities of their formula eligibility and allocation amounts and EMSA service areas annually.

[57 FR 61740, Dec. 28, 1992, as amended at 59 FR 17199, Apr. 11, 1994; 60 FR 1917, Jan. 5, 1995]

§ 574.110 Overview of formula allocations.

The formula grants are awarded upon submission and approval of a consolidated plan, pursuant to 24 CFR part 91, that covers the assistance to be provided under this part. Certain states and cities that are the most populous unit of general local government in eligible metropolitan statistical areas will receive formula allocations based on their State or metropolitan population and proportionate number of cases of persons with AIDS. They will receive funds under this part (providing they comply with 24 CFR part 91) for eligible activities that address the housing needs of persons with AIDS or related diseases and their families (see § 574.130(b)).

[61 FR 7963, Feb. 29, 1996]

§ 574.120 Responsibility of applicant to serve EMSA.

The EMSA's applicant shall serve eligible persons who live anywhere within the EMSA, except that housing assistance shall be provided only in localities within the EMSA that have a consolidated plan prepared, submitted, and approved in accordance with 24 CFR part 91 that covers the assistance to be provided under this part. In allocating grant amounts among eligible activities, the EMSA's applicant shall address needs of eligible persons who reside within the metropolitan statistical area, including those not within the jurisdiction of the applicant.

[60 FR 1917, Jan. 5, 1995]

§ 574.130 Formula allocations.

(a) *Data sources.* HUD will allocate funds based on the number of cases of acquired immunodeficiency syndrome reported to and confirmed by the Director of the Centers for Disease Control, and on population data provided by the U.S. Census. The number of cases of acquired immunodeficiency syndrome used for this purpose shall be the number reported as of March 31 of the fiscal year immediately preceding the fiscal year for which the amounts are appropriated and allocated.

(b) *Distribution of appropriated funds for entitlement awards.* (1) Seventy-five percent of the funds allocated under the formula is distributed to qualifying cities and eligible States, as described in § 574.100, based on each metropolitan statistical area's or State's proportionate share of the cumulative number of AIDS cases in all eligible metropolitan statistical areas and eligible States.

(2) The remaining twenty-five percent is allocated among qualifying cities, but not States, where the per capita incidence of AIDS for the year, April 1 through March 31, preceding the fiscal year of the appropriation is higher than the average for all metropolitan statistical areas with more than 500,000 population. Each qualifying city's allocation reflects its EMSA's proportionate share of the high incidence factor among EMSA's with higher than average per capita incidence of AIDS. The high incidence factor is computed by multiplying the population of the metropolitan statistical area by the difference between its twelve-month-per-capita-incidence rate and the average rate for all metropolitan statistical areas with more than 500,000 population. The EMSA's proportionate share is determined by dividing its high incidence factor by the sum of the high incidence factors for all EMSA's with higher than average per capita incidence of AIDS.

(c) *Minimum grant.* No grant awarded under paragraph (b) of this section shall be less than $200,000. Therefore, if the calculations under paragraph (b) of this section would result in any eligible metropolitan statistical area or eligible State receiving less than $200,000, the amount allocated to that entity is increased to $200,000 and allocations to entities in excess of $200,000 are proportionately reduced by the amount of the increase.

§574.190 Reallocation of grant amounts.

If an eligible State or qualifying city does not submit a consolidated plan in a timely fashion, in accordance with 24 CFR part 91, that provides for use of its allocation of funding under this part, the funds allocated to that jurisdiction will be added to the funds available for formula allocations to other jurisdictions in the current fiscal year. Any formula funds that become available as a result of deobligations or the imposition of sanctions as provided for in §574.540 will be added to the funds available for formula allocations in the next fiscal year.

[57 FR 61740, Dec. 28, 1992, as amended at 60 FR 1918, Jan. 5, 1995]

Subpart C—Competitive Grants

§574.200 Amounts available for competitive grants.

(a) The Department will set aside 10 percent of the amounts appropriated under this program to fund on a competitive basis:

(1) Special projects of national significance; and

(2) Other projects submitted by States and localities that do not qualify for formula grants.

(b) Any competitively awarded funds that become available as a result of deobligations or the imposition of sanctions, as provided in §574.540, will be added to the funds available for competitive grants in the next fiscal year.

(c) The competitive grants are awarded based on applications, as described in subpart C of this part, submitted in response to a Notice of Funding Availability published in the FEDERAL REGISTER. All States and units of general local government and nonprofit organizations are eligible to apply for competitive grants to fund projects of national significance. Only those States and units of general local government that do not qualify for formula allocations are eligible to apply for competitive grants to fund other projects.

(d) If HUD makes a procedural error in a funding competition that, when corrected, would warrant funding of an otherwise eligible application, HUD will select that application for potential funding when sufficient funds become available.

[57 FR 61740, Dec. 28, 1992, as amended at 61 FR 7963, Feb. 29, 1996]

§574.210 Eligible applicants.

(a) All States, units of general local government, and nonprofit organizations, may apply for grants for projects of national significance.

(b) Only those States and units of general local government that do not qualify for formula grants, as described in §574.100; may apply for grants for other projects as described in §574.200(a)(2).

(c) Except for grants for projects of national significance, nonprofit organizations are not eligible to apply directly to HUD for a grant but may receive funding as a project sponsor under contract with a grantee.

§574.240 Application requirements.

Applications must comply with the provisions of the Department's Notice of Funding Availability (NOFA) for the fiscal year published in the FEDERAL REGISTER in accordance with 24 CFR part 12. The rating criteria, including the point value for each, are described in the NOFA, including criteria determined by the Secretary.

[61 FR 7963, Feb. 29, 1996]

§574.260 Amendments.

(a) After an application has been selected for funding, any change that will significantly alter the scope, location, service area, or objectives of an activity or the number of eligible persons served must be justified to HUD and approved by HUD. Whenever any other amendment to the application is made, the grantee must provide a copy to HUD.

(b) Each amendment request must contain a description of the revised proposed use of funds. Funds may not be expended for the revised proposed use of funds until:

(1) HUD accepts the revised proposed use; and

(2) For amendments to acquire, rehabilitate, convert, lease, repair or construct properties to provide housing, an environmental review of the revised proposed use of funds has been completed in accordance with § 574.510.

(Approved by the Office of Management and Budget under control number 2506–0133)

Subpart D—Uses of Grant Funds

§ 574.300 Eligible activities.

(a) *General.* Subject to applicable requirements described in §§ 574.310, 574.320, 574.330, and 574.340, HOPWA funds may be used to assist all forms of housing designed to prevent homelessness including emergency housing, shared housing arrangements, apartments, single room occupancy (SRO) dwellings, and community residences. Appropriate supportive services, as required by § 574.310(a), must be provided as part of any HOPWA assisted housing, but HOPWA funds may also be used to provide services independently of any housing activity.

(b) *Activities.* The following activities may be carried out with HOPWA funds:

(1) Housing information services including, but not limited to, counseling, information, and referral services to assist an eligible person to locate, acquire, finance, and maintain housing. This may also include fair housing guidance for eligible persons who may encounter discrimination on the basis of race, color, religion, sex, age, national origin, familial status, or handicap. Housing counseling, as defined in § 5.100, that is funded with or provided in connection with HOPWA funds must be carried out in accordance with § 5.111. When grantees provide housing services to eligible persons (including persons undergoing relocation) that are incidental to a larger set of holistic case management services, these services do not meet the definition of Housing counseling, as defined in § 5.100, and therefore are not required to be carried out in accordance with the certification requirements of § 5.111;

(2) Resource identification to establish, coordinate and develop housing assistance resources for eligible persons (including conducting preliminary research and making expenditures necessary to determine the feasibility of specific housing-related initiatives);

(3) Acquisition, rehabilitation, conversion, lease, and repair of facilities to provide housing and services;

(4) New construction (for single room occupancy (SRO) dwellings and community residences only).

(5) Project- or tenant-based rental assistance, including assistance for shared housing arrangements;

(6) Short-term rent, mortgage, and utility payments to prevent the homelessness of the tenant or mortgagor of a dwelling;

(7) Supportive services including, but not limited to, health, mental health, assessment, permanent housing placement, drug and alcohol abuse treatment and counseling, day care, personal assistance, nutritional services, intensive care when required, and assistance in gaining access to local, State, and Federal government benefits and services, except that health services may only be provided to individuals with acquired immunodeficiency syndrome or related diseases and not to family members of these individuals;

(8) Operating costs for housing including maintenance, security, operation, insurance, utilities, furnishings, equipment, supplies, and other incidental costs;

(9) Technical assistance in establishing and operating a community residence, including planning and other pre-development or pre-construction expenses and including, but not limited to, costs relating to community outreach and educational activities regarding AIDS or related diseases for persons residing in proximity to the community residence;

(10) Administrative expenses:

(i) Each grantee may use not more than 3 percent of the grant amount for its own administrative costs relating to administering grant amounts and allocating such amounts to project sponsors; and

(ii) Each project sponsor receiving amounts from grants made under this program may use not more than 7 percent of the amounts received for administrative costs.

(11) For competitive grants only, any other activity proposed by the applicant and approved by HUD.

(c) *Equal participation of faith-based organizations.* The HUD program requirements in §5.109 of this title apply to the HOPWA program, including the requirements regarding disposition and change in use of real property by a faith-based organization.

[57 FR 61740, Dec. 28, 1992, as amended at 59 FR 17200, Apr. 11, 1994; 68 FR 56405, Sept. 30, 2003; 80 FR 75938, Dec. 7, 2015; 81 19418, Apr. 4, 2016; 81 FR 90659, Dec. 14, 2016]

§574.310 General standards for eligible housing activities.

All grantees using grant funds to provide housing must adhere to the following standards:

(a)(1) *General.* The grantee shall ensure that qualified service providers in the area make available appropriate supportive services to the individuals assisted with housing under this subpart. Supportive services are described in §574.300(b)(7). For any individual with acquired immunodeficiency syndrome or a related disease who requires more intensive care than can be provided in housing assisted under this subpart, the grantee shall provide for locating a care provider who can appropriately care for the individual and for referring the individual to the care provider.

(2) *Payments.* The grantee shall ensure that grant funds will not be used to make payments for health services for any item or service to the extent that payment has been made, or can reasonably be expected to be made, with respect to that item or service:

(i) Under any State compensation program, under an insurance policy, or under any Federal or State health benefits program; or

(ii) By an entity that provides health services on a prepaid basis.

(b) *Housing quality standards.* The following standards apply for all housing for which HOPWA funds are used under §574.300(b)(3), (4), (5), and (8).

(1) *State and local requirements.* Each recipient of assistance under this part must provide safe and sanitary housing that is in compliance with all applicable State and local housing codes, licensing requirements, and any other requirements in the jurisdiction in which the housing is located regarding the condition of the structure and the operation of the housing.

(2) *HUD housing standards.* Except for such variations as are proposed by the grantee and approved by HUD, the housing must meet the standards for HUD housing in 24 CFR 5.703, except that:

(i) As applied to HOPWA, "HUD housing" in 24 CFR 5.703 means the units eligible persons occupy or will occupy, systems equipment that directly services those units, items and components within the primary and secondary means of egress from those units' doors to the public way, and common features related to the residential use of the building (e.g., the laundry room, community room, mail room).

(ii) Housing that continues to meet the HOPWA housing quality standards that applied when the eligible person(s) moved into that housing shall not be required to meet new or different standards under 24 CFR 5.703.

(3) The requirements of 24 CFR 5.705 through 5.713 do not apply.

(c) *Minimum use period for structures.* (1) Any building or structure assisted with amounts under this part must be maintained as a facility to provide housing or assistance for individuals with acquired immunodeficiency syndrome or related diseases:

(i) For a period of not less than 10 years, in the case of assistance provided under an activity eligible under §574.300(b) (3) and (4) involving new construction, substantial rehabilitation or acquisition of a building or structure; or

(ii) For a period of not less than 3 years in the cases involving non-substantial rehabilitation or repair of a building or structure.

(2) Waiver of minimum use period. HUD may waive the minimum use period of a building or structure as stipulated in paragraph (c)(1) of this section if the grantee can demonstrate, to the satisfaction of HUD, that:

(i) The assisted structure is no longer needed to provide supported housing or assistance, or the continued operation of the structure for such purposes is no longer feasible; and

(ii) The structure will be used to benefit individuals or families whose incomes do not exceed 80 percent of the median income for the area, as determined by HUD with adjustments for smaller and larger families, if the Secretary finds that such variations are necessary because of construction costs or unusually high or low family incomes.

(d) *Resident rent payment.* Except for persons in short-term supported housing, each person receiving rental assistance under this program or residing in any rental housing assisted under this program must pay as rent, including utilities, an amount which is the higher of:

(1) 30 percent of the family's monthly adjusted income;

(2) Ten percent of the family's monthly income; or

(3) If the family is receiving payments for welfare assistance from a public agency and a part of the payments, adjusted in accordance with the family's actual housing costs, is specifically designated by the agency to meet the family's housing costs, the portion of the payment that is designated for housing costs.

(e) *Calculating income to determine resident rent payment*—(1) *In general.* When determining resident rent payments, the family's monthly income and monthly adjusted income must be calculated as provided by §§ 5.609 and 5.611 of this title, respectively, except that:

(i) As with the references to "grantee" and "grantees" in paragraphs (e), (f), and (h) of this section, the references to "PHA" and "responsible entity" in §§ 5.609 and 5.611 of this title refer to the "grantee" or "project sponsor" that is determining income;

(ii) References in § 5.609(c) of this title to an interim reexamination of family income under §§ 5.657(c), 960.257(b), or 982.516(c) of this title refer to an interim reexamination provided under paragraph (e)(4) of this section;

(iii) References in § 5.609(c) of this title to a streamlined income determination under §§ 5.657(d), 960.257(c), or 982.516(b) of this title refer to a streamlined income determination provided under paragraph (e)(5) of this section;

(iv) Section 5.611(b) of this title does not apply;

(v) The grantee may choose to grant financial hardship exemptions in accordance with the process described in §§ 5.611(c) through (e);

(vi) During the period that § 5.617 of this title remains in effect, the calculation of monthly adjusted income must also include the disallowance of earned income as provided by § 5.617 of this title.

(2) *Annual reexaminations.* For purposes of determining resident rent payments, grantees will conduct a reexamination and redetermination of family income and family composition every year.

(3) *Third-party verification.* (i) Except as provided in paragraph (e)(3)(ii) of this section, the grantee must obtain and document in the tenant file third-party verification of the following factors, or must document in the tenant file why third-party verification was not available:

(A) Reported family annual income;

(B) The value of assets;

(C) Expenses related to deductions from annual income; and

(D) Other factors that affect the determination of adjusted income.

(ii) For a family with net family assets (as the term is defined in paragraph (f) of this section) equal to or less than $50,000, which amount will be adjusted annually in accordance with the Consumer Price Index for Urban Wage Earners and Clerical Worker, the grantee may accept, for purposes of recertification of income, a family's declaration under § 5.618(b) of this title, except that the grantee must obtain third-party verification of all family assets every 3 years.

(iii) The grantee must establish procedures that are appropriate and necessary to require that income data provided by applicant or participant families is complete and accurate.

(4) *Interim reexaminations*—(i) *Generally.* A family may request an interim reexamination of family income or composition because of any changes since the last determination. The grantee must make any interim reexamination within a reasonable period

of time after the family's request or when the grantee becomes aware of an increase in family adjusted income under paragraph (e)(4)(iii) of this section. What qualifies as a "reasonable time" may vary based on the amount of time it takes to verify information, but generally should not exceed 30 days from the date a family reports changes in income to a grantee.

(ii) *Decreases in the family's annual adjusted income.* Grantees may decline to conduct an interim reexamination of family income if the grantee estimates that the family's adjusted income will decrease by an amount that is less than ten percent of the family's annual adjusted income (or a lower amount established by HUD through notice), or a lower threshold established by the grantee.

(iii) *Increases in the family's annual adjusted income.* Grantees must conduct the interim reexamination of family income when the grantee becomes aware that the family's adjusted income has changed by an amount that the grantee estimates will result in an increase of ten percent or more in annual adjusted income or such other amount established by HUD through notice, except:

(A) The grantee may not consider any increase in the earned income of the family when estimating or calculating whether the family's adjusted income has increased unless the family has previously received an interim reduction under paragraph (e)(4)(i) of this section during the certification period; and

(B) The grantee may choose not to conduct an interim reexamination in the last three months of a certification period.

(iv) *Policies on reporting changes in family income or composition.* The grantee must adopt policies consistent with this section prescribing when and under what conditions the family must report a change in family income or composition.

(v) *Effective date of rent changes.* (A) If the family has reported a change in family income or composition in a timely manner according to the grantee's policies, the grantee must provide the family with 30 days advance notice of any rent increase, and such rent increase will be effective the first day of the month beginning after the end of that 30-day period. Rent decreases will be effective on the first day of the first month after the date of the actual change leading to the interim reexamination of family income.

(B) If the family has failed to report a change in family income or composition in a timely manner according to the grantee's policies, grantees must implement any resulting rent increases retroactively to the first of the month following the date of the change leading to the interim reexamination of family income. Any resulting rent decrease must be implemented no later than the first rent period following completion of the reexamination. However, rent decreases may be applied retroactively at the discretion of the grantee, in accordance with the grantee's conditions as established in written policy, and subject to paragraph (e)(4)(v)(C) of this section.

(C) A retroactive rent decrease may not be applied by the grantee prior to the later of the first of the month following:

(*1*) The date of the change leading to the interim reexamination of family income; or

(*2*) The effective date of the family's most recent previous interim or annual reexamination (or initial examination if that was the family's last examination).

(5) *Streamlined income determinations*—(i) *Generally.* A grantee may elect to apply a streamlined income determination to families receiving fixed income as described in paragraph (e)(5)(iii) of this section.

(ii) *Definition of fixed income.* For purposes of this section, "fixed income" means periodic payments at reasonably predictable levels from one or more of the following sources:

(A) Social Security, Supplemental Security Income, Supplemental Disability Insurance.

(B) Federal, state, local, or private pension plans.

(C) Annuities or other retirement benefit programs, insurance policies, disability or death benefits, or other similar types of periodic receipts.

(D) Any other source of income subject to adjustment by a verifiable Cost-of-Living Adjustment (COLA) or current rate of interest.

(iii) *Method of streamlined income determination.* Grantees using the streamlined income determination must adjust a family's income according to the percentage of a family's unadjusted income that is from fixed income.

(A) When 90 percent or more of a family's unadjusted income consists of fixed income, grantees using streamlined income determinations must apply a COLA or COLAs to the family's fixed-income sources, provided that the family certifies both that 90 percent or more of their unadjusted income is fixed income and that their sources of fixed income have not changed from the previous year. For non-fixed income, grantees may choose, but are not required, to make appropriate adjustments pursuant to paragraph (e)(2) of this section.

(B) When less than 90 percent of a family's unadjusted income consists of fixed income, grantees using streamlined income determinations must apply a COLA to each of the family's sources of fixed income. Grantees must determine all other income pursuant to paragraph (e)(2) of this section.

(iv) *COLA rate applied by grantees.* Grantees using streamlined income determinations must adjust a family's fixed income using a COLA or current interest rate that applies to each specific source of fixed income and is available from a public source or through tenant-provided, third-party-generated documentation. If no public verification or tenant-provided documentation is available, then the grantee must obtain third-party verification of the income amounts in order to calculate the change in income for the source.

(v) *Triennial verification.* For any income determined pursuant to a streamlined income determination, a grantee must obtain third-party verification of all income amounts every 3 years.

(f) *Net family assets and restriction on assistance to families based on assets.* The "net family assets" definition in § 5.603 of this section applies for purposes of calculating resident rent payments under this section and applying the asset-based restrictions in §§ 5.618(a) through (d) this title. The "net family assets" definition in § 5.603 of this section may also apply where a grantee elects to apply § 5.609 of this title alone or in combination with § 5.611(a) of this title for other purposes under this part; however, the value of real property a family owns and occupies as its primary residence must be excluded from the calculation of "net family assets" for purposes of assistance for which homeowners are eligible under this part. The asset-based restrictions in §§ 5.618(a) through (d) of this title apply only to housing activities subject to the resident rent payment requirements in this section. References to "PHA" in §§ 5.618(a) through (d) of this title refer to the grantee or project sponsor that is determining the asset-based restrictions.

(g) *Termination of assistance*—(1) *Surviving family members.* With respect to the surviving member or members of a family who were living in a unit assisted under the HOPWA program with the person with AIDS at the time of his or her death, housing assistance and supportive services under the HOPWA program shall continue for a grace period following the death of the person with AIDS. The grantee or project sponsor shall establish a reasonable grace period for continued participation by a surviving family member, but that period may not exceed one year from the death of the family member with AIDS. The grantee or project sponsor shall notify the family of the duration of their grace period and may assist the family with information on other available housing programs and with moving expenses.

(2) *Violation of requirements*— (i) *Basis.* Assistance to participants who reside in housing programs assisted under this part may be terminated if the participant violates program requirements or conditions of occupancy, subject to the VAWA protections in 24 CFR 5.2005(b) and 24 CFR 5.2005(c). Grantees must ensure that supportive services are provided, so that a participant's assistance is terminated only in the most severe cases.

(ii) *Procedure.* In terminating assistance to any program participant for violation of requirements, grantees must provide a formal process that recognizes the rights of individuals receiving assistance to due process of law. This process at minimum, must consist of:

(A) Serving the participant with a written notice containing a clear statement of the reasons for termination;

(B) Permitting the participant to have a review of the decision, in which the participant is given the opportunity to confront opposing witnesses, present written objections, and be represented by their own counsel, before a person other than the person (or a subordinate of that person) who made or approved the termination decision; and

(C) Providing prompt written notification of the final decision to the participant.

(h) *De minimis errors.* The grantee will not be considered out of compliance with the requirements in paragraphs (e)(2), (e)(4), or (e)(5) of this section due solely to de minimis errors in calculating family income but is still obligated to correct errors once the grantee becomes aware of the errors. A de minimis error is an error where the grantee's determination of family income varies from the correct income determination by no more than $30 per month in monthly adjusted income ($360 in annual adjusted income) per family.

(1) The grantee must take any corrective action necessary to credit or repay a family if the family has been overcharged for their resident rent payment as a result of the de minimis error in the income determination. Families will not be required to repay the grantee in instances where the grantee has miscalculated income resulting in a family being undercharged for their resident rent payment.

(2) HUD may revise the amount of de minimis error in this paragraph (h) through a rulemaking published in the FEDERAL REGISTER for public comment.

(Paragraph (c) approved by the Office of Management and Budget under control number 2506–0133)

[57 FR 61740, Dec. 28, 1992, as amended at 59 FR 17200, Apr. 11, 1994; 61 FR 7963, Feb. 29, 1996; 66 FR 6225, Jan. 19, 2001; 81 FR 80806, Nov. 16, 2016; 88 FR 30498, May 11, 2023; 88 FR 9665, Feb. 14, 2023]

§574.320 Additional standards for rental assistance.

(a) If grant funds are used to provide rental assistance, the following additional standards apply:

(1) *Maximum subsidy.* The amount of grant funds used to pay monthly assistance for an eligible person may not exceed the difference between:

(i) The lower of the rent standard or reasonable rent for the unit; and

(ii) The resident's rent payment calculated under §574.310(d).

(2) *Rent standard.* The rent standard shall be established by the grantee and shall be no more than the published section 8 fair market rent (FMR) or the HUD-approved community-wide exception rent for the unit size. However, on a unit by unit basis, the grantee may increase that amount by up to 10 percent for up to 20 percent of the units assisted.

(3) *Rent reasonableness.* The rent charged for a unit must be reasonable in relation to rents currently being charged for comparable units in the private unassisted market and must not be in excess of rents currently being charged by the owner for comparable unassisted units.

(b) With respect to shared housing arrangements, the rent charged for an assisted family or individual shall be in relation to the size of the private space for that assisted family or individual in comparison to other private space in the shared unit, excluding common space. An assisted family or individual may be assigned a pro rata portion based on the ratio derived by dividing the number of bedrooms in their private space by the number of bedrooms in the unit. Participation in shared housing arrangements shall be voluntary.

[57 FR 61740, Dec. 28, 1992, as amended at 61 FR 7963, Feb. 29, 1996]

§574.330 Additional standards for short-term supported housing.

Short-term supported housing includes facilities to provide temporary shelter to eligible individuals as well as rent, mortgage, and utilities payments to enable eligible individuals to remain in their own dwellings. If grant funds are used to provide such short-term supported housing assistance, the following additional standards apply:

(a) *Time limits.* (1) A short-term supported housing facility may not provide residence to any individual for more than 60 days during any six month period. Rent, mortgage, and utilities payments to prevent the homelessness of the tenant or mortgagor of a dwelling may not be provided to such an individual for these costs accruing over a period of more than 21 weeks in any 52 week period. These limitations do not apply to rental assistance provided under § 574.300(b)(5).

(2) *Waiver of time limitations.* HUD may waive, as it determines appropriate, the limitations of paragraph (a)(1) and will favorably consider a waiver based on the good faith effort of a project sponsor to provide permanent housing under subsection (c).

(b) *Residency limitations*—(1) *Residency.* A short-term supported facility may not provide shelter or housing at any single time for more than 50 families or individuals;

(2) *Waiver of residency limitations.* HUD may waive, as it determines appropriate, the limitations of paragraph (b)(1) of this section.

(c) *Placement.* A short-term supported housing facility assisted under this part must, to the maximum extent practicable, provide each individual living in such housing the opportunity for placement in permanent housing or in a living environment appropriate to his or her health and social needs.

(d) *Assistance to continue independent living.* In addition to the supportive services provided when an individual is relocated to a short-term supported housing facility, supportive services may be provided to individuals when they remain in their residence because the residence is appropriate to the needs of the individual. In the latter case, a rent, mortgage and utilities payments program assisted under this part shall provide, when reasonable, supportive services specifically designed to maintain the individual in such residence.

(e) *Case management services.* A program assisted under this section shall provide each assisted individual with an opportunity, if eligible, to receive case management services from the appropriate social service agencies.

(Paragraph (b) approved by the Office of Management and Budget under control number 2506–0133)

[57 FR 61740, Dec. 28, 1992, as amended at 59 FR 17200, Apr. 11, 1994]

§ 574.340 Additional standards for community residences.

(a) A community residence is a multiunit residence designed for eligible persons to provide a lower cost residential alternative to institutional care; to prevent or delay the need for such care; to provide a permanent or transitional residential setting with appropriate services to enhance the quality of life for those who are unable to live independently; and to enable such persons to participate as fully as possible in community life.

(b) If grant funds are used to provide a community residence, except for planning and other expenses preliminary to construction or other physical improvement for a community residence, the grantee must, prior to the expenditure of such funds, obtain and keep on file the following certifications:

(1) *A services agreement.* (i) A certification that the grantee will itself provide services as required by § 574.310(a) to eligible persons assisted by the community residence; or

(ii) A certification that the grantee has entered into a written agreement with a project sponsor or contracted service provider to provide services as required by § 574.310(a) to eligible persons assisted by the community residence;

(2) *The adequacy of funding.* (i) A certification that the grantee has acquired sufficient funding for these services; or

(ii) A certification that the grantee has on file an analysis of the service level needed for each community residence, a statement of which grantee agency, project sponsor, or service provider will provide the needed services, and a statement of how the services will be funded; and

(3) *Capability.* (i) A certification that the grantee is qualified to provide the services; or

(ii) A certification that the project sponsor or the service provider is qualified to provide the services.

[57 FR 61740, Dec. 28, 1992, as amended at 59 FR 17200, Apr. 11, 1994]

§574.350 Additional standards for broadband infrastructure.

Any new construction or substantial rehabilitation, as substantial rehabilitation is defined by 24 CFR 574.3, of a building with more than 4 rental units, for which HOPWA funds are first obligated by the grantee or project sponsor on or after January 19, 2017 must include installation of broadband infrastructure, as this term is defined in 24 CFR 5.100, except where the grantee or project sponsor determines and, in accordance with §574.530, documents the determination that:

(a) The location of the new construction or substantial rehabilitation makes installation of broadband infrastructure infeasible;

(b) The cost of installing broadband infrastructure would result in a fundamental alteration in the nature of its program or activity or in an undue financial burden; or

(c) The structure of the housing to be substantially rehabilitated makes installation of broadband infrastructure infeasible.

[81 FR 92637, Dec. 20, 2016]

Subpart E—Special Responsibilities of Grantees and Project Sponsors

§574.400 Prohibition of substitution of funds.

Amounts received from grants under this part may not be used to replace other amounts made available or designated by State or local governments through appropriations for use for the purposes of this part.

§574.410 Capacity.

The grantee shall ensure that any project sponsor with which the grantee contracts to carry out an activity under this part has the capacity and capability to effectively administer the activity.

§574.420 Cooperation.

(a) The grantee shall agree, and shall ensure that each project sponsor agrees, to cooperate and coordinate in providing assistance under this part with the agencies of the relevant State and local governments responsible for services in the area served by the grantee for eligible persons and other public and private organizations and agencies providing services for such eligible persons.

(b) A grantee that is a State shall obtain the approval of the unit of general local government in which a project is to be located before entering into a contract with a project sponsor to carry out an activity authorized under this part.

(c) A grantee that is a city receiving a formula allocation for an EMSA shall coordinate with other units of general local government located within the metropolitan statistical area to address needs within that area.

§574.430 Fee prohibitions.

The grantee shall agree, and shall ensure that each project sponsor agrees, that no fee, except rent, will be charged of any eligible person for any housing or services provided with amounts from a grant under this part.

§574.440 Confidentiality.

The grantee shall agree, and shall ensure that each project sponsor agrees, to ensure the confidentiality of the name of any individual assisted under this part and any other information regarding individuals receiving assistance.

§574.450 Financial records.

The grantee shall agree, and shall ensure that each project sponsor agrees, to maintain and make available to HUD for inspection financial records sufficient, in HUD's determination, to ensure proper accounting and disbursing of amounts received from a grant under this part.

§ 574.460 Remaining participants following bifurcation of a lease or eviction as a result of domestic violence, dating violence, sexual assault, or stalking.

When a covered housing provider exercises the option to bifurcate a lease, as provided in 24 CFR 5.2009(a), in order to evict, remove, terminate occupancy rights, or terminate assistance to a person with AIDS or related diseases that receives rental assistance or resides in rental housing assisted under the HOPWA program for engaging in criminal activity directly relating to domestic violence, dating violence, sexual assault or stalking, the covered housing provider shall provide the remaining persons residing in the unit a reasonable grace period to establish eligibility to receive HOPWA assistance or find alternative housing. The grantee or project sponsor shall set the reasonable grace period, which shall be no less than 90 calendar days, and not more than one year, from the date of the bifurcation of the lease. Housing assistance and supportive services under the HOPWA program shall continue for the remaining persons residing in the unit during the grace period. The grantee or project sponsor shall notify the remaining persons residing in the unit of the duration of the reasonable grace period and may assist them with information on other available housing programs and with moving expenses.

[81 FR 80806, Nov. 16, 2016]

Subpart F—Grant Administration

§ 574.500 Responsibility for grant administration.

(a) *General.* Grantees are responsible for ensuring that grants are administered in accordance with the requirements of this part and other applicable laws. Grantees are responsible for ensuring that their respective project sponsors carry out activities in compliance with all applicable requirements.

(b) *Grant agreement.* The grant agreement will provide that the grantee agrees, and will ensure that each project sponsor agrees, to:

(1) Operate the program in accordance with the provisions of these regulations and other applicable HUD regulations;

(2) Conduct an ongoing assessment of the housing assistance and supportive services required by the participants in the program;

(3) Assure the adequate provision of supportive services to the participants in the program; and

(4) Comply with such other terms and conditions, including recordkeeping and reports (which must include racial and ethnic data on participants) for program monitoring and evaluation purposes, as HUD may establish for purposes of carrying out the program in an effective and efficient manner.

(c) *Enforcement.* HUD will enforce the obligations in the grant agreement in accordance with the provisions of 2 CFR part 200, subpart D. A grantee will be provided an opportunity for informal consultation before HUD will exercise any remedies authorized in 2 CFR 200.338.

[57 FR 61740, Dec. 28, 1992, as amended at 80 FR 75938, Dec. 7, 2015]

§ 574.510 Environmental procedures and standards.

(a) Activities under this part are subject to HUD environmental regulations in part 58 of this title, except that HUD will perform an environmental review in accordance with part 50 of this title for any competitive grant for Fiscal Year 2000.

(b) The recipient, its project partners and their contractors may not acquire, rehabilitate, convert, lease, repair, dispose of, demolish, or construct property for a project under this part, or commit or expend HUD or local funds for such eligible activities under this part, until the responsible entity (as defined in § 58.2 of this title) has completed the environmental review procedures required by part 58 and the environmental certification and RROF have been approved (or HUD has performed an environmental review and the recipient has received HUD approval of the property). HUD will not release grant funds if the recipient or any other party commits grant funds (*i.e.*, incurs any costs or expenditures to be paid or reimbursed with such funds) before the recipient submits and

HUD approves its RROF (where such submission is required).

(c) For activities under a grant to a nonprofit entity that would generally be subject to review under part 58, HUD may make a finding in accordance with §58.11(d) and may itself perform the environmental review under the provisions of part 50 of this title if the recipient nonprofit entity objects in writing to the responsible entity's performing the review under part 58. Irrespective of whether the responsible entity in accord with part 58 (or HUD in accord with part 50) performs the environmental review, the recipient shall supply all available, relevant information necessary for the responsible entity (or HUD, if applicable) to perform for each property any environmental review required by this part. The recipient also shall carry out mitigating measures required by the responsible entity (or HUD, if applicable) or select alternate eligible property.

[68 FR 56130, Sept. 29, 2003]

§574.520 Performance reports.

(a) *Formula grants.* For a formula grant recipient, the performance reporting requirements are specified in 24 CFR part 91.

(b) *Competitive grants.* A grantee shall submit to HUD annually a report describing the use of the amounts received, including the number of individuals assisted, the types of assistance provided, data on emergency transfers requested under 24 CFR 5.2005(e), pertaining to victims of domestic violence, dating violence, sexual assault, or stalking, including data on the outcomes of such requests, and any other information that HUD may require. Annual reports are required until all grant funds are expended.

[60 FR 1918, Jan. 5, 1995, as amended at 81 FR 80806, Nov. 16, 2016]

§574.530 Recordkeeping.

Each grantee must ensure that records are maintained for a 4-year period to document compliance with the provisions of this part. Grantees must maintain the following:

(a) Current and accurate data on the race and ethnicity of program participants.

(b) Documentation of the actions the grantee has taken to affirmatively further fair housing, pursuant to §§5.151 and 5.152 of this title.

(c) Data on emergency transfers requested under 24 CFR 5.2005(e), pertaining to victims of domestic violence, dating violence, sexual assault, or stalking, including data on the outcomes of such requests.

[80 FR 42368, July 16, 2015, as amended at 81 FR 80806, Nov. 16, 2016; 85 FR 47911, Aug. 7, 2020; 86 FR 30792, June 10, 2021]

EFFECTIVE DATE NOTE: At 90 FR 11024, Mar. 3, 2025, §574.530 was amended, effective Apr. 2, 2025.

§574.540 Deobligation of funds.

HUD may deobligate all or a portion of the amounts approved for eligible activities if such amounts are not expended in a timely manner, or the proposed activity for which funding was approved is not provided in accordance with the approved application or action plan and the requirements of this regulation. HUD may deobligate any amount of grant funds that have not been expended within a three-year period from the date of the signing of the grant agreement. The grant agreement may set forth other circumstances under which funds may be deobligated or sanctions imposed.

[61 FR 7963, Feb. 29, 1996]

Subpart G—Other Federal Requirements

§574.600 Cross-reference.

The Federal requirements set forth in 24 CFR part 5 and part 75 apply to this program as specified in this subpart.

[61 FR 5209, Feb. 9, 1996, as amended at 85 FR 61567, Sept. 29, 2020]

§574.603 Nondiscrimination and equal opportunity.

Within the population eligible for this program, the nondiscrimination and equal opportunity requirements set forth in 24 CFR part 5 and the following requirements apply:

(a) *Fair housing requirements.* (1) Grantees and project sponsors shall comply with the applicable provisions of the Americans with Disabilities Act

(42 U.S.C. 12101–12213) and implementing regulations at 28 CFR part 35 (States and local government grantees) and part 36 (public accommodations and requirements for certain types of short-term housing assistance).

(2) Executive Order 11246, as amended by Executive Orders 11375, 11478, 12086, and 12107 (3 CFR, 1964–1965 Comp., p. 339; 3 CFR, 1966–1970 Comp., p. 684; 3 CFR, 1966–1970 Comp., p. 803; 3 CFR 1978 Comp., p. 230; and 3 CFR, 1978 Comp., p. 264) (Equal Employment Opportunity) does not apply to this program.

(b) *Affirmative outreach.* A grantee or project sponsor must adopt procedures to ensure that all persons who qualify for the assistance, regardless of their race, color, religion, sex, age, national origin, familial status, or handicap, know of the availability of the HOPWA program, including facilities and services accessible to persons with a handicap, and maintain evidence of implementation of the procedures.

[57 FR 61740, Dec. 28, 1992, as amended at 59 FR 33894, June 30, 1994. Redesignated and amended at 61 FR 5209, Feb. 9, 1996; 61 FR 7964, Feb. 29, 1996]

§ 574.604 Protections for victims of domestic violence, dating violence, sexual assault, and stalking.

(a) *General*—(1) *Applicability of VAWA requirements.* Except as provided in paragraph (a)(2) of this section, the Violence Against Women Act (VAWA) requirements set forth in 24 CFR part 5, subpart L (Protection for Victims of Domestic Violence, Dating Violence, Sexual Assault, or Stalking), apply to housing assisted with HOPWA grant funds for acquisition, rehabilitation, conversion, lease, and repair of facilities to provide housing; new construction; and operating costs, as provided in § 574.300. The requirements set forth in 24 CFR part 5, subpart L, also apply to project-based and tenant-based rental assistance, as provided in §§ 574.300 and 574.320, and community residences, as provided in § 574.340.

(2) Limited applicability of VAWA requirements. The VAWA requirements set forth in 24 CFR part 5, subpart L do not apply to short-term supported housing, as provided in § 574.330, except that no individual may be denied admission to or removed from the short-term supported housing on the basis or as a direct result of the fact that the individual is or has been a victim of domestic violence, dating violence, sexual assault, or stalking, if the individual otherwise qualifies for admission or occupancy.

(3) The terms "affiliated individual," "dating violence," "domestic violence," "sexual assault," and "stalking" are defined in 24 CFR 5.2003.

(b) *Covered housing provider.* As used in this part, the term, "covered housing provider," which is defined in 24 CFR 5.2003, refers to the HOPWA grantee, project sponsor, or housing or facility owner, or manager, as described in this section.

(1)(i) For housing assisted with HOPWA grant funds for acquisition, rehabilitation, conversion, lease, and repair of facilities to provide housing; new construction; operating costs; community residences; and project-based rental assistance, the HOPWA grantee is responsible for ensuring that each project sponsor undertakes the following actions (or, if administering the HOPWA assistance directly, the grantee shall undertake the following actions):

(A) Sets a policy for determining the "reasonable grace period" for remaining persons residing in the unit to establish eligibility for HOPWA assistance or find alternative housing, which period shall be no less than 90 calendar days nor more than one year from the date of bifurcation of a lease, consistent with 24 CFR 574.460;

(B) Provides notice of occupancy rights and the certification form at the times listed in paragraph (d) of this section;

(C) Adopts and administers an emergency transfer plan, as developed by the grantee in accordance with 24 CFR 5.2005(e) of this section, and facilitates emergency transfers; and

(D) Maintains the confidentiality of documentation submitted by tenants requesting emergency transfers and of each tenant's housing location consistent with § 574.440 and 24 CFR 5.2007(c).

(ii)(A) If a tenant seeks VAWA protections, set forth in 24 CFR part 5, subpart L, the tenant must submit such request through the project sponsor (or the grantee if the grantee is directly administering HOPWA assistance). Grantees and project sponsors will work with the housing or facility owner or manager to facilitate protections on the tenant's behalf. Project sponsors must follow the documentation specifications in 24 CFR 5.2007, including the confidentiality requirements in 24 CFR 5.2007(c).

(B) The grantee or project sponsor is responsible for ensuring that the housing or facility owner or manager develops and uses a HOPWA lease addendum with VAWA protections and is made aware of the option to bifurcate a lease in accordance with §574.460 and 24 CFR 5.2009.

(2)(i) For tenant-based rental assistance, the HOPWA grantee is responsible for ensuring that each project sponsor providing tenant-based rental assistance undertakes the following actions (or, if administering the HOPWA assistance directly, the grantee shall undertake the following actions):

(A) Sets policy for determining the "reasonable grace period" for remaining persons residing in the unit to establish eligibility for HOPWA assistance or find alternative housing, which period shall be no less than 90 calendar days and no more than one year from the date of bifurcation of a lease, consistent with 24 CFR 574.460;

(B) Provides notice of occupancy rights and the certification form at the times listed in paragraph (d) of this section;

(C) Adopts and administers an emergency transfer plan, as developed by the grantee in accordance with 24 CFR 5.2005(e) of this section, and facilitates emergency transfers; and

(D) Maintains the confidentiality of documentation submitted by tenants requesting emergency transfers and of each tenant's housing location consistent with §574.440 and 24 CFR 5.2007(c).

(ii)(A) If a tenant seeks VAWA protections set forth in 24 CFR part 5, subpart L, the tenant must submit such request through the project sponsor (or the grantee if the grantee is directly administering HOPWA assistance). The project sponsor will work with the housing owner or manager to facilitate protections on the tenant's behalf. Project sponsors must follow the documentation specifications in 24 CFR 5.2007, including the confidentiality requirements in 24 CFR 5.2007(c). The project sponsor (or the grantee if the grantee is directly administering HOPWA assistance) is also responsible for determining on a case-by-case basis whether to provide new tenant-based rental assistance to a remaining tenant if lease bifurcation or an emergency transfer results in division of the household.

(B) The grantee or project sponsor is responsible for ensuring that the housing owner or manager develops and uses a HOPWA lease addendum with VAWA protections and is made aware of the option to bifurcate a lease in accordance with §574.460 and 24 CFR 5.2009.

(c) *Effective date.* The core statutory protections of VAWA that prohibit denial or termination of assistance or eviction because an applicant or tenant is a victim of domestic violence, dating violence, sexual assault, or stalking applied upon enactment of VAWA 2013 on March 7, 2013. For formula grants, compliance with the VAWA regulatory requirements under this section and 24 CFR part 5, subpart L, are required for any project covered under §574.604(a) for which the date of the HOPWA funding commitment is made on or after *December 16, 2016*. For competitive grants, compliance with the VAWA regulatory requirements under this section and 24 CFR part 5, subpart L, are required for awards made on or after *December 16, 2016*.

(d) *Notification requirements.* (1) As provided in paragraph (b) of this section, the grantee is responsible for ensuring that the notice of occupancy rights and certification form described in 24 CFR 5.2005(a) is provided to each person receiving project-based or tenant-based rental assistance under HOPWA or residing in rental housing assisted under the eligible activities described in §574.604(a) at the following times:

(i) At the time the person is denied rental assistance or admission to a HOPWA-assisted unit;

(ii) At the time the person is admitted to a HOPWA-assisted unit or is provided rental assistance;

(iii) With any notification of eviction from the HOPWA-assisted unit or notification of termination of rental assistance; and

(iv) During the 12-month period following December 16, 2016, either during annual recertification or lease renewal, whichever is applicable, or, if there will be no recertification or lease renewal for a tenant during the first year after the rule takes effect, through other means.

(2) The grantee is responsible for ensuring that, for each tenant receiving HOPWA tenant-based rental assistance, the owner or manager of the tenant's housing unit commits to provide the notice of occupancy rights and certification form described in 24 CFR 5.2005 with any notification of eviction that the owner or manager provides to the tenant during the period for which the tenant is receiving HOPWA tenant-based rental assistance. This commitment, as well as the confidentiality requirements under 24 CFR 5.2007(c), must be set forth in the VAWA lease term/addendum required under paragraph (f) of this section.

(e) *Definition of reasonable time.* For the purpose of 24 CFR 5.2009(b), the reasonable time to establish eligibility or find alternative housing following bifurcation of a lease is the reasonable grace period described in § 574.460.

(f) *VAWA lease term/addendum.* As provided in paragraph (b) of this section, the grantee or project sponsor is responsible for ensuring that the housing or facility owner or manager, as applicable, develops and uses a VAWA lease term/addendum to incorporate all requirements that apply to the housing or facility owner or manager under 24 CFR part 5, subpart L, and this section, including the prohibited bases for eviction under 24 CFR 5.2005(b), the provisions regarding construction of lease terms and terms of assistance under 24 CFR 5.2005(c), and the confidentiality of documentation submitted by tenants requesting emergency transfers and of each tenant's housing location consistent with 24 CFR 5.2007(c). The VAWA lease term/addendum must also provide that the tenant may terminate the lease without penalty if a determination is made that the tenant has met the conditions for an emergency transfer under 24 CFR 5.2005(e). The grantee or project sponsor is responsible for ensuring that the housing or facility owner, or manager, as applicable, adds the VAWA lease term/addendum to the leases for all HOPWA-assisted units and the leases for all eligible persons receiving HOPWA tenant-based rental assistance.

[81 FR 80806, Nov. 16, 2016]

§ 574.605 Applicability of uniform administrative requirements, cost principles, and audit requirements for Federal awards.

The provisions of 2 CFR part 200, "Uniform Administrative Requirements, Cost Principles, and Audit Requirements for Federal Awards", apply to HOPWA grants.

[80 FR 75938, Dec. 7, 2015]

§ 574.625 Conflict of interest.

(a) In addition to the conflict of interest requirements in 2 CFR 200.317 (for recipients and subrecipients that are States) and 2 CFR 200.318 (for recipients and subrecipients that are not States), no person who is an employee, agent, consultant, officer, or elected or appointed official of the grantee or project sponsor and who exercises or has exercised any functions or responsibilities with respect to assisted activities, or who is in a position to participate in a decision making process or gain inside information with regard to such activities, may obtain a financial interest or benefit from the activity, or have an interest in any contract, subcontract, or agreement with respect thereto, or the proceeds thereunder, either for himself or herself or for those with whom he or she has family or business ties, during his or her tenure or for one year thereafter.

(b) *Exceptions: Threshold requirements.* Upon the written request of the recipient, HUD may grant an exception to the provisions of paragraph (a) of this section when it determines that the exception will serve to further the purposes of the HOPWA program and the effective and efficient administration of the recipient's program or project.

An exception may be considered only after the recipient has provided the following:

(1) A disclosure of the nature of the conflict, accompanied by an assurance that there has been public disclosure of the conflict and a description of how the public disclosure was made; and

(2) An opinion of the recipient's attorney that the interest for which the exception is sought would not violate State or local law.

(c) *Factors to be considered for exceptions.* In determining whether to grant a requested exception after the recipient has satisfactorily met the requirements of paragraph (b) of this section, HUD will consider the cumulative effect of the following factors, where applicable:

(1) Whether the exception would provide a significant cost benefit or an essential degree of expertise to the program or project that would otherwise not be available;

(2) Whether the person affected is a member of a group or class of eligible persons and the exception will permit such person to receive generally the same interests or benefits as are being made available or provided to the group or class;

(3) Whether the affected person has withdrawn from his or her functions or responsibilities, or the decisionmaking process with respect to the specific assisted activity in question;

(4) Whether the interest or benefit was present before the affected person was in a position as described in paragraph (a) of this section;

(5) Whether undue hardship will result either to the recipient or the person affected when weighed against the public interest served by avoiding the prohibited conflict; and

(6) Any other relevant considerations.

[57 FR 61740, Dec. 28, 1992, as amended at 80 FR 75938, Dec. 7, 2015]

§574.630 Displacement, relocation and real property acquisition.

(a) *Minimizing displacement.* Consistent with the other goals and objectives of this part, grantees and project sponsors must assure that they have taken all reasonable steps to minimize the displacement of persons (families, individuals, businesses, nonprofit organizations, and farms) as a result of a project assisted under this part.

(b) *Relocation assistance for displaced persons.* A displaced person (defined in paragraph (f) of this section) must be provided relocation assistance at the levels described in, and in accordance with the requirements of, the Uniform Relocation Assistance and Real Property Acquisition Policies Act of 1970 (URA) (42 U.S.C. 4601–4655) and implementing regulations at 49 CFR part 24.

(c) *Real property acquisition requirements.* The acquisition of real property for a project is subject to the URA and the requirements described in 49 CFR part 24, subpart B.

(d) *Appeals.* A person who disagrees with the grantee's or project sponsor's determination concerning whether the person qualifies as a "displaced person," or the amount of relocation assistance for which the person is eligible, may file a written appeal of that determination with the grantee. A low-income person who is dissatisfied with the grantee's determination on his or her appeal may submit a written request for review of that determination to the HUD Field Office.

(e) *Responsibility of grantee.* (1) Each grantee shall certify (i.e., provide assurance of compliance as required by 49 CFR part 24) that it will comply with the URA, the regulations at 49 CFR part 24, and the requirements of this section, and shall ensure such compliance notwithstanding any third party's contractual obligation to the grantee to comply with these provisions.

(2) The cost of required relocation assistance is an eligible project cost in the same manner and to the same extent as other project costs. Such costs also may be paid for with funds available from other sources.

(3) The grantee shall maintain records in sufficient detail to demonstrate compliance with these provisions.

(f) *Definition of displaced person.* (1) For purposes of this section, the term "displaced person" means a person (family, individual, business, nonprofit organization, or farm) that moves from real property, or moves personal property from real property, permanently, as a direct result of acquisition, rehabilitation, or demolition for a project assisted under this part. This includes any permanent, involuntary move for an assisted project including any permanent move for an assisted project, including any permanent move from the real property that is made:

(i) After notice by the grantee, project sponsor, or property owner to move permanently from the property, if the move occurs on or after the date that the grantee submits to HUD an application for assistance that is later approved and funded;

(ii) Before the submission of the application to HUD, if the grantee, project sponsor, or HUD determines that the displacement resulted directly from acquisition, rehabilitation, or demolition for the assisted project; or

(iii) By a tenant-occupant of a dwelling unit, if any one of the following three situations occurs:

(A) The tenant moves after the "initiation of negotiations" and the move occurs before the tenant has been provided written notice offering him or her the opportunity to lease and occupy a suitable, decent, safe and sanitary dwelling in the same building/complex, under reasonable terms and conditions, upon completion of the project. Such reasonable terms and conditions include a monthly rent and estimated average monthly utility costs that do not exceed the greater of:

(*1*) The tenant's monthly rent before the initiation of negotiations and estimated average utility costs, or

(*2*) 30 percent of gross household income; or

(B) The tenant is required to relocate temporarily, does not return to the building/complex and either:

(*1*) The tenant is not offered payment for all reasonable out-of-pocket expenses incurred in connection with the temporary relocation, or

(*2*) Other conditions of the temporary relocation are not reasonable; or

(C) The tenant is required to move to another unit in the same building/complex but is not offered reimbursement for all reasonable out-of-pocket expenses incurred in connection with the move, or other conditions of the move are not reasonable.

(2) Notwithstanding the provisions of paragraph (f)(1) of this section, a person does not qualify as a "displaced person" (and is not eligible for relocation assistance under the URA or this section), if:

(i) The person has been evicted for serious or repeated violation of the terms and conditions of the lease or occupancy agreement, violation or applicable Federal, State or local law, or other good cause, and HUD determines that the eviction was not undertaken for the purposes of evading the obligation to provide relocation assistance;

(ii) The person moved into the property after the submission of the application and, before signing a lease and commencing occupancy, was provided written notice of the project, its possible impact on the person (e.g., the person may be displaced, temporarily relocated, or suffer a rent increase) and the fact that the person would not qualify as a "displaced person" (or for any assistance provided under this section), if the project is approved;

(iii) The person is ineligible under 49 CFR 24.2(g)(2); or

(iv) HUD determines that the person was not displaced as a direct result of acquisition, rehabilitation, or demolition for the project.

(3) The grantee or project sponsor may request, at any time, HUD's determination of whether a displacement is or would be covered under this section.

(g) *Definition of initiation of negotiations.* For purposes of determining the formula for computing the replacement housing assistance to be provided to a residential tenant displaced as a direct result of privately undertaken rehabilitation, demolition, or acquisition of the real property, the term "initiation of negotiations" means the execution of the agreement between the grantee and the project sponsor.

§ 574.635 Lead-based paint.

The Lead-Based Paint Poisoning Prevention Act (42 U.S.C. 4821–4846), the Residential Lead-Based Paint Hazard Reduction Act of 1992 (42 U.S.C. 4851–4856), and implementing regulations at part 35, subparts A, B, H, J, K, M, and R of this part apply to activities under this program.

[64 FR 50226, Sept. 15, 1999]

§ 574.640 Flood insurance protection.

No property to be assisted under this part may be located in an area that has been identified by the Federal Emergency Management Agency (FEMA) as having special flood hazards, unless:

(a)(1) The community in which the area is situated is participating in the National Flood Insurance Program and the regulations thereunder (44 CFR parts 59 through 79); or

(2) Less than a year has passed since FEMA notification regarding such hazards; and

(b) The grantee will ensure that flood insurance on the structure is obtained in compliance with section 102(a) of the Flood Disaster Protection Act of 1973 (42 U.S.C. 4001 *et seq.*).

§ 574.645 Coastal barriers.

In accordance with the Coastal Barrier Resources Act, 16 U.S.C. 3501, no financial assistance under this part may be made available within the Coastal Barrier Resources System.

§ 574.650 Audit.

Grantees and project sponsors are subject to the audit requirements set forth in 2 CFR part 200, subpart F.

[80 FR 75938, Dec. 7, 2015]

§ 574.655 Wage rates.

The provisions of the Davis-Bacon Act (40 U.S.C. 276a–276a–5) do not apply to this program, except where funds received under this part are combined with funds from other Federal programs that are subject to the Act.

[59 FR 17201, Apr. 11, 1994]

§ 574.660 Housing counseling.

Housing counseling, as defined in § 5.100, that is funded with or provided in connection with HOPWA funds must be carried out in accordance with § 5.111. When grantees provide housing services to eligible persons (including persons undergoing relocation) that are incidental to a larger set of holistic case management services, these services do not meet the definition of housing counseling, as defined in § 5.100, and therefore are not required to be carried out in accordance with the certification requirements of § 5.111.

[81 FR 90659, Dec. 14, 2016, as amended at 82 FR 8811, Jan. 31, 2017]

PART 576—EMERGENCY SOLUTIONS GRANTS PROGRAM

Subpart A—General Provisions

Sec.

Subpart B—Program Components and Eligible Activities

Subpart C—Award and Use of Funds

Subpart D—Reallocations

Subpart E—Program Requirements

AUTHORITY: 12 U.S.C. 1701x, 1701 x–1; 42 U.S.C. 11371 *et seq.*, 42 U.S.C. 3535(d).

SOURCE: 76 FR 75974, Dec. 5, 2011, unless otherwise noted.

Subpart A—General Provisions

§ 576.1 Applicability and purpose.

This part implements the Emergency Solutions Grants (ESG) program authorized by subtitle B of title IV of the McKinney-Vento Homeless Assistance Act (42 U.S.C. 11371–11378). The program authorizes the Department of Housing and Urban Development (HUD) to make grants to States, units of general purpose local government, and territories for the rehabilitation or conversion of buildings for use as emergency shelter for the homeless, for the payment of certain expenses related to operating emergency shelters, for essential services related to emergency shelters and street outreach for the homeless, and for homelessness prevention and rapid re-housing assistance.

§ 576.2 Definitions.

At risk of homelessness means: (1) An individual or family who:

(i) Has an annual income below 30 percent of median family income for the area, as determined by HUD;

(ii) Does not have sufficient resources or support networks, *e.g.*, family, friends, faith-based or other social networks, immediately available to prevent them from moving to an emergency shelter or another place described in paragraph (1) of the "homeless" definition in this section; and

(iii) Meets one of the following conditions:

(A) Has moved because of economic reasons two or more times during the 60 days immediately preceding the application for homelessness prevention assistance;

(B) Is living in the home of another because of economic hardship;

(C) Has been notified in writing that their right to occupy their current housing or living situation will be terminated within 21 days after the date of application for assistance;

(D) Lives in a hotel or motel and the cost of the hotel or motel stay is not paid by charitable organizations or by Federal, State, or local government programs for low-income individuals;

(E) Lives in a single-room occupancy or efficiency apartment unit in which there reside more than two persons or lives in a larger housing unit in which there reside more than 1.5 persons reside per room, as defined by the U.S. Census Bureau;

(F) Is exiting a publicly funded institution, or system of care (such as a health-care facility, a mental health facility, foster care or other youth facility, or correction program or institution); or

(G) Otherwise lives in housing that has characteristics associated with instability and an increased risk of homelessness, as identified in the recipient's approved consolidated plan;

(2) A child or youth who does not qualify as "homeless" under this section, but qualifies as "homeless" under section 387(3) of the Runaway and Homeless Youth Act (42 U.S.C. 5732a(3)), section 637(11) of the Head Start Act (42 U.S.C. 9832(11)), section 41403(6) of the Violence Against Women Act of 1994 (42 U.S.C. 14043e–2(6)), section 330(h)(5)(A) of the Public Health Service Act (42 U.S.C. 254b(h)(5)(A)), section 3(m) of the Food and Nutrition Act of 2008 (7 U.S.C. 2012(m)), or section 17(b)(15) of the Child Nutrition Act of 1966 (42 U.S.C. 1786(b)(15)); or

(3) A child or youth who does not qualify as "homeless" under this section, but qualifies as "homeless" under section 725(2) of the McKinney-Vento Homeless Assistance Act (42 U.S.C. 11434a(2)), and the parent(s) or guardian(s) of that child or youth if living with her or him.

Consolidated plan means a plan prepared in accordance with 24 CFR part 91. An *approved consolidated* plan means a consolidated plan that has been approved by HUD in accordance with 24 CFR part 91.

Continuum of Care means the group composed of representatives of relevant organizations, which generally includes nonprofit homeless providers; victim service providers; faith-based organizations; governments; businesses; advocates; public housing agencies; school districts; social service providers; mental health agencies; hospitals; universities; affordable housing developers; law enforcement; organizations that serve homeless and formerly homeless veterans, and homeless and formerly homeless persons that are organized to plan for and provide, as necessary, a system of outreach, engagement, and assessment; emergency shelter; rapid re-housing; transitional housing; permanent housing; and prevention strategies to address the various needs of homeless persons and persons at risk of homelessness for a specific geographic area.

Emergency shelter means any facility, the primary purpose of which is to provide a temporary shelter for the homeless in general or for specific populations of the homeless and which does not require occupants to sign leases or occupancy agreements. Any project funded as an emergency shelter under a Fiscal Year 2010 Emergency Solutions grant may continue to be funded under ESG.

Homeless means:

(1) An individual or family who lacks a fixed, regular, and adequate nighttime residence, meaning:

(i) An individual or family with a primary nighttime residence that is a public or private place not designed for or ordinarily used as a regular sleeping accommodation for human beings, including a car, park, abandoned building, bus or train station, airport, or camping ground;

(ii) An individual or family living in a supervised publicly or privately operated shelter designated to provide temporary living arrangements (including congregate shelters, transitional housing, and hotels and motels paid for by charitable organizations or by federal, state, or local government programs for low-income individuals); or

(iii) An individual who is exiting an institution where he or she resided for 90 days or less and who resided in an emergency shelter or place not meant for human habitation immediately before entering that institution;

(2) An individual or family who will imminently lose their primary nighttime residence, provided that:

(i) The primary nighttime residence will be lost within 14 days of the date of application for homeless assistance;

(ii) No subsequent residence has been identified; and

(iii) The individual or family lacks the resources or support networks, *e.g.*, family, friends, faith-based or other social networks, needed to obtain other permanent housing;

(3) Unaccompanied youth under 25 years of age, or families with children and youth, who do not otherwise qualify as homeless under this definition, but who:

(i) Are defined as homeless under section 387 of the Runaway and Homeless Youth Act (42 U.S.C. 5732a), section 637 of the Head Start Act (42 U.S.C. 9832), section 41403 of the Violence Against Women Act of 1994 (42 U.S.C. 14043e–2), section 330(h) of the Public Health Service Act (42 U.S.C. 254b(h)), section 3 of the Food and Nutrition Act of 2008 (7 U.S.C. 2012), section 17(b) of the Child Nutrition Act of 1966 (42 U.S.C. 1786(b)) or section 725 of the McKinney-Vento Homeless Assistance Act (42 U.S.C. 11434a);

(ii) Have not had a lease, ownership interest, or occupancy agreement in permanent housing at any time during the 60 days immediately preceding the date of application for homeless assistance;

(iii) Have experienced persistent instability as measured by two moves or more during the 60-day period immediately preceding the date of applying for homeless assistance; and

(iv) Can be expected to continue in such status for an extended period of time because of chronic disabilities, chronic physical health or mental health conditions, substance addiction, histories of domestic violence or childhood abuse (including neglect), the presence of a child or youth with a disability, or two or more barriers to employment, which include the lack of a high school degree or General Education Development (GED), illiteracy, low English proficiency, a history of incarceration or detention for criminal activity, and a history of unstable employment; or

(4) Any individual or family who:

(i) Is fleeing, or is attempting to flee, domestic violence, dating violence, sexual assault, stalking, or other dangerous or life-threatening conditions that relate to violence against the individual or a family member, including a child, that has either taken place within the individual's or family's primary nighttime residence or has made the individual or family afraid to return to their primary nighttime residence;

(ii) Has no other residence; and

(iii) Lacks the resources or support networks, *e.g.*, family, friends, faith-based or other social networks, to obtain other permanent housing.

Homeless Management Information System (HMIS) means the information system designated by the Continuum of Care to comply with the HUD's data collection, management, and reporting standards and used to collect client-level data and data on the provision of housing and services to homeless individuals and families and persons at-risk of homelessness.

Metropolitan city means a city that was classified as a metropolitan city under 42 U.S.C. 5302(a) for the fiscal year immediately preceding the fiscal year for which ESG funds are made available. This term includes the District of Columbia.

Private nonprofit organization means a private nonprofit organization that is a secular or religious organization described in section 501(c) of the Internal Revenue Code of 1986 and which is exempt from taxation under subtitle A of the Code, has an accounting system and a voluntary board, and practices nondiscrimination in the provision of assistance. A private nonprofit organization does not include a governmental organization, such as a public housing agency or housing finance agency.

Program income shall have the meaning provided in 2 CFR 200.80. Program income includes any amount of a security or utility deposit returned to the recipient or subrecipient.

Program participant means an individual or family who is assisted under ESG program.

Program year means the consolidated program year established by the recipient under 24 CFR part 91.

Recipient means any State, territory, metropolitan city, or urban county, or in the case of reallocation, any unit of general purpose local government that is approved by HUD to assume financial responsibility and enters into a grant agreement with HUD to administer assistance under this part.

State means each of the several States and the Commonwealth of Puerto Rico.

Subrecipient means a unit of general purpose local government or private nonprofit organization to which a recipient makes available ESG funds.

Territory means each of the following: the Virgin Islands, Guam, American Samoa, and the Northern Mariana Islands.

Unit of general purpose local government means any city, county, town, township, parish, village, or other general purpose political subdivision of a State.

Urban county means a county that was classified as an urban county under 42 U.S.C. 5302(a) for the fiscal year immediately preceding the fiscal year for which ESG funds are made available.

Victim service provider means a private nonprofit organization whose primary mission is to provide services to victims of domestic violence, dating violence, sexual assault, or stalking. This term includes rape crisis centers, battered women's shelters, domestic violence transitional housing programs, and other programs.

[76 FR 75974, Dec. 5, 2011, as amended at 80 FR 75939, Dec. 7, 2015]

§ 576.3 Allocation of funding.

(a) *Territories.* HUD will set aside for allocation to the territories up to 0.2 percent, but not less than 0.1 percent, of the total amount of each appropriation under this part in any fiscal year. HUD will allocate this set-aside amount to each territory based on its proportionate share of the total population of all territories and its rate of compliance with the most recent expenditure deadline under § 576.203.

(b) *States, metropolitan cities, and urban counties.* HUD will allocate the amounts that remain after the set-aside to territories under paragraph (a) of this section to States, metropolitan cities, and urban counties, as follows:

(1) HUD will provide that the percentage of the total amount available for allocation to each State, metropolitan city, or urban county is equal to the percentage of the total amount available under section 106 of the Housing and Community Development Act of 1974 for the prior fiscal year that was allocated to that State, metropolitan city, or urban county.

(2) Except as otherwise provided by law, if the amount a metropolitan city or urban county would be allocated under paragraph (b)(1) is less than 0.05 percent of the total fiscal year appropriation for ESG, that amount will be added to the allocation for the State in which the city or county is located.

(c) *Notification of allocation amount.* HUD will notify each State, metropolitan city, urban county, and territory that is eligible to receive an allocation under this section of the amount of its allocation.

Subpart B—Program Components and Eligible Activities

§576.100 General provisions and expenditure limits.

(a) ESG funds may be used for five program components: street outreach, emergency shelter, homelessness prevention, rapid re-housing assistance, and HMIS; as well as administrative activities. The five program components and the eligible activities that may be funded under each are set forth in §576.101 through §576.107. Eligible administrative activities are set forth in §576.108.

(b) The total amount of the recipient's fiscal year grant that may be used for street outreach and emergency shelter activities cannot exceed the greater of:

(1) 60 percent of the recipient's fiscal year grant; or

(2) The amount of Fiscal Year 2010 grant funds committed for homeless assistance activities.

(c) The total amount of ESG funds that may be used for administrative activities cannot exceed 7.5 percent of the recipient's fiscal year grant.

(d) Subject to the cost principles in 2 CFR part 200, subpart E, and other requirements in this part, employee compensation and other overhead costs directly related to carrying out street outreach, emergency shelter, homelessness prevention, rapid re-housing, and HMIS are eligible costs of those program components. These costs are not subject to the expenditure limit in paragraph (c) of this section.

[76 FR 75974, Dec. 5, 2011, as amended at 80 FR 75939, Dec. 7, 2015]

§576.101 Street outreach component.

(a) *Eligible costs.* Subject to the expenditure limit in §576.100(b), ESG funds may be used for costs of providing essential services necessary to reach out to unsheltered homeless people; connect them with emergency shelter, housing, or critical services; and provide urgent, nonfacility-based care to unsheltered homeless people who are unwilling or unable to access emergency shelter, housing, or an appropriate health facility. For the purposes of this section, the term "unsheltered homeless people" means individuals and families who qualify as homeless under paragraph (1)(i) of the "homeless" definition under §576.2. The eligible costs and requirements for essential services consist of:

(1) *Engagement.* The costs of activities to locate, identify, and build relationships with unsheltered homeless people and engage them for the purpose of providing immediate support, intervention, and connections with homeless assistance programs and/or mainstream social services and housing programs. These activities consist of making an initial assessment of needs and eligibility; providing crisis counseling; addressing urgent physical needs, such as providing meals, blankets, clothes, or toiletries; and actively connecting and providing information and referrals to programs targeted to homeless people and mainstream social services and housing programs, including emergency shelter, transitional housing, community-based services, permanent supportive housing, and rapid re-housing programs. Eligible costs include the cell phone costs of outreach workers during the performance of these activities.

(2) *Case management.* The cost of assessing housing and service needs, arranging, coordinating, and monitoring the delivery of individualized services to meet the needs of the program participant. Eligible services and activities are as follows: using the centralized or coordinated assessment system as required under §576.400(d); conducting the initial evaluation required under §576.401(a), including verifying and documenting eligibility; counseling; developing, securing and coordinating services; obtaining Federal, State, and local benefits; monitoring and evaluating program participant progress; providing information and referrals to other providers; and developing an individualized housing and service plan, including planning a path to permanent housing stability.

(3) *Emergency health services.* (i) Eligible costs are for the direct outpatient treatment of medical conditions and are provided by licensed medical professionals operating in community-based settings, including streets, parks, and other places where unsheltered homeless people are living.

(ii) ESG funds may be used only for these services to the extent that other appropriate health services are inaccessible or unavailable within the area.

(iii) Eligible treatment consists of assessing a program participant's health problems and developing a treatment plan; assisting program participants to understand their health needs; providing directly or assisting program participants to obtain appropriate emergency medical treatment; and providing medication and follow-up services.

(4) *Emergency mental health services.* (i) Eligible costs are the direct outpatient treatment by licensed professionals of mental health conditions operating in community-based settings, including streets, parks, and other places where unsheltered people are living.

(ii) ESG funds may be used only for these services to the extent that other appropriate mental health services are inaccessible or unavailable within the community.

(iii) Mental health services are the application of therapeutic processes to personal, family, situational, or occupational problems in order to bring about positive resolution of the problem or improved individual or family functioning or circumstances.

(iv) Eligible treatment consists of crisis interventions, the prescription of psychotropic medications, explanation about the use and management of medications, and combinations of therapeutic approaches to address multiple problems.

(5) *Transportation.* The transportation costs of travel by outreach workers, social workers, medical professionals, or other service providers are eligible, provided that this travel takes place during the provision of services eligible under this section. The costs of transporting unsheltered people to emergency shelters or other service facilities are also eligible. These costs include the following:

(i) The cost of a program participant's travel on public transportation;

(ii) If service workers use their own vehicles, mileage allowance for service workers to visit program participants;

(iii) The cost of purchasing or leasing a vehicle for the recipient or subrecipient in which staff transports program participants and/or staff serving program participants, and the cost of gas, insurance, taxes and maintenance for the vehicle; and

(iv) The travel costs of recipient or subrecipient staff to accompany or assist program participants to use public transportation.

(6) *Services for special populations.* ESG funds may be used to provide services for homeless youth, victim services, and services for people living with HIV/AIDS, so long as the costs of providing these services are eligible under paragraphs (a)(1) through (a)(5) of this section. The term *victim services* means services that assist program participants who are victims of domestic violence, dating violence, sexual assault, or stalking, including services offered by rape crisis centers and domestic violence shelters, and other organizations with a documented history of effective work concerning domestic violence, dating violence, sexual assault, or stalking.

(b) *Minimum period of use.* The recipient or subrecipient must provide services to homeless individuals and families for at least the period during which ESG funds are provided.

(c) *Maintenance of effort.* (1) If the recipient or subrecipient is a unit of general purpose local government, its ESG funds cannot be used to replace funds the local government provided for street outreach and emergency shelter services during the immediately preceding 12-month period, unless HUD determines that the unit of general purpose local government is in a severe financial deficit.

(2) Upon the recipient's request, HUD will determine whether the unit of general purpose local government is in a severe financial deficit, based on the recipient's demonstration of each of the following:

(i) The average poverty rate in the unit of general purpose local government's jurisdiction was equal to or greater than 125 percent of the average national poverty rate, during the calendar year for which the most recent data are available, as determined according to information from the U.S. Census Bureau.

(ii) The average per-capita income in the unit of general purpose local government's jurisdiction was less than 75 percent of the average national per-capita income, during the calendar year for which the most recent data are available, as determined according to information from the Census Bureau.

(iii) The unit of general purpose local government has a current annual budget deficit that requires a reduction in funding for services for homeless people.

(iv) The unit of general purpose local government has taken all reasonable steps to prevent a reduction in funding of services for homeless people. Reasonable steps may include steps to increase revenue generation, steps to maximize cost savings, or steps to reduce expenditures in areas other than services for homeless people.

§576.102 Emergency shelter component.

(a) *General.* Subject to the expenditure limit in §576.100(b), ESG funds may be used for costs of providing essential services to homeless families and individuals in emergency shelters, renovating buildings to be used as emergency shelter for homeless families and individuals, and operating emergency shelters.

(1) *Essential services.* ESG funds may be used to provide essential services to individuals and families who are in an emergency shelter, as follows:

(i) *Case management.* The cost of assessing, arranging, coordinating, and monitoring the delivery of individualized services to meet the needs of the program participant is eligible. Component services and activities consist of:

(A) Using the centralized or coordinated assessment system as required under §576.400(d);

(B) Conducting the initial evaluation required under §576.401(a), including verifying and documenting eligibility;

(C) Counseling;

(D) Developing, securing, and coordinating services and obtaining Federal, State, and local benefits;

(E) Monitoring and evaluating program participant progress;

(F) Providing information and referrals to other providers;

(G) Providing ongoing risk assessment and safety planning with victims of domestic violence, dating violence, sexual assault, and stalking; and

(H) Developing an individualized housing and service plan, including planning a path to permanent housing stability.

(ii) *Child care.* The costs of child care for program participants, including providing meals and snacks, and comprehensive and coordinated sets of appropriate developmental activities, are eligible. The children must be under the age of 13, unless they are disabled. Disabled children must be under the age of 18. The child-care center must be licensed by the jurisdiction in which it operates in order for its costs to be eligible.

(iii) *Education services.* When necessary for the program participant to obtain and maintain housing, the costs of improving knowledge and basic educational skills are eligible. Services include instruction or training in consumer education, health education, substance abuse prevention, literacy,

English as a Second Language, and General Educational Development (GED). Component services or activities are screening, assessment and testing; individual or group instruction; tutoring; provision of books, supplies and instructional material; counseling; and referral to community resources.

(iv) *Employment assistance and job training.* The costs of employment assistance and job training programs are eligible, including classroom, online, and/or computer instruction; on-the-job instruction; and services that assist individuals in securing employment, acquiring learning skills, and/or increasing earning potential. The cost of providing reasonable stipends to program participants in employment assistance and job training programs is an eligible cost. Learning skills include those skills that can be used to secure and retain a job, including the acquisition of vocational licenses and/or certificates. Services that assist individuals in securing employment consist of employment screening, assessment, or testing; structured job skills and job-seeking skills; special training and tutoring, including literacy training and prevocational training; books and instructional material; counseling or job coaching; and referral to community resources.

(v) *Outpatient health services.* Eligible costs are for the direct outpatient treatment of medical conditions and are provided by licensed medical professionals. Emergency Solutions Grant (ESG) funds may be used only for these services to the extent that other appropriate health services are unavailable within the community. Eligible treatment consists of assessing a program participant's health problems and developing a treatment plan; assisting program participants to understand their health needs; providing directly or assisting program participants to obtain appropriate medical treatment, preventive medical care, and health maintenance services, including emergency medical services; providing medication and follow-up services; and providing preventive and noncosmetic dental care.

(vi) *Legal services.* (A) Eligible costs are the hourly fees for legal advice and representation by attorneys licensed and in good standing with the bar association of the State in which the services are provided, and by person(s) under the supervision of the licensed attorney, regarding matters that interfere with the program participant's ability to obtain and retain housing.

(B) Emergency Solutions Grant (ESG) funds may be used only for these services to the extent that other appropriate legal services are unavailable or inaccessible within the community.

(C) Eligible subject matters are child support, guardianship, paternity, emancipation, and legal separation, orders of protection and other civil remedies for victims of domestic violence, dating violence, sexual assault, and stalking, appeal of veterans and public benefit claim denials, and the resolution of outstanding criminal warrants.

(D) Component services or activities may include client intake, preparation of cases for trial, provision of legal advice, representation at hearings, and counseling.

(E) Fees based on the actual service performed (*i.e.*, fee for service) are also eligible, but only if the cost would be less than the cost of hourly fees. Filing fees and other necessary court costs are also eligible. If the subrecipient is a legal services provider and performs the services itself, the eligible costs are the subrecipient's employees' salaries and other costs necessary to perform the services.

(F) Legal services for immigration and citizenship matters and issues relating to mortgages are ineligible costs. Retainer fee arrangements and contingency fee arrangements are ineligible costs.

(vii) *Life skills training.* The costs of teaching critical life management skills that may never have been learned or have been lost during the course of physical or mental illness, domestic violence, substance use, and homelessness are eligible costs. These services must be necessary to assist the program participant to function independently in the community. Component life skills training are budgeting resources, managing money, managing a household, resolving conflict, shopping for food and needed items, improving nutrition, using public transportation, and parenting.

(viii) *Mental health services.* (A) Eligible costs are the direct outpatient treatment by licensed professionals of mental health conditions.

(B) ESG funds may only be used for these services to the extent that other appropriate mental health services are unavailable or inaccessible within the community.

(C) Mental health services are the application of therapeutic processes to personal, family, situational, or occupational problems in order to bring about positive resolution of the problem or improved individual or family functioning or circumstances. Problem areas may include family and marital relationships, parent-child problems, or symptom management.

(D) Eligible treatment consists of crisis interventions; individual, family, or group therapy sessions; the prescription of psychotropic medications or explanations about the use and management of medications; and combinations of therapeutic approaches to address multiple problems.

(ix) *Substance abuse treatment services.* (A) Eligible substance abuse treatment services are designed to prevent, reduce, eliminate, or deter relapse of substance abuse or addictive behaviors and are provided by licensed or certified professionals.

(B) ESG funds may only be used for these services to the extent that other appropriate substance abuse treatment services are unavailable or inaccessible within the community.

(C) Eligible treatment consists of client intake and assessment, and outpatient treatment for up to 30 days. Group and individual counseling and drug testing are eligible costs. Inpatient detoxification and other inpatient drug or alcohol treatment are not eligible costs.

(x) *Transportation.* Eligible costs consist of the transportation costs of a program participant's travel to and from medical care, employment, child care, or other eligible essential services facilities. These costs include the following:

(A) The cost of a program participant's travel on public transportation;

(B) If service workers use their own vehicles, mileage allowance for service workers to visit program participants;

(C) The cost of purchasing or leasing a vehicle for the recipient or subrecipient in which staff transports program participants and/or staff serving program participants, and the cost of gas, insurance, taxes, and maintenance for the vehicle; and

(D) The travel costs of recipient or subrecipient staff to accompany or assist program participants to use public transportation.

(xi) *Services for special populations.* ESG funds may be used to provide services for homeless youth, victim services, and services for people living with HIV/AIDS, so long as the costs of providing these services are eligible under paragraphs (a)(1)(i) through (a)(1)(x) of this section. The term *victim services* means services that assist program participants who are victims of domestic violence, dating violence, sexual assault, or stalking, including services offered by rape crisis centers and domestic violence shelters, and other organizations with a documented history of effective work concerning domestic violence, dating violence, sexual assault, or stalking.

(2) *Renovation.* Eligible costs include labor, materials, tools, and other costs for renovation (including major rehabilitation of an emergency shelter or conversion of a building into an emergency shelter). The emergency shelter must be owned by a government entity or private nonprofit organization.

(3) *Shelter operations.* Eligible costs are the costs of maintenance (including minor or routine repairs), rent, security, fuel, equipment, insurance, utilities, food, furnishings, and supplies necessary for the operation of the emergency shelter. Where no appropriate emergency shelter is available for a homeless family or individual, eligible costs may also include a hotel or motel voucher for that family or individual.

(4) *Assistance required under the Uniform Relocation Assistance and Real Property Acquisition Policies Act of 1970 (URA).* Eligible costs are the costs of providing URA assistance under §576.408, including relocation payments and other assistance to persons displaced by a project assisted with ESG

funds. Persons that receive URA assistance are not considered "program participants" for the purposes of this part, and relocation payments and other URA assistance are not considered "rental assistance" or "housing relocation and stabilization services" for the purposes of this part.

(b) *Prohibition against involuntary family separation.* The age, of a child under age 18 must not be used as a basis for denying any family's admission to an emergency shelter that uses Emergency Solutions Grant (ESG) funding or services and provides shelter to families with children under age 18.

(c) *Minimum period of use.* (1) *Renovated buildings.* Each building renovated with ESG funds must be maintained as a shelter for homeless individuals and families for not less than a period of 3 or 10 years, depending on the type of renovation and the value of the building. The "value of the building" is the reasonable monetary value assigned to the building, such as the value assigned by an independent real estate appraiser. The minimum use period must begin on the date the building is first occupied by a homeless individual or family after the completed renovation. A minimum period of use of 10 years, required for major rehabilitation and conversion, must be enforced by a recorded deed or use restriction.

(i) *Major rehabilitation.* If the rehabilitation cost of an emergency shelter exceeds 75 percent of the value of the building before rehabilitation, the minimum period of use is 10 years.

(ii) *Conversion.* If the cost to convert a building into an emergency shelter exceeds 75 percent of the value of the building after conversion, the minimum period of use is 10 years.

(iii) *Renovation other than major rehabilitation or conversion.* In all other cases where ESG funds are used for renovation, the minimum period of use is 3 years.

(2) *Essential services and shelter operations.* Where the recipient or subrecipient uses ESG funds solely for essential services or shelter operations, the recipient or subrecipient must provide services or shelter to homeless individuals and families at least for the period during which the ESG funds are provided. The recipient or subrecipient does not need to limit these services or shelter to a particular site or structure, so long as the site or structure serves the same type of persons originally served with the assistance (*e.g.*, families with children, unaccompanied youth, disabled individuals, or victims of domestic violence) or serves homeless persons in the same area where the recipient or subrecipient originally provided the services or shelter.

(d) *Maintenance of effort.* The maintenance of effort requirements under § 576.101(c), which apply to the use of ESG funds for essential services related to street outreach, also apply for the use of such funds for essential services related to emergency shelter.

§ 576.103 Homelessness prevention component.

ESG funds may be used to provide housing relocation and stabilization services and short- and/or medium-term rental assistance necessary to prevent an individual or family from moving into an emergency shelter or another place described in paragraph (1) of the "homeless" definition in § 576.2. This assistance, referred to as homelessness prevention, may be provided to individuals and families who meet the criteria under the "at risk of homelessness" definition, or who meet the criteria in paragraph (2), (3), or (4) of the "homeless" definition in § 576.2 and have an annual income below 30 percent of median family income for the area, as determined by HUD. The costs of homelessness prevention are only eligible to the extent that the assistance is necessary to help the program participant regain stability in the program participant's current permanent housing or move into other permanent housing and achieve stability in that housing. Homelessness prevention must be provided in accordance with the housing relocation and stabilization services requirements in § 576.105, the short-term and medium-term rental assistance requirements in § 576.106, and the written standards and procedures established under § 576.400.

§576.104 Rapid re-housing assistance component.

ESG funds may be used to provide housing relocation and stabilization services and short- and/or medium-term rental assistance as necessary to help a homeless individual or family move as quickly as possible into permanent housing and achieve stability in that housing. This assistance, referred to as rapid re-housing assistance, may be provided to program participants who meet the criteria under paragraph (1) of the "homeless" definition in §576.2 or who meet the criteria under paragraph (4) of the "homeless" definition and live in an emergency shelter or other place described in paragraph (1) of the "homeless" definition. The rapid re-housing assistance must be provided in accordance with the housing relocation and stabilization services requirements in §576.105, the short- and medium-term rental assistance requirements in §576.106, and the written standards and procedures established under §576.400.

§576.105 Housing relocation and stabilization services.

(a) *Financial assistance costs.* Subject to the general conditions under §576.103 and §576.104, ESG funds may be used to pay housing owners, utility companies, and other third parties for the following costs:

(1) *Rental application fees.* ESG funds may pay for the rental housing application fee that is charged by the owner to all applicants.

(2) *Security deposits.* ESG funds may pay for a security deposit that is equal to no more than 2 months' rent.

(3) *Last month's rent.* If necessary to obtain housing for a program participant, the last month's rent may be paid from ESG funds to the owner of that housing at the time the owner is paid the security deposit and the first month's rent. This assistance must not exceed one month's rent and must be included in calculating the program participant's total rental assistance, which cannot exceed 24 months during any 3-year period.

(4) *Utility deposits.* ESG funds may pay for a standard utility deposit required by the utility company for all customers for the utilities listed in paragraph (5) of this section.

(5) *Utility payments.* ESG funds may pay for up to 24 months of utility payments per program participant, per service, including up to 6 months of utility payments in arrears, per service. A partial payment of a utility bill counts as one month. This assistance may only be provided if the program participant or a member of the same household has an account in his or her name with a utility company or proof of responsibility to make utility payments. Eligible utility services are gas, electric, water, and sewage. No program participant shall receive more than 24 months of utility assistance within any 3-year period.

(6) *Moving costs.* ESG funds may pay for moving costs, such as truck rental or hiring a moving company. This assistance may include payment of temporary storage fees for up to 3 months, provided that the fees are accrued after the date the program participant begins receiving assistance under paragraph (b) of this section and before the program participant moves into permanent housing. Payment of temporary storage fees in arrears is not eligible.

(7) If a program participant receiving short- or medium-term rental assistance under §576.106 meets the conditions for an emergency transfer under 24 CFR 5.2005(e), ESG funds may be used to pay amounts owed for breaking a lease to effect an emergency transfer. These costs are not subject to the 24-month limit on rental assistance under §576.106.

(b) *Services costs.* Subject to the general restrictions under §576.103 and §576.104, ESG funds may be used to pay the costs of providing the following services:

(1) *Housing search and placement.* Services or activities necessary to assist program participants in locating, obtaining, and retaining suitable permanent housing, include the following:

(i) Assessment of housing barriers, needs, and preferences;

(ii) Development of an action plan for locating housing;

(iii) Housing search;

(iv) Outreach to and negotiation with owners;

(v) Assistance with submitting rental applications and understanding leases;

(vi) Assessment of housing for compliance with Emergency Solutions Grant (ESG) requirements for habitability, lead-based paint, and rent reasonableness;

(vii) Assistance with obtaining utilities and making moving arrangements; and

(viii) Tenant counseling.

(2) *Housing stability case management.* ESG funds may be used to pay cost of assessing, arranging, coordinating, and monitoring the delivery of individualized services to facilitate housing stability for a program participant who resides in permanent housing or to assist a program participant in overcoming immediate barriers to obtaining housing. This assistance cannot exceed 30 days during the period the program participant is seeking permanent housing and cannot exceed 24 months during the period the program participant is living in permanent housing. Component services and activities consist of:

(A) Using the centralized or coordinated assessment system as required under § 576.400(d), to evaluate individuals and families applying for or receiving homelessness prevention or rapid re-housing assistance;

(B) Conducting the initial evaluation required under § 576.401(a), including verifying and documenting eligibility, for individuals and families applying for homelessness prevention or rapid re-housing assistance;

(C) Counseling;

(D) Developing, securing, and coordinating services and obtaining Federal, State, and local benefits;

(E) Monitoring and evaluating program participant progress;

(F) Providing information and referrals to other providers;

(G) Developing an individualized housing and service plan, including planning a path to permanent housing stability; and

(H) Conducting re-evaluations required under § 576.401(b).

(3) *Mediation.* ESG funds may pay for mediation between the program participant and the owner or person(s) with whom the program participant is living, provided that the mediation is necessary to prevent the program participant from losing permanent housing in which the program participant currently resides.

(4) *Legal services.* ESG funds may pay for legal services, as set forth in § 576.102(a)(1)(vi), except that the eligible subject matters also include landlord/tenant matters, and the services must be necessary to resolve a legal problem that prohibits the program participant from obtaining permanent housing or will likely result in the program participant losing the permanent housing in which the program participant currently resides.

(5) *Credit repair.* ESG funds may pay for credit counseling and other services necessary to assist program participants with critical skills related to household budgeting, managing money, accessing a free personal credit report, and resolving personal credit problems. This assistance does not include the payment or modification of a debt.

(c) *Maximum amounts and periods of assistance.* The recipient may set a maximum dollar amount that a program participant may receive for each type of financial assistance under paragraph (a) of this section. The recipient may also set a maximum period for which a program participant may receive any of the types of assistance or services under this section. However, except for housing stability case management, the total period for which any program participant may receive the services under paragraph (b) of this section must not exceed 24 months during any 3-year period. The limits on the assistance under this section apply to the total assistance an individual receives, either as an individual or as part of a family.

(d) *Use with other subsidies.* Financial assistance under paragraph (a) of this section cannot be provided to a program participant who is receiving the same type of assistance through other public sources or to a program participant who has been provided with replacement housing payments under the URA, during the period of time covered by the URA payments.

(e) *Housing counseling.* Housing counseling, as defined in § 5.100, that is funded with or provided in connection with

ESG funds must be carried out in accordance with § 5.111. When recipients or subrecipients provide housing services to eligible persons that are incidental to a larger set of holistic case management services, these services do not meet the definition of housing counseling, as defined in § 5.100, and therefore are not required to be carried out in accordance with the certification requirements of § 5.111

[76 FR 75974, Dec. 5, 2011,, as amended at 81 FR 80808, Nov. 16, 2016; 81 FR 90659, Dec. 14, 2016]

§ 576.106 Short-term and medium-term rental assistance.

(a) *General provisions.* Subject to the general conditions under § 576.103 and § 576.104, the recipient or subrecipient may provide a program participant with up to 24 months of rental assistance during any 3-year period. This assistance may be short-term rental assistance, medium-term rental assistance, payment of rental arrears, or any combination of this assistance.

(1) Short-term rental assistance is assistance for up to 3 months of rent.

(2) Medium-term rental assistance is assistance for more than 3 months but not more than 24 months of rent.

(3) Payment of rental arrears consists of a one-time payment for up to 6 months of rent in arrears, including any late fees on those arrears.

(4) Rental assistance may be tenant-based or project-based, as set forth in paragraphs (h) and (i) of this section.

(b) *Discretion to set caps and conditions.* Subject to the requirements of this section, the recipient may set a maximum amount or percentage of rental assistance that a program participant may receive, a maximum number of months that a program participant may receive rental assistance, or a maximum number of times that a program participant may receive rental assistance. The recipient may also require program participants to share in the costs of rent.

(c) *Use with other subsidies.* Except for a one-time payment of rental arrears on the tenant's portion of the rental payment, rental assistance cannot be provided to a program participant who is receiving tenant-based rental assistance, or living in a housing unit receiving project-based rental assistance or operating assistance, through other public sources. Rental assistance may not be provided to a program participant who has been provided with replacement housing payments under the URA during the period of time covered by the URA payments.

(d) *Rent restrictions.* (1) Rental assistance cannot be provided unless the rent does not exceed the Fair Market Rent established by HUD, as provided under 24 CFR part 888, and complies with HUD's standard of rent reasonableness, as established under 24 CFR 982.507.

(2) For purposes of calculating rent under this section, the rent shall equal the sum of the total monthly rent for the unit, any fees required for occupancy under the lease (other than late fees and pet fees) and, if the tenant pays separately for utilities, the monthly allowance for utilities (excluding telephone) established by the public housing authority for the area in which the housing is located.

(e) *Rental assistance agreement.* The recipient or subrecipient may make rental assistance payments only to an owner with whom the recipient or subrecipient has entered into a rental assistance agreement. The rental assistance agreement must set forth the terms under which rental assistance will be provided, including the requirements that apply under this section. The rental assistance agreement must provide that, during the term of the agreement, the owner must give the recipient or subrecipient a copy of any notice to the program participant to vacate the housing unit or any complaint used under State or local law to commence an eviction action against the program participant. Each rental assistance agreement that is executed or renewed on or after *December 16, 2016* must include all protections that apply to tenants and applicants under 24 CFR part 5, subpart L, as supplemented by § 576.409, except for the emergency transfer plan requirements under 24 CFR 5.2005(e) and 576.409(d). If the housing is not assisted under another "covered housing program", as defined in 24 CFR 5.2003, the agreement may provide that the owner's obligations under 24 CFR part 5, subpart L (Protection for Victims of Domestic Violence, Dating

Violence, Sexual Assault, or Stalking), expire at the end of the rental assistance period.

(f) *Late payments*. The recipient or subrecipient must make timely payments to each owner in accordance with the rental assistance agreement. The rental assistance agreement must contain the same payment due date, grace period, and late payment penalty requirements as the program participant's lease. The recipient or subrecipient is solely responsible for paying late payment penalties that it incurs with non-ESG funds.

(g) *Lease*. Each program participant receiving rental assistance must have a legally binding, written lease for the rental unit, unless the assistance is solely for rental arrears. The lease must be between the owner and the program participant. Where the assistance is solely for rental arrears, an oral agreement may be accepted in place of a written lease, if the agreement gives the program participant an enforceable leasehold interest under state law and the agreement and rent owed are sufficiently documented by the owner's financial records, rent ledgers, or canceled checks. For program participants living in housing with project-based rental assistance under paragraph (i) of this section, the lease must have an initial term of 1 year. Each lease executed on or after *December 16, 2016* must include a lease provision or incorporate a lease addendum that includes all requirements that apply to tenants, the owner or lease under 24 CFR part 5, subpart L (Protection for Victims of Domestic Violence, Dating Violence, Sexual Assault, or Stalking), as supplemented by 24 CFR 576.409, including the prohibited bases for eviction and restrictions on construing lease terms under 24 CFR 5.2005(b) and (c). If the housing is not assisted under another "covered housing program," as defined in 24 CFR 5.2003, the lease provision or lease addendum may be written to expire at the end of the rental assistance period.

(h) *Tenant-based rental assistance*. (1) A program participant who receives tenant-based rental assistance may select a housing unit in which to live and may move to another unit or building and continue to receive rental assistance, as long as the program participant continues to meet the program requirements.

(2) The recipient may require that all program participants live within a particular area for the period in which the rental assistance is provided.

(3) The rental assistance agreement with the owner must terminate and no further rental assistance payments under that agreement may be made if:

(i) The program participant moves out of the housing unit for which the program participant has a lease;

(ii) The lease terminates and is not renewed; or

(iii) The program participant becomes ineligible to receive ESG rental assistance.

(i) *Project-based rental assistance*. If the recipient or subrecipient identifies a permanent housing unit that meets ESG requirements and becomes available before a program participant is identified to lease the unit, the recipient or subrecipient may enter into a rental assistance agreement with the owner to reserve the unit and subsidize its rent in accordance with the following requirements:

(1) The rental assistance agreement may cover one or more permanent housing units in the same building. Each unit covered by the rental assistance agreement ("assisted unit") may only be occupied by program participants, except as provided under paragraph (i)(4) of this section.

(2) The recipient or subrecipient may pay up to 100 percent of the first month's rent, provided that a program participant signs a lease and moves into the unit before the end of the month for which the first month's rent is paid. The rent paid before a program participant moves into the unit must not exceed the rent to be charged under the program participant's lease and must be included when determining that program participant's total rental assistance.

(3) The recipient or subrecipient may make monthly rental assistance payments only for each whole or partial month an assisted unit is leased to a program participant. When a program participant moves out of an assisted unit, the recipient or subrecipient may pay the next month's rent, *i.e.*, the first

month's rent for a new program participant, as provided in paragraph (i)(2) of this section.

(4) The program participant's lease must not condition the term of occupancy to the provision of rental assistance payments. If the program participant is determined ineligible or reaches the maximum number of months over which rental assistance can be provided, the recipient or subrecipient must suspend or terminate the rental assistance payments for the unit. If the payments are suspended, the individual or family may remain in the assisted unit as permitted under the lease, and the recipient or subrecipient may resume payments if the individual or family again becomes eligible and needs further rental assistance. If the payments are terminated, the rental assistance may be transferred to another available unit in the same building, provided that the other unit meets all ESG requirements.

(5) The rental assistance agreement must have an initial term of one year. When a new program participant moves into an assisted unit, the term of the rental assistance agreement may be extended to cover the initial term of the program participant's lease. If the program participant's lease is renewed, the rental assistance agreement may be renewed or extended, as needed, up to the maximum number of months for which the program participant remains eligible. However, under no circumstances may the recipient or subrecipient commit ESG funds to be expended beyond the expenditure deadline in §576.203 or commit funds for a future ESG grant before the grant is awarded.

(j) *Changes in household composition.* The limits on the assistance under this section apply to the total assistance an individual receives, either as an individual or as part of a family.

[76 FR 75974, Dec. 5, 2011,, as amended at 81 FR 80808, Nov. 16, 2016]

§576.107 HMIS component.

(a) *Eligible costs.* (1) The recipient or subrecipient may use ESG funds to pay the costs of contributing data to the HMIS designated by the Continuum of Care for the area, including the costs of:

(i) Purchasing or leasing computer hardware;

(ii) Purchasing software or software licenses;

(iii) Purchasing or leasing equipment, including telephones, fax machines, and furniture;

(iv) Obtaining technical support;

(v) Leasing office space;

(vi) Paying charges for electricity, gas, water, phone service, and high-speed data transmission necessary to operate or contribute data to the HMIS;

(vii) Paying salaries for operating HMIS, including:

(A) Completing data entry;

(B) Monitoring and reviewing data quality;

(C) Completing data analysis;

(D) Reporting to the HMIS Lead;

(F) Training staff on using the HMIS or comparable database; and

(G) Implementing and complying with HMIS requirements;

(viii) Paying costs of staff to travel to and attend HUD-sponsored and HUD-approved training on HMIS and programs authorized by Title IV of the McKinney-Vento Homeless Assistance Act;

(ix) Paying staff travel costs to conduct intake; and

(x) Paying participation fees charged by the HMIS Lead, if the recipient or subrecipient is not the HMIS Lead. The HMIS Lead is the entity designated by the Continuum of Care to operate the area's HMIS.

(2) If the recipient is the HMIS lead agency, as designated by the Continuum of Care in the most recent fiscal year Continuum of Care Homeless Assistance Grants Competition, it may also use ESG funds to pay the costs of:

(i) Hosting and maintaining HMIS software or data;

(ii) Backing up, recovering, or repairing HMIS software or data;

(iii) Upgrading, customizing, and enhancing the HMIS;

(iv) Integrating and warehousing data, including development of a data warehouse for use in aggregating data from subrecipients using multiple software systems;

(v) Administering the system;

(vi) Reporting to providers, the Continuum of Care, and HUD; and

(vii) Conducting training on using the system or a comparable database, including traveling to the training.

(3) If the subrecipient is a victim services provider or a legal services provider, it may use ESG funds to establish and operate a comparable database that collects client-level data over time (*i.e.*, longitudinal data) and generates unduplicated aggregate reports based on the data. Information entered into a comparable database must not be entered directly into or provided to an HMIS.

(b) *General restrictions.* Activities funded under this section must comply with HUD's standards on participation, data collection, and reporting under a local HMIS.

§ 576.108 Administrative activities.

(a) *Eligible costs.* The recipient may use up to 7.5 percent of its ESG grant for the payment of administrative costs related to the planning and execution of ESG activities. This does not include staff and overhead costs directly related to carrying out activities eligible under § 576.101 through § 576.107, because those costs are eligible as part of those activities. Eligible administrative costs include:

(1) *General management, oversight and coordination.* Costs of overall program management, coordination, monitoring, and evaluation. These costs include, but are not limited to, necessary expenditures for the following:

(i) Salaries, wages, and related costs of the recipient's staff, the staff of subrecipients, or other staff engaged in program administration. In charging costs to this category, the recipient may either include the entire salary, wages, and related costs allocable to the program of each person whose *primary* responsibilities with regard to the program involve program administration assignments, or the pro rata share of the salary, wages, and related costs of each person whose job includes *any* program administration assignments. The recipient may use only one of these methods for each fiscal year grant. Program administration assignments include the following:

(A) Preparing program budgets and schedules, and amendments to those budgets and schedules;

(B) Developing systems for assuring compliance with program requirements;

(C) Developing interagency agreements and agreements with subrecipients and contractors to carry out program activities;

(D) Monitoring program activities for progress and compliance with program requirements;

(E) Preparing reports and other documents directly related to the program for submission to HUD;

(F) Coordinating the resolution of audit and monitoring findings;

(G) Evaluating program results against stated objectives; and

(H) Managing or supervising persons whose primary responsibilities with regard to the program include such assignments as those described in paragraph (a)(1)(i)(A) through (G) of this section.

(ii) Travel costs incurred for monitoring of subrecipients;

(iii) Administrative services performed under third-party contracts or agreements, including general legal services, accounting services, and audit services; and

(iv) Other costs for goods and services required for administration of the program, including rental or purchase of equipment, insurance, utilities, office supplies, and rental and maintenance (but not purchase) of office space.

(2) *Training on ESG requirements.* Costs of providing training on ESG requirements and attending HUD-sponsored ESG trainings.

(3) *Consolidated plan.* Costs of preparing and amending the ESG and homelessness-related sections of the consolidated plan in accordance with ESG requirements and 24 CFR part 91.

(4) *Environmental review.* Costs of carrying out the environmental review responsibilities under § 576.407.

(b) *Sharing requirement.* (1) *States.* If the recipient is a State, the recipient must share its funds for administrative costs with its subrecipients that are units of general purpose local government. The amount shared must be reasonable under the circumstances. The recipient may share its funds for administrative costs with its subrecipients that are private nonprofit organizations.

(2) *Territories, metropolitan cities, and urban counties.* If the recipient is a territory, metropolitan city, or urban county, the recipient may share its funds for administrative costs with its subrecipients.

§576.109 Indirect costs.

(a) *In general.* ESG grant funds may be used to pay indirect costs in accordance with 2 CFR part 200, subpart E.

(b) *Allocation.* Indirect costs may be allocated to each eligible activity under §576.101 through §576.108, so long as that allocation is consistent with 2 CFR part 200, subpart E.

(c) *Expenditure limits.* The indirect costs charged to an activity subject to an expenditure limit under §576.100 must be added to the direct costs charged for that activity when determining the total costs subject to the expenditure limit.

[76 FR 75974, Dec. 5, 2011, as amended at 80 FR 75939, Dec. 7, 2015]

Subpart C—Award and Use of Funds

§576.200 Submission requirements and grant approval.

(a) *Application submission and approval.* In addition to meeting the application submission requirements in 24 CFR part 5, subpart K, each State, urban county, or metropolitan city must submit and obtain HUD approval of a consolidated plan in accordance with the requirements in 24 CFR part 91, and each territory must submit and obtain HUD approval of a consolidated plan in accordance with the requirements that apply to local governments under 24 CFR part 91. As provided under 2 CFR 200.207, HUD may impose special conditions or restrictions on a grant, if the recipient is determined to be high risk.

(b) *Amendments.* The recipient must amend its approved consolidated plan in order to make a change in its allocation priorities; make a change in its method of distributing funds; carry out an activity not previously described in the plan; or change the purpose, scope, location, or beneficiaries of an activity. The amendment must be completed and submitted to HUD in accordance with the requirements under 24 CFR 91.505.

[76 FR 75974, Dec. 5, 2011, as amended at 80 FR 75939, Dec. 7, 2015]

§576.201 Matching requirement.

(a) The recipient must make matching contributions to supplement the recipient's ESG program in an amount that equals the recipient's fiscal year grant for ESG. This amount may include contributions to any project under the recipient's ESG program, including any subrecipient's ESG project, if the requirements in this section are met. The first $100,000 of a State's fiscal year grant is not required to be matched, but the benefit of this exception must pass to the state's subrecipients that are least capable of providing matching contributions. The match requirements under this section do not apply if the recipient is a territory.

(b) To be recognized as match for ESG, each contribution must meet the requirements under 2 CFR 200.306, except that:

(1) Notwithstanding 2 CFR 200.306(b)(4), matching contributions are not subject to the expenditure limits in §576.100; and

(2) Notwithstanding 2 CFR 200.306(b)(5), the recipient may use funds from another Federal program as match for ESG, unless doing so would violate a specific statutory prohibition or the recipient or subrecipient counts ESG funds as match for that program.

(c) The recipient may count as match the value specified in 2 CFR 200.306(d) for any building the recipient or subrecipient donates for long-term use in the recipient's ESG program, provided that depreciation on the building is not counted as match or charged to any Federal award. If a third party donates a building to the recipient or subrecipient, the recipient may count as match either depreciation of the building and fair rental charges for the land for each year the building is used for the recipient's ESG program or, if the building is donated for long-term use in the recipient's ESG program, the fair market value of the capital assets, as specified in 2 CFR 200.306(h)(2), (i), and (j). To qualify as a donation for long-term use, the donation must be evidenced by a recorded deed or use restriction that is effective for at least 10 years after the donation date. If the donated building is renovated with ESG funds, the minimum period of use under § 576.102(c) may increase the period for which the building must be used in the recipient's ESG program.

(d) *Eligible types of matching contributions.* The matching requirement may be met by one or both of the following:

(1) *Cash contributions.* Cash expended for allowable costs, as defined in OMB Circulars A–87 (2 CFR part 225) and A–122 (2 CFR part 230), of the recipient or subrecipient.

(2) *Noncash contributions.* The value of any real property, equipment, goods, or services contributed to the recipient's or subrecipient's ESG program, provided that if the recipient or subrecipient had to pay for them with grant funds, the costs would have been allowable. Noncash contributions may also include the purchase value of any donated building.

(e) *Calculating the amount of noncash contributions.* (1) To determine the value of any donated material or building, or of any lease, the recipient must use a method reasonably calculated to establish the fair market value.

(2) Services provided by individuals must be valued at rates consistent with those ordinarily paid for similar work in the recipient's or subrecipient's organization. If the recipient or subrecipient does not have employees performing similar work, the rates must be consistent with those ordinarily paid by other employers for similar work in the same labor market.

(3) Some noncash contributions are real property, equipment, goods, or services that, if the recipient or subrecipient had to pay for them with grant funds, the payments would have been indirect costs. Matching credit for these contributions must be given only if the recipient or subrecipient has established, along with its regular indirect cost rate, a special rate for allocating to individual projects or programs the value of those contributions.

(f) *Costs paid by program income.* Costs paid by program income shall count toward meeting the recipient's matching requirements, provided the costs are eligible ESG costs that supplement the recipient's ESG program.

[76 FR 75974, Dec. 5, 2011, as amended at 80 FR 75939, Dec. 7, 2015]

§ 576.202 Means of carrying out grant activities.

(a) *States.* If the recipient is a State, the recipient may use an amount consistent with the restrictions in § 576.100 and § 576.108 to carry out administrative activities through its employees or procurement contracts. If the recipient is a State, and has been identified as the HMIS lead by the Continuum of Care, the State may use funds to carry out HMIS activities set forth in § 576.107(a)(2). The recipient must subgrant the remaining funds in its fiscal year grant to:

(1) Units of general purpose local government in the State, which may include metropolitan cities and urban counties that receive ESG funds directly from HUD; or

(2) Private nonprofit organizations, provided that for emergency shelter activities the recipient obtains a certification of approval from the unit of general purpose local government for the geographic area in which those activities are to be carried out.

(b) *Recipients other than States; subrecipients.* The recipient, if it is not a State, and all subrecipients may carry out all eligible activities through their employees, procurement contracts, or subgrants to private nonprofit organizations. If the recipient is an urban county, it may carry out activities through any of its member governments, so long as the county applies to its members the same requirements that are applicable to local government subrecipients under this part.

§ 576.203 Obligation, expenditure, and payment requirements.

(a) *Obligation of funds.* (1) *Funds allocated to States.* (i) Within 60 days from the date that HUD signs the grant agreement with the State (or grant amendment for reallocated funds), the recipient must obligate the entire grant, except the amount for its administrative costs. This requirement is met by a subgrant agreement with, or a letter of award requiring payment from the grant to, a subrecipient.

(ii) Within 120 days after the date that the State obligates its funds to a unit of general purpose local government, the subrecipient must obligate all of those funds by a subgrant agreement with, or a letter of award requiring payment to, a private nonprofit organization; a procurement contract; or the written designation of a department within the government of the subrecipient to directly carry out an eligible activity.

(2) *Funds allocated to metropolitan cities, urban counties, and territories.* Within 180 days after the date that HUD signs the grant agreement (or a grant amendment for reallocation of funds) with the metropolitan city, urban county, or territory, the recipient must obligate all the grant amount, except the amount for its administrative costs. This requirement is met by an agreement with, or a letter of award requiring payment to, a subrecipient; a procurement contract; or a written designation of a department within the government of the recipient to directly carry out an eligible activity. If the recipient is an urban county, this requirement may also be met with an agreement with, or letter of award requiring payment to, a member government, which has designated a department to directly carry out an eligible activity.

(b) *Expenditures.* The recipient must draw down and expend funds from each year's grant not less than once during each quarter of the recipient's program year. All of the recipient's grant must be expended for eligible activity costs within 24 months after the date HUD signs the grant agreement with the recipient. For the purposes of this paragraph, expenditure means either an actual cash disbursement for a direct charge for a good or service or an indirect cost or the accrual of a direct charge for a good or service or an indirect cost.

(c) *Payments to subrecipients.* The recipient must pay each subrecipient for allowable costs within 30 days after receiving the subrecipient's complete payment request. This requirement also applies to each subrecipient that is a unit of general purpose local government.

Subpart D—Reallocations

§ 576.300 In general.

(1) Funds not awarded by HUD due to failure by the recipient to submit and obtain HUD approval of a consolidated plan will be reallocated in accordance with §§ 576.301 through 576.303.

(2) Recaptured funds will be awarded by formula. In October and April each year, HUD will determine if the amount of recaptured funds is at least 30 percent of the most recent fiscal year appropriation. If so, HUD will amend all existing grants and reallocate the funds. If the amount is less than 30 percent of the most recent fiscal year appropriation, the funds will be reallocated in conjunction with the next fiscal year's allocation of funding.

§ 576.301 Metropolitan cities and urban counties.

Grant funds returned by a metropolitan city or urban county will be reallocated as follows:

(a) *Eligible recipient.* HUD will make the funds available to the State in which the city or county is located.

(b) *Notification of availability.* HUD will promptly notify the State of the availability of the amounts to be reallocated.

(c) *Application requirement.* Within 45 days after the date of notification, the State must submit to HUD a substantial amendment to its consolidated plan in accordance with 24 CFR part 91.

(d) *Restrictions that apply to reallocated amounts.* The same requirements that apply to grant funds allocated under § 576.3 apply to grant funds reallocated under this section, except that the State must distribute the reallocated funds:

(1) To private nonprofit organizations and units of general purpose local government in the geographic area in which the metropolitan city or urban county is located;

(2) If funds remain, to private nonprofit organizations and units of general purpose local government located throughout the State.

§ 576.302 States.

Grant funds returned by a State will be reallocated as follows:

(a) *Eligible recipients.* HUD will make the funds available:

(1) To metropolitan cities and urban counties in the State that were not allocated funds under § 576.3 because the amount they would have been allocated did not meet the minimum requirement under § 576.3(b)(2);

(2) If funds remain, to county governments in the State other than urban counties;

(3) Then, if funds remain, to metropolitan cities and urban counties in the State that were allocated funds under § 576.3.

(b) *Notification of availability.* HUD will notify eligible recipients of the availability of the funds by a notification letter or FEDERAL REGISTER notice, which will specify how the awards of funds will be made.

(c) *Application requirements.* Within 45 days after the date of notification, the eligible recipient must submit to HUD:

(1) A substantial amendment to its approved consolidated plan in accordance with 24 CFR part 91; or

(2) If the eligible recipient does not have an approved consolidated plan, an abbreviated consolidated plan that meets the requirements in the FEDERAL REGISTER notice or notification letter from HUD.

(d) *Restrictions that apply to reallocated amounts.* The same requirements that apply to grant funds allocated under § 576.3 apply to grant funds reallocated under this section.

§ 576.303 Territories.

(a) *General.* Grant funds returned by a territory will be reallocated to other territories, then if funds remain, to States.

(b) *Allocation method.* The funds will be allocated as follows:

(1) For territories, the funds will be allocated among the territories in direct proportion with each territory's share of the total population of all of the eligible territories. If HUD determines that a territory failed to spend its funds in accordance with ESG requirements, then HUD may exclude the territory from the allocation of reallocation amounts under this section.

(2) For States, the funds will be allocated to each State in direct proportion with each State's share of the total amount of funds allocated to States under § 576.3.

(c) *Notification of availability.* HUD will notify eligible recipients of the availability of the fund by a letter or FEDERAL REGISTER notice, which will specify how the awards of funds will be made.

(d) *Application requirements.* Within 45 days after the date of notification, the eligible recipient must submit to HUD a substantial amendment to its consolidated plan in accordance with 24 CFR part 91.

(e) *Restrictions that apply to reallocated amounts.* The same requirements that apply to grant funds allocated under § 576.3 apply to grant funds reallocated under this section.

Subpart E—Program Requirements

§ 576.400 Area-wide systems coordination requirements.

(a) *Consultation with Continuums of Care.* The recipient must consult with each Continuum of Care that serves the recipient's jurisdiction in determining how to allocate ESG funds each program year; developing the performance standards for, and evaluating the outcomes of, projects and activities assisted by ESG funds; and developing funding, policies, and procedures for the administration and operation of the HMIS.

(b) *Coordination with other targeted homeless services.* The recipient and its subrecipients must coordinate and integrate, to the maximum extent practicable, ESG-funded activities with other programs targeted to homeless people in the area covered by the Continuum of Care or area over which the services are coordinated to provide a strategic, community-wide system to prevent and end homelessness for that area. These programs include:

(1) Shelter Plus Care Program (24 CFR part 582);

(2) Supportive Housing Program (24 CFR part 583);

(3) Section 8 Moderate Rehabilitation Program for Single Room Occupancy Program for Homeless Individuals (24 CFR part 882);

(4) HUD—Veterans Affairs Supportive Housing (HUD–VASH) (division K, title II, Consolidated Appropriations Act, 2008, Pub. L. 110–161 (2007), 73 FR 25026 (May 6, 2008));

(5) Education for Homeless Children and Youth Grants for State and Local Activities (title VII–B of the McKinney-Vento Homeless Assistance Act (42 U.S.C. 11431 *et seq.*));

(6) Grants for the Benefit of Homeless Individuals (section 506 of the Public Health Services Act (42 U.S.C. 290aa–5));

(7) Healthcare for the Homeless (42 CFR part 51c);

(8) Programs for Runaway and Homeless Youth (Runaway and Homeless Youth Act (42 U.S.C. 5701 *et seq.*));

(9) Projects for Assistance in Transition from Homelessness (part C of title V of the Public Health Service Act (42 U.S.C. 290cc–21 *et seq.*));

(10) Services in Supportive Housing Grants (section 520A of the Public Health Service Act);

(11) Emergency Food and Shelter Program (title III of the McKinney-Vento Homeless Assistance Act (42 U.S.C. 11331 *et seq.*));

(12) Transitional Housing Assistance Grants for Victims of Sexual Assault, Domestic Violence, Dating Violence, and Stalking Program (section 40299 of the Violent Crime Control and Law Enforcement Act (42 U.S.C. 13975));

(13) Homeless Veterans Reintegration Program (section 5(a)(1)) of the Homeless Veterans Comprehensive Assistance Act (38 U.S.C. 2021);

(14) Domiciliary Care for Homeless Veterans Program (38 U.S.C. 2043);

(15) VA Homeless Providers Grant and Per Diem Program (38 CFR part 61);

(16) Health Care for Homeless Veterans Program (38 U.S.C. 2031);

(17) Homeless Veterans Dental Program (38 U.S.C. 2062);

(18) Supportive Services for Veteran Families Program (38 CFR part 62); and

(19) Veteran Justice Outreach Initiative (38 U.S.C. 2031).

(c) *System and program coordination with mainstream resources.* The recipient and its subrecipients must coordinate and integrate, to the maximum extent practicable, ESG-funded activities with mainstream housing, health, social services, employment, education, and youth programs for which families and individuals at risk of homelessness and homeless individuals and families may be eligible. Examples of these programs include:

(1) Public housing programs assisted under section 9 of the U.S. Housing Act of 1937 (42 U.S.C. 1437g) (24 CFR parts 905, 968, and 990);

(2) Housing programs receiving tenant-based or project-based assistance under section 8 of the U.S. Housing Act of 1937 (42 U.S.C. 1437f) (respectively 24 CFR parts 982 and 983);

(3) Supportive Housing for Persons with Disabilities (Section 811) (24 CFR part 891);

(4) HOME Investment Partnerships Program (24 CFR part 92);

(5) Temporary Assistance for Needy Families (TANF) (45 CFR parts 260–265);

(6) Health Center Program (42 CFR part 51c);

(7) State Children's Health Insurance Program (42 CFR part 457):

(8) Head Start (45 CFR chapter XIII, subchapter B);

(9) Mental Health and Substance Abuse Block Grants (45 CFR part 96); and

(10) Services funded under the Workforce Investment Act (29 U.S.C. 2801 *et seq.*).

(d) *Centralized or coordinated assessment.* Once the Continuum of Care has developed a centralized assessment system or a coordinated assessment system in accordance with requirements to be established by HUD, each ESG-funded program or project within the Continuum of Care's area must use that assessment system. The recipient and subrecipient must work with the Continuum of Care to ensure the screening, assessment and referral of program participants are consistent with the written standards required by paragraph (e) of this section. A victim service provider may choose not to use the Continuum of Care's centralized or coordinated assessment system.

(e) *Written standards for providing ESG assistance.* (1) If the recipient is a metropolitan city, urban county, or territory, the recipient must have written standards for providing Emergency Solutions Grant (ESG) assistance and must consistently apply those standards for all program participants. The recipient must describe these standards in its consolidated plan.

(2) If the recipient is a state:

(i) The recipient must establish and consistently apply, or require that its subrecipients establish and consistently apply, written standards for providing ESG assistance. If the written standards are established by the subrecipients, the recipient may require these written standards to be:

(A) Established for each area covered by a Continuum of Care or area over which the services are coordinated and followed by each subrecipient providing assistance in that area; or

(B) Established by each subrecipient and applied consistently within the subrecipient's program.

(ii) Written standards developed by the state must be included in the state's Consolidated Plan. If the written standards are developed by its subrecipients, the recipient must describe its requirements for the establishment and implementation of these standards in the state's Consolidated Plan.

(3) At a minimum these written standards must include:

(i) Standard policies and procedures for evaluating individuals' and families' eligibility for assistance under Emergency Solutions Grant (ESG);

(ii) Standards for targeting and providing essential services related to street outreach;

(iii) Policies and procedures for admission, diversion, referral, and discharge by emergency shelters assisted under ESG, including standards regarding length of stay, if any, and safeguards to meet the safety and shelter needs of special populations, *e.g.*, victims of domestic violence, dating violence, sexual assault, and stalking; and individuals and families who have the highest barriers to housing and are likely to be homeless the longest;

(iv) Policies and procedures for assessing, prioritizing, and reassessing individuals' and families' needs for essential services related to emergency shelter;

(v) Policies and procedures for coordination among emergency shelter providers, essential services providers, homelessness prevention, and rapid re-housing assistance providers; other homeless assistance providers; and mainstream service and housing providers (see § 576.400(b) and (c) for a list of programs with which ESG-funded activities must be coordinated and integrated to the maximum extent practicable);

(vi) Policies and procedures for determining and prioritizing which eligible families and individuals will receive homelessness prevention assistance and which eligible families and individuals will receive rapid re-housing assistance (these policies must include the emergency transfer priority required under § 576.409);

(vii) Standards for determining what percentage or amount of rent and utilities costs each program participant must pay while receiving homelessness prevention or rapid re-housing assistance;

(viii) Standards for determining how long a particular program participant will be provided with rental assistance and whether and how the amount of that assistance will be adjusted over time; and

(ix) Standards for determining the type, amount, and duration of housing stabilization and/or relocation services to provide to a program participant, including the limits, if any, on the homelessness prevention or rapid re-housing assistance that each program participant may receive, such as the maximum amount of assistance, maximum number of months the program participant receive assistance; or the maximum number of times the program participant may receive assistance.

(f) *Participation in HMIS.* The recipient must ensure that data on all persons served and all activities assisted under ESG are entered into the applicable community-wide HMIS in the area in which those persons and activities are located, or a comparable database, in accordance with HUD's standards on participation, data collection, and reporting under a local HMIS. If the subrecipient is a victim service provider or a legal services provider, it may use a comparable database that collects client-level data over time (*i.e.*, longitudinal data) and generates unduplicated aggregate reports based on the data. Information entered into a comparable database must not be entered directly into or provided to an HMIS.

[76 FR 75974, Dec. 5, 2011, as amended at 81 FR 80808, Nov. 16, 2016]

§576.401 Evaluation of program participant eligibility and needs.

(a) *Evaluations.* The recipient or its subrecipient must conduct an initial evaluation to determine the eligibility of each individual or family's eligibility for ESG assistance and the amount and types of assistance the individual or family needs to regain stability in permanent housing. These evaluations must be conducted in accordance with the centralized or coordinated assessment requirements set forth under §576.400(d) and the written standards established under §576.400(e).

(b) *Re-evaluations for homelessness prevention and rapid re-housing assistance.* (1) The recipient or subrecipient must re-evaluate the program participant's eligibility and the types and amounts of assistance the program participant needs not less than once every 3 months for program participants receiving homelessness prevention assistance, and not less than once annually for program participants receiving rapid re-housing assistance. At a minimum, each re-evaluation of eligibility must establish that:

(i) The program participant does not have an annual income that exceeds 30 percent of median family income for the area, as determined by HUD; and

(ii) The program participant lacks sufficient resources and support networks necessary to retain housing without ESG assistance.

(2) The recipient or subrecipient may require each program participant receiving homelessness prevention or rapid re-housing assistance to notify the recipient or subrecipient regarding changes in the program participant's income or other circumstances (*e.g.*, changes in household composition) that affect the program participant's need for assistance under ESG. When notified of a relevant change, the recipient or subrecipient must re-evaluate the program participant's eligibility and the amount and types of assistance the program participant needs.

(c) *Annual income.* When determining the annual income of an individual or family, the recipient or subrecipient must use the standard for calculating annual income under 24 CFR 5.609.

(d) *Connecting program participants to mainstream and other resources.* The recipient and its subrecipients must assist each program participant, as needed, to obtain:

(1) Appropriate supportive services, including assistance in obtaining permanent housing, medical health treatment, mental health treatment, counseling, supervision, and other services essential for achieving independent living; and

(2) Other Federal, State, local, and private assistance available to assist the program participant in obtaining housing stability, including:

(i) Medicaid (42 CFR chapter IV, subchapter C):

(ii) Supplemental Nutrition Assistance Program (7 CFR parts 271–283);

(iii) Women, Infants and Children (WIC) (7 CFR part 246);

(iv) Federal-State Unemployment Insurance Program (20 CFR parts 601–603, 606, 609, 614–617, 625, 640, 650);

(v) Social Security Disability Insurance (SSDI) (20 CFR part 404);

(vi) Supplemental Security Income (SSI) (20 CFR part 416);

(vii) Child and Adult Care Food Program (42 U.S.C. 1766(t) (7 CFR part 226));

(viii) Other assistance available under the programs listed in §576.400(c).

(e) *Housing stability case management.* (1) While providing homelessness prevention or rapid re-housing assistance to a program participant, the recipient or subrecipient must:

(i) Require the program participant to meet with a case manager not less than once per month to assist the program participant in ensuring long-term housing stability; and

(ii) Develop a plan to assist the program participant to retain permanent housing after the ESG assistance ends, taking into account all relevant considerations, such as the program participant's current or expected income and expenses; other public or private assistance for which the program participant will be eligible and likely to receive; and the relative affordability of available housing in the area.

(2) The recipient or subrecipient is exempt from the requirement under paragraph (e)(1)(i) of this section if the Violence Against Women Act of 1994 (42 U.S.C. 13701 *et seq.*) or the Family Violence Prevention and Services Act (42 U.S.C. 10401 *et seq.*) prohibits that recipient or subrecipient from making its shelter or housing conditional on the participant's acceptance of services.

§ 576.402 Terminating assistance.

(a) *In general.* If a program participant violates program requirements, the recipient or subrecipient may terminate the assistance in accordance with a formal process established by the recipient or subrecipient that recognizes the rights of individuals affected. The recipient or subrecipient must exercise judgment and examine all extenuating circumstances in determining when violations warrant termination so that a program participant's assistance is terminated only in the most severe cases.

(b) *Program participants receiving rental assistance or housing relocation and stabilization services.* To terminate rental assistance or housing relocation and stabilization services to a program participant, the required formal process, at a minimum, must consist of:

(1) Written notice to the program participant containing a clear statement of the reasons for termination;

(2) A review of the decision, in which the program participant is given the opportunity to present written or oral objections before a person other than the person (or a subordinate of that person) who made or approved the termination decision; and

(3) Prompt written notice of the final decision to the program participant.

(c) *Ability to provide further assistance.* Termination under this section does not bar the recipient or subrecipient from providing further assistance at a later date to the same family or individual.

§ 576.403 Shelter and housing standards.

(a) *Lead-based paint remediation and disclosure.* The Lead-Based Paint Poisoning Prevention Act (42 U.S.C. 4821–4846), the Residential Lead-Based Paint Hazard Reduction Act of 1992 (42 U.S.C. 4851–4856), and implementing regulations in 24 CFR part 35, subparts A, B, H, J, K, M, and R apply to all shelters assisted under ESG program and all housing occupied by program participants.

(b) *Minimum standards for emergency shelters.* Any building for which Emergency Solutions Grant (ESG) funds are used for conversion, major rehabilitation, or other renovation, must meet state or local government safety and sanitation standards, as applicable, and the following minimum safety, sanitation, and privacy standards. Any emergency shelter that receives assistance for shelter operations must also meet the following minimum safety, sanitation, and privacy standards. The recipient may also establish standards that exceed or add to these minimum standards.

(1) *Structure and materials.* The shelter building must be structurally sound to protect residents from the elements and not pose any threat to health and safety of the residents. Any renovation (including major rehabilitation and conversion) carried out with ESG assistance must use Energy Star and WaterSense products and appliances.

(2) *Access.* The shelter must be accessible in accordance with Section 504 of the Rehabilitation Act (29 U.S.C. 794) and implementing regulations at 24 CFR part 8; the Fair Housing Act (42 U.S.C. 3601 *et seq.*) and implementing regulations at 24 CFR part 100; and Title II of the Americans with Disabilities Act (42 U.S.C. 12131 *et seq.*) and 28 CFR part 35; where applicable.

(3) *Space and security.* Except where the shelter is intended for day use only, the shelter must provide each program participant in the shelter with an acceptable place to sleep and adequate space and security for themselves and their belongings.

(4) *Interior air quality.* Each room or space within the shelter must have a natural or mechanical means of ventilation. The interior air must be free of pollutants at a level that might threaten or harm the health of residents.

(5) *Water supply.* The shelter's water supply must be free of contamination.

(6) *Sanitary facilities.* Each program participant in the shelter must have access to sanitary facilities that are in proper operating condition, are private, and are adequate for personal cleanliness and the disposal of human waste.

(7) *Thermal environment.* The shelter must have any necessary heating/cooling facilities in proper operating condition.

(8) *Illumination and electricity.* The shelter must have adequate natural or artificial illumination to permit normal indoor activities and support health and safety. There must be sufficient electrical sources to permit the safe use of electrical appliances in the shelter.

(9) *Food preparation.* Food preparation areas, if any, must contain suitable space and equipment to store, prepare, and serve food in a safe and sanitary manner.

(10) *Sanitary conditions.* The shelter must be maintained in a sanitary condition.

(11) *Fire safety.* There must be at least one working smoke detector in each occupied unit of the shelter. Where possible, smoke detectors must be located near sleeping areas. The fire alarm system must be designed for hearing-impaired residents. All public areas of the shelter must have at least one working smoke detector. There must also be a second means of exiting the building in the event of fire or other emergency.

(c) *Minimum standards for permanent housing.* When ESG funds are used for permanent housing under 24 CFR 576.105 or 576.106, the minimum standards in 24 CFR 5.703 apply, except that:

(1) *Definition of HUD housing.* For the purposes of ESG, "HUD housing" in 24 CFR 5.703 means the program participant's unit, systems equipment that directly services those units, items and components within the primary and secondary means of egress from those units' doors to the public way, and common features related to the program participant's use of the building (e.g., the laundry room, community room, mail room).

(2) *Housing inspections.* For the first 30 days in which a program participant receives homelessness prevention assistance, the recipient or subrecipient may provide services under 24 CFR 576.105(b) to help the program participant remain in their unit without inspecting the unit to determine whether it meets the minimum standards identified in this paragraph (c), except that the recipient or subrecipient must still comply with the requirements under 24 CFR part 35. Before otherwise using ESG funds under 24 CFR 576.105 or 576.106 to help a program participant remain in or move into specific housing, however, the recipient or subrecipient must inspect that housing to confirm that it meets the requirements in this section. In addition, recipient or subrecipient must inspect the housing at least once every 12 months during the period of assistance to confirm the housing continues to meet the minimum standards in this paragraph (c).

(3) *Correction of deficiencies.* If an inspection reveals one or more deficiencies that prevent the housing from meeting the requirements in this section, ESG funds must not be used under 24 CFR 576.105 or 576.106 with respect to that housing unless the owner corrects the deficiencies within 30 days from the date of the initial inspection and the recipient or subrecipient verifies that all deficiencies have been corrected.

(4) *Rental arrears.* Housing for which rental arrears are paid is only subject to the requirements in this section, if a program participant is seeking to stay in that housing.

(5) *Additional standards.* The recipient may also add standards that exceed these minimum standards.

(6) *Other exemptions from 24 CFR part 5, subpart G.* The requirements in 24 CFR 5.703(b)(2) and (d)(6) and 5.705 through 5.713 do not apply.

[76 FR 75974, Dec. 5, 2011, as amended at 88 FR 30498, May 11, 2023]

§ 576.404 Conflicts of interest.

(a) *Organizational conflicts of interest.* The provision of any type or amount of ESG assistance may not be conditioned on an individual's or family's acceptance or occupancy of emergency shelter or housing owned by the recipient, the subrecipient, or a parent or subsidiary of the subrecipient. No subrecipient may, with respect to individuals or families occupying housing owned by the subrecipient, or any parent or subsidiary of the subrecipient, carry out the initial evaluation required under § 576.401 or administer homelessness prevention assistance under § 576.103. Recipients and subrecipients must also maintain written standards of conduct covering organizational conflicts of interest required under 2 CFR 200.318.

(b) *Individual conflicts of interest.* For the procurement of goods and services, the recipient and its subrecipients must comply with 2 CFR 200.317 and 200.318. For all other transactions and activities, the following restrictions apply:

(1) *Conflicts prohibited.* No person described in paragraph (b)(2) of this section who exercises or has exercised any functions or responsibilities with respect to activities assisted under the ESG program, or who is in a position to participate in a decision-making process or gain inside information with regard to activities assisted under the program, may obtain a financial interest or benefit from an assisted activity; have a financial interest in any contract, subcontract, or agreement with respect to an assisted activity; or have a financial interest in the proceeds derived from an assisted activity, either for him or herself or for those with whom he or she has family or business ties, during his or her tenure or during the one-year period following his or her tenure.

(2) *Persons covered.* The conflict-of-interest provisions of paragraph (b)(1) of this section apply to any person who is an employee, agent, consultant, officer, or elected or appointed official of the recipient or its subrecipients.

(3) *Exceptions.* Upon the written request of the recipient, HUD may grant an exception to the provisions of this subsection on a case-by-case basis, taking into account the cumulative effects of the criteria in paragraph (b)(3)(ii) of this section, provided that the recipient has satisfactorily met the threshold requirements of paragraph (b)(3)(i) of this section.

(i) *Threshold requirements.* HUD will consider an exception only after the recipient has provided the following documentation:

(A) If the recipient or subrecipient is a government, disclosure of the nature of the conflict, accompanied by an assurance that there has been public disclosure of the conflict and a description of how the public disclosure was made; and

(B) An opinion of the recipient's attorney that the interest for which the exception is sought would not violate state or local law.

(ii) *Factors to be considered for exceptions.* In determining whether to grant a requested exception after the recipient has satisfactorily met the threshold requirements under paragraph (b)(3)(i) of this section, HUD must conclude that the exception will serve to further the purposes of the ESG program and the effective and efficient administration of the recipient's or subrecipient's program or project, taking into account the cumulative effect of the following factors, as applicable:

(A) Whether the exception would provide a significant cost benefit or an essential degree of expertise to the program or project that would otherwise not be available;

(B) Whether an opportunity was provided for open competitive bidding or negotiation;

(C) Whether the affected person has withdrawn from his or her functions, responsibilities or the decision-making process with respect to the specific activity in question;

(D) Whether the interest or benefit was present before the affected person was in the position described in paragraph (b)(1) of this section;

(E) Whether undue hardship results to the recipient, the subrecipient, or the person affected, when weighed against the public interest served by avoiding the prohibited conflict; and

(F) Any other relevant considerations.

(c) *Contractors.* All contractors of the recipient or subrecipient must comply with the same requirements that apply to subrecipients under this section.

[76 FR 75974, Dec. 5, 2011, as amended at 80 FR 75939, Dec. 7, 2015]

§576.405 Homeless participation.

(a) Unless the recipient is a State, the recipient must provide for the participation of not less than one homeless individual or formerly homeless individual on the board of directors or other equivalent policy-making entity of the recipient, to the extent that the entity considers and makes policies and decisions regarding any facilities, services, or other assistance that receive funding under Emergency Solutions Grant (ESG).

(b) If the recipient is unable to meet requirement under paragraph (a), it must instead develop and implement a plan to consult with homeless or formerly homeless individuals in considering and making policies and decisions regarding any facilities, services, or other assistance that receive funding under Emergency Solutions Grant (ESG). The plan must be included in the annual action plan required under 24 CFR 91.220.

(c) To the maximum extent practicable, the recipient or subrecipient must involve homeless individuals and families in constructing, renovating, maintaining, and operating facilities assisted under ESG, in providing services assisted under ESG, and in providing services for occupants of facilities assisted under ESG. This involvement may include employment or volunteer services.

§576.406 Equal participation of faith-based organizations.

The HUD program requirements in §5.109 of this title apply to the ESG program, including the requirements regarding disposition and change in use of real property by a faith-based organization.

[81 FR 19418, Apr. 4, 2016]

§576.407 Other Federal requirements.

(a) *General.* The requirements in 24 CFR part 5, subpart A are applicable, including the nondiscrimination and equal opportunity requirements at 24 CFR 5.105(a) and the housing counseling requirements at 24 CFR 5.111. Section 3 of the Housing and Urban Development Act of 1968, 12 U.S.C. 1701u, and implementing regulations at 24 CFR part 75apply, except that homeless individuals have priority over other Section 3 residents in accordance with §576.405(c).

(b) *Affirmative outreach.* The recipient or subrecipient must make known that use of the facilities, assistance, and services are available to all on a nondiscriminatory basis. If it is unlikely that the procedures that the recipient or subrecipient intends to use to make known the availability of the facilities, assistance, and services will to reach persons of any particular race, color, religion, sex, age, national origin, familial status, or disability who may qualify for those facilities and services, the recipient or subrecipient must establish additional procedures that ensure that those persons are made aware of the facilities, assistance, and services. The recipient and its subrecipients must take appropriate steps to ensure effective communication with persons with disabilities including, but not limited to, adopting procedures that will make available to interested persons information concerning the location of assistance, services, and facilities that are accessible to persons with disabilities. Consistent with Title VI and Executive Order 13166, recipients and subrecipients are also required to take reasonable steps to ensure meaningful access to programs and activities for limited English proficiency (LEP) persons.

(c) *Uniform requirements.* The requirements of 2 CFR part 200 apply to the recipient and subrecipients, and:

(1) Program income may be used as matching contributions, subject to the requirements in §576.201;

(2) The disposition of real property for which ESG funds are used for major rehabilitation, conversion, or other renovation under §576.102 is governed by the minimum period of use requirements under §576.102(c).

(d) *Environmental review responsibilities.* (1) Activities under this part are subject to environmental review by HUD under 24 CFR part 50. The recipient shall supply all available, relevant information necessary for HUD to perform for each property any environmental review required by 24 CFR part 50. The recipient also shall carry out mitigating measures required by HUD or select alternate eligible property.

HUD may eliminate from consideration any application that would require an Environmental Impact Statement (EIS).

(2) The recipient or subrecipient, or any contractor of the recipient or subrecipient, may not acquire, rehabilitate, convert, lease, repair, dispose of, demolish, or construct property for a project under this part, or commit or expend HUD or local funds for eligible activities under this part, until HUD has performed an environmental review under 24 CFR part 50 and the recipient has received HUD approval of the property.

(e) *Davis-Bacon Act.* The provisions of the Davis-Bacon Act (40 U.S.C. 276a to 276a–5) do not apply to the ESG program.

(f) *Procurement of Recovered Materials.* The recipient and its contractors must comply with Section 6002 of the Solid Waste Disposal Act, as amended by the Resource Conservation and Recovery Act. The requirements of Section 6002 include procuring only items designated in guidelines of the Environmental Protection Agency (EPA) at 40 CFR part 247 that contain the highest percentage of recovered materials practicable, consistent with maintaining a satisfactory level of competition, where the purchase price of the item exceeds $10,000 or the value of the quantity acquired by the preceding fiscal year exceeded $10,000; procuring solid waste management services in a manner that maximizes energy and resource recovery; and establishing an affirmative procurement program for procurement of recovered materials identified in the EPA guidelines.

[76 FR 75974, Dec. 5, 2011, as amended at 80 FR 75939, Dec. 7, 2015; 81 FR 90660, Dec. 14, 2016; 85 FR 61568, Sept. 29, 2020]

§ 576.408 Displacement, relocation, and acquisition.

(a) *Minimizing displacement.* Consistent with the other goals and objectives of Emergency Solutions Grant (ESG), the recipient and its subrecipients must assure that they have taken all reasonable steps to minimize the displacement of persons (families, individuals, businesses, nonprofit organizations, and farms) as a result of a project assisted under Emergency Solutions Grant (ESG).

(b) *Temporary relocation not permitted.* No tenant-occupant of housing (a dwelling unit) that is converted into an emergency shelter may be required to relocate temporarily for a project assisted with ESG funds, or be required to move to another unit in the same building/complex. When a tenant moves for a project assisted with ESG funds under conditions that trigger the Uniform Relocation Assistance and Real Property Acquisition Policies Act of 1970 (URA), 42 U.S.C. 4601–4655, as described in paragraph (c) of this section, the tenant should be treated as permanently displaced and offered relocation assistance and payments consistent with that paragraph.

(c) *Relocation assistance for displaced persons.* (1) *In general.* A displaced person (defined in paragraph (c)(2) of this section) must be provided relocation assistance at the levels described in, and in accordance with, the URA and 49 CFR part 24. A displaced person must be advised of his or her rights under the Fair Housing Act (42 U.S.C. 3601 *et seq.*). Whenever possible, minority persons shall be given reasonable opportunities to relocate to comparable and suitable decent, safe, and sanitary replacement dwellings, not located in an area of minority concentration, that are within their financial means. This policy, however, does not require providing a person a larger payment than is necessary to enable a person to relocate to a comparable replacement dwelling. (See 49 CFR 24.205(c)(2)(ii)(D).) As required by Section 504 of the Rehabilitation Act (29 U.S.C. 794) and 49 CFR part 24, replacement dwellings must also contain the accessibility features needed by displaced persons with disabilities.

(2) *Displaced Person.* (i) For purposes of paragraph (c) of this section, the term "displaced person" means any person (family, individual, business, nonprofit organization, or farm, including any corporation, partnership, or association) that moves from real property, or moves personal property from real property, permanently, as a direct result of acquisition, rehabilitation, or demolition for a project assisted under the ESG program. This includes any

permanent, involuntary move for an assisted project, including any permanent move from the real property that is made:

(A) After the owner (or person in control of the site) issues a notice to move permanently from the property or refuses to renew an expiring lease, if the move occurs on or after:

(I) The date of the submission by the recipient (or subrecipient, as applicable) of an application for assistance to HUD (or the recipient, as applicable) that is later approved and funded if the recipient (or subrecipient, as applicable) has site control as evidenced by a deed, sales contract, or option contract to acquire the property; or

(II) The date on which the recipient (or subrecipient, as applicable) selects the applicable site, if the recipient (or subrecipient, as applicable) does not have site control at the time of the application, provided that the recipient (or subrecipient, as applicable) eventually obtains control over the site;

(B) Before the date described in paragraph (c)(2)(i)(A) of this section, if the recipient or HUD determines that the displacement resulted directly from acquisition, rehabilitation, or demolition for the project; or

(C) By a tenant-occupant of a dwelling unit and the tenant moves after execution of the agreement covering the acquisition, rehabilitation, or demolition of the property for the project.

(ii) Notwithstanding paragraph (c)(2)(i) of this section, a person does not qualify as a displaced person if:

(A) The person has been evicted for cause based upon a serious or repeated violation of the terms and conditions of the lease or occupancy agreement; violation of applicable Federal, State or local law, or other good cause; and the recipient determines that the eviction was not undertaken for the purpose of evading the obligation to provide relocation assistance.

(B) The person moved into the property after the submission of the application but, before signing a lease and commencing occupancy, was provided written notice of the project, its possible impact on the person (*e.g.*, the person may be displaced), and the fact that the person would not qualify as a "displaced person" (or for any assistance under this section) as a result of the project;

(C) The person is ineligible under 49 CFR 24.2(a)(9)(ii); or

(D) HUD determines that the person was not displaced as a direct result of acquisition, rehabilitation, or demolition for the project.

(iii) The recipient or subrecipient may, at any time, request that HUD to determine whether a displacement is or would be covered by this rule.

(3) *Initiation of negotiations.* For purposes of determining the type of replacement housing payment assistance to be provided to a displaced person pursuant to this section:

(i) If the displacement is the direct result of privately undertaken rehabilitation, demolition, or acquisition of the real property, "initiation of negotiations" means the execution of the agreement between the recipient and the subrecipient or the agreement between the recipient (or subrecipient, as applicable) and the person owning or controlling the property;

(ii) If site control is only evidenced by an option contract to acquire the property, the "initiation of negotiations" does not become effective until the execution of a written agreement that creates a legally enforceable commitment to proceed with the purchase, such as a sales contract.

(d) *Real property acquisition requirements.* The acquisition of real property, whether funded privately or publicly, for a project assisted with Emergency Solutions Grant (ESG) funds is subject to the URA and Federal governmentwide regulations at 49 CFR part 24, subpart B.

(e) *Appeals.* A person who disagrees with the recipient's (or subrecipient's, if applicable) determination concerning whether the person qualifies as a displaced person, or the amount of relocation assistance for which the person may be eligible, may file a written appeal of that determination with the recipient under 49 CFR 24.10. A low-income person who disagrees with the recipient's determination may submit a written request for review of that determination by the appropriate HUD field office.

§ 576.409 Protection for victims of domestic violence, dating violence, sexual assault, or stalking.

(a) *Applicability of VAWA protections.* The core statutory protections of VAWA that prohibit denial or termination of assistance or eviction solely because an applicant or tenant is a victim of domestic violence, dating violence, sexual assault, or stalking applied upon enactment of VAWA 2013 on March 7, 2013. The VAWA regulatory requirements under 24 CFR part 5, subpart L, as supplemented by this section, apply to all eligibility and termination decisions that are made with respect to ESG rental assistance on or after *December 16, 2016*. The recipient must ensure that the requirements under 24 CFR part 5, subpart L, are included or incorporated into rental assistance agreements and leases as provided in § 576.106(e) and (g).

(b) *Covered housing provider.* For the ESG program, "covered housing provider," as such term is used in HUD's regulations in 24 CFR part 5, subpart L, refers to:

(1) The recipient or subrecipient that administers the rental assistance for the purposes of 24 CFR 5.2005(e);

(2) The housing owner for the purposes of 24 CFR 5.2005(d)(1), (d)(3), and (d)(4) and 5.2009(a);

(3) The housing owner and the recipient or subrecipient that administers the rental assistance for the purposes of 24 CFR 5.2005(d)(2); and

(4) The housing owner and the recipient or subrecipient that administers the rental assistance for the purposes of 24 CFR 5.2007. However, the recipient or subrecipient may limit documentation requests under 24 CFR 5.2007 to only the recipient or subrecipient, provided that:

(i) This limitation is made clear in both the notice described under 24 CFR 5.2005(a)(1) and the rental assistance agreement;

(ii) The entity designated to receive documentation requests determines whether the program participant is entitled to protection under VAWA and immediately advise the program participant of the determination; and

(iii) If the program participant is entitled to protection, the entity designated to receive documentation requests must notify the owner in writing that the program participant is entitled to protection under VAWA and work with the owner on the program participant's behalf. Any further sharing or disclosure of the program participant's information will be subject to the requirements in 24 CFR 5.2007.

(c) *Notification.* As provided under 24 CFR 5.2005(a) each recipient or subrecipient that determines eligibility for or administers ESG rental assistance is responsible for ensuring that the notice and certification form described under 24 CFR 5.2005(a)(1) is provided to each applicant for ESG rental assistance and each program participant receiving ESG rental assistance at each of the following times:

(1) When an individual or family is denied ESG rental assistance;

(2) When an individual or family's application for a unit receiving project-based rental assistance is denied;

(3) When a program participant begins receiving ESG rental assistance;

(4) When a program participant is notified of termination of ESG rental assistance; and

(5) When a program participant receives notification of eviction.

(d) *Emergency transfer plan.* (1) The recipient must develop the emergency transfer plan under 24 CFR 5.2005(e) or, if the recipient is a state, require its subrecipients that administer ESG rental assistance to develop the emergency transfer plan(s) required under 24 CFR 5.2005(e). If the state's subrecipients are required to develop the plan(s), the recipient must specify whether an emergency transfer plan is to be developed for:

(i) The state as a whole;

(ii) Each area within the state that is covered by a Continuum of Care; or

(iii) Each subrecipient that administers ESG rental assistance.

(2) Once the applicable plan is developed in accordance with this section, the recipient and each subrecipient that administers ESG rental assistance must implement the plan in accordance with 24 CFR 5.2005(e).

(3) Each emergency transfer plan must meet the requirements in 24 CFR 5.2005(e) and include the following program requirements:

(i) For families living in units receiving project-based rental assistance (assisted units), the required policies must provide that if a program participant qualifies for an emergency transfer, but a safe unit is not immediately available for an internal emergency transfer, that program participant shall have priority over all other applicants for tenant-based rental assistance, utility assistance, and units for which project-based rental assistance is provided.

(ii) For families receiving tenant-based rental assistance, the required policies must specify what will happen with respect to the non-transferring family member(s), if the family separates in order to effect an emergency transfer.

(e) *Bifurcation.* For the purposes of this part, the following requirements shall apply in place of the requirements at 24 CFR 5.2009(b):

(1) When a family receiving tenant-based rental assistance separates under 24 CFR 5.2009(a), the family's tenant-based rental assistance and utility assistance, if any, shall continue for the family member(s) who are not evicted or removed.

(2) If a family living in a unit receiving project-based rental assistance separates under 24 CFR 5.2009(a), the family member(s) who are not evicted or removed can remain in the assisted unit without interruption to the rental assistance or utility assistance provided for the unit.

(f) *Emergency shelters.* The following requirements apply to emergency shelters funded under § 576.102:

(1) No individual or family may be denied admission to or removed from the emergency shelter on the basis or as a direct result of the fact that the individual or family is or has been a victim of domestic violence, dating violence, sexual assault, or stalking, if the individual or family otherwise qualifies for admission or occupancy.

(2) The terms "affiliated individual," "dating violence," "domestic violence," "sexual assault," and "stalking" are defined in 24 CFR 5.2003.

[81 FR 80808, Nov. 16, 2016]

Subpart F—Grant Administration

§ 576.500 Recordkeeping and reporting requirements.

(a) *In general.* The recipient must have policies and procedures to ensure the requirements of this part are met, including those required by 2 CFR part 200. The policies and procedures must be established in writing and implemented by the recipient and its subrecipients to ensure that ESG funds are used in accordance with the requirements. In addition, sufficient records must be established and maintained to enable the recipient and HUD to determine whether ESG requirements are being met.

(b) *Homeless status.* The recipient must maintain and follow written intake procedures to ensure compliance with the homeless definition in § 576.2. The procedures must require documentation at intake of the evidence relied upon to establish and verify homeless status. The procedures must establish the order of priority for obtaining evidence as third-party documentation first, intake worker observations second, and certification from the person seeking assistance third. However, lack of third-party documentation must not prevent an individual or family from being immediately admitted to emergency shelter, receiving street outreach services, or being immediately admitted to shelter or receiving services provided by a victim service provider. Records contained in an HMIS or comparable database used by victim service or legal service providers are acceptable evidence of third-party documentation and intake worker observations if the HMIS retains an auditable history of all entries, including the person who entered the data, the date of entry, and the change made; and if the HMIS prevents overrides or changes of the dates on which entries are made.

(1) If the individual or family qualifies as homeless under paragraph (1)(i) or (ii) of the homeless definition in § 576.2, acceptable evidence includes a written observation by an outreach worker of the conditions where the individual or family was living, a written referral by another housing or service

provider, or a certification by the individual or head of household seeking assistance.

(2) If the individual qualifies as homeless under paragraph (1)(iii) of the homeless definition in § 576.2, because he or she resided in an emergency shelter or place not meant for human habitation and is exiting an institution where he or she resided for 90 days or less, acceptable evidence includes the evidence described in paragraph (b)(1) of this section and one of the following:

(i) Discharge paperwork or a written or oral referral from a social worker, case manager, or other appropriate official of the institution, stating the beginning and end dates of the time residing in the institution. All oral statements must be recorded by the intake worker; or

(ii) Where the evidence in paragraph (b)(2)(i) of this section is not obtainable, a written record of the intake worker's due diligence in attempting to obtain the evidence described in paragraph (b)(2)(i) and a certification by the individual seeking assistance that states he or she is exiting or has just exited an institution where he or she resided for 90 days or less.

(3) If the individual or family qualifies as homeless under paragraph (2) of the homeless definition in § 576.2, because the individual or family will imminently lose their housing, the evidence must include:

(i)(A) A court order resulting from an eviction action that requires the individual or family to leave their residence within 14 days after the date of their application for homeless assistance; or the equivalent notice under applicable state law, a Notice to Quit, or a Notice to Terminate issued under state law;

(B) For individuals and families whose primary nighttime residence is a hotel or motel room not paid for by charitable organizations or federal, state, or local government programs for low-income individuals, evidence that the individual or family lacks the resources necessary to reside there for more than 14 days after the date of application for homeless assistance; or

(C) An oral statement by the individual or head of household that the owner or renter of the housing in which they currently reside will not allow them to stay for more than 14 days after the date of application for homeless assistance. The intake worker must record the statement and certify that it was found credible. To be found credible, the oral statement must either: (I) be verified by the owner or renter of the housing in which the individual or family resides at the time of application for homeless assistance and documented by a written certification by the owner or renter or by the intake worker's recording of the owner or renter's oral statement; or (II) if the intake worker is unable to contact the owner or renter, be documented by a written certification by the intake worker of his or her due diligence in attempting to obtain the owner or renter's verification and the written certification by the individual or head of household seeking assistance that his or her statement was true and complete;

(ii) Certification by the individual or head of household that no subsequent residence has been identified; and

(iii) Certification or other written documentation that the individual or family lacks the resources and support networks needed to obtain other permanent housing.

(4) If the individual or family qualifies as homeless under paragraph (3) of the homeless definition in § 576.2, because the individual or family does not otherwise qualify as homeless under the homeless definition but is an unaccompanied youth under 25 years of age, or homeless family with one or more children or youth, and is defined as homeless under another Federal statute or section 725(2) of the McKinney-Vento Homeless Assistance Act (42 U.S.C. 11434a(2)), the evidence must include:

(i) For paragraph (3)(i) of the homeless definition in § 576.2, certification of homeless status by the local private nonprofit organization or state or local governmental entity responsible for administering assistance under the Runaway and Homeless Youth Act (42 U.S.C. 5701 *et seq.*), the Head Start Act (42 U.S.C. 9831 *et seq.*), subtitle N of the Violence Against Women Act of 1994 (42 U.S.C. 14043e *et seq.*), section 330 of the Public Health Service Act (42 U.S.C.

254b), the Food and Nutrition Act of 2008 (7 U.S.C. 2011 *et seq.*), section 17 of the Child Nutrition Act of 1966 (42 U.S.C. 1786), or subtitle B of title VII of the McKinney-Vento Homeless Assistance Act (42 U.S.C. 11431 *et seq.*), as applicable;

(ii) For paragraph (3)(ii) of the homeless definition in § 576.2, referral by a housing or service provider, written observation by an outreach worker, or certification by the homeless individual or head of household seeking assistance;

(iii) For paragraph (3)(iii) of the homeless definition in § 576.2, certification by the individual or head of household and any available supporting documentation that the individual or family moved two or more times during the 60-day period immediately preceding the date of application for homeless assistance, including: recorded statements or records obtained from each owner or renter of housing, provider of shelter or housing, or social worker, case worker, or other appropriate official of a hospital or institution in which the individual or family resided; or, where these statements or records are unobtainable, a written record of the intake worker's due diligence in attempting to obtain these statements or records. Where a move was due to the individual or family fleeing domestic violence, dating violence, sexual assault, or stalking, then the intake worker may alternatively obtain a written certification from the individual or head of household seeking assistance that they were fleeing that situation and that they resided at that address; and

(iv) For paragraph (3)(iv) of the homeless definition in § 576.2, written diagnosis from a professional who is licensed by the state to diagnose and treat that condition (or intake staff-recorded observation of disability that within 45 days of date of the application for assistance is confirmed by a professional who is licensed by the state to diagnose and treat that condition); employment records; department of corrections records; literacy, English proficiency tests; or other reasonable documentation of the conditions required under paragraph (3)(iv) of the homeless definition.

(5) If the individual or family qualifies under paragraph (4) of the homeless definition in § 576.2, because the individual or family is fleeing domestic violence, dating violence, sexual assault, stalking, or other dangerous or life-threatening conditions related to violence, then acceptable evidence includes an oral statement by the individual or head of household seeking assistance that they are fleeing that situation, that no subsequent residence has been identified and that they lack the resources or support networks, *e.g.*, family, friends, faith-based or other social networks, needed to obtain other housing. If the individual or family is receiving shelter or services provided by a victim service provider, the oral statement must be documented by either a certification by the individual or head of household; or a certification by the intake worker. Otherwise, the oral statement that the individual or head of household seeking assistance has not identified a subsequent residence and lacks the resources or support networks, *e.g.*, family, friends, faith-based or other social networks, needed to obtain housing must be documented by a certification by the individual or head of household that the oral statement is true and complete, and, where the safety of the individual or family would not be jeopardized, the domestic violence, dating violence, sexual assault, stalking, or other dangerous or life-threatening condition must be verified by a written observation by the intake worker or a written referral by a housing or service provider, social worker, legal assistance provider, health-care provider, law enforcement agency, legal assistance provider, pastoral counselor, or any other organization from whom the individual or head of household has sought assistance for domestic violence, dating violence, sexual assault, or stalking. The written referral or observation need only include the minimum amount of information necessary to document that the individual or family is fleeing, or attempting to flee domestic violence, dating violence, sexual assault, and stalking.

(c) *At risk of homelessness status.* For each individual or family who receives Emergency Solutions Grant (ESG) homelessness prevention assistance, the records must include the evidence relied upon to establish and verify the individual or family's "at risk of homelessness" status. This evidence must include an intake and certification form that meets HUD specifications and is completed by the recipient or subrecipient. The evidence must also include:

(1) If the program participant meets the criteria under paragraph (1) of the "at risk of homelessness" definition in § 576.2:

(i) The documentation specified under this section for determining annual income;

(ii) The program participant's certification on a form specified by HUD that the program participant has insufficient financial resources and support networks; *e.g.*, family, friends, faith-based or other social networks, immediately available to attain housing stability and meets one or more of the conditions under paragraph (1)(iii) of the definition of "at risk of homelessness" in § 576.2;

(iii) The most reliable evidence available to show that the program participant does not have sufficient resources or support networks; *e.g.*, family, friends, faith-based or other social networks, immediately available to prevent them from moving to an emergency shelter or another place described in paragraph (1) of the "homeless" definition. Acceptable evidence includes:

(A) Source documents (*e.g.*, notice of termination from employment, unemployment compensation statement, bank statement, health-care bill showing arrears, utility bill showing arrears);

(B) To the extent that source documents are unobtainable, a written statement by the relevant third party (*e.g.*, former employer, public administrator, relative) or the written certification by the recipient's or subrecipient's intake staff of the oral verification by the relevant third party that the applicant meets one or both of the criteria under paragraph (1)(ii) of the definition of "at risk of homelessness" in § 576.2; or

(C) To the extent that source documents and third-party verification are unobtainable, a written statement by the recipient's or subrecipient's intake staff describing the efforts taken to obtain the required evidence; and

(iv) The most reliable evidence available to show that the program participant meets one or more of the conditions under paragraph (1)(iii) of the definition of "at risk of homelessness" in § 576.2. Acceptable evidence includes:

(A) Source documents that evidence one or more of the conditions under paragraph (1)(iii) of the definition (*e.g.*, eviction notice, notice of termination from employment, bank statement);

(B) To the extent that source documents are unobtainable, a written statement by the relevant third party (*e.g.*, former employer, owner, primary leaseholder, public administrator, hotel or motel manager) or the written certification by the recipient's or subrecipient's intake staff of the oral verification by the relevant third party that the applicant meets one or more of the criteria under paragraph (1)(iii) of the definition of "at risk of homelessness"; or

(C) To the extent that source documents and third-party verification are unobtainable, a written statement by the recipient's or subrecipient's intake staff that the staff person has visited the applicant's residence and determined that the applicant meets one or more of the criteria under paragraph (1)(iii) of the definition or, if a visit is not practicable or relevant to the determination, a written statement by the recipient's or subrecipient's intake staff describing the efforts taken to obtain the required evidence; or

(2) If the program participant meets the criteria under paragraph (2) or (3) of the "at risk of homelessness" definition in § 576.2, certification of the child or youth's homeless status by the agency or organization responsible for administering assistance under the Runaway and Homeless Youth Act (42 U.S.C. 5701 *et seq.*), the Head Start Act (42 U.S.C. 9831 *et seq.*), subtitle N of the Violence Against Women Act of 1994 (42 U.S.C. 14043e *et seq.*), section 330 of the Public Health Service Act (42 U.S.C. 254b), the Food and Nutrition Act of 2008 (7 U.S.C. 2011 *et seq.*), section 17 of the Child Nutrition Act of 1966 (42 U.S.C. 1786) or subtitle B of title VII of

the McKinney-Vento Homeless Assistance Act (42 U.S.C. 11431 *et seq.*), as applicable.

(d) *Determinations of ineligibility.* For each individual and family determined ineligible to receive Emergency Solutions Grant (ESG) assistance, the record must include documentation of the reason for that determination.

(e) *Annual income.* For each program participant who receives homelessness prevention assistance, or who receives rapid re-housing assistance longer than one year, the following documentation of annual income must be maintained:

(1) Income evaluation form containing the minimum requirements specified by HUD and completed by the recipient or subrecipient; and

(2) Source documents for the assets held by the program participant and income received over the most recent period for which representative data is available before the date of the evaluation (*e.g.*, wage statement, unemployment compensation statement, public benefits statement, bank statement);

(3) To the extent that source documents are unobtainable, a written statement by the relevant third party (*e.g.*, employer, government benefits administrator) or the written certification by the recipient's or subrecipient's intake staff of the oral verification by the relevant third party of the income the program participant received over the most recent period for which representative data is available; or

(4) To the extent that source documents and third party verification are unobtainable, the written certification by the program participant of the amount of income the program participant received for the most recent period representative of the income that the program participant is reasonably expected to receive over the 3-month period following the evaluation.

(f) *Program participant records.* In addition to evidence of homeless status or "at risk of homelessness" status, as applicable, records must be kept for each program participant that document:

(1) The services and assistance provided to that program participant, including, as applicable, the security deposit, rental assistance, and utility payments made on behalf of the program participant;

(2) Compliance with the applicable requirements for providing services and assistance to that program participant under the program components and eligible activities provisions at §576.101 through §576.106, the provision on determining eligibility and amount and type of assistance at §576.401(a) and (b), and the provision on using appropriate assistance and services at §576.401(d) and (e); and

(3) Where applicable, compliance with the termination of assistance requirement in §576.402.

(g) *Centralized or coordinated assessment systems and procedures.* The recipient and its subrecipients must keep documentation evidencing the use of, and written intake procedures for, the centralized or coordinated assessment system(s) developed by the Continuum of Care(s) in accordance with the requirements established by HUD.

(h) *Rental assistance agreements and payments.* The records must include copies of all leases and rental assistance agreements for the provision of rental assistance, documentation of payments made to owners for the provision of rental assistance, and supporting documentation for these payments, including dates of occupancy by program participants.

(i) *Utility allowance.* The records must document the monthly allowance for utilities (excluding telephone) used to determine compliance with the rent restriction.

(j) *Shelter and housing standards.* The records must include documentation of compliance with the shelter and housing standards in §576.403, including inspection reports.

(k) *Emergency shelter facilities.* The recipient must keep records of the emergency shelters assisted under the ESG program, including the amount and type of assistance provided to each emergency shelter. As applicable, the recipient's records must also include documentation of the value of the building before the rehabilitation of an existing emergency shelter or after the conversion of a building into an emergency shelter and copies of the recorded deed or use restrictions.

(l) *Services and assistance provided.* The recipient must keep records of the types of essential services, rental assistance, and housing stabilization and relocation services provided under the recipient's program and the amounts spent on these services and assistance. The recipient and its subrecipients that are units of general purpose local government must keep records to demonstrate compliance with the maintenance of effort requirement, including records of the unit of the general purpose local government's annual budgets and sources of funding for street outreach and emergency shelter services.

(m) *Coordination with Continuum(s) of Care and other programs.* The recipient and its subrecipients must document their compliance with the requirements of § 576.400 for consulting with the Continuum(s) of Care and coordinating and integrating ESG assistance with programs targeted toward homeless people and mainstream service and assistance programs.

(n) *HMIS.* The recipient must keep records of the participation in HMIS or a comparable database by all projects of the recipient and its subrecipients.

(o) *Matching.* The recipient must keep records of the source and use of contributions made to satisfy the matching requirement in § 576.201. The records must indicate the particular fiscal year grant for which each matching contribution is counted. The records must show how the value placed on third-party, noncash contributions was derived. To the extent feasible, volunteer services must be supported by the same methods that the organization uses to support the allocation of regular personnel costs.

(p) *Conflicts of interest.* The recipient and its subrecipients must keep records to show compliance with the organizational conflicts-of-interest requirements in § 576.404(a), a copy of the personal conflicts of interest policy or codes of conduct developed and implemented to comply with the requirements in § 576.404(b), and records supporting exceptions to the personal conflicts of interest prohibitions.

(q) *Homeless participation.* The recipient must document its compliance with the homeless participation requirements under § 576.405.

(r) *Faith-based activities.* The recipient and its subrecipients must document their compliance with the faith-based activities requirements under § 576.406.

(s) *Other Federal requirements.* The recipient and its subrecipients must document their compliance with the Federal requirements in § 576.407 and § 576.409, as applicable, including:

(1) Records demonstrating compliance with the nondiscrimination and equal opportunity requirements under § 576.407(a) and the affirmative outreach requirements in § 576.407(b), including:

(i) Data concerning race, ethnicity, disability status, sex, and family characteristics of persons and households who are applicants for, or program participants in, any program or activity funded in whole or in part with ESG funds; and

(ii) Documentation of the actions that the recipient has taken to affirmatively further fair housing, pursuant to §§ 5.151 and 5.152 of this title.

(2) Records demonstrating compliance with the uniform administrative requirements in 2 CFR part 200.

(3) Records demonstrating compliance with the environmental review requirements, including flood insurance requirements.

(4) Certifications and disclosure forms required under the lobbying and disclosure requirements in 24 CFR part 87.

(5) Data on emergency transfers requested under § 576.409, pertaining to victims of domestic violence, dating violence, sexual assault, or stalking, including data on the outcomes of such requests.

(t) *Relocation.* The records must include documentation of compliance with the displacement, relocation, and acquisition requirements in § 576.408.

(u) *Financial records.* (1) The recipient must retain supporting documentation for all costs charged to the ESG grant.

(2) The recipient and its subrecipients must keep documentation showing that ESG grant funds were spent on allowable costs in accordance with the requirements for eligible activities under "§§ 576.101 through 576.109, financial management in 2 CFR 200.302, and

the cost principles in 2 CFR part 200, subpart E.

(3) The recipient and its subrecipients must retain records of the receipt and use of program income.

(4) The recipient must keep documentation of compliance with the expenditure limits in §576.100 and the expenditure deadline in §576.203.

(v) *Subrecipients and contractors.* (1) The recipient must retain copies of all solicitations of and agreements with subrecipients, records of all payment requests by and dates of payments made to subrecipients, and documentation of all monitoring and sanctions of subrecipients, as applicable. If the recipient is a State, the recipient must keep records of each recapture and distribution of recaptured funds under §576.501.

(2) The recipient and its subrecipients must retain copies of all procurement contracts and documentation of compliance with the procurement requirements in 2 CFR part 200, subpart D.

(3) The recipient must ensure that its subrecipients comply with the recordkeeping requirements specified by the recipient and HUD notice or regulations.

(w) *Other records specified by HUD.* The recipient must keep other records specified by HUD.

(x) *Confidentiality.* (1) The recipient and its subrecipients must develop and implement written procedures to ensure:

(i) All records containing personally identifying information (as defined in HUD's standards for participation, data collection, and reporting in a local HMIS) of any individual or family who applies for and/or receives ESG assistance will be kept secure and confidential;

(ii) The address or location of any domestic violence, dating violence, sexual assault, or stalking shelter project assisted under the ESG will not be made public, except with written authorization of the person responsible for the operation of the shelter; and

(iii) The address or location of any housing of a program participant will not be made public, except as provided under a preexisting privacy policy of the recipient or subrecipient and consistent with state and local laws regarding privacy and obligations of confidentiality.

(2) The confidentiality procedures of the recipient and its subrecipients must be in writing and must be maintained in accordance with this section.

(y) *Period of record retention.* All records pertaining to each fiscal year of ESG funds must be retained for the greater of 5 years or the period specified below. Copies made by microfilming, photocopying, or similar methods may be substituted for the original records.

(1) Documentation of each program participant's qualification as a family or individual at risk of homelessness or as a homeless family or individual and other program participant records must be retained for 5 years after the expenditure of all funds from the grant under which the program participant was served;

(2) Where ESG funds are used for the renovation of an emergency shelter involves costs charged to the ESG grant that exceed 75 percent of the value of the building before renovation, records must be retained until 10 years after the date that ESG funds are first obligated for the renovation; and

(3) Where ESG funds are used to convert a building into an emergency shelter and the costs charged to the ESG grant for the conversion exceed 75 percent of the value of the building after conversion, records must be retained until 10 years after the date that ESG funds are first obligated for the conversion.

(z) *Access to records.* (1) *Federal Government rights.* Notwithstanding the confidentiality procedures established under paragraph (x) of this section, the recipient and its subrecipients must comply with the requirements for access to records in 2 CFR 200.336.

(2) *Public rights.* The recipient must provide citizens, public agencies, and other interested parties with reasonable access (consistent with state and local laws regarding privacy and obligations of confidentiality and the confidentiality requirements in this part) to records regarding any uses of ESG funds the recipient received during the preceding 5 years.

(aa) *Reports.* The recipient must collect and report data on its use of ESG funds in the Integrated Disbursement and Information System (IDIS) and other reporting systems, as specified by HUD. The recipient must also comply with the reporting requirements in 2 CFR part 200 and 24 CFR part 91 and the reporting requirements under the Federal Funding Accountability and Transparency Act of 2006, (31 U.S.C. 6101 note), which are set forth in appendix A to 2 CFR part 170.

[76 FR 75974, Dec. 5, 2011, as amended at 80 FR 42368, July 16, 2015; 80 FR 75939, Dec. 7, 2015; 81 FR 80809, Nov. 16, 2016; 85 FR 47911, Aug. 7, 2020; 86 FR 30792, June 10, 2021]

EFFECTIVE DATE NOTE: At 90 FR 11024, Mar. 3, 2025, § 576.500 was amended, effective Apr. 2, 2025.

§ 576.501 Enforcement.

(a) *Performance reviews.* (1) HUD will review the performance of each recipient in carrying out its responsibilities under this part whenever determined necessary by HUD, but at least annually. In conducting performance reviews, HUD will rely primarily on information obtained from the records and reports from the recipient and, when appropriate, its subrecipients, as well as information from onsite monitoring, audit reports, and information from IDIS and HMIS. Where applicable, HUD may also consider relevant information pertaining to the recipient's performance gained from other sources, including citizen comments, complaint determinations, and litigation. Reviews to determine compliance with specific requirements of this part will be conducted as necessary, with or without prior notice to the recipient.

(2) If HUD determines preliminarily that the recipient or one of its subrecipients has not complied with an ESG program requirement, HUD will give the recipient notice of this determination and an opportunity to demonstrate, within the time prescribed by HUD and on the basis of substantial facts and data, that the recipient has complied with Emergency Solutions Grant (ESG) requirements. HUD may change the method of payment to require the recipient to obtain HUD's prior approval each time the recipient draws down Emergency Solutions Grant (ESG) funds. To obtain prior approval, the recipient may be required to manually submit its payment requests and supporting documentation to HUD in order to show that the funds to be drawn down will be expended on eligible activities in accordance with all ESG program requirements.

(3) If the recipient fails to demonstrate to HUD's satisfaction that the activities were carried out in compliance with ESG program requirements, HUD will take one or more of the remedial actions or sanctions specified in paragraph (b) of this section.

(b) *Remedial actions and sanctions.* Remedial actions and sanctions for a failure to meet an ESG program requirement will be designed to prevent a continuation of the deficiency; mitigate, to the extent possible, its adverse effects or consequences; and prevent its recurrence.

(1) HUD may instruct the recipient to submit and comply with proposals for action to correct, mitigate, and prevent noncompliance with ESG requirements, including:

(i) Preparing and following a schedule of actions for carrying out activities affected by the noncompliance, including schedules, timetables, and milestones necessary to implement the affected activities;

(ii) Establishing and following a management plan that assigns responsibilities for carrying out the remedial actions;

(iii) Canceling or revising activities likely to be affected by the noncompliance, before expending ESG funds for the activities;

(iv) Reprogramming ESG funds that have not yet been expended from affected activities to other eligible activities;

(v) Suspending disbursement of ESG funds for some or all activities;

(vi) Reducing or terminating the remaining grant of a subrecipient and reallocating those funds to other subrecipients; and

(vii) Making matching contributions before or as draws are made from the recipient's ESG grant.

(2) HUD may change the method of payment to a reimbursement basis.

(3) HUD may suspend payments to the extent HUD deems it necessary to

preclude the further expenditure of funds for affected activities.

(4) HUD may remove the recipient from participation in reallocations of funds under subpart D of this part.

(5) HUD may deny matching credit for all or part of the cost of the affected activities and require the recipient to make further matching contributions to make up for the contribution determined to be ineligible.

(6) HUD may require the recipient to reimburse its line of credit in an amount equal to the funds used for the affected activities.

(7) HUD may reduce or terminate the remaining grant of a recipient and reallocate those funds to other recipients in accordance with subpart D of this part.

(8) HUD may condition a future grant.

(9) HUD may take other remedies that are legally available.

(c) *Recipient sanctions.* If the recipient determines that a subrecipient is not complying with an ESG program requirement or its subgrant agreement, the recipient must take appropriate actions, as prescribed for HUD in paragraphs (a) and (b) of this section. If the recipient is a State and funds become available as a result of an action under this section, the recipient must reallocate those funds to other subrecipients as soon as practicable. If the recipient is a unit of general purpose local government of territory, it must either reallocate those funds to other subrecipients or reprogram the funds for other activities to be carried out by the recipient as soon as practicable. The recipient must amend its Consolidated Plan in accordance with its citizenship participation plan if funds become available and are reallocated or reprogrammed under this section. The reallocated or reprogrammed funds must be used by the expenditure deadline in §576.203.

PART 578—CONTINUUM OF CARE PROGRAM

Subpart A—General Provisions

Subpart B—Establishing and Operating a Continuum of Care

Subpart C—Application and Grant Award Process

Subpart D—Program Components and Eligible Costs

Subpart E—High-Performing Communities

Subpart F—Program Requirements

AUTHORITY: 12 U.S.C. 1701x, 1701 x–1; 42 U.S.C. 11381 *et seq.*, 42 U.S.C. 3535(d).

SOURCE: 77 FR 45442, July 31, 2012, unless otherwise noted.

Subpart A—General Provisions

§ 578.1 Purpose and scope.

(a) The Continuum of Care program is authorized by subtitle C of title IV of the McKinney-Vento Homeless Assistance Act (42 U.S.C. 11381–11389).

(b) The program is designed to:

(1) Promote communitywide commitment to the goal of ending homelessness;

(2) Provide funding for efforts by nonprofit providers, States, and local governments to quickly rehouse homeless individuals (including unaccompanied youth) and families, while minimizing the trauma and dislocation caused to homeless individuals, families, and communities by homelessness;

(3) Promote access to and effective utilization of mainstream programs by homeless individuals and families; and

(4) Optimize self-sufficiency among individuals and families experiencing homelessness.

§ 578.3 Definitions.

As used in this part:

Act means the McKinney-Vento Homeless Assistance Act as amended (42 U.S.C. 11371 *et seq.*).

Annual renewal amount means the amount that a grant can be awarded on an annual basis when renewed. It includes funds only for those eligible activities (operating, supportive services, leasing, rental assistance, HMIS, and administration) that were funded in the original grant (or the original grant as amended), less the unrenewable activities (acquisition, new construction, rehabilitation, and any administrative costs related to these activities).

Applicant means an eligible applicant that has been designated by the Continuum of Care to apply for assistance under this part on behalf of that Continuum.

At risk of homelessness. (1) An individual or family who:

(i) Has an annual income below 30 percent of median family income for the area, as determined by HUD;

(ii) Does not have sufficient resources or support networks, *e.g.*, family, friends, faith-based or other social networks, immediately available to prevent them from moving to an emergency shelter or another place described in paragraph (1) of the "Homeless" definition in this section; and

(iii) Meets one of the following conditions:

(A) Has moved because of economic reasons two or more times during the 60 days immediately preceding the application for homelessness prevention assistance;

(B) Is living in the home of another because of economic hardship;

(C) Has been notified in writing that their right to occupy their current housing or living situation will be terminated within 21 days of the date of application for assistance;

(D) Lives in a hotel or motel and the cost of the hotel or motel stay is not paid

by charitable organizations or by federal, State, or local government programs for low-income individuals;

(E) Lives in a single-room occupancy or efficiency apartment unit in which there reside more than two persons, or lives in a larger housing unit in which there reside more than 1.5 people per room, as defined by the U.S. Census Bureau;

(F) Is exiting a publicly funded institution, or system of care (such as a health-care facility, a mental health facility, foster care or other youth facility, or correction program or institution); or

(G) Otherwise lives in housing that has characteristics associated with instability and an increased risk of homelessness, as identified in the recipient's approved consolidated plan;

(2) A child or youth who does not qualify as "homeless" under this section, but qualifies as "homeless" under section 387(3) of the Runaway and Homeless Youth Act (42 U.S.C. 5732a(3)), section 637(11) of the Head Start Act (42 U.S.C. 9832(11)), section 41403(6) of the Violence Against Women Act of 1994 (42 U.S.C. 14043e–2(6)), section 330(h)(5)(A) of the Public Health Service Act (42 U.S.C. 254b(h)(5)(A)), section 3(m) of the Food and Nutrition Act of 2008 (7 U.S.C. 2012(m)), or section 17(b)(15) of the Child Nutrition Act of 1966 (42 U.S.C. 1786(b)(15)); or

(3) A child or youth who does not qualify as "homeless" under this section, but qualifies as "homeless" under section 725(2) of the McKinney-Vento Homeless Assistance Act (42 U.S.C. 11434a(2)), and the parent(s) or guardian(s) of that child or youth if living with her or him.

Centralized or coordinated assessment system means a centralized or coordinated process designed to coordinate program participant intake assessment and provision of referrals. A centralized or coordinated assessment system covers the geographic area, is easily accessed by individuals and families seeking housing or services, is well advertized, and includes a comprehensive and standardized assessment tool.

Chronically homeless means:

(1) A "homeless individual with a disability," as defined in section 401(9) of the McKinney-Vento Homeless Assistance Act (42 U.S.C. 11360(9)), who:

(i) Lives in a place not meant for human habitation, a safe haven, or in an emergency shelter; and

(ii) Has been homeless and living as described in paragraph (1)(i) of this definition continuously for at least 12 months or on at least 4 separate occasions in the last 3 years, as long as the combined occasions equal at least 12 months and each break in homelessness separating the occasions included at least 7 consecutive nights of not living as described in paragraph (1)(i). Stays in institutional care facilities for fewer than 90 days will not constitute as a break in homelessness, but rather such stays are included in the 12-month total, as long as the individual was living or residing in a place not meant for human habitation, a safe haven, or an emergency shelter immediately before entering the institutional care facility;

(2) An individual who has been residing in an institutional care facility, including a jail, substance abuse or mental health treatment facility, hospital, or other similar facility, for fewer than 90 days and met all of the criteria in paragraph (1) of this definition, before entering that facility; or

(3) A family with an adult head of household (or if there is no adult in the family, a minor head of household) who meets all of the criteria in paragraph (1) or (2) of this definition, including a family whose composition has fluctuated while the head of household has been homeless.

Collaborative applicant means the eligible applicant that has been designated by the Continuum of Care to apply for a grant for Continuum of Care planning funds under this part on behalf of the Continuum.

Consolidated plan means the HUD-approved plan developed in accordance with 24 CFR 91.

Continuum of Care and Continuum means the group organized to carry out the responsibilities required under this part and that is composed of representatives of organizations, including nonprofit homeless providers, victim service providers, faith-based organizations, governments, businesses, advocates, public housing agencies, school districts, social service providers, mental health agencies, hospitals, universities, affordable housing developers, law enforcement, organizations that serve homeless and formerly homeless veterans, and homeless and formerly homeless persons to the extent these groups are represented within the geographic area and are available to participate.

Developmental disability means, as defined in section 102 of the Developmental Disabilities Assistance and Bill of Rights Act of 2000 (42 U.S.C. 15002):

(1) A severe, chronic disability of an individual that—

(i) Is attributable to a mental or physical impairment or combination of mental and physical impairments;

(ii) Is manifested before the individual attains age 22;

(iii) Is likely to continue indefinitely;

(iv) Results in substantial functional limitations in three or more of the following areas of major life activity:

(A) Self-care;

(B) Receptive and expressive language;

(C) Learning;

(D) Mobility;

(E) Self-direction;

(F) Capacity for independent living;

(G) Economic self-sufficiency.

(v) Reflects the individual's need for a combination and sequence of special, interdisciplinary, or generic services, individualized supports, or other forms of assistance that are of lifelong or extended duration and are individually planned and coordinated.

(2) An individual from birth to age 9, inclusive, who has a substantial developmental delay or specific congenital or acquired condition, may be considered to have a developmental disability without meeting three or more of the criteria described in paragraphs (1)(i) through (v) of the definition of "developmental disability" in this section if the individual, without services and supports, has a high probability of meeting these criteria later in life.

Eligible applicant means a private nonprofit organization, State, local government, or instrumentality of State and local government.

Emergency shelter is defined in 24 CFR part 576.

Emergency Solutions Grants (ESG) means the grants provided under 24 CFR part 576.

Fair Market Rent (FMR) means the Fair Market Rents published in the FEDERAL REGISTER annually by HUD.

High-performing community (HPC) means a Continuum of Care that meets the standards in subpart E of this part and has been designated as a high-performing community by HUD.

Homeless means:

(1) An individual or family who lacks a fixed, regular, and adequate nighttime residence, meaning:

(i) An individual or family with a primary nighttime residence that is a public or private place not designed for or ordinarily used as a regular sleeping accommodation for human beings, including a car, park, abandoned building, bus or train station, airport, or camping ground;

(ii) An individual or family living in a supervised publicly or privately operated shelter designated to provide temporary living arrangements (including congregate shelters, transitional housing, and hotels and motels paid for by charitable organizations or by federal, State, or local government programs for low-income individuals); or

(iii) An individual who is exiting an institution where he or she resided for 90 days or less and who resided in an emergency shelter or place not meant for human habitation immediately before entering that institution;

(2) An individual or family who will imminently lose their primary nighttime residence, provided that:

(i) The primary nighttime residence will be lost within 14 days of the date of application for homeless assistance;

(ii) No subsequent residence has been identified; and

(iii) The individual or family lacks the resources or support networks, *e.g.*, family, friends, faith-based or other social networks, needed to obtain other permanent housing;

(3) Unaccompanied youth under 25 years of age, or families with children and youth, who do not otherwise qualify as homeless under this definition, but who:

(i) Are defined as homeless under section 387 of the Runaway and Homeless Youth Act (42 U.S.C. 5732a), section 637 of the Head Start Act (42 U.S.C. 9832), section 41403 of the Violence Against Women Act of 1994 (42 U.S.C. 14043e–2), section 330(h) of the Public Health Service Act (42 U.S.C. 254b(h)), section 3 of the Food and Nutrition Act of 2008 (7 U.S.C. 2012), section 17(b) of the Child Nutrition Act of 1966 (42 U.S.C. 1786(b)), or section 725 of the McKinney-Vento Homeless Assistance Act (42 U.S.C. 11434a);

(ii) Have not had a lease, ownership interest, or occupancy agreement in permanent housing at any time during the 60 days immediately preceding the date of application for homeless assistance;

(iii) Have experienced persistent instability as measured by two moves or more during the 60-day period immediately preceding the date of applying for homeless assistance; and

(iv) Can be expected to continue in such status for an extended period of time because of chronic disabilities; chronic physical health or mental health conditions; substance addiction; histories of domestic violence or childhood abuse (including neglect); the presence of a child or youth with a disability; or two or more barriers to employment, which include the lack of a high school degree or General Education Development (GED), illiteracy, low English proficiency, a history of incarceration or detention for criminal activity, and a history of unstable employment; or

(4) Any individual or family who:

(i) Is fleeing, or is attempting to flee, domestic violence, dating violence, sexual assault, stalking, or other dangerous or life-threatening conditions that relate to violence against the individual or a family member, including a child, that has either taken place within the individual's or family's primary nighttime residence or has made the individual or family afraid to return to their primary nighttime residence;

(ii) Has no other residence; and

(iii) Lacks the resources or support networks, *e.g.*, family, friends, and faith-based or other social networks, to obtain other permanent housing.

Homeless Management Information System (HMIS) means the information system designated by the Continuum of Care to comply with the HMIS requirements prescribed by HUD.

HMIS Lead means the entity designated by the Continuum of Care in accordance with this part to operate the Continuum's HMIS on its behalf.

Permanent housing means community-based housing without a designated length of stay, and includes both permanent supportive housing and rapid rehousing. To be permanent housing, the program participant must be the tenant on a lease for a term of at least one year, which is renewable for terms that are a minimum of one month long, and is terminable only for cause.

Permanent supportive housing means permanent housing in which supportive services are provided to assist homeless persons with a disability to live independently.

Point-in-time count means a count of sheltered and unsheltered homeless persons carried out on one night in the last 10 calendar days of January or at such other time as required by HUD.

Private nonprofit organization means an organization:

(1) No part of the net earnings of which inure to the benefit of any member, founder, contributor, or individual;

(2) That has a voluntary board;

(3) That has a functioning accounting system that is operated in accordance with generally accepted accounting principles, or has designated a fiscal agent that will maintain a functioning accounting system for the organization in accordance with generally accepted accounting principles; and

(4) That practices nondiscrimination in the provision of assistance.

A private nonprofit organization does not include governmental organizations, such as public housing agencies.

Program participant means an individual (including an unaccompanied youth) or family who is assisted with Continuum of Care program funds.

Project means a group of eligible activities, such as HMIS costs, identified as a project in an application to HUD for Continuum of Care funds and includes a structure (or structures) that is (are) acquired, rehabilitated, constructed, or leased with assistance provided under this part or with respect to which HUD provides rental assistance or annual payments for operating costs, or supportive services under this subtitle.

Recipient means an applicant that signs a grant agreement with HUD.

Safe haven means, for the purpose of defining chronically homeless, supportive housing that meets the following:

(1) Serves hard to reach homeless persons with severe mental illness who came from the streets and have been unwilling or unable to participate in supportive services;

(2) Provides 24-hour residence for eligible persons for an unspecified period;

(3) Has an overnight capacity limited to 25 or fewer persons; and

(4) Provides low-demand services and referrals for the residents.

State means each of the 50 States, the District of Columbia, the Commonwealth of Puerto Rico, American Samoa, Guam, the Commonwealth of the Northern Marianas, and the Virgin Islands.

Subrecipient means a private nonprofit organization, State, local government, or instrumentality of State or local government that receives a subgrant from the recipient to carry out a project.

Transitional housing means housing, where all program participants have signed a lease or occupancy agreement, the purpose of which is to facilitate the movement of homeless individuals and families into permanent housing within 24 months or such longer period as HUD determines necessary. The program participant must have a lease or occupancy agreement for a term of at least one month that ends in 24 months and cannot be extended.

Unified Funding Agency (UFA) means an eligible applicant selected by the Continuum of Care to apply for a grant for the entire Continuum, which has the capacity to carry out the duties in § 578.11(b), which is approved by HUD and to which HUD awards a grant.

Victim service provider means a private nonprofit organization whose primary mission is to provide services to victims of domestic violence, dating violence, sexual assault, or stalking. This term includes rape crisis centers, battered women's shelters, domestic violence transitional housing programs, and other programs.

Subpart B—Establishing and Operating a Continuum of Care

§ 578.5 Establishing the Continuum of Care.

(a) *The Continuum of Care.* Representatives from relevant organizations within a geographic area shall establish a Continuum of Care for the geographic area to carry out the duties of this part. Relevant organizations include nonprofit homeless assistance providers, victim service providers, faith-based organizations, governments, businesses, advocates, public housing agencies, school districts, social service providers, mental health agencies, hospitals, universities, affordable housing developers, law enforcement, and organizations that serve veterans and homeless and formerly homeless individuals.

(b) *The board.* The Continuum of Care must establish a board to act on behalf of the Continuum using the process established as a requirement by § 578.7(a)(3) and must comply with the conflict-of-interest requirements at § 578.95(b). The board must:

(1) Be representative of the relevant organizations and of projects serving homeless subpopulations; and

(2) Include at least one homeless or formerly homeless individual.

(c) *Transition.* Continuums of Care shall have 2 years after August 30, 2012 to comply with the requirements of paragraph (b) of this section.

§ 578.7 Responsibilities of the Continuum of Care.

(a) *Operate the Continuum of Care.* The Continuum of Care must:

(1) Hold meetings of the full membership, with published agendas, at least semi-annually;

(2) Make an invitation for new members to join publicly available within the geographic at least annually;

(3) Adopt and follow a written process to select a board to act on behalf of the Continuum of Care. The process must be reviewed, updated, and approved by the Continuum at least once every 5 years;

(4) Appoint additional committees, subcommittees, or workgroups;

(5) In consultation with the collaborative applicant and the HMIS Lead, develop, follow, and update annually a governance charter, which will include all procedures and policies needed to comply with subpart B of this part and with HMIS requirements as prescribed by HUD; and a code of conduct and recusal process for the board, its chair(s), and any person acting on behalf of the board;

(6) Consult with recipients and subrecipients to establish performance targets appropriate for population and

program type, monitor recipient and subrecipient performance, evaluate outcomes, and take action against poor performers;

(7) Evaluate outcomes of projects funded under the Emergency Solutions Grants program and the Continuum of Care program, and report to HUD;

(8) In consultation with recipients of Emergency Solutions Grants program funds within the geographic area, establish and operate either a centralized or coordinated assessment system that provides an initial, comprehensive assessment of the needs of individuals and families for housing and services. The Continuum must develop a specific policy to guide the operation of the centralized or coordinated assessment system on how its system will address the needs of individuals and families who are fleeing, or attempting to flee, domestic violence, dating violence, sexual assault, or stalking, but who are seeking shelter or services from non-victim service providers. This system must comply with any requirements established by HUD by Notice.

(9) In consultation with recipients of Emergency Solutions Grants program funds within the geographic area, establish and consistently follow written standards for providing Continuum of Care assistance. At a minimum, these written standards must include:

(i) Policies and procedures for evaluating individuals' and families' eligibility for assistance under this part;

(ii) Policies and procedures for determining and prioritizing which eligible individuals and families will receive transitional housing assistance (these policies must include the emergency transfer priority required under § 578.99(j)(8));

(iii) Policies and procedures for determining and prioritizing which eligible individuals and families will receive rapid rehousing assistance (these policies must include the emergency transfer priority required under § 578.99(j)(8));

(iv) Standards for determining what percentage or amount of rent each program participant must pay while receiving rapid rehousing assistance;

(v) Policies and procedures for determining and prioritizing which eligible individuals and families will receive permanent supportive housing assistance (these policies must include the emergency transfer priority required under § 578.99(j)(8)); and

(vi) Where the Continuum is designated a high-performing community, as described in subpart G of this part, policies and procedures set forth in 24 CFR 576.400(e)(3)(vi), (e)(3)(vii), (e)(3)(viii), and (e)(3)(ix).

(b) *Designating and operating an HMIS.* The Continuum of Care must:

(1) Designate a single Homeless Management Information System (HMIS) for the geographic area;

(2) Designate an eligible applicant to manage the Continuum's HMIS, which will be known as the HMIS Lead;

(3) Review, revise, and approve a privacy plan, security plan, and data quality plan for the HMIS.

(4) Ensure consistent participation of recipients and subrecipients in the HMIS; and

(5) Ensure the HMIS is administered in compliance with requirements prescribed by HUD.

(c) *Continuum of Care planning.* The Continuum must develop a plan that includes:

(1) Coordinating the implementation of a housing and service system within its geographic area that meets the needs of the homeless individuals (including unaccompanied youth) and families. At a minimum, such system encompasses the following:

(i) Outreach, engagement, and assessment;

(ii) Shelter, housing, and supportive services;

(iii) Prevention strategies.

(2) Planning for and conducting, at least biennially, a point-in-time count of homeless persons within the geographic area that meets the following requirements:

(i) Homeless persons who are living in a place not designed or ordinarily used as a regular sleeping accommodation for humans must be counted as unsheltered homeless persons.

(ii) Persons living in emergency shelters and transitional housing projects must be counted as sheltered homeless persons.

(iii) Other requirements established by HUD by Notice.

(3) Conducting an annual gaps analysis of the homeless needs and services available within the geographic area;

(4) Providing information required to complete the Consolidated Plan(s) within the Continuum's geographic area;

(5) Consulting with State and local government Emergency Solutions Grants program recipients within the Continuum's geographic area on the plan for allocating Emergency Solutions Grants program funds and reporting on and evaluating the performance of Emergency Solutions Grants program recipients and subrecipients.

(d) *VAWA emergency transfer plan.* The Continuum of Care must develop the emergency transfer plan for the Continuum of Care that meets the requirements under § 578.99(j)(8).

[77 FR 45442, July 31, 2012,as amended at 81 FR 80809, Nov. 16, 2016]

§ 578.9 Preparing an application for funds.

(a) The Continuum must:

(1) Design, operate, and follow a collaborative process for the development of applications and approve the submission of applications in response to a NOFA published by HUD under § 578.19 of this subpart;

(2) Establish priorities for funding projects in the geographic area;

(3) Determine if one application for funding will be submitted for all projects within the geographic area or if more than one application will be submitted for the projects within the geographic area;

(i) If more than one application will be submitted, designate an eligible applicant to be the collaborative applicant that will collect and combine the required application information from all applicants and for all projects within the geographic area that the Continuum has selected funding. The collaborative applicant will also apply for Continuum of Care planning activities. If the Continuum is an eligible applicant, it may designate itself;

(ii) If only one application will be submitted, that applicant will be the collaborative applicant and will collect and combine the required application information from all projects within the geographic area that the Continuum has selected for funding and apply for Continuum of Care planning activities;

(b) The Continuum retains all of its responsibilities, even if it designates one or more eligible applicants other than itself to apply for funds on behalf of the Continuum. This includes approving the Continuum of Care application.

§ 578.11 Unified Funding Agency.

(a) *Becoming a Unified Funding Agency.* To become designated as the Unified Funding Agency (UFA) for a Continuum, a collaborative applicant must be selected by the Continuum to apply to HUD to be designated as the UFA for the Continuum.

(b) *Criteria for designating a UFA.* HUD will consider these criteria when deciding whether to designate a collaborative applicant a UFA:

(1) The Continuum of Care it represents meets the requirements in § 578.7;

(2) The collaborative applicant has financial management systems that meet the standards set forth in 2 CFR 200.302;

(3) The collaborative applicant demonstrates the ability to monitor subrecipients; and

(4) Such other criteria as HUD may establish by NOFA.

(c) *Requirements.* HUD-designated UFAs shall:

(1) Apply to HUD for funding for all of the projects within the geographic area and enter into a grant agreement with HUD for the entire geographic area.

(2) Enter into legally binding agreements with subrecipients, and receive and distribute funds to subrecipients for all projects within the geographic area.

(3) Require subrecipients to establish fiscal control and accounting procedures as necessary to assure the proper disbursal of and accounting for federal funds in accordance with the requirements of 2 CFR part 200, subpart D.

(4) Obtain approval of any proposed grant agreement amendments by the Continuum of Care before submitting a request for an amendment to HUD.

[77 FR 45442, July 31, 2012, as amended at 80 FR 75939, Dec. 7, 2015]

§578.13 Remedial action.

(a) If HUD finds that the Continuum of Care for a geographic area does not meet the requirements of the Act or its implementing regulations, or that there is no Continuum for a geographic area, HUD may take remedial action to ensure fair distribution of grant funds within the geographic area. Such measures may include:

(1) Designating a replacement Continuum of Care for the geographic area;

(2) Designating a replacement collaborative applicant for the Continuum's geographic area; and

(3) Accepting applications from other eligible applicants within the Continuum's geographic area.

(b) HUD must provide a 30-day prior written notice to the Continuum and its collaborative applicant and give them an opportunity to respond.

Subpart C—Application and Grant Award Process

§578.15 Eligible applicants.

(a) *Who may apply.* Nonprofit organizations, States, local governments, and instrumentalities of State or local governments are eligible to apply for grants.

(b) *Designation by the Continuum of Care.* Eligible applicant(s) must have been designated by the Continuum of Care to submit an application for grant funds under this part. The designation must state whether the Continuum is designating more than one applicant to apply for funds and, if it is, which applicant is being designated as the collaborative applicant. If the Continuum is designating only one applicant to apply for funds, the Continuum must designate that applicant to be the collaborative applicant.

(c) *Exclusion.* For-profit entities are not eligible to apply for grants or to be subrecipients of grant funds.

§578.17 Overview of application and grant award process.

(a) *Formula.* (1) After enactment of the annual appropriations act for each fiscal year, and issuance of the NOFA, HUD will publish, on its Web site, the Preliminary Pro Rata Need (PPRN) assigned to metropolitan cities, urban counties, and all other counties.

(2) HUD will apply the formula used to determine PPRN established in paragraph (a)(3) of this section, to the amount of funds being made available under the NOFA. That amount is calculated by:

(i) Determining the total amount for the Continuum of Care competition in accordance with section 413 of the Act or as otherwise directed by the annual appropriations act;

(ii) From the amount in paragraph (a)(2)(i) of this section, deducting the amount published in the NOFA as being set aside to provide a bonus to geographic areas for activities that have proven to be effective in reducing homelessness generally or for specific subpopulations listed in the NOFA or achieving homeless prevention and independent living goals established in the NOFA and to meet policy priorities set in the NOFA; and

(iii) Deducting the amount of funding necessary for Continuum of Care planning activities and UFA costs.

(3) PPRN is calculated on the amount determined under paragraph (a)(2) of this section by using the following formula:

(i) Two percent will be allocated among the four insular areas (American Samoa, Guam, the Commonwealth of the Northern Marianas, and the Virgin Islands) on the basis of the ratio of the population of each insular area to the population of all insular areas.

(ii) Seventy-five percent of the remaining amount will be allocated, using the Community Development Block Grant (CDBG) formula, to metropolitan cities and urban counties that have been funded under either the Emergency Shelter Grants or Emergency Solutions Grants programs in any one year since 2004.

(iii) The amount remaining after the allocation under paragraphs (a)(1) and (2) of this section will be allocated, using the CDBG formula, to metropolitan cities and urban counties that have not been funded under the Emergency Solutions Grants program in any year since 2004 and all other counties in the United States and Puerto Rico.

(4) If the calculation in paragraph (a)(2) of this section results in an

amount less than the amount required to renew all projects eligible for renewal in that year for at least one year, after making adjustments proportional to increases in fair market rents for the geographic area for leasing, operating, and rental assistance for permanent housing, HUD will reduce, proportionately, the total amount required to renew all projects eligible for renewal in that year for at least one year, for each Continuum of Care. HUD will publish, via the NOFA, the total dollar amount that every Continuum will be required to deduct from renewal projects Continuum-wide.

(b) *Calculating a Continuum of Care's maximum award amount.* (1) *Establish the PPRN amount.* First, HUD will total the PPRN amounts for each metropolitan city, urban county, other county, and insular area claimed by the Continuum as part of its geographic area, excluding any counties applying for or receiving funding from the Rural Housing Stability Assistance program under 24 CFR part 579.

(2) *Establishing renewal demand.* Next, HUD will determine the renewal demand within the Continuum's geographic area. Renewal demand is the sum of the annual renewal amounts of all projects within the Continuum eligible to apply for renewal in that fiscal year's competition, before any adjustments to rental assistance, leasing, and operating line items based on FMR changes.

(3) *Establishing FPRN.* The higher of PPRN or renewal demand for the Continuum of Care is the FPRN, which is the base for the maximum award amount for the Continuum.

(4) *Establishing the maximum award amount.* The maximum award amount for the Continuum is the FPRN amount plus any additional eligible amounts for Continuum planning; UFA costs; adjustments to leasing, operating and rental assistance line items based on changes to FMR; and available bonuses.

§ 578.19 Application process.

(a) *Notice of Funding Availability.* After enactment of the annual appropriations act for the fiscal year, HUD will issue a NOFA in accordance with the requirements of 24 CFR part 4.

(b) *Applications.* All applications to HUD, including applications for grant funds and requests for designation as a UFA or HPC, must be submitted at such time and in such manner as HUD may require, and contain such information as HUD determines necessary. At a minimum, an application for grant funds must contain a list of the projects for which it is applying for funds; a description of the projects; a list of the projects that will be carried out by subrecipients and the names of the subrecipients; a description of the subpopulations of homeless or at risk of homelessness to be served by projects; the number of units to be provided and/or the number of persons to be served by each project; a budget request by project; and reasonable assurances that the applicant, or the subrecipient, will own or have control of a site for the proposed project not later than the expiration of the 12-month period beginning upon notification of an award for grant assistance.

§ 578.21 Awarding funds.

(a) *Selection.* HUD will review applications in accordance with the guidelines and procedures provided in the NOFA and will award funds to recipients through a national competition based on selection criteria as defined in section 427 of the Act.

(b) *Announcement of awards.* HUD will announce awards and notify selected applicants of any conditions imposed on awards. Conditions must be satisfied before HUD will execute a grant agreement with the applicant.

(c) *Satisfying conditions.* HUD will withdraw an award if the applicant does not satisfy all conditions imposed on it. Correcting all issues and conditions attached to an award must be completed within the time frame established in the NOFA. Proof of site control, match, environmental review, and the documentation of financial feasibility must be completed within 12 months of the announcement of the award, or 24 months in the case of funds for acquisition, rehabilitation, or new construction. The 12-month deadline may be extended by HUD for up to 12 additional months upon a showing of compelling reasons for delay due to factors beyond the control of the recipient or subrecipient.

§578.23 Executing grant agreements.

(a) *Deadline*. No later than 45 days from the date when all conditions are satisfied, the recipient and HUD must execute the grant agreement.

(b) *Grant agreements*. (1) *Multiple applicants for one Continuum*. If a Continuum designates more than one applicant for the geographic area, HUD will enter into a grant agreement with each designated applicant for which an award is announced.

(2) *One applicant for a Continuum*. If a Continuum designates only one applicant for the geographic area, after awarding funds, HUD may enter into a grant agreement with that applicant for new awards, if any, and one grant agreement for renewals, Continuum of Care planning, and UFA costs, if any. These two grants will cover the entire geographic area. A default by the recipient under one of those grant agreements will also be a default under the other.

(3) *Unified Funding Agencies*. If a Continuum is a UFA that HUD has approved, then HUD will enter into one grant agreement with the UFA for new awards, if any, and one grant agreement for renewals, Continuum of Care planning and UFA costs, if any. These two grants will cover the entire geographic area. A default by the UFA under one of those grant agreements will also be a default under the other.

(c) *Required agreements*. Recipients will be required to sign a grant agreement in which the recipient agrees:

(1) To ensure the operation of the project(s) in accordance with the provisions of the McKinney-Veto Act and all requirements under 24 CFR part 578;

(2) To monitor and report the progress of the project(s) to the Continuum of Care and HUD;

(3) To ensure, to the maximum extent practicable, that individuals and families experiencing homelessness are involved, through employment, provision of volunteer services, or otherwise, in constructing, rehabilitating, maintaining, and operating facilities for the project and in providing supportive services for the project;

(4) To require certification from all subrecipients that:

(i) Subrecipients will maintain the confidentiality of records pertaining to any individual or family that was provided family violence prevention or treatment services through the project;

(ii) The address or location of any family violence project assisted under this part will not be made public, except with written authorization of the person responsible for the operation of such project;

(iii) Subrecipients will establish policies and practices that are consistent with, and do not restrict, the exercise of rights provided by subtitle B of title VII of the Act and other laws relating to the provision of educational and related services to individuals and families experiencing homelessness;

(iv) In the case of projects that provide housing or services to families, that subrecipients will designate a staff person to be responsible for ensuring that children being served in the program are enrolled in school and connected to appropriate services in the community, including early childhood programs such as Head Start, part C of the Individuals with Disabilities Education Act, and programs authorized under subtitle B of title VII of the Act;

(v) The subrecipient, its officers, and employees are not debarred or suspended from doing business with the Federal Government; and

(vi) Subrecipients will provide information, such as data and reports, as required by HUD; and

(5) To establish such fiscal control and accounting procedures as may be necessary to assure the proper disbursal of, and accounting for grant funds in order to ensure that all financial transactions are conducted, and records maintained in accordance with generally accepted accounting principles, if the recipient is a UFA;

(6) To monitor subrecipient match and report on match to HUD;

(7) To take the educational needs of children into account when families are placed in housing and will, to the maximum extent practicable, place families with children as close as possible to their school of origin so as not to disrupt such children's education;

(8) To monitor subrecipients at least annually;

(9) To use the centralized or coordinated assessment system established by the Continuum of Care as set forth in § 578.7(a)(8). A victim service provider may choose not to use the Continuum of Care's centralized or coordinated assessment system, provided that victim service providers in the area use a centralized or coordinated assessment system that meets HUD's minimum requirements and the victim service provider uses that system instead;

(10) To follow the written standards for providing Continuum of Care assistance developed by the Continuum of Care, including the minimum requirements set forth in § 578.7(a)(9);

(11) Enter into subrecipient agreements requiring subrecipients to operate the project(s) in accordance with the provisions of this Act and all requirements under 24 CFR part 578; and

(12) To comply with such other terms and conditions as HUD may establish by NOFA.

§ 578.25 Site control.

(a) *In general.* When grant funds will be used for acquisition, rehabilitation, new construction, operating costs, or to provide supportive services, the recipient or subrecipient must demonstrate that it has site control within the time frame established in section § 578.21 before HUD will execute a grant agreement. This requirement does not apply to funds used for housing that will eventually be owned or controlled by the individuals or families served or for supportive services provided at sites not operated by the recipient or subrecipient.

(b) *Evidence.* Acceptable evidence of site control is a deed or lease. If grant funds will be used for acquisition, acceptable evidence of site control will be a purchase agreement. The owner, lessee, and purchaser shown on these documents must be the selected applicant or intended subrecipient identified in the application for assistance.

(c) *Tax credit projects.* (1) Applicants that plan to use the low-income housing tax credit authorized under 26 U.S.C. 42 to finance a project must prove to HUD's satisfaction that the applicant or subrecipient identified in the application is in control of the limited partnership or limited liability corporation that has a deed or lease for the project site.

(i) To have control of the limited partnership, the applicant or subrecipient must be the general partner of the limited partnership or have a 51 percent controlling interest in that general partner.

(ii) To have control of the limited liability company, the applicant or subrecipient must be the sole managing member.

(2) If grant funds are to be used for acquisition, rehabilitation, or new construction, the recipient or subrecipient must maintain control of the partnership or corporation and must ensure that the project is operated in compliance with law and regulation for 15 years from the date of initial occupancy or initial service provision. The partnership or corporation must own the project site throughout the 15-year period. If grant funds were not used for acquisition, rehabilitation, or new construction, then the recipient or subrecipient must maintain control for the term of the grant agreement and any renewals thereof.

§ 578.27 Consolidated plan.

(a) *States or units of general local government.* An applicant that is a State or a unit of general local government must have a HUD-approved, complete or abbreviated, consolidated plan in accordance with 24 CFR part 91. The applicant must submit a certification that the application for funding is consistent with the HUD-approved consolidated plan(s) for the jurisdiction(s) in which the proposed project will be located. Funded applicants must certify in a grant agreement that they are following the HUD-approved consolidated plan.

(b) *Other applicants.* Applicants that are not States or units of general local government must submit a certification by the jurisdiction(s) in which the proposed project will be located that the applicant's application for funding is consistent with the jurisdiction's HUD-approved consolidated plan. The certification must be made by the unit of general local government or the

State, in accordance with the consistency certification provisions under 24 CFR part 91, subpart F. If the jurisdiction refuses to provide a certification of consistency, the applicant may appeal to HUD under §578.35.

(c) *Timing of consolidated plan certification submissions.* The required certification that the application for funding is consistent with the HUD-approved consolidated plan must be submitted by the funding application submission deadline announced in the NOFA.

§578.29 Subsidy layering.

HUD may provide assistance under this program only in accordance with HUD subsidy layering requirements in section 102 of the Housing and Urban Development Reform Act of 1989 (42 U.S.C. 3545) and 24 CFR part 4, subpart A. An applicant must submit information in its application on other sources of governmental assistance that the applicant has received, or reasonably expects to receive, for a proposed project or activities. HUD's review of this information is intended to prevent excessive public assistance for proposed project or activities by combining (layering) assistance under this program with other governmental housing assistance from federal, State, or local agencies, including assistance such as tax concessions or tax credits.

§578.31 Environmental review.

(a) Activities under this part are subject to environmental review by HUD under 24 CFR part 50. The recipient or subrecipient shall supply all available, relevant information necessary for HUD to perform, for each property, any environmental review required by 24 CFR part 50. The recipient or subrecipient must carry out mitigating measures required by HUD or select an alternate eligible property. HUD may eliminate from consideration any application that would require an Environmental Impact Statement.

(b) The recipient or subrecipient, its project partners, and their contractors may not acquire, rehabilitate, convert, lease, repair, dispose of, demolish, or construct property for a project under this part, or commit or expend HUD or local funds for such eligible activities under this part, until HUD has performed an environmental review under 24 CFR part 50 and the recipient or subrecipient has received HUD approval of the property.

§578.33 Renewals.

(a) *In general.* Awards made under this part and title IV of the Act, as in effect before August 30, 2012 (the Supportive Housing Program and the Shelter Plus Care program), may be renewed to continue ongoing leasing, operations, supportive services, rental assistance, HMIS, and administration beyond the initial funding period. To be considered for funding, recipients must submit a request in a form specified by HUD, must meet the requirements of this part, and must submit the request within the time frame established by HUD.

(b) *Length of renewal.* HUD may award up to 3 years of funds for supportive services, leasing, HMIS, and operating costs. Renewals of tenant-based and sponsor-based rental assistance may be for up to one year of rental assistance. Renewals of project-based rental assistance may be for up to 15 years of rental assistance, subject to availability of annual appropriations.

(c) *Assistance available.* (1) Assistance during each year of a renewal period may be for:

(i) Up to 100 percent of the amount for supportive services and HMIS costs in the final year of the prior funding period;

(ii) Up to 100 percent of the amount for leasing and operating in the final year of the prior funding period adjusted in proportion to changes in the FMR for the geographic area; and

(iii) For rental assistance, up to 100 percent of the result of multiplying the number and unit size(s) in the grant agreement by the number of months in the renewal grant term and the applicable FMR.

(d) *Review criteria.* (1) Awards made under title IV of the Act, as in effect before August 30, 2012 are eligible for renewal in the Continuum of Care program even if the awardees would not be eligible for a new grant under the program, so long as they continue to serve the same population and the same number of persons or units in the same type of housing as identified in their most recently amended grant agreement signed before August 30, 2012. Grants will be renewed if HUD receives a certification from the Continuum that there is a demonstrated need for the project, and HUD finds that the project complied with program requirements applicable before August 30, 2012. For purposes of meeting the requirements of this part, a project will continue to be administered in accordance with 24 CFR 582.330, if the project received funding under the Shelter Plus Care program, or 24 CFR 583.325, if the project received funding under the Supportive Housing Program.

(2) *Renewal of awards made after August 30, 2012.* Review criteria for competitively awarded renewals made after August 30, 2012 will be described in the NOFA.

(e) *Unsuccessful projects.* HUD may renew a project that was eligible for renewal in the competition and was part of an application that was not funded despite having been submitted on time, in the manner required by HUD, and containing the information required by HUD, upon a finding that the project meets the purposes of the Continuum of Care program. The renewal will not exceed more than one year and will be under such conditions as HUD deems appropriate.

(f) *Annual Performance Report condition.* HUD may terminate the renewal of any grant and require the recipient to repay the renewal grant if:

(1) The recipient fails to timely submit a HUD Annual Performance Report (APR) for the grant year immediately prior to renewal; or

(2) The recipient submits an APR that HUD deems unacceptable or shows noncompliance with the requirements of the grant and this part.

§ 578.35 Appeal.

(a) *In general.* Failure to follow the procedures or meet the deadlines established in this section will result in denial of the appeal.

(b) *Solo applicants.* (1) *Who may appeal.* Nonprofits, States, and local governments, and instrumentalities of State or local governments that attempted to participate in the Continuum of Care planning process in the geographic area in which they operate, that believe they were denied the right to participate in a reasonable manner, and that submitted a solo application for funding by the application deadline established in the NOFA, may appeal the decision of the Continuum to HUD.

(2) *Notice of intent to appeal.* The solo applicant must submit a written notice of intent to appeal, with a copy to the Continuum, with their funding application.

(3) *Deadline for submitting proof.* No later than 30 days after the date that HUD announces the awards, the solo applicant shall submit in writing, with a copy to the Continuum, all relevant evidence supporting its claim, in such manner as HUD may require by Notice.

(4) *Response from the Continuum of Care.* The Continuum shall have 30 days from the date of its receipt of the solo applicant's evidence to respond to HUD in writing and in such manner as HUD may require, with a copy to the solo applicant.

(5) *Decision.* HUD will notify the solo applicant and the Continuum of its decision within 60 days of receipt of the Continuum's response.

(6) *Funding.* If HUD finds that the solo applicant was not permitted to participate in the Continuum of Care planning process in a reasonable manner, then HUD may award a grant to the solo applicant when funds next become available and may direct the Continuum of Care to take remedial steps to ensure reasonable participation in the future. HUD may also reduce the award to the Continuum's applicant(s).

(c) *Denied or decreased funding.* (1) *Who may appeal.* Eligible applicants that are denied funds by HUD, or that requested more funds than HUD awarded to them, may appeal the award by filing a written appeal, in such form and manner as HUD may require by Notice, within 45 days of the date of HUD's announcement of the award.

(2) *Decision.* HUD will notify the applicant of its decision on the appeal within 60 days of HUD's receipt of the written appeal. HUD will reverse a decision only when the applicant can show that HUD error caused the denial or decrease.

(3) *Funding.* Awards and increases to awards made upon appeal will be made from next available funds.

(d) *Competing Continuums of Care.* (1) *In general.* If more than one Continuum of Care claims the same geographic area, HUD will award funds to the Continuum applicant(s) whose application(s) has the highest total score. No projects will be funded from the lower scoring Continuum. No projects that are submitted in two or more competing Continuum of Care applications will be funded.

(2) *Who may appeal.* The designated applicant(s) for the lower scoring Continuum may appeal HUD's decision to fund the application(s) from the competing Continuum by filing a written appeal, in such form and manner as HUD may require by Notice, within 45 days of the date of HUD's announcement of the award.

(3) *Decision.* HUD will notify the applicant(s) of its decision on the appeal within 60 days of the date of HUD's receipt of the written appeal. HUD will reverse a decision only upon a showing by the applicant that HUD error caused the denial.

(e) *Consolidated plan certification.* (1) *In general.* An applicant may appeal to HUD a jurisdiction's refusal to provide a certification of consistency with the Consolidated Plan.

(2) *Procedure.* The applicant must submit a written appeal with its application to HUD and send a copy of the appeal to the jurisdiction that denied the certification of consistency. The appeal must include, at a minimum:

(i) A copy of the applicant's request to the jurisdiction for the certification of consistency with the Consolidated Plan;

(ii) A copy of the jurisdiction's response stating the reasons for denial, including the reasons the proposed project is not consistent with the jurisdiction's Consolidated Plan in accordance with 24 CFR 91.500(c); and

(iii) A statement of the reasons why the applicant believes its project is consistent with the jurisdiction's Consolidated Plan.

(3) *Jurisdiction response.* The jurisdiction that refused to provide the certification of consistency with the jurisdiction's Consolidated Plan shall have 10 days after receipt of a copy of the appeal to submit a written explanation of the reasons originally given for refusing to provide the certification and a written rebuttal to any claims made by the applicant in the appeal.

(4) *HUD review.* (i) HUD will issue its decision within 45 days of the date of HUD's receipt of the jurisdiction's response. As part of its review, HUD will consider:

(A) Whether the applicant submitted the request to the appropriate political jurisdiction; and

(B) The reasonableness of the jurisdiction's refusal to provide the certificate.

(ii) If the jurisdiction did not provide written reasons for refusal, including the reasons why the project is not consistent with the jurisdiction's Consolidated Plan in its initial response to the applicant's request for a certification, HUD will find for the applicant without further inquiry or response from the political jurisdiction.

Subpart D—Program Components and Eligible Costs

§578.37 Program components and uses of assistance.

(a) Continuum of Care funds may be used to pay for the eligible costs listed in §578.39 through §578.63 when used to establish and operate projects under five program components: permanent housing; transitional housing; supportive services only; HMIS; and, in some cases, homelessness prevention. Although grant funds may be used by recipients and subrecipients in all components for the eligible costs of contributing data to the HMIS designated by the Continuum of Care, only HMIS Leads may use grant funds for an HMIS component. Administrative costs are eligible for all components. All components are subject to the restrictions on combining funds for certain eligible activities in a single project found in §578.87(c). The eligible program components are:

(1) *Permanent housing (PH).* Permanent housing is community-based housing, the purpose of which is to provide housing without a designated length of

stay. Grant funds may be used for acquisition, rehabilitation, new construction, leasing, rental assistance, operating costs, and supportive services. PH includes:

(i) *Permanent supportive housing for persons with disabilities (PSH).* PSH can only provide assistance to individuals with disabilities and families in which one adult or child has a disability. Supportive services designed to meet the needs of the program participants must be made available to the program participants.

(ii) *Rapid rehousing.* Continuum of Care funds may provide supportive services, as set forth in §578.53, and/or short-term (up to 3 months) and/or medium-term (for 3 to 24 months) tenant-based rental assistance, as set forth in §578.51(c), as necessary to help a homeless individual or family, with or without disabilities, move as quickly as possible into permanent housing and achieve stability in that housing. When providing short-term and/or medium-term rental assistance to program participants, the rental assistance is subject to §578.51(a)(1), but not §578.51(a)(1)(i) and (ii); (a)(2); (c) and (f) through (i); and (l)(1). These projects:

(A) Must follow the written policies and procedures established by the Continuum of Care for determining and prioritizing which eligible families and individuals will receive rapid rehousing assistance, as well as the amount or percentage of rent that each program participant must pay.

(B) May set a maximum amount or percentage of rental assistance that a program participant may receive, a maximum number of months that a program participant may receive rental assistance, and/or a maximum number of times that a program participant may receive rental assistance. The recipient or subrecipient may also require program participants to share in the costs of rent. For the purposes of calculating rent for rapid rehousing, the rent shall equal the sum of the total monthly rent for the unit and, if the tenant pays separately for utilities, the monthly allowance for utilities (excluding telephone) established by the public housing authority for the area in which the housing is located.

(C) Limit rental assistance to no more than 24 months to a household.

(D) May provide supportive services for no longer than 6 months after rental assistance stops.

(E) Must re-evaluate, not less than once annually, that the program participant lacks sufficient resources and support networks necessary to retain housing without Continuum of Care assistance and the types and amounts of assistance that the program participant needs to retain housing. The recipient or subrecipient may require each program participant receiving assistance to notify the recipient or subrecipient of changes in the program participant's income or other circumstances (*e.g.*, changes in household composition) that affect the program participant's need for assistance. When notified of a relevant change, the recipient or subrecipient must reevaluate the program participant's eligibility and the amount and types of assistance that the program participant needs.

(F) Require the program participant to meet with a case manager not less than once per month to assist the program participant in ensuring long-term housing stability. The project is exempt from this requirement if the Violence Against Women Act of 1994 (42 U.S.C. 13925 *et seq.*) or the Family Violence Prevention and Services Act (42 U.S.C. 10401 *et seq.*) prohibits the recipient carrying out the project from making its housing conditional on the participant's acceptance of services.

(2) *Transitional Housing (TH).* Transitional housing facilitates the movement of homeless individuals and families to PH within 24 months of entering TH. Grant funds may be used for acquisition, rehabilitation, new construction, leasing, rental assistance, operating costs, and supportive services.

(3) *Supportive Service Only (SSO).* Funds may be used for acquisition, rehabilitation, relocation costs, or leasing of a facility from which supportive services will be provided, and supportive services in order to provide supportive services to unsheltered and sheltered homeless persons for whom the recipient or subrecipient is not providing housing or housing assistance. SSO includes street outreach.

(4) *HMIS.* Funds may be used by HMIS Leads to lease a structure in which the HMIS is operated or as operating funds to operate a structure in which the HMIS is operated, and for other costs eligible in §578.57.

(5) *Homelessness prevention.* Funds may be used by recipients in Continuums of Care-designated high-performing communities for housing relocation and stabilization services, and short- and/or medium-term rental assistance, as described in 24 CFR 576.105 and 24 CFR 576.106, that are necessary to prevent an individual or family from becoming homeless.

(b) *Uses of assistance.* Funds are available to pay for the eligible costs listed in §578.39 through §578.63 when used to:

(1) Establish new housing or new facilities to provide supportive services;

(2) Expand existing housing and facilities in order to increase the number of homeless persons served;

(3) Bring existing housing and facilities into compliance with State and local government health and safety standards, as described in §578.87;

(4) Preserve existing permanent housing and facilities that provide supportive services;

(5) Provide supportive services for residents of supportive housing or for homeless persons not residing in supportive housing;

(6) Continue funding permanent housing when the recipient has received funding under this part for leasing, supportive services, operating costs, or rental assistance;

(7) Establish and operate an HMIS or comparable database; and

(8) Establish and carry out a Continuum of Care planning process and operate a Continuum of Care.

(c) *Multiple purposes.* Structures used to provide housing, supportive housing, supportive services, or as a facility for HMIS activities may also be used for other purposes. However, assistance under this part will be available only in proportion to the use of the structure for supportive housing or supportive services. If eligible and ineligible activities are carried out in separate portions of the same structure or in separate structures, grant funds may not be used to pay for more than the actual cost of acquisition, construction, or rehabilitation of the portion of the structure or structures used for eligible activities. If eligible and ineligible activities are carried out in the same structure, the costs will be prorated based on the amount of time that the space is used for eligible versus ineligible activities.

§578.39 Continuum of Care planning activities.

(a) *In general.* Collaborative applicants may use up to 3 percent of their FPRN, or a maximum amount to be established by the NOFA, for costs of:

(1) Designing and carrying out a collaborative process for the development of an application to HUD;

(2) Evaluating the outcomes of projects for which funds are awarded in the geographic area under the Continuum of Care and the Emergency Solutions Grants programs; and

(3) Participating in the consolidated plan(s) for the geographic area(s).

(b) *Continuum of Care planning activities.* Eligible planning costs include the costs of:

(1) Developing a communitywide or regionwide process involving the coordination of nonprofit homeless providers, victim service providers, faith-based organizations, governments, businesses, advocates, public housing agencies, school districts, social service providers, mental health agencies, hospitals, universities, affordable housing developers, law enforcement, organizations that serve veterans, and homeless and formerly homeless individuals;

(2) Determining the geographic area that the Continuum of Care will serve;

(3) Developing a Continuum of Care system;

(4) Evaluating the outcomes of projects for which funds are awarded in the geographic area, including the Emergency Solutions Grants program;

(5) Participating in the consolidated plan(s) of the jurisdiction(s) in the geographic area; and

(6) Preparing and submitting an application to HUD on behalf of the entire Continuum of Care membership, including conducting a sheltered and unsheltered point-in-time count and other data collection as required by HUD.

(c) *Monitoring costs.* The costs of monitoring recipients and subrecipients and enforcing compliance with program requirements are eligible.

§ 578.41 Unified Funding Agency costs.

(a) *In general.* UFAs may use up to 3 percent of their FPRN, or a maximum amount to be established by the NOFA, whichever is less, for fiscal control and accounting costs necessary to assure the proper disbursal of, and accounting for, federal funds awarded to subrecipients under the Continuum of Care program.

(b) *UFA costs.* UFA costs include costs of ensuring that all financial transactions carried out under the Continuum of Care program are conducted and records are maintained in accordance with generally accepted accounting principles, including arranging for an annual survey, audit, or evaluation of the financial records of each project carried out by a subrecipient funded by a grant received through the Continuum of Care program.

(c) *Monitoring costs.* The costs of monitoring subrecipients and enforcing compliance with program requirements are eligible for costs.

§ 578.43 Acquisition.

Grant funds may be used to pay up to 100 percent of the cost of acquisition of real property selected by the recipient or subrecipient for use in the provision of housing or supportive services for homeless persons.

§ 578.45 Rehabilitation.

(a) *Use.* Grant funds may be used to pay up to 100 percent of the cost of rehabilitation of structures to provide housing or supportive services to homeless persons.

(b) *Eligible costs.* Eligible rehabilitation costs include installing cost-effective energy measures, and bringing an existing structure to State and local government health and safety standards.

(c) *Ineligible costs.* Grant funds may not be used for rehabilitation of leased property.

(d) *Broadband infrastructure.* Any substantial rehabilitation, as defined by 24 CFR 5.100, of a building with more than 4 rental units and funded by a grant awarded after January 19, 2017 must include installation of broadband infrastructure, as this term is also defined in 24 CFR 5.100, except where the grantee determines and, in accordance with § 578.103, documents the determination that:

(1) The location of the substantial rehabilitation makes installation of broadband infrastructure infeasible;

(2) The cost of installing broadband infrastructure would result in a fundamental alteration in the nature of its program or activity or in an undue financial burden; or

(3) The structure of the housing to be substantially rehabilitated makes installation of broadband infrastructure infeasible.

[77 FR 45442, July 31, 2012, as amended at 81 FR 92637, Dec. 20, 2016]

§ 578.47 New construction.

(a) *Use.* Grant funds may be used to:

(1) Pay up to 100 percent of the cost of new construction, including the building of a new structure or building an addition to an existing structure that increases the floor area by 100 percent or more, and the cost of land associated with that construction, for use as housing.

(2) If grant funds are used for new construction, the applicant must demonstrate that the costs of new construction are substantially less than the costs of rehabilitation or that there is a lack of available appropriate units that could be rehabilitated at a cost less than new construction. For purposes of this cost comparison, costs of rehabilitation or new construction may include the cost of real property acquisition.

(b) *Ineligible costs.* Grant funds may not be used for new construction on leased property.

(c) *Broadband infrastructure.* Any new construction of a building with more than 4 rental units and funded by a grant awarded after January 19, 2017 must include installation of broadband infrastructure, as this term is defined in 24 CFR 5.100, except where the grantee determines and, in accordance with § 578.103, documents the determination that:

(1) The location of the new construction makes installation of broadband infrastructure infeasible; or

(2) The cost of installing broadband infrastructure would result in a fundamental alteration in the nature of its program or activity or in an undue financial burden.

[77 FR 45442, July 31, 2012, as amended at 81 FR 92637, Dec. 20, 2016]

§578.49 Leasing.

(a) *Use.* (1) Where the recipient or subrecipient is leasing the structure, or portions thereof, grant funds may be used to pay for 100 percent of the costs of leasing a structure or structures, or portions thereof, to provide housing or supportive services to homeless persons for up to 3 years. Leasing funds may not be used to lease units or structures owned by the recipient, subrecipient, their parent organization(s), any other related organization(s), or organizations that are members of a partnership, where the partnership owns the structure, unless HUD authorized an exception for good cause.

(2) Any request for an exception must include the following:

(i) A description of how leasing these structures is in the best interest of the program;

(ii) Supporting documentation showing that the leasing charges paid with grant funds are reasonable for the market; and

(iii) A copy of the written policy for resolving disputes between the landlord and tenant, including a recusal for officers, agents, and staff who work for both the landlord and tenant.

(b) *Requirements.* (1) *Leasing structures.* When grants are used to pay rent for all or part of a structure or structures, the rent paid must be reasonable in relation to rents being charged in the area for comparable space. In addition, the rent paid may not exceed rents currently being charged by the same owner for comparable unassisted space.

(2) *Leasing individual units.* When grants are used to pay rent for individual housing units, the rent paid must be reasonable in relation to rents being charged for comparable units, taking into account the location, size, type, quality, amenities, facilities, and management services. In addition, the rents may not exceed rents currently being charged for comparable units, and the rent paid may not exceed HUD-determined fair market rents.

(3) *Utilities.* If electricity, gas, and water are included in the rent, these utilities may be paid from leasing funds. If utilities are not provided by the landlord, these utility costs are an operating cost, except for supportive service facilities. If the structure is being used as a supportive service facility, then these utility costs are a supportive service cost.

(4) *Security deposits and first and last month's rent.* Recipients and subrecipients may use grant funds to pay security deposits, in an amount not to exceed 2 months of actual rent. An advance payment of the last month's rent may be provided to the landlord in addition to the security deposit and payment of the first month's rent.

(5) *Occupancy agreements and subleases.* Occupancy agreements and subleases are required as specified in §578.77(a).

(6) *Calculation of occupancy charges and rent.* Occupancy charges and rent from program participants must be calculated as provided in §578.77.

(7) *Program income.* Occupancy charges and rent collected from program participants are program income and may be used as provided under §578.97.

(8) *Transition.* Beginning in the first year awards are made under the Continuum of Care program, renewals of grants for leasing funds entered into under the authority of title IV, subtitle D of the Act as it existed before May 20, 2009, will be renewed either as grants for leasing or as rental assistance, depending on the characteristics of the project. Leasing funds will be renewed as rental assistance if the funds are used to pay rent on units where the lease is between the program participant and the landowner or sublessor. Projects requesting leasing funds will be renewed as leasing if the funds were used to lease a unit or structure and the lease is between the recipient or subrecipient and the landowner.

§ 578.51 Rental assistance.

(a) *Use.* (1) Grant funds may be used for rental assistance for homeless individuals and families. Rental assistance cannot be provided to a program participant who is already receiving rental assistance, or living in a housing unit receiving rental assistance or operating assistance through other federal, State, or local sources.

(i) The rental assistance may be short-term, up to 3 months of rent; medium-term, for 3 to 24 months of rent; or long-term, for longer than 24 months of rent and must be administered in accordance with the policies and procedures established by the Continuum as set forth in § 578.7(a)(9) and this section.

(ii) The rental assistance may be tenant-based, project-based, or sponsor-based, and may be for transitional or permanent housing.

(2) Grant funds may be used for security deposits in an amount not to exceed 2 months of rent. An advance payment of the last month's rent may be provided to the landlord, in addition to the security deposit and payment of first month's rent.

(b) *Rental assistance administrator.* Rental assistance must be administered by a State, unit of general local government, or a public housing agency.

(c) *Tenant-based rental assistance.* Tenant-based rental assistance is rental assistance in which program participants choose housing of an appropriate size in which to reside. Up to 5 years' worth of rental assistance may be awarded to a project in one competition.

(1) When necessary to facilitate the coordination of supportive services, recipients and subrecipients may require program participants to live in a specific area for their entire period of participation, or in a specific structure for the first year and in a specific area for the remainder of their period of participation. Program participants who are receiving rental assistance in transitional housing may be required to live in a specific structure for their entire period of participation in transitional housing.

(2) Program participants who have complied with all program requirements during their residence retain the rental assistance if they move.

(3) Program participants who have complied with all program requirements during their residence, who have been a victim of domestic violence, dating violence, sexual assault, or stalking, who reasonably believe they are imminently threatened by harm from further domestic violence, dating violence, sexual assault, or stalking (which would include threats from a third party, such as a friend or family member of the perpetrator of the violence) if they remain in the assisted unit, and who are able to document the violence and basis for their belief, may retain the rental assistance and move to a different Continuum of Care geographic area if they move out of the assisted unit to protect their health and safety. These program participants may move to a different Continuum of Care's geographic service area even if the recipient or subrecipient cannot meet all regulatory requirements of this part in the new geographic area where the unit is located. The recipient or subrecipient, however, must be able to meet all statutory requirements of the Continuum of Care program either directly or through a third-party contract or agreement.

(4) Program participants other than those described in paragraph (c)(3) of this section may choose housing outside of the Continuum of Care's geographic area if the recipient or subrecipient, through its employees or contractors, is able to meet all requirements of this part in the geographic area where the program participant chooses housing. If the recipient or subrecipient is unable to meet the requirements of this part, either directly or through a third-party contract or agreement, the recipient or subrecipient may refuse to permit the program participant to retain the tenant-based rental assistance if the program participant chooses to move outside of the Continuum of Care's geographic area.

(d) *Sponsor-based rental assistance.* Sponsor-based rental assistance is provided through contracts between the recipient and sponsor organization. A sponsor may be a private, nonprofit organization, or a community mental health agency established as a public nonprofit organization. Program participants must reside in housing owned or leased by the sponsor. Up to 5 years worth of rental assistance may be awarded to a project in one competition.

(e) *Project-based rental assistance.* Project-based rental assistance is provided through a contract with the owner of an existing structure, where the owner agrees to lease the subsidized units to program participants. Program participants will not retain rental assistance if they move. Up to 15 years of rental assistance may be awarded in one competition.

(f) *Grant amount.* The amount of rental assistance in each project will be based on the number and size of units proposed by the applicant to be assisted over the grant period. The amount of rental assistance in each project will be calculated by multiplying the number and size of units proposed by the FMR of each unit on the date the application is submitted to HUD, by the term of the grant.

(g) *Rent reasonableness.* HUD will only provide rental assistance for a unit if the rent is reasonable. The recipient or subrecipient must determine whether the rent charged for the unit receiving rental assistance is reasonable in relation to rents being charged for comparable unassisted units, taking into account the location, size, type, quality, amenities, facilities, and management and maintenance of each unit. Reasonable rent must not exceed rents currently being charged by the same owner for comparable unassisted units.

(h) *Payment of grant.* (1) The amount of rental assistance in each project will be reserved for rental assistance over the grant period. An applicant's request for rental assistance in each grant is an estimate of the amount needed for rental assistance. Recipients will make draws from the grant funds to pay the actual costs of rental assistance for program participants.

(2) For tenant-based rental assistance, on demonstration of need:

(i) Up to 25 percent of the total rental assistance awarded may be spent in any year of a 5-year grant term; or

(ii) A higher percentage if approved in advance by HUD, if the recipient provides evidence satisfactory to HUD that it is financially committed to providing the housing assistance described in the application for the full 5-year period.

(3) A recipient must serve at least as many program participants as shown in its application for assistance.

(4) If the amount in each grant reserved for rental assistance over the grant period exceeds the amount that will be needed to pay the actual costs of rental assistance, due to such factors as contract rents being lower than FMRs and program participants being able to pay a portion of the rent, recipients or subrecipients may use the excess funds for covering the costs of rent increases, or for serving a greater number of program participants.

(i) *Vacancies.* If a unit assisted under this section is vacated before the expiration of the lease, the assistance for the unit may continue for a maximum of 30 days from the end of the month in which the unit was vacated, unless occupied by another eligible person. No additional assistance will be paid until the unit is occupied by another eligible person. Brief periods of stays in institutions, not to exceed 90 days for each occurrence, are not considered vacancies.

(j) *Property damage.* Recipients and subrecipients may use grant funds in an amount not to exceed one month's rent to pay for any damage to housing due to the action of a program participant. This shall be a one-time cost per participant, incurred at the time a participant exits a housing unit.

(k) *Resident rent.* Rent must be calculated as provided in §578.77. Rents collected from program participants are program income and may be used as provided under §578.97.

(l) *Leases.* (1) *Initial lease.* For project-based, sponsor-based, or tenant-based rental assistance, program participants must enter into a lease agreement for a term of at least one year, which is terminable for cause. The leases must be automatically renewable upon expiration for terms that are a minimum of one month long, except on prior notice by either party.

(2) *Initial lease for transitional housing.* Program participants in transitional

housing must enter into a lease agreement for a term of at least one month. The lease must be automatically renewable upon expiration, except on prior notice by either party, up to a maximum term of 24 months.

(m) *VAWA emergency transfer plan costs.* Recipients and subrecipients of grants for tenant-based rental assistance may use grant funds to pay amounts owed for breaking the lease if the family qualifies for an emergency transfer under the emergency transfer plan established under § 578.99(j)(8).

[77 FR 45442, July 31, 2012, as amended at 81 FR 38584, June 14, 2016; 81 FR 80810, Nov. 16, 2016]

§ 578.53 Supportive services.

(a) *In general.* Grant funds may be used to pay the eligible costs of supportive services that address the special needs of the program participants. If the supportive services are provided in a supportive service facility not contained in a housing structure, the costs of day-to-day operation of the supportive service facility, including maintenance, repair, building security, furniture, utilities, and equipment are eligible as a supportive service.

(1) Supportive services must be necessary to assist program participants obtain and maintain housing.

(2) Recipients and subrecipients shall conduct an annual assessment of the service needs of the program participants and should adjust services accordingly.

(b) *Duration.* (1) For a transitional housing project, supportive services must be made available to residents throughout the duration of their residence in the project.

(2) Permanent supportive housing projects must provide supportive services for the residents to enable them to live as independently as is practicable throughout the duration of their residence in the project.

(3) Services may also be provided to former residents of transitional housing and current residents of permanent housing who were homeless in the prior 6 months, for no more than 6 months after leaving transitional housing or homelessness, respectively, to assist their adjustment to independent living.

(4) Rapid rehousing projects must require the program participant to meet with a case manager not less than once per month as set forth in § 578.37(a)(1)(ii)(F), to assist the program participant in maintaining long-term housing stability.

(c) *Special populations.* All eligible costs are eligible to the same extent for program participants who are unaccompanied homeless youth; persons living with HIV/AIDS; and victims of domestic violence, dating violence, sexual assault, or stalking.

(d) *Ineligible costs.* Any cost that is not described as an eligible cost under this section is not an eligible cost of providing supportive services using Continuum of Care program funds. Staff training and the costs of obtaining professional licenses or certifications needed to provide supportive services are not eligible costs.

(e) *Eligible costs.* (1) *Annual Assessment of Service Needs.* The costs of the assessment required by § 578.53(a)(2) are eligible costs.

(2) *Assistance with moving costs.* Reasonable one-time moving costs are eligible and include truck rental and hiring a moving company.

(3) *Case management.* The costs of assessing, arranging, coordinating, and monitoring the delivery of individualized services to meet the needs of the program participant(s) are eligible costs. Component services and activities consist of:

(i) Counseling;

(ii) Developing, securing, and coordinating services;

(iii) Using the centralized or coordinated assessment system as required under § 578.23(c)(9).

(iv) Obtaining federal, State, and local benefits;

(v) Monitoring and evaluating program participant progress;

(vi) Providing information and referrals to other providers;

(vii) Providing ongoing risk assessment and safety planning with victims of domestic violence, dating violence, sexual assault, and stalking; and

(viii) Developing an individualized housing and service plan, including planning a path to permanent housing stability.

(4) *Child care.* The costs of establishing and operating child care, and providing child-care vouchers, for children from families experiencing homelessness, including providing meals and snacks, and comprehensive and coordinated developmental activities, are eligible.

(i) The children must be under the age of 13, unless they are disabled children.

(ii) Disabled children must be under the age of 18.

(iii) The child-care center must be licensed by the jurisdiction in which it operates in order for its costs to be eligible.

(5) *Education services.* The costs of improving knowledge and basic educational skills are eligible.

(i) Services include instruction or training in consumer education, health education, substance abuse prevention, literacy, English as a Second Language, and General Educational Development (GED).

(ii) Component services or activities are screening, assessment and testing; individual or group instruction; tutoring; provision of books, supplies, and instructional material; counseling; and referral to community resources.

(6) *Employment assistance and job training.* The costs of establishing and operating employment assistance and job training programs are eligible, including classroom, online and/or computer instruction, on-the-job instruction, services that assist individuals in securing employment, acquiring learning skills, and/or increasing earning potential. The cost of providing reasonable stipends to program participants in employment assistance and job training programs is also an eligible cost.

(i) Learning skills include those skills that can be used to secure and retain a job, including the acquisition of vocational licenses and/or certificates.

(ii) Services that assist individuals in securing employment consist of:

(A) Employment screening, assessment, or testing;

(B) Structured job skills and job-seeking skills;

(C) Special training and tutoring, including literacy training and pre-vocational training;

(D) Books and instructional material;

(E) Counseling or job coaching; and

(F) Referral to community resources.

(7) *Food.* The cost of providing meals or groceries to program participants is eligible.

(8) *Housing search and counseling services.* Costs of assisting eligible program participants to locate, obtain, and retain suitable housing are eligible.

(i) Component services or activities are tenant counseling; assisting individuals and families to understand leases; securing utilities; and making moving arrangements.

(ii) Other eligible costs are:

(A) Mediation with property owners and landlords on behalf of eligible program participants;

(B) Credit counseling, accessing a free personal credit report, and resolving personal credit issues; and

(C) The payment of rental application fees.

(iii) Housing counseling, as defined in §5.100, that is funded with or provided in connection with grant funds must be carried out in accordance with §5.111. When recipients or subrecipients provide housing services to eligible persons that are incidental to a larger set of holistic case management services, these services do not meet the definition of Housing counseling, as defined in §5.100, and therefore are not required to be carried out in accordance with the certification requirements of §5.111.

(9) *Legal services.* Eligible costs are the fees charged by licensed attorneys and by person(s) under the supervision of licensed attorneys, for advice and representation in matters that interfere with the homeless individual or family's ability to obtain and retain housing.

(i) Eligible subject matters are child support; guardianship; paternity; emancipation; legal separation; orders of protection and other civil remedies for victims of domestic violence, dating violence, sexual assault, and stalking; appeal of veterans and public benefit claim denials; landlord tenant disputes; and the resolution of outstanding criminal warrants.

(ii) Component services or activities may include receiving and preparing cases for trial, provision of legal advice, representation at hearings, and counseling.

(iii) Fees based on the actual service performed (i.e., fee for service) are also eligible, but only if the cost would be less than the cost of hourly fees. Filing fees and other necessary court costs are also eligible. If the subrecipient is a legal services provider and performs the services itself, the eligible costs are the subrecipient's employees' salaries and other costs necessary to perform the services.

(iv) Legal services for immigration and citizenship matters and issues related to mortgages and homeownership are ineligible. Retainer fee arrangements and contingency fee arrangements are ineligible.

(10) *Life skills training*. The costs of teaching critical life management skills that may never have been learned or have been lost during the course of physical or mental illness, domestic violence, substance abuse, and homelessness are eligible. These services must be necessary to assist the program participant to function independently in the community. Component life skills training are the budgeting of resources and money management, household management, conflict management, shopping for food and other needed items, nutrition, the use of public transportation, and parent training.

(11) *Mental health services*. Eligible costs are the direct outpatient treatment of mental health conditions that are provided by licensed professionals. Component services are crisis interventions; counseling; individual, family, or group therapy sessions; the prescription of psychotropic medications or explanations about the use and management of medications; and combinations of therapeutic approaches to address multiple problems.

(12) *Outpatient health services*. Eligible costs are the direct outpatient treatment of medical conditions when provided by licensed medical professionals including:

(i) Providing an analysis or assessment of an individual's health problems and the development of a treatment plan;

(ii) Assisting individuals to understand their health needs;

(iii) Providing directly or assisting individuals to obtain and utilize appropriate medical treatment;

(iv) Preventive medical care and health maintenance services, including in-home health services and emergency medical services;

(v) Provision of appropriate medication;

(vi) Providing follow-up services; and

(vii) Preventive and noncosmetic dental care.

(13) *Outreach services*. The costs of activities to engage persons for the purpose of providing immediate support and intervention, as well as identifying potential program participants, are eligible.

(i) Eligible costs include the outreach worker's transportation costs and a cell phone to be used by the individual performing the outreach.

(ii) Component activities and services consist of: initial assessment; crisis counseling; addressing urgent physical needs, such as providing meals, blankets, clothes, or toiletries; actively connecting and providing people with information and referrals to homeless and mainstream programs; and publicizing the availability of the housing and/or services provided within the geographic area covered by the Continuum of Care.

(14) *Substance abuse treatment services*. The costs of program participant intake and assessment, outpatient treatment, group and individual counseling, and drug testing are eligible. Inpatient detoxification and other inpatient drug or alcohol treatment are ineligible.

(15) *Transportation*. Eligible costs are:

(i) The costs of program participant's travel on public transportation or in a vehicle provided by the recipient or subrecipient to and from medical care, employment, child care, or other services eligible under this section.

(ii) Mileage allowance for service workers to visit program participants and to carry out housing quality inspections;

(iii) The cost of purchasing or leasing a vehicle in which staff transports program participants and/or staff serving program participants;

(iv) The cost of gas, insurance, taxes, and maintenance for the vehicle;

(v) The costs of recipient or subrecipient staff to accompany or assist program participants to utilize public transportation; and

(vi) If public transportation options are not sufficient within the area, the recipient may make a one-time payment on behalf of a program participant needing car repairs or maintenance required to operate a personal vehicle, subject to the following:

(A) Payments for car repairs or maintenance on behalf of the program participant may not exceed 10 percent of the Blue Book value of the vehicle (Blue Book refers to the guidebook that compiles and quotes prices for new and used automobiles and other vehicles of all makes, models, and types);

(B) Payments for car repairs or maintenance must be paid by the recipient or subrecipient directly to the third party that repairs or maintains the car; and

(C) The recipients or subrecipients may require program participants to share in the cost of car repairs or maintenance as a condition of receiving assistance with car repairs or maintenance.

(16) *Utility deposits.* This form of assistance consists of paying for utility deposits. Utility deposits must be a one-time fee, paid to utility companies.

(17) *Direct provision of services.* If the service described in paragraphs (e)(1) through (e)(16) of this section is being directly delivered by the recipient or subrecipient, eligible costs for those services also include:

(i) The costs of labor or supplies, and materials incurred by the recipient or subrecipient in directly providing supportive services to program participants; and

(ii) The salary and benefit packages of the recipient and subrecipient staff who directly deliver the services.

[77 FR 45442, July 31, 2012, as amended at 81 FR 90660, Dec. 14, 2016]

§578.55 Operating costs.

(a) *Use.* Grant funds may be used to pay the costs of the day-to-day operation of transitional and permanent housing in a single structure or individual housing units.

(b) *Eligible costs.* (1) The maintenance and repair of housing;

(2) Property taxes and insurance;

(3) Scheduled payments to a reserve for replacement of major systems of the housing (provided that the payments must be based on the useful life of the system and expected replacement cost);

(4) Building security for a structure where more than 50 percent of the units or area is paid for with grant funds;

(5) Electricity, gas, and water;

(6) Furniture; and

(7) Equipment.

(c) *Ineligible costs.* Program funds may not be used for rental assistance and operating costs in the same project. Program funds may not be used for the operating costs of emergency shelter- and supportive service-only facilities. Program funds may not be used for the maintenance and repair of housing where the costs of maintaining and repairing the housing are included in the lease.

§578.57 Homeless Management Information System.

(a) *Eligible costs.* (1) The recipient or subrecipient may use Continuum of Care program funds to pay the costs of contributing data to the HMIS designated by the Continuum of Care, including the costs of:

(i) Purchasing or leasing computer hardware;

(ii) Purchasing software or software licenses;

(iii) Purchasing or leasing equipment, including telephones, fax machines, and furniture;

(iv) Obtaining technical support;

(v) Leasing office space;

(vi) Paying charges for electricity, gas, water, phone service, and high-speed data transmission necessary to operate or contribute data to the HMIS;

(vii) Paying salaries for operating HMIS, including:

(A) Completing data entry;

(B) Monitoring and reviewing data quality;

(C) Completing data analysis;

(D) Reporting to the HMIS Lead;

(E) Training staff on using the HMIS; and

(F) Implementing and complying with HMIS requirements;

(viii) Paying costs of staff to travel to and attend HUD-sponsored and HUD-approved training on HMIS and programs authorized by Title IV of the McKinney-Vento Homeless Assistance Act;

(ix) Paying staff travel costs to conduct intake; and

(x) Paying participation fees charged by the HMIS Lead, as authorized by HUD, if the recipient or subrecipient is not the HMIS Lead.

(2) If the recipient or subrecipient is the HMIS Lead, it may also use Continuum of Care funds to pay the costs of:

(i) Hosting and maintaining HMIS software or data;

(ii) Backing up, recovering, or repairing HMIS software or data;

(iii) Upgrading, customizing, and enhancing the HMIS;

(iv) Integrating and warehousing data, including development of a data warehouse for use in aggregating data from subrecipients using multiple software systems;

(v) Administering the system;

(vi) Reporting to providers, the Continuum of Care, and HUD; and

(vii) Conducting training on using the system, including traveling to the training.

(3) If the recipient or subrecipient is a victim services provider, or a legal services provider, it may use Continuum of Care funds to establish and operate a comparable database that complies with HUD's HMIS requirements.

(b) *General restrictions.* Activities funded under this section must comply with the HMIS requirements.

§ 578.59 Project administrative costs.

(a) *Eligible costs.* The recipient or subrecipient may use up to 10 percent of any grant awarded under this part, excluding the amount for Continuum of Care Planning Activities and UFA costs, for the payment of project administrative costs related to the planning and execution of Continuum of Care activities. This does not include staff and overhead costs directly related to carrying out activities eligible under § 578.43 through § 578.57, because those costs are eligible as part of those activities. Eligible administrative costs include:

(1) *General management, oversight, and coordination.* Costs of overall program management, coordination, monitoring, and evaluation. These costs include, but are not limited to, necessary expenditures for the following:

(i) Salaries, wages, and related costs of the recipient's staff, the staff of subrecipients, or other staff engaged in program administration. In charging costs to this category, the recipient may include the entire salary, wages, and related costs allocable to the program of each person whose primary responsibilities with regard to the program involve program administration assignments, or the pro rata share of the salary, wages, and related costs of each person whose job includes any program administration assignments. The recipient may use only one of these methods for each fiscal year grant. Program administration assignments include the following:

(A) Preparing program budgets and schedules, and amendments to those budgets and schedules;

(B) Developing systems for assuring compliance with program requirements;

(C) Developing agreements with subrecipients and contractors to carry out program activities;

(D) Monitoring program activities for progress and compliance with program requirements;

(E) Preparing reports and other documents directly related to the program for submission to HUD;

(F) Coordinating the resolution of audit and monitoring findings;

(G) Evaluating program results against stated objectives; and

(H) Managing or supervising persons whose primary responsibilities with regard to the program include such assignments as those described in paragraph (a)(1)(i)(A) through (G) of this section.

(ii) Travel costs incurred for monitoring of subrecipients;

(iii) Administrative services performed under third-party contracts or agreements, including general legal services, accounting services, and audit services; and

(iv) Other costs for goods and services required for administration of the program, including rental or purchase of equipment, insurance, utilities, office supplies, and rental and maintenance (but not purchase) of office space.

(2) *Training on Continuum of Care requirements.* Costs of providing training on Continuum of Care requirements and attending HUD-sponsored Continuum of Care trainings.

(3) *Environmental review.* Costs of carrying out the environmental review responsibilities under §578.31.

(b) *Sharing requirement.* (1) *UFAs.* If the recipient is a UFA that carries out a project, it may use up to 10 percent of the grant amount awarded for the project on project administrative costs. The UFA must share the remaining project administrative funds with its subrecipients.

(2) *Recipients that are not UFAs.* If the recipient is not a UFA, it must share at least 50 percent of project administrative funds with its subrecipients.

§578.61 Relocation costs.

(a) *In general.* Relocation costs under the Uniform Relocation Assistance and Real Property Acquisition Policies Act of 1970 are eligible.

(b) *Eligible relocation costs.* Eligible costs are costs to provide relocation payments and other assistance to persons displaced by a project assisted with grant funds in accordance with §578.83.

§578.63 Indirect costs.

(a) *In general.* Continuum of Care funds may be used to pay indirect costs in accordance with 2 CFR part 200, subpart E.

(b) *Allocation.* Indirect costs may be allocated to each eligible activity as provided in this subpart, so long as that allocation is consistent with an indirect cost rate proposal developed in accordance with 2 CFR part 200, subpart E.

(c) *Expenditure limits.* The indirect costs charged to an activity subject to an expenditure limit under §§578.39, 578.41, and 578.59 must be added to the direct costs charged for that activity when determining the total costs subject to the expenditure limits.

[77 FR 45442, July 31, 2012, as amended at 80 FR 75939, Dec. 7, 2015]

Subpart E—High-Performing Communities

§578.65 Standards.

(a) *In general.* The collaborative applicant for a Continuum may apply to HUD to have the Continuum be designated a high-performing community (HPC). The designation shall be for grants awarded in the same competition in which the designation is applied for and made.

(b) *Applying for HPC designation.* The application must be submitted at such time and in such manner as HUD may require, must use HMIS data where required to show the standards for qualifying are met, and must contain such information as HUD requires, including at a minimum:

(1) A report showing how the Continuum of Care program funds received in the preceding year were expended;

(2) A specific plan for how grant funds will be expended; and

(3) Information establishing that the Continuum of Care meets the standards for HPCs.

(c) *Standards for qualifying as an HPC.* To qualify as an HPC, a Continuum must demonstrate through:

(1) Reliable data generated by the Continuum of Care's HMIS that it meets all of the following standards:

(i) *Mean length of homelessness.* Either the mean length of episode of homelessness within the Continuum's geographic area is fewer than 20 days, or the mean length of episodes of homelessness for individuals or families in similar circumstances was reduced by at least 10 percent from the preceding federal fiscal year.

(ii) *Reduced recidivism.* Of individuals and families who leave homelessness, less than 5 percent become homeless again at any time within the next 2 years; or the percentage of individuals and families in similar circumstances who become homeless again within 2 years after leaving homelessness was decreased by at least 20 percent from the preceding federal fiscal year.

(iii) *HMIS coverage.* The Continuum's HMIS must have a bed coverage rate of 80 percent and a service volume coverage rate of 80 percent as calculated in accordance with HUD's HMIS requirements.

(iv) *Serving families and youth.* With respect to Continuums that served homeless families and youth defined as homeless under other federal statutes in paragraph (3) of the definition of homeless in § 576.2:

(A) 95 percent of those families and youth did not become homeless again within a 2-year period following termination of assistance; or

(B) 85 percent of those families achieved independent living in permanent housing for at least 2 years following termination of assistance.

(2) Reliable data generated from sources other than the Continuum's HMIS that is provided in a narrative or other form prescribed by HUD that it meets both of the following standards:

(i) *Community action.* All the metropolitan cities and counties within the Continuum's geographic area have a comprehensive outreach plan, including specific steps for identifying homeless persons and referring them to appropriate housing and services in that geographic area.

(ii) *Renewing HPC status.* If the Continuum was designated an HPC in the previous federal fiscal year and used Continuum of Care grant funds for activities described under § 578.71, that such activities were effective at reducing the number of individuals and families who became homeless in that community.

§ 578.67 Publication of application.

HUD will publish the application to be designated an HPC through the HUD Web site, for public comment as to whether the Continuum seeking designation as an HPC meets the standards for being one.

§ 578.69 Cooperation among entities.

An HPC must cooperate with HUD in distributing information about its successful efforts to reduce homelessness.

§ 578.71 HPC-eligible activities.

In addition to using grant funds for the eligible costs described in subpart D of this part, recipients and subrecipients in Continuums of Care designated as HPCs may also use grant funds to provide housing relocation and stabilization services and short- and/or medium-term rental assistance to individuals and families at risk of homelessness as set forth in 24 CFR 576.103 and 24 CFR 576.104, if necessary to prevent the individual or family from becoming homeless. Activities must be carried out in accordance with the plan submitted in the application. When carrying out housing relocation and stabilization services and short- and/or medium-term rental assistance, the written standards set forth in § 578.7(a)(9)(v) and recordkeeping requirements of 24 CFR 576.500 apply.

Subpart F—Program Requirements

§ 578.73 Matching requirements.

(a) *In general.* The recipient or subrecipient must match all grant funds, except for leasing funds, with no less than 25 percent of funds or in-kind contributions from other sources. For Continuum of Care geographic areas in which there is more than one grant agreement, the 25 percent match must be provided on a grant-by-grant basis. Recipients that are UFAs or are the sole recipient for their Continuum, may provide match on a Continuum-wide basis. Cash match must be used for the costs of activities that are eligible under subpart D of this part, except that HPCs may use such match for the costs of activities that are eligible under § 578.71.

(b) *Cash sources.* Notwithstanding 2 CFR 200.306(b)(5), a recipient or subrecipient may use funds from any source, including any other federal sources (excluding Continuum of Care program funds), as well as State, local, and private sources, provided that funds from the source are not statutorily prohibited to be used as a match.

The recipient must ensure that any funds used to satisfy the matching requirements of this section are eligible under the laws governing the funds in order to be used as matching funds for a grant awarded under this program.

(c) *In-kind contributions.* (1) The recipient or subrecipient may use the value of any real property, equipment, goods, or services contributed to the project as match, provided that if the recipient or subrecipient had to pay for them with grant funds, the costs would have been eligible under Subpart D, or, in the case of HPCs, eligible under §578.71.

(2) The requirements of 2 CFR 200.306, with the exception of §200.306(b)(5) apply.

(3) Before grant execution, services to be provided by a third party must be documented by a memorandum of understanding (MOU) between the recipient or subrecipient and the third party that will provide the services. Services provided by individuals must be valued at rates consistent with those ordinarily paid for similar work in the recipient's or subrecipient's organization. If the recipient or subrecipient does not have employees performing similar work, the rates must be consistent with those ordinarily paid by other employers for similar work in the same labor market.

(i) The MOU must establish the unconditional commitment, except for selection to receive a grant, by the third party to provide the services, the specific service to be provided, the profession of the persons providing the service, and the hourly cost of the service to be provided.

(ii) During the term of the grant, the recipient or subrecipient must keep and make available, for inspection, records documenting the service hours provided.

[77 FR 45442, July 31, 2012, as amended at 80 FR 75940, Dec. 7, 2015]

§578.75 General operations.

(a) *State and local requirements.* (1) Housing and facilities constructed or rehabilitated with assistance under this part must meet State or local building codes, and in the absence of State or local building codes, the International Residential Code or International Building Code (as applicable to the type of structure) of the International Code Council.

(2) Services provided with assistance under this part must be provided in compliance with all applicable State and local requirements, including licensing requirements.

(b) *Housing standards.* Housing leased with Continuum of Care program funds, or for which rental assistance payments are made with Continuum of Care program funds, must meet the applicable standards under 24 CFR 5.703, except that the carbon monoxide detection requirement at 24 CFR 5.703(b)(2) and (d)(6) shall not apply. For housing that is occupied by program participants receiving tenant-based rental assistance, 24 CFR part 35, subparts A, B, M, and R apply. For housing rehabilitated with funds under this part, the lead-based paint requirements in 24 CFR part 35, subparts A, B, J, and R apply. For housing that receives project-based or sponsor-based rental assistance, 24 CFR part 35, subparts A, B, H, and R apply. For residential property for which funds under this part are used for acquisition, leasing, services, or operating costs, 24 CFR part 35, subparts A, B, K, and R apply. Additionally, for tenant-based rental assistance, for leasing of individual units, and for sponsor based rental assistance where not all units in a structure are or will be assisted, the standards apply only to the unit itself, and to the means of ingress and egress from the unit to the public way and to the building's common areas.

(1) Before any assistance will be provided on behalf of a program participant, the recipient, or subrecipient, must physically inspect each unit to assure that the unit meets 24 CFR 5.703. Assistance will not be provided for units that fail to meet 24 CFR 5.703, unless the owner corrects any deficiencies within 30 days from the date of the initial inspection and the recipient or subrecipient verifies that all deficiencies have been corrected.

(2) Recipients or subrecipients must inspect all units at least annually during the grant period to ensure that the units continue to meet 24 CFR 5.703.

(3) The requirements in 24 CFR 5.705 through 5.713 do not apply.

(c) *Suitable dwelling size.* The dwelling unit must have at least one bedroom or living/sleeping room for each two persons.

(1) Children of opposite sex, other than very young children, may not be required to occupy the same bedroom or living/sleeping room.

(2) If household composition changes during the term of assistance, recipients and subrecipients may relocate the household to a more appropriately sized unit. The household must still have access to appropriate supportive services.

(d) *Meals.* Each recipient and subrecipient of assistance under this part who provides supportive housing for homeless persons with disabilities must provide meals or meal preparation facilities for residents.

(e) *Ongoing assessment of supportive services.* To the extent practicable, each project must provide supportive services for residents of the project and homeless persons using the project, which may be designed by the recipient or participants. Each recipient and subrecipient of assistance under this part must conduct an ongoing assessment of the supportive services needed by the residents of the project, the availability of such services, and the coordination of services needed to ensure long-term housing stability and must make adjustments, as appropriate.

(f) *Residential supervision.* Each recipient and subrecipient of assistance under this part must provide residential supervision as necessary to facilitate the adequate provision of supportive services to the residents of the housing throughout the term of the commitment to operate supportive housing. Residential supervision may include the employment of a full- or part-time residential supervisor with sufficient knowledge to provide or to supervise the provision of supportive services to the residents.

(g) *Participation of homeless individuals.* (1) Each recipient and subrecipient must provide for the participation of not less than one homeless individual or formerly homeless individual on the board of directors or other equivalent policymaking entity of the recipient or subrecipient, to the extent that such entity considers and makes policies and decisions regarding any project, supportive services, or assistance provided under this part. This requirement is waived if a recipient or subrecipient is unable to meet such requirement and obtains HUD approval for a plan to otherwise consult with homeless or formerly homeless persons when considering and making policies and decisions.

(2) Each recipient and subrecipient of assistance under this part must, to the maximum extent practicable, involve homeless individuals and families through employment; volunteer services; or otherwise in constructing, rehabilitating, maintaining, and operating the project, and in providing supportive services for the project.

(h) *Supportive service agreement.* Recipients and subrecipients may require the program participants to take part in supportive services that are not disability-related services provided through the project as a condition of continued participation in the program. Examples of disability-related services include, but are not limited to, mental health services, outpatient health services, and provision of medication, which are provided to a person with a disability to address a condition caused by the disability. Notwithstanding this provision, if the purpose of the project is to provide substance abuse treatment services, recipients and subrecipients may require program participants to take part in such services as a condition of continued participation in the program.

(i) *Retention of assistance after death, incarceration, or institutionalization for more than 90 days of qualifying member.* For permanent supportive housing projects surviving, members of any household who were living in a unit assisted under this part at the time of the qualifying member's death, long-term incarceration, or long-term institutionalization, have the right to rental assistance under this section until the expiration of the lease in effect at the time of the qualifying member's death, long-term incarceration, or long-term institutionalization.

(j) *Remaining program participants following bifurcation of a lease or eviction as a result of domestic violence.* For permanent supportive housing projects, members of any household who were living in a unit assisted under this part at the time of a qualifying member's eviction from the unit because the qualifying member was found to have engaged in criminal activity directly relating to domestic violence, dating violence, sexual assault, or stalking, have the right to rental assistance under this section until the expiration of the lease in effect at the time of the qualifying member's eviction.

[77 FR 45442, July 31, 2012, as amended at 81 FR 80810, Nov. 16, 2016; 88 FR 30499, May 11, 2023]

§578.77 Calculating occupancy charges and rent.

(a) *Occupancy agreements and leases.* Recipients and subrecipients must have signed occupancy agreements or leases (or subleases) with program participants residing in housing.

(b) *Calculation of occupancy charges.* Recipients and subrecipients are not required to impose occupancy charges on program participants as a condition of residing in the housing. However, if occupancy charges are imposed, they may not exceed the highest of:

(1) 30 percent of the family's monthly adjusted income (adjustment factors include the number of people in the family, age of family members, medical expenses, and child-care expenses);

(2) 10 percent of the family's monthly income; or

(3) If the family is receiving payments for welfare assistance from a public agency and a part of the payments (adjusted in accordance with the family's actual housing costs) is specifically designated by the agency to meet the family's housing costs, the portion of the payments that is designated for housing costs.

(4) *Income.* Income must be calculated in accordance with 24 CFR 5.609 and 24 CFR 5.611(a). Recipients and subrecipients must examine a program participant's income initially, and if there is a change in family composition (*e.g.*, birth of a child) or a decrease in the resident's income during the year, the resident may request an interim reexamination, and the occupancy charge will be adjusted accordingly.

(c) *Resident rent.* (1) *Amount of rent.* (i) Each program participant on whose behalf rental assistance payments are made must pay a contribution toward rent in accordance with section 3(a)(1) of the U.S. Housing Act of 1937 (42 U.S.C. 1437a(a)(1)).

(ii) Income of program participants must be calculated in accordance with 24 CFR 5.609 and 24 CFR 5.611(a).

(2) *Review.* Recipients or subrecipients must examine a program participant's income initially, and at least annually thereafter, to determine the amount of the contribution toward rent payable by the program participant. Adjustments to a program participant's contribution toward the rental payment must be made as changes in income are identified.

(3) *Verification.* As a condition of participation in the program, each program participant must agree to supply the information or documentation necessary to verify the program participant's income. Program participants must provide the recipient or subrecipient with information at any time regarding changes in income or other circumstances that may result in changes to a program participant's contribution toward the rental payment.

§578.79 Limitation on transitional housing.

A homeless individual or family may remain in transitional housing for a period longer than 24 months, if permanent housing for the individual or family has not been located or if the individual or family requires additional time to prepare for independent living. However, HUD may discontinue assistance for a transitional housing project if more than half of the homeless individuals or families remain in that project longer than 24 months.

§578.81 Term of commitment, repayment of grants, and prevention of undue benefits.

(a) *In general.* All recipients and subrecipients receiving grant funds for acquisition, rehabilitation, or new construction must operate the housing or provide supportive services in accordance with this part, for at least 15 years from the date of initial occupancy or date of initial service provision. Recipient and subrecipients must execute and record a HUD-approved Declaration of Restrictive Covenants before receiving payment of grant funds.

(b) *Conversion.* Recipients and subrecipients carrying out a project that provides transitional or permanent housing or supportive services in a structure may submit a request to HUD to convert a project for the direct benefit of very low-income persons. The request must be made while the project is operating as homeless housing or supportive services for homeless individuals and families, must be in writing, and must include an explanation of why the project is no longer needed to provide transitional or permanent housing or supportive services. The primary factor in HUD's decision on the proposed conversion is the unmet need for transitional or permanent housing or supportive services in the Continuum of Care's geographic area.

(c) *Repayment of grant funds.* If a project is not operated as transitional or permanent housing for 10 years following the date of initial occupancy, HUD will require repayment of the entire amount of the grant used for acquisition, rehabilitation, or new construction, unless conversion of the project has been authorized under paragraph (b) of this section. If the housing is used for such purposes for more than 10 years, the payment amount will be reduced by 20 percentage points for each year, beyond the 10-year period in which the project is used for transitional or permanent housing.

(d) *Prevention of undue benefits.* Except as provided under paragraph (e) of this section, upon any sale or other disposition of a project site that received grant funds for acquisition, rehabilitation, or new construction, occurring before the 15-year period, the recipient must comply with such terms and conditions as HUD may prescribe to prevent the recipient or subrecipient from unduly benefiting from such sale or disposition.

(e) *Exception.* A recipient or subrecipient will not be required to comply with the terms and conditions prescribed under paragraphs (c) and (d) of this section if:

(1) The sale or disposition of the property used for the project results in the use of the property for the direct benefit of very low-income persons;

(2) All the proceeds are used to provide transitional or permanent housing that meet the requirements of this part;

(3) Project-based rental assistance or operating cost assistance from any federal program or an equivalent State or local program is no longer made available and the project is meeting applicable performance standards, provided that the portion of the project that had benefitted from such assistance continues to meet the tenant income and rent restrictions for low-income units under section 42(g) of the Internal Revenue Code of 1986; or

(4) There are no individuals and families in the Continuum of Care geographic area who are homeless, in which case the project may serve individuals and families at risk of homelessness.

§ 578.83 Displacement, relocation, and acquisition.

(a) *Minimizing displacement.* Consistent with the other goals and objectives of this part, recipients and subrecipients must ensure that they have taken all reasonable steps to minimize the displacement of persons (families, individuals, businesses, nonprofit organizations, and farms) as a result of projects assisted under this part. "Project," as used in this section, means any activity or series of activities assisted with Continuum of Care funds received or anticipated in any phase of an undertaking.

(b) *Temporary relocation.* (1) *Existing Building Not Assisted under Title IV of the McKinney-Vento Act.* No tenant may be required to relocate temporarily for a project if the building in which the project is being undertaken or will be undertaken is not currently assisted under Title IV of the McKinney-Vento Act. The absence of such assistance to the building means the tenants are not homeless and the tenants are therefore not eligible to receive assistance under the Continuum of Care program. When a tenant moves for such a project under conditions that cause the Uniform Relocation Assistance and Real Property Acquisition Policies Act of 1970 (URA), 42 U.S.C. 4601–4655, to apply, the tenant must be treated as permanently displaced and offered relocation assistance and payments consistent with paragraph (c) of this section.

(2) *Existing Transitional Housing or Permanent Housing Projects Assisted Under Title IV of the McKinney-Vento Act.* Consistent with paragraph (c)(2)(ii) of this section, no program participant may be required to relocate temporarily for a project if the person cannot be offered a decent, safe, and sanitary unit in the same building or complex upon project completion under reasonable terms and conditions. The length of occupancy requirements in §578.79 may prevent a program participant from returning to the property upon completion (See paragraph (c)(2)(iii)(D) of this section). Any program participant who has been temporarily relocated for a period beyond one year must be treated as permanently displaced and offered relocation assistance and payments consistent with paragraph (c) of this section. Program participants temporarily relocated in accordance with the policies described in this paragraph must be provided:

(i) Reimbursement for all reasonable out-of-pocket expenses incurred in connection with the temporary relocation, including the cost of moving to and from the temporarily occupied housing and any increase in monthly rent/occupancy charges and utility costs; and

(ii) Appropriate advisory services, including reasonable advance written notice of:

(A) The date and approximate duration of the temporary relocation;

(B) The location of the suitable, decent, safe, and sanitary dwelling to be made available for the temporary period;

(C) The reasonable terms and conditions under which the program participant will be able to occupy a suitable, decent, safe, and sanitary dwelling in the building or complex upon completion of the project; and

(D) The provisions of paragraph (b)(2)(i) of this section.

(c) *Relocation assistance for displaced persons.* (1) *In general.* A displaced person (defined in paragraph (c)(2) of this section) must be provided relocation assistance in accordance with the requirements of the URA and implementing regulations at 49 CFR part 24. A displaced person must be advised of his or her rights under the Fair Housing Act. Whenever possible, minority persons must be given reasonable opportunities to relocate to decent, safe, and sanitary replacement dwellings, not located in an area of minority concentration, that are within their financial means. This policy, however, does not require providing a person a larger payment than is necessary to enable a person to relocate to a comparable replacement dwelling. See 49 CFR 24.205(c)(2)(ii)(D).

(2) *Displaced person.* (i) For the purposes of paragraph (c) of this section, the term "displaced person" means any person (family, individual, business, nonprofit organization, or farm) that moves from real property, or moves personal property from real property, permanently, as a direct result of acquisition, rehabilitation, or demolition for a project. This includes any permanent, involuntary move for a project, including any permanent move from the real property that is made:

(A) After the owner (or person in control of the site) issues a notice to move permanently from the property, or refuses to renew an expiring lease, if the move occurs after the date of the submission by the recipient or subrecipient of an application for assistance to HUD (or the recipient, as applicable) that is later approved and funded and the recipient or subrecipient has site control as evidenced in accordance with §578.25(b); or

(B) After the owner (or person in control of the site) issues a notice to move permanently from the property, or refuses to renew an expiring lease, if the move occurs after the date the recipient or subrecipient obtains site control, as evidenced in accordance with §578.25(b), if that occurs after the application for assistance; or

(C) Before the date described under paragraph (c)(2)(i)(A) or (B) of this section, if the recipient or HUD determines that the displacement resulted directly from acquisition, rehabilitation, or demolition for the project; or

(D) By a tenant of a building that is not assisted under Title IV of the McKinney-Vento Act, if the tenant moves after execution of the agreement covering the acquisition, rehabilitation, or demolition of the property for the project; or

(ii) For the purposes of paragraph (c) of this section, the term "displaced person" means any person (family, individual, business, nonprofit organization, or farm) that moves from real property, or moves personal property from real property, permanently, as a direct result of acquisition, rehabilitation, or demolition for a project. This includes any permanent, involuntary move for a project that is made by a program participant occupying transitional housing or permanent housing assisted under Title IV of the McKinney-Vento Act, if any one of the following three situations occurs:

(A) The program participant moves after execution of the agreement covering the acquisition, rehabilitation, or demolition of the property for the project and is either not eligible to return upon project completion or the move occurs before the program participant is provided written notice offering the program participant an opportunity to occupy a suitable, decent, safe, and sanitary dwelling in the same building or complex upon project completion under reasonable terms and conditions. Such reasonable terms and conditions must include a lease (or occupancy agreement, as applicable) consistent with Continuum of Care program requirements, including a monthly rent or occupancy charge and monthly utility costs that does not exceed the maximum amounts established in § 578.77; or

(B) The program participant is required to relocate temporarily, does not return to the building or complex, and any one of the following situations occurs:

(*1*) The program participant is not offered payment for all reasonable out-of-pocket expenses incurred in connection with the temporary relocation;

(*2*) The program participant is not eligible to return to the building or complex upon project completion; or

(*3*) Other conditions of the temporary relocation are not reasonable; or

(C) The program participant is required to move to another unit in the same building or complex, and any one of the following situations occurs:

(*1*) The program participant is not offered reimbursement for all reasonable out-of-pocket expenses incurred in connection with the move;

(*2*) The program participant is not eligible to remain in the building or complex upon project completion; or

(*3*) Other conditions of the move are not reasonable.

(iii) Notwithstanding the provisions of paragraph (c)(2)(i) or (ii) of this section, a person does not qualify as a "displaced person" if:

(A) The person has been evicted for serious or repeated violation of the terms and conditions of the lease or occupancy agreement; the eviction complied with applicable federal, State, or local requirements (see § 578.91); and the recipient or subrecipient determines that the eviction was not undertaken for the purpose of evading the obligation to provide relocation assistance;

(B) The person moved into the property after the submission of the application but, before signing a lease or occupancy agreement and commencing occupancy, was provided written notice of the project's possible impact on the person (*e.g.*, the person may be displaced, temporarily relocated, or incur a rent increase) and the fact that the person would not qualify as a "displaced person" (or for any relocation assistance provided under this section), as a result of the project;

(C) The person is ineligible under 49 CFR 24.2(a)(9)(ii));

(D) The person is a program participant occupying transitional housing or permanent housing assisted under Title IV of the Act who must move as a direct result of the length-of- occupancy restriction under § 578.79; or

(E) HUD determines that the person was not displaced as a direct result of acquisition, rehabilitation, or demolition for the project.

(iv) The recipient may request, at any time, HUD's determination of whether a displacement is or would be covered under this section.

(3) *Initiation of negotiations*. For purposes of determining the formula for computing replacement housing payment assistance to be provided to a displaced person pursuant to this section, if the displacement is a direct result of privately undertaken rehabilitation, demolition, or acquisition of the real property, "initiation of negotiations" means the execution of the agreement between the recipient and the subrecipient, or between the recipient (or subrecipient, as applicable) and the person owning or controlling the property. In the case of an option contract to acquire property, the initiation of negotiations does not become effective until execution of a written agreement that creates a legally enforceable commitment to proceed with the purchase, such as a purchase agreement.

(d) *Real property acquisition requirements*. Except for acquisitions described in 49 CFR 24.101(b)(1) through (5), the URA and the requirements of 49 CFR part 24, subpart B apply to any acquisition of real property for a project where there are Continuum of Care funds in any part of the project costs.

(e) *Appeals*. A person who disagrees with the recipient's (or subrecipient's, if applicable) determination concerning whether the person qualifies as a displaced person, or the amount of relocation assistance for which the person is eligible, may file a written appeal of that determination with the recipient (see 49 CFR 24.10). A low-income person who is dissatisfied with the recipient's determination on his or her appeal may submit a written request for review of that determination to the local HUD field office.

§578.85 Timeliness standards.

(a) *In general*. Recipients must initiate approved activities and projects promptly.

(b) *Construction activities*. Recipients of funds for rehabilitation or new construction must meet the following standards:

(1) Construction activities must begin within 9 months of the later of signing of the grant agreement or of signing an addendum to the grant agreement authorizing use of grant funds for the project.

(2) Construction activities must be completed within 24 months of signing the grant agreement.

(3) Activities that cannot begin until after construction activities are completed must begin within 3 months of the date that construction activities are completed.

(c) *Distribution*. A recipient that receives funds through this part must:

(1) Distribute the funds to subrecipients (in advance of expenditures by the subrecipients);

(2) Distribute the appropriate portion of the funds to a subrecipient no later than 45 days after receiving an approvable request for such distribution from the subrecipient; and

(3) Draw down funds at least once per quarter of the program year, after eligible activities commence.

§578.87 Limitation on use of funds.

(a) *Maintenance of effort*. No assistance provided under this part (or any State or local government funds used to supplement this assistance) may be used to replace State or local funds previously used, or designated for use, to assist homeless persons.

(b) *Equal participation of faith-based organizations*. The HUD program requirements in §5.109 apply to the Continuum of Care program, including the requirements regarding disposition and change in use of real property by a faith-based organization.

(c) *Restriction on combining funds*. In a single structure or housing unit, the following types of assistance may not be combined:

(1) Leasing and acquisition, rehabilitation, or new construction;

(2) Tenant-based rental assistance and acquisition, rehabilitation, or new construction;

(3) Short- or medium-term rental assistance and acquisition, rehabilitation, or new construction;

(4) Rental assistance and leasing; or

(5) Rental assistance and operating.

(d) *Program fees*. Recipients and subrecipients may not charge program participants program fees.

[77 FR 45442, July 31, 2012, as amended at 80 FR 75804, Dec. 4, 2015;80 FR 75940, Dec. 7, 2015; 81 FR 19418, Apr. 4, 2016]

§ 578.89 Limitation on use of grant funds to serve persons defined as homeless under other federal laws.

(a) *Application requirement.* Applicants that intend to serve unaccompanied youth and families with children and youth defined as homeless under other federal laws in paragraph (3) of the homeless definition in § 576.2 must demonstrate in their application, to HUD's satisfaction, that the use of grant funds to serve such persons is an equal or greater priority than serving persons defined as homeless under paragraphs (1), (2), and (4) of the definition of homeless in § 576.2. To demonstrate that it is of equal or greater priority, applicants must show that it is equally or more cost effective in meeting the overall goals and objectives of the plan submitted under section 427(b)(1)(B) of the Act, especially with respect to children and unaccompanied youth.

(b) *Limit.* No more than 10 percent of the funds awarded to recipients within a single Continuum of Care's geographic area may be used to serve such persons.

(c) *Exception.* The 10 percent limitation does not apply to Continuums in which the rate of homelessness, as calculated in the most recent point-in-time count, is less than one-tenth of one percent of the total population.

§ 578.91 Termination of assistance to program participants.

(a) *Termination of assistance.* The recipient or subrecipient may terminate assistance to a program participant who violates program requirements or conditions of occupancy. Termination under this section does not bar the recipient or subrecipient from providing further assistance at a later date to the same individual or family.

(b) *Due process.* In terminating assistance to a program participant, the recipient or subrecipient must provide a formal process that recognizes the rights of individuals receiving assistance under the due process of law. This process, at a minimum, must consist of:

(1) Providing the program participant with a written copy of the program rules and the termination process before the participant begins to receive assistance;

(2) Written notice to the program participant containing a clear statement of the reasons for termination;

(3) A review of the decision, in which the program participant is given the opportunity to present written or oral objections before a person other than the person (or a subordinate of that person) who made or approved the termination decision; and

(4) Prompt written notice of the final decision to the program participant.

(c) *Hard-to-house populations.* Recipients and subrecipients that are providing permanent supportive housing for hard-to-house populations of homeless persons must exercise judgment and examine all extenuating circumstances in determining when violations are serious enough to warrant termination so that a program participant's assistance is terminated only in the most severe cases.

§ 578.93 Fair Housing and Equal Opportunity.

(a) *Nondiscrimination and equal opportunity requirements.* The nondiscrimination and equal opportunity requirements set forth in 24 CFR 5.105(a) are applicable.

(b) *Housing for specific subpopulations.* Recipients and subrecipients may exclusively serve a particular homeless subpopulation in transitional or permanent housing if the housing addresses a need identified by the Continuum of Care for the geographic area and meets one of the following:

(1) The housing may be limited to one sex where such housing consists of a single structure with shared bedrooms or bathing facilities such that the considerations of personal privacy and the physical limitations of the configuration of the housing make it appropriate for the housing to be limited to one sex;

(2) The housing may be limited to a specific subpopulation, so long as admission does not discriminate against any protected class under federal nondiscrimination laws in 24 CFR 5.105 (*e.g.*, the housing may be limited to homeless veterans, victims of domestic violence and their children, or chronically homeless persons and families).

(3) The housing may be limited to families with children.

(4) If the housing has in residence at least one family with a child under the age of 18, the housing may exclude registered sex offenders and persons with a criminal record that includes a violent crime from the project so long as the child resides in the housing.

(5) Sober housing may exclude persons who refuse to sign an occupancy agreement or lease that prohibits program participants from possessing, using, or being under the influence of illegal substances and/or alcohol on the premises.

(6) If the housing is assisted with funds under a federal program that is limited by federal statute or Executive Order to a specific subpopulation, the housing may be limited to that subpopulation (*e.g.*, housing also assisted with funding from the Housing Opportunities for Persons with AIDS program under 24 CFR part 574 may be limited to persons with acquired immunodeficiency syndrome or related diseases).

(7) Recipients may limit admission to or provide a preference for the housing to subpopulations of homeless persons and families who need the specialized supportive services that are provided in the housing (*e.g.*, substance abuse addiction treatment, domestic violence services, or a high intensity package designed to meet the needs of hard-to-reach homeless persons). While the housing may offer services for a particular type of disability, no otherwise eligible individuals with disabilities or families including an individual with a disability, who may benefit from the services provided may be excluded on the grounds that they do not have a particular disability.

(c) *Affirmatively furthering fair housing.* A recipient must implement its programs in a manner that affirmatively furthers fair housing, which means that the recipient must:

(1) Affirmatively market their housing and supportive services to eligible persons regardless of race, color, national origin, religion, sex, age, familial status, or handicap who are least likely to apply in the absence of special outreach, and maintain records of those marketing activities;

(2) Where a recipient encounters a condition or action that impedes fair housing choice for current or prospective program participants, provide such information to the jurisdiction that provided the certification of consistency with the Consolidated Plan; and

(3) Provide program participants with information on rights and remedies available under applicable federal, State and local fair housing and civil rights laws.

(d) *Accessibility and integrative housing and services for persons with disabilities.* Recipients and subrecipients must comply with the accessibility requirements of the Fair Housing Act (24 CFR part 100), Section 504 of the Rehabilitation Act of 1973 (24 CFR part 8), and Titles II and III of the Americans with Disabilities Act, as applicable (28 CFR parts 35 and 36). In accordance with the requirements of 24 CFR 8.4(d), recipients must ensure that their program's housing and supportive services are provided in the most integrated setting appropriate to the needs of persons with disabilities.

(e) *Prohibition against involuntary family separation.* The age and gender of a child under age 18 must not be used as a basis for denying any family's admission to a project that receives funds under this part.

§578.95 Conflicts of interest.

(a) *Procurement.* For the procurement of property (goods, supplies, or equipment) and services, the recipient and its subrecipients must comply with the standards of conduct and conflict-of-interest requirements under 2 CFR 200.317 and 200.318.

(b) *Continuum of Care board members.* No Continuum of Care board member may participate in or influence discussions or resulting decisions concerning the award of a grant or other financial benefits to the organization that the member represents.

(c) *Organizational conflict.* An organizational conflict of interest arises when, because of activities or relationships with other persons or organizations, the recipient or subrecipient is unable or potentially unable to render impartial assistance in the provision of any type or amount of assistance under this part, or when a covered person's, as in paragraph (d)(1) of this section, objectivity in performing work with respect to any activity assisted under this part is or might be otherwise impaired. Such an organizational conflict would arise when a board member of an applicant participates in decision of the applicant concerning the award of a grant, or provision of other financial benefits, to the organization that such member represents. It would also arise when an employee of a recipient or subrecipient participates in making rent reasonableness determinations under § 578.49(b)(2) and § 578.51(g) and housing quality inspections of property under § 578.75(b) that the recipient, subrecipient, or related entity owns.

(d) *Other conflicts.* For all other transactions and activities, the following restrictions apply:

(1) No covered person, meaning a person who is an employee, agent, consultant, officer, or elected or appointed official of the recipient or its subrecipients and who exercises or has exercised any functions or responsibilities with respect to activities assisted under this part, or who is in a position to participate in a decision-making process or gain inside information with regard to activities assisted under this part, may obtain a financial interest or benefit from an assisted activity, have a financial interest in any contract, subcontract, or agreement with respect to an assisted activity, or have a financial interest in the proceeds derived from an assisted activity, either for him or herself or for those with whom he or she has immediate family or business ties, during his or her tenure or during the one-year period following his or her tenure.

(2) *Exceptions.* Upon the written request of the recipient, HUD may grant an exception to the provisions of this section on a case-by-case basis, taking into account the cumulative effects of the criteria in paragraph (d)(2)(ii) of this section, provided that the recipient has satisfactorily met the threshold requirements of paragraph (d)(2)(ii) of this section.

(i) *Threshold requirements.* HUD will consider an exception only after the recipient has provided the following documentation:

(A) Disclosure of the nature of the conflict, accompanied by a written assurance, if the recipient is a government, that there has been public disclosure of the conflict and a description of how the public disclosure was made; and if the recipient is a private nonprofit organization, that the conflict has been disclosed in accordance with their written code of conduct or other conflict-of-interest policy; and

(B) An opinion of the recipient's attorney that the interest for which the exception is sought would not violate State or local law, or if the subrecipient is a private nonprofit organization, the exception would not violate the organization's internal policies.

(ii) *Factors to be considered for exceptions.* In determining whether to grant a requested exception after the recipient has satisfactorily met the threshold requirements under paragraph (c)(3)(i) of this section, HUD must conclude that the exception will serve to further the purposes of the Continuum of Care program and the effective and efficient administration of the recipient's or subrecipient's project, taking into account the cumulative effect of the following factors, as applicable:

(A) Whether the exception would provide a significant cost benefit or an essential degree of expertise to the program or project that would otherwise not be available;

(B) Whether an opportunity was provided for open competitive bidding or negotiation;

(C) Whether the affected person has withdrawn from his or her functions, responsibilities, or the decision-making process with respect to the specific activity in question;

(D) Whether the interest or benefit was present before the affected person was in the position described in paragraph (c)(1) of this section;

(E) Whether undue hardship will result to the recipient, the subrecipient, or the person affected, when weighed against the public interest served by avoiding the prohibited conflict;

(F) Whether the person affected is a member of a group or class of persons intended to be the beneficiaries of the assisted activity, and the exception will permit such person to receive generally the same interests or benefits as are being made available or provided to the group or class; and

(G) Any other relevant considerations.

[77 FR 45442, July 31, 2012, as amended at 80 FR 75940, Dec. 7, 2015]

§ 578.97 Program income.

(a) *Defined.* Program income is the income received by the recipient or subrecipient directly generated by a grant-supported activity.

(b) *Use.* Program income earned during the grant term shall be retained by the recipient, and added to funds committed to the project by HUD and the recipient, used for eligible activities in accordance with the requirements of this part. Costs incident to the generation of program income may be deducted from gross income to calculate program income, provided that the costs have not been charged to grant funds.

(c) *Rent and occupancy charges.* Rents and occupancy charges collected from program participants are program income. In addition, rents and occupancy charges collected from residents of transitional housing may be reserved, in whole or in part, to assist the residents from whom they are collected to move to permanent housing.

§ 578.99 Applicability of other Federal requirements.

In addition to the requirements set forth in 24 CFR part 5, use of assistance provided under this part must comply with the following federal requirements:

(a) *Environmental review.* Activities under this part are subject to environmental review by HUD under 24 CFR part 50 as noted in § 578.31.

(b) *Section 6002 of the Solid Waste Disposal Act.* State agencies and agencies of a political subdivision of a state that are using assistance under this part for procurement, and any person contracting with such an agency with respect to work performed under an assisted contract, must comply with the requirements of Section 6003 of the Solid Waste Disposal Act, as amended by the Resource Conservation and Recovery Act. In accordance with Section 6002, these agencies and persons must:

(1) Procure items designated in guidelines of the Environmental Protection Agency (EPA) at 40 CFR part 247 that contain the highest percentage of recovered materials practicable, consistent with maintaining a satisfactory level of competition, where the purchase price of the item exceeds $10,000 or the value of the quantity acquired in the preceding fiscal year exceeded $10,000;

(2) Procure solid waste management services in a manner that maximizes energy and resource recovery; and

(3) Must have established an affirmative procurement program for the procurement of recovered materials identified in the EPA guidelines.

(c) *Transparency Act Reporting.* Section 872 of the Duncan Hunter Defense Appropriations Act of 2009, and additional requirements published by the Office of Management and Budget (OMB), requires recipients to report subawards made either as pass-through awards, subrecipient awards, or vendor awards in the Federal Government Web site *www.fsrs.gov* or its successor system. The reporting of award and subaward information is in accordance with the requirements of the Federal Financial Assistance Accountability and Transparency Act of 2006, as amended by section 6202 of Public Law 110–252 and in OMB Policy Guidance issued to the federal agencies on September 14, 2010 (75 FR 55669).

(d) *The Coastal Barrier Resources Act of 1982* (16 U.S.C. 3501 *et seq.*) may apply to proposals under this part, depending on the assistance requested.

(e) *Applicability of uniform administrative requirements, cost principles, and audit requirements for Federal awards.* The requirements of 2 CFR part 200 apply to recipients and subrecipients, except where inconsistent with the provisions of the McKinney-Vento Act or this part.

(f) *Lead-based paint.* The Lead-Based Paint Poisoning Prevention Act (42 U.S.C. 4821–4846), the Residential Lead-Based Paint Hazard Reduction Act of 1992 (42 U.S.C. 4851–4856), and implementing regulations at 24 CFR part 35, subparts A, B, H, J, K, M, and R apply to activities under this program.

(g) *Audit.* Recipients and subrecipients must comply with the audit requirements of 2 CFR part 200, subpart F.

(h) *Davis-Bacon Act.* The provisions of the Davis-Bacon Act do not apply to this program.

(i) *Section 3 of the Housing and Urban Development Act.* Recipients and subrecipients must, as applicable, comply with Section 3 of the Housing and Urban Development Act of 1968 and its implementing regulations at 24 CFR part 75, as applicable.

(j) *Protections for victims of domestic violence, dating violence, sexual assault, or stalking*—(1) *General.* The requirements set forth in 24 CFR part 5, subpart L (Protection for Victims of Domestic Violence, Dating Violence, Sexual Assault, or Stalking), implementing the requirements of VAWA apply to all permanent housing and transitional housing for which Continuum of Care program funds are used for acquisition, rehabilitation, new construction, leasing, rental assistance, or operating costs. The requirements also apply where funds are used for homelessness prevention, but only where the funds are used to provide short- and/or medium-term rental assistance. Safe havens are subject only to the requirements in paragraph (j)(9) of this section.

(2) *Definition of covered housing provider.* For the Continuum of Care program, "covered housing provider," as such term is used in HUD's regulations in 24 CFR part 5, subpart L refers to:

(i) The owner or landlord, which may be the recipient or subrecipient, for purposes of 24 CFR 5.2005(d)(1) and 5.2009(a);

(ii) The recipient, subrecipient, and owner or landlord for purposes of 24 CFR 5.2005(d)(2) through (d)(4); and

(iii) The recipient, subrecipient, and owner or landlord for purposes of 24 CFR 5.2007. However, the recipient or subrecipient may limit documentation requests under § 5.2007 to only the recipient or subrecipient, provided that:

(A) This limitation is made clear in both the notice described under 24 CFR 5.2005(a)(1) and the rental assistance agreement;

(B) The entity designated to receive documentation requests determines whether the program participant is entitled to protection under VAWA and immediately advise the program participant of the determination; and

(C) If the program participant is entitled to protection, the entity designated to receive documentation requests must notify the owner in writing that the program participant is entitled to protection under VAWA and work with the owner on the program participant's behalf. Any further sharing or disclosure of the program participant's information will be subject to the requirements in 24 CFR 5.2007.

(3) *Effective date.* The core statutory protections of VAWA that prohibit denial or termination of assistance or eviction solely because an applicant or tenant is a victim of domestic violence, dating violence, sexual assault, or stalking, applied upon enactment of VAWA 2013 on March 7, 2013. Compliance with the VAWA regulatory requirements under this section and at 24 CFR part 5, subpart L, is required for grants awarded pursuant to NOFAs published on or after December 16, 2016.

(4) *Notification requirements.* (i) The recipient or subrecipient must provide each individual or family applying for permanent housing and transitional housing and each program participant the notice and the certification form described in 24 CFR 5.2005 at each of the following times:

(A) When an individual or family is denied permanent housing or transitional housing;

(B) When a program participant is admitted to permanent housing or transitional housing;

(C) When a program participant receives notification of eviction; and

(D) When a program participant is notified of termination of assistance.

(ii) When grant funds are used for rental assistance, the recipient or subrecipient must ensure that the owner or manager of the housing provides the notice and certification form described in 24 CFR 5.2005(a) to the program participant with any notification of eviction. This commitment and the confidentiality requirements under 24 CFR 5.2007(c) must be set forth in a contract with the owner or landlord.

(5) *Contract, lease, and occupancy agreement provisions.* (i) Recipients and

subrecipients must include in any contracts and leases between the recipient or subrecipient, and an owner or landlord of the housing:

(A) The requirement to comply with 24 CFR part 5, subpart L; and

(B) Where the owner or landlord of the housing will have a lease with a program participant, the requirement to include a lease provision that include all requirements that apply to tenants, the owner or the lease under 24 CFR part 5, subpart L, as supplemented by this part, including the prohibited bases for eviction and restrictions on construing lease terms under 24 CFR 5.2005(b) and (c).

(ii) The recipient or subrecipient must include in any lease, sublease, and occupancy agreement with the program participant a provision that include all requirements that apply to tenants, the owner or the lease under 24 CFR part 5, subpart L, as supplemented by this part, including the prohibited bases for eviction and restrictions on construing lease terms under 24 CFR 5.2005(b) and (c). The lease, sublease, and occupancy agreement may specify that the protections under 24 CFR part 5, subpart L, apply only during the period of assistance under the Continuum of Care Program. The period of assistance for housing where grant funds were used for acquisition, construction, or rehabilitation is 15 years from the date of initial occupancy or date of initial service provision.

(iii) Except for tenant-based rental assistance, recipients and subrecipients must require that any lease, sublease, or occupancy agreement with a program participant permits the program participant to terminate the lease, sublease, or occupancy agreement without penalty if the recipient or subrecipient determines that the program participant qualifies for an emergency transfer under the emergency transfer plan established under paragraph (j)(8) of this section.

(iv) For tenant-based rental assistance, the recipient or subrecipient must enter into a contract with the owner or landlord of the housing that:

(A) Requires the owner or landlord of the housing to comply with the provisions of 24 CFR part 5, subpart L; and

(B) Requires the owner or landlord of the housing to include a lease provision that include all requirements that apply to tenants, the owner or the lease under 24 CFR part 5, subpart L, as supplemented by this part, including the prohibited bases for eviction and restrictions on construing lease terms under 24 CFR 5.005(b) and (c). The lease may specify that the protections under 24 CFR part 5, subpart L, only apply while the program participant receives tenant-based rental assistance under the Continuum of Care Program.

(6) *Transition.* (i) The recipient or subrecipient must ensure that the requirements set forth in paragraph (j)(5) of this section apply to any contracts, leases, subleases, or occupancy agreements entered into, or renewed, following the expiration of an existing term, on or after the effective date in paragraph (j)(2) of this section. This obligation includes any contracts, leases, subleases, and occupancy agreements that will automatically renew on or after the effective date in paragraph (j)(3) of this section.

(ii) For leases for tenant-based rental assistance existing prior to the effective date in paragraph (j)(2) of this section, recipients and subrecipients must enter into a contract under paragraph (j)(6)(iv) of this section before the next renewal of the lease.

(7) *Bifurcation.* For the purposes of this part, the following requirements shall apply in place of the requirements at 24 CFR 5.2009(b):

(i) If a family who is receiving tenant-based rental assistance under this part separates under 24 CFR 5.2009(a), the family's tenant-based rental assistance and any utility assistance shall continue for the family member(s) who are not evicted or removed.

(ii) If a family living in permanent supportive housing separates under 24 CFR 5.2009(a), and the family's eligibility for the housing was based on the evicted individual's disability or chronically homeless status, the remaining tenants may stay in the project as provided under §578.75(i)(2). Otherwise, if a family living in a project funded under this part separates under 24 CFR 5.2009(a), the remaining tenant(s) will be eligible to remain in the project.

(8) *Emergency transfer plan.* The Continuum of Care must develop an emergency transfer plan for the Continuum of Care, and recipients and subrecipients in the Continuum of Care must follow that plan. The plan must comply with 24 CFR 5.2005(e) and include the following program requirements:

(i) For families receiving tenant-based rental assistance, the plan must specify what will happen with respect to the non-transferring family member(s), if the family separates in order to effect an emergency transfer.

(ii) For families living in units that are otherwise assisted under this part (assisted units), the required policies must provide that for program participants who qualify for an emergency transfer but a safe unit is not immediately available for an internal emergency transfer, the individual or family shall have priority over all other applicants for rental assistance, transitional housing, and permanent supportive housing projects funded under this part, provided that: The individual or family meets all eligibility criteria required by Federal law or regulation or HUD NOFA; and the individual or family meets any additional criteria or preferences established in accordance with § 578.93(b)(1), (4), (6), or (7). The individual or family shall not be required to meet any other eligibility criteria or preferences for the project. The individual or family shall retain their original homeless or chronically homeless status for the purposes of the transfer.

(9) *Protections with respect to safe havens.* The following requirements apply to safe havens funded under this part:

(i) No individual may be denied admission to or removed from the safe haven on the basis or as a direct result of the fact that the individual is or has been a victim of domestic violence, dating violence, sexual assault, or stalking, if the individual otherwise qualifies for admission or occupancy.

(iii) The terms "affiliated individual," "dating violence," "domestic violence," "sexual assault," and "stalking" are defined in 24 CFR 5.2003.

[77 FR 45442, July 31, 2012, as amended at 80 FR 75940, Dec. 7, 2015; 81 FR 80810, Nov. 16, 2016; 81 FR 87812, Dec. 6, 2016; 85 FR 61568, Sept. 29, 2020]

Subpart G—Grant Administration

§ 578.101 Technical assistance.

(a) *Purpose.* The purpose of Continuum of Care technical assistance is to increase the effectiveness with which Continuums of Care, eligible applicants, recipients, subrecipients, and UFAs implement and administer their Continuum of Care planning process; improve their capacity to prepare applications; prevent the separation of families in projects funded under the Emergency Solutions Grants, Continuum of Care, and Rural Housing Stability Assistance programs; and adopt and provide best practices in housing and services for persons experiencing homelessness.

(b) *Defined.* Technical assistance means the transfer of skills and knowledge to entities that may need, but do not possess, such skills and knowledge. The assistance may include, but is not limited to, written information such as papers, manuals, guides, and brochures; person-to-person exchanges; web-based curriculums, training and Webinars, and their costs.

(c) *Set-aside.* HUD may set aside funds annually to provide technical assistance, either directly by HUD staff or indirectly through third-party providers.

(d) *Awards.* From time to time, as HUD determines the need, HUD may advertise and competitively select providers to deliver technical assistance. HUD may enter into contracts, grants, or cooperative agreements, when necessary, to implement the technical assistance. HUD may also enter into agreements with other federal agencies for awarding the technical assistance funds.

§ 578.103 Recordkeeping requirements.

(a) *In general.* The recipient and its subrecipients must establish and maintain standard operating procedures for ensuring that Continuum of Care program funds are used in accordance with the requirements of this part and must establish and maintain sufficient records to enable HUD to determine whether the recipient and its subrecipients are meeting the requirements of this part, including:

(1) *Continuum of Care records.* Each collaborative applicant must keep the following documentation related to establishing and operating a Continuum of Care:

(i) Evidence that the Board selected by the Continuum of Care meets the requirements of §578.5(b);

(ii) Evidence that the Continuum has been established and operated as set forth in subpart B of this part, including published agendas and meeting minutes, an approved Governance Charter that is reviewed and updated annually, a written process for selecting a board that is reviewed and updated at least once every 5 years, evidence required for designating a single HMIS for the Continuum, and monitoring reports of recipients and subrecipients;

(iii) Evidence that the Continuum has prepared the application for funds as set forth in §578.9, including the designation of the eligible applicant to be the collaborative applicant.

(2) *Unified funding agency records.* UFAs that requested grant amendments from HUD, as set forth in §578.105, must keep evidence that the grant amendment was approved by the Continuum. This evidence may include minutes of meetings at which the grant amendment was discussed and approved.

(3) *Homeless status.* Acceptable evidence of the homeless as status is set forth in 24 CFR 576.500(b).

(4) *Chronically homeless status.* The recipient must maintain and follow written intake procedures to ensure compliance with the chronically homeless definition in §578.3. The procedures must require documentation at intake of the evidence relied upon to establish and verify chronically homeless status. The procedures must establish the order of priority for obtaining evidence as third-party documentation first, intake worker observations second, and certification from the person seeking assistance third. Records contained in an HMIS, or comparable database used by victim service or legal service providers, are acceptable evidence of third-party documentation and intake worker observations if the HMIS, or comparable database, retains an auditable history of all entries, including the person who entered the data, the date of entry, and the change made, and if the HMIS prevents overrides or changes of the dates on which entries are made.

(i) For paragraph (1) of the "Chronically homeless" definition in §578.3, evidence that the individual is a "homeless individual with a disability" as defined in section 401(9) of the McKinney-Vento Homeless Assistance Act (42 U.S.C. 11360(9)) must include:

(A) Evidence of homeless status as set forth in paragraph (a)(3) of this section; and

(B) Evidence of a disability. In addition to the documentation required under paragraph (a)(4)(i)(A) of this section, the procedures must require documentation at intake of the evidence relied upon to establish and verify the disability of the person applying for homeless assistance. The recipient must keep these records for 5 years after the end of the grant term. Acceptable evidence of the disability includes:

(*1*) Written verification of the disability from a professional licensed by the state to diagnose and treat the disability and his or her certification that the disability is expected to be long-continuing or of indefinite duration and substantially impedes the individual's ability to live independently;

(*2*) Written verification from the Social Security Administration;

(*3*) The receipt of a disability check (*e.g.*, Social Security Disability Insurance check or Veteran Disability Compensation);

(*4*) Intake staff-recorded observation of disability that, no later than 45 days from the application for assistance, is confirmed and accompanied by evidence in paragraph (a)(4)(i)(B)(*1*), (*2*), (*3*), or (*5*) of this section; or

(*5*) Other documentation approved by HUD.

(ii) For paragraph (1)(i) of the "Chronically homeless" definition in §578.3, evidence that the individual lives in a place not meant for human habitation, a safe haven, or an emergency shelter, which includes:

(A) An HMIS record or record from a comparable database;

(B) A written observation by an outreach worker of the conditions where the individual was living;

(C) A written referral by another housing or service provider; or

(D) Where evidence in paragraphs (a)(4)(ii)(A) through (C) of this section cannot be obtained, a certification by the individual seeking assistance, which must be accompanied by the intake worker's documentation of the living situation of the individual or family seeking assistance and the steps taken to obtain evidence in paragraphs (a)(4)(ii)(A) through (C).

(iii) For paragraph (1)(ii) of the "Chronically homeless" definition in § 578.3, evidence must include a combination of the evidence described in paragraphs (a)(4)(ii)(A) through (D) of this section, subject to the following conditions:

(A) Third-party documentation of a single encounter with a homeless service provider on a single day within 1 month is sufficient to consider an individual as homeless and living or residing in a place not meant for human habitation, a safe haven, or an emergency shelter for the entire calendar month (e.g., an encounter on May 5, 2015, counts for May 1—May 31, 2015), unless there is evidence that there have been at least 7 consecutive nights not living or residing in a place not meant for human habitation, a safe haven, or an emergency shelter during that month (e.g., evidence in HMIS of a stay in transitional housing);

(B) Each break in homelessness of at least 7 consecutive nights not living or residing in a place not meant for human habitation, a safe haven, or in an emergency shelter between separate occasions must be documented with the evidence described in paragraphs (a)(4)(ii)(A) through (D) of this section;

(C) Evidence of stays in institutional care facilities fewer than 90 days included in the total of at least 12 months of living or residing in a place not meant for human habitation, a safe haven, or an emergency shelter must include the evidence in paragraphs (a)(4)(iv)(A) through (B) of this section and evidence described in paragraphs (a)(4)(ii)(A) through (D) of this section that the individual was living or residing in a place not meant for human habitation, a safe haven, or an emergency shelter immediately prior to entering the institutional care facility; and

(D) For at least 75 percent of the chronically homeless individuals and families assisted by a recipient in a project during an operating year, no more than 3 months of living or residing in a place not meant for human habitation, a safe haven, or an emergency shelter may be documented using the evidence in paragraph (a)(4)(ii)(D) of this section for each assisted chronically homeless individual or family. This limitation does not apply to documentation of breaks in homelessness between separate occasions, which may be documented entirely based on a self-report by the individual seeking assistance.

(iv) If an individual qualifies as chronically homeless under paragraph (2) of the "Chronically homeless" definition in § 578.3 because he or she has been residing in an institutional care facility for fewer than 90 days and met all of the criteria in paragraph (1) of the definition, before entering that facility, evidence must include the following:

(A) Discharge paperwork or a written or oral referral from a social worker, case manager, or other appropriate official of the institutional care facility stating the beginning and end dates of the time residing in the institutional care facility. All oral statements must be recorded by the intake worker; or

(B) Where the evidence in paragraph (a)(4)(iv)(A) of this section is not obtainable, a written record of the intake worker's due diligence in attempting to obtain the evidence described in paragraph (a)(4)(iv)(A) and a certification by the individual seeking assistance that states that he or she is exiting or has just exited an institutional care facility where he or she resided for fewer than 90 days; and

(C) Evidence as set forth in paragraphs (a)(4)(i) through (iii) of this section that the individual met the criteria in paragraph (1) of the definition for "Chronically homeless" in § 578.3, immediately prior to entry into the institutional care facility.

(v) If a family qualifies as chronically homeless under paragraph (3) of the "Chronically homeless" definition in §578.3, evidence must include the evidence as set forth in paragraphs (a)(4)(i) through (iv) of this section that the adult head of household (or if there is no adult in the family, a minor head of household) met all of the criteria in paragraph (1) or (2) of the definition.

(5) *At risk of homelessness status.* For those recipients and subrecipients that serve persons at risk of homelessness, the recipient or subrecipient must keep records that establish "at risk of homelessness" status of each individual or family who receives Continuum of Care homelessness prevention assistance. Acceptable evidence is found in 24 CFR 576.500(c).

(6) *Moves for victims of domestic violence, dating violence, sexual assault, and stalking.*

(i) For each program participant who moved to a different Continuum of Care due to imminent threat of further domestic violence, dating violence, sexual assault, or stalking under §578.51(c)(3), each recipient or subrecipient of assistance under this part must retain:

(A) Documentation of the original incidence of domestic violence, dating violence, sexual assault, or stalking, only if the original violence is not already documented in the program participant's case file. This may be written observation of the housing or service provider; a letter or other documentation from a victim service provider, social worker, legal assistance provider, pastoral counselor, mental health provider, or other professional from whom the victim has sought assistance; medical or dental records; court records or law enforcement records; or written certification by the program participant to whom the violence occurred or by the head of household.

(B) Documentation of the reasonable belief of imminent threat of further domestic violence, dating violence, or sexual assault or stalking, which would include threats from a third-party, such as a friend or family member of the perpetrator of the violence. This may be written observation by the housing or service provider; a letter or other documentation from a victim service provider, social worker, legal assistance provider, pastoral counselor, mental health provider, or other professional from whom the victim has sought assistance; current restraining order; recent court order or other court records; law enforcement report or records; communication records from the perpetrator of the violence or family members or friends of the perpetrator of the violence, including emails, voicemails, text messages, and social media posts; or a written certification by the program participant to whom the violence occurred or the head of household.

(ii) Data on emergency transfers requested under 24 CFR 5.2005(e) and §578.99, pertaining to victims of domestic violence, dating violence, sexual assault, or stalking, including data on the outcomes of such requests.

(7) *Annual income.* For each program participant who receives housing assistance where rent or an occupancy charge is paid by the program participant, the recipient or subrecipient must keep the following documentation of annual income:

(i) Income evaluation form specified by HUD and completed by the recipient or subrecipient; and

(ii) Source documents (*e.g.*, most recent wage statement, unemployment compensation statement, public benefits statement, bank statement) for the assets held by the program participant and income received before the date of the evaluation;

(iii) To the extent that source documents are unobtainable, a written statement by the relevant third party (*e.g.*, employer, government benefits administrator) or the written certification by the recipient's or subrecipient's intake staff of the oral verification by the relevant third party of the income the program participant received over the most recent period; or

(iv) To the extent that source documents and third-party verification are unobtainable, the written certification by the program participant of the amount of income that the program participant is reasonably expected to receive over the 3-month period following the evaluation.

(8) *Program participant records.* In addition to evidence of "homeless" status or "at-risk-of-homelessness" status, as applicable, the recipient or subrecipient must keep records for each program participant that document:

(i) The services and assistance provided to that program participant, including evidence that the recipient or subrecipient has conducted an annual assessment of services for those program participants that remain in the program for more than a year and adjusted the service package accordingly, and including case management services as provided in § 578.37(a)(1)(ii)(F); and

(ii) Where applicable, compliance with the termination of assistance requirement in § 578.91.

(9) *Housing standards.* The recipient or subrecipient must retain documentation of compliance with the housing standards in § 578.75(b), including inspection reports.

(10) *Services provided.* The recipient or subrecipient must document the types of supportive services provided under the recipient's program and the amounts spent on those services. The recipient or subrecipient must keep record that these records were reviewed at least annually and that the service package offered to program participants was adjusted as necessary.

(11) *Match.* The recipient must keep records of the source and use of contributions made to satisfy the match requirement in § 578.73. The records must indicate the grant and fiscal year for which each matching contribution is counted. The records must show how the value placed on third party in-kind contributions was derived. To the extent feasible, volunteer services must be supported by the same methods that the organization uses to support the allocation of regular personnel costs.

(12) *Conflicts of interest.* The recipient and its subrecipients must keep records to show compliance with the organizational conflict-of-interest requirements in § 578.95(c), the Continuum of Care board conflict-of-interest requirements in § 578.95(b), the other conflict requirements in § 578.95(d), a copy of the personal conflict-of-interest policy developed and implemented to comply with the requirements in § 578.95, and records supporting exceptions to the personal conflict-of-interest prohibitions.

(13) *Homeless participation.* The recipient or subrecipient must document its compliance with the homeless participation requirements under § 578.75(g).

(14) *Faith-based activities.* The recipient and its subrecipients must document their compliance with the faith-based activities requirements under § 578.87(b).

(15) *Affirmatively Furthering Fair Housing.* Recipients and subrecipients must maintain copies of their marketing, outreach, and other materials used to inform eligible persons of the program to document compliance with the requirements in § 578.93(c).

(16) *Other federal requirements.* The recipient and its subrecipients must document their compliance with the federal requirements in § 578.99, as applicable.

(17) *Subrecipients and contractors.* (i) The recipient must retain copies of all solicitations of and agreements with subrecipients, records of all payment requests by and dates of payments made to subrecipients, and documentation of all monitoring and sanctions of subrecipients, as applicable.

(ii) The recipient must retain documentation of monitoring subrecipients, including any monitoring findings and corrective actions required.

(iii) The recipient and its subrecipients must retain copies of all procurement contracts and documentation of compliance with the procurement requirements in 2 CFR part 200, subpart D.

(18) *Other records specified by HUD.* The recipient and subrecipients must keep other records specified by HUD.

(b) *Confidentiality.* In addition to meeting the specific confidentiality and security requirements for HMIS data, the recipient and its subrecipients must develop and implement written procedures to ensure:

(1) All records containing protected identifying information of any individual or family who applies for and/or receives Continuum of Care assistance will be kept secure and confidential;

(2) The address or location of any family violence project assisted with Continuum of Care funds will not be

made public, except with written authorization of the person responsible for the operation of the project; and

(3) The address or location of any housing of a program participant will not be made public, except as provided under a preexisting privacy policy of the recipient or subrecipient and consistent with State and local laws regarding privacy and obligations of confidentiality;

(c) *Period of record retention.* All records pertaining to Continuum of Care funds must be retained for the greater of 5 years or the period specified below. Copies made by microfilming, photocopying, or similar methods may be substituted for the original records.

(1) Documentation of each program participant's qualification as a family or individual at risk of homelessness or as a homeless family or individual and other program participant records must be retained for 5 years after the expenditure of all funds from the grant under which the program participant was served; and

(2) Where Continuum of Care funds are used for the acquisition, new construction, or rehabilitation of a project site, records must be retained until 15 years after the date that the project site is first occupied, or used, by program participants.

(d) *Access to records.* (1) *Federal Government rights.* Notwithstanding the confidentiality procedures established under paragraph (b) of this section, HUD, the HUD Office of the Inspector General, and the Comptroller General of the United States, or any of their authorized representatives, must have the right of access to all books, documents, papers, or other records of the recipient and its subrecipients that are pertinent to the Continuum of Care grant, in order to make audits, examinations, excerpts, and transcripts. These rights of access are not limited to the required retention period, but last as long as the records are retained.

(2) *Public rights.* The recipient must provide citizens, public agencies, and other interested parties with reasonable access to records regarding any uses of Continuum of Care funds the recipient received during the preceding 5 years, consistent with State and local laws regarding privacy and obligations of confidentiality and confidentiality requirements in this part.

(e) *Reports.* In addition to the reporting requirements in 2 CFR part 200, subpart D, the recipient must collect and report data on its use of Continuum of Care funds in an Annual Performance Report (APR), as well as in any additional reports as and when required by HUD. Projects receiving grant funds only for acquisition, rehabilitation, or new construction must submit APRs for 15 years from the date of initial occupancy or the date of initial service provision, unless HUD provides an exception under §578.81(e).

[77 FR 45442, July 31, 2012, as amended at 80 FR 75804, Dec. 4, 2015; 80 FR 75940, Dec. 7, 2015; 80 FR 80258, Dec. 24, 2015; 81 FR 80811, Nov. 16, 2016]

§578.105 Grant and project changes.

(a) *For Unified Funding Agencies and Continuums having only one recipient.* (1) The recipient may not make any significant changes without prior HUD approval, evidenced by a grant amendment signed by HUD and the recipient. Significant grant changes include a change of recipient, a shift in a single year of more than 10 percent of the total amount awarded under the grant for one approved eligible activity category to another activity and a permanent change in the subpopulation served by any one project funded under the grant, as well as a permanent proposed reduction in the total number of units funded under the grant.

(2) Approval of substitution of the recipient is contingent on the new recipient meeting the capacity criteria in the NOFA under which the grant was awarded, or the most recent NOFA. Approval of shifting funds between activities and changing subpopulations is contingent on the change being necessary to better serve eligible persons within the geographic area and ensuring that the priorities established under the NOFA in which the grant was originally awarded, or the most recent NOFA, are met.

(b) *For Continuums having more than one recipient.* (1) The recipients or subrecipients may not make any significant changes to a project without prior HUD approval, evidenced by a grant amendment signed by HUD and the recipient. Significant changes include a change of recipient, a change of project site, additions or deletions in the types of eligible activities approved for a project, a shift of more than 10 percent from one approved eligible activity to another, a reduction in the number of units, and a change in the subpopulation served.

(2) Approval of substitution of the recipient is contingent on the new recipient meeting the capacity criteria in the NOFA under which the grant was awarded, or the most recent NOFA. Approval of shifting funds between activities and changing subpopulations is contingent on the change being necessary to better serve eligible persons within the geographic area and ensuring that the priorities established under the NOFA in which the grant was originally awarded, or the most recent NOFA, are met.

(c) *Documentation of changes not requiring a grant amendment.* Any other changes to an approved grant or project must be fully documented in the recipient's or subrecipient's records.

§ 578.107 Sanctions.

(a) *Performance reviews.* (1) HUD will review the performance of each recipient in carrying out its responsibilities under this part, with or without prior notice to the recipient. In conducting performance reviews, HUD will rely primarily on information obtained from the records and reports from the recipient and subrecipients, as well as information from on-site monitoring, audit reports, and information generated from HUD's financial and reporting systems (*e.g.*, LOCCS and e-snaps) and HMIS. Where applicable, HUD may also consider relevant information pertaining to the recipient's performance gained from other sources, including citizen comments, complaint determinations, and litigation.

(2) If HUD determines preliminarily that the recipient or one of its subrecipients has not complied with a program requirement, HUD will give the recipient notice of this determination and an opportunity to demonstrate, within the time prescribed by HUD and on the basis of substantial facts and data that the recipient has complied with the requirements. HUD may change the method of payment to require the recipient to submit documentation before payment and obtain HUD's prior approval each time the recipient draws down funds. To obtain prior approval, the recipient may be required to manually submit its payment requests and supporting documentation to HUD in order to show that the funds to be drawn down will be expended on eligible activities in accordance with all program requirements.

(3) If the recipient fails to demonstrate to HUD's satisfaction that the activities were carried out in compliance with program requirements, HUD may take one or more of the remedial actions or sanctions specified in paragraph (b) of this section.

(b) *Remedial actions and sanctions.* Remedial actions and sanctions for a failure to meet a program requirement will be designed to prevent a continuation of the deficiency; to mitigate, to the extent possible, its adverse effects or consequences; and to prevent its recurrence.

(1) HUD may instruct the recipient to submit and comply with proposals for action to correct, mitigate, and prevent noncompliance with program requirements, including:

(i) Preparing and following a schedule of actions for carrying out activities and projects affected by the noncompliance, including schedules, timetables, and milestones necessary to implement the affected activities and projects;

(ii) Establishing and following a management plan that assigns responsibilities for carrying out the remedial actions;

(iii) Canceling or revising activities or projects likely to be affected by the noncompliance, before expending grant funds for them;

(iv) Reprogramming grant funds that have not yet been expended from affected activities or projects to other eligible activities or projects;

(v) Suspending disbursement of grant funds for some or all activities or projects;

(vi) Reducing or terminating the remaining grant of a subrecipient and either reallocating those funds to other subrecipients or returning funds to HUD; and

(vii) Making matching contributions before or as draws are made from the recipient's grant.

(2) HUD may change the method of payment to a reimbursement basis.

(3) HUD may suspend payments to the extent HUD determines necessary to preclude the further expenditure of funds for affected activities or projects.

(4) HUD may continue the grant with a substitute recipient of HUD's choosing.

(5) HUD may deny matching credit for all or part of the cost of the affected activities and require the recipient to make further matching contributions to make up for the contribution determined to be ineligible.

(6) HUD may require the recipient to reimburse the recipient's line of credit in an amount equal to the funds used for the affected activities.

(7) HUD may reduce or terminate the remaining grant of a recipient.

(8) HUD may condition a future grant.

(9) HUD may take other remedies that are legally available.

(c) *Recipient sanctions.* If the recipient determines that a subrecipient is not complying with a program requirement or its subrecipient agreement, the recipient must take one of the actions listed in paragraphs (a) and (b) of this section.

(d) *Deobligation.* HUD may deobligate funds for the following reasons:

(1) If the timeliness standards in §578.85 are not met;

(2) If HUD determines that delays completing construction activities for a project will mean that the funds for other funded activities cannot reasonably be expected to be expended for eligible costs during the remaining term of the grant;

(3) If the actual total cost of acquisition, rehabilitation, or new construction for a project is less than the total cost agreed to in the grant agreement;

(4) If the actual annual leasing costs, operating costs, supportive services costs, rental assistance costs, or HMIS costs are less than the total cost agreed to in the grant agreement for a one-year period;

(5) Program participants have not moved into units within 3 months of the time that the units are available for occupancy; and

(6) The grant agreement may set forth in detail other circumstances under which funds may be deobligated and other sanctions may be imposed.

§578.109 Closeout.

(a) *In general.* Grants will be closed out in accordance with the requirements of 2 CFR part 200, subpart D, and closeout procedures established by HUD.

(b) *Reports.* Applicants must submit all reports required by HUD no later than 90 days from the date of the end of the project's grant term.

(c) *Closeout agreement.* Any obligations remaining as of the date of the closeout must be covered by the terms of a closeout agreement. The agreement will be prepared by HUD in consultation with the recipient. The agreement must identify the grant being closed out, and include provisions with respect to the following:

(1) Identification of any closeout costs or contingent liabilities subject to payment with Continuum of Care program funds after the closeout agreement is signed;

(2) Identification of any unused grant funds to be deobligated by HUD;

(3) Identification of any program income on deposit in financial institutions at the time the closeout agreement is signed;

(4) Description of the recipient's responsibility after closeout for:

(i) Compliance with all program requirements in using program income on deposit at the time the closeout agreement is signed and in using any other remaining Continuum of Care program funds available for closeout costs and contingent liabilities;

(ii) Use of real property assisted with Continuum of Care program funds in accordance with the terms of commitment and principles;

(iii) Use of personal property purchased with Continuum of Care program funds; and

(iv) Compliance with requirements governing program income received subsequent to grant closeout.

(5) Other provisions appropriate to any special circumstances of the grant closeout, in modification of or in addition to the obligations in paragraphs (c)(1) through (4) of this section.

[77 FR 45442, July 31, 2012, as amended at 80 FR 75940, Dec. 7, 2015]

PART 581—USE OF FEDERAL REAL PROPERTY TO ASSIST THE HOMELESS

Sec.

AUTHORITY: 42 U.S.C. 11411 note; 42 U.S.C. 3535(d).

SOURCE: 56 FR 23794, 23795, May 24, 1991, unless otherwise noted.

§ 581.1 Definitions.

Applicant means any eligible organization that has submitted an application to the Department of Health and Human Services to obtain use of a certain suitable property to assist the homeless.

Checklist or property checklist means the form developed by HUD for use by landholding agencies to report the information to be used by HUD in making determinations of suitability.

Classification means a property's designation as unutilized, underutilized, excess, or surplus.

Day means one calendar day including weekends and holidays.

Eligible organization means a State or local government agency, or a private, non-profit organization that provides assistance to the homeless, and that is authorized under the State law in which the property is located to carry out the activity for which it requests property and enter into an agreement with the Federal Government for use of property for the purposes of this part. Eligible organizations that are private, non-profit organizations interested in applying for suitable property must be tax exempt under section 501(c)(3) of the Internal Revenue Code at the time of application and remain tax exempt throughout the time the Federal Government retains a reversionary interest in the property.

Encumbrance means any non-approved use by a transferee or a third party that limits the full utilization of the transferred property, regardless of time period, and includes liens, easements, restrictive covenants, licenses, leases, mortgages, informal agreements, and unaddressed trespass.

Excess property means any property under the control of a Federal executive agency that the head of the agency determines is not required to meet the agency's needs or responsibilities, pursuant to 40 U.S.C. 524.

GSA means the General Services Administration.

HHS means the Department of Health and Human Services.

Homeless is defined in 42 U.S.C. 11302. This term is synonymous with "homeless individual" and "homeless person."

HUD means the Department of Housing and Urban Development.

HUD website means a website maintained by HUD providing information about HUD, including any successor websites or technologies that are equally accessible and available to the public.

Landholding agency means the Federal department or agency with statutory authority to control property. For purposes of this part, the landholding agency is typically the Federal department or agency that had custody and accountability on behalf of the Federal

Government, of a certain piece of property at the time that such property was reported to HUD for a suitability determination pursuant to 42 U.S.C. 11411.

Lease means an agreement in writing between either HHS for surplus property or landholding agencies for underutilized and unutilized properties and the applicant giving rise to the relationship of lessor and lessee for the use of Federal property for a term of at least one year under the conditions set forth in the lease document.

Non-profit organization means an organization recognized as a non-profit by the State in which the organization operates, no part of the net earnings of which inures to the benefit of any member, founder, contributor, or individual; that has a voluntary board; that has an accounting system or has designated an entity that will maintain a functioning accounting system for the organization in accordance with generally accepted accounting procedures; and that practices nondiscrimination in the provision of assistance.

Permit means a license granted by a landholding agency to use unutilized or underutilized property for a specific amount of time, usually one year or less, under terms and conditions determined by the landholding agency. A permit does not grant to the recipient an estate in land or any interest in the property.

Property means real property consisting of vacant land or buildings, or a portion thereof, that is excess, surplus, or designated as unutilized or underutilized in surveys by the heads of landholding agencies conducted pursuant to 40 U.S.C. 524.

Related personal property means any personal property that is located on real property and is either an integral part of or useful in the operation of that property or is determined by GSA to be otherwise related to the property.

Representative of the homeless means a State or local government agency, or private nonprofit organization which provides, or proposes to provide, services to the homeless.

Screen means the process by which GSA surveys Federal executive agencies to determine if they have an interest in using excess Federal property to carry out a particular agency mission, and then surveys State, local, and nonprofit entities, to determine if any such entity has an interest in using surplus Federal property to carry out a specific public use.

State means a State of the United States, and includes the District of Columbia, the Commonwealth of Puerto Rico, and the Territories and possessions of the United States.

Suitable property means that HUD has determined that a certain property satisfies the criteria listed in §581.6.

Surplus property means any excess property not required by any Federal landholding agency for its needs or the discharge of its responsibilities, as determined by GSA.

Transfer document means a lease, deed, or permit transferring surplus, unutilized, or underutilized property.

Transferee means an eligible entity that acquires Federal property by lease, deed, or permit.

Underutilized means an entire property or portion thereof, with or without improvements which is used only at irregular periods or intermittently by the accountable landholding agency for current program purposes of that agency, or which is used for current program purposes that can be satisfied with only a portion of the property.

Unsuitable property means that HUD has determined that a particular property does not satisfy the criteria in §581.6.

Unutilized property means an entire property or portion thereof, with or without improvements, not occupied for current program purposes for the accountable executive agency or occupied in caretaker status only.

[56 FR 23794, 23795, May 24, 1991, as amended at 89 FR 89880, Nov. 13, 2024]

§581.2 Applicability.

(a) This part applies to Federal property that has been designated by Federal landholding agencies as unutilized, underutilized, excess, or surplus and is therefore subject to the provisions of Title V of the McKinney Act, as amended (42 U.S.C. 11411).

(b) The following categories of properties are not subject to this part (regardless of whether they may be unutilized or underutilized):

(1) Buildings and property at military installations that were approved for closure under the Defense Base Closure and Realignment Act of 1990 (part A of title XXIX of Pub. L. 101–510; 10 U.S.C. 2687 note) after October 25, 1994.

(2) Machinery and equipment not determined to be related personal property by the landholding agency or GSA or determined to be related personal property that the landholding agency or GSA chooses to dispose of separate from real property.

(3) Government-owned, contractor-operated machinery, equipment, land, and other facilities reported excess for sale only to the using contractor and subject to a continuing military requirement.

(4) Properties subject to special legislation directing a particular action.

(5) Properties subject to a court order that is binding on the Federal Government and, for any reason, precludes transfer for use to assist the homeless under the authority of 42 U.S.C. 11411.

(6) Property not subject to Federal Real Property Council reporting requirements in accordance with 40 U.S.C. 623(i).

(7) Mineral rights interests independent of surface rights.

(8) Air space interests independent of surface rights.

(9) Indian Reservation land subject to 40 U.S.C. 523.

(10) Property interests subject to reversion.

(11) Easements.

(12) Any building or fixture that is excess, or surplus, that is on land under the control of a landholding agency, where the underlying land is not excess or surplus.

(13) Property purchased in whole or in part with Federal funds if title to the property is not held by a Federal landholding agency as defined in this part.

[89 FR 89881, Nov. 13, 2024]

§ 581.3 Collecting the information.

(a) *Canvass of landholding agencies.* On a quarterly basis, HUD will canvass each landholding agency to collect information about property described as unutilized, underutilized, excess or surplus in accordance with 40 U.S.C. 524; however, HUD will accept property information between canvasses. Each canvass will collect information on properties not previously reported, and about property reported previously where the status or classification of the property has changed, or improvements have been made to the property. HUD will request descriptive information on properties sufficient to make a reasonable determination, under the criteria described in this section, of the suitability of a property for use to assist the homeless. Landholding agencies must report property information to HUD using the property checklist developed by HUD for that purpose. Property checklists submitted in response to a canvass must be submitted to HUD within 25 days of receipt of the canvass.

(b) *Agency annual suitable property report.* By December 31 of each year, each landholding agency must notify HUD of the current availability status and classification of each property controlled by the agency that:

(1) Was included in a list of suitable properties published that year by HUD; and

(2) Remains available for application for use to assist the homeless or has become available for application during that year.

(c) *GSA inventory.* HUD will collect information, in the same manner as described in paragraph (a) of this section, from GSA regarding property that is in GSA's current inventory of excess or surplus property.

(d) *Change in status.* If the information provided on the property checklist changes subsequent to HUD's determination of suitability, including any improvements or other alterations to the physical condition of the land or the buildings on the property, and the property remains unutilized, underutilized, excess, or surplus, the landholding agency must submit a revised property checklist in response to the next quarterly canvass. HUD will review for suitability and, if it differs from the previous determination, repost the property information on the HUD website. For example, property determined unsuitable due to extensive deterioration may have had improvements, or property determined suitable may subsequently be found to be extensively deteriorated.

[89 FR 89881, Nov. 13, 2024]

§581.4 Suitability determination.

(a) *Suitability determination.* Within 30 days after the receipt of a completed property checklist from landholding agencies either in response to a quarterly canvass, or between canvasses, HUD will determine, using the criteria set forth in §581.6 whether a property is suitable for use to assist the homeless and report its determination to the landholding agency. Properties that are under lease, contract, license, or agreement by which a Federal agency retains a real property interest or which are scheduled to become unutilized or underutilized will be reviewed for suitability no earlier than six months prior to the expected date when the property will become unutilized or underutilized.

(b) *Scope of suitability.* HUD will determine the suitability of a property for use to assist the homeless without regard to any particular use.

(c) *Environmental information.* HUD will evaluate the environmental information contained in property checklists forwarded to HUD by the landholding agencies solely for the purpose of determining suitability of properties under the criteria in §581.6.

(d) *Record of suitability determination.* HUD will assign an identification number to each property reviewed for suitability. HUD will maintain a public record of the following:

(1) The suitability determination for a particular piece of property, and the reasons for that determination; and

(2) The landholding agency's response to the determination pursuant to the requirements of §581.7(a).

(e) *Property determined unsuitable.* Property that is reviewed by HUD under this section and that is determined unsuitable for use to assist the homeless may not be made available for any other purpose for 20 days after publication of a notice of unsuitability on the HUD website.

(f) *Procedures for appealing unsuitability determinations.* (1) To request review of a determination of unsuitability, a representative of the homeless must contact HUD, in writing, through the U.S. Mail, email, or the HUD website, or such other method as HUD may require, within 20 days of publication of the notice of unsuitability.

(2) Requests for review of a determination of unsuitability may be made only by representatives of the homeless.

(3) The request for review must specify the grounds on which it is based, *i.e.*, HUD has improperly applied the criteria or HUD has relied on incorrect or incomplete information in making the determination (*e.g.*, that property is in a floodplain but not in a floodway).

(4) Upon receipt of a request to review a determination of unsuitability, HUD will notify the landholding agency or GSA that such a request has been made. The landholding agency or GSA shall have 20 days from receipt of the notice from HUD, or an extended period agreed to between HUD and the landholding agency or GSA, to provide any information pertinent to the review. The landholding agency or GSA must refrain from initiating disposal procedures until HUD has completed its reconsideration regarding unsuitability. If the landholding agency or GSA fails to meet the deadline, HUD will move forward with the appeal review with the property information it already has and information submitted in the appeal request provided by the representative of the homeless.

(i) HUD will act on all requests for review within 30 days of receipt of the landholding agency's or GSA's response, or, if the landholding agency or GSA failed to meet the deadline, within 30 days of such deadline, and will notify the representative of the homeless and the landholding agency or GSA in writing of its decision.

(ii) If a property is determined suitable as a result of the review, HUD will request the landholding agency's or GSA's determination of availability pursuant to §581.7, upon receipt of which HUD will promptly publish the determination on the HUD website.

[89 FR 89881, Nov. 13, 2024]

§ 581.5 Real property reported excess to GSA.

(a) Each landholding agency must submit a report to GSA of properties it determines excess. Each landholding agency must also provide a copy of HUD's suitability determination, if any, including HUD's identification number for the property.

(b) If a landholding agency reports an excess property to GSA that HUD has already determined to be suitable for use to assist the homeless, GSA will screen the property pursuant to paragraph (h) of this section and will advise HUD of the availability of the property for use by the homeless as provided in paragraph (e) of this section. In lieu of the preceding sentence, GSA may submit a new checklist to HUD and follow the procedures in paragraphs (c) through (h) of this section.

(c) If a landholding agency reports an excess property to GSA that has not been reviewed by HUD for homeless assistance suitability, GSA will complete a property checklist, based on information provided by the landholding agency, and will forward this checklist to HUD for a suitability determination. This checklist will reflect any change in classification, such as from unutilized or underutilized to excess or surplus.

(d) Within 30 days after GSA's submission, HUD will advise GSA of the suitability determination.

(e) When GSA receives notification from HUD listing suitable excess properties, GSA will transmit a response to HUD within 45 days regarding the availability of the property. GSA's response will include the following for each identified property:

(1) A statement that there is no other compelling Federal need for the property and, therefore, the property will be determined surplus; or

(2) A statement that there is further and compelling Federal need for the property (including a full explanation of such need) and that, therefore, the property is not presently available for use to assist the homeless.

(f) When GSA submits a checklist to HUD in accordance with paragraphs (b) and (c) of this section, the information regarding the availability of the property, as specified in paragraph (e)(1) and (2) of this section, may be included with the checklist if it is known at the time of submittal.

(g) When a surplus property is determined as suitable, confirmed as available by GSA, and notice is published on the HUD website, GSA will concurrently notify HHS, State and local government units, and known homeless assistance providers that have expressed interest in the particular property, and other organizations, as appropriate, concerning suitable properties.

(h) Upon submission of a Report of Excess to GSA, GSA may screen the property for Federal use. In addition, GSA may screen State and local governmental units and eligible non-profit organizations to determine interest in the property in accordance with 41 CFR part 102–75. (See 41 CFR 102–75.1220, 102–75.255, and 102–75.350.)

(i) The landholding agency will retain custody and accountability and will protect and maintain any property that is reported excess to GSA as provided in 41 CFR 102–75.965.

[89 FR 89881, Nov. 13, 2024]

§ 581.6 Suitability criteria.

(a) In general, properties will be determined suitable unless a property's characteristics include one or more of the following conditions:

(1) *Flammable or explosive hazards.* Property located less than an acceptable separation distance (under the standards in 24 CFR part 51, subpart C, and the HUD Guidebook, "Siting of HUD-Assisted Projects Near Hazardous Facilities" or successor guidebook) from any stationary above-ground container or facility which stores, handles, or processes hazardous substances of an explosive or fire prone nature (excluding containers and facilities that are not hazards as defined in 24 CFR 51.201), unless HUD can determine during the review period based on information provided by the landholding agency that appropriate mitigating measures, as defined in 24 CFR 51.205, are already in place.

(2) *Coastal barriers.* Property located in a System Unit, as defined at 16 U.S.C. 3502(7), under the Coastal Barrier Resources Act, as amended (16 U.S.C. 3501 *et seq.*).

(3) *Site safety conditions.* Property with a documented and extensive condition(s) that represents a clear threat to personal physical safety or health. Such conditions may include, but are not limited to, significant contamination from hazardous substances, as defined by 42 U.S.C. 9601, periodic flooding, sinkholes, or landslides.

(b) In the cases in paragraphs (b)(1) through (4) of this section, properties will be determined unsuitable, unless the landholding agencies provide information to enable HUD to determine the property is suitable:

(1) *Inaccessible.* Property that is inaccessible, meaning that the property is not accessible by road (including property on small offshore islands) or is landlocked (*e.g.*, can be reached only by crossing private property and there is no established right or means of entry).

(2) *National security.* Property located in an area to which the general public is denied access in the interest of national security (*e.g.*, where a special pass or security clearance is a condition of entry to the property), unless there is an alternative method to gain access without compromising national security.

(3) *Runway clear zones.* Property located within a runway clear zone or a military airfield clear zone.

(4) *Floodway.* Property located in a floodway, unless only an incidental portion of the property is in the floodway and that incidental portion does not affect the use of the remainder of the property to assist the homeless.

[89 FR 89881, Nov. 13, 2024]

§581.7 Determination of availability for suitable properties.

Within 45 days after receipt of notification from HUD pursuant to §581.4(a) that a property has been determined to be suitable, each landholding agency or GSA must transmit to HUD a statement of one of the following:

(a) In the case of unutilized or underutilized property—

(1) An intention to declare the property excess;

(2) An intention to make the property available for use to assist the homeless; or

(3) The reasons why the property cannot be declared excess or made available for use to assist the homeless. The reasons given must be different from those listed as suitability criteria in §581.6.

(b) In the case of excess property which has been reported to GSA—

(1) A statement that there is no compelling Federal need for the property, and, therefore, the property will be determined surplus; or

(2) A statement that there is a further and compelling Federal need for the property (including a full explanation of such need) and therefore, the property is not presently available for use to assist the homeless.

[89 FR 89881, Nov. 13, 2024]

§581.8 Public notice of determination.

(a) No later than 15 days after the most recent 45-day period has elapsed for receiving responses from the landholding agencies or GSA regarding availability, HUD will post on the HUD website a list of all properties reviewed, including a description of the property, its address, and classification. The following designations will be made:

(1) Properties that are suitable and available.

(2) Properties that are suitable and unavailable.

(3) Properties that are suitable and to be declared excess.

(4) Properties that are unsuitable.

(b) HUD will establish and maintain a toll-free number for the public to obtain specific information about properties in paragraph (a) of this section.

(c) No later than 15 days after the most recent 45-day period has elapsed for receiving responses from the landholding agencies or GSA regarding availability, HUD will transmit to the United States Interagency Council on Homelessness (USICH) a copy of the list of all properties in paragraph (a) of this section. The USICH will immediately distribute to all State and regional homeless coordinators area-relevant portions of the list. The USICH will encourage the State and regional homeless coordinators to disseminate this information widely.

(d) No later than February 15 of each year, HUD will publish in the FEDERAL

REGISTER a list of all properties in the agency annual suitable property reports, reported to HUD pursuant to § 581.3(b).

(e) HUD will publish an annual list of properties determined suitable, but which agencies reported unavailable including the reasons such properties are not available.

[89 FR 89881, Nov. 13, 2024]

§ 581.9 General policies of HHS.

(a) It is the policy of HHS to foster and assure maximum utilization of surplus property for homeless assistance purposes.

(b) Transfers may be made only to eligible organizations.

(c) Property will be requested for assignment only when HUD has made a final determination that the property is suitable for use to assist the homeless, GSA has determined it is available, and HHS has determined it is needed for homeless assistance purposes. The amount of real and related personal property to be transferred shall not exceed normal operating requirements of the applicant. Such property will not be requested for assignment unless it is needed at the time of application for homeless assistance purposes or will be so needed within the immediate or foreseeable future.

(d) Transfers by deed will be made only after the applicant's financial plan is approved and the applicant provides certification that the proposed program is permissible under all applicable State and local zoning restrictions, building codes, and similar limitations.

(e) In instances of noncompliance, transferees are provided an opportunity to cure the noncompliance pursuant to 45 CFR 12a.10.

[89 FR 89881, Nov. 13, 2024]

§ 581.10 Expression of interest process.

(a) Properties published by HUD as suitable and available, pursuant to § 581.8, for application for use to assist the homeless shall not be available for any other purpose for a period of 30 days beginning on the date the list of properties is published on the HUD website. Any eligible organization interested in any underutilized, unutilized, excess, or surplus property for use to assist the homeless must send HHS a written expression of interest in that property within 30 days after the property has been published on the HUD website.

(b) Although a property may be determined suitable by HUD, HUD's determination does not mean a property is necessarily fit for use for the purpose(s) stated in the application, nor does it guarantee subsequent conveyance or transfer of a property.

(c) If a written expression of interest to apply for suitable property for use to assist the homeless is received by HHS within the 30-day holding period, such property may not be made available for any other purpose until the date HHS or the appropriate landholding agency has completed action on the application submitted pursuant to that expression of interest.

(d)(1) The expression of interest should identify the specific property, briefly describe the proposed use, include the name of the organization, and indicate whether it is a public body or a private, non-profit organization. The expression of interest must be sent to HHS by email, *rpb@psc.hhs.gov*, or by mail at the following address: Department of Health and Human Services, Program Manager, Federal Real Property Assistance Program, Real Estate Logistics and Operations, 5600 Fishers Lane, Rockville, Maryland 20852.

(2) HHS will notify the landholding agency (for unutilized and underutilized properties) or GSA (for excess and surplus properties) when an expression of interest has been received for a certain property.

(e) An expression of interest may be sent to and accepted by HHS any time after the 30-day holding period has expired only if the property remains available as determined by GSA or the landholding agency for application to assist the homeless. In such a case, an application submitted pursuant to this expression of interest may be approved for use by the homeless if:

(1) There are no pending applications or written expressions of interest made under any law for use of the property for any purpose; and

(2) In the case of excess or surplus property, GSA has not received a bona fide offer to purchase that property or advertised for the sale of the property by public auction.

[89 FR 89881, Nov. 13, 2024]

§581.11 Application process and requirements.

(a) Upon receipt of an expression of interest, HHS will send an application packet to the interested entity. The application packet requires the applicant to provide certain information, including the following—

(1) *Acquisition type.* The applicant must state whether it is requesting acquisition of the property by lease, deed, or permit. A lease of one year, extendable at HHS's discretion, with the concurrence of GSA or the landholding agency, may be granted when the applicant's initial application is approved and the applicant's final application outlining the applicant's financial plan is found to be otherwise reasonable based on the criteria in paragraph (a)(7) of this section, but either a change in zoning is required or the financial plan proposes to utilize Low-Income Housing Tax Credits or other funding sources that typically take longer to process than other forms of financing. Applicants that initially apply for transfer by lease or permit and subsequently request transfer by deed will follow the same bifurcated application process, including deadlines, contained in 42 U.S.C. 11411. Should an applicant wish to transition from acquisition by lease to acquisition by deed, HHS will issue a letter of commitment to a lessee indicating that, provided its application meets all application criteria, including securing of all necessary financing that complies with Federal Government requirements, HHS will issue a deed.

(2) *Description of the applicant organization.* The applicant must document that it satisfies the definition of an *eligible organization* as specified in §581.1.

(3) *Description of the property desired.* The applicant must describe the listed property desired, including existing zoning. Applicants must certify that any modification(s) made to and use of the property will conform to all applicable building codes, and local use restrictions, or similar limitations. In accordance with GSA policy, determinations regarding parcelization are made prior to screening. Therefore, expressions of interest and applications for portions of listed properties will not be accepted.

(4) *Description of the proposed program.* The applicant must fully describe the proposed program and plan of use, including implementation plans.

(5) *Demonstration of need.* The applicant must demonstrate that the property is needed for homeless assistance purposes at the time of application and how the program will address the needs of the homeless population to be assisted. The applicant must demonstrate that it has an immediate need and ability to utilize all of the property for which it is applying.

(6) *Demonstrate that the property is suitable and adaptable for the proposed program and plan of use.* The applicant must fully explain why the property is suitable and describe what, if any, modification(s) will be made to the property before the program becomes operational.

(7) *Ability to finance and operate the proposed program.* If the applicant's initial application is approved, the applicant must set forth a reasonable plan to finance the approved program within 45 days of the initial approval. To be considered reasonable, the plan must, at a minimum:

(i) Specifically describe all anticipated costs and sources of funding for the proposed program, including any property modifications;

(ii) Be accompanied by supporting documentation which demonstrates that the proposed plan is likely to succeed;

(iii) Demonstrate that the applicant is ready, willing, able, and authorized to assume care, custody, and maintenance of the property;

(iv) Demonstrate that it has secured the necessary dedicated funds, or will obtain such funds, to carry out the approved proposed program and plan of use for the property, including administrative expenses incident to the transfer by deed, lease, or permit;

(v) Not diminish the value of the Federal Government's interest in the property nor impair the Federal Government's ability to revert and immediately dispose of the property free of any and all liens, encumbrances, or anything else which renders the property unmarketable. Deed transfers will only be made after an applicant demonstrates its financial plan adequately protects the Federal Government's interest in the property; and

(vi) Neither subject the Federal Government's interest in the property to foreclosure nor impose obligations (*e.g.*, extended use agreements) on the Federal Government.

(8) *Compliance with non-discrimination requirements.* Each applicant under this part must certify in writing that it will comply with all requirements of Federal law and HHS policy, as amended, relating to non-discrimination, including the following: the Fair Housing Act (42 U.S.C. 3601–3619) and implementing regulations at 24 CFR part 100; and, as applicable, Executive Order 11063 (Equal Opportunity in Housing) and implementing regulations at 24 CFR part 107; Title VI of the Civil Rights Act of 1964 (42 U.S.C. 2000d to d–4) (Nondiscrimination in Federally Assisted Programs) and implementing regulations at 24 CFR part 1; section 1557 of the Affordable Care Act and implementing regulations at 45 CFR part 92; the prohibitions against discrimination on the basis of age under the Age Discrimination Act of 1975 (42 U.S.C. 6101–6107) and implementing regulations at 24 CFR part 146; and the prohibitions against discrimination against otherwise qualified individuals with disabilities under section 504 of the Rehabilitation Act of 1973 (29 U.S.C. 794) and implementing regulations at 24 CFR part 8; and Titles II or III of the Americans with Disabilities Act and implementing regulations at 28 CFR part 35 or 36, as applicable. The applicant must maintain the required records to demonstrate compliance with all applicable Federal laws and HHS policies related to non-discrimination.

(9) *Insurance and indemnification.* The applicant must certify that it will insure the property against loss, damage, or destruction to protect the residual financial interest of the United States. The United States shall be named as an additional insured. Applicants must provide proof of insurance annually or upon request. Failure to maintain sufficient insurance may result in adverse action, including reversion of the property, at the discretion of HHS. In the event of a covered loss, the transferee must hold all insurance proceeds in trust and obtain written concurrence from HHS before disbursing the funds. Applicants, and all affiliated parties utilizing the property, as approved by HHS, must indemnify the United States and hold the United States harmless for all actions involving use of the property.

(10) *Historic preservation.* Where applicable, the applicant must provide information that will enable HHS to comply with Federal historic preservation requirements.

(11) *Environmental information.* The applicant must provide sufficient information to allow HHS to analyze the potential impact of the applicant's proposal on the environment, in accordance with the instructions provided with the application packet. HHS will assist applicants in obtaining any pertinent environmental information in the possession of HUD, GSA, or the landholding agency. However, the burden is on the applicant to submit sufficient documentation for analysis by HHS.

(12) *Local government notification.* The applicant must certify that it has notified the applicable unit of general local government responsible for sewer, water, police, and fire services, in writing, of its proposed program for the specific property and submit a copy of that written notification.

(13) *Zoning and local use restrictions.* An applicant requesting a deed must certify that it has consulted all State and local governmental entities that will have jurisdiction over the property and that the proposed use will comply with all applicable zoning and local use restrictions, including local building code requirements. An applicant that applies for a lease or permit is not required to comply with local zoning requirements, as long as the Federal Government retains ownership of the property. Deed transfers will only be made after the applicant has provided

acceptable written proof that the proposed program is not in conflict with State or local zoning laws and restrictions, building codes, or similar limitations.

(b) *Scope of evaluations.* Due to the short time frame imposed by statute for evaluating applications, HHS's evaluation will, generally, be limited to the information contained in the application. It is therefore incumbent on applicants to provide thorough and complete applications.

(c) *Deadline for initial application.* An initial application must be received by HHS, at the email address in §581.10(d)(1) or other address indicated by HHS, within 75 days after an expression of interest is received from a particular applicant for that property. Upon written request from the applicant, HHS may, in its discretion, grant extensions authorized by 42 U.S.C. 11411(e)(2)(A), provided that the appropriate landholding agency or GSA concurs with the extension.

(d) *Evaluation of initial application.* (1) Upon receipt of an initial application, HHS will review it for completeness, and, if incomplete and time permits, may, in its discretion, return it or ask the applicant to furnish any missing or additional required information prior to final evaluation of the initial application.

(2) HHS will evaluate each initial application within 10 days of receipt and will promptly advise the applicant of its decision. All initial applications will be reviewed on the basis of the following elements:

(i) *Services offered.* The extent and range of proposed services, such as meals, shelter, job training, and counseling.

(ii) *Need.* The demand for the program, the program's ability to satisfy unmet needs of the community, and the degree to which the available property will be fully utilized.

(iii) *Experience.* Demonstrated ability to provide the services, such as prior success in operating similar programs and recommendations attesting to that fact by Federal, State, and local authorities.

(e) *Deadline and evaluation of final application.* (1) If HHS approves an initial application, HHS will notify the applicant and provide the applicant 45 days in which to provide a final application. The final application shall set forth a reasonable plan to finance, as specified in paragraph (a)(7) of this section, the approved program as set forth in the initial application. Applicants may not modify the approved initial application within its final application proposal.

(2) Upon receipt of the final application, HHS will make a determination within 15 days and notify the applicant.

(3) Unlike with initial applications, requests for extensions are not authorized by 42 U.S.C. 11411 and thus will not be considered for final applications.

(4) Applications are evaluated on a first-come, first-served basis. HHS will notify all organizations that have submitted expressions of interest for a particular property whether an earlier application received for that property has been approved.

(f) *Competing applications.* If HHS receives more than one final application simultaneously, HHS will evaluate all applications and make a determination based on each application's merit. HHS will rank approved applications based on the elements listed in paragraph (a) of this section, and notify the landholding agency, or GSA, as appropriate, of the approved applicant.

[89 FR 89881, Nov. 13, 2024]

§581.12 Action on approved applications.

(a) *Unutilized and underutilized properties.* (1) When HHS approves an application, it will so notify the applicant and forward a copy of the application to the landholding agency. The landholding agency will execute the lease, or permit document, as appropriate, in consultation with the applicant.

(2) The landholding agency maintains the discretion to decide the following:

(i) The length of time the property will be available.

(ii) The terms and conditions of the lease or permit document (except that a landholding agency may not charge any fees or impose any costs).

(b) *Excess and surplus properties.* (1) When HHS approves an application, it will so notify the applicant and request that GSA assign the property to HHS for transfer. Requests to GSA for the assignment of surplus property to HHS for homeless assistance purposes will be based on the following conditions:

(i) HHS has a fully approved application for the property;

(ii) The applicant is able, willing, and authorized to assume immediate care, custody, and maintenance of the property;

(iii) The applicant is able, willing and authorized to pay the administrative expenses incident to the transfer; and

(iv) The applicant has secured the necessary funds, or had demonstrated the ability to obtain such funds, to carry out the approved program of use of the property.

(2) Upon receipt of an acceptable assignment, HHS will execute the transfer document in accordance with the procedures and requirements set out in this part and any other terms and conditions HHS and GSA determine are appropriate or necessary. Custody and accountability of the property will remain throughout the lease term with the landholding agency (*i.e.*, the agency which initially reported the property as excess) and throughout the deed term with the transferee.

(3) Prior to assignment to HHS, GSA may consider other Federal uses and other important national needs in deciding the disposition of surplus property. Priority of consideration will normally be given to uses to assist the homeless. However, both GSA and HHS may consider any competing request for the property made under 40 U.S.C. 550 that is so meritorious and compelling that it outweighs the needs of the homeless.

(4) Whenever GSA or HHS decides in favor of a competing request over a request for property for homeless assistance, the agency making the decision will transmit to the appropriate committees of Congress an explanatory statement which details the need satisfied by conveyance of the surplus property, and the reasons for determining that such need was so meritorious and compelling as to outweigh the needs of the homeless.

[89 FR 89881, Nov. 13, 2024]

§ 581.13 Waivers.

The Secretary may waive any requirement of this part that is not required by law, whenever it is determined that undue hardship would result from applying the requirement, or where application of the requirement would adversely affect the purposes of the program. Each waiver will be in writing and will be supported by documentation of the pertinent facts and grounds. The Secretary periodically will publish notice of granted waivers in the FEDERAL REGISTER.

§ 581.14 Surplus property transfer documents.

(a) Surplus property may be conveyed to eligible organizations pursuant to 40 U.S.C. 550(d) and 42 U.S.C. 11411, as amended, by lease or deed, at the applicant's discretion.

(b) Transfers of surplus property for homeless assistance purposes are in exchange for the transferee's agreement to fully utilize the property for homeless assistance purposes in accordance with the terms specified in the transfer document.

(c) A transfer of surplus property for homeless assistance purposes is subject to the disapproval of GSA within 30 days after notice is given to GSA of the proposed transfer.

(d) Surplus property transferred pursuant to this part will be disposed on an "as is, where is" basis without warranty of any kind except as may be stated in the transfer document.

(e) Unless excepted by GSA in its assignment, the disposal of property includes mineral rights associated with the surface estate.

(f) Transfers of surplus property under this part will be made with the following general terms and conditions:

(1) For the period provided in the transfer document, the transferee shall utilize all the surplus property it receives solely and continuously for the approved program and plan of use, in accordance with 42 U.S.C. 11411 and this part, except that:

(i) The transferee has 12 months from the date of transfer to place the surplus property into use, if HHS did not approve in writing, construction of new facilities or major renovation of the property when it approved the final application;

(ii) The transferee has 48 months from the date of transfer to place the surplus property into use, if the transferee proposes construction of new facilities or major renovation of the property and HHS approves it in writing at the time it approves the final application;

(iii) If the applicable time limitation is not met, the transferee shall either commence payments in cash to the Federal Government for each month thereafter during which the proposed use has not been implemented or take such other action as set forth at §581.18 as is deemed appropriate by HHS. Such monthly payments shall be computed on the basis of the current fair market value of the property, as conveyed, at the time of the first payment and dividing it by 360 months. At HHS's discretion, the payment may be waived if the transferee makes a sufficient showing of continued progress to place the property into use or if an unforeseeable event occurs which prevents the property from being put into use within the applicable timeframe; and

(iv) HHS may permit use of surplus property at any time during the period of restriction by an entity other than the transferee in accordance with §581.19.

(2) The transferee will not be permitted to encumber, or dispose of the property, or impair full utilization thereof, without the prior written authorization of HHS. In the event the property is encumbered, sold, or disposed of, or is used for any purposes other than those set forth in an approved plan without the written consent of HHS, all revenues or the reasonable value of other benefits received by the transferee directly or indirectly from such use, as determined by HHS, will be considered to have been received and held in trust by the transferee for the account of the United States and will be subject to the direction and control of HHS. The provisions of this paragraph (f)(2) shall not impair or affect the rights reserved to the United States in paragraph (f)(8) of this section, or the right of HHS to impose conditions to its consent.

(3) The transferee will file with HHS such reports on its maintenance and use of the transferred property and any other reports or information deemed necessary by HHS.

(4) The transferee shall pay all administrative costs incidental to the transfer, including but not limited to—transfer taxes; surveys; appraisals; title searches; the transferee's legal fees; and recordation expenses. Transferee is solely responsible for such costs and may not seek reimbursement from the Federal Government for any reason.

(5) The transferee shall protect, preserve, maintain, and repair the property to ensure that the property remains in as good a condition as when received.

(6) The transferee shall protect the residual financial interest of the United States in the surplus property by insurance or such other means as HHS directs.

(7) The transferee shall abide by all applicable Federal civil rights laws including those specified in the covenants and conditions contained in the transfer document, prohibiting the transferee from discriminating on the basis of, including but not limited to, race, color, national origin, religion, sex, familial status, or disability in the use of the property.

(8) In the event of noncompliance with any conditions of the deed as determined by HHS, whether caused by the legal or other inability of the transferee, its successors and assigns, to perform any of the obligations of the transfer document, the Federal Government has an immediate right of reentry thereon, and to cause all right, title, and interest in and to the property to revert to the United States, and the transferee shall forfeit all right, title, and interest in and to the property. In such event, transferee shall execute a quitclaim deed and take all other actions necessary to return the property to the United States within ninety (90) days of a written request from the Federal Government, extended only at the discretion of the Federal Government. Transferee shall cooperate with the United States in the event of a reversion and agrees that the United States need not seek judicial intervention before exercising its right to revert, reenter, and reconvey the property.

(9) In the event title is reverted to the United States for noncompliance or

voluntarily reconveyed to the United States, the transferee shall, at the option of HHS, be required to: reimburse the United States for the decrease in value of the property not due to market conditions, reasonable wear and tear, acts of God, or approved alterations completed by the transferee to adapt the property to the homeless use for which the property was transferred; and reimburse the United States for any costs incurred in reverting title to or possession of the property, including reasonable attorneys' fees.

(10) With respect to leased property, in the event of noncompliance with any of the conditions of the lease, as determined by HHS or the landholding agency, the right of occupancy and possession shall, at the option of HHS or the landholding agency, be terminated. In the event a leasehold is terminated by the United States for noncompliance or is voluntarily surrendered, the lessee shall be required, at the option of HHS, to reimburse the United States for the decrease in value of the property not due to market conditions, reasonable wear and tear, acts of God, or approved alterations completed by the lessee to adapt the property to the homeless use for which the property was leased. With respect to any termination of leasehold resulting from noncompliance, the United States, shall, in addition thereto, be reimbursed for such costs as may be incurred in recovering possession of the property, including reasonable attorneys' fees.

(11) Any other term or condition that HHS and GSA determine appropriate or necessary.

(12) With respect to surplus property transferred by deed, the terms and conditions including those in this paragraph (f), apply for a period of three hundred sixty (360) months of use in accordance with a program of use approved in writing by HHS. The three hundred sixty months (360) period may, in HHS's sole discretion, be extended or restarted in the event the property is not fully utilized or is retransferred to a successor entity. Expiration of the terms and conditions in this paragraph (f) does not release the transferee from continuing compliance, as appropriate, with any conditions that may run with the land, *e.g.*, environmental conditions and/or historic preservation covenants. Such conditions will continue to be the responsibility of the transferee and successors.

(13) With respect to surplus property transferred by lease, the terms and conditions including those in this paragraph (f), extend for the entire initial lease and for any subsequent renewal periods, unless specifically excluded in writing by HHS.

(g) Related personal property may be transferred or leased as a part of the realty and in accordance with real property procedures.

(h) Transferees will be responsible for the protection and maintenance of the property during the time that they possess the property. Upon termination of the lease term or reversion of title to the United States, the transferee will be responsible for removing improvements made to the property if directed to by the United States and, in such event, will be responsible for restoration of the property or the costs associated with restoring the property. If improvements made by the transferee are not voluntarily removed by the transferee and the United States consents, they will become the property of the United States. If the United States does not consent, the transferee shall reimburse the United States for reasonable costs of removal. GSA or the landholding agency, as appropriate, will assume responsibility for protection and maintenance of a property when the lease terminates or title reverts.

(i) Transferees, by obtaining the written consent of HHS, may abrogate the restrictions set forth in paragraph (f) of this section for all or any portion of the property in accordance with the provisions of § 581.20.

[89 FR 89886, Nov. 13, 2024]

§ 581.15 Unsuitable properties.

The landholding agency or GSA will defer action to dispose of properties determined unsuitable for homeless assistance for 20 days after the date that notice of a property is posted on the HUD website. HUD will inform landholding agencies or GSA if an appeal of an unsuitability determination is filed by a representative of the homeless pursuant to § 581.4(f). HUD will advise the agency to refrain from initiating disposal procedures until HUD has completed its reconsideration process regarding unsuitability. Thereafter, or if no appeal has been filed after 20 days, GSA or the appropriate landholding agency may proceed with disposal action in accordance with applicable law.

[89 FR 89886, Nov. 13, 2024]

§581.16 Compliance with the National Environmental Policy Act of 1969 and other related Acts (environmental impact).

(a) HHS, prior to making a final decision to convey or lease, or to amend, reform, or grant an approval or release with respect to a previous conveyance or lease of, surplus property for homeless purposes, will act in accordance with applicable provisions of the National Environmental Policy Act of 1969, the National Historic Preservation Act of 1966, the National Archeological Data Preservation Act, and other related acts. No lease to use surplus property shall allow the lessee to make, or cause to be made, any irreversible change in the conditions of said property, and no lease shall be employed for the purpose of delaying or avoiding compliance with the requirements of these Acts, unless approved by the United States.

(b) Applicants shall be required to provide such information as HHS deems necessary to make an assessment of the impact of the proposed Federal action on the human environment. Materials contained in the applicant's official request, responses to a standard questionnaire prescribed by HHS, as well as other relevant information, will be used by HHS in making said assessment.

(c) If the assessment reveals:

(1) That the proposed Federal action involved properties of historical significance which are listed, or eligible for listing, in the National Register of Historic Places; or

(2) That a more than insignificant impact on the human environment is reasonably foreseeable as a result of the proposed action; or

(3) That the proposed Federal action could result in irreparable loss or destruction of archeologically significant items or data, HHS will, except as provided for in paragraph (d) of this section, prepare and distribute, or cause to be prepared or distributed, such notices and statements and obtain such approvals as are required by the Acts cited in paragraph (a) of this section.

(d) If a proposed action involves other Federal agencies in a sequence of actions, or a group of actions, directly related to each other because of their functional interdependence, HHS may enter into and support a lead agency agreement to designate a single lead agency which will assume primary responsibility for coordinating the assessment of environmental effects of proposed Federal actions, preparing and distributing such notices and statements, or obtaining such approvals, as are required by the Acts cited in paragraph (a) of this section. The procedures of the designated lead agency will be utilized in conducting the environmental assessment. In the event of disagreement between HHS and another Federal agency, HHS will reserve the right to abrogate the lead agency agreement with the other Federal agency.

[89 FR 89886, Nov. 13, 2024]

§581.17 No applications approved.

(a) At the end of the 30-day holding period described in §581.10(a), HHS will notify GSA, or the landholding agency, as appropriate, if an expression of interest has been received for a certain property. Where there is no expression of interest, GSA or the landholding agency, as appropriate, will proceed with disposal in accordance with applicable law.

(b) Upon notice from HHS that all applications have been disapproved, or if no initial applications have been received within 75 days after an expression of interest, or no final application has been received within 45 days after an approved initial application, disposal may proceed in accordance with applicable law.

[89 FR 89886, Nov. 13, 2024]

§581.18 Utilization and enforcement.

(a) *Sanctions.* For instances of noncompliance relating to surplus property transfers, HHS may impose, after providing an opportunity to cure to the transferee, any or all of the following sanctions in its sole discretion, as applicable:

(1) Where property or any portion thereof was not used or is not being used for the purposes for which transferred, or is sold, leased or subleased, encumbered, disposed of, or used for purposes other than those in the approved program and plan of use, without the prior written consent of HHS, HHS may require the transferee to—

(i) Place the property into immediate use for an approved purpose and extend the period of restriction in the transfer document for an additional term as determined by HHS;

(ii) Hold in trust all revenues and the reasonable value of other benefits received by the transferee directly or indirectly from that use for the United States subject to the direction and control of HHS;

(iii) Return title to such property to the United States or to relinquish any leasehold interest therein;

(iv) Abrogate the conditions and restrictions of the transfer, as set forth in § 581.20;

(v) Make cash payments to the United States, as directed by HHS, equivalent to the current fair market rental value of the surplus property, as transferred, for each month during which the program and plan of use has not been implemented and continues to not be implemented; or

(vi) Any other remedy that HHS determines appropriate or necessary.

(2) Where the transferee desires to place the property into temporary use to assist the homeless other than that for which the property was transferred, written approval from HHS must be obtained, and will be conditioned upon HHS's authority to permit the use and such terms as HHS may impose.

(3) If HHS or the landholding agency determines that a lessee or sublessee of a transferee is in noncompliance with a term or condition of the lease, or if the lessee voluntarily surrenders the premises, HHS may require termination of the lease and impose sanctions described in paragraph (a)(1) of this section, as appropriate.

(b) *Reversion*. When HHS recommends reversion of the property for noncompliance, HHS will seek GSA's concurrence. GSA will respond to HHS's concurrence request within 30 days of its receipt. If GSA concurs, GSA will work with HHS to complete the reversion of the property. If GSA does not concur to the reversion recommendation, GSA will issue, to HHS, a written determination: stating the reason(s) for the disapproval; and acknowledging that HHS has recommended reversion and, therefore, the property is no longer within HHS's Title V program. The Federal Government will implement a response to the noncompliance that is in its best interests.

[89 FR 89886, Nov. 13, 2024]

§ 581.19 Other uses.

(a) A transferee may permit the use of all or a portion of the surplus property by another eligible entity as described in § 581.1 for homeless assistance purposes, only upon those terms and conditions HHS determines appropriate, if:

(1) The transferee submits a written request to HHS explaining the purpose of and need for another eligible entity's use of the property, program plan, and other relevant information requested by HHS;

(2) HHS determines that the proposed use would not substantially limit the program and plan of use by the transferee and that the use will not unduly burden the Federal Government;

(3) HHS's written consent is obtained by the transferee in advance;

(4) HHS approves the use instrument in advance and in writing;

(5) The transferee agrees to lengthen the period of restrictions as determined by HHS; and

(6) HHS advises GSA and there is no disapproval by GSA within thirty (30) days.

(b) A transferee that does not follow paragraph (a) of this section will be deemed to be not in compliance with the terms and conditions of the Title V program and subject to enforcement action, including reversion of the property.

[89 FR 89886, Nov. 13, 2024]

§ 581.20 Abrogation.

(a) HHS may abrogate the conditions and restrictions in the transfer document if:

(1) The transferee submits to HHS a written request that HHS abrogate the conditions and restrictions in the transfer document as to all or any portion of the surplus property;

(2) HHS determines the terms and conditions of the proposed abrogation and determines that the proposed abrogation is in the best interest of the United States; and

(3) HHS transmits the abrogation request to GSA and there is no disapproval by GSA within 30 days after notice is given. If GSA disapproves, GSA will state, in writing, to HHS the reason(s) for the disapproval.

(b) HHS abrogates the conditions and restrictions in the transfer document only upon receipt of the appropriate consideration, including cash payment, to the United States, as directed by HHS, which is based on the formula contained in the transfer document, and any other terms and conditions HHS deems appropriate to protect the interest of the United States.

[89 FR 89886, Nov. 13, 2024]

§ 581.21 Compliance inspections and reports.

Transferees are required to allow HHS to conduct compliance inspections and to submit such compliance reports and actions as are deemed necessary by HHS. At a minimum, the transferee will be required to submit an annual utilization report regarding the operation and maintenance of the property, including current images of the entire property and such information as HHS shall require.

[89 FR 89886, Nov. 13, 2024]

§ 581.22 No right of administrative review for agency decisions.

There is no right to administrative review within HHS, including requests for reconsideration or appeal, of agency decisions on applications and other discretionary decisions.

[89 FR 89886, Nov. 13, 2024]

§ 581.23 Severability.

Any provision of this part held to be invalid or unenforceable with respect to certain parties or circumstances shall be construed so as to continue to give the maximum effect to the provision permitted by law unless such holding is that the provision of this part is invalid and unenforceable in all circumstances, in which event the provision shall be severable from the remainder of this part and shall not affect the remainder thereof.

[89 FR 89886, Nov. 13, 2024]

PART 582—SHELTER PLUS CARE

Subpart A—General

Subpart B—Assistance Provided

Subpart C—Application and Grant Award

Subpart D—Program Requirements

Subpart E—Administration

AUTHORITY: 42 U.S.C. 3535(d) and 11403–11407b.

SOURCE: 58 FR 13892, Mar. 15, 1993, unless otherwise noted.

Subpart A—General

§ 582.1 Purpose and scope.

(a) *General.* The Shelter Plus Care program (S+C) is authorized by title IV, subtitle F, of the Stewart B. McKinney Homeless Assistance Act (the McKinney Act) (42 U.S.C. 11403–11407b). S+C is designed to link rental assistance to supportive services for hard-to-serve homeless persons with disabilities (primarily those who are seriously mentally ill; have chronic problems with alcohol, drugs, or both; or have acquired immunodeficiency syndrome (AIDS) and related diseases) and their families. The program provides grants to be used for rental assistance for permanent housing for homeless persons with disabilities. Rental assistance grants must be matched in the aggregate by supportive services that are equal in value to the amount of rental assistance and appropriate to the needs of the population to be served. Recipients are chosen on a competitive basis nationwide.

(b) *Components.* Rental assistance is provided through four components described in § 582.100. Applicants may apply for assistance under any one of the four components, or a combination.

[58 FR 13892, Mar. 15, 1993, as amended at 61 FR 51169, Sept. 30, 1996; 80 FR 75804, Dec. 4, 2015]

§ 582.5 Definitions.

The terms *Fair Market Rent (FMR), HUD, Public Housing Agency (PHA), Indian Housing Authority (IHA),* and *Secretary* are defined in 24 CFR part 5.

As used in this part:

Acquired immunodeficiency syndrome (AIDS) and related diseases has the meaning given in section 853 of the AIDS Housing Opportunity Act (42 U.S.C. 12902).

Applicant has the meaning given in section 462 of the McKinney Act (42 U.S.C. 11403g).

Developmental disability means, as defined in section 102 of the Developmental Disabilities Assistance and Bill of Rights Act of 2000 (42 U.S.C. 15002):

(1) A severe, chronic disability of an individual that—

(i) Is attributable to a mental or physical impairment or combination of mental and physical impairments;

(ii) Is manifested before the individual attains age 22;

(iii) Is likely to continue indefinitely;

(iv) Results in substantial functional limitations in three or more of the following areas of major life activity:

(A) Self-care;

(B) Receptive and expressive language;

(C) Learning;

(D) Mobility;

(E) Self-direction;

(F) Capacity for independent living;

(G) Economic self-sufficiency; and

(v) Reflects the individual's need for a combination and sequence of special, interdisciplinary, or generic services, individualized supports, or other forms of assistance that are of lifelong or extended duration and are individually planned and coordinated.

(2) An individual from birth to age 9, inclusive, who has a substantial developmental delay or specific congenital or acquired condition, may be considered to have a developmental disability without meeting three or more of the criteria described in paragraphs (1)(i) through (v) of the definition of "developmental disability" in this section if the individual, without services and supports, has a high probability of meeting those criteria later in life.

Eligible person means a homeless person with disabilities (primarily persons who are seriously mentally ill; have chronic problems with alcohol, drugs, or both; or have AIDS and related diseases) and, if also homeless, the family of such a person. To be eligible for assistance, persons must be very low income, except that low-income individuals may be assisted under the SRO component in accordance with 24 CFR 813.105(b).

Homeless means:

(1) An individual or family who lacks a fixed, regular, and adequate nighttime residence, meaning:

(i) An individual or family with a primary nighttime residence that is a public or private place not designed for or ordinarily used as a regular sleeping accommodation for human beings, including a car, park, abandoned building, bus or train station, airport, or camping ground;

(ii) An individual or family living in a supervised publicly or privately operated shelter designated to provide temporary living arrangements (including congregate shelters, transitional housing, and hotels and motels paid for by charitable organizations or by federal, state, or local government programs for low-income individuals); or

(iii) An individual who is exiting an institution where he or she resided for 90 days or less and who resided in an emergency shelter or place not meant for human habitation immediately before entering that institution;

(2) An individual or family who will imminently lose their primary nighttime residence, provided that:

(i) The primary nighttime residence will be lost within 14 days of the date of application for homeless assistance;

(ii) No subsequent residence has been identified; and

(iii) The individual or family lacks the resources or support networks, e.g., family, friends, faith-based or other social networks, needed to obtain other permanent housing;

(3) Unaccompanied youth under 25 years of age, or families with children and youth, who do not otherwise qualify as homeless under this definition, but who:

(i) Are defined as homeless under section 387 of the Runaway and Homeless Youth Act (42 U.S.C. 5732a), section 637 of the Head Start Act (42 U.S.C. 9832), section 41403 of the Violence Against Women Act of 1994 (42 U.S.C. 14043e–2), section 330(h) of the Public Health Service Act (42 U.S.C. 254b(h)), section 3 of the Food and Nutrition Act of 2008 (7 U.S.C. 2012), section 17(b) of the Child Nutrition Act of 1966 (42 U.S.C. 1786(b)), or section 725 of the McKinney-Vento Homeless Assistance Act (42 U.S.C. 11434a);

(ii) Have not had a lease, ownership interest, or occupancy agreement in permanent housing at any time during the 60 days immediately preceding the date of application for homeless assistance;

(iii) Have experienced persistent instability as measured by two moves or more during the 60-day period immediately preceding the date of applying for homeless assistance; and

(iv) Can be expected to continue in such status for an extended period of time because of chronic disabilities; chronic physical health or mental health conditions; substance addiction; histories of domestic violence or childhood abuse (including neglect); the presence of a child or youth with a disability; or two or more barriers to employment, which include the lack of a high school degree or General Education Development (GED), illiteracy, low English proficiency, a history of incarceration or detention for criminal activity, and a history of unstable employment; or

(4) Any individual or family who:

(i) Is fleeing, or is attempting to flee, domestic violence, dating violence, sexual assault, stalking, or other dangerous or life-threatening conditions that relate to violence against the individual or a family member, including a child, that has either taken place within the individual's or family's primary nighttime residence or has made the individual or family afraid to return to their primary nighttime residence;

(ii) Has no other residence; and

(iii) Lacks the resources or support networks, e.g., family, friends, and faith-based or other social networks, to obtain other permanent housing.

Indian tribe has the meaning given in section 102 of the Housing and Community Development Act of 1974 (42 U.S.C. 5302).

Low-income means an annual income not in excess of 80 percent of the median income for the area, as determined by HUD. HUD may establish income limits higher or lower than 80 percent of the median income for the area on the basis of its finding that such variations are necessary because of the prevailing levels of construction costs or unusually high or low family incomes.

Nonprofit organization has the meaning given in section 104 of the Cranston-Gonzalez National Affordable Housing Act (42 U.S.C. 12704). The term nonprofit organization also includes a community mental health center established as a public nonprofit organization.

Participant means an eligible person who has been selected to participate in S+C.

Person with disabilities means a household composed of one or more persons at least one of whom is an adult who has a disability.

(1) A person shall be considered to have a disability if he or she has a disability that:

(i) Is expected to be long-continuing or of indefinite duration;

(ii) Substantially impedes the individual's ability to live independently;

(iii) Could be improved by the provision of more suitable housing conditions; and

(iv) Is a physical, mental, or emotional impairment, including an impairment caused by alcohol or drug abuse, post-traumatic stress disorder, or brain injury.

(2) A person will also be considered to have a disability if he or she has a developmental disability, as defined in this section.

(3) A person will also be considered to have a disability if he or she has acquired immunodeficiency syndrome (AIDS) or any conditions arising from the etiologic agent for acquired immunodeficiency syndrome, including infection with the human immunodeficiency virus (HIV).

(4) Notwithstanding the preceding provisions of this definition, the term person with disabilities includes, except in the case of the SRO component, two or more persons with disabilities living together, one or more such persons living with another person who is determined to be important to their care or well-being, and the surviving member or members of any household described in the first sentence of this definition who were living, in a unit assisted under this part, with the deceased member of the household at the time of his or her death. (In any event, with respect to the surviving member or members of a household, the right to rental assistance under this part will terminate at the end of the grant period under which the deceased member was a participant.)

Recipient means an applicant approved to receive a S+C grant.

Seriously mentally ill has the meaning given in section 462 of the McKinney Act (42 U.S.C. 11403g).

Single room occupancy (SRO) housing means a unit for occupancy by one person, which need not but may contain food preparation or sanitary facilities, or both.

Sponsor means a nonprofit organization which owns or leases dwelling units and has contracts with a recipient to make such units available to eligible homeless persons and receives rental assistance payments under the SRA component.

State has the meaning given in section 462 of the McKinney Act (42 U.S.C. 11403g).

Supportive service provider, or *service provider*, means a person or organization licensed or otherwise qualified to provide supportive services, either for profit or not for profit.

Supportive services means assistance that—

(1) Addresses the special needs of eligible persons; and

(2) Provides appropriate services or assists such persons in obtaining appropriate services, including health care, mental health treatment, alcohol and other substance abuse services, child care services, case management services, counseling, supervision, education, job training, and other services essential for achieving and maintaining independent living.

(Inpatient acute hospital care does not qualify as a supportive service.).

Unit of general local government has the meaning given in section 102 of the Housing and Community Development Act of 1974 (42 U.S.C. 5302).

Very low-income means an annual income not in excess of 50 percent of the median income for the area, as determined by HUD, with adjustments for smaller and larger families. HUD may establish income limits higher or lower than 50 percent of the median income for the area on the basis of its finding that such variations are necessary because of unusually high or low family incomes.

[61 FR 51169, Sept. 30, 1996; 62 FR 13539, Mar. 21, 1997; 76 FR 76014, Dec. 5, 2011]

Subpart B—Assistance Provided

§ 582.100 Program component descriptions.

(a) *Tenant-based rental assistance (TRA).* Tenant-based rental assistance provides grants for rental assistance which permit participants to choose housing of an appropriate size in which to reside. Participants retain the rental assistance if they move. Where necessary to facilitate the coordination of supportive services, grant recipients may require participants to live in a specific area for their entire period of participation or in a specific structure for the first year and in a specific area for the remainder of their period of participation. Recipients may not define the area in a way that violates the Fair Housing Act or the Rehabilitation Act of 1973. The term of the grant between HUD and the grant recipient for TRA is five years.

(b) *Project-based rental assistance (PRA).* Project-based rental assistance provides grants for rental assistance to the owner of an existing structure, where the owner agrees to lease the subsidized units to participants. Participants do not retain rental assistance if they move. Rental subsidies are provided to the owner for a period of either five or ten years. To qualify for ten years of rental subsidies, the owner must complete at least $3,000 of eligible rehabilitation for each unit (including the unit's prorated share of work to be accomplished on common areas or systems), to make the structure decent, safe and sanitary. This rehabilitation must be completed with in 12 months of the grant award.

(c) *Sponsor-based rental assistance (SRA).* Sponsor-based rental assistance provides grants for rental assistance through contracts between the grant recipient and sponsor organizations. A sponsor may be a private, nonprofit organization or a community mental health agency established as a public nonprofit organization. Participants reside in housing owned or leased by the sponsor. The term of the grant between HUD and the grant recipient for SRA is five years.

(d) *Moderate rehabilitation for single room occupancy dwellings (SRO).* (1) The SRO component provides grants for rental assistance in connection with the moderate rehabilitation of single room occupancy housing units. Resources to initially fund the cost of rehabilitating the dwellings must be obtained from other sources. However, the rental assistance covers operating expenses of the rehabilitated SRO units occupied by homeless persons, including debt service to retire the cost of the moderate rehabilitation over a ten-year period.

(2) SRO housing must be in need of moderate rehabilitation and must meet the requirements of 24 CFR 882.803(a). Costs associated with rehabilitation of common areas may be included in the calculation of the cost for assisted units based on the proportion of the number of units to be assisted under this part to the total number of units.

(3) SRO assistance may also be used for efficiency units selected for rehabilitation under this program, but the gross rent (contract rent plus any utility allowance) for those units will be no higher than for SRO units (i.e., 75 percent of the 0-bedroom Moderate Rehabilitation Fair Market Rent).

(4) The requirements regarding maintenance, operation, and inspections described in 24 CFR 882.806(b)(4) and 882.808(n) must be met.

(5) *Governing regulations.* Except where there is a conflict with any requirement under this part or where specifically provided, the SRO component will be governed by the regulations set forth in 24 CFR part 882, subpart H.

§582.105 Rental assistance amounts and payments.

(a) *Eligible activity.* S+C grants may be used for providing rental assistance for housing occupied by participants in the program and administrative costs as provided for in paragraph (e) of this section, except that the housing may not be currently receiving Federal funding for rental assistance or operating costs under other HUD programs. Recipients may design a housing program that includes a range of housing types with differing levels of supportive services. Rental assistance may include security deposits on units in an amount up to one month's rent.

(b) *Amount of the grant.* The amount of the grant is based on the number and size of units proposed by the applicant to be assisted over the grant period. The grant amount is calculated by multiplying the number of units proposed times the applicable Fair

prospective program beneficiary on the basis of religion or religious belief.

(5) If a State or local government voluntarily contributes its own funds to supplement federally funded activities, the State or local government has the option to segregate the Federal funds or commingle them. However, if the funds are commingled, this section applies to all of the commingled funds.

(d) *Maintenance of effort.* No assistance received under this part (or any State or local government funds used to supplement this assistance) may be used to replace funds provided under any State or local government assistance programs previously used, or designated for use, to assist persons with disabilities, homeless persons, or homeless persons with disabilities.

[58 FR 13892, Mar. 15, 1993, as amended at 68 FR 56407, Sept. 30, 2003]

§ 582.120 Consolidated plan.

(a) *Applicants that are States or units of general local government.* The applicant must have a HUD-approved complete or abbreviated consolidated plan, in accordance with 24 CFR part 91, and must submit a certification that the application for funding is consistent with the HUD-approved consolidated plan. Funded applicants must certify in a grant agreement that they are following the HUD-approved consolidated plan. If the applicant is a State, and the project will be located in a unit of general local government that is required to have, or has, a complete consolidated plan, or that is applying for Shelter Plus Care assistance under the same Notice of Fund Availability (NOFA) and will have an abbreviated consolidated plan with respect to that application, the State also must submit a certification by the unit of general local government that the State's application is consistent with the unit of general local government's HUD-approved consolidated plan.

(b) *Applicants that are not States or units of general local government.* The applicant must submit a certification by the jurisdiction in which the proposed project will be located that the jurisdiction is following its HUD-approved consolidated plan and the applicant's application for funding is consistent with the jurisdiction's HUD-approved consolidated plan. The certification must be made by the unit of general local government or the State, in accordance with the consistency certification provisions of the consolidated plan regulations, 24 CFR part 91, subpart F.

(c) *Indian tribes and the Insular Areas of Guam, the U.S. Virgin Islands, American Samoa, and the Northern Mariana Islands.* These entities are not required to have a consolidated plan or to make consolidated plan certifications. An application by an Indian tribe or other applicant for a project that will be located on a reservation of an Indian tribe will not require a certification by the tribe or the State. However, where an Indian tribe is the applicant for a project that will not be located on a reservation, the requirement for a certification under paragraph (b) of this section will apply.

(d) *Timing of consolidated plan certification submissions.* Unless otherwise set forth in the NOFA, the required certification that the application for funding is consistent with the HUD-approved consolidated plan must be submitted by the funding application submission deadline announced in the NOFA.

[60 FR 16379, Mar. 30, 1995]

Subpart C—Application and Grant Award

§ 582.200 Application and grant award.

(a) *Review.* When funds are made available for assistance, HUD will publish a notice of fund availability in the FEDERAL REGISTER in accordance with the requirements of 24 CFR part 4. Applications will be reviewed and screened in accordance with the guidelines, rating criteria and procedures published in the notice.

(b) *Rating criteria.* HUD will award funds based on the criteria specified in section 455(a)(1) through (8) of the McKinney Act (42 U.S.C. 11403d(1)—11403d(8)) and on the following criteria authorized by section 455(a)(9) of the McKinney Act (42 U.S.C. 11403d(9)):

(1) The extent to which the applicant has demonstrated coordination with other Federal, State, local, private and other entities serving homeless persons

in the planning and operation of the project, to the extent practicable;

(2) Extent to which the project targets homeless persons living in emergency shelters, supportive housing for homeless persons, or in places not designed for, or ordinarily used as, a regular sleeping accommodation for human beings;

(3) Quality of the project; and

(4) Extent to which the program will serve homeless persons who are seriously mentally ill, have chronic alcohol and/or drug abuse problems, or have AIDS and related diseases.

(Approved by the Office of Management and Budget under control number 2506–0118)

[61 FR 51170, Sept. 30, 1996]

§582.230 Environmental review.

(a) Activities under this part are subject to HUD environmental regulations in part 58 of this title, except that HUD will perform an environmental review in accordance with part 50 of this title prior to its approval of any conditionally selected applications from PHAs for Fiscal Year 2000 and prior years for other than the SRO component. For activities under a grant to a PHA that generally would be subject to review under part 58, HUD may make a finding in accordance with §58.11(d) and may itself perform the environmental review under the provisions of part 50 of this title if the recipient PHA objects in writing to the responsible entity's performing the review under part 58. Irrespective of whether the responsible entity in accord with part 58 (or HUD in accord with part 50) performs the environmental review, the recipient shall supply all available, relevant information necessary for the responsible entity (or HUD, if applicable) to perform for each property any environmental review required by this part. The recipient also shall carry out mitigating measures required by the responsible entity (or HUD, if applicable) or select alternate eligible property. HUD may eliminate from consideration any application that would require an Environmental Impact Statement (EIS).

(b) The recipient, its project partners and their contractors may not acquire, rehabilitate, convert, lease, repair, dispose of, demolish, or construct property for a project under this part, or commit or expend HUD or local funds for such eligible activities under this part, until the responsible entity (as defined in §58.2 of this title) has completed the environmental review procedures required by part 58 and the environmental certification and RROF have been approved or HUD has performed an environmental review under part 50 and the recipient has received HUD approval of the property. HUD will not release grant funds if the recipient or any other party commits grant funds (*i.e.*, incurs any costs or expenditures to be paid or reimbursed with such funds) before the recipient submits and HUD approves its RROF (where such submission is required).

[68 FR 56130, Sept. 29, 2003]

Subpart D—Program Requirements

§582.300 General operation.

(a) *Participation of homeless individuals.* (1) Each recipient must provide for the consultation and participation of not less than one homeless individual or formerly homeless individual on the board of directors or other equivalent policy-making entity of the recipient, to the extent that the entity considers and makes policies and decisions regarding any housing assisted under this part or services for the participants. This requirement is waived if the applicant is unable to meet the requirement and presents a plan, which HUD approves, to otherwise consult with homeless or formerly homeless individuals in considering and making such policies and decisions. Participation by such an individual who also is a participant under the program does not constitute a conflict of interest under §582.340(b) of this part.

(2) To the maximum extent practicable, each recipient must involve homeless individuals and families, through employment, volunteer services, or otherwise, in constructing or rehabilitating housing assisted under this part and in providing supportive services required under §582.215 of this part.

(b) *Ongoing assessment of housing and supportive services.* Each recipient of assistance must conduct an ongoing assessment of the housing assistance and supportive services required by the participants, and make adjustments as appropriate.

(c) *Adequate supportive services.* Each recipient must assure that adequate supportive services are available to participants in the program.

(d) *Records and reports.* (1) Each recipient must keep any records and, within the timeframe required, make any reports (including those pertaining to race, ethnicity, gender, and disability status data) that HUD may require.

(2) Each recipient must keep on file, and make available to the public on request, a description of the procedures used to select sponsors under the SRA component and buildings under the SRO, SRA, and PRA components.

(3) Each recipient must develop, and make available to the public upon request, its procedures for managing the rental housing assistance funds provided by HUD. At a minimum, such procedures must describe how units will be identified and selected; how the responsibility for inspections will be handled; the process for deciding which unit a participant will occupy; how participants will be placed in, or assisted in finding appropriate housing; how rent calculations will be made and the amount of rental assistance payments determined; and what safeguards will be used to prevent the misuse of funds.

(Approved by the Office of Management and Budget under control number 2506–0118)

[58 FR 13892, Mar. 15, 1993, as amended at 61 FR 51171, Sept. 30, 1996]

§ 582.301 Recordkeeping.

(a) [Reserved]

(b) *Homeless status.* The recipient must maintain and follow written intake procedures to ensure compliance with the homeless definition in § 582.5. The procedures must require documentation at intake of the evidence relied upon to establish and verify homeless status. The procedures must establish the order of priority for obtaining evidence as third-party documentation first, intake worker observations second, and certification from the person seeking assistance third. However, lack of third-party documentation must not prevent an individual or family from being immediately admitted to emergency shelter, receiving street outreach services, or being immediately admitted to shelter or receiving services provided by a victim service provider, as defined in section 401(32) of the McKinney-Vento Homeless Assistance Act, as amended by the HEARTH Act. Records contained in an HMIS or comparable database used by victim service or legal service providers are acceptable evidence of third-party documentation and intake worker observations if the HMIS retains an auditable history of all entries, including the person who entered the data, the date of entry, and the change made; and if the HMIS prevents overrides or changes of the dates entries are made.

(1) If the individual or family qualifies as homeless under paragraph (1)(i) or (ii) of the homeless definition in § 582.5, acceptable evidence includes a written observation by an outreach worker of the conditions where the individual or family was living, a written referral by another housing or service provider, or a certification by the individual or head of household seeking assistance.

(2) If the individual qualifies as homeless under paragraph (1)(iii) of the homeless definition in § 582.5, because he or she resided in an emergency shelter or place not meant for human habitation and is exiting an institution where he or she resided for 90 days or less, acceptable evidence includes the evidence described in paragraph (b)(1) of this section and one of the following:

(i) Discharge paperwork or a written or oral referral from a social worker, case manager, or other appropriate official of the institution, stating the beginning and end dates of the time residing in the institution. All oral statements must be recorded by the intake worker; or

(ii) Where the evidence in paragraph (b)(2)(i) of this section is not obtainable, a written record of the intake worker's due diligence in attempting to obtain the evidence described in paragraph (b)(2)(i) and a certification by the individual seeking assistance that states he or she is exiting or has just exited an institution where he or she resided for 90 days or less.

(3) If the individual or family qualifies as homeless under paragraph (2) of the homeless definition in §582.5, because the individual or family will imminently lose their housing, the evidence must include:

(i)(A) A court order resulting from an eviction action that requires the individual or family to leave their residence within 14 days after the date of their application for homeless assistance; or the equivalent notice under applicable state law, a Notice to Quit, or a Notice to Terminate issued under state law;

(B) For individuals and families whose primary nighttime residence is a hotel or motel room not paid for by charitable organizations or federal, state, or local government programs for low-income individuals, evidence that the individual or family lacks the resources necessary to reside there for more than 14 days after the date of application for homeless assistance; or

(C) An oral statement by the individual or head of household that the owner or renter of the housing in which they currently reside will not allow them to stay for more than 14 days after the date of application for homeless assistance. The intake worker must record the statement and certify that it was found credible. To be found credible, the oral statement must either: (I) Be verified by the owner or renter of the housing in which the individual or family resides at the time of application for homeless assistance and be documented by a written certification by the owner or renter or by the intake worker's recording of the owner or renter's oral statement; or (II) if the intake worker is unable to contact the owner or renter, be documented by a written certification by the intake worker of his or her due diligence in attempting to obtain the owner or renter's verification and the written certification by the individual or head of household seeking assistance that his or her statement was true and complete;

(ii) Certification by the individual or head of household that no subsequent residence has been identified; and

(iii) Certification or other written documentation that the individual or family lacks the resources and support networks needed to obtain other permanent housing.

(4) If the individual or family qualifies as homeless under paragraph (3) of the homeless definition in §582.5, because the individual or family does not otherwise qualify as homeless under the homeless definition but is an unaccompanied youth under 25 years of age, or homeless family with one or more children or youth, and is defined as homeless under another Federal statute or section 725(2) of the McKinney-Vento Homeless Assistance Act (42 U.S.C. 11434a(2)), the evidence must include:

(i) For paragraph (3)(i) of the homeless definition in §582.5, certification of homeless status by the local private nonprofit organization or state or local governmental entity responsible for administering assistance under the Runaway and Homeless Youth Act (42 U.S.C. 5701 *et seq.*), the Head Start Act (42 U.S.C. 9831 *et seq.*), subtitle N of the Violence Against Women Act of 1994 (42 U.S.C. 14043e *et seq.*), section 330 of the Public Health Service Act (42 U.S.C. 254b), the Food and Nutrition Act of 2008 (7 U.S.C. 2011 *et seq.*), section 17 of the Child Nutrition Act of 1966 (42 U.S.C. 1786), or subtitle B of title VII of the McKinney-Vento Homeless Assistance Act (42 U.S.C. 11431 *et seq.*), as applicable;

(ii) For paragraph (3)(ii) of the homeless definition in §582.5, referral by a housing or service provider, written observation by an outreach worker, or certification by the homeless individual or head of household seeking assistance;

(iii) For paragraph (3)(iii) of the homeless definition in §582.5, certification by the individual or head of household and any available supporting documentation that the individual or family moved two or more times during the 60-day period immediately preceding the date of application for homeless assistance, including: Recorded statements or records obtained from each owner or renter of housing, provider of shelter or housing, or social worker, case worker, or other appropriate official of a hospital or institution in which the individual or family resided; or, where these statements or records are unobtainable, a written record of the intake worker's due diligence in attempting to obtain these statements or records. Where a move was due to the individual or family fleeing domestic violence, dating violence, sexual assault, or stalking, then the intake worker may alternatively obtain a written certification from the individual or head of household seeking assistance that they were fleeing that situation and that they resided at that address; and

(iv) For paragraph (3)(iv) of the homeless definition in § 582.5, written diagnosis from a professional who is licensed by the state to diagnose and treat that condition (or intake staff-recorded observation of disability that within 45 days of the date of application for assistance is confirmed by a professional who is licensed by the state to diagnose and treat that condition); employment records; department of corrections records; literacy, English proficiency tests; or other reasonable documentation of the conditions required under paragraph (3)(iv) of the homeless definition.

(5) If the individual or family qualifies under paragraph (4) of the homeless definition in § 582.5, because the individual or family is fleeing domestic violence, dating violence, sexual assault, stalking, or other dangerous or life-threatening conditions related to violence, then acceptable evidence includes an oral statement by the individual or head of household seeking assistance that they are fleeing that situation, that no subsequent residence has been identified, and that they lack the resources or support networks, e.g., family, friends, faith-based or other social networks, needed to obtain other housing. If the individual or family is receiving shelter or services provided by a victim service provider, as defined in section 401(32) of the McKinney-Vento-Homeless Assistance Act, as amended by the HEARTH Act, the oral statement must be documented by either a certification by the individual or head of household, or a certification by the intake worker. Otherwise, the oral statement that the individual or head of household seeking assistance has not identified a subsequent residence and lacks the resources or support networks, e.g., family, friends, faith-based or other social networks, needed to obtain housing must be documented by a certification by the individual or head of household that the oral statement is true and complete, and, where the safety of the individual or family would not be jeopardized, the domestic violence, dating violence, sexual assault, stalking or other dangerous or life-threatening condition must be verified by a written observation by the intake worker or a written referral by a housing or service provider, social worker, health-care provider, law enforcement agency, legal assistance provider, pastoral counselor, or any other organization from whom the individual or head of household has sought assistance for domestic violence, dating violence, sexual assault, or stalking. The written referral or observation need only include the minimum amount of information necessary to document that the individual or family is fleeing, or attempting to flee domestic violence, dating violence, sexual assault, and stalking.

(c) *Disability.*—Each recipient of assistance under this part must maintain and follow written intake procedures to ensure that the assistance benefits persons with disabilities, as defined in § 582.5. In addition to the documentation required under paragraph (b), the procedures must require documentation at intake of the evidence relied upon to establish and verify the disability of the person applying for homeless assistance. The recipient must keep these records for 5 years after the end of the grant term. Acceptable evidence of the disability includes:

(1) Written verification of the disability from a professional licensed by the state to diagnose and treat the disability and his or her certification that the disability is expected to be long-continuing or of indefinite duration and substantially impedes the individual's ability to live independently;

(2) Written verification from the Social Security Administration;

(3) The receipt of a disability check (e.g., Social Security Disability Insurance check or Veteran Disability Compensation);

(4) Intake staff-recorded observation of disability that, no later than 45 days of the application for assistance, is confirmed and accompanied by evidence in paragraph (c)(1), (2), (3), or (4) of this section; or

(5) Other documentation approved by HUD.

[76 FR 76015, Dec. 5, 2011]

§582.305 Housing quality standards; rent reasonableness.

(a) *Housing quality standards.* Housing assisted under this part must meet the applicable housing quality standards (HQS) under §982.401 of this title—except that §982.401(j) of this title does not apply and instead part 35, subparts A, B, K and R of this title apply—and, for SRO under §882.803(b) of this title. Before any assistance will be provided on behalf of a participant, the recipient, or another entity acting on behalf of the recipient (other than the owner of the housing), must physically inspect each unit to assure that the unit meets the HQS. Assistance will not be provided for units that fail to meet the HQS, unless the owner corrects any deficiencies within 30 days from the date of the lease agreement and the recipient verifies that all deficiencies have been corrected. Recipients must also inspect all units at least annually during the grant period to ensure that the units continue to meet the HQS.

(b) *Rent reasonableness.* HUD will only provide assistance for a unit for which the rent is reasonable. For TRA, PRA, and SRA, it is the responsibility of the recipient to determine whether the rent charged for the unit receiving rental assistance is reasonable in relation to rents being charged for comparable unassisted units, taking into account the location, size, type, quality, amenities, facilities, and management and maintenance of each unit, as well as not in excess of rents currently being charged by the same owner for comparable unassisted units. For SRO, rents are calculated in accordance with 24 CFR 882.805(g).

[58 FR 13892, Mar. 15, 1993, as amended at 61 FR 51171, Sept. 30, 1996; 64 FR 50226, Sept. 15, 1999]

§582.310 Resident rent.

(a) *Amount of rent.* Each participant must pay rent in accordance with section 3(a)(1) of the U.S. Housing Act of 1937 (42 U.S.C. 1437a(a)(1)), except that in determining the rent of a person occupying an intermediate care facility assisted under title XIX of the Social Security Act, the gross income of this person is the same as if the person were being assisted under title XVI of the Social Security Act.

(b) *Calculating income.* (1) Income of participants must be calculated in accordance with 24 CFR 5.609 and 24 CFR 5.611(a).

(2) Recipients must examine a participant's income initially, and at least annually thereafter, to determine the amount of rent payable by the participant. Adjustments to a participant's rental payment must be made as necessary.

(3) As a condition of participation in the program, each participant must agree to supply the information or documentation necessary to verify the participant's income. Participants must provide the recipient information at any time regarding changes in income or other circumstances that may result in changes to a participant's rental payment.

[66 FR 6225, Jan. 19, 2001]

§582.315 Occupancy agreements.

(a) *Initial occupancy agreement.* Participants must enter into an occupancy agreement for a term of at least one month. The occupancy agreement must be automatically renewable upon expiration, except on prior notice by either party.

(b) *Terms of agreement.* In addition to standard lease provisions, the occupancy agreement may also include a provision requiring the participant to take part in the supportive services provided through the program as a condition of continued occupancy.

§ 582.320 Termination of assistance to participants.

(a) *Termination of assistance.* The recipient may terminate assistance to a participant who violates program requirements or conditions of occupancy. Recipients must exercise judgment and examine all extenuating circumstances in determining when violations are serious enough to warrant termination, so that a participant's assistance is terminated only in the most severe cases. Recipients are not prohibited from resuming assistance to a participant whose assistance has been terminated.

(b) *Due process.* In terminating assistance to a participant, the recipient must provide a formal process that recognizes the rights of individuals receiving assistance to due process of law. This process, at a minimum, must consist of:

(1) Written notice to the participant containing a clear statement of the reasons for termination;

(2) A review of the decision, in which the participant is given the opportunity to present written or oral objections before a person other than the person (or a subordinate of that person) who made or approved the termination decision; and

(3) Prompt written notice of the final decision to the participant.

§ 582.325 Outreach activities.

Recipients must use their best efforts to ensure that eligible hard-to-reach persons are served by S+C. Recipients are expected to make sustained efforts to engage eligible persons so that they may be brought into the program. Outreach should be primarily directed toward eligible persons who have a nighttime residence that is an emergency shelter or a public or private place not designed for, or ordinarily used as, a regular sleeping accommodation for human beings (*e.g.*, persons living in cars, streets, and parks). Outreach activities are considered to be a supportive service, and the value of such activities that occur after the execution of the grant agreement may be included in meeting the matching requirement.

§ 582.330 Nondiscrimination and equal opportunity requirements.

(a) *General.* Recipients may establish a preference as part of their admissions procedures for one or more of the statutorily targeted populations (*i.e.*, seriously mentally ill, alcohol or substance abusers, or persons with AIDS and related diseases). However, other eligible disabled homeless persons must be considered for housing designed for the target population unless the recipient can demonstrate that there is sufficient demand by the target population for the units, and other eligible disabled homeless persons would not benefit from the primary supportive services provided.

(b) *Compliance with requirements.* (1) In addition to the nondiscrimination and equal opportunity requirements set forth in 24 CFR part 5, recipients serving a designated population of homeless persons must, within the designated population, comply with the prohibitions against discrimination against handicapped individuals under section 503 of the Rehabilitation Act of 1973 (29 U.S.C. 794) and implementing regulations at 41 CFR chapter 60–741.

(2) The nondiscrimination and equal opportunity requirements set forth at part 5 of this title are modified as follows:

(i) The Indian Civil Rights Act (25 U.S.C. 1301 *et seq.*) applies to tribes when they exercise their powers of self-government, and to IHAs when established by the exercise of such powers. When an IHA is established under State law, the applicability of the Indian Civil Rights Act will be determined on a case-by-case basis. Projects subject to the Indian Civil Rights Act must be developed and operated in compliance with its provisions and all implementing HUD requirements, instead of title VI and the Fair Housing Act and their implementing regulations.

(ii) [Reserved]

(c) *Affirmative outreach.* (1) If the procedures that the recipient intends to use to make known the availability of the program are unlikely to reach persons of any particular race, color, religion, sex, age, national origin, familial status, or handicap who may qualify for assistance, the recipient must establish additional procedures that will ensure that interested persons can obtain information concerning the assistance.

(2) The recipient must adopt procedures to make available information on the existence and locations of facilities and services that are accessible to persons with a handicap and maintain evidence of implementation of the procedures.

(d) The accessibility requirements, reasonable modification, and accommodation requirements of the Fair Housing Act and of section 504 of the Rehabilitation Act of 1973, as amended.

[58 FR 13892, Mar. 15, 1993, as amended at 61 FR 5210, Feb. 9, 1996]

§582.335 Displacement, relocation, and real property acquisition.

(a) *Minimizing displacement.* Consistent with the other goals and objectives of this part, recipients must assure that they have taken all reasonable steps to minimize the displacement of persons (families, individuals, businesses, nonprofit organizations, and farms) as a result of supportive housing assisted under this part.

(b) *Relocation assistance for displaced persons.* A displaced person (defined in paragraph (f) of this section) must be provided relocation assistance at the levels described in, and in accordance with, the requirements of the Uniform Relocation Assistance and Real Property Acquisition Policies Act of 1970 (URA) (42 U.S.C. 4601–4655) and implementing regulations at 49 CFR part 24.

(c) *Real property acquisition requirements.* The acquisition of real property for supportive housing is subject to the URA and the requirements described in 49 CFR part 24, subpart B.

(d) *Responsibility of recipient.* (1) The recipient must certify (*i.e.*, provide assurance of compliance) that it will comply with the URA, the regulations at 49 CFR part 24, and the requirements of this section, and must ensure such compliance notwithstanding any third party's contractual obligation to the recipient to comply with these provisions.

(2) The cost of required relocation assistance is an eligible project cost in the same manner and to the same extent as other project costs. Such costs also may be paid for with local public funds or funds available from other sources.

(3) The recipient must maintain records in sufficient detail to demonstrate compliance with provisions of this section.

(e) *Appeals.* A person who disagrees with the recipient's determination concerning whether the person qualifies as a "displaced person," or the amount of relocation assistance for which the person is eligible, may file a written appeal of that determination with the recipient. A low-income person who is dissatisfied with the recipient's determination on his or her appeal may submit a written request for review of that determination to the HUD field office.

(f) *Definition of displaced person.* (1) For purposes of this section, the term "displaced person" means a person (family, individual, business, nonprofit organization, or farm) that moves from real property, or moves personal property from real property permanently as a direct result of acquisition, rehabilitation, or demolition for supportive housing project assisted under this part. The term "displaced person" includes, but may not be limited to:

(i) A person that moves permanently from the real property after the property owner (or person in control of the site) issues a vacate notice or refuses to renew an expiring lease, if the move occurs on or after:

(A) The date that the recipient submits to HUD an application for assistance that is later approved and funded, if the recipient has control of the project site; or

(B) The date that the recipient obtains control of the project site, if such control is obtained after the submission of the application to HUD.

(ii) Any person, including a person who moves before the date described in paragraph (f)(1)(i) of this section, if the recipient or HUD determines that the displacement resulted directly from acquisition, rehabilitation, or demolition for the assisted project.

(iii) A tenant-occupant of a dwelling unit who moves permanently from the building/complex on or after the date of the "initiation of negotiations" (see paragraph (g) of this section) if the move occurs before the tenant has been provided written notice offering him or her the opportunity to lease and occupy a suitable, decent, safe and sanitary dwelling in the same building/complex, under reasonable terms and conditions, upon completion of the project. Such reasonable terms and conditions must include a monthly rent and estimated average monthly utility costs that do not exceed the greater of:

(A) The tenant's monthly rent before the initiation of negotiations and estimated average utility costs, or

(B) 30 percent of gross household income. If the initial rent is at or near the maximum, there must be a reasonable basis for concluding at the time the project is initiated that future rent increases will be modest.

(iv) A tenant of a dwelling who is required to relocate temporarily, but does not return to the building/complex, if either:

(A) A tenant is not offered payment for all reasonable out-of-pocket expenses incurred in connection with the temporary relocation, or

(B) Other conditions of the temporary relocation are not reasonable.

(v) A tenant of a dwelling who moves from the building/complex permanently after he or she has been required to move to another unit in the same building/complex, if either:

(A) The tenant is not offered reimbursement for all reasonable out-of-pocket expenses incurred in connection with the move; or

(B) Other conditions of the move are not reasonable.

(2) Notwithstanding the provisions of paragraph (f)(1) of this section, a person does not qualify as a "displaced person" (and is not eligible for relocation assistance under the URA or this section), if:

(i) The person has been evicted for serious or repeated violation of the terms and conditions of the lease or occupancy agreement, violation of applicable Federal, State, or local or tribal law, or other good cause, and HUD determines that the eviction was not undertaken for the purpose of evading the obligation to provide relocation assistance;

(ii) The person moved into the property after the submission of the application and, before signing a lease and commencing occupancy, was provided written notice of the project, its possible impact on the person (e.g., the person may be displaced, temporarily relocated, or suffer a rent increase) and the fact that the person would not qualify as a "displaced person" (or for any assistance provided under this section), if the project is approved;

(iii) The person is ineligible under 49 CFR 24.2(g)(2); or

(iv) HUD determines that the person was not displaced as a direct result of acquisition, rehabilitation, or demolition for the project.

(3) The recipient may request, at any time, HUD's determination of whether a displacement is or would be covered under this section.

(g) *Definition of initiation of negotiations.* For purposes of determining the formula for computing the replacement housing assistance to be provided to a residential tenant displaced as a direct result of privately undertaken rehabilitation, demolition, or acquisition of the real property, the term "initiation of negotiations" means the execution of the agreement between the recipient and HUD, or selection of the project site, if later.

§ 582.340 Other Federal requirements.

In addition to the Federal requirements set forth in 24 CFR part 5, the following requirements apply to this program:

(a) *Uniform requirements.* (1) The policies, guidelines, and requirements of 24 CFR part 85 (as revised April 1, 2013) apply to the acceptance and use of assistance under the program by governmental entities and 24 CFR part 84 (as revised April 1, 2013) apply to the acceptance and use of assistance by private nonprofit organizations, except where inconsistent with provisions of the McKinney Act, other Federal statutes, or this part.

(2) The financial management systems used by recipients under this program must provide for audits in accordance with the provisions of 2 CFR part 200, subpart F. Private nonprofit organizations who are subrecipients are subject to the audit requirements

of 2 CFR part 200, subpart F. HUD may perform or require additional audits as it finds necessary or appropriate.

(b) *Conflict of interest.* (1) In addition to the conflict of interest requirements in 24 CFR part 85 (as revised April 1, 2013), no person who is an employee, agent, consultant, officer, or elected or appointed official of the recipient and who exercises or has exercised any functions or responsibilities with respect to assisted activities, or who is in a position to participate in a decisionmaking process or gain inside information with regard to such activities, may obtain a personal or financial interest or benefit from the activity, or have an interest in any contract, subcontract, or agreement with respect thereto, or the proceeds thereunder, either for himself or herself or for those with whom he or she has family or business ties, during his or her tenure or for one year thereafter. Participation by homeless individuals who also are participants under the program in policy or decisionmaking under §582.300 of this part does not constitute a conflict of interest.

(2) Upon the written request of the recipient, HUD may grant an exception to the provisions of paragraph (b)(1) of this section on a case-by-case basis when it determine that the exception will serve to further the purposes of the program and the effective and efficient administration of the recipient's project. An exception may be considered only after the recipient has provided the following:

(i) For States, units of general local governments, PHAs and IHAs, a disclosure of the nature of the conflict, accompanied by an assurance that there has been public disclosure of the conflict and a description of how the public disclosure was made; and

(ii) For all recipients, an opinion of the recipient's attorney that the interest for which the exception is sought would not violate State or local law.

(3) In determining whether to grant a requested exception after the recipient has satisfactorily met the requirement of paragraph (b)(2) of this section, HUD will consider the cumulative effect of the following factors, where applicable:

(i) Whether the exception would provide a significant cost benefit or an essential degree of expertise to the project which would otherwise not be available;

(ii) Whether the person affected is a member of a group or class of eligible persons and the exception will permit such person to receive generally the same interests or benefits as are being made available or provided to the group or class;

(iii) Whether the affected person has withdrawn from his or her functions or responsibilities, or the decisionmaking process with respect to the specific assisted activity in question;

(iv) Whether the interest or benefit was present before the affected person was in a position as described in paragraph (b)(1) of this section;

(v) Whether undue hardship will result either to the recipient or the person affected when weighed against the public interest served by avoiding the prohibited conflict; and

(vi) Any other relevant considerations.

[58 FR 13892, Mar. 15, 1993, as amended at 61 FR 5210, Feb. 9, 1996; 61 FR 51171, Sept. 30, 1996; 62 FR 13539, Mar. 21, 1997; 80 FR 75940, Dec. 7, 2015]

Subpart E—Administration

§582.400 Grant agreement.

(a) *General.* The grant agreement will be between HUD and the recipient. HUD will hold the recipient responsible for the overall administration of the program, including overseeing any subrecipients or contractors. Under the grant agreement, the recipient must agree to operate the program in accordance with the provisions of this part and other applicable HUD regulations.

(b) *Enforcement.* HUD will enforce the obligations in the grant agreement through such action as may be necessary, including recapturing assistance awarded under the program.

§582.405 Program changes.

(a) *Changes.* HUD must approve, in writing, any significant changes to an approved program. Significant changes that require approval include, but are not limited to, a change in sponsor , a change in the project site for SRO or PRA with rehabilitation projects, and a change in the type of persons with disabilities to be served. Depending on the nature of the change, HUD may require a new certification of consistency with the CHAS (see § 582.120).

(b) *Approval.* Approval for such changes is contingent upon the application ranking remaining high enough to have been competitively selected for funding in the year the application was selected.

§ 582.410 Obligation and deobligation of funds.

(a) *Obligation of funds.* When HUD and the applicant execute a grant agreement, HUD will obligate funds to cover the amount of the approved grant. The recipient will be expected to carry out the activities as proposed in the application. After the initial obligation of funds, HUD is under no obligation to make any upward revisions to the grant amount for any approved assistance.

(b) *Deobligation.* (1) HUD may deobligate all or a portion of the approved grant amount if such amount is not expended in a timely manner, or the proposed housing for which funding was approved or the supportive services proposed in the application are not provided in accordance with the approved application, the requirements of this part, and other applicable HUD regulations. The grant agreement may set forth other circumstances under which funds may be deobligated, and other sanctions may be imposed.

(2) HUD may readvertise, in a notice of fund availability, the availability of funds that have been deobligated, or may reconsider applications that were submitted in response to the most recently published notice of fund availability and select applications for funding with the deobligated funds. Such selections would be made in accordance with the selection process described in § 582.220 of this part. Any selections made using deobligated funds will be subject to applicable appropriation act requirements governing the use of deobligated funding authority.

(Approved by the Office of Management and Budget under control number 2506–0118)

PART 583—SUPPORTIVE HOUSING PROGRAM

AUTHORITY: 42 U.S.C. 11389 and 3535(d).

SOURCE: 58 FR 13871, Mar. 15, 1993, unless otherwise noted.

Subpart A—General

§ 583.1 Purpose and scope.

(a) *General.* The Supportive Housing Program is authorized by title IV of the Stewart B. McKinney Homeless Assistance Act (the McKinney Act) (42

U.S.C. 11381–11389). The Supportive Housing program is designed to promote the development of supportive housing and supportive services, including innovative approaches to assist homeless persons in the transition from homelessness, and to promote the provision of supportive housing to homeless persons to enable them to live as independently as possible.

(b) *Components*. Funds under this part may be used for:

(1) Transitional housing to facilitate the movement of homeless individuals and families to permanent housing;

(2) Permanent housing that provides long-term housing for homeless persons with disabilities;

(3) Housing that is, or is part of, a particularly innovative project for, or alternative methods of, meeting the immediate and long-term needs of homeless persons; or

(4) Supportive services for homeless persons not provided in conjunction with supportive housing.

[58 FR 13871, Mar. 15, 1993, as amended at 61 FR 51175, Sept. 30, 1996]

§583.5 Definitions.

As used in this part:

Applicant is defined in section 422(1) of the McKinney Act (42 U.S.C. 11382(1)). For purposes of this definition, governmental entities include those that have general governmental powers (such as a city or county), as well as those that have limited or special powers (such as public housing agencies).

Consolidated plan means the plan that a jurisdiction prepares and submits to HUD in accordance with 24 CFR part 91.

Date of initial occupancy means the date that the supportive housing is initially occupied by a homeless person for whom HUD provides assistance under this part. If the assistance is for an existing homeless facility, the *date of initial occupancy* is the date that services are first provided to the residents of supportive housing with funding under this part.

Date of initial service provision means the date that supportive services are initially provided with funds under this part to homeless persons who do not reside in supportive housing. This definition applies only to projects funded under this part that do not provide supportive housing.

Developmental disability means, as defined in section 102 of the Developmental Disabilities Assistance and Bill of Rights Act of 2000 (42 U.S.C. 15002):

(1) A severe, chronic disability of an individual that—

(i) Is attributable to a mental or physical impairment or combination of mental and physical impairments;

(ii) Is manifested before the individual attains age 22;

(iii) Is likely to continue indefinitely;

(iv) Results in substantial functional limitations in three or more of the following areas of major life activity:

(A) Self-care;

(B) Receptive and expressive language;

(C) Learning;

(D) Mobility;

(E) Self-direction;

(F) Capacity for independent living;

(G) Economic self-sufficiency; and

(v) Reflects the individual's need for a combination and sequence of special, interdisciplinary, or generic services, individualized supports, or other forms of assistance that are of lifelong or extended duration and are individually planned and coordinated.

(2) An individual from birth to age 9, inclusive, who has a substantial developmental delay or specific congenital or acquired condition, may be considered to have a developmental disability without meeting three or more of the criteria described in paragraphs (1)(i) through (v) of the definition of "developmental disability" in this section if the individual, without services and supports, has a high probability of meeting those criteria later in life.

Disability means:

(1) A condition that:

(i) Is expected to be long-continuing or of indefinite duration;

(ii) Substantially impedes the individual's ability to live independently;

(iii) Could be improved by the provision of more suitable housing conditions; and

(iv) Is a physical, mental, or emotional impairment, including an impairment caused by alcohol or drug abuse, post-traumatic stress disorder, or brain injury;

(2) A developmental disability, as defined in this section; or

(3) The disease of acquired immunodeficiency syndrome (AIDS) or any conditions arising from the etiologic agent for acquired immunodeficiency syndrome, including infection with the human immunodeficiency virus (HIV).

Homeless means:

(1) An individual or family who lacks a fixed, regular, and adequate nighttime residence, meaning:

(i) An individual or family with a primary nighttime residence that is a public or private place not designed for or ordinarily used as a regular sleeping accommodation for human beings, including a car, park, abandoned building, bus or train station, airport, or camping ground;

(ii) An individual or family living in a supervised publicly or privately operated shelter designated to provide temporary living arrangements (including congregate shelters, transitional housing, and hotels and motels paid for by charitable organizations or by federal, state, or local government programs for low-income individuals); or

(iii) An individual who is exiting an institution where he or she resided for 90 days or less and who resided in an emergency shelter or place not meant for human habitation immediately before entering that institution;

(2) An individual or family who will imminently lose their primary nighttime residence, provided that:

(i) The primary nighttime residence will be lost within 14 days of the date of application for homeless assistance;

(ii) No subsequent residence has been identified; and

(iii) The individual or family lacks the resources or support networks, e.g., family, friends, faith-based or other social networks, needed to obtain other permanent housing;

(3) Unaccompanied youth under 25 years of age, or families with children and youth, who do not otherwise qualify as homeless under this definition, but who:

(i) Are defined as homeless under section 387 of the Runaway and Homeless Youth Act (42 U.S.C. 5732a), section 637 of the Head Start Act (42 U.S.C. 9832), section 41403 of the Violence Against Women Act of 1994 (42 U.S.C. 14043e–2), section 330(h) of the Public Health Service Act (42 U.S.C. 254b(h)), section 3 of the Food and Nutrition Act of 2008 (7 U.S.C. 2012), section 17(b) of the Child Nutrition Act of 1966 (42 U.S.C. 1786(b)), or section 725 of the McKinney-Vento Homeless Assistance Act (42 U.S.C. 11434a);

(ii) Have not had a lease, ownership interest, or occupancy agreement in permanent housing at any time during the 60 days immediately preceding the date of application for homeless assistance;

(iii) Have experienced persistent instability as measured by two moves or more during the 60-day period immediately preceding the date of applying for homeless assistance; and

(iv) Can be expected to continue in such status for an extended period of time because of chronic disabilities, chronic physical health or mental health conditions, substance addiction, histories of domestic violence or childhood abuse (including neglect), the presence of a child or youth with a disability, or two or more barriers to employment, which include the lack of a high school degree or General Education Development (GED), illiteracy, low English proficiency, a history of incarceration or detention for criminal activity, and a history of unstable employment; or

(4) Any individual or family who:

(i) Is fleeing, or is attempting to flee, domestic violence, dating violence, sexual assault, stalking, or other dangerous or life-threatening conditions that relate to violence against the individual or a family member, including a child, that has either taken place within the individual's or family's primary nighttime residence or has made the individual or family afraid to return to their primary nighttime residence;

(ii) Has no other residence; and

(iii) Lacks the resources or support networks, e.g., family, friends, and faith-based or other social networks, to obtain other permanent housing.

Metropolitan city is defined in section 102(a)(4) of the Housing and Community Development Act of 1974 (42 U.S.C. 5302(a)(4)). In general, metropolitan cities are those cities that are eligible for an entitlement grant under 24 CFR part 570, subpart D.

New construction means the building of a structure where none existed or an addition to an existing structure that increases the floor area by more than 100 percent.

Operating costs is defined in section 422(5) of the McKinney Act (42 U.S.C. 11382(5)).

Outpatient health services is defined in section 422(6) of the McKinney Act (42 U.S.C. 11382(6)).

Permanent housing for homeless persons with disabilities is defined in section 424(c) of the McKinney Act (42 U.S.C. 11384(c)).

Private nonprofit organization is defined in section 422(7) (A), (B), and (D) of the McKinney Act (42 U.S.C. 11382(7) (A), (B), and (D)). The organization must also have a functioning accounting system that is operated in accordance with generally accepted accounting principles, or designate an entity that will maintain a functioning accounting system for the organization in accordance with generally accepted accounting principles.

Project is defined in sections 422(8) and 424(d) of the McKinney Act (42 U.S.C. 11382(8), 11384(d)).

Recipient is defined in section 422(9) of the McKinney Act (42 U.S.C. 11382(9)).

Rehabilitation means the improvement or repair of an existing structure or an addition to an existing structure that does not increase the floor area by more than 100 percent. Rehabilitation does not include minor or routine repairs.

State is defined in section 422(11) of the McKinney Act (42 U.S.C. 11382(11)).

Supportive housing is defined in section 424(a) of the McKinney Act (42 U.S.C. 11384(a)).

Supportive services is defined in section 425 of the McKinney Act (42 U.S.C. 11385).

Transitional housing is defined in section 424(b) of the McKinney Act (42 U.S.C. 11384(b)). See also §583.300(j).

Tribe is defined in section 102 of the Housing and Community Development Act of 1974 (42 U.S.C. 5302).

Urban county is defined in section 102(a)(6) of the Housing and Community Development Act of 1974 (42 U.S.C. 5302(a)(6)). In general, urban counties are those counties that are eligible for an entitlement grant under 24 CFR part 570, subpart D.

[61 FR 51175, Sept. 30, 1996, as amended at 76 FR 76016, Dec. 5, 2011]

Subpart B—Assistance Provided

§583.100 Types and uses of assistance.

(a) *Grant assistance.* Assistance in the form of grants is available for acquisition of structures, rehabilitation of structures, acquisition and rehabilitation of structures, new construction, leasing, operating costs for supportive housing, and supportive services, as described in §§583.105 through 583.125. Applicants may apply for more than one type of assistance.

(b) *Uses of grant assistance.* Grant assistance may be used to:

(1) Establish new supportive housing facilities or new facilities to provide supportive services;

(2) Expand existing facilities in order to increase the number of homeless persons served;

(3) Bring existing facilities up to a level that meets State and local government health and safety standards;

(4) Provide additional supportive services for residents of supportive housing or for homeless persons not residing in supportive housing;

(5) Purchase HUD-owned single family properties currently leased by the applicant for use as a homeless facility under 24 CFR part 291; and

(6) Continue funding supportive housing where the recipient has received funding under this part for leasing, supportive services, or operating costs.

(c) *Structures used for multiple purposes.* Structures used to provide supportive housing or supportive services may also be used for other purposes, except that assistance under this part will be available only in proportion to the use of the structure for supportive housing or supportive services.

(d) *Technical assistance.* HUD may offer technical assistance, as described in §583.140.

[58 FR 13871, Mar. 15, 1993, as amended at 59 FR 36891, July 19, 1994]

§ 583.105 Grants for acquisition and rehabilitation.

(a) *Use.* HUD will grant funds to recipients to:

(1) Pay a portion of the cost of the acquisition of real property selected by the recipients for use in the provision of supportive housing or supportive services, including the repayment of any outstanding debt on a loan made to purchase property that has not been used previously as supportive housing or for supportive services;

(2) Pay a portion of the cost of rehabilitation of structures, including cost-effective energy measures, selected by the recipients to provide supportive housing or supportive services; or

(3) Pay a portion of the cost of acquisition and rehabilitation of structures, as described in paragraphs (a)(1) and (2) of this section.

(b) *Amount.* The maximum grant available for acquisition, rehabilitation, or acquisition and rehabilitation is the lower of:

(1) $200,000; or

(2) The total cost of the acquisition, rehabilitation, or acquisition and rehabilitation minus the applicant's contribution toward the cost.

(c) *Increased amounts.* In areas determined by HUD to have high acquisition and rehabilitation costs, grants of more than $200,000, but not more than $400,000, may be available.

§ 583.110 Grants for new construction.

(a) *Use.* HUD will grant funds to recipients to pay a portion of the cost of new construction, including cost-effective energy measures and the cost of land associated with that construction, for use in the provision of supportive housing. If the grant funds are used for new construction, the applicant must demonstrate that the costs associated with new construction are substantially less than the costs associated with rehabilitation or that there is a lack of available appropriate units that could be rehabilitated at a cost less than new construction. For purposes of this cost comparison, costs associated with rehabilitation or new construction may include the cost of real property acquisition.

(b) *Amount.* The maximum grant available for new construction is the lower of:

(1) $400,000; or

(2) The total cost of the new construction, including the cost of land associated with that construction, minus the applicant's contribution toward the cost of same.

§ 583.115 Grants for leasing.

(a) *General.* HUD will provide grants to pay (as described in § 583.130 of this part) for the actual costs of leasing a structure or structures, or portions thereof, used to provide supportive housing or supportive services for up to five years.

(b)(1) *Leasing structures.* Where grants are used to pay rent for all or part of structures, the rent paid must be reasonable in relation to rents being charged in the area for comparable space. In addition, the rent paid may not exceed rents currently being charged by the same owner for comparable space.

(2) *Leasing individual units.* Where grants are used to pay rent for individual housing units, the rent paid must be reasonable in relation to rents being charged for comparable units, taking into account the location, size, type, quality, amenities, facilities, and management services. In addition, the rents may not exceed rents currently being charged by the same owner for comparable unassisted units, and the portion of rents paid with grant funds may not exceed HUD-determined fair market rents. Recipients may use grant funds in an amount up to one month's rent to pay the non-recipient landlord for any damages to leased units by homeless participants.

[58 FR 13871, Mar. 15, 1993, as amended at 59 FR 36891, July 19, 1994]

§ 583.120 Grants for supportive services costs.

(a) *General.* HUD will provide grants to pay (as described in § 583.130 of this part) for the actual costs of supportive services for homeless persons for up to five years. All or part of the supportive services may be provided directly by the recipient or by arrangement with public or private service providers.

(b) *Supportive services costs.* Costs associated with providing supportive services include salaries paid to providers of supportive services and any other costs directly associated with providing such services. For a transitional housing project, supportive services costs also include the costs of services provided to former residents of transitional housing to assist their adjustment to independent living. Such services may be provided for up to six months after they leave the transitional housing facility.

[58 FR 13871, Mar. 15, 1993, as amended at 59 FR 36891, July 19, 1994]

§583.125 Grants for operating costs.

(a) *General.* HUD will provide grants to pay a portion (as described in §583.130) of the actual operating costs of supportive housing for up to five years.

(b) *Operating costs.* Operating costs are those associated with the day-to-day operation of the supportive housing. They also include the actual expenses that a recipient incurs for conducting on-going assessments of the supportive services needed by residents and the availability of such services; relocation assistance under §583.310, including payments and services; and insurance.

(c) *Recipient match requirement for operating costs.* Assistance for operating costs will be available for up to 75 percent of the total cost in each year of the grant term. The recipient must pay the percentage of the actual operating costs not funded by HUD. At the end of each operating year, the recipient must demonstrate that it has met its match requirement of the costs for that year.

[58 FR 13871, Mar. 15, 1993, as amended at 61 FR 51175, Sept. 30, 1996; 65 FR 30823, May 12, 2000]

§583.130 Commitment of grant amounts for leasing, supportive services, and operating costs.

Upon execution of a grant agreement covering assistance for leasing, supportive services, or operating costs, HUD will obligate amounts for a period not to exceed five operating years. The total amount obligated will be equal to an amount necessary for the specified years of operation, less the recipient's share of operating costs.

(Approved by the Office of Management and Budget under OMB control number 2506–0112)

[59 FR 36891, July 19, 1994]

§583.135 Administrative costs.

(a) *General.* Up to five percent of any grant awarded under this part may be used for the purpose of paying costs of administering the assistance.

(b) *Administrative costs.* Administrative costs include the costs associated with accounting for the use of grant funds, preparing reports for submission to HUD, obtaining program audits, similar costs related to administering the grant after the award, and staff salaries associated with these administrative costs. They do not include the costs of carrying out eligible activities under §§583.105 through 583.125.

[58 FR 13871, Mar. 15, 1993, as amended at 61 FR 51175, Sept. 30, 1996]

§583.140 Technical assistance.

(a) *General.* HUD may set aside funds annually to provide technical assistance, either directly by HUD staff or indirectly through third-party providers, for any supportive housing project. This technical assistance is for the purpose of promoting the development of supportive housing and supportive services as part of a continuum of care approach, including innovative approaches to assist homeless persons in the transition from homelessness, and promoting the provision of supportive housing to homeless persons to enable them to live as independently as possible.

(b) *Uses of technical assistance.* HUD may use these funds to provide technical assistance to prospective applicants, applicants, recipients, or other providers of supportive housing or services for homeless persons, for supportive housing projects. The assistance may include, but is not limited to, written information such as papers, monographs, manuals, guides, and brochures; person-to-person exchanges; and training and related costs.

(c) *Selection of providers.* From time to time, as HUD determines the need, HUD may advertise and competitively select providers to deliver technical assistance. HUD may enter into contracts, grants, or cooperative agreements, when necessary, to implement the technical assistance.

[59 FR 36892, July 19, 1994]

§ 583.145 Matching requirements.

(a) *General.* The recipient must match the funds provided by HUD for grants for acquisition, rehabilitation, and new construction with an equal amount of funds from other sources.

(b) *Cash resources.* The matching funds must be cash resources provided to the project by one or more of the following: the recipient, the Federal government, State and local governments, and private resources, in accordance with 42 U.S.C. 11386. This statute provides that a recipient may use funds from any source, including any other Federal source (but excluding the specific statutory subtitle from which Supportive Housing Program funds are provided), as well as State, local, and private sources, provided that funds from the other source are not statutorily prohibited to be used as a match. It is the responsibility of the recipient to ensure that any funds used to satisfy the matching requirements of this section are eligible under the laws governing the funds to be used as matching funds for a grant awarded under this program.

(c) *Maintenance of effort.* State or local government funds used in the matching contribution are subject to the maintenance of effort requirements described at § 583.150(a).

[58 FR 13871, Mar. 15, 1993, as amended at 73 FR 75326, Dec. 11, 2008]

§ 583.150 Limitations on use of assistance.

(a) *Maintenance of effort.* No assistance provided under this part (or any State or local government funds used to supplement this assistance) may be used to replace State or local funds previously used, or designated for use, to assist homeless persons.

(b) *Faith-based activities.* (1) Organizations that are religious or faith-based are eligible, on the same basis as any other organization, to participate in the Supportive Housing Program. Neither the Federal government nor a State or local government receiving funds under Supportive Housing programs shall discriminate against an organization on the basis of the organization's religious character or affiliation.

(2) Organizations that are directly funded under the Supportive Housing Program may not engage in inherently religious activities, such as worship, religious instruction, or proselytization as part of the programs or services funded under this part. If an organization conducts such activities, the activities must be offered separately, in time or location, from the programs or services funded under this part, and participation must be voluntary for the beneficiaries of the HUD-funded programs or services.

(3) A religious organization that participates in the Supportive Housing Program will retain its independence from Federal, State, and local governments, and may continue to carry out its mission, including the definition, practice, and expression of its religious beliefs, provided that it does not use direct Supportive Housing Program funds to support any inherently religious activities, such as worship, religious instruction, or proselytization. Among other things, faith-based organizations may use space in their facilities to provide Supportive Housing Program-funded services, without removing religious art, icons, scriptures, or other religious symbols. In addition, a Supportive Housing Program-funded religious organization retains its authority over its internal governance, and it may retain religious terms in its organization's name, select its board members on a religious basis, and include religious references in its organization's mission statements and other governing documents.

(4) An organization that participates in the Supportive Housing Program shall not, in providing program assistance, discriminate against a program beneficiary or prospective program beneficiary on the basis of religion or religious belief.

(5) Program funds may not be used for the acquisition, construction, or rehabilitation of structures to the extent that those structures are used for inherently religious activities. Program

funds may be used for the acquisition, construction, or rehabilitation of structures only to the extent that those structures are used for conducting eligible activities under this part. Where a structure is used for both eligible and inherently religious activities, program funds may not exceed the cost of those portions of the acquisition, construction, or rehabilitation that are attributable to eligible activities in accordance with the cost accounting requirements applicable to Supportive Housing Program funds in this part. Sanctuaries, chapels, or other rooms that a Supportive Housing Program-funded religious congregation uses as its principal place of worship, however, are ineligible for Supportive Housing Program-funded improvements. Disposition of real property after the term of the grant, or any change in use of the property during the term of the grant, is subject to government-wide regulations governing real property disposition (*see* 24 CFR parts 84 and 85 (as revised April 1, 2013)).

(6) If a State or local government voluntarily contributes its own funds to supplement federally funded activities, the State or local government has the option to segregate the Federal funds or commingle them. However, if the funds are commingled, this section applies to all of the commingled funds.

(c) *Participant control of site.* Where an applicant does not propose to have control of a site or sites but rather proposes to assist a homeless family or individual in obtaining a lease, which may include assistance with rent payments and receiving supportive services, after which time the family or individual remains in the same housing without further assistance under this part, that applicant may not request assistance for acquisition, rehabilitation, or new construction.

[58 FR 13871, Mar. 15, 1993, as amended at 59 FR 36892, July 19, 1993; 68 FR 56407, Sept. 30, 2003; 80 FR 75940, Dec. 7, 2015]

§583.155 Consolidated plan.

(a) *Applicants that are States or units of general local government.* The applicant must have a HUD-approved complete or abbreviated consolidated plan, in accordance with 24 CFR part 91, and must submit a certification that the application for funding is consistent with the HUD-approved consolidated plan. Funded applicants must certify in a grant agreement that they are following the HUD-approved consolidated plan.

(b) *Applicants that are not States or units of general local government.* The applicant must submit a certification by the jurisdiction in which the proposed project will be located that the applicant's application for funding is consistent with the jurisdiction's HUD-approved consolidated plan. The certification must be made by the unit of general local government or the State, in accordance with the consistency certification provisions of the consolidated plan regulations, 24 CFR part 91, subpart F.

(c) *Indian tribes and the Insular Areas of Guam, the U.S. Virgin Islands, American Samoa, and the Northern Mariana Islands.* These entities are not required to have a consolidated plan or to make consolidated plan certifications. An application by an Indian tribe or other applicant for a project that will be located on a reservation of an Indian tribe will not require a certification by the tribe or the State. However, where an Indian tribe is the applicant for a project that will not be located on a reservation, the requirement for a certification under paragraph (b) of this section will apply.

(d) *Timing of consolidated plan certification submissions.* Unless otherwise set forth in the NOFA, the required certification that the application for funding is consistent with the HUD-approved consolidated plan must be submitted by the funding application submission deadline announced in the NOFA.

[60 FR 16380, Mar. 30, 1995]

Subpart C—Application and Grant Award Process

§583.200 Application and grant award.

When funds are made available for assistance, HUD will publish a notice of funding availability (NOFA) in the FEDERAL REGISTER, in accordance with the requirements of 24 CFR part 4. HUD will review and screen applications in accordance with the requirements in section 426 of the McKinney Act (42 U.S.C. 11386) and the guidelines, rating criteria, and procedures published in the NOFA.

[61 FR 51176, Sept. 30, 1996]

§ 583.230 Environmental review.

(a) Activities under this part are subject to HUD environmental regulations in part 58 of this title, except that HUD will perform an environmental review in accordance with part 50 of this title prior to its approval of any conditionally selected applications for Fiscal Year 2000 and prior years that were received directly from private nonprofit entities and governmental entities with special or limited purpose powers. For activities under a grant that generally would be subject to review under part 58, HUD may make a finding in accordance with § 58.11(d) and may itself perform the environmental review under the provisions of part 50 of this title if the recipient objects in writing to the responsible entity's performing the review under part 58. Irrespective of whether the responsible entity in accord with part 58 (or HUD in accord with part 50) performs the environmental review, the recipient shall supply all available, relevant information necessary for the responsible entity (or HUD, if applicable) to perform for each property any environmental review required by this part. The recipient also shall carry out mitigating measures required by the responsible entity (or HUD, if applicable) or select alternate eligible property. HUD may eliminate from consideration any application that would require an Environmental Impact Statement (EIS).

(b) The recipient, its project partners and their contractors may not acquire, rehabilitate, convert, lease, repair, dispose of, demolish or construct property for a project under this part, or commit or expend HUD or local funds for such eligible activities under this part, until the responsible entity (as defined in § 58.2 of this title) has completed the environmental review procedures required by part 58 and the environmental certification and RROF have been approved or HUD has performed an environmental review under part 50 and the recipient has received HUD approval of the property. HUD will not release grant funds if the recipient or any other party commits grant funds (*i.e.*, incurs any costs or expenditures to be paid or reimbursed with such funds) before the recipient submits and HUD approves its RROF (where such submission is required).

[68 FR 56131, Sept. 29, 2003]

§ 583.235 Renewal grants.

(a) *General.* Grants made under this part, and grants made under subtitles C and D (the Supportive Housing Demonstration and SAFAH, respectively) of the Stewart B. McKinney Homeless Assistance Act as in effect before October 28, 1992, may be renewed on a noncompetitive basis to continue ongoing leasing, operations, and supportive services for additional years beyond the initial funding period. To be considered for renewal funding for leasing, operating costs, or supportive services, recipients must submit a request for such funding in the form specified by HUD, must meet the requirements of this part, and must submit requests within the time period established by HUD.

(b) *Assistance available.* The first renewal will be for a period of time not to exceed the difference between the end of the initial funding period and ten years from the date of initial occupancy or the date of initial service provision, as applicable. Any subsequent renewal will be for a period of time not to exceed five years. Assistance during each year of the renewal period, subject to maintenance of effort requirements under § 583.150(a) may be for:

(1) Up to 50 percent of the actual operating and leasing costs in the final year of the initial funding period;

(2) Up to the amount of HUD assistance for supportive services in the final year of the initial funding period; and

(3) An allowance for cost increases.

(c) *HUD review.* (1) HUD will review the request for renewal and will evaluate the recipient's performance in previous years against the plans and goals established in the initial application for assistance, as amended. HUD will approve the request for renewal unless the recipient proposes to serve a population that is not homeless, or the recipient has not shown adequate progress as evidenced by an unacceptably slow expenditure of funds, or the recipient has been unsuccessful in assisting participants in achieving and maintaining independent living. In determining the recipient's success in assisting participants to achieve and maintain independent living, consideration will be given to the level and type of problems of participants. For recipients with a poor record of success, HUD will also consider the recipient's willingness to accept technical assistance and to make changes suggested by technical assistance providers. Other factors which will affect HUD's decision to approve a renewal request include the following: a continuing history of inadequate financial management accounting practices, indications of mismanagement on the part of the recipient, a drastic reduction in the population served by the recipient, program changes made by the recipient without prior HUD approval, and loss of project site.

(2) HUD reserves the right to reject a request from any organization with an outstanding obligation to HUD that is in arrears or for which a payment schedule has not been agreed to, or whose response to an audit finding is overdue or unsatisfactory.

(3) HUD will notify the recipient in writing that the request has been approved or disapproved.

(Approved by the Office of Management and Budget under control number 2506–0112)

Subpart D—Program Requirements

§583.300 General operation.

(a) *State and local requirements.* Each recipient of assistance under this part must provide housing or services that are in compliance with all applicable State and local housing codes, licensing requirements, and any other requirements in the jurisdiction in which the project is located regarding the condition of the structure and the operation of the housing or services.

(b) *Habitability standards.* Except for such variations as are proposed by the recipient and approved by HUD, supportive housing must meet the following requirements:

(1) *Structure and materials.* The structures must be structurally sound so as not to pose any threat to the health and safety of the occupants and so as to protect the residents from the elements.

(2) *Access.* The housing must be accessible and capable of being utilized without unauthorized use of other private properties. Structures must provide alternate means of egress in case of fire.

(3) *Space and security.* Each resident must be afforded adequate space and security for themselves and their belongings. Each resident must be provided an acceptable place to sleep.

(4) *Interior air quality.* Every room or space must be provided with natural or mechanical ventilation. Structures must be free of pollutants in the air at levels that threaten the health of residents.

(5) *Water supply.* The water supply must be free from contamination.

(6) *Sanitary facilities.* Residents must have access to sufficient sanitary facilities that are in proper operating condition, may be used in privacy, and are adequate for personal cleanliness and the disposal of human waste.

(7) *Thermal environment.* The housing must have adequate heating and/or cooling facilities in proper operating condition.

(8) *Illumination and electricity.* The housing must have adequate natural or artificial illumination to permit normal indoor activities and to support the health and safety of residents. Sufficient electrical sources must be provided to permit use of essential electrical appliances while assuring safety from fire.

(9) *Food preparation and refuse disposal.* All food preparation areas must contain suitable space and equipment to store, prepare, and serve food in a sanitary manner.

(10) *Sanitary condition.* The housing and any equipment must be maintained in sanitary condition.

(11) *Fire safety.* (i) Each unit must include at least one battery-operated or hard-wired smoke detector, in proper working condition, on each occupied level of the unit. Smoke detectors must be located, to the extent practicable, in a hallway adjacent to a bedroom. If the unit is occupied by hearing-impaired persons, smoke detectors

must have an alarm system designed for hearing-impaired persons in each bedroom occupied by a hearing-impaired person.

(ii) The public areas of all housing must be equipped with a sufficient number, but not less than one for each area, of battery-operated or hard-wired smoke detectors. Public areas include, but are not limited to, laundry rooms, community rooms, day care centers, hallways, stairwells, and other common areas.

(c) *Meals.* Each recipient of assistance under this part who provides supportive housing for homeless persons with disabilities must provide meals or meal preparation facilities for residents.

(d) *Ongoing assessment of supportive services.* Each recipient of assistance under this part must conduct an ongoing assessment of the supportive services required by the residents of the project and the availability of such services, and make adjustments as appropriate.

(e) *Residential supervision.* Each recipient of assistance under this part must provide residential supervision as necessary to facilitate the adequate provision of supportive services to the residents of the housing throughout the term of the commitment to operate supportive housing. Residential supervision may include the employment of a full- or part-time residential supervisor with sufficient knowledge to provide or to supervise the provision of supportive services to the residents.

(f) *Participation of homeless persons.* (1) Each recipient must provide for the participation of homeless persons as required in section 426(g) of the McKinney Act (42 U.S.C. 11386(g)). This requirement is waived if an applicant is unable to meet it and presents a plan for HUD approval to otherwise consult with homeless or formerly homeless persons in considering and making policies and decisions. See also § 583.330(e).

(2) Each recipient of assistance under this part must, to the maximum extent practicable, involve homeless individuals and families, through employment, volunteer services, or otherwise, in constructing, rehabilitating, maintaining, and operating the project and in providing supportive services for the project.

(g) *Records and reports.* Each recipient of assistance under this part must keep any records and make any reports (including those pertaining to race, ethnicity, gender, and disability status data) that HUD may require within the timeframe required.

(h) *Confidentiality.* Each recipient that provides family violence prevention or treatment services must develop and implement procedures to ensure:

(1) The confidentiality of records pertaining to any individual services; and

(2) That the address or location of any project assisted will not be made public, except with written authorization of the person or persons responsible for the operation of the project.

(i) *Termination of housing assistance.* The recipient may terminate assistance to a participant who violates program requirements. Recipients should terminate assistance only in the most severe cases. Recipients may resume assistance to a participant whose assistance was previously terminated. In terminating assistance to a participant, the recipient must provide a formal process that recognizes the rights of individuals receiving assistance to due process of law. This process, at a minimum, must consist of:

(1) Written notice to the participant containing a clear statement of the reasons for termination;

(2) A review of the decision, in which the participant is given the opportunity to present written or oral objections before a person other than the person (or a subordinate of that person) who made or approved the termination decision; and

(3) Prompt written notice of the final decision to the participant.

(j) *Limitation of stay in transitional housing.* A homeless individual or family may remain in transitional housing for a period longer than 24 months, if permanent housing for the individual or family has not been located or if the individual or family requires additional time to prepare for independent living. However, HUD may discontinue assistance for a transitional housing project if more than half of the homeless individuals or families remain in that project longer than 24 months.

(k) *Outpatient health services.* Outpatient health services provided by the recipient must be approved as appropriate by HUD and the Department of Health and Human Services (HHS). Upon receipt of an application that proposes the provision of outpatient health services, HUD will consult with HHS with respect to the appropriateness of the proposed services.

(l) *Annual assurances.* Recipients who receive assistance only for leasing, operating costs or supportive services costs must provide an annual assurance for each year such assistance is received that the project will be operated for the purpose specified in the application.

(Approved by the Office of Management and Budget under control number 2506–0112)

[58 FR 13871, Mar. 15, 1993, as amended at 59 FR 36892, July 19, 1994; 61 FR 51176, Sept. 30, 1996]

§ 583.301 Recordkeeping.

(a) [Reserved]

(b) *Homeless status.* The recipient must maintain and follow written intake procedures to ensure compliance with the homeless definition in § 583.5. The procedures must require documentation at intake of the evidence relied upon to establish and verify homeless status. The procedures must establish the order of priority for obtaining evidence as third-party documentation first, intake worker observations second, and certification from the person seeking assistance third. However, lack of third-party documentation must not prevent an individual or family from being immediately admitted to emergency shelter, receiving street outreach services, or being immediately admitted to shelter or receiving services provided by a victim service provider, as defined in section 401(32) of the McKinney-Vento Homeless Assistance Act, as amended by the HEARTH Act. Records contained in an HMIS or comparable database used by victim service or legal service providers are acceptable evidence of third-party documentation and intake worker observations if the HMIS retains an auditable history of all entries, including the person who entered the data, the date of entry, and the change made; and if the HMIS prevents overrides or changes of the dates on which entries are made.

(1) If the individual or family qualifies as homeless under paragraph (1)(i) or (ii) of the homeless definition in § 583.5, acceptable evidence includes a written observation by an outreach worker of the conditions where the individual or family was living, a written referral by another housing or service provider, or a certification by the individual or head of household seeking assistance.

(2) If the individual qualifies as homeless under paragraph (1)(iii) of the homeless definition in § 583.5, because he or she resided in an emergency shelter or place not meant for human habitation and is exiting an institution where he or she resided for 90 days or less, acceptable evidence includes the evidence described in paragraph (b)(1) of this section and one of the following:

(i) Discharge paperwork or a written or oral referral from a social worker, case manager, or other appropriate official of the institution, stating the beginning and end dates of the time residing in the institution. All oral statements must be recorded by the intake worker; or

(ii) Where the evidence in paragraph (b)(2)(i) of this section is not obtainable, a written record of the intake worker's due diligence in attempting to obtain the evidence described in paragraph (b)(2)(i) and a certification by the individual seeking assistance that states he or she is exiting or has just exited an institution where he or she resided for 90 days or less.

(3) If the individual or family qualifies as homeless under paragraph (2) of the homeless definition in § 583.5, because the individual or family will imminently lose their housing, the evidence must include:

(i)(A) A court order resulting from an eviction action that requires the individual or family to leave their residence within 14 days after the date of their application for homeless assistance; or the equivalent notice under applicable state law, a Notice to Quit, or a Notice to Terminate issued under state law;

in accordance with this part and with sections 423 (b)(1) and (b)(3) of the McKinney Act (42 U.S.C. 11383(b)(1), 11383(b)(3)).

(b) *Repayment of grant and prevention of undue benefits.* In accordance with section 423(c) of the McKinney Act (42 U.S.C. 11383(c)), HUD will require recipients to repay the grant unless HUD has authorized conversion of the project under section 423(b)(3) of the McKinney Act (42 U.S.C. 11383(b)(3)).

[61 FR 51176, Sept. 30, 1996]

§583.310 Displacement, relocation, and acquisition.

(a) *Minimizing displacement.* Consistent with the other goals and objectives of this part, recipients must assure that they have taken all reasonable steps to minimize the displacement of persons (families, individuals, businesses, nonprofit organizations, and farms) as a result of supportive housing assisted under this part.

(b) *Relocation assistance for displaced persons.* A displaced person (defined in paragraph (f) of this section) must be provided relocation assistance at the levels described in, and in accordance with, the requirements of the Uniform Relocation Assistance and Real Property Acquisition Policies Act of 1970 (URA) (42 U.S.C. 4601–4655) and implementing regulations at 49 CFR part 24.

(c) *Real property acquisition requirements.* The acquisition of real property for supportive housing is subject to the URA and the requirements described in 49 CFR part 24, subpart B.

(d) *Responsibility of recipient.* (1) The recipient must certify (*i.e.*, provide assurance of compliance) that it will comply with the URA, the regulations at 49 CFR part 24, and the requirements of this section, and must ensure such compliance notwithstanding any third party's contractual obligation to the recipient to comply with these provisions.

(2) The cost of required relocation assistance is an eligible project cost in the same manner and to the same extent as other project costs. Such costs also may be paid for with local public funds or funds available from other sources.

(3) The recipient must maintain records in sufficient detail to demonstrate compliance with provisions of this section.

(e) *Appeals.* A person who disagrees with the recipient's determination concerning whether the person qualifies as a "displaced person," or the amount of relocation assistance for which the person is eligible, may file a written appeal of that determination with the recipient. A low-income person who is dissatisfied with the recipient's determination on his or her appeal may submit a written request for review of that determination to the HUD field office.

(f) *Definition of displaced person.* (1) For purposes of this section, the term "displaced person" means a person (family, individual, business, nonprofit organization, or farm) that moves from real property, or moves personal property from real property permanently as a direct result of acquisition, rehabilitation, or demolition for supportive housing projects assisted under this part. The term "displaced person" includes, but may not be limited to:

(i) A person that moves permanently from the real property after the property owner (or person in control of the site) issues a vacate notice, or refuses to renew an expiring lease in order to evade the responsibility to provide relocation assistance, if the move occurs on or after the date the recipient submits to HUD the application or application amendment designating the project site.

(ii) Any person, including a person who moves before the date described in paragraph (f)(1)(i) of this section, if the recipient or HUD determines that the displacement resulted directly from acquisition, rehabilitation, or demolition for the assisted project.

(iii) A tenant-occupant of a dwelling unit who moves permanently from the building/complex on or after the date of the "initiation of negotiations" (see paragraph (g) of this section) if the move occurs before the tenant has been provided written notice offering him or her the opportunity to lease and occupy a suitable, decent, safe and sanitary dwelling in the same building/complex, under reasonable terms and conditions, upon completion of the project. Such reasonable terms and conditions must include a monthly rent and estimated average monthly utility costs that do not exceed the greater of:

(A) The tenant's monthly rent before the initiation of negotiations and estimated average utility costs, or

(B) 30 percent of gross household income. If the initial rent is at or near the maximum, there must be a reasonable basis for concluding at the time the project is initiated that future rent increases will be modest.

(iv) A tenant of a dwelling who is required to relocate temporarily, but does not return to the building/complex, if either:

(A) A tenant is not offered payment for all reasonable out-of-pocket expenses incurred in connection with the temporary relocation, or

(B) Other conditions of the temporary relocation are not reasonable.

(v) A tenant of a dwelling who moves from the building/complex permanently after he or she has been required to move to another unit in the same building/complex, if either:

(A) The tenant is not offered reimbursement for all reasonable out-of-pocket expenses incurred in connection with the move; or

(B) Other conditions of the move are not reasonable.

(2) Notwithstanding the provisions of paragraph (f)(1) of this section, a person does not qualify as a "displaced person" (and is not eligible for relocation assistance under the URA or this section), if:

(i) The person has been evicted for serious or repeated violation of the terms and conditions of the lease or occupancy agreement, violation of applicable Federal, State, or local or tribal law, or other good cause, and HUD determines that the eviction was not undertaken for the purpose of evading the obligation to provide relocation assistance;

(ii) The person moved into the property after the submission of the application and, before signing a lease and commencing occupancy, was provided written notice of the project, its possible impact on the person (e.g., the person may be displaced, temporarily relocated, or suffer a rent increase) and the fact that the person would not qualify as a "displaced person" (or for any assistance provided under this section), if the project is approved;

(iii) The person is ineligible under 49 CFR 24.2(g)(2); or

(iv) HUD determines that the person was not displaced as a direct result of acquisition, rehabilitation, or demolition for the project.

(3) The recipient may request, at any time, HUD's determination of whether a displacement is or would be covered under this section.

(g) *Definition of initiation of negotiations.* For purposes of determining the formula for computing the replacement housing assistance to be provided to a residential tenant displaced as a direct result of privately undertaken rehabilitation, demolition, or acquisition of the real property, the term "initiation of negotiations" means the execution of the agreement between the recipient and HUD.

(h) *Definition of project.* For purposes of this section, the term "project" means an undertaking paid for in whole or in part with assistance under this part. Two or more activities that are integrally related, each essential to the others, are considered a single project, whether or not all component activities receive assistance under this part.

[58 FR 13871, Mar. 15, 1993, as amended at 59 FR 36892, July 19, 1994]

§583.315 Resident rent.

(a) *Calculation of resident rent.* Each resident of supportive housing may be required to pay as rent an amount determined by the recipient which may not exceed the highest of:

(1) 30 percent of the family's monthly adjusted income (adjustment factors include the number of people in the family, age of family members, medical expenses and child care expenses). The calculation of the family's monthly adjusted income must include the expense deductions provided in 24 CFR 5.611(a), and for persons with disabilities, the calculation of the family's monthly adjusted income also must include the disallowance of earned income as provided in 24 CFR 5.617, if applicable;

(2) 10 percent of the family's monthly gross income; or

(3) If the family is receiving payments for welfare assistance from a public agency and a part of the payments, adjusted in accordance with the family's actual housing costs, is specifically designated by the agency to meet the family's housing costs, the portion of the payment that is designated for housing costs.

(b) *Use of rent.* Resident rent may be used in the operation of the project or may be reserved, in whole or in part, to assist residents of transitional housing in moving to permanent housing.

(c) *Fees.* In addition to resident rent, recipients may charge residents reasonable fees for services not paid with grant funds.

[58 FR 13871, Mar. 15, 1993, as amended at 59 FR 36892, July 19, 1994; 66 FR 6225, Jan. 19, 2001]

§ 583.320 Site control.

(a) *Site control.* (1) Where grant funds will be used for acquisition, rehabilitation, or new construction to provide supportive housing or supportive services, or where grant funds will be used for operating costs of supportive housing, or where grant funds will be used to provide supportive services except where an applicant will provide services at sites not operated by the applicant, an applicant must demonstrate site control before HUD will execute a grant agreement (*e.g.*, through a deed, lease, executed contract of sale). If such site control is not demonstrated within one year after initial notification of the award of assistance under this part, the grant will be deobligated as provided in paragraph (c) of this section.

(2) Where grant funds will be used to lease all or part of a structure to provide supportive housing or supportive services, or where grant funds will be used to lease individual housing units for homeless persons who will eventually control the units, site control need not be demonstrated.

(b) *Site change.* (1) A recipient may obtain ownership or control of a suitable site different from the one specified in its application. Retention of an assistance award is subject to the new site's meeting all requirements under this part for suitable sites.

(2) If the acquisition, rehabilitation, acquisition and rehabilitation, or new construction costs for the substitute site are greater than the amount of the grant awarded for the site specified in the application, the recipient must provide for all additional costs. If the recipient is unable to demonstrate to HUD that it is able to provide for the difference in costs, HUD may deobligate the award of assistance.

(c) *Failure to obtain site control within one year.* HUD will recapture or deobligate any award for assistance under this part if the recipient is not in control of a suitable site before the expiration of one year after initial notification of an award.

§ 583.325 Nondiscrimination and equal opportunity requirements.

(a) *General.* Notwithstanding the permissibility of proposals that serve designated populations of disabled homeless persons, recipients serving a designated population of disabled homeless persons are required, within the designated population, to comply with these requirements for nondiscrimination on the basis of race, color, religion, sex, national origin, age, familial status, and disability.

(b) *Nondiscrimination and equal opportunity requirements.* The nondiscrimination and equal opportunity requirements set forth at part 5 of this title apply to this program. The Indian Civil Rights Act (25 U.S.C. 1301 *et seq.*) applies to tribes when they exercise their powers of self-government, and to Indian housing authorities (IHAs) when established by the exercise of such powers. When an IHA is established under State law, the applicability of the Indian Civil Rights Act will be determined on a case-by-case basis. Projects subject to the Indian Civil Rights Act must be developed and operated in compliance with its provisions and all implementing HUD requirements, instead of title VI and the Fair Housing Act and their implementing regulations.

(c) *Procedures.* (1) If the procedures that the recipient intends to use to make known the availability of the supportive housing are unlikely to reach persons of any particular race, color, religion, sex, age, national origin, familial status, or handicap who may qualify for admission to the housing, the recipient must establish additional procedures that will ensure that such persons can obtain information concerning availability of the housing.

(2) The recipient must adopt procedures to make available information on the existence and locations of facilities and services that are accessible to persons with a handicap and maintain evidence of implementation of the procedures.

(d) *Accessibility requirements.* The recipient must comply with the new construction accessibility requirements of the Fair Housing Act and section 504 of the Rehabilitation Act of 1973, and the reasonable accommodation and rehabilitation accessibility requirements of section 504 as follows:

(1) All new construction must meet the accessibility requirements of 24 CFR 8.22 and, as applicable, 24 CFR 100.205.

(2) Projects in which costs of rehabilitation are 75 percent or more of the replacement cost of the building must meet the requirements of 24 CFR 8.23(a). Other rehabilitation must meet the requirements of 24 CFR 8.23(b).

[58 FR 13871, Mar. 15, 1993, as amended at 59 FR 33894, June 30, 1994; 61 FR 5210, Feb. 9, 1996; 61 FR 51176, Sept. 30, 1996]

§583.330 Applicability of other Federal requirements.

In addition to the requirements set forth in 24 CFR part 5, use of assistance provided under this part must comply with the following Federal requirements:

(a) *Flood insurance.* (1) The Flood Disaster Protection Act of 1973 (42 U.S.C. 4001–4128) prohibits the approval of applications for assistance for acquisition or construction (including rehabilitation) for supportive housing located in an area identified by the Federal Emergency Management Agency (FEMA) as having special flood hazards, unless:

(i) The community in which the area is situated is participating in the National Flood Insurance Program (see 44 CFR parts 59 through 79), or less than a year has passed since FEMA notification regarding such hazards; and

(ii) Flood insurance is obtained as a condition of approval of the application.

(2) Applicants with supportive housing located in an area identified by FEMA as having special flood hazards and receiving assistance for acquisition or construction (including rehabilitation) are responsible for assuring that flood insurance under the National Flood Insurance Program is obtained and maintained.

(b) The Coastal Barrier Resources Act of 1982 (16 U.S.C. 3501 *et seq.*) may apply to proposals under this part, depending on the assistance requested.

(c) *Uniform requirements.* The policies, guidelines, and requirements of 24 CFR part 85 (as revised April 1, 2013) apply to the award, acceptance, and use of assistance under the program by governmental entities, and 24 CFR part 84 (as revised April 1, 2013) apply to the acceptance and use of assistance by private nonprofit organizations, except where inconsistent with the provisions of the McKinney Act, other Federal statutes, or this part.

(d) *Lead-based paint.* The Lead-Based Paint Poisoning Prevention Act (42 U.S.C. 4821–4846), the Residential Lead-Based Paint Hazard Reduction Act of 1992 (42 U.S.C. 4851–4856), and implementing regulations at part 35, subparts A, B, J, K, and R of this title apply to activities under this program.

(e) *Conflicts of interest.* (1) In addition to the conflict of interest requirements in 24 CFR part 85 (as revised April 1, 2013), no person who is an employee, agent, consultant, officer, or elected or appointed official of the recipient and who exercises or has exercised any functions or responsibilities with respect to assisted activities, or who is in a position to participate in a decision-making process or gain inside information with regard to such activities, may obtain a personal or financial interest or benefit from the activity, or have an interest in any contract, subcontract, or agreement with respect thereto, or the proceeds thereunder, either for himself or herself or for those with whom he or she has family or business ties, during his or her tenure or for one year thereafter. Participation by homeless individuals who also are participants under the program in policy or decisionmaking under § 583.300(f) does not constitute a conflict of interest.

(2) Upon the written request of the recipient, HUD may grant an exception to the provisions of paragraph (e)(1) of this section on a case-by-case basis when it determines that the exception will serve to further the purposes of the program and the effective and efficient administration of the recipient's project. An exception may be considered only after the recipient has provided the following:

(i) For States and other governmental entities, a disclosure of the nature of the conflict, accompanied by an assurance that there has been public disclosure of the conflict and a description of how the public disclosure was made; and

(ii) For all recipients, an opinion of the recipient's attorney that the interest for which the exception is sought would not violate State or local law.

(3) In determining whether to grant a requested exception after the recipient has satisfactorily met the requirement of paragraph (e)(2) of this section, HUD will consider the cumulative effect of the following factors, where applicable:

(i) Whether the exception would provide a significant cost benefit or an essential degree of expertise to the project which would otherwise not be available;

(ii) Whether the person affected is a member of a group or class of eligible persons and the exception will permit such person to receive generally the same interests or benefits as are being made available or provided to the group or class;

(iii) Whether the affected person has withdrawn from his or her functions or responsibilities, or the decisionmaking process with respect to the specific assisted activity in question;

(iv) Whether the interest or benefit was present before the affected person was in a position as described in paragraph (e)(1) of this section;

(v) Whether undue hardship will result either to the recipient or the person affected when weighed against the public interest served by avoiding the prohibited conflict; and

(vi) Any other relevant considerations.

(f) *Audit.* The financial management systems used by recipients under this program must provide for audits in accordance with 2 CFR part 200, subpart F. HUD may perform or require additional audits as it finds necessary or appropriate.

(g) Davis-Bacon Act. The provisions of the Davis-Bacon Act do not apply to this program.

[58 FR 13871, Mar. 15, 1993, as amended at 61 FR 5211, Feb. 9, 1996; 64 FR 50226, Sept. 15, 1999; 80 FR 75940, Dec. 7, 2015]

Subpart E—Administration

§ 583.400 Grant agreement.

(a) *General.* The duty to provide supportive housing or supportive services in accordance with the requirements of this part will be incorporated in a grant agreement executed by HUD and the recipient.

(b) *Enforcement.* HUD will enforce the obligations in the grant agreement through such action as may be appropriate, including repayment of funds that have already been disbursed to the recipient.

§ 583.405 Program changes.

(a) *HUD approval.* (1) A recipient may not make any significant changes to an approved program without prior HUD approval. Significant changes include, but are not limited to, a change in the recipient, a change in the project site, additions or deletions in the types of activities listed in § 583.100 of this part approved for the program or a shift of more than 10 percent of funds from one approved type of activity to another, and a change in the category of participants to be served. Depending on the nature of the change, HUD may require a new certification of consistency with the consolidated plan (see § 583.155).

(2) Approval for changes is contingent upon the application ranking remaining high enough after the approved change to have been competitively selected for funding in the year the application was selected.

(b) *Documentation of other changes.* Any changes to an approved program that do not require prior HUD approval must be fully documented in the recipient's records.

[58 FR 13871, Mar. 15, 1993, as amended at 61 FR 51176, Sept. 30, 1996]

§583.410 Obligation and deobligation of funds.

(a) *Obligation of funds.* When HUD and the applicant execute a grant agreement, funds are obligated to cover the amount of the approved assistance under subpart B of this part. The recipient will be expected to carry out the supportive housing or supportive services activities as proposed in the application.

(b) *Increases.* After the initial obligation of funds, HUD will not make revisions to increase the amount obligated.

(c) *Deobligation.* (1) HUD may deobligate all or parts of grants for acquisition, rehabilitation, acquisition and rehabilitation, or new construction:

(i) If the actual total cost of acquisition, rehabilitation, acquisition and rehabilitation, or new construction is less than the total cost anticipated in the application; or

(ii) If proposed activities for which funding was approved are not begun within three months or residents do not begin to occupy the facility within nine months after grant execution.

(2) HUD may deobligate the amounts for annual leasing costs, operating costs or supportive services in any year:

(i) If the actual leasing costs, operating costs or supportive services for that year are less than the total cost anticipated in the application; or

(ii) If the proposed supportive housing operations are not begun within three months after the units are available for occupancy.

(3) The grant agreement may set forth in detail other circumstances under which funds may be deobligated, and other sanctions may be imposed.

(4) HUD may:

(i) Readvertise the availability of funds that have been deobligated under this section in a notice of fund availability under §583.200, or

(ii) Award deobligated funds to applications previously submitted in response to the most recently published notice of fund availability, and in accordance with subpart C of this part.

PART 586—REVITALIZING BASE CLOSURE COMMUNITIES AND COMMUNITY ASSISTANCE—COMMUNITY REDEVELOPMENT AND HOMELESS ASSISTANCE

Sec.

AUTHORITY: 10 U.S.C. 2687 *note;* 42 U.S.C. 3535(d).

SOURCE: 62 FR 37479, July 11, 1997, unless otherwise noted.

§586.1 Purpose.

This part implements the Base Closure Community Redevelopment and Homeless Assistance Act, as amended (10 U.S.C. 2687 *note*), which instituted a new community-based process for addressing the needs of the homeless at base closure and realignment sites. In this process, Local Redevelopment Authorities (LRAs) identify interest from homeless providers in installation property and develop a redevelopment plan for the installation that balances the economic redevelopment and other development needs of the communities in the vicinity of the installation with the needs of the homeless in those communities. The Department of Housing and Urban Development (HUD) reviews the LRA's plan to see that an appropriate balance is achieved. This part also implements the process for identifying interest from State and local entities for property under a public benefit transfer. The LRA is responsible for concurrently identifying interest from homeless providers and State and local entities interested in property under a public benefit transfer.

§586.5 Definitions.

As used in this part:

CERCLA. Comprehensive Environmental Response, Compensation, and Liability Act (42 U.S.C. 9601 *et seq.*).

Communities in the vicinity of the installation. The communities that constitute the political jurisdictions (other than the State in which the installation is located) that comprise the LRA for the installation. If no LRA is formed at the local level, and the State is serving in that capacity, the communities in the vicinity of the installation are deemed to be those political jurisdiction(s) (other than the State) in which the installation is located.

Consolidated Plan. The plan prepared in accordance with the requirements of 24 CFR part 91.

Continuum of care system.

(1) A comprehensive homeless assistance system that includes:

(i) A system of outreach and assessment for determining the needs and condition of an individual or family who is homeless, or whether assistance is necessary to prevent an individual or family from becoming homeless;

(ii) Emergency shelters with appropriate supportive services to help ensure that homeless individuals and families receive adequate emergency shelter and referral to necessary service providers or housing finders;

(iii) Transitional housing with appropriate supportive services to help those homeless individuals and families who are not prepared to make the transition to independent living;

(iv) Housing with or without supportive services that has no established limitation on the amount of time of residence to help meet long-term needs of homeless individuals and families; and

(v) Any other activity that clearly meets an identified need of the homeless and fills a gap in the continuum of care.

(2) Supportive services are services that enable homeless persons and families to move through the continuum of care toward independent living. These services include, but are not limited to, case management, housing counseling, job training and placement, primary health care, mental health services, substance abuse treatment, child care, transportation, emergency food and clothing, family violence services, education services, moving services, assistance in obtaining entitlements, and referral to veterans services and legal services.

Day. One calendar day including weekends and holidays.

DoD. Department of Defense.

HHS. Department of Health and Human Services.

Homeless person. (1) An individual or family who lacks a fixed, regular, and adequate nighttime residence; and

(2) An individual or family who has a primary nighttime residence that is:

(i) A supervised publicly or privately operated shelter designed to provide temporary living accommodations (including welfare hotels, congregate shelters and transitional housing for the mentally ill);

(ii) An institution that provides a temporary residence for individuals intended to be institutionalized; or

(iii) A public or private place not designed for, or ordinarily used as, a regular sleeping accommodation for human beings.

(3) This term does not include any individual imprisoned or otherwise detained under an Act of the Congress or a State law.

HUD. Department of Housing and Urban Development.

Installation. A base, camp, post, station, yard, center, homeport facility for any ship or other activity under the jurisdiction of DoD, including any leased facility, that is approved for closure or realignment under the Base Closure and Realignment Act of 1988 (Pub. L. 100–526), as amended, or the Defense Base Closure and Realignment Act of 1990 (Pub. L. 101–510), as amended (both at 10 U.S.C. 2687, *note*).

Local redevelopment authority (LRA). Any authority or instrumentality established by State or local government and recognized by the Secretary of Defense, through the Office of Economic Adjustment, as the entity responsible for developing the redevelopment plan with respect to the installation or for directing implementation of the plan.

NEPA. National Environmental Policy Act of 1969 (42 U.S.C. 4320).

OEA. Office of Economic Adjustment, Department of Defense.

Private nonprofit organization. An organization, no part of the net earnings of which inures to the benefit of any member, founder, contributor, or individual; that has a voluntary board; that has an accounting system or has designated an entity that will maintain a functioning accounting system for the organization in accordance with generally accepted accounting procedures; and that practices nondiscrimination in the provision of assistance.

Public benefit transfer. The transfer of surplus military property for a specified public purpose at up to a 100 percent discount in accordance with 40 U.S.C. 471 *et seq*., or 49 U.S.C. 47151-47153.

Redevelopment plan. A plan that is agreed to by the LRA with respect to the installation and provides for the reuse or redevelopment of the real property and personal property of the installation that is available for such reuse and redevelopment as a result of the closure of the installation.

Representative(s) of the homeless. A State or local government agency or private nonprofit organization, including a homeless assistance planning board, that provides or proposes to provide services to the homeless.

Substantially equivalent. Property that is functionally suitable to substitute for property referred to in an approved Title V application. For example, if the representative of the homeless had an approved Title V application for a building that would accommodate 100 homeless persons in an emergency shelter, the replacement facility would also have to accommodate 100 at a comparable cost for renovation.

Substantially equivalent funding. Sufficient funding to acquire a substantially equivalent facility.

Surplus property. Any excess property not required for the needs and the discharge of the responsibilities of all Federal Agencies. Authority to make this determination, after screening with all Federal Agencies, rests with the Military Departments.

Title V. Title V of the Stewart B. McKinney Homeless Assistance Act of 1987 (42 U.S.C 11411) as amended by the National Defense Authorization Act for Fiscal Year 1994 (Pub. L. 103–160).

Urban county. A county within a metropolitan area as defined at 24 CFR 570.3.

§586.10 Applicability.

(a) *General*. This part applies to all installations that are approved for closure/realignment by the President and Congress under Pub. L. 101–510 after October 25, 1994.

(b) *Request for inclusion under this process*. This part also applies to installations that were approved for closure/realignment under either Public Law 100–526 or Public Law 101–510 prior to October 25, 1994 and for which an LRA submitted a request for inclusion under this part to DoD by December 24, 1994. A list of such requests was published in the FEDERAL REGISTER on May 30, 1995 (60 FR 28089).

(1) For installations with Title V applications pending but not approved before October 25, 1994, the LRA shall consider and specifically address any application for use of buildings and property to assist the homeless that were received by HHS prior to October 25, 1994, and were pending with the Secretary of HHS on that date. These pending requests shall be addressed in the LRA's homeless assistance submission.

(2) For installations with Title V applications approved before October 25, 1994 where there is an approved Title V application, but property has not been assigned or otherwise disposed of by the Military Department, the LRA must ensure that its homeless assistance submission provides the Title V applicant with:

(i) The property requested;

(ii) Properties, on or off the installation, that are substantially equivalent to those requested;

(iii) Sufficient funding to acquire such substantially equivalent properties;

(iv) Services and activities that meet the needs identified in the application; or

(v) A combination of the properties, funding, and services and activities described in §586.10(b)(2)(i) through (iv).

(c) *Revised Title V process*. All other installations approved for closure or realignment under either Public Law 100–526 or Public Law 101–510 prior to

October 25, 1994, for which there was no request for consideration under this part, are covered by the process stipulated under Title V. Buildings or property that were transferred or leased for homeless use under Title V prior to October 25, 1994, may not be reconsidered under this part.

§ 586.15 Waivers and extensions of deadlines.

(a) After consultation with the LRA and HUD, and upon a finding that it is in the interest of the communities affected by the closure/realignment of the installation, DoD, through the Director of the Office of Economic Adjustment, may extend or postpone any deadline contained in this part.

(b) Upon completion of a determination and finding of good cause, and except for deadlines and actions required on the part of DoD, HUD may waive any provision of §§ 586.20 through 586.45 in any particular case, subject only to statutory limitations.

§ 586.20 Overview of the process.

(a) *Recognition of the LRA.* As soon as practicable after the list of installations recommended for closure or realignment is approved, DoD, through OEA, will recognize an LRA for the installation. Upon recognition, OEA shall publish the name, address, and point of contact for the LRA in the FEDERAL REGISTER and in a newspaper of general circulation in the communities in the vicinity of the installation.

(b) *Responsibilities of the Military Department.* The Military Department shall make installation properties available to other DoD components and Federal agencies in accordance with the procedures set out at 32 CFR part 175. The Military Department will keep the LRA informed of other Federal interest in the property during this process. Upon completion of this process the Military Department will notify HUD and either the LRA, or the Chief Executive Officer of the State, as appropriate, and publish a list of surplus property on the installation that will be available for reuse in the FEDERAL REGISTER and a newspaper of general circulation in the communities in the vicinity of the installation.

(c) *Responsibilities of the LRA.* The LRA should begin to conduct outreach efforts with respect to the installation as soon as is practicable after the date of approval of closure/realignment of the installation. The local reuse planning process must begin no later than the date of the Military Department's FEDERAL REGISTER publication of available property described at § 586.20(b). For those installations that began the process described in this part prior to August 17, 1995, HUD will, on a case by case basis, determine whether the statutory requirements have been fulfilled and whether any additional requirements listed in this part should be required. Upon the FEDERAL REGISTER publication described in § 586.20(b), the LRA shall:

(1) Publish, within 30 days, in a newspaper of general circulation in the communities in the vicinity of the installation, the time period during which the LRA will receive notices of interest from State and local governments, representatives of the homeless, and other interested parties. This publication shall include the name, address, telephone number and the point of contact for the LRA who can provide information on the prescribed form and contents of the notices of interest. The LRA shall notify DoD of the deadline specified for receipt of notices of interest. LRAs are strongly encouraged to make this publication as soon as possible within the permissible 30 day period in order to expedite the closure process.

(i) In addition, the LRA has the option to conduct an informal solicitation of notices of interest from public and non-profit entities interested in obtaining property via a public benefit transfer other than a homeless assistance conveyance under either 40 U.S.C. 471 *et seq.*, or 49 U.S.C. 47151–47153. As part of such a solicitation, the LRA may wish to request that interested entities submit a description of the proposed use to the LRA and the sponsoring Federal agency.

(ii) For all installations selected for closure or realignment prior to 1995 that elected to proceed under Public Law 103–421, the LRA shall accept notices of interest for not less than 30 days.

(iii) For installations selected for closure or realignment in 1995 or thereafter, notices of interest shall be accepted for a minimum of 90 days and not more than 180 days after the LRA's publication under §586.20(c)(1).

(2) Prescribe the form and contents of notices of interest.

(i) The LRA may not release to the public any information regarding the capacity of the representative of the homeless to carry out its program, a description of the organization, or its financial plan for implementing the program, without the consent of the representative of the homeless concerned, unless such release is authorized under Federal law and under the law of the State and communities in which the installation concerned is located. The identity of the representative of the homeless may be disclosed.

(ii) The notices of interest from representatives of the homeless must include:

(A) A description of the homeless assistance program proposed, including the purposes to which the property or facility will be put, which may include uses such as supportive services, job and skills training, employment programs, shelters, transitional housing or housing with no established limitation on the amount of time of residence, food and clothing banks, treatment facilities, or any other activity which clearly meets an identified need of the homeless and fills a gap in the continuum of care;

(B) A description of the need for the program;

(C) A description of the extent to which the program is or will be coordinated with other homeless assistance programs in the communities in the vicinity of the installation;

(D) Information about the physical requirements necessary to carry out the program including a description of the buildings and property at the installation that are necessary to carry out the program;

(E) A description of the financial plan, the organization, and the organizational capacity of the representative of the homeless to carry out the program; and

(F) An assessment of the time required to start carrying out the program.

(iii) The notices of interest from entities other than representatives of the homeless should specify the name of the entity and specific interest in property or facilities along with a description of the planned use.

(3) In addition to the notice required under §586.20(c)(1), undertake outreach efforts to representatives of the homeless by contacting local government officials and other persons or entities that may be interested in assisting the homeless within the vicinity of the installation.

(i) The LRA may invite persons and organizations identified on the HUD list of representatives of the homeless and any other representatives of the homeless with which the LRA is familiar, operating in the vicinity of the installation, to the workshop described in §586.20(c)(3)(ii).

(ii) The LRA, in coordination with the Military Department and HUD, shall conduct at least one workshop where representatives of the homeless have an opportunity to:

(A) Learn about the closure/realignment and disposal process;

(B) Tour the buildings and properties available either on or off the installation;

(C) Learn about the LRA's process and schedule for receiving notices of interest as guided by §586.20(c)(2); and

(D) Learn about any known land use constraints affecting the available property and buildings.

(iii) The LRA should meet with representatives of the homeless that express interest in discussing possible uses for these properties to alleviate gaps in the continuum of care.

(4) Consider various properties in response to the notices of interest. The LRA may consider property that is located off the installation.

(5) Develop an application, including the redevelopment plan and homeless assistance submission, explaining how the LRA proposes to address the needs of the homeless. This application shall consider the notices of interest received from State and local governments, representatives of the homeless, and other interested parties. This shall

include, but not be limited to, entities eligible for public benefit transfers under either 40 U.S.C. 471 *et seq.*, or 49 U.S.C. 47151–47153; representatives of the homeless; commercial, industrial, and residential development interests; and other interests. From the deadline date for receipt of notices of interest described at § 586.20(c)(1), the LRA shall have 270 days to complete and submit the LRA application to the appropriate Military Department and HUD. The application requirements are described at § 586.30.

(6) Make the draft application available to the public for review and comment periodically during the process of developing the application. The LRA must conduct at least one public hearing on the application prior to its submission to HUD and the appropriate Military Department. A summary of the public comments received during the process of developing the application shall be included in the application when it is submitted.

(d) *Public benefit transfer screening.* The LRA should, while conducting its outreach efforts, work with the Federal agencies that sponsor public benefit transfers under either 40 U.S.C. 471 *et seq.* or 49 U.S.C. 47151–47153. Those agencies can provide a list of parties in the vicinity of the installation that might be interested in and eligible for public benefit transfers. The LRA should make a reasonable effort to inform such parties of the availability of the property and incorporate their interests within the planning process. Actual recipients of property are to be determined by the sponsoring Federal agency. The Military Departments shall notify sponsoring Federal agencies about property that is available based on the community redevelopment plan and keep the LRA apprised of any expressions of interest. Such expressions of interest are not required to be incorporated into the redevelopment plan, but must be considered.

§ 586.25 HUD's negotiations and consultations with the LRA.

HUD may negotiate and consult with the LRA before and during the course of preparation of the LRA's application and during HUD's review thereof with a view toward avoiding any preliminary determination that the application does not meet any requirement of this part. LRAs are encouraged to contact HUD for a list of persons and organizations that are representatives of the homeless operating in the vicinity of the installation.

§ 586.30 LRA application.

(a) *Redevelopment plan.* A copy of the redevelopment plan shall be part of the application.

(b) *Homeless assistance submission.* This component of the application shall include the following:

(1) Information about homelessness in the communities in the vicinity of the installation.

(i) A list of all the political jurisdictions which comprise the LRA.

(ii) A description of the unmet need in the continuum of care system within each political jurisdiction, which should include information about any gaps that exist in the continuum of care for particular homeless subpopulations. The source for this information shall depend upon the size and nature of the political jurisdictions(s) that comprise the LRA. LRAs representing:

(A) Political jurisdictions that are required to submit a Consolidated Plan shall include a copy of their Homeless and Special Needs Population Table (table 1), Priority Homeless Needs Assessment Table (table 2), and narrative description thereof from that Consolidated Plan, including the inventory of facilities and services that assist the homeless in the jurisdiction.

(B) Political jurisdictions that are part of an urban county that is required to submit a Consolidated Plan shall include a copy of their Homeless and Special Needs Population Table (table 1), Priority Homeless Needs Assessment Table (table 2), and narrative description thereof from that Consolidated Plan, including the inventory of facilities and services that assist the homeless in the jurisdiction. In addition, the LRA shall explain what portion of the homeless population and subpopulations described in the Consolidated Plan are attributable to the political jurisdiction it represents.

(C) A political jurisdiction not described by § 586.30(b)(1)(ii)(A) or

§586.30(b)(1)(ii)(B) shall submit a narrative description of what it perceives to be the homeless population within the jurisdiction and a brief inventory of the facilities and services that assist homeless persons and families within the jurisdiction. LRAs that represent these jurisdictions are not required to conduct surveys of the homeless population.

(2) Notices of interest proposing assistance to homeless persons and/or families.

(i) A description of the proposed activities to be carried out on or off the installation and a discussion of how these activities meet a portion or all of the needs of the homeless by addressing the gaps in the continuum of care. The activities need not be limited to expressions of interest in property, but may also include discussions of how economic redevelopment may benefit the homeless;

(ii) A copy of each notice of interest from representatives of the homeless for use of buildings and property and a description of the manner in which the LRA's application addresses the need expressed in each notice of interest. If the LRA determines that a particular notice of interest should not be awarded property, an explanation of why the LRA determined not to support that notice of interest, the reasons for which may include the impact of the program contained in the notice of interest on the community as described in §586.30(b)(2)(iii); and

(iii) A description of the impact that the implemented redevelopment plan will have on the community. This shall include information on how the LRA's redevelopment plan might impact the character of existing neighborhoods adjacent to the properties proposed to be used to assist the homeless and should discuss alternative plans. Impact on schools, social services, transportation, infrastructure, and concentration of minorities and/or low income persons shall also be discussed.

(3) Legally binding agreements for buildings, property, funding, and/or services.

(i) A copy of the legally binding agreements that the LRA proposes to enter into with the representative(s) of the homeless selected by the LRA to implement homeless programs that fill gaps in the existing continuum of care. The legally binding agreements shall provide for a process for negotiating alternative arrangements in the event that an environmental analysis conducted under §586.45(b) indicates that any property identified for transfer in the agreement is not suitable for the intended purpose. Where the balance determined in accordance with §586.30(b)(4) provides for the use of installation property as a homeless assistance facility, legally binding agreements must provide for the reversion or transfer, either to the LRA or to another entity or entities, of the buildings and property in the event they cease to be used for the homeless. In cases where the balance proposed by the LRA does not include the use of buildings or property on the installation, the legally binding agreements need not be tied to the use of specific real property and need not include a reverter clause. Legally binding agreements shall be accompanied by a legal opinion of the chief legal advisor of the LRA or political jurisdiction or jurisdictions which will be executing the legally binding agreements that the legally binding agreements, when executed, will constitute legal, valid, binding, and enforceable obligations on the parties thereto;

(ii) A description of how buildings, property, funding, and/or services either on or off the installation will be used to fill some of the gaps in the current continuum of care system and an explanation of the suitability of the buildings and property for that use; and

(iii) Information on the availability of general services such as transportation, police, and fire protection, and a discussion of infrastructure such as water, sewer, and electricity in the vicinity of the proposed homeless activity at the installation.

(4) An assessment of the balance with economic and other development needs.

(i) An assessment of the manner in which the application balances the expressed needs of the homeless and the needs of the communities comprising the LRA for economic redevelopment and other development; and

(ii) An explanation of how the LRA's application is consistent with the appropriate Consolidated Plan(s) or any other existing housing, social service, community, economic, or other development plans adopted by the jurisdictions in the vicinity of the installation.

(5) A description of the outreach undertaken by the LRA. The LRA shall explain how the outreach requirements described at § 586.20(c)(1) and § 586.20(c)(3) have been fulfilled. This explanation shall include a list of the representatives of the homeless the LRA contacted during the outreach process.

(c) *Public comments.* The LRA application shall include the materials described at § 586.20(c)(6). These materials shall be prefaced with an overview of the citizen participation process observed in preparing the application.

§ 586.35 HUD's review of the application.

(a) *Timing.* HUD shall complete a review of each application no later than 60 days after its receipt of a completed application.

(b) *Standards of review.* The purpose of the review is to determine whether the application is complete and, with respect to the expressed interest and requests of representatives of the homeless, whether the application:

(1) *Need.* Takes into consideration the size and nature of the homeless population in the communities in the vicinity of the installation, the availability of existing services in such communities to meet the needs of the homeless in such communities, and the suitability of the buildings and property covered by the application for use and needs of the homeless in such communities. HUD will take into consideration the size and nature of the installation in reviewing the needs of the homeless population in the communities in the vicinity of the installation.

(2) *Impact of notices of interest.* Takes into consideration any economic impact of the homeless assistance under the plan on the communities in the vicinity of the installation, including:

(i) Whether the plan is feasible in light of demands that would be placed on available social services, police and fire protection, and infrastructure in the community; and,

(ii) Whether the selected notices of interest are consistent with the Consolidated Plan(s) or any other existing housing, social service, community, economic, or other development plans adopted by the political jurisdictions in the vicinity of the installation.

(3) *Legally binding agreements.* Specifies the manner in which the buildings, property, funding, and/or services on or off the installation will be made available for homeless assistance purposes. HUD will review each legally binding agreement to verify that:

(i) They include all the documents legally required to complete the transactions necessary to realize the homeless use(s) described in the application;

(ii) They include all appropriate terms and conditions;

(iii) They address the full range of contingencies including those described at § 586.30(b)(3)(i);

(iv) They stipulate that the buildings, property, funding, and/or services will be made available to the representatives of the homeless in a timely fashion; and

(v) They are accompanied by a legal opinion of the chief legal advisor of the LRA or political jurisdiction or jurisdictions which will be executing the legally binding agreements that the legally binding agreements will, when executed, constitute legal, valid, binding, and enforceable obligations on the parties thereto.

(4) *Balance.* Balances in an appropriate manner a portion or all of the needs of the communities in the vicinity of the installation for economic redevelopment and other development with the needs of the homeless in such communities.

(5) *Outreach.* Was developed in consultation with representatives of the homeless and the homeless assistance planning boards, if any, in the communities in the vicinity of the installation and whether the outreach requirements described at § 586.20(c)(1) and § 586.20(c)(3) have been fulfilled by the LRA.

(c) *Notice of determination.* (1) HUD shall, no later than the 60th day after its receipt of the application, unless such deadline is extended pursuant to

§ 586.15(a), send written notification both to DoD and the LRA of its preliminary determination that the application meets or fails to meet the requirements of § 586.35(b). If the application fails to meet the requirements, HUD will send the LRA:

(i) A summary of the deficiencies in the application;

(ii) An explanation of the determination; and

(iii) A statement of how the LRA must address the determinations.

(2) In the event that no application is submitted and no extension is requested as of the deadline specified in § 586.20(c)(5), and the State does not accept within 30 days a DoD written request to become recognized as the LRA, the absence of such application will trigger an adverse determination by HUD effective on the date of the lapsed deadline. Under these conditions, HUD will follow the process described at § 586.40.

(d) *Opportunity to cure.* (1) The LRA shall have 90 days from its receipt of the notice of preliminary determination under § 586.35(c)(1) within which to submit to HUD and DoD a revised application which addresses the determinations listed in the notice. Failure to submit a revised application shall result in a final determination, effective 90 days from the LRA's receipt of the preliminary determination, that the redevelopment plan fails to meet the requirements of § 586.35(b).

(2) HUD shall, within 30 days of its receipt of the LRA's resubmission, send written notification of its final determination of whether the application meets the requirements of § 586.35(b) to both DOD and the LRA.

§ 586.40 Adverse determinations.

(a) *Review and consultation.* If the resubmission fails to meet the requirements of § 586.35(b), or if no resubmission is received, HUD will review the original application, including the notices of interest submitted by representatives of the homeless. In addition, in such instances or when no original application has been submitted, HUD:

(1) Shall consult with the representatives of the homeless, if any, for purposes of evaluating the continuing interest of such representatives in the use of buildings or property at the installation to assist the homeless;

(2) May consult with the applicable Military Department regarding the suitability of the buildings and property at the installation for use to assist the homeless; and

(3) May consult with representatives of the homeless and other parties as necessary.

(b) *Notice of decision.* (1) Within 90 days of receipt of an LRA's revised application which HUD determines does not meet the requirements of § 586.35(b), HUD shall, based upon its reviews and consultations under § 586.40(a):

(i) Notify DoD and the LRA of the buildings and property at the installation that HUD determines are suitable for use to assist the homeless; and

(ii) Notify DoD and the LRA of the extent to which the revised redevelopment plan meets the criteria set forth in § 586.35(b).

(2) In the event that an LRA does not submit a revised redevelopment plan under § 586.35(d), HUD shall, based upon its reviews and consultations under § 586.40(a), notify DoD and the LRA of the buildings and property at the installation that HUD determines are suitable for use to assist the homeless, either

(i) Within 190 days after HUD sends its notice of preliminary adverse determination under § 586.35(c)(1), if an LRA has not submitted a revised redevelopment plan; or

(ii) Within 390 days after the Military Department's FEDERAL REGISTER publication of available property under § 586.20(b), if no redevelopment plan has been received and no extension has been approved.

§ 586.45 Disposal of buildings and property.

(a) *Public benefit transfer screening.* Not later than the LRA's submission of its redevelopment plan to DoD and HUD, the Military Department will conduct an official public benefit transfer screening in accordance with the Federal Property Management Regulations (41 CFR part 101–47.303–2) based upon the uses identified in the redevelopment plan. Federal sponsoring agencies shall notify eligible applicants that any request for property must be consistent with the uses identified in the redevelopment plan. At the request of the LRA, the Military Department may conduct the official State and local public benefit screening at any time after the publication of available property described at § 586.20(b).

(b) *Environmental analysis.* Prior to disposal of any real property, the Military Department shall, consistent with NEPA and section 2905 of the Defense Base Closure and Realignment Act of 1990, as amended (10 U.S.C. 2687 *note*), complete an environmental impact analysis of all reasonable disposal alternatives. The Military Department shall consult with the LRA throughout the environmental impact analysis process to ensure both that the LRA is provided the most current environmental information available concerning the installation, and that the Military Department receives the most current information available concerning the LRA's redevelopment plans for the installation.

(c) *Disposal.* Upon receipt of a notice of approval of an application from HUD under § 586.35(c)(1) or § 586.35(d)(2), DoD shall dispose of buildings and property in accordance with the record of decision or other decision document prepared under § 586.45(b). Disposal of buildings and property to be used as homeless assistance facilities shall be to either the LRA or directly to the representative(s) of the homeless and shall be without consideration. Upon receipt of a notice from HUD under § 586.40(b), DoD will dispose of the buildings and property at the installation in consultation with HUD and the LRA.

(d) *LRA's responsibility.* The LRA shall be responsible for the implementation of and compliance with legally binding agreements under the application.

(e) *Reversions to the LRA.* If a building or property reverts to the LRA under a legally binding agreement under the application, the LRA shall take appropriate actions to secure, to the maximum extent practicable, the utilization of the building or property by other homeless representatives to assist the homeless. An LRA may not be required to utilize the building or property to assist the homeless.

PART 594—JOHN HEINZ NEIGHBORHOOD DEVELOPMENT PROGRAM

Subpart A—General

Subpart B—Eligibility

Subpart C—Funding Allocation and Criteria

Subpart D—Award and Use of Grant Amounts

AUTHORITY: 42 U.S.C. 3535(d) and 5318a.

SOURCE: 60 FR 16359, Mar. 29, 1995, unless otherwise noted.

Subpart A—General

§ 594.1 Applicability and purpose.

(a) *General.* This part establishes as a permanent program the John Heinz Neighborhood Development Program, as authorized by section 832 of the Housing and Community Development Act of 1992. Previously, the program had been administered by the Department as a demonstration program under section 123 of the Housing and Urban-Rural Recovery Act of 1983 (42 U.S.C. 5318 note).

(b) *Purpose.* The program is intended to assist communities to become more viable, by providing incentive funds to carry out neighborhood development activities that benefit low- and moderate-income families. The program objectives are to increase the capacity of neighborhood organizations, promote long-term financial support for their neighborhood projects, and encourage greater participation of neighborhood organizations with private and public institutions.

§594.3 Definitions.

Empowerment zone means an area designated by HUD as an Empowerment Zone under 26 U.S.C. 1391–1393.

Enterprise community means an area designated by HUD as an Enterprise Community under 26 U.S.C. 1391–1393.

Grantee means an eligible neighborhood organization that executes a grant agreement with HUD under this part.

Low- and moderate-income persons means families and individuals whose incomes do not exceed 80 percent of the median income for the area, as determined by the Secretary of HUD in accordance with 42 U.S.C. 5302(a)(20).

Neighborhood development funding organization means:

(1) A depository institution, the accounts of which are insured pursuant to the Federal Deposit Insurance Act, 12 U.S.C. 1811 *et seq.*, or the Federal Credit Union Act, 12 U.S.C. 1751 *et seq.*, and any subsidiary (as such term is defined in 12 U.S.C. 1813(w)) thereof;

(2) A depository institution holding company and any subsidiary (as such term is defined in 12 U.S.C. 1813(w)) thereof; or

(3) A company at least 75 percent of the common stock of which is owned by one or more insured depository institutions or depository institution holding companies.

Neighborhood development organization means the same as the term is defined in §594.5.

Rural neighborhoods. In small cities with under 10,000 in population and in rural areas, a neighborhood area can be the same unit as the unit of general local government.

Unit of general local government means a city, town, township, county, parish, village, or other general purpose political subdivision of a State; an urban county; the Federated States of Micronesia; the Marshall Islands; or a general purpose political subdivision thereof.

[60 FR 16359, Mar. 29, 1995, as amended at 61 FR 5211, Feb. 9, 1996]

Subpart B—Eligibility

§594.5 Eligible applicants.

(a) *General requirements.* To be eligible under this program, a neighborhood development organization must be located within the neighborhood for which assistance is to be provided. It cannot be a city-wide consortium, or, in general, an organization serving a large area of the city. The applicant must meet all of the following requirements:

(1) The organization must be incorporated as a private, voluntary, nonprofit corporation under the laws of the State in which it operates;

(2) The organization must be responsible through a governing body to the residents of the neighborhood it serves, and not less than 51 percent of the members of the governing body must be residents of the neighborhood;

(3) The organization must have conducted business for at least one year;

(4) The organization must operate within an area that meets at least one of the following criteria:

(i) The area meets the requirements for Federal assistance under section 119 of the Housing and Community Development Act of 1974, 42 U.S.C. 5318;

(ii) The area is designated as an Enterprise Community or Empowerment Zone under Federal law as enacted;

(iii) The area is designated as an enterprise zone under State law and is recognized by the Secretary as a State enterprise zone for purposes of this part; or

(iv) The area is a qualified distressed community within the meaning of section 233(b)(1) of the Bank Enterprise Act of 1991, 12 U.S.C. 1834a(b)(1); and

(5) The organization must have conducted one or more eligible neighborhood development activities that primarily benefit low- and moderate-income persons.

(b) *Special eligibility.* Any facility that provides small entrepreneurial business with affordable shared support services and business development services and that meets the requirements of paragraph (a) of this section may also be eligible to participate in this program.

§ 594.7 Other threshold requirements.

In addition, an applicant must meet the following threshold requirements:

(a) Specify a management business plan for accomplishing one or more of the eligible activities specified in § 594.10;

(b) Specify a strategy for achieving greater long-term private sector support, especially in cooperation with a neighborhood development funding organization; and

(c) Specify a strategy for increasing the capacity of the applicant.

§ 594.10 Eligible activities.

Eligible activities include, but are not limited to, the following:

(a) Developing economic development activities that include:

(1) Creating permanent jobs in the neighborhood; or

(2) Establishing or expanding businesses within the neighborhood;

(b) Developing new housing, rehabilitating existing housing, or managing housing stock within the neighborhood;

(c) Developing delivery mechanisms for essential services that have lasting benefits to the neighborhood; and

(d) Planning, promoting, or financing voluntary neighborhood improvement efforts.

Subpart C—Funding Allocation and Criteria

§ 594.15 Allocation amounts.

(a) *Amounts and match requirement.* HUD will make grants, in the form of matching funds, to eligible neighborhood development organizations. HUD reserves the right to make grants for less than the maximum amount established by statute, and to limit the number of times a previous grantee can receive funding. A Federal matching ratio will be established for each grantee in accordance with the statutory requirement that the highest ratios be established for neighborhoods having the greatest degree of economic distress or the smallest number of households.

(b) *Administrative costs.* The Secretary may use no more than 5 percent of the funds appropriated for the program for administrative or other expenses in connection with the program.

§ 594.17 General criteria for competitive selection.

(a) *Criteria.* HUD will use the following general criteria for selecting and ranking applications for all competitions for John Heinz Neighborhood Development Program funds. The relative values for the criteria will be indicated in each NOFA:

(1) The degree of economic distress and the benefit to low- and moderate-income residents of the neighborhood;

(2) The past performance in carrying out eligible activities, and staff capability;

(3) The quality of the Management/Business Plan;

(4) The evidence of coordination and resident participation; and

(5) The quality of the strategy to increase the capacity of the organization and the strategy developed for meeting long-term financial needs.

(b) *Geographic diversity.* The Department also reserves the right to fund applicants in other than rank order, for the purpose of achieving geographic balance.

Subpart D—Award and Use of Grant Amounts

§ 594.20 Submission procedures.

(a) *Use of NOFAs.* The Department will publish a Notice of Funding Availability (NOFA) in the FEDERAL REGISTER for each funding competition under this program, indicating the objective of the competition; the amount of funding available; the application procedures, including the eligible applicants and activities to be funded; and any special conditions applicable to the competition, including the requirements for the match. The NOFA also will describe the maximum points to be awarded under each evaluation criterion, for the purpose of ranking applications, and any special factors to be considered in assigning the points to each criterion.

(b) Applications shall be submitted in accordance with the time, place, and content described in the NOFA.

(Approved by the Office of Management and Budget under control number 2535–0084)

§ 594.23 Approval and certification procedures.

(a) *Approval of application.* HUD's acceptance of an application for review does not imply a commitment to provide funding. HUD will provide notification of whether a project will be funded in accordance with the criteria and procedures set out in the applicable NOFA.

(b) *Certifications.* In the absence of independent evidence that tends to challenge in a substantial manner the certifications made by the applicant pursuant to § 594.30, the required certifications will be accepted by HUD.

However, if independent evidence is available that tends to challenge in a substantial manner an applicant's certification, HUD may require further information or assurances to be submitted in order to determine whether the applicant's certification is satisfactory.

§ 594.25 Project administration.

Project administration will be governed by the terms of the grant agreement.

§ 594.28 Environmental reviews.

(a) For all proposed actions or activities that are not considered categorically excluded under 24 CFR 50.20, HUD will perform the appropriate environmental reviews under the National Environmental Policy Act (NEPA).

(b) Whether the action or activity is categorically excluded from NEPA review or not, HUD will comply also with other applicable requirements of environmental statutes, Executive Orders, and HUD standards listed in 24 CFR 50.4. The environmental reviews will be performed before award of a grant. Grantees shall adhere to all assurances applicable to environmental concerns as contained in the RFGA and grant agreements.

§ 594.30 Equal opportunity and other Federal requirements.

Each participating neighborhood development organization must certify that it will carry out activities assisted under the program in compliance with the nondiscrimination and equal opportunity requirements set forth in 24 CFR part 5 and:

(a) The requirements at 24 CFR part 200, subpart M;

(b) The prohibitions against discrimination and related requirements of section 109 of the Housing and Community Development Act of 1974 (42 U.S.C. 5309);

(c) The requirements of the Americans with Disabilities Act (42 U.S.C. 12181–12189) and implementing regulations at 28 CFR part 36, as applicable;

(d) The Consolidated Plan of the appropriate unit of general local government; and

(e) Other Federal requirements as specified in the applicable NOFA and application kit.

[60 FR 16359, Mar. 29, 1995, as amended at 61 FR 5211, Feb. 9, 1996]

PART 599—RENEWAL COMMUNITIES

Subpart A—General Provisions

Subpart B—Eligibility Requirements for Nomination of Renewal Communities

Subpart C—Procedures for Nomination of Renewal Communities

AUTHORITY: 26 U.S.C. 1400E; 42 U.S.C. 3535(d).

SOURCE: 66 FR 35855, July 9, 2001, unless otherwise noted.

Subpart A—General Provisions

§ 599.1 Applicability and scope.

(a) This part establishes requirements and procedures applicable to the designation of Renewal Communities (RCs) through December 31, 2001, authorized under Subchapter X of the Internal Revenue Code of 1986 (26 U.S.C. 1400E, *et seq.*). HUD may choose to use these requirements and procedures in whole or in part for any future Renewal Community designations that may be authorized.

(b) This part contains provisions relating to area requirements, the nomination process for Renewal Communities, and the evaluation and designation of nominated areas by HUD.

§ 599.3 Definitions.

In addition to the definitions of "HUD" and "Secretary" found in 24 CFR 5.100, the following definitions apply to this part:

Census tract means a census tract, as the term is used by the Bureau of the Census, or, if census tracts are not defined for the area, a block numbering area.

Designation means the process by which the Secretary designates areas as Renewal Communities eligible for tax incentives and credits established by Subchapter X of the Internal Revenue Code of 1986, as amended (26 U.S.C. 1400E, *et seq.*) and for any additional assistance that may be made available.

Empowerment Zone (EZ) means an area so designated by the Secretary in accordance with 24 CFR part 597 or 24 CFR part 598.

Enterprise Community (EC) means an area so designated by the Secretary in accordance with 24 CFR part 597.

Local government means any county, city, town, township, parish, village, or other general purpose political subdivision of a State, and any combination of these political subdivisions that is recognized by the Secretary.

Metropolitan Area (MA) means an area as defined to be a Metropolitan Statistical Area or Primary Metropolitan Statistical Area by the Office of Management and Budget on June 30, 1999.

Nominated area means an area with a population of not more than 200,000 that is nominated by one or more local governments and the State or States in which it is located, or the governing body of the Indian reservation in which it is located, for designation in accordance with this part.

Renewal Community (RC) means an area so designated by HUD in accordance with this part.

Rural area means a nominated area:

(1) Which is within a local government jurisdiction or jurisdictions with a population of less than 50,000; or

(2) Which is outside of an MA; or

(3) Which is determined by HUD, after consultation with the Secretary of Commerce, to be a rural area. An area may qualify as a rural area under this paragraph (3) of this definition if:

(i) It is a nominated area that crosses jurisdictional boundaries;

(ii) The total population of the nominated area does not exceed 200,000;

(iii) The nominated area as a whole would not satisfy the requirements of either paragraph (1) or (2) of this definition;

(iv) Each portion of the nominated area that is located within a separate jurisdiction meets the requirements of either paragraph (1) or (2) of this definition; and

(v) The area is specifically nominated as a rural area; or

(4) Which does not meet the requirements of either paragraph (1), (2), or (3) of this definition but which is determined by HUD on a case-by-case basis, after consultation with the Secretary of Commerce, to be a rural area based on information submitted to demonstrate that the nominated area should be considered as a rural area.

State means any State of the United States.

Urban area means a nominated area that is not a rural area.

§ 599.5 Data used for eligibility determinations.

(a) *Source of data.* The data to be used in determining the population, poverty rate, unemployment rate and household income distribution information of an area is from the 1990 Decennial Census.

(b) *Geographic boundaries.* The boundary of an area that is nominated for designation as an Renewal Community must coincide with the boundaries of census tracts, as defined in § 599.3 except in the case of Indian reservation areas where the use of census tracts would tend to include areas outside the jurisdiction of the reservation governing body and such body is not making the nomination in concert with another jurisdiction.

Subpart B—Eligibility Requirements for Nomination of Renewal Communities

§ 599.101 Eligibility to submit nominations.

(a) *In general.* Except as provided in paragraph (b) of this section, a nomination for the designation of an area as a Renewal Community must be submitted by one or more local governments and the State or States in which the nominated area is located.

(b) *Nominated areas on Indian reservations.* In the case of a nominated area on an Indian reservation, the reservation governing body (as determined by the Secretary of the Interior) must submit the nomination and shall be treated as being both the State and local governments with respect to the area for purposes of this part.

(c) *Responsible official.* The submission of an application, and any other action required of a nominating government under this part, such as the submission of a certification, must be performed by an official or employee authorized to act on behalf of the government for that purpose.

§ 599.103 Geographic and population requirements for a nominated area.

(a) *Geographic requirements.* A nominated area must meet the following geographic requirements to be eligible for designation as a Renewal Community:

(1) The area must be within the jurisdiction of one or more local governments.

(2) The boundary of the area must be continuous.

(i) The boundary line of the nominated area may be interrupted by jurisdictional boundaries, such as State or county lines, or natural boundaries, such as rivers, as long as the resulting area is entirely within the boundary line except for the interruptions.

(ii) The nominated area may enclose an area or areas that are excluded from the nominated area, as long as each enclosed area to be excluded is within a continuous boundary line.

(3) The nominated area may be any size, as long as it meets all of the requirements of this part.

(b) *Population requirements*—(1) *In general.* Except as provided in paragraph (b)(2) of this section, a nominated area must have a population of not more than 200,000 and at least:

(i) 4,000 if any portion of the area (other than a nominated rural area) is located within an MA which has a population of 50,000 or greater; or

(ii) 1,000 in any other case.

(2) *Nominated areas on Indian reservations.* A nominated area that is entirely within an Indian reservation (as determined by the Secretary of the Interior) is not subject to the population requirements of paragraph (b)(1) of this section.

§ 599.105 Economic condition requirements for a nominated area.

(a) *Certification for economic requirements.* An official or officials authorized to do so by the nominating State and local governments must certify in writing for HUD's acceptance that the nominated area is an area of pervasive poverty, unemployment, and general distress, and that the nominated area meets the requirements of paragraphs (b), (c) and, in the case of urban areas, paragraph (d) of this section. HUD's acceptance of the certification is subject to a review of data supporting the certification, as provided in paragraph (e) of this section.

(b) *Unemployment requirement.* A nominated area meets the unemployment requirement if the unemployment rate in the nominated area taken as a whole was at least one and one-half times (150% of) the national unemployment rate for the period to which such data relate.

(c) *Poverty requirement.* A nominated area meets the poverty requirement if the poverty rate for each population census tract within the nominated area is at least 20 percent. In the case of a nominated area that is within an Indian reservation, and cannot equivalently be described with census tracts, the poverty rate of the nominated area taken as a whole is considered for purposes of making this determination.

(d) *Income requirement for urban areas.* In the case of a nominated urban area, at least 70 percent of the households living in the nominated area must have incomes below 80 percent of the median income of households within the jurisdiction of the local government or governments in which the nominated area is located. The number of households below 80 percent of the median income in each census tract shall be the number of households with incomes below 80 percent of the Household Adjusted Median Family Income (HAMFI) in each census tract as determined by HUD.

(e) *HUD review of supporting data*—(1) *Unemployment, poverty and income.* HUD will review 1990 census data to determine whether to accept a certification that a nominated area meets the requirements of paragraphs (b), (c) and (d) of this section.

(2) *Pervasive poverty, unemployment and general distress*—(i) *Pervasive poverty.* Pervasive poverty is demonstrated by evidence that:

(A) Poverty, as indicated by the number of persons listed as being in poverty in the 1990 Decennial Census, is widespread throughout the nominated area; or

(B) Poverty, as described in paragraph (e)(2)(i)(A) of this section, has become entrenched or intractable over time (through comparison of 1980 and 1990 census data or other relevant evidence).

(ii) *Unemployment.* Unemployment is demonstrated by:

(A) The most recent data available indicating that the annual rate of unemployment for the nominated area is not less than the national annual average rate of unemployment; or

(B) Evidence of especially severe economic conditions, such as military base or plant closings or other conditions that have brought about significant job dislocation within the nominated area.

(iii) *General distress.* General distress is evidenced by describing adverse conditions within the nominated urban area other than those of pervasive poverty and unemployment. Below average or decline in per capita income, earnings per worker, number of persons on welfare, per capita property tax base, average years of school completed, substantial population decline, and a high or rising incidence of crime, narcotics use, homelessness, high incidence of AIDS, abandoned housing, deteriorated infrastructure, school dropouts, teen pregnancy, incidence of domestic violence, incidence of certain health conditions and illiteracy are examples of appropriate indicators of general distress.

§ 599.107 Required State and local commitments.

(a) *Commitment to a course of action*—(1) *Agreement of State and local governments.* The nominating State and local governments must agree in writing that, for any period during which the area is a Renewal Community, the governments will follow a specified course of action which meets the requirements of paragraph (a)(2) of this section. If each nominating State and local government is a signatory to a course of action under paragraph (a)(2) of this section, a separate written agreement is not necessary to meet the requirements of this paragraph.

(2) *Course of action requirements*—(i) *In general.* A course of action is a written document, signed by the nominated area's State and/or local governments and community-based organizations which commits each signatory to undertake and achieve measurable goals and actions within the nominated area upon its designation as a Renewal Community.

(ii) *Community-based organizations.* For purposes of the course of action, "community-based organizations" includes for-profit and non-profit private entities, businesses and business organizations, neighborhood organizations, and community groups. Community-based organizations are not required to be located in the nominated area as long as they commit to achieving the goals of the course of action in the Renewal Community.

(iii) *Timetable.* The course of action must include a timetable that identifies the significant steps and target dates for implementing the goals and actions.

(iv) *Performance measures.* The course of action must include a description of how the performance of the course of action will be measured and evaluated.

(v) *Required goals and actions.* The course of action must include at least four of the following:

(A) A reduction of tax rates or fees applying within the Renewal Community;

(B) An increase in the level of efficiency of local services within the Renewal Community, such as services for residents funded through the Federal Temporary Assistance for Needy Families program and related Federal programs including, for example, job support services, child care and after school care for children of working residents, employment training, transportation services and other services that help residents become economically self-sufficient;

(C) Crime reduction strategies, such as crime prevention, including the provision of crime prevention services by nongovernmental entities;

(D) Actions to reduce, remove, simplify, or streamline governmental requirements applying within the Renewal Community, such as:

(*1*) *Density bonus.* Permission to develop or redevelop real property at a higher density level than otherwise permitted under the zoning ordinance, e.g., increased height or increased number of residential or business units;

(*2*) *Incentive zoning.* Providing a density bonus or other real property-related incentive for the development, redevelopment, or preservation of a parcel in the designated area;

(*3*) *Comprehensive or one-stop permit.* Streamlining construction or other development permitting processes, rather than requiring multiple applications for multiple permits, e.g., for demolition, site preparation, and construction, the developer or redeveloper submits a single application that is circulated for the necessary reviews by the various planning, engineering, and other departments in the county or municipality;

(*4*) *Variance and exception policies.* Counties or municipalities may pass ordinancesthat permit variances to or exceptions from certain zoning or other land use limitations. Examples include a reduced building set-back requirement or a reduced requirement for the provision of parking. Thepolicy may be limited to a particular geographic area;

(*5*) *Voluntary environmental compliance program.* A shared or limited environmental liability program, with limited liability from certain legal or administrative action in exchange for undertaking an approved program of environmental investigation, hazard control, and on-going risk reduction activities. Typically, the liability limitation is for future environmental cleanup (and not against lawsuit for damages). Risk of cleanup may be shared by the developer or property owner and the government;

(E) Involvement in economic development activities by private entities, organizations, neighborhood organizations, and community groups, particularly those in the Renewal Community, including a commitment from such private entities to provide jobs and job training for, and technical, financial, or other assistance to, employers, employees, and residents from the Renewal Community;

(F) The gift or sale at below fair market value of surplus real property held by State or local governments, such as land, homes, and commercial or industrial structures in the Renewal Community to neighborhood organizations, community development corporations, or private companies.

(3) *Certification requirement for crime incidence.* If preference points are being sought for the nominated area because it qualifies for preference points in accordance with § 599.303(c)(1), the course of action must contain a certification by each nominating State and local government of the 1999 Local Crime Index rate per 100,000 inhabitants (LCI) determined for the nominated area. The offenses used in determining the LCI are the violent crimes of murder and nonnegligent manslaughter, forcible rape, robbery, and aggravated assault, and the property crimes of burglary, larceny-theft, and motor vehicle theft.

(b) *Economic growth promotion requirements*—(1) *Required certification.* The State and local governments in which a nominated area is located must certify in writing that they have repealed or reduced, will not enforce, or will reduce within the nominated area at least four of the following:

(i) Licensing requirements for occupations that do not ordinarily require a professional degree;

(ii) Zoning restrictions on home-based businesses which do not create a public nuisance;

(iii) Permit requirements for street vendors who do not create a public nuisance;

(iv) Zoning or other restrictions that impede the formation of schools or child care centers; and

(v) Franchises or other restrictions on competition for businesses providing public services, including taxicabs, jitneys, cable television, or trash hauling.

(2) *Exception.* The requirements of paragraph (b)(1) of this section do not apply to the extent that a regulation of businesses and occupations is necessary for and well-tailored to the protection of health and safety. The certifications required under paragraph (b)(1) of this section may be limited to exclude or include specific businesses and occupations.

(c) *Recognition of past efforts.* The course of action and economic growth requirements under paragraphs (a) and (b), respectively, of this section are not limited to future goals and actions. Past efforts within the previous eight years, either completed or on-going, of the nominating State or local governments to undertake any of the goals or actions listed in paragraph (a)(2)(v) or (b)(1) of this section qualify to meet these requirements. If past efforts are used, the nominating governments must identify which of the required goals and actions listed in paragraph (a)(2)(v) or (b)(1) of this section they address; the timetable for their continued implementation, if on-going; and the community-based organizations involved, if any.

[66 FR 35855, July 9, 2001, as amended at 66 FR 52675, Oct. 17, 2001]

Subpart C—Procedures for Nomination of Renewal Communities

§ 599.201 Initiation of application process.

(a) *Federal Register notice.* To initiate the nomination process for Renewal Communities, HUD will publish a notice inviting applications for the designation of Renewal Communities in the FEDERAL REGISTER.

(b) *Contents.* The notice inviting applications will include specific information as to due dates and submission requirements.

§ 599.203 Basic application submission requirements.

The basic application submission requirements for nominating an area as a Renewal Community are:

(a) *Identification of the nominated area.* An application must identify the census tracts that constitute the nominated area. The nominated area must meet all of the eligibility requirements of subpart B of this part.

(b) *State and local commitments.* An application must include the documents evidencing compliance with State and local commitments required by § 599.107.

(c) *Public notice certification.* An application must include a certification, signed by a responsible official or employee of each nominating State and local government, that the public was provided notice of, and an opportunity to participate in, the application development process. Notice and opportunity to participate may include procedures such as placing announcements in newspapers or other media, holding public meetings, and soliciting comments.

Subpart D—Evaluation of Applications Nominating Renewal Communities

§ 599.301 Initial determination of threshold requirements.

(a) *Two threshold requirements.* Before rating and ranking an application, HUD will review it to determine if the application meets both of the following thresholds:

(1) *Eligibility of the nominated area.* This threshold is met if HUD determines that the nominated area as identified in the application meets all of the area eligibility requirements of subpart B of this part.

(2) *Adequacy of State and local commitments.* This threshold is met if HUD determines that the documents in the application evidencing compliance with the required State and local commitments meet all of the course of action and economic growth promotion requirements of § 599.107.

(b) *Failure to meet threshold requirements*—(1) *No rating or ranking.* An application that does not meet both of the threshold requirements by the application due date specified in the published notice inviting applications will not be rated or ranked for further Renewal Community consideration.

(2) *Opportunity to correct failure.* HUD will notify an applicant of the threshold deficiencies in its application. An applicant may submit additional information and take any other action required to correct the deficiencies and meet the threshold requirements until the due date for applications specified in the published notice inviting applications.

§ 599.303 Rating of applications.

(a) *In general.* Each application that qualifies by meeting the threshold requirements will receive a score based on its ranking, as described in paragraph (b) of this section, plus any preference points, as described in paragraph (c) of this section.

(b) *Ranking score.* Each nominated area meeting the minimum thresholds will be ranked from highest to lowest according to the area poverty rate, area unemployment rate, and for urban areas, the percentage of families below 80 percent of area median income. Urban nominated areas will be ranked separately from rural nominated areas. The percentile rank will be determined by dividing these rankings by the total number of nominated areas ranked and multiplying the result by 100. The average ranking will be determined by computing the simple average of the percentile ranks for each nominated area. To create a 100 point scale, the average rankings will be subtracted from 100.

(c) *Preference points*—(1) *Incidence of crime.* A nominated area may receive a maximum of 1, 2, or 4 crime incidence preference points as follows:

(i) *Number of points awarded.* A nominated area will receive 1 additional point if its 1999 Local Crime Index (LCI), as determined on the basis of data from each State and local law enforcement authority with jurisdiction in the nominated area, does not exceed by more than 25% the nation-wide 1999 Crime Index rate per 100,000 inhabitants (CI) prepared as part of the FBI's Uniform Crime Reporting (UCR) Program. A preference of 2 points will be added to the score of a nominated area with an LCI that does not exceed the CI by more than 10 percent. A nominated area that has an LCI that is less than the CI will receive 4 preference points.

(ii) *Qualifying for preference points.* To qualify for preference points based on the incidence of crime, the nominating governments must determine and then certify to the LCI determined for the nominated area, in accordance with § 599.107(a)(3)

(2) *Preference points for certain census tracts.* A nominated area will receive one preference point if any of its census tracts is a census tract identified in GAO Report RCED–98–158R, dated May 12, 1998. (The GAO Report is available from U.S. General Accounting Office, P.O. Box 37050, Washington, DC 20013 or *http://www.gao.gov.*)

Subpart E—Selection of Nominated Areas To Be Renewal Communities

§ 599.401 Ranking of applications.

(a) *Ranking order.* Rural and urban applications will be ranked according to their final scores as determined in accordance with § 599.303, with the highest scoring applications ranked first.

(b) *Separate ranking categories.* After initial ranking, both rural and urban applications will be separated into two ranking categories:

(1) *Category 1.* Applications for designation of nominated areas that are Enterprise Communities or Empowerment Zones will be placed into Category 1 in rank order.

(2) *Category 2.* Applications for designation of nominated areas that are not placed into or selected from Category 1 will be placed into Category 2 in rank order.

§ 599.403 Number of Renewal Communities to be designated.

(a) *In general.* Except as provided in paragraph (b) of this section, the total number of Renewal Communities to be designated and the distribution of designations between urban and rural areas are as follows:

(1) *Total number.* The total number of nominated areas to be selected for designation as Renewal Communities is 40.

(2) *Rural areas.* HUD will select at least 12 rural areas for designation as Renewal Communities. If HUD does not receive at least 12 eligible rural area applications for Renewal Community designation, the number of rural area designations will be the number of eligible rural area applications received by HUD.

(3) *Urban areas.* The number of urban areas selected for designation as Renewal Communities will be the number remaining after subtracting the number of rural areas selected from 40.

(b) *Less than 40 eligible applications.* If HUD receives fewer than 40 eligible applications nominating areas, the total number of nominated areas to be selected for designation as Renewal Communities will be the total number of eligible applications.

§ 599.405 Selection of Renewal Communities.

(a) *Selection of Category 1 applications*—(1) *Six or less rural nominations.* If there are six or fewer Category 1 rural area nominations, HUD will select all of the nominated rural areas in Category 1 for designation as Renewal Communities. HUD will then select the highest ranking Category 1 urban area nominations, but will not exceed a total of 20 Category 1 designations.

(2) *More than six rural nominations.* If there are more than six Category 1 rural area nominations, HUD will select the six highest ranked Category 1 rural applications, and will then select, in rank order, the highest ranking Category 1 area nominations, whether urban or rural, until not more than a total of 20 Category 1 designations is made.

(b) *Selection of Category 2 applications.* After not more than 20 Category 1 designations are made in accordance with paragraph (a) of this section, any remaining Category 1 applications will be placed back in rank order into Category 2, with selections for a combined Category 1 and Category 2 total of not more than 40 designations made as follows:

(1) *Less than six Category 1 rural applications.* If the number of rural area applications selected in Category 1 is less than six, HUD will select the highest ranking rural area applications in Category 2 until the total number of rural areas selected is 12. The remaining designations will be made from both rural

and urban areas in rank order. If there are fewer than 12 eligible rural applications overall, counting both Category 1 and Category 2, all of the eligible rural applications will be selected.

(2) *Six or more Category 1 rural applications.* If the number of rural area applications selected in Category 1 is six or more, HUD will select the six highest Category 2 rural applications. The remaining designations will be made from both rural and urban areas in rank order.

(c) *Effective date of designation.* The effective date of designation as a Renewal Community is the date a nominated area is selected in accordance with this section.

§ 599.407 Notification of Renewal Community designations.

(a) *Notification of applicant.* HUD will notify each applicant of the designation of its nominated area as a Renewal Community.

(b) *Federal Register publication.* In addition to any other form of notification, HUD will publish a notice of the designation of Renewal Communities in the FEDERAL REGISTER.

Subpart F—Post-Designation Requirements

§ 599.501 Period for which Renewal Community designation is in effect.

Any designation of an area as a Renewal Community will remain in effect during the period beginning on January 1, 2002, and ending on the earliest of:

(a) December 31, 2009;

(b) The termination date designated by the State and local governments in their nomination application, if any; or

(c) The date HUD revokes the designation.

§ 599.503 Effect of Renewal Community designation on an EZ/EC.

The designation of any area as an Empowerment Zone or Enterprise Community shall cease to be in effect as of the date that the designation of any portion of such area as a Renewal Community takes effect.

§ 599.505 Coordinating responsible authority (CoRA).

Within 30 days of the Renewal Community designation, the State and local governments in which the area is located must submit to HUD information identifying the coordinating responsible authority (CoRA), which is the entity, organization or persons with the responsibility and authority to achieve the State and local government commitments made at the time of application as required by § 599.107 and to undertake the development and administration of policies, procedures and activities to implement and maximize the Federal, State and local benefits made available in the Renewal Community.

§ 599.507 Tax incentives utilization plan.

(a) *Preliminary plan.* Within six months of designation, the CoRA must prepare and submit to HUD a preliminary tax incentives utilization plan for achieving the State and local commitments made at the time of application as required by § 599.107 and implementing and maximizing the Federal, State and local benefits made available in the Renewal Community.

(b) *Final plan.* Within twelve months of designation, the CoRA must prepare and submit to HUD the final tax incentives utilization plan for achieving the State and local commitments made at the time of application as required by § 599.107 and implementing and maximizing the Federal, State and local benefits made available in the Renewal Community.

(c) *Community participation.* The CoRA must ensure that the preliminary and final tax incentives utilizations plans are developed with the participation of the residents and community organizations in the Renewal Community.

(d) *Coordination with Consolidated Plan and Indian Housing Plan.* The tax incentives utilization plan must include a certification that it is consistent with the Consolidated Plan prepared in accordance with 24 CFR part 91 or the Indian Housing Plan prepared in accordance with 24 CFR part 1000, as applicable.

(e) *HUD technical assistance.* HUD will provide technical assistance as authorized to assist the CoRA in preparing the required tax incentives utilization plans.

§ 599.509 Modification of commitments and plans.

The CoRA may submit requests to HUD to modify the State and local commitments made at the time of application as required by § 599.107 and the tax incentives utilization plans required by § 599.505. Requests must provide evidence to support the proposed modifications. HUD will review the proposed modification for consistency with regulatory and statutory requirements and approve, suggest additional or alternate modifications or deny the request within 30 days.

§ 599.511 Reports and other information.

The CoRA and the State or local governments in which the Renewal Community is located must submit such periodic reports and provide such additional information as HUD may require.

§ 599.513 Revocation of designation.

(a) *Basis for revocation.* HUD may revoke the Renewal Community designation of an area if HUD determines that the CoRA or the State or local governments in which the area is located:

(1) Have modified the boundaries of the area; or

(2) Are not complying substantially with, or fail to make progress in achieving the State and local commitments made at the time of application as required by § 599.107.

(b) *Letter of warning.* Before revoking the Renewal Community designation of an area, HUD will issue a letter of warning to the CoRa and the State and local governments in which the area is located, with a copy to all affected Federal agencies of which HUD is aware:

(1) Advising that HUD has determined that the CoRA and/or State and/or local governments in which the area is located have:

(i) Modified the boundaries of the area without written approval from HUD; or

(ii) Are not complying substantially with, or have failed to make progress in achieving the State and local commitments made at the time of application as required by § 599.107; and

(2) Requesting a reply from the CoRa and State and local governments in which the area is located within 90 days of the receipt of this letter of warning.

(c) *Notice of revocation.* To revoke the designation, HUD must issue a final notice of revocation of the designation of the area as a Renewal Community, after allowing 90 days from the date of receipt of the letter of warning for response, and after making a determination in accordance with paragraph (a) of this section.

(d) *Notice to affected Federal agencies.* HUD will notify all affected Federal agencies of which it is aware, of its determination to revoke any designation in accordance with this section.

(e) *Effect of revocation.* Upon revocation of a Renewal Community designation, the designation and applicable benefits cease to be available in the area.

(f) *Publication.* The final notice of revocation of designation will be published in the FEDERAL REGISTER, and the revocation will be effective on the date of publication.

CHAPTER VI—OFFICE OF ASSISTANT SECRETARY FOR COMMUNITY PLANNING AND DEVELOPMENT, DEPARTMENT OF HOUSING AND URBAN DEVELOPMENT [RESERVED]

PARTS 600–699 [RESERVED]

FINDING AIDS

A list of CFR titles, subtitles, chapters, subchapters and parts and an alphabetical list of agencies publishing in the CFR are included in the CFR Index and Finding Aids volume to the Code of Federal Regulations which is published separately and revised annually.

Table of CFR Titles and Chapters

(Revised as of April 1, 2025)

Title 1—General Provisions

Title 2—Federal Financial Assistance

Chap.	
XXIV	Department of Housing and Urban Development (Parts 2400—2499)
XXV	National Science Foundation (Parts 2500—2599)
XXVI	National Archives and Records Administration (Parts 2600—2699)
XXVII	Small Business Administration (Parts 2700—2799)
XXVIII	Department of Justice (Parts 2800—2899)
XXIX	Department of Labor (Parts 2900—2999)
XXX	Department of Homeland Security (Parts 3000—3099)
XXXI	Institute of Museum and Library Services (Parts 3100—3199)
XXXII	National Endowment for the Arts (Parts 3200—3299)
XXXIII	National Endowment for the Humanities (Parts 3300—3399)
XXXIV	Department of Education (Parts 3400—3499)
XXXV	Export-Import Bank of the United States (Parts 3500—3599)
XXXVI	Office of National Drug Control Policy, Executive Office of the President (Parts 3600—3699)
XXXVII	Peace Corps (Parts 3700—3799)
LVIII	Election Assistance Commission (Parts 5800—5899)
LIX	Gulf Coast Ecosystem Restoration Council (Parts 5900—5999)
LX	Federal Communications Commission (Parts 6000—6099)

Title 3—The President

I	Executive Office of the President (Parts 100—199)

Title 4—Accounts

I	Government Accountability Office (Parts 1—199)

Title 5—Administrative Personnel

I	Office of Personnel Management (Parts 1—1199)
II	Merit Systems Protection Board (Parts 1200—1299)
III	Office of Management and Budget (Parts 1300—1399)
IV	Office of Personnel Management and Office of the Director of National Intelligence (Parts 1400—1499)
V	The International Organizations Employees Loyalty Board (Parts 1500—1599)
VI	Federal Retirement Thrift Investment Board (Parts 1600—1699)
VIII	Office of Special Counsel (Parts 1800—1899)
IX	Appalachian Regional Commission (Parts 1900—1999)
XI	Armed Forces Retirement Home (Parts 2100—2199)
XIV	Federal Labor Relations Authority, General Counsel of the Federal Labor Relations Authority and Federal Service Impasses Panel (Parts 2400—2499)
XVI	Office of Government Ethics (Parts 2600—2699)
XXI	Department of the Treasury (Parts 3100—3199)
XXII	Federal Deposit Insurance Corporation (Parts 3200—3299)

Chap.	
XXIII	Department of Energy (Parts 3300—3399)
XXIV	Federal Energy Regulatory Commission (Parts 3400—3499)
XXV	Department of the Interior (Parts 3500—3599)
XXVI	Department of Defense (Parts 3600—3699)
XXVIII	Department of Justice (Parts 3800—3899)
XXIX	Federal Communications Commission (Parts 3900—3999)
XXX	Farm Credit System Insurance Corporation (Parts 4000—4099)
XXXI	Farm Credit Administration (Parts 4100—4199)
XXXIII	U.S. International Development Finance Corporation (Parts 4300—4399)
XXXIV	Securities and Exchange Commission (Parts 4400—4499)
XXXV	Office of Personnel Management (Parts 4500—4599)
XXXVI	Department of Homeland Security (Parts 4600—4699)
XXXVII	Federal Election Commission (Parts 4700—4799)
XL	Interstate Commerce Commission (Parts 5000—5099)
XLI	Commodity Futures Trading Commission (Parts 5100—5199)
XLII	Department of Labor (Parts 5200—5299)
XLIII	National Science Foundation (Parts 5300—5399)
XLV	Department of Health and Human Services (Parts 5500—5599)
XLVI	Postal Rate Commission (Parts 5600—5699)
XLVII	Federal Trade Commission (Parts 5700—5799)
XLVIII	Nuclear Regulatory Commission (Parts 5800—5899)
XLIX	Federal Labor Relations Authority (Parts 5900—5999)
L	Department of Transportation (Parts 6000—6099)
LII	Export-Import Bank of the United States (Parts 6200—6299)
LIII	Department of Education (Parts 6300—6399)
LIV	Environmental Protection Agency (Parts 6400—6499)
LV	National Endowment for the Arts (Parts 6500—6599)
LVI	National Endowment for the Humanities (Parts 6600—6699)
LVII	General Services Administration (Parts 6700—6799)
LVIII	Board of Governors of the Federal Reserve System (Parts 6800—6899)
LIX	National Aeronautics and Space Administration (Parts 6900—6999)
LX	United States Postal Service (Parts 7000—7099)
LXI	National Labor Relations Board (Parts 7100—7199)
LXII	Equal Employment Opportunity Commission (Parts 7200—7299)
LXIII	Inter-American Foundation (Parts 7300—7399)
LXIV	Merit Systems Protection Board (Parts 7400—7499)
LXV	Department of Housing and Urban Development (Parts 7500—7599)
LXVI	National Archives and Records Administration (Parts 7600—7699)
LXVII	Institute of Museum and Library Services (Parts 7700—7799)
LXVIII	Commission on Civil Rights (Parts 7800—7899)
LXIX	Tennessee Valley Authority (Parts 7900—7999)

Title 7—Agriculture—Continued

Chap.	
XXXVI	National Agricultural Statistics Service, Department of Agriculture (Parts 3600—3699)
XXXVII	Economic Research Service, Department of Agriculture (Parts 3700—3799)
XXXVIII	World Agricultural Outlook Board, Department of Agriculture (Parts 3800—3899)
XLI	[Reserved]
XLII	Rural Business-Cooperative Service, Department of Agriculture (Parts 4200—4299)
L	Rural Business-Cooperative Service, Rural Housing Service, and Rural Utilities Service, Department of Agriculture (Parts 5000—5099)

Title 8—Aliens and Nationality

I	Department of Homeland Security (Parts 1—499)
V	Executive Office for Immigration Review, Department of Justice (Parts 1000—1399)

Title 9—Animals and Animal Products

I	Animal and Plant Health Inspection Service, Department of Agriculture (Parts 1—199)
II	Agricultural Marketing Service (Fair Trade Practices Program), Department of Agriculture (Parts 200—299)
III	Food Safety and Inspection Service, Department of Agriculture (Parts 300—599)

Title 10—Energy

I	Nuclear Regulatory Commission (Parts 0—199)
II	Department of Energy (Parts 200—699)
III	Department of Energy (Parts 700—999)
X	Department of Energy (General Provisions) (Parts 1000—1099)
XIII	Nuclear Waste Technical Review Board (Parts 1300—1399)
XVII	Defense Nuclear Facilities Safety Board (Parts 1700—1799)
XVIII	Northeast Interstate Low-Level Radioactive Waste Commission (Parts 1800—1899)

Title 11—Federal Elections

I	Federal Election Commission (Parts 1—9099)
II	Election Assistance Commission (Parts 9400—9499)

Title 12—Banks and Banking

I	Comptroller of the Currency, Department of the Treasury (Parts 1—199)
II	Federal Reserve System (Parts 200—299)

Title 12—Banks and Banking—Continued

Title 13—Business Credit and Assistance

Title 14—Aeronautics and Space

Title 15—Commerce and Foreign Trade

Title 15—Commerce and Foreign Trade—Continued

Title 16—Commercial Practices

Title 17—Commodity and Securities Exchanges

Title 18—Conservation of Power and Water Resources

Title 19—Customs Duties

Chap.

I U.S. Customs and Border Protection, Department of Homeland Security; Department of the Treasury (Parts 0—199)

II United States International Trade Commission (Parts 200—299)

III International Trade Administration, Department of Commerce (Parts 300—399)

IV U.S. Immigration and Customs Enforcement, Department of Homeland Security (Parts 400—599) [Reserved]

Title 20—Employees' Benefits

I Office of Workers' Compensation Programs, Department of Labor (Parts 1—199)

II Railroad Retirement Board (Parts 200—399)

III Social Security Administration (Parts 400—499)

IV Employees' Compensation Appeals Board, Department of Labor (Parts 500—599)

V Employment and Training Administration, Department of Labor (Parts 600—699)

VI Office of Workers' Compensation Programs, Department of Labor (Parts 700—799)

VII Benefits Review Board, Department of Labor (Parts 800—899)

VIII Joint Board for the Enrollment of Actuaries (Parts 900—999)

IX Office of the Assistant Secretary for Veterans' Employment and Training Service, Department of Labor (Parts 1000—1099)

Title 21—Food and Drugs

I Food and Drug Administration, Department of Health and Human Services (Parts 1—1299)

II Drug Enforcement Administration, Department of Justice (Parts 1300—1399)

III Office of National Drug Control Policy (Parts 1400—1499)

Title 22—Foreign Relations

I Department of State (Parts 1—199)

II Agency for International Development (Parts 200—299)

III Peace Corps (Parts 300—399)

IV International Joint Commission, United States and Canada (Parts 400—499)

V United States Agency for Global Media (Parts 500—599)

VII U.S. International Development Finance Corporation (Parts 700—799)

IX Foreign Service Grievance Board (Parts 900—999)

X Inter-American Foundation (Parts 1000—1099)

XI International Boundary and Water Commission, United States and Mexico, United States Section (Parts 1100—1199)

Title 22—Foreign Relations—Continued

Title 23—Highways

Title 24—Housing and Urban Development

Title 25—Indians

Title 26—Internal Revenue

Title 27—Alcohol, Tobacco Products and Firearms

Chap.

II Bureau of Alcohol, Tobacco, Firearms, and Explosives, Department of Justice (Parts 400—799)

Title 28—Judicial Administration

I Department of Justice (Parts 0—299)

III Federal Prison Industries, Inc., Department of Justice (Parts 300—399)

V Bureau of Prisons, Department of Justice (Parts 500—599)

VI Offices of Independent Counsel, Department of Justice (Parts 600—699)

VII Office of Independent Counsel (Parts 700—799)

VIII Court Services and Offender Supervision Agency for the District of Columbia (Parts 800—899)

IX National Crime Prevention and Privacy Compact Council (Parts 900—999)

XI Department of Justice and Department of State (Parts 1100—1199)

Title 29—Labor

SUBTITLE A—OFFICE OF THE SECRETARY OF LABOR (PARTS 0—99)

SUBTITLE B—REGULATIONS RELATING TO LABOR

I National Labor Relations Board (Parts 100—199)

II Office of Labor-Management Standards, Department of Labor (Parts 200—299)

III National Railroad Adjustment Board (Parts 300—399)

IV Office of Labor-Management Standards, Department of Labor (Parts 400—499)

V Wage and Hour Division, Department of Labor (Parts 500—899)

IX Construction Industry Collective Bargaining Commission (Parts 900—999)

X National Mediation Board (Parts 1200—1299)

XII Federal Mediation and Conciliation Service (Parts 1400—1499)

XIV Equal Employment Opportunity Commission (Parts 1600—1699)

XVII Occupational Safety and Health Administration, Department of Labor (Parts 1900—1999)

XX Occupational Safety and Health Review Commission (Parts 2200—2499)

XXV Employee Benefits Security Administration, Department of Labor (Parts 2500—2599)

XXVII Federal Mine Safety and Health Review Commission (Parts 2700—2799)

XL Pension Benefit Guaranty Corporation (Parts 4000—4999)

Title 30—Mineral Resources

Title 31—Money and Finance: Treasury

Title 32—National Defense

Title 32—National Defense—Continued

Chap.

XX Information Security Oversight Office, National Archives and Records Administration (Parts 2000—2099)

XXI National Security Council (Parts 2100—2199)

XXIV Office of Science and Technology Policy (Parts 2400—2499)

XXVII Office for Micronesian Status Negotiations (Parts 2700—2799)

XXVIII Office of the Vice President of the United States (Parts 2800—2899)

Title 33—Navigation and Navigable Waters

I Coast Guard, Department of Homeland Security (Parts 1—199)

II Corps of Engineers, Department of the Army, Department of Defense (Parts 200—399)

IV Great Lakes St. Lawrence Seaway Development Corporation, Department of Transportation (Parts 400—499)

Title 34—Education

SUBTITLE A—OFFICE OF THE SECRETARY, DEPARTMENT OF EDUCATION (PARTS 1—99)

SUBTITLE B—REGULATIONS OF THE OFFICES OF THE DEPARTMENT OF EDUCATION

I Office for Civil Rights, Department of Education (Parts 100—199)

II Office of Elementary and Secondary Education, Department of Education (Parts 200—299)

III Office of Special Education and Rehabilitative Services, Department of Education (Parts 300—399)

IV Office of Career, Technical, and Adult Education, Department of Education (Parts 400—499)

V Office of Bilingual Education and Minority [Reserved]

VI Office of Postsecondary Education, Department of Education (Parts 600—699)

VII Office of Educational Research and Improvement, Department of Education (Parts 700—799) [Reserved]

SUBTITLE C—REGULATIONS RELATING TO EDUCATION

XI [Reserved]

XII National Council on Disability (Parts 1200—1299)

Title 35 [Reserved]

Title 36—Parks, Forests, and Public Property

I National Park Service, Department of the Interior (Parts 1—199)

II Forest Service, Department of Agriculture (Parts 200—299)

III Corps of Engineers, Department of the Army (Parts 300—399)

IV American Battle Monuments Commission (Parts 400—499)

V Smithsonian Institution (Parts 500—599)

VI [Reserved]

Title 36—Parks, Forests, and Public Property—Continued

Chap.

Chap.	
VII	Library of Congress (Parts 700—799)
VIII	Advisory Council on Historic Preservation (Parts 800—899)
IX	Pennsylvania Avenue Development Corporation (Parts 900—999)
X	Presidio Trust (Parts 1000—1099)
XI	Architectural and Transportation Barriers Compliance Board (Parts 1100—1199)
XII	National Archives and Records Administration (Parts 1200—1299)
XV	Oklahoma City National Memorial Trust (Parts 1500—1599)
XVI	Morris K. Udall Scholarship and Excellence in National Environmental Policy Foundation (Parts 1600—1699)

Title 37—Patents, Trademarks, and Copyrights

I	United States Patent and Trademark Office, Department of Commerce (Parts 1—199)
II	U.S. Copyright Office, Library of Congress (Parts 200—299)
III	Copyright Royalty Board, Library of Congress (Parts 300—399)
IV	National Institute of Standards and Technology, Department of Commerce (Parts 400—599)

Title 38—Pensions, Bonuses, and Veterans' Relief

I	Department of Veterans Affairs (Parts 0—199)
II	Armed Forces Retirement Home (Parts 200—299)

Title 39—Postal Service

I	United States Postal Service (Parts 1—999)
III	Postal Regulatory Commission (Parts 3000—3099)

Title 40—Protection of Environment

I	Environmental Protection Agency (Parts 1—1099)
IV	Environmental Protection Agency and Department of Justice (Parts 1400—1499)
V	Council on Environmental Quality (Parts 1500—1599)
VI	Chemical Safety and Hazard Investigation Board (Parts 1600—1699)
VII	Environmental Protection Agency and Department of Defense; Uniform National Discharge Standards for Vessels of the Armed Forces (Parts 1700—1799)
VIII	Gulf Coast Ecosystem Restoration Council (Parts 1800—1899)
IX	Federal Permitting Improvement Steering Council (Part 1900)

Title 41—Public Contracts and Property Management

SUBTITLE A—FEDERAL PROCUREMENT REGULATIONS SYSTEM [NOTE]

Title 42—Public Health

Title 43—Public Lands: Interior

Chap.

Title 43—Public Lands: Interior—Continued

SUBTITLE B—REGULATIONS RELATING TO PUBLIC LANDS

I Bureau of Reclamation, Department of the Interior (Parts 400—999)

II Bureau of Land Management, Department of the Interior (Parts 1000—9999)

III Utah Reclamation Mitigation and Conservation Commission (Parts 10000—10099)

Title 44—Emergency Management and Assistance

I Federal Emergency Management Agency, Department of Homeland Security (Parts 0—399)

IV Department of Commerce and Department of Transportation (Parts 400—499)

Title 45—Public Welfare

SUBTITLE A—DEPARTMENT OF HEALTH AND HUMAN SERVICES (PARTS 1—199)

SUBTITLE B—REGULATIONS RELATING TO PUBLIC WELFARE

II Office of Family Assistance (Assistance Programs), Administration for Children and Families, Department of Health and Human Services (Parts 200—299)

III Office of Child Support Services, Administration of Families and Services, Department of Health and Human Services (Parts 300—399)

IV Office of Refugee Resettlement, Administration for Children and Families, Department of Health and Human Services (Parts 400—499)

V Foreign Claims Settlement Commission of the United States, Department of Justice (Parts 500—599)

VI National Science Foundation (Parts 600—699)

VII Commission on Civil Rights (Parts 700—799)

VIII Office of Personnel Management (Parts 800—899)

IX Denali Commission (Parts 900—999)

X Office of Community Services, Administration for Children and Families, Department of Health and Human Services (Parts 1000—1099)

XI National Foundation on the Arts and the Humanities (Parts 1100—1199)

XII Corporation for National and Community Service (Parts 1200—1299)

XIII Administration for Children and Families, Department of Health and Human Services (Parts 1300—1399)

XVI Legal Services Corporation (Parts 1600—1699)

XVII National Commission on Libraries and Information Science (Parts 1700—1799)

XVIII Harry S. Truman Scholarship Foundation (Parts 1800—1899)

XXI Commission of Fine Arts (Parts 2100—2199)

Title 45—Public Welfare—Continued

Chap.	
XXIII	Arctic Research Commission (Parts 2300—2399)
XXIV	James Madison Memorial Fellowship Foundation (Parts 2400—2499)
XXV	Corporation for National and Community Service (Parts 2500—2599)

Title 46—Shipping

I	Coast Guard, Department of Homeland Security (Parts 1—199)
II	Maritime Administration, Department of Transportation (Parts 200—399)
III	Coast Guard (Great Lakes Pilotage), Department of Homeland Security (Parts 400—499)
IV	Federal Maritime Commission (Parts 500—599)

Title 47—Telecommunication

I	Federal Communications Commission (Parts 0—199)
II	Office of Science and Technology Policy and National Security Council (Parts 200—299)
III	National Telecommunications and Information Administration, Department of Commerce (Parts 300—399)
IV	National Telecommunications and Information Administration, Department of Commerce, and National Highway Traffic Safety Administration, Department of Transportation (Parts 400—499)
V	The First Responder Network Authority (Parts 500—599)

Title 48—Federal Acquisition Regulations System

1	Federal Acquisition Regulation (Parts 1—99)
2	Defense Acquisition Regulations System, Department of Defense (Parts 200—299)
3	Health and Human Services (Parts 300—399)
4	Department of Agriculture (Parts 400—499)
5	General Services Administration (Parts 500—599)
6	Department of State (Parts 600—699)
7	Agency for International Development (Parts 700—799)
8	Department of Veterans Affairs (Parts 800—899)
9	Department of Energy (Parts 900—999)
10	Department of the Treasury (Parts 1000—1099)
12	Department of Transportation (Parts 1200—1299)
13	Department of Commerce (Parts 1300—1399)
14	Department of the Interior (Parts 1400—1499)
15	Environmental Protection Agency (Parts 1500—1599)
16	Office of Personnel Management, Federal Employees Health Benefits Acquisition Regulation (Parts 1600—1699)
17	Office of Personnel Management (Parts 1700—1799)

Chap.

18 National Aeronautics and Space Administration (Parts 1800—1899)

19 Broadcasting Board of Governors (Parts 1900—1999)

20 Nuclear Regulatory Commission (Parts 2000—2099)

21 Office of Personnel Management, Federal Employees Group Life Insurance Federal Acquisition Regulation (Parts 2100—2199)

23 Social Security Administration (Parts 2300—2399)

24 Department of Housing and Urban Development (Parts 2400—2499)

25 National Science Foundation (Parts 2500—2599)

28 Department of Justice (Parts 2800—2899)

29 Department of Labor (Parts 2900—2999)

30 Department of Homeland Security, Homeland Security Acquisition Regulation (HSAR) (Parts 3000—3099)

34 Department of Education Acquisition Regulation (Parts 3400—3499)

51 Department of the Army Acquisition Regulations (Parts 5100—5199) [Reserved]

52 Department of the Navy Acquisition Regulations (Parts 5200—5299)

53 Department of the Air Force Federal Acquisition Regulation Supplement (Parts 5300—5399) [Reserved]

54 Defense Logistics Agency, Department of Defense (Parts 5400—5499)

57 African Development Foundation (Parts 5700—5799)

61 Civilian Board of Contract Appeals, General Services Administration (Parts 6100—6199)

99 Cost Accounting Standards Board, Office of Federal Procurement Policy, Office of Management and Budget (Parts 9900—9999)

Title 49—Transportation

SUBTITLE A—OFFICE OF THE SECRETARY OF TRANSPORTATION (PARTS 1—99)

SUBTITLE B—OTHER REGULATIONS RELATING TO TRANSPORTATION

I Pipeline and Hazardous Materials Safety Administration, Department of Transportation (Parts 100—199)

II Federal Railroad Administration, Department of Transportation (Parts 200—299)

III Federal Motor Carrier Safety Administration, Department of Transportation (Parts 300—399)

IV Coast Guard, Department of Homeland Security (Parts 400—499)

V National Highway Traffic Safety Administration, Department of Transportation (Parts 500—599)

VI Federal Transit Administration, Department of Transportation (Parts 600—699)

VII National Railroad Passenger Corporation (AMTRAK) (Parts 700—799)

Title 49—Transportation—Continued

Chap.	
VIII	National Transportation Safety Board (Parts 800—999)
X	Surface Transportation Board (Parts 1000—1399)
XI	Research and Innovative Technology Administration, Department of Transportation (Parts 1400—1499) [Reserved]
XII	Transportation Security Administration, Department of Homeland Security (Parts 1500—1699)

Title 50—Wildlife and Fisheries

I	United States Fish and Wildlife Service, Department of the Interior (Parts 1—199)
II	National Marine Fisheries Service, National Oceanic and Atmospheric Administration, Department of Commerce (Parts 200—299)
III	International Fishing and Related Activities (Parts 300—399)
IV	Joint Regulations (United States Fish and Wildlife Service, Department of the Interior and National Marine Fisheries Service, National Oceanic and Atmospheric Administration, Department of Commerce); Endangered Species Committee Regulations (Parts 400—499)
V	Marine Mammal Commission (Parts 500—599)
VI	Fishery Conservation and Management, National Oceanic and Atmospheric Administration, Department of Commerce (Parts 600—699)

Alphabetical List of Agencies Appearing in the CFR

(Revised as of April 1, 2025)

Agency	CFR Title, Subtitle or Chapter
Administrative Conference of the United States	1, III
Advisory Council on Historic Preservation	36, VIII
Advocacy and Outreach, Office of	7, XXV
Afghanistan Reconstruction, Special Inspector General for	5, LXXXIII
African Development Foundation	22, XV
Federal Acquisition Regulation	48, 57
Agency for International Development	2, VII; 22, II
Federal Acquisition Regulation	48, 7
Agricultural Marketing Service	7, I, VIII, IX, X, XI; 9, II
Agricultural Research Service	7, V
Agriculture, Department of	2, IV; 5, LXXIII
Advocacy and Outreach, Office of	7, XXV
Agricultural Marketing Service	7, I, VIII, IX, X, XI; 9, II
Agricultural Research Service	7, V
Animal and Plant Health Inspection Service	7, III; 9, I
Chief Financial Officer, Office of	7, XXX
Commodity Credit Corporation	7, XIV
Economic Research Service	7, XXXVII
Energy and Environmental Policy, Office of	7, XXI
Energy Policy and New Uses, Office of	2, IX; 7, XXIX
Environmental Quality, Office of	7, XXXI
Farm Service Agency	7, VII, XVIII
Federal Acquisition Regulation	48, 4
Federal Crop Insurance Corporation	7, IV
Food and Nutrition Service	7, II
Food Safety and Inspection Service	9, III
Foreign Agricultural Service	7, XV
Forest Service	36, II
Information Resources Management, Office of	7, XXVII
Inspector General, Office of	7, XXVI
National Agricultural Library	7, XLI
National Agricultural Statistics Service	7, XXXVI
National Institute of Food and Agriculture	7, XXXIV
Natural Resources Conservation Service	7, VI
Operations, Office of	7, XXVIII
Procurement and Property Management, Office of	7, XXXII
Rural Business-Cooperative Service	7, XVIII, XLII
Rural Development Administration	7, XLII
Rural Housing Service	7, XVIII, XXXV
Rural Utilities Service	7, XVII, XVIII, XLII
Secretary of Agriculture, Office of	7, Subtitle A
Transportation, Office of	7, XXXIII
World Agricultural Outlook Board	7, XXXVIII
Air Force, Department of	32, VII
Federal Acquisition Regulation Supplement	48, 53
Air Transportation Stabilization Board	14, VI
Alcohol and Tobacco Tax and Trade Bureau	27, I
Alcohol, Tobacco, Firearms, and Explosives, Bureau of	27, II
AMTRAK	49, VII
American Battle Monuments Commission	36, IV
American Indians, Office of the Special Trustee	25, VII
Animal and Plant Health Inspection Service	7, III; 9, I
Appalachian Regional Commission	5, IX

Agency	CFR Title, Subtitle or Chapter
Architectural and Transportation Barriers Compliance Board	36, XI
Arctic Research Commission	45, XXIII
Armed Forces Retirement Home	5, XI; 38, II
Army, Department of	32, V
Engineers, Corps of	33, II; 36, III
Federal Acquisition Regulation	48, 51
Benefits Review Board	20, VII
Bilingual Education and Minority Languages Affairs, Office of	34, V
Blind or Severely Disabled, Committee for Purchase from People Who Are	41, 51
Broadcasting Board of Governors	
Federal Acquisition Regulation	48, 19
Career, Technical, and Adult Education, Office of	34, IV
Census Bureau	15, I
Centers for Medicare & Medicaid Services	42, IV
Central Intelligence Agency	32, XIX
Chemical Safety and Hazard Investigation Board	40, VI
Chief Financial Officer, Office of	7, XXX
Child Support Services, Office of	45, III
Children and Families, Administration for	45, II, IV, X, XIII
Civil Rights, Commission on	5, LXVIII; 45, VII
Civil Rights, Office for	34, I
Coast Guard	33, I; 46, I; 49, IV
Coast Guard (Great Lakes Pilotage)	46, III
Commerce, Department of	2, XIII; 44, IV; 50, VI
Census Bureau	15, I
Economic Affairs, Office of the Under-Secretary for	15, XV
Economic Analysis, Bureau of	15, VIII
Economic Development Administration	13, III
Emergency Management and Assistance	44, IV
Federal Acquisition Regulation	48, 13
Foreign-Trade Zones Board	15, IV
Industry and Security, Bureau of	15, VII
International Trade Administration	15, III; 19, III
National Institute of Standards and Technology	15, II; 37, IV
National Marine Fisheries Service	50, II, IV
National Oceanic and Atmospheric Administration	15, IX; 50, II, III, IV, VI
National Technical Information Service	15, XI
National Telecommunications and Information Administration	15, XXIII; 47, III, IV
National Weather Service	15, IX
Patent and Trademark Office, United States	37, I
Secretary of Commerce, Office of	15, Subtitle A
Commercial Space Transportation	14, III
Commodity Credit Corporation	7, XIV
Commodity Futures Trading Commission	5, XLI; 17, I
Community Planning and Development, Office of Assistant Secretary for	24, V, VI
Community Services, Office of	45, X
Comptroller of the Currency	12, I
Construction Industry Collective Bargaining Commission	29, IX
Consumer Financial Protection Bureau	5, LXXXIV; 12, X
Consumer Product Safety Commission	5, LXXI; 16, II
Copyright Royalty Board	37, III
Corporation for National and Community Service	2, XXII; 45, XII, XXV
Cost Accounting Standards Board	48, 99
Council on Environmental Quality	40, V
Council of the Inspectors General on Integrity and Efficiency	5, XCVIII
Court Services and Offender Supervision Agency for the District of Columbia	5, LXX; 28, VIII
Customs and Border Protection	19, I
Defense, Department of	2, XI; 5, XXVI; 32, Subtitle A; 40, VII
Advanced Research Projects Agency	32, I
Air Force Department	32, VII
Army Department	32, V; 33, II; 36, III; 48, 51

Agency	CFR Title, Subtitle or Chapter
Defense Acquisition Regulations System	48, 2
Defense Intelligence Agency	32, I
Defense Logistics Agency	32, I, XII; 48, 54
Engineers, Corps of	33, II; 36, III
National Imagery and Mapping Agency	32, I
Navy, Department of	32, VI; 48, 52
Secretary of Defense, Office of	2, XI; 32, I
Defense Contract Audit Agency	32, I
Defense Intelligence Agency	32, I
Defense Logistics Agency	32, XII; 48, 54
Defense Nuclear Facilities Safety Board	10, XVII
Delaware River Basin Commission	18, III
Denali Commission	45, IX
Disability, National Council on	5, C; 34, XII
District of Columbia, Court Services and Offender Supervision Agency for the	5, LXX; 28, VIII
Drug Enforcement Administration	21, II
East-West Foreign Trade Board	15, XIII
Economic Affairs, Office of the Under-Secretary for	15, XV
Economic Analysis, Bureau of	15, VIII
Economic Development Administration	13, III
Economic Research Service	7, XXXVII
Education, Department of	2, XXXIV; 5, LIII
Bilingual Education and Minority Languages Affairs, Office of	34, V
Career, Technical, and Adult Education, Office of	34, IV
Civil Rights, Office for	34, I
Educational Research and Improvement, Office of	34, VII
Elementary and Secondary Education, Office of	34, II
Federal Acquisition Regulation	48, 34
Postsecondary Education, Office of	34, VI
Secretary of Education, Office of	34, Subtitle A
Special Education and Rehabilitative Services, Office of	34, III
Educational Research and Improvement, Office of	34, VII
Election Assistance Commission	2, LVIII; 11, II
Elementary and Secondary Education, Office of	34, II
Emergency Oil and Gas Guaranteed Loan Board	13, V
Emergency Steel Guarantee Loan Board	13, IV
Employee Benefits Security Administration	29, XXV
Employees' Compensation Appeals Board	20, IV
Employees Loyalty Board	5, V
Employment and Training Administration	20, V
Employment Policy, National Commission for	1, IV
Employment Standards Administration	20, VI
Endangered Species Committee	50, IV
Energy, Department of	2, IX; 5, XXIII; 10, II, III, X
Federal Acquisition Regulation	48, 9
Federal Energy Regulatory Commission	5, XXIV; 18, I
Property Management Regulations	41, 109
Energy, Office of	7, XXIX
Energy and Environmental Policy, Office of	7, XXI
Engineers, Corps of	33, II; 36, III
Engraving and Printing, Bureau of	31, VI
Environmental Protection Agency	2, XV; 5, LIV; 40, I, IV, VII
Federal Acquisition Regulation	48, 15
Property Management Regulations	41, 115
Environmental Quality, Office of	7, XXXI
Equal Employment Opportunity Commission	5, LXII; 29, XIV
Equal Opportunity, Office of Assistant Secretary for	24, I
Executive Office of the President	3, I
Environmental Quality, Council on	40, V
Management and Budget, Office of	2, Subtitle A; 5, III, LXXVII; 14, VI; 48, 99
National Drug Control Policy, Office of	2, XXXVI; 21, III
National Security Council	32, XXI; 47, II

Agency	CFR Title, Subtitle or Chapter
Presidential Documents	3
Science and Technology Policy, Office of	32, XXIV; 47, II
Trade Representative, Office of the United States	15, XX
Export-Import Bank of the United States	2, XXXV; 5, LII; 12, IV
Families and Services, Administration of	45, III
Family Assistance, Office of	45, II
Farm Credit Administration	5, XXXI; 12, VI
Farm Credit System Insurance Corporation	5, XXX; 12, XIV
Farm Service Agency	7, VII, XVIII
Federal Acquisition Regulation	48, 1
Federal Acquisition Security Council	41, 201
Federal Aviation Administration	14, I
Commercial Space Transportation	14, III
Federal Claims Collection Standards	31, IX
Federal Communications Commission	2, LX; 5, XXIX; 47, I
Federal Contract Compliance Programs, Office of	41, 60
Federal Crop Insurance Corporation	7, IV
Federal Deposit Insurance Corporation	5, XXII; 12, III
Federal Election Commission	5, XXXVII; 11, I
Federal Emergency Management Agency	44, I
Federal Employees Group Life Insurance Federal Acquisition Regulation	48, 21
Federal Employees Health Benefits Acquisition Regulation	48, 16
Federal Energy Regulatory Commission	5, XXIV; 18, I
Federal Financial Institutions Examination Council	12, XI
Federal Financing Bank	12, VIII
Federal Highway Administration	23, I, II
Federal Home Loan Mortgage Corporation	1, IV
Federal Housing Enterprise Oversight Office	12, XVII
Federal Housing Finance Agency	5, LXXX; 12, XII
Federal Labor Relations Authority	5, XIV, XLIX; 22, XIV
Federal Law Enforcement Training Center	31, VII
Federal Management Regulation	41, 102
Federal Maritime Commission	46, IV
Federal Mediation and Conciliation Service	5, CIII; 29, XII
Federal Mine Safety and Health Review Commission	5, LXXIV; 29, XXVII
Federal Motor Carrier Safety Administration	49, III
Federal Permitting Improvement Steering Council	40, IX
Federal Prison Industries, Inc.	28, III
Federal Procurement Policy Office	48, 99
Federal Property Management Regulations	41, 101
Federal Railroad Administration	49, II
Federal Register, Administrative Committee of	1, I
Federal Register, Office of	1, II
Federal Reserve System	12, II
Board of Governors	5, LVIII
Federal Retirement Thrift Investment Board	5, VI, LXXVI
Federal Service Impasses Panel	5, XIV
Federal Trade Commission	5, XLVII; 16, I
Federal Transit Administration	49, VI
Federal Travel Regulation System	41, Subtitle F
Financial Crimes Enforcement Network	31, X
Financial Research Office	12, XVI
Financial Stability Oversight Council	12, XIII
Fine Arts, Commission of	45, XXI
Fiscal Service	31, II
Fish and Wildlife Service, United States	50, I, IV
Food and Drug Administration	21, I
Food and Nutrition Service	7, II
Food Safety and Inspection Service	9, III
Foreign Agricultural Service	7, XV
Foreign Assets Control, Office of	31, V
Foreign Claims Settlement Commission of the United States	45, V
Foreign Service Grievance Board	22, IX
Foreign Service Impasse Disputes Panel	22, XIV
Foreign Service Labor Relations Board	22, XIV
Foreign-Trade Zones Board	15, IV

Agency	CFR Title, Subtitle or Chapter
Forest Service	36, II
General Services Administration	5, LVII; 41, 105
Contract Appeals, Board of	48, 61
Federal Acquisition Regulation	48, 5
Federal Management Regulation	41, 102
Federal Property Management Regulations	41, 101
Federal Travel Regulation System	41, Subtitle F
General	41, 300
Payment From a Non-Federal Source for Travel Expenses	41, 304
Payment of Expenses Connected With the Death of Certain Employees	41, 303
Relocation Allowances	41, 302
Temporary Duty (TDY) Travel Allowances	41, 301
Geological Survey	30, IV
Government Accountability Office	4, I
Government Ethics, Office of	5, XVI
Government National Mortgage Association	24, III
Grain Inspection, Packers and Stockyards Administration	7, VIII; 9, II
Great Lakes St. Lawrence Seaway Development Corporation	33, IV
Gulf Coast Ecosystem Restoration Council	2, LIX; 40, VIII
Harry S. Truman Scholarship Foundation	45, XVIII
Health and Human Services, Department of	2, III; 5, XLV; 45, Subtitle A
Centers for Medicare & Medicaid Services	42, IV
Child Support Services, Office of	45, III
Children and Families, Administration for	45, II, IV, X, XIII
Community Services, Office of	45, X
Families and Services, Administration of	45, III
Family Assistance, Office of	45, II
Federal Acquisition Regulation	48, 3
Food and Drug Administration	21, I
Indian Health Service	25, V
Inspector General (Health Care), Office of	42, V
Public Health Service	42, I
Refugee Resettlement, Office of	45, IV
Homeland Security, Department of	2, XXX; 5, XXXVI; 6, I; 8, I
Coast Guard	33, I; 46, I; 49, IV
Coast Guard (Great Lakes Pilotage)	46, III
Customs and Border Protection	19, I
Federal Emergency Management Agency	44, I
Human Resources Management and Labor Relations Systems	5, XCVII
Immigration and Customs Enforcement Bureau	19, IV
Transportation Security Administration	49, XII
HOPE for Homeowners Program, Board of Directors of	24, XXIV
Housing and Urban Development, Department of	2, XXIV; 5, LXV; 24, Subtitle B
Community Planning and Development, Office of Assistant Secretary for	24, V, VI
Equal Opportunity, Office of Assistant Secretary for	24, I
Federal Acquisition Regulation	48, 24
Federal Housing Enterprise Oversight, Office of	12, XVII
Government National Mortgage Association	24, III
Housing—Federal Housing Commissioner, Office of Assistant Secretary for	24, II, VIII, X, XX
Housing, Office of, and Multifamily Housing Assistance Restructuring, Office of	24, IV
Inspector General, Office of	24, XII
Public and Indian Housing, Office of Assistant Secretary for	24, IX
Secretary, Office of	24, Subtitle A, VII
Housing—Federal Housing Commissioner, Office of Assistant Secretary for	24, II, VIII, X, XX
Housing, Office of, and Multifamily Housing Assistance Restructuring, Office of	24, IV
Immigration and Customs Enforcement Bureau	19, IV
Immigration Review, Executive Office for	8, V

Agency	CFR Title, Subtitle or Chapter
Independent Counsel, Office of	28, VII
Independent Counsel, Offices of	28, VI
Indian Affairs, Bureau of	25, I, V
Indian Affairs, Office of the Assistant Secretary	25, VI
Indian Arts and Crafts Board	25, II
Indian Health Service	25, V
Industry and Security, Bureau of	15, VII
Information Resources Management, Office of	7, XXVII
Information Security Oversight Office, National Archives and Records Administration	32, XX
Inspector General	
Agriculture Department	7, XXVI
Health and Human Services Department	42, V
Housing and Urban Development Department	24, XII, XV
Institute of Peace, United States	22, XVII
Intellectual Property Enforcement Coordinator, Office of	5, CIV
Inter-American Foundation	5, LXIII; 22, X
Interior, Department of	2, XIV
American Indians, Office of the Special Trustee	25, VII
Endangered Species Committee	50, IV
Federal Acquisition Regulation	48, 14
Federal Property Management Regulations System	41, 114
Fish and Wildlife Service, United States	50, I, IV
Geological Survey	30, IV
Indian Affairs, Bureau of	25, I, V
Indian Affairs, Office of the Assistant Secretary	25, VI
Indian Arts and Crafts Board	25, II
Land Management, Bureau of	43, II
National Indian Gaming Commission	25, III
National Park Service	36, I
Natural Resource Revenue, Office of	30, XII
Ocean Energy Management, Bureau of	30, V
Reclamation, Bureau of	43, I
Safety and Environmental Enforcement, Bureau of	30, II
Secretary of the Interior, Office of	2, XIV; 43, Subtitle A
Surface Mining Reclamation and Enforcement, Office of	30, VII
Internal Revenue Service	26, I
International Boundary and Water Commission, United States and Mexico, United States Section	22, XI
International Development, United States Agency for	22, II
Federal Acquisition Regulation	48, 7
International Development Cooperation Agency, United States	22, XII
International Development Finance Corporation, U.S.	2, XVI; 5, XXXIII; 22, VII
International Joint Commission, United States and Canada	22, IV
International Organizations Employees Loyalty Board	5, V
International Trade Administration	15, III; 19, III
International Trade Commission, United States	19, II
Interstate Commerce Commission	5, XL
Investment Security, Office of	31, VIII
James Madison Memorial Fellowship Foundation	45, XXIV
Japan–United States Friendship Commission	22, XVI
Joint Board for the Enrollment of Actuaries	20, VIII
Justice, Department of	2, XXVIII; 5, XXVIII; 28, I, XI; 40, IV
Alcohol, Tobacco, Firearms, and Explosives, Bureau of	27, II
Drug Enforcement Administration	21, II
Federal Acquisition Regulation	48, 28
Federal Claims Collection Standards	31, IX
Federal Prison Industries, Inc.	28, III
Foreign Claims Settlement Commission of the United States	45, V
Immigration Review, Executive Office for	8, V
Independent Counsel, Offices of	28, VI
Prisons, Bureau of	28, V
Property Management Regulations	41, 128

Agency	CFR Title, Subtitle or Chapter
Labor, Department of	2, XXIX; 5, XLII
Benefits Review Board	20, VII
Employee Benefits Security Administration	29, XXV
Employees' Compensation Appeals Board	20, IV
Employment and Training Administration	20, V
Federal Acquisition Regulation	48, 29
Federal Contract Compliance Programs, Office of	41, 60
Federal Procurement Regulations System	41, 50
Labor-Management Standards, Office of	29, II, IV
Mine Safety and Health Administration	30, I
Occupational Safety and Health Administration	29, XVII
Public Contracts	41, 50
Secretary of Labor, Office of	29, Subtitle A
Veterans' Employment and Training Service, Office of the Assistant Secretary for	41, 61; 20, IX
Wage and Hour Division	29, V
Workers' Compensation Programs, Office of	20, I, VI
Labor-Management Standards, Office of	29, II, IV
Land Management, Bureau of	43, II
Legal Services Corporation	45, XVI
Libraries and Information Science, National Commission on	45, XVII
Library of Congress	36, VII
Copyright Royalty Board	37, III
U.S. Copyright Office	37, II
Management and Budget, Office of	2, Subpart A; 5, III, LXXVII; 14, VI; 48, 99
Marine Mammal Commission	50, V
Maritime Administration	46, II
Merit Systems Protection Board	5, II, LXIV
Micronesian Status Negotiations, Office for	32, XXVII
Military Compensation and Retirement Modernization Commission	5, XCIX
Millennium Challenge Corporation	22, XIII
Mine Safety and Health Administration	30, I
Minority Business Development Agency	15, XIV
Miscellaneous Agencies	1, IV
Monetary Offices	31, I
Morris K. Udall Scholarship and Excellence in National Environmental Policy Foundation	36, XVI
Museum and Library Services, Institute of	2, XXXI
National Aeronautics and Space Administration	2, XVIII; 5, LIX; 14, V
Federal Acquisition Regulation	48, 18
National Agricultural Library	7, XLI
National Agricultural Statistics Service	7, XXXVI
National and Community Service, Corporation for	2, XXII; 45, XII, XXV
National Archives and Records Administration	2, XXVI; 5, LXVI; 36, XII
Information Security Oversight Office	32, XX
National Capital Planning Commission	1, IV, VI
National Counterintelligence Center	32, XVIII
National Credit Union Administration	5, LXXXVI; 12, VII
National Crime Prevention and Privacy Compact Council	28, IX
National Drug Control Policy, Office of	2, XXXVI; 21, III
National Endowment for the Arts	2, XXXII
National Endowment for the Humanities	2, XXXIII
National Foundation on the Arts and the Humanities	45, XI
National Geospatial-Intelligence Agency	32, I
National Highway Traffic Safety Administration	23, II, III; 47, VI; 49, V
National Imagery and Mapping Agency	32, I
National Indian Gaming Commission	25, III
National Institute of Food and Agriculture	7, XXXIV
National Institute of Standards and Technology	15, II; 37, IV
National Intelligence, Office of Director of	5, IV; 32, XVII
National Labor Relations Board	5, LXI; 29, I
National Marine Fisheries Service	50, II, IV
National Mediation Board	5, CI; 29, X
National Oceanic and Atmospheric Administration	15, IX; 50, II, III, IV, VI

Agency	CFR Title, Subtitle or Chapter
National Park Service	36, I
National Railroad Adjustment Board	29, III
National Railroad Passenger Corporation (AMTRAK)	49, VII
National Science Foundation	2, XXV; 5, XLIII; 45, VI
Federal Acquisition Regulation	48, 25
National Security Council	32, XXI; 47, II
National Technical Information Service	15, XI
National Telecommunications and Information Administration	15, XXIII; 47, III, IV, V
National Transportation Safety Board	49, VIII
Natural Resource Revenue, Office of	30, XII
Natural Resources Conservation Service	7, VI
Navajo and Hopi Indian Relocation, Office of	25, IV
Navy, Department of	32, VI
Federal Acquisition Regulation	48, 52
Neighborhood Reinvestment Corporation	24, XXV
Northeast Interstate Low-Level Radioactive Waste Commission	10, XVIII
Nuclear Regulatory Commission	2, XX; 5, XLVIII; 10, I
Federal Acquisition Regulation	48, 20
Occupational Safety and Health Administration	29, XVII
Occupational Safety and Health Review Commission	29, XX
Ocean Energy Management, Bureau of	30, V
Oklahoma City National Memorial Trust	36, XV
Operations Office	7, XXVIII
Patent and Trademark Office, United States	37, I
Payment From a Non-Federal Source for Travel Expenses	41, 304
Payment of Expenses Connected With the Death of Certain Employees	41, 303
Peace Corps	2, XXXVII; 22, III
Pennsylvania Avenue Development Corporation	36, IX
Pension Benefit Guaranty Corporation	29, XL
Personnel Management, Office of	5, I, IV, XXXV; 45, VIII
Federal Acquisition Regulation	48, 17
Federal Employees Group Life Insurance Federal Acquisition Regulation	48, 21
Federal Employees Health Benefits Acquisition Regulation	48, 16
Human Resources Management and Labor Relations Systems, Department of Homeland Security	5, XCVII
Pipeline and Hazardous Materials Safety Administration	49, I
Postal Regulatory Commission	5, XLVI; 39, III
Postal Service, United States	5, LX; 39, I
Postsecondary Education, Office of	34, VI
President's Commission on White House Fellowships	1, IV
Presidential Documents	3
Presidio Trust	36, X
Prisons, Bureau of	28, V
Privacy and Civil Liberties Oversight Board	6, X
Procurement and Property Management, Office of	7, XXXII
Public and Indian Housing, Office of Assistant Secretary for	24, IX
Public Contracts, Department of Labor	41, 50
Public Health Service	42, I
Railroad Retirement Board	20, II
Reclamation, Bureau of	43, I
Refugee Resettlement, Office of	45, IV
Relocation Allowances	41, 302
Research and Innovative Technology Administration	49, XI
Rural Business-Cooperative Service	7, XVIII, XLII, L
Rural Housing Service	7, XVIII, XXXV, L
Rural Utilities Service	7, XVII, XVIII, XLII, L
Safety and Environmental Enforcement, Bureau of	30, II
Science and Technology Policy, Office of	32, XXIV; 47, II
Secret Service	31, IV
Securities and Exchange Commission	5, XXXIV; 17, II
Selective Service System	32, XVI
Small Business Administration	2, XXVII; 13, I
Smithsonian Institution	36, V

List of CFR Sections Affected

All changes in this volume of the Code of Federal Regulations (CFR) that were made by documents published in the FEDERAL REGISTER since January 1, 2020 are enumerated in the following list. Entries indicate the nature of the changes effected. Page numbers refer to FEDERAL REGISTER pages. The user should consult the entries for chapters, parts and subparts as well as sections for revisions.

For changes to this volume of the CFR prior to this listing, consult the annual edition of the monthly List of CFR Sections Affected (LSA). The LSA is available at *www.govinfo.gov*. For changes to this volume of the CFR prior to 2001, see the "List of CFR Sections Affected, 1949–1963, 1964–1972, 1973–1985, and 1986–2000" published in 11 separate volumes. The "List of CFR Sections Affected 1986–2000" is available at *www.govinfo.gov*.

2020

24 CFR

85 FR Page

Chapter V

570 Notification 52479
570.3 Introductory text revised 47910
570.205 (a)(4)(vii) removed; (a)(4)(viii) redesignated as new (a)(4)(vii) and revised 47910
570.441 (b) introductory text, (2), (3), (c) heading, (1), (d), and (e) revised 47910
570.487 (b) revised 47911
570.487 (d) amended 61567
570.490 (a)(1) and (b) revised 47911
570.506 (g)(1) revised 47911
570.601 (a)(2) revised 47911
570.607 (b) amended 61567
574.530 (b) revised 47911
574.600 Amended 61567
576.407 (a) amended 61568
576.500 (s)(1)(ii) revised 47911
578.99 Heading and (i) amended 61568

2021

24 CFR

86 FR Page

Chapter V

570 Notification 59302
570.487 (b) revised; interim 30792
570.506 (g)(1) revised; interim 30792
570.601 (a)(2) revised; interim 30792
574.530 (b) revised; interim 30792

24 CFR—Continued

86 FR Page

Chapter V—Continued

576.500 (s)(1)(ii) revised; interim 30792

2022

24 CFR

87 FR Page

Chapter V

570 Announcement 53662
570.496 (d)(1)(iii) amended 8197

2023

24 CFR

88 FR Page

Chapter V

570 Notification 73532
570.3 (1)(i) amended; eff. 1-1-24 9665
570.208 (b)(1)(iv) revised 30498
574.310 (d)(1) and (2) revised; (e) redesignated as (g); new (e), (f), and (h) added; eff. 1-1-24 9665
574.310 (b) introductory text and (2) revised; (b)(3) added 30498
576.403 (c) revised 30498
578.75 (b) revised 30499

2024

24 CFR

89 FR Page

Chapter V

570 Notification 78239

24 CFR—Continued

2025

(Regulations published from January 1, 2025, through April 1, 2025)

24 CFR

○

www.ingramcontent.com/pod-product-compliance
Ingram Content Group UK Ltd.
Pitfield, Milton Keynes, MK11 3LW, UK
UKHW020127290926
15471UKWH00003B/341

9 798892 058247

application; it might, for instance, be used to assess the degree of risk of a new disease being successfully introduced into a particular climatic area. This application involves two further assumptions. One is that the agent of disease retains the same environmental requirements in space and time. The question of the acclimatisation of parasites or pests, or their adaption to changed climatic conditions, is controversial (Parry 1979). It is, however, an important consideration; if, for instance, the Japanese beetle adapted itself to conditions radically different from those previously found necessary, it would negate the deductions illustrated in Figure 13.1. The second assumption is that no effective climatic change or sustained fluctuation radically alters the position *vis-à-vis* the pathogen (see p. 273).

13.4 Climate and the diseases of agricultural plants: in particular, potato blight

Practical attempts to use climatology and meteorology in the fight against a number of plant diseases date from the end of the First World War. In the following six decades, considerable progress has been made, which is fully described in a number of review articles (Miller & O'Brien 1952, 1957, Bourke 1955, 1970, World Meteorological Organization 1963, 1969, Krause & Massie 1975, Miller 1967).

Potato blight (*Phytophthora infestans*) has been chosen as a representative example to outline the progress achieved. It is a major plant disease, in the impact of which climate plays a dominant part; indeed, in the 1840s when blight first appeared in Europe, it was almost universally diagnosed as being an effect of the weather alone (Graham 1847). It was not until some 20 years later that the fact that blight was due to a fungus won general acceptance.

The first attempt to define the climatic conditions which favour the blight fungus was carried out in a pioneer investigation in the Netherlands in the years 1919–23 (Bourke 1955). Miss Löhnis tried without success to correlate outbreaks of the disease in those five years with individual weather parameters. Professor van Everdingen (then Director of the Royal Netherlands Meteorological Institute) reworked the same data with various groupings of the weather factors, and concluded that the following four conditions were always met within the two weeks which preceded an outbreak of potato blight:

(a) at least four hours of dew in the course of a night;
(b) minimum temperature not below 10°C during the same night;
(c) mean cloudiness in the following day at least 8/10ths;
(d) a rainfall of not less than 0.1 mm in the 24 hours following the dew night.

These rules, operated with the help of a network of special weather-observing stations located within or very close to the potato fields of the main growing areas, were the foundation on which the pioneer Dutch potato blight warning system operated with some success for 20 years.

Nowadays, the primary defect of van Everdingen's rules would be seen to be a certain cumbrousness arising from their complexity, and the recurrent problem of near misses, in which three of the rules were met while the fourth was narrowly missed. In general, approximate models serve best when they are kept as simple as possible. Again, the use of special weather observations within the growing crop, while often necessary at the research stage, imposes a heavy burden in costs and communications if they are to be continued during the operational stage. Indeed, investigations into the microclimate of potato crops have shown that while in sunny weather there can be wide divergence between conditions in the meteorological instrument screen and those within the growing crop, they approximate closely in the cloudy and moist weather critical for potato blight (Broadbent 1949). Today, almost all practical forecast systems for potato blight and other plant diseases make use of standard meteorological observations.

The first reaction of Beaumont (1940, 1947), who tested van Everdingen's rules in Devonshire for the ten years 1929–38, was to add yet one further requirement in order to ensure that the foliage wetness caused by dew lasted well into the following day:

(e) relative humidity at 1500 h on the afternoon after the dew night must be at least 75%.

Further work convinced him that relative humidity was the crucial factor, and, abandoning the first, third and fourth of the Dutch rules, he evolved the critical period which bears his name and which, with minor changes, was used until quite recently as the basis for the British potato blight warning service. In modified form, a Beaumont period was defined as commencing with a spell of 48 hours during which the air temperature had been 10°C or more and the relative humidity 75% or above on at least 46 of the 48 hourly observations. The period continued until two consecutive hourly observations failed to meet one or both of the Beaumont criteria.

Initially, both the Dutch and British rules were designed as automatic warnings, following which an outbreak of potato blight was to be expected within two weeks. Indeed, an automatic recording instrument for the use of farmers was developed in Scotland which measured dry and wet bulb temperatures within or near the potato crop, and enabled the grower to see at a glance when a Beaumont 'critical period' had occurred, and to take countermeasures against the expected onset of disease (Grainger 1953).

The general trend in countries with longer experience in applying weather data to plant disease forecasting, such as Holland, UK and Ireland, has been to move away from a rigid or mechanistic application of a set of rules, and towards a more flexible approach which regards the rules as merely one stage in meteopathological analysis. The correct interpretation of the data calls for considerable experience, skill and judgement. Constant reference to the course of disease in response to weather conditions in past seasons, as well as local knowledge and expertise are required (Billing 1980). Best results follow from close collaboration between meteorologists and plant pathologists. A review of the success of Beaumont's rule when it was the basis of the British blight forecasting system made no extreme claims: 'although the occurrence of weather that satisfies the rule, whether recorded in screens or in crops, is not invariably followed by blight outbreaks, when the rule is combined with experience and knowledge of the state of potato crops and the behaviour of the fungus it provides a workable basis for forecasting' (Hirst & Stedman 1956).

Tests of the Beaumont rule in the more maritime climate of Ireland proved disappointing: in particular, on the west coast, where the average relative humidity is high, it is possible for the afternoon values in a long series of successive days not to fall below 75% without any appreciable change in the blight situation. Nor was it possible to develop an alternative empirical model in the absence of an adequate series of annual disease reports. It was decided to attempt to base a model on available laboratory determination of the meteorological requirements of the pathogen (as represented by curve P in Fig. 13.2). A comprehensive American report on the relationship between weather conditions and the development of blight on potato foliage had been published by Crosier (1934). The blight–weather model which was developed in Ireland in 1949 on the basis of Crosier's work makes use of hourly weather reports from standard meteorological observing stations, and requires as an absolute minimum:

(a) a humid period of at least 12 hours with the temperature not falling below 10°C nor the relative humidity below 90% (conditions favourable for the formation of sporangia to begin);
(b) free water on the leaves for a subsequent period of at least 4 hours (conditions favourable for the germination of sporangia and for reinfection).

The second requirement usually follows automatically because of persistent rain or drizzle when condition (a) has been met. Should there be no precipitation ('dry cases', normally of fog), the alternative requirement is a further 4 hours beyond the initial 12 in which the relative humidity remains at 90% or above.

Each period in which the rules are met is considered to correspond to a single generation of the fungus. Between three and five generations are normally required before the disease is visible in the potato fields (Bourke 1953).

The rules were tested and found satisfactory in the 1950 and 1951 Irish potato growing seasons, and were introduced as the basis of a public blight warning system in 1952. They have continued in successful operation without modification since that time. Their method of derivation suggests that they might be valid in diverse climatic regions, and in fact they have been successfully used in Chile and Tasmania. A model, which despite some differences of emphasis is basically similar, was independently derived by Wallin (1962) from Crosier's data.

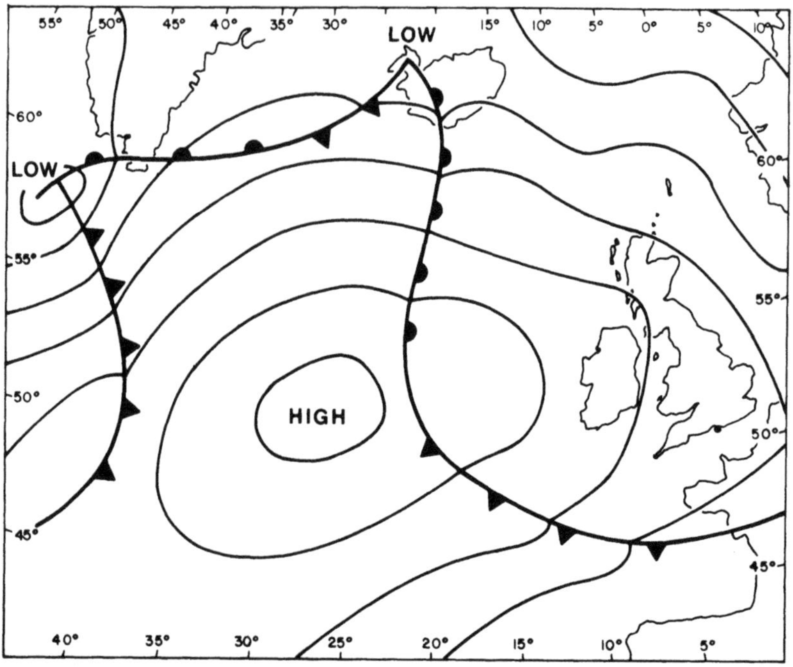

Figure 13.3 Surface synoptic weather chart for 06.00 GMT 4 July 1964, on the basis of which a potato late blight warning for Ireland was issued.

Two aspects of the Irish system of blight forecasting which were novel when first introduced have proved of value in other localities, and in respect of other diseases and pests. One is the emphasis on fairly lengthy periods of 90% or higher relative humidities in the screen as a measure of the duration of air saturation within the crop. The criterion of 90% relative humidity has been widely adopted; it is, for example, used in the blight forecasting technique which has replaced the Beaumont rule in the UK.

A more important innovation was the use of synoptic weather map and airmass analysis as an aid to phytopathological forecasting (Bourke 1957). The fact that conditions favourable to potato blight in the coastal fringe of north-west Europe are associated mainly with incursions of broad currents of moist warm air of tropical or subtropical origin (maritime tropical airmasses), provides a basis for converting disease warnings into true forecasts, and thereby considerably improving their value. On 4 July 1964, for example, it was clear that the synoptic situation (Fig. 13.3) which had earlier been unfavourable to potato blight was about to change to a set-up which would locate tropical air over Ireland at intervals during the next two weeks. On this basis, a spraying recommendation was issued which gave a full four days' notice of the onset of recurrent blight weather in Ireland (Fig. 13.4). It is a typical example of how a confident, broad long-term weather forecast, in terms adequate for plant disease

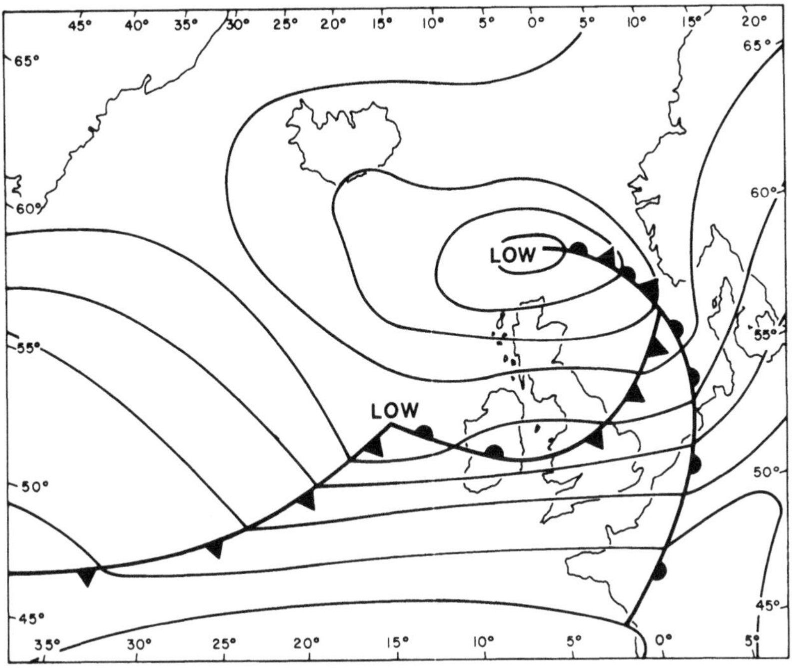

Figure 13.4 One of the successive weather situations highly favourable to potato late blight, which developed in the 2 weeks following 4 July 1964.

epidemiology, is often possible in situations where the precise timing necessary for a day-to-day forecast would be extremely difficult.

The use of weather map analysis in forecasting potato blight (as well as the occurrence of other plant diseases and pests) has proved fruitful elsewhere, particularly in the USA. The direction of upper air winds, as deduced from upper level charts, can indicate the possibility of an influx of maritime tropical air, favouring potato blight and similar diseases (Wallin & Riley 1960). Long-term prognostic weather charts have also been found useful in phytopathological forecasting.

An unexpected feedback from the use of weather map analysis as an aid to plant disease epidemiology has been the development of improved numerical models of the disease–weather relationship. Scarpa and Raniere (1964) found that outbreaks of downy mildew on lima beans in New Jersey depend on the frequency and persistence of incursions of maritime tropical air over the region, and, relating this to the conservative property of dewpoint values in this airmass, evolved a rule which calls for 40 or more hours of dewpoint values greater than 20°C.

The frequent recurrence of outbreaks of maritime tropical air seems to favour not only many fungal diseases (notably the downy mildews), but also certain plant pests. Huff (1963) found that a sustained flow of tropical air from the Gulf of Mexico into the American Midwest led to an influx into the area of numbers of potato leafhoppers (*Empoasca fabae*).

In the last few years, the wide availability of microcomputers has led almost inevitably to a potentially less happy development. There has been a tendency to return to the use of simple disease–weather models as automatic mechanised disease predictors from which programmes of the measures which should be taken against the disease can be derived. In the early 1970s, 'Blitecast' was developed as a computer program which incorporated two previous forecasting systems for the onset and development of potato blight, and which also drew up a recommended programme of fungicide applications (Krause *et al.* 1975). A similar electronic instrument has been designed to monitor temperature, relative humidity, and leaf wetness in apple orchards, and to detect primary infection periods of apple scab, *Venturia inaequalis* (Jones *et al.* 1980). Goltz *et al.* (1978) have developed a similar computerised device to measure temperature, relative humidity, and rainfall as a basis for predicting *Phytophthora* blight of tomatoes, and for scheduling spray applications against the disease. Adaptations of this basic system are outlined as a basis for drawing up spray programmes for other plant diseases.

The trend towards the complete computerisation of the disease–weather relationship and the control programme, without seasonal access to the skill and experience of plant pathologists and meteorologists, is not without its dangers.

13.5 Climate and the diseases of livestock; in particular, liver fluke

Although it has long been recognised that climate has a considerable influence on many diseases of farm animals, it was not until quite recently that attention has focused on making practical use of the relationship to help veterinarians in their work. Attempts to draw up usable climatic models of animal diseases have taken place mainly in the last 30 years. There are a number of excellent summaries of progress to date, much of which has occurred in the UK (Smith 1970, Taylor & Muller 1974, Gibson 1978, Gettinby & Gardiner 1980).

The major pioneering work in this connection was undertaken by Ollerenshaw (of the UK Central Veterinary Laboratory), who had noted that liver fluke disease caused by *Fasciola hepatica* is most severe after a wet summer. He set out to quantify the connection in order to forecast the extent of the countermeasures which would be necessary (Ollerenshaw & Rowlands 1959). The stage in the life-cycle of the parasite during which weather is critical is clearly that when it no longer shelters safely within the body of the farm animal, having been passed out of the host as eggs in its dung. The eggs hatch in a few weeks, given favourable conditions of moisture and temperature. At this vulnerable stage, the larvae must find a suitable mud snail in which to take refuge while they develop further. They emerge from the snail in their final form, attach themselves to grass or other convenient vegetation, and are taken once again into the bodies of grazing animals to complete their damaging life-cycle.

The same environmental conditions favour the hatching of the eggs which have been deposited in dung and the breeding of a large population of the snails which give the larvae temporary refuge, i.e. temperature of at least 10°C and a suitably high level of soil moisture. The temperature requirement is consistent with the fact that the disease does not cause problems in the cool sheep-raising areas of Iceland and northern Scandinavia. The moisture requirement for big thriving snails capable of supporting a large parasite population is that the upper layer of soil under pasture should have a consistently high water content without being permanently waterlogged.

Initial trials were made of the index $R - P$ as a rough parameter for measuring each month's disease potential, where R = rainfall amount as measured, and P = potential evapotranspiration as calculated by Penman's formula. The method showed distinct promise but it was found necessary to take into account the distribution, as well as the total amount, of rain during the month. This was achieved by introducing the number of days of appreciable rain into the analysis. An arbitrary constant was added to $R - P$ to avoid the inconvenience of negative values. The final Ollerenshaw monthly index for liver fluke potential took the form $(R - P + 5)n$, where n = number of days during the month on which at least 0.01 inches of rain fell.

Summed over the months during which average air temperature is 10°C or above, this index, when applied to climatic data for England and Wales, helps to explain the broad pattern of liver fluke occurrence in these countries. The disease is not a serious problem in southern and eastern England, where summer rainfall rarely exceeds potential evapotranspiration. Over high country where rainfall is heavy, waterlogging tends to occur; this, combined with the acidity of peatlands which is inimical to mud snails, restricts the impact of the disease. The disease is endemic in the rainy lowlands of Wales and western England, the actual level varying considerably with weather conditions from year to year. It is in the latter areas that the index, summed over the appropriate months, shows a close relationship with later disease levels, and has proved valuable in advising farmers on the extent and nature of desirable control measures. The Ollerenshaw system has now been in operation in England and Wales for over 20 years; it has also been adopted in Ireland, and a similar approach has been employed with success in France and the USSR. A simpler system, based entirely on the number of raindays, was later developed by Ross (1970) in Northern Ireland and was found to be valid also in Scotland.

The establishment of a numerical interconnection between meteorological data and the level of liver fluke disease has encouraged similar developments in the case of a number of other parasitic diseases of livestock.

13.6 Towards a climatology of disease potential

A quantitative weather–disease index which has proved its value in assessing the seasonal course of a disease or pest may, when averaged over a number of years, serve as a basis for drawing up a climatology of the weather-induced risk of damage by that disease or pest in a given area. At first sight, it might appear that information on the actual occurrence of attacks of the pathogen would serve the purpose better, but in fact such occurrence depends on a complex of factors apart from climate – density of crops, cultivars in use and their susceptibility, dates of sowing and emergence, management practices, countermeasures taken etc. – so that reports of actual damage by disease or pest frequently obscure the basic suitability of a given area to facilitate or discourage epidemic development. On the other hand, the demarcation of climate zones on the basis of a valid weather–pathogen model is related exclusively to the *potential* for disease or pest impact which is inherent in the climate of an area. Such climatic zoning of disease risks can be of value in larger scale planning of agricultural land use and in developing control strategies.

Figure 13.5 shows the distribution of climatic suitability in Ireland for the development of (a) liver fluke, measured in terms of the mean Ollerenshaw index for the months May–October, 1957–81, and (b) potato blight, measured in terms of the mean duration in hours of effective periods of blight weather, as determined by the Irish rules during the months May–September, 1957–81. For weighting humid spells of different lengths which meet the Irish rules, the 'effective' length of the minimum period of 12 hours is, by convention, taken as 1; accordingly, the 'effective period' in longer cases is determined by deducting 11 hours from the total duration when rain or drizzle occurs, or 15 hours in dry cases.

13.7 Meteorology and the transport of inoculum

The rôle of the wind is a climatic factor which is important in the case of certain pests and diseases (Hirst & Hurst 1967, Johnson 1969, Gregory 1973). The flight activity of many insects is greatly reduced in windy conditions, a fact which can restrict the damage they cause either directly or as vectors of disease. In the case of haematophagous insects, wind can even affect population levels, since the suppression of flight restricts blood-feeding, and thus reduces the insects' reproductive capacity (Service 1980). As in the case of the desert locust and the potato leafhopper, suitable wind patterns can assist in dispersal and in the colonisation of new areas.

That many plant diseases are spread locally on the wind has long been known; more recently, the important rôle of the wind in the short-distance extension of animal diseases such as fowl pest and foot-and-mouth has been established in England.

While the local movement of airborne pathogens is significant when seeking out and destroying secondary infections in the course of a disease outbreak, greater overall importance attaches to the long-distance transport of viable disease spores or insect pests which might thus be carried from one continent to another.

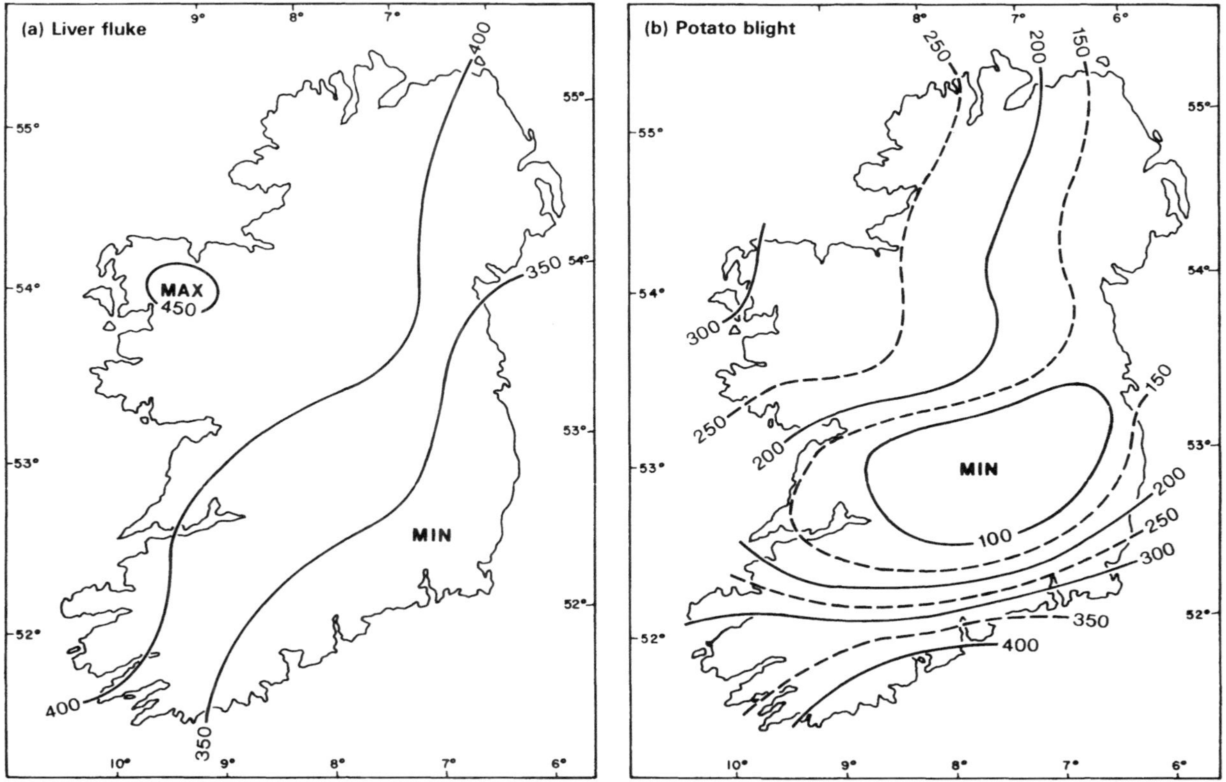

Figure 13.5 Distribution of climatic susceptibility to (a) liver fluke, measured in terms of the mean Ollerenshaw index for May to October 1957–81, and (b) potato blight, measured in terms of mean duration of effective 'blight weather' for May to September, 1957–81.

The best established regular long-distance commuter among disease spores is the black or stem rust of wheat, *Puccinia graminis* (Zadoks 1965, 1967). Hogg (1970) described the wind trajectories which have been shown to bring black rust spores from continental Europe to England, a country not subject to the disease except when inoculum is imported from elsewhere. Each instance of uredospore introduction was found to involve a precise synchronisation of liberation and deposition with the movement of weather systems and the speed of the winds within them. A similar atmospheric mechanism underlies the familiar south–north movement of rust inoculum in North America.

The broader European situation has been summarised by Zadoks (1965), who differentiates two main summer migration tracks of black rust in Europe. The western track, in a region where the prevailing winds are southwesterly, follows the general direction of the Atlantic coastline from Morocco to Britain, and possibly on to Scandinavia. The eastern track has its probable source in the lower Danube plains, from which a lesser branch reaches westwards to the middle and upper Danube plains, while the main track fans out over the Ukraine and Poland and continues northwards into Scandinavia. Clearly, any climatic change which substantially changed the frequency and strength of the relevant winds in Europe could lead to major changes in the impact of this important grain disease.

The long-distance transport of spores along tracks which are mainly over land can be confirmed by surveys made *en route*, and, if the host crop is generally grown in the countries traversed, the journey may be facilitated by being broken down into shorter stages as the crops are consecutively infected along the route. This is not possible if the journey is mainly over the sea, and considerable controversy surrounds the question of whether viable crossings of the great oceans such as the Atlantic are possible for spores or pests.

A plausible case for an airborne crossing of the North Atlantic by an insect is made by Hirst and Hurst (1967). An American moth, *Phytometra biloba*, was caught in Wales in July 1954. Back tracking the journey of the moth, on the basis of winds between the surface and 600 m, led back to South Virginia, and suggested a passage time of just over three days. An interesting feature (in a synoptic situation broadly similar to that of Fig. 13.4) was that the moth would have made an air-conditioned flight throughout in maritime tropical air. But did the moth perhaps cheat by making at least part of its journey on board ship?

Even more controversy has been aroused by the discovery in part of Brazil in 1970 of the devastating coffee rust disease, *Himeleia vastatrix* (Schieber 1972). This fungal disease had long been spreading and ravaging coffee crops in Asia and Africa, and when the impact of the disease in coastal West Africa became marked, Rayner (1960) wrote that coffee rust disease 'presented a threat to the coffee-growing regions of the New World as uredospores might be carried there from Africa by the north-east trade winds'. Bowden *et al.* (1971) calculated that the trade winds could plausibly have transported spores across the South Atlantic in 5–7 days, from Angola, where the disease was active in 1966, to Bahia in Brazil where it made its first appearance in South America.

The subsequent progress of the disease in Latin America from its initial foothold in Bahia has been generally consistent with atmospheric dissemination by wind and storms.

13.8 Climatic change and the impact of disease

In recent years, there has been a growing awareness that the climate of a region is far from being a fixed entity. There are obvious implications for plant protection in even temporary fluctuations of climate; an unusual series of mild winters, for example, may lead to a greater survival rate for insect pests, and a progressive build-up over several years to abnormal levels of population. Some 20 years ago, Whyte drew attention to the risk that a change of climate may radically alter the frequency and virulence of crop disease attacks, and characterised the problem as 'an aspect of great economic significance to land use and agricultural production which merits a full review by a competent authority' (Whyte 1963).

No such comprehensive review has yet been undertaken, although accounts of some scattered evidence of change have appeared. It is normally difficult to segregate with certainty the rôle played by the atmosphere as distinct from other factors of importance for disease, e.g. changes in acreage, cultural practices, cultivars, crop protection measures etc. (Coakley 1978, 1979). The fact that common rust of maize has become a bigger problem in Britain in recent years is due in large measure to intensive maize cultivation (Mahindapala 1978). Increased use of weedkillers has removed one reason for earthing up potato crops; failure to carry out this operation has increased the exposure of tubers to potato blight.

A reasonably convincing case of weather-induced disease is related to the succession of hot summers in north-west Europe which began in 1933, and to which is confidently attributed the sudden spread and increased destruction of rust disease of snapdragon (Moore 1940). Slow climatic change is held by Woods (1953) to have been largely responsible, firstly, for permitting the extension of the geographical distribution of the American chestnut and, later, in the period 1825–75, for the virtual elimination of the tree from the southern states of the USA by reason of *Phytophthora* root rot. The damaging upsurge of coffee berry disease in East Africa in the early 1960s has been attributed to 'a number of changing factors, probably the most important being a climatic change towards wetter, cooler conditions which favour infection' (Bent 1969). In the coffee-growing areas of tropical Africa 'the disease hazards will vary with the occurrence of wet and dry weather cycles' (Nutman & Roberts 1969).

The most spectacular cases of climatic control of disease or pest are clearly to be sought in areas which are marginal for the parasites and where any drift towards or away from critical threshold values of the relevant meteorological elements may be expected to have significant consequences. Iceland, where, despite the low summer temperatures and comparatively short growing season, potatoes are an important food crop, provides a remarkable example of the climatic control of potato blight. When Cox and Large (1960) carried out their comprehensive review of potato blight epidemics throughout the world, they commented (p. 89) that 'the occurrence of potato blight in Iceland is of special interest as the temperature conditions are here at the lower limit for any epidemic development of the disease'. The review indicated that, under favourable humidity conditions, the disease attacked the crop when the mean daily temperatures in July and August reached about 12–13°C, but appeared to be inhibited when these temperatures ranged about 10–11°C. Indeed, an examination of the disease data included in the report shows that even the crude indicators of mean monthly temperature could serve to differentiate the years of serious damage. In the period 1936–56, there were six years of severe blight; in fact, this was the period when the disease became a serious and recurrent problem in Iceland. In the six years of severe blight, the mean air temperatures were consistently higher in July (average 12.3°C) and in August (average 11.7°C) than they were in the years of little or no disease (11.2°C and 10.7°C respectively).

The shape of later developments in the potato blight situation in Iceland is clearly foreshadowed in Table 13.1, which gives mean monthly air temperatures during the potato-growing season in Reykjavik for each decade in the present century.

The gradual rise of temperature early in the century to the peak of warmth in the 1930s stands out clearly, as does the subsequent cooling, gradual at first, but sharp since 1960. Indeed, the mean July-August temperatures in each of the last two decades were markedly lower than those of the preceding years of the century. Simultaneously, the impact of potato blight in Iceland has dropped spectacularly, so that in the last few years the disease has been difficult to detect at all. Does this constitute a remarkable case of the success of a climatic fluctuation in wiping out a troublesome plant disease? Experience elsewhere suggests that the disease almost certainly lives on in Iceland at a subclinical level, ready to build up again if and when suitable climatic conditions return.

A point of some importance in this connection is that a successful pathogen

Table 13.1 Mean monthly air temperatures (°C) during the summer half-year in Reykjavik in successive decades, 1901–80.

	May	June	July	August	September	October
1901–10	6.2	9.8	11.4	10.3	8.4	4.2
1911–20	6.6	9.8	11.6	11.0	7.8	4.9
1921–30	6.1	9.2	11.1	10.4	7.2	3.7
1931–40	7.6	9.9	12.0	11.3	9.2	4.9
1941–50	6.8	9.8	11.5	11.1	8.3	5.1
1951–60	6.8	9.6	11.2	10.7	8.7	5.1
1961–70	6.7	9.6	10.6	10.5	7.8	4.8
1971–80	6.2	8.7	10.6	10.2	7.4	4.7

tends to have a life pattern well adapted to the growth cycle of its host (Billing 1980); consequently, conditions which are trying for the pathogen are unlikely to favour the crop upon which it feeds. The temperature drop which has blunted the edge of blight in Iceland has simultaneously reduced crop yields because of a shortened growing period. A similar phenomenon occurs in potato-growing areas, where soil moisture is apt to be the element in short supply: here, the wet years increase the potential yield, but also lead to more severe blight attacks (Cox & Large 1960). It is therefore not in areas where the crop is grown, and the parasite survives, in climatic conditions close to certain borderline values that the net consequences of climatic change may be greatest. It is, in fact, in regions where the climatic situation looks superficially more secure that the greater danger may lie. The advent of still-moister weather to a potato-growing area which is already moist enough for maximum potential yield will increase losses due to blight without benefiting the potential harvest, and may indeed put it at further risk by reason of waterlogging.

The marked rise of mean temperature which occurred in many northern areas in the first half of the present century has had consequences for the distribution of pests as well as plant diseases. In the case of insects, the controlling factor is often the intensity of winter cold and its effect on the survival rate of the pests. An insect pest of forest trees, the European pine shoot (*Rhyacionia buoliana*), was observed to spread northwards in Ontario in the period 1925–50; afterwards, it apparently ceased to expand. The northern limit of continuous distribution approximates to the −26°C isotherm for mean annual minimum temperature (MacHattie 1979).

A recent increase in the frequency and severity of epidemics of yellow rust, *Puccinia striiformis*, on winter wheat crops in the Pacific Northwest of the USA has been attributed to climatic change (Coakley 1978, 1979). Mean air temperatures in January–February averaged 1.2°C higher in 1961–74 compared with the period 1935–60, whereas mean April temperatures averaged 1.3°C lower in the later period. The milder winters helped the survival of the fungus and shortened its latent period. The effect of colder springs is on the host crop. The cultivars which are grown need springtime warmth to trigger their resistance mechanism; accordingly, the consequence of the lower April temperatures was to render the crop more vulnerable to disease.

13.9 The future

It seems certain that the struggle to counter the major diseases and pests of agriculture will intensify sharply in the coming years. Avoidable losses in production will become increasingly intolerable as the demand for food rises. Further, there is the paradox that the risk of serious loss caused by plant parasites has been increased by many of the practices which are being used today to promote food production: the introduction of new cultivars for widespread use, more intensive cropping, the growing of more than one crop per year, the wider use of irrigation, and increased fertiliser application. There is further danger in the fact that many of the new cultivars, finely tuned to a narrow belt of temperature and water needs, are bred to give much enhanced yields in the climatic conditions for which they are programmed, but are likely, in more extreme weather, to fare worse than the older 'fail-safe' varieties which they replaced. A climatic fluctuation which simultaneously depressed yields over a wide area while favouring losses due to disease or pest could be disastrous. It is a risk for which students of climatic change should be alert.

References

Aspliden, C. I. H. and R. C. Rainey 1961. Desert Locust control. *WMO Bulletin* **10**, 155–61.

Beaumont, A. 1940. Potato blight and the weather. *Abstr. Trans Br. Mycol Soc.* **24**, 266.

Beaumont, A. 1947. The dependence on the weather of the dates of outbreak of potato blight epidemics. *Trans Br. Mycol Soc.* **31**, 45–53.

Bent, K. J. 1969. Fungicides in perspective. *Endeavour* **28**, 129–34.

Billing, E. 1980. Fireblight (*Erwinia Amylora*) and weather: a comparison of warning systems. *Ann. Appl. Biol.* **95**, 365–77.

Bourke, P. M. A. 1953. *Potato blight and the weather: a fresh approach*. Irish Met. Serv. Tech. Note 12.

Bourke, P. M. A. 1955. *The forecasting from weather data of potato blight and other plant diseases and pests*. WMO Tech. Note 10.

Bourke, P. M. A. 1957. *The use of synoptic weather maps in potato blight epidemiology*. Irish Met. Serv. Tech. Note 23.

Bourke, P. M. A. 1961. *Climatic aspects of the possible establishment of the Japanese beetle in Europe*. WMO Tech. Note 41.

Bourke, P. M. A. 1970. Use of weather information in the prediction of plant disease epiphytotics. *Ann. Rev. Phytopathol.* **12**, 345–70.

Bowden, J., P. H. Gregory and C. G. Johnson 1971. Possible wind transport of coffee leaf rust across the Atlantic Ocean. *Nature* (Lond.) **229**, 500–01.

Broadbent, L. 1949. Potatoes and the weather. *Q. J. R. Met. Soc.* **75**, 302–09.

Coakley, S. M. 1978. The effect of climate variability on stripe rust of wheat in the Pacific Northwest. *Phytopathology* **68**, 207–12.

Coakley, S. M. 1979. Climatic variability in the Pacific Northwest and its effect on stripe rust disease of winter wheat. *Climatic Change* **2**, 33–51.

Cox, A. E. and E. C. Large 1960. *Potato blight epidemics throughout the world*. Agriculture Handbook No 174. Washington, DC: US Department of Agriculture.

Crosier, W. 1934. *Studies in the biology of* Phytophthora infestans *(Mont.) de Bary*. Cornell University Agric. Exp. Sta. Memoir 155.

Dubey, R. C. and T. S. Godvindaswamy 1978. Regions in India favourable for the incidence and establishment of the Colorado beetle. *Ind. J. Met. Hydrol. Geophys.* **29**, 564–5.

Dubey, R. C. and S. Venkataraman 1980. A note on the likely areas of establishment of the Japanese beetle in India. *Mausam* **31**, 175–7.

Gettinby, G. and W. P. Gardiner 1980. Disease and incidence forecasts by means of climatic data. *Biomet.* **7**, 87–103.

Gibson, T. E. (ed.) 1978. *Weather and parasite animal disease*. WMO Tech. Note 159.

Goltz, S. M., F. Manzer and H. G. Schimmelpfennig 1978. Microcomputers – an application to potato late blight forecasting. *Am. Met. Soc. Bull.* **59**, 1511.

Graham, F. J. 1847. The potato disease. *J. R. Agric. Soc. Eng.* **7**, 357–91.
Grainger, J. 1953. Potato blight forecasting and its mechanism. *Nature* (Lond.) **171**, 1012–14.
Gregory, P. H. 1973. *Microbiology of the atmosphere.* London: Leonard Hill.
Hirst, J. M. and G. W. Hurst 1967. Long-distance spore transport. *Symp. Soc. Gen. Microbiol.* **17**, 307–44.
Hirst, J. M. and O. J. Stedman 1956. The effect of height of observation in forecasting potato blight by Beaumont's method. *Plant Pathol.* **5**, 35–40.
Hogg, W. H. 1970. Weather, climate and plant disease. *Met Mag.* **99**, 317–26.
Huff, F. A. 1963. Relation between leafhopper influxes and synoptic weather conditions. *J. Appl. Met.* **2**, 39–43.
Hurst, G. W. 1975. *Meteorology and the Colorado potato beetle.* WMO Tech. Note 137.
Johnson, C. G. 1969. *Migration and dispersal of insects by flight.* London: Methuen.
Jones, A. L., S. L. Lillevik, P. D. Fisher and T. C. Stebtaus 1980. A micro-computer based instrument to predict primary apple scab infection periods. *Plant Dis.* **64**, 69–71.
Krause, R. A. and L. B. Massie 1975. Predictive systems: modern approaches to disease control. *Ann. Rev. Phytopathol* **13**, 31–47.
Krause, R. A., L. B. Massie and R. A. Hyre 1975. Blitecast: a computerized forecast of potato late blight. *Plant Dis. Reptr.* **59**, 95–98.
MacHattie, L. B. 1979. Meteorology and forest insect control in Canada. *WMO Symp. on Forest Met.* **527**, 139–52.
Mahindapala, R. 1978. Epidemiology of maize rust. *Ann. Appl. Biol.* **90**, 155–61.
Miller, P. R. 1953. The effect of weather on diseases. *US Department of Agriculture Yearbook 1953*, 83–93.
Miller, P. R. 1964. Disease warning system organised for blue mold control. *Agricultural Chemicals* **19**(4), 22–3 and 131.
Miller, P. R. 1967. Plant disease epidemics: their analysis and forecasting. In *Papers presented at FAO Symposium Crop losses, Rome 1967*, 9–37.
Miller, P. R. and M. O'Brien 1952. Plant disease forecasting. *Bot. Rev.* **18**, 547–601.
Miller, P. R. and M. O'Brien 1957. Prediction of plant disease epidemics. *Ann. Rev. Microbiol.* **11**, 77–110.
Moore, W. C. 1940. Weather in relation to plant disease survey records. *Abstr. Trans Br. Mycol Soc.* **24**, 264.
Nutman, F. J. and F. M. Roberts 1969. Climatic conditions in relation to the spread of coffee berry disease since 1962 in the East Rift districts of Kenya. *E. Afr. Agric. & Forest J.* **37**, 118–27.
Ollerenshaw, C. B. and W. T. Rowlands 1959. A method of forecasting the incidence of fascioliasis in Anglesey. *Vet. Rec.* **71**, 591.
Omar, M. H. 1980. *Meteorological factors affecting the epidemiology of the cotton leaf worm and the pink bollworm.* WMO Tech. Note **167**.
Parry, W. H. 1979. Acclimatisation in the green spruce aphid. *Ann. Appl. Biol.* **92**, 299–306.
Pedgley, D. E. 1979. Weather during desert locust plague upsurges. *Phil Trans R. Soc. Lond.* 287, 387–91.
Populer, Ch. 1964. Le comportement des épidémies de mildiou du tabac, *Peronospera tabacina* Adam. Part 1 la situation en Europe. *Bull. Inst. Agr. et Stat. Rech. Gembloux* **32**, 339–78.
Rainey, R. C. 1963. *Meteorology and the migration of desert locusts.* WMO Tech. Note 54.
Rayner, R. W. 1960. Rust disease of coffee. III. Spread of the disease. *World Crops* **12**, 222–4.

Ross, J. G. 1970. The Stormont 'wet day' forecasting system for fascioliasis *Br. Vet. J.* **126**, 401–08.

Scarpa, M. J. and L. C. Raniere 1964. The use of consecutive hourly dewpoints in forecasting downy mildew of lima beans. *Plant Dis. Reptr.* **48**, 77–81.

Schieber, E. 1972. Economic impact of coffee rust in Latin America. *Ann. Rev. Phytopathol.* **10**, 491–512.

Service, M. W. 1980. Effects of wind on the behaviour and distribution of mosquitoes and blackflies. *Int. J. Biomet.* **24**, 347–53.

Smith, L. P. 1970. *Weather and animal diseases.* WMO Tech. Note 113.

Sutton, T. B. and A. L. Jones 1975. Monitoring *Erwinia amylorara* populations on apple in relation to disease incidence. *Phytopathol.* **65**, 1009–12.

Taylor, A. E. R. and R. Muller (eds) 1974. The effect of meteorological factors upon parasites. *Symp. Brit. Soc. Parasit.* **12**.

Wallin, J. R. 1962. Summary of recent progress in predicting late blight epidemics in United States and Canada. *Am. Potato J.* **39**, 306–12.

Wallin, J. R. and J. A. Riley, 1960. Weather map analysis – an aid in forecasting potato late blight. *Plant Dis. Reptr.* **44**, 227–34.

Whyte, R. O. 1963. The significance of climatic change for natural vegetation and agriculture. In *Changes of climate*, UNESCO Arid Zone Res. Series. **20**, 381–6.

Woods, F. W. 1953. Disease as a factor in the evolution of forest composition. *J. Forest.* **51**, 871–3.

World Meteorological Organization 1963. *The influence of weather conditions on the occurrence of apple scab.* WMO Tech. Note 55.

World Meteorological Organization 1965. *Meteorology and the desert locust.* WMO Tech. Note 69.

World Meteorological Organization 1969. *Meteorological factors affecting the epidemiology of wheat rusts.* WMO Tech. Note 99.

Zadoks, J. C. 1965. Epidemiology of wheat rusts in Europe. *FAO Plant Prot. Bull.* **13**, 97–108.

Zadoks, J. C. 1967. International dispersal of fungi. *Neth. J. Plant Path.* **73** Suppl., 61–81.

Bibliography of papers by Professor Gordon Manley

GILLIAN M. SHEAIL, JOAN M. KENWORTHY and MICHAEL J. TOOLEY

This bibliography is based on a search in three libraries: Cambridge University Library, Durham University Library, and the National Meteorological Library, Bracknell. It extends the bibliography attached to the obituary in the *Transactions of the Institute of British Geographers* (1980, New Series Vol.5, No.4, 513–17). The absence of references for particular years led to a redoubled effort that was invariably rewarded, but there are probably gaps. The catalogued deposit of Professor Manley's papers in Cambridge University Library has yielded papers published in hitherto unsuspected places, as well as much unpublished material. Attention is drawn to this rich resource, and to the unpublished material in the National Meteorological Library (Manley 1969a, b, c, 1973). It had been hoped also to list all Professor Manley's contributions to *The Manchester Guardian* and *The Guardian* but the index to *The Guardian* ends in 1962, and the list at the end of the bibliography must be regarded as provisional.

1927 Appendix I. Survey. In Wordie, J. M. The Cambridge expedition to East Greenland in 1926. *Geog. J.* **70**, 241–4.

1927 Appendix IV. Weather. In Wordie, J. M. The Cambridge expedition to East Greenland in 1926. *Geog. J.* **70**, 249–52.

1927 Appendix VII. The pendulum observations. In Wordie, J. M. The Cambridge expedition to East Greenland in 1926. *Geog. J.* **70**, 260–62.

1930 Appendix III. Meteorology. In Wordie, J. M. Cambridge East Greenland expedition 1929: ascent of Petermann Peak. *Geog. J.* **75**, 498–502.

1931 Some notes on the maps of the county of Durham in the University Library. *Durham Univ. J.* **27** (2), 127–33.

1932 Pendulum observations at Sabine Island. *Meddr Grønland* **92**(2), 1–16.

1932 The weather of the High Pennines. *Durham Univ. J.* **28**(1), 31–2.

1932 Meteorological records from the northern Pennines. *Met. Mag., Lond.* **67**, 206–8.

1933 Notes on the weather in Upper Teesdale, 1933. *Durham Univ. J.* **28**(4), 304–7.

1933 Further records from the northern Pennines. *Met. Mag., Lond.* **68**, 180–81.

1934 On a means of transport. *Durham Univ. J.* **28**(6), 481–4.

1934 Saxton's survey of northern England. *Geog. J.* **83**, 308–16.

1934 The Plancius map of England, Wales and Ireland, 1592. *Geog. J.* **83**, 252–3.

1935 Some notes on the climate of north-east England. *Q. J. R. Met. Soc.* **61**, 405–10.

1936 The climate of the northern Pennines: the coldest part of England. *Q. J. R. Met. Soc.* **62**, 103–13; Discussion. *ibid.* 114–15.

1936 On atlases. *Durham Univ. J.* **29**(6), 439–43.

1936 On the instrumental climatology of the Durham district. *Durham Univ. J.* **30**(1), 43–8.

1936 The earliest extant map of the County of Durham. *Trans Archaeol. Antiq. Soc. Durham* **7**, 278–87.
1937 Appendix III. Meteorology. In Wager, L. R. The Kangerdlugssuak region of East Greenland. *Geog. J.* **90**, 418–20.
1937 Snowfall in Scotland: problems and suggestions. *Scott. Geog. Mag.* **53**, 394–7.
1937 The weather of 1936 in the northern Pennines. *Met. Mag., Lond.* **72**, 8–10.
1937 Systematic records of British snowfall. *Met. Mag., Lond.* **72**, 231–2.
1938 Scottish snow. *Scott. Mountaineering Club J.* **21**, 366–7.
1938 Meteorological observations of the British East Greenland Expedition, 1935–1936, at Kangerdlugssuak, 68°10′N, 31°44′W. *Q. J. R. Met. Soc.* **64**, 253–76.
1938 The weather of 1937 in the northern Pennines. *Met. Mag., Lond.* **73**, 69–72.
1938 Appendix: snowfall and its relation to transport problems, with special reference to northern England. In RGS evidence to the Royal Commission. Memorandum on the geographical factors relevant to the location of industry. *Geog. J.* **92**, 522–6.
1938 Observations on the early cartography of the English hills. In *Comptes Rendus du Congrèss International de Geographie*, Tome 11, Section IV, E. J. Brill (ed.), 36–42. Leiden: E. J. Brill.
1938 The City of Durham. *Geography* **23**, 147–55.
1939 On the occurrence of snow-cover in Great Britain. *Q. J. R. Met. Soc.* **65**, 2–24; Discussion. *ibid.* 25–7.
1939 The frequency of snow in Great Britain. *Wat. & Wat. Engng* **41**, 22–3.
1939 The helm wind of Crossfell. *Nature, Lond.* **143**, 377.
1939 High altitude records from the northern Pennines, 1938–39. *Met. Mag., Lond,* **74**, 114–17.
1939 Report on the snow survey of the British Hills, July 1938–July 1939. *Association for the study of Snow and Ice, Papers and Discussions* **1**, 18–20.
1940 The helm wind of the northern Pennines. *Met. Office Misc.* **387** (unpublished).
1940 Snowfall in the British Isles. *Met. Mag., Lond.* **75**, 41–48.
1941 Observations of snow-cover on the British mountains. *Q. J. R. Met. Soc.* **67**, 1–4.
1941 The Durham meteorological record 1847–1940. *Q. J. R. Met. Soc.* **67**, 363–80.
1941 Climate and agriculture in County Durham. In *The land of Britain. The report of the Land Utilisation Survey of Britain. Part 47. County Durham,* Ada Temple (ed.), 193–200. London: Geographical Publications.
1942 Meteorological observations on Dun Fell. *Q. J. R. Met. Soc.* **68**, 151–62; Discussion. *ibid.* 162–5.
1943 Further climatological averages for the northern Pennines, with a note on topographical effects. *Q. J. R. Met. Soc.* **69**, 251–61.
1943 Snow cover in the British Isles. *Met. Mag., Lond.* Limited typescript edition, 1–12. Repr. 1947 *Met. Mag., Lond.* **76**, 28–36.
1943 The climate of Cumberland and Westmorland. In *The land of Britain. The Report of the Land Utilisation Survey of Britain. Parts 49 and 50. Cumberland and Westmorland,* L. D. Stamp, G. Manley and E. Davies (eds), 274–80. London: Geographical Publications.
1944 Topographical features and the climate of Britain: a review of some outstanding effects. *Geog. J.* **103**, 241–58; Discussion. *ibid.* 258–63.
1944 John Dalton: 1766–1844. *Q. J. R. Met. Soc.* **70**, 235–9.
1944 Some recent contributions to the study of climatic change. *Q. J. R. Met. Soc.* **70**, 197–219.

1945 The effective rate of altitudinal change in temperate Atlantic climates. *Geog. Rev.* **35**, 408–17.
1945 Has the climate of N. W. Scotland deteriorated since 1700? *Q. J. R. Met. Soc.* **71**, 154–6.
1945 The helm wind of Crossfell 1937–1939. *Q. J. R. Met Soc.* **71**, 197–215; Discussion. *ibid.* 215–19.
1945 Problems of Scottish climatology. *Scott Geogr. Mag.* **61**, 73–6.
1946 Temperature trend in Lancashire, 1735–1945. *Q. J. R. Met. Soc.* **72**, 1–13.
1946 Variations in the length of the frost-free season. *Q. J. R. Met. Soc.* **72**, 180–84.
1946 Recent antarctic discoveries and some speculations thereupon. *Q. J. R. Met. Soc.* **72**, 307–17.
1946 Foreword by the President of the Royal Meteorological Society. *Weather, Lond.* **1**, 1.
1946 The centenary of rainfall observations at Seathwaite. *Weather, Lond.* **1**, 163–8.
1946 The climate of Northumberland, with notes on agriculture. In *The land of Britain. The report of the Land Utilisation Survey of Britain. Part 52. Northumberland*, L. D. Stamp (ed.), 429–39. London: Geographical Publications.
1946 The climate of Lancashire – past and present. *Trans Rochdale Lit. Sci. Soc.* **22**, 84–9.
1946 The climate of Lancashire. *Mem. Proc. Manchr. Lit. Phil Soc.* **87**, 73–95.
1947 A remarkable winter day on the High Pennines. *Weather, Lond.* **2**, 6–8.
1947 Snowfall and snow cover in the British Isles. *Weather, Lond.* **2**, 149.
1947 Tornadoes in England. *Weather, Lond.* **2**, 238–40.
1947 Looking back at last winter (a) February 1947: its place in meteorological history. *Weather, Lond.* **2**, 267–72.
1947 Dorothy Wordsworth's weather. *Weather, Lond.* **2**, 361–4.
1947 The geographer's contribution to meteorology. *Q. J. R. Met. Soc.* **73**, 1–10.
1948 Records of snow cover on the Scottish mountains. *Met. Mag., Lond.* **77**, 270–72.
1948 On the trend of temperature in N. W. Europe, 1720–1750. *Q. J. R. Met. Soc.* **74**, 119–22.
1948 Glacier variations and climatic fluctuations in Britain, U.G.G.I. *Assoc. Hydrol. Sci., Assoc. Gen., Oslo* **2**, 304–05.
1948 George Smith the geographer and his ascent of Crossfell. *Trans Cumb. Westm. Antiq. Archaeol Soc.* **48**, 135–44.
1949 Microclimatology – local variations of climate likely to affect the design and siting of buildings. *J. R. Inst. Br. Archit.* **56**, 317–23.
1949 The snowline in Britain. *Geog. Annlr.* **31**, 179–93.
1941 The extent of the fluctuations shown during the 'instrumental' period in relation to post-glacial events in N. W. Europe. *Q. J. R. Met Soc.* **75**, 165–71.
1949 Fanaråken: the mountain station in Norway. *Weather, Lond.* **4**, 352–4.
1949 Part I. The atmosphere. In *Physical geography*, 2nd edn, P. Lake, (ed.), revised and enlarged by J. A. Steers, W. V. Lewis and G. Manley, 3–137. Cambridge: Cambridge University Press.
1949 Glaciological research on the North Atlantic coasts: a review. *Geog. Rev.* **39**, 136–8.
1950 *Degrees of freedom. An inaugural lecture given at Bedford College for Women, January 27th 1949.* London: Christopher Johnson.
1950 Some consequences of the relation between glacier variations and climatic fluctuations in Britain. *J. Glaciol.* **1**, 352–6.

1950 On British climatic fluctuations since Queen Elizabeth's day. *Weather, Lond*, **5**, 312–18.

1950 Discussion: climatic change. In *Centenary Proceedings of the Royal Meteorological Society*, 225–8. London.

1951 The range of variation of the British climate. Part I: climatic fluctuations in modern times. Part II: the dimensions of the changes in the British climate before the 'climatic optimum'. *Geog. J.* **117**, 43–65; Discussion. *ibid.* 65–8.

1951 Climatic fluctuations: a review. *Geog. Rev.* **41**, 656–60.

1951 Royal Society's Conversazione, 24 May 1951. Conversazione included item 26 'Past climatic change as revealed by deep sea cores'. *Weather, Lond.* **6**, 208–09.

1952 John Dalton's snowdrift. *Weather, Lond.* **7**, 210–12.

1952 *Climate and the British scene.* London: Collins.

1952 Thomas Barker's meteorological journals, 1748–63 and 1777–89. *Q. J. R. Met. Soc.* **78**, 255–9.

1952 Britain's sunshine. *Geog. Mag.* **25**, 59–63.

1952 Variations in the mean temperature of Britain since glacial times. *Geol Rdsch.* **40**, 125–7.

1952 The weather and diseases: some 18th century contributions to observational meteorology. *Notes and Records. Royal Society of London* **9**, 300–07.

1952 A warm decade. *Weather, Lond.* **7**, 242–3.

1953 The mean temperature of central England, 1698–1952. *Q. J. R. Met. Soc.* **79**, 242–261; Discussion. *ibid.* 558–67.

1953 A prospect of winter. *Weather, Lond.* **8**, 357–60.

1953 Reviews of modern meteorology – 9. Climatic variation. *Q. J. R. Met Soc.* **79**, 185–209.

1953 (with Whiten, A. J.) World-wide distribution of pressure. *Q. J. R. Met Soc.* **79**, 419.

1954 Climatic change: the problem of transatlantic correlation. In *Proceedings of the Toronto Meteorological Conference 1953*, 199–206. London: Royal Meteorological Society, and Boston, Mass: American Meteorological Society.

1954 Changes in world glaciation. A geophysical discussion of the Royal Astronomical Society in conjunction with the British Glaciological Society held on January 29, 1954. *Nature, Lond.* **173**, 1206–08.

1954 The winter of 1798–9. *Weather, Lond.* **9**, 254.

1955 A climatological survey of the retreat of the Laurentide Ice Sheet. *Am. J. Sci.* **253**, 256–73.

1955 On the occurrence of ice domes and permanently snow-covered summits. *J. Glaciol.* **2**, 453–6.

1955 Constantia Orlebar's weather book 1786–1808. *Q. J. R. Met. Soc.* **81**, 622–5.

1955 The remarkable weather of 1954. *Manchr Guardian Weekly* **72**(1), 14.

1955 Arctic air over England. *Manchr Guardian Weekly* **72**(11), 7.

1955 On disappointing summers. *Scott. Mountaineering Club J.* **25**, 334–41.

1956 The climate at Malham Tarn. In *Annual Report of the Field Studies Council, 1955–1956*, 43–53.

1956 Future lines of progress in glaciology. *J. Glaciol.* **2**, 697–8.

1956 British summers of the past. *Weather, Lond.* **11**, 335.

1956 (with Jackson, P. S.) Severe winters in 1813 and 1860. *Weather, Lond.* **11**, 134–5.

1957 Climatic fluctuations and fuel requirements. *Scott. Geog. Mag.* **73**, 19–28.

1957 Climatic fluctuations and fuel requirements. *Advmt Sci., Lond.* **13**, 324–6.

1957 Glaciers and the changing climate. *New Scientist* **1** (17), 33–5.
1957 The Meteorological Office Report for 1955–56. *Nature, Lond.* **179**, 765–6.
1958 On the frequency of snowfall in metropolitan England. *Q. J. R. Met. Soc.* **84**, 70–72.
1958 Early meteorological journals; some further notes. *Q. J. R. Met. Soc.* **84**, 75–7.
1958 (with Bonacina, L. C. W.) Snowfall frequency in metropolitan England. *Q. J. R. Met. Soc.* **84**, 283–4.
1958 Bad summers. *New Scientist* **4**, 1054–6.
1958 Nuclear tests and the weather, reply by Professor Gordon Manley. *New Scientist* **4** 1339.
1958 The great winter of 1740. *Weather, Lond.* **13**, 11–17.
1958 The revival of climatic determinism. *Geog. Rev.* **48**, 98–105.
1958 Studies on the frequency of snowfall in England, 1668–1956, UGGI. *Assoc. Int. Hydrol. Sci. C. R. Rapp. Assoc. Gen. Toronto, 1957* **4**, 40–45.
1959 Temperature trends in England, 1698–1957. *Arch. Met. Geophys. Bioklim. Ser. B* **9**, 413–33.
1959 The Late-Glacial climate of north-west England. *Lpool Manchr Geol J.* **2**, 188–215.
1960 Climate and the International Geophysical Year. *Science Survey* **1**, 267–78.
1961 Late and Postglacial climatic fluctuations and their relationship to those shown by the instrumental record of the past 300 years. *Ann. NY Acad. Sci.* **95**, 162–72.
1961 A preliminary note on early meteorological observations in the London region, 1680–1717, with estimates of the monthly mean temperatures, 1680–1706. *Met. Mag., Lond.* **90**, 303–10.
1961 The Earth's climate. In *Discovery, fifteen talks given on television in the Discovery Series for the Granada Television Network*, 87–97. London: Methuen.
1961 Meteorological factors in the great glacier advance (1690–1720), UGGI. *Assoc. Int. Hydrol. Sci. Assoc. Gen. Helsinki, 1960* **54**, 388–91.
1961 Solar variations, climatic change and related geophysical problems. *Nature, Lond.* **190**, 967–8.
1961 *Geography: our planet, its peoples and resources*, G. Manley, Sir Gerald Barry, J. Bronowski, J. Fisher and Sir Julian Huxley (eds). London: Macdonald.
1961 Geographers at work. In *Geography, our planet, its people and resources*, G. Manley *et al.* (eds), 317–18. London: Macdonald.
1962 Early meteorological observations and the study of climatic fluctuation. *Endeavour* **21**, 43–50.
1962 The Late-Glacial climate of the Lake District. *Weather, Lond.* **17**, 60–4.
1962 A venturesome Victorian. *Weather, Lond.* **17**, 340–1.
1962 A Victorian explorer of the upper air. *New Scientist* **15**, 607–9.
1963 Seventeenth-century London temperatures: some further experiments. *Weather, Lond.* **18**, 98–105.
1963 The climatologist's view. In *The long winter 1962–3*, 14–18. Manchester: Manchester Guardian.
1963 Glaciology in the last 25 years. *Geog. Mag.* **35**, 729–38.
1963 Snowfall in Britain. *New Scientist* **17**, 68–70.
1963 The weather in Britain. *Anglia* **8**, 34–43 (in Russian).
1964 The evolution of the climatic environment. In *The British Isles: a systematic geography*, J. W. Watson and J. B. Sissons (eds), 152–76. London: Nelson.
1964 Cold winters in Manchester. *Weather, Lond.* **19**, 96.

1965 Possible climatic agencies in the development of Post-Glacial habitats. *Proc. R. Soc. Ser. B* **161**, 363–75.

1966 Climate and landscape architecture. *J. Inst. Landscape Archit.* **74**, 4–7.

1966 The problem of the climatic optimum: the contribution of glaciology. In *World climate from 8000 to 0 BC*, J. S. Sawyer (ed.), 34–9. London: Royal Meteorological Society.

1967 *Weather* comes of age. *Weather, Lond.* **22**, 171–3.

1967 This North-western environment. In *Inaugural lectures 1965–1967, University of Lancaster*, 1–11. Lancaster: University.

1967 Climate in Britain. In *Congress Proceedings of the 20th International Geographical Congress*, J. W. Watson (ed.), 34–45. London: Nelson.

1968 Dalton's accomplishment in meteorology. In *John Dalton and the progress of science*, D. S. L. Cardwell (ed.), 140–58. Manchester: University Press.

1968 Climatic variation (climatic change). In *Encyclopaedic Dictionary of Physics* vol.3, 25–8. London: Pergamon.

1969a *Corrected temperature data 1771–1798 at Lyndon in Rutland, taken from Thomas Barker's observations.* National Meteorological Library, Bracknell (unpublished).

1969b *Daily observations 1782–1796 kept by William Godschell at Albury near Guildford and at Huxham near Plymouth 1725–1752.* National Meteorological Library, Bracknell (unpublished).

1969c *Monthly means 1786–1833, kept by 'Cary in the Strand'.* National Meteorological Library, Bracknell (unpublished).

1969 Snowfall in Britain over the past 300 years. *Weather, Lond.* 24, 428–37.

1970 Climate in Britain over 10 000 years. *Geog. Mag.* 43, 100–7.

1970 The climate of the British Isles. *World Survey of Climatology* **5**, 81–133.

1971 The mountain snows of Britain. *Weather, Lond.* **26**, 192–200.

1971 Interpreting the meteorology of the Late and Post-Glacial. *Palaeogeogr., Palaeoclimatol., Palaeoecol.* **10**, 163–75.

1971 Scotland's semi-permanent snows. *Weather, Lond.* **26**, 458–71.

1972 Manchester rainfall since 1765. *Mem. Proc. Manchr Lit. Phil Soc.* **114**, 70–89.

1972 The Society's headquarters. *Weather, Lond.* **27**, 88–9.

1972 Scotland's semi-permanent snows. *Scott. Mountaineering Club J.* **30**, 4–15.

1972 Foreword (introductory preface). In *Times of feast, times of famine: a history of climate since the year 1000*, E. Le Roy Ladurie. xiii–xvi. London: George Allen & Unwin.

1973 Climate. In *The Lake District*, W. H. Pearsall and W. Pennington, 106–20. London: Collins.

1973 *Snow in London 1669–1958.* National Meteorological Library. Bracknell (unpublished).

1973 Climate in Britain over 10 000 years. In *Man made the land*, A. R. H. Baker and J. B. Harley (eds), 9–21. Newton Abbot: David and Charles.

1974 *Enjoy Cumbria's climate.* Windermere: Cumbria Tourist Board.

1974 Central England temperatures; monthly means 1659–1973. *Q. J. R. Met. Soc.* **100**, 389–405.

1975 Reply to 'Central England temperatures; monthly means of the Radcliffe Meteorological Station, Oxford' C. G. Smith. *Q. J. R. Met. Soc.* **101**, 387–9.

1975 Fluctuations of snowfall and persistence of snow-cover in marginal oceanic climates. In *Proceedings of the WMO/IAMP Symposium on Long Term Climatic Fluctuations, Norwich, 18–23 August 1975*, 183–7. Geneva: WMO.

1975 Snowfalls in June. *Weather, Lond.* **30**, 308.
1975 1684: the coldest winter in the English instrumental record. *Weather, Lond.* **30**, 382–8.
1975 Weather and climate of the Lake Counties. In *Lake District. National Park guide* No. **6**. Countryside Commission (ed.), 129–38. London: HMSO.
1975 Manchester rainfall since 1765: further comments, meteorological and social. *Mem. Proc. Manchr Lit. Phil Soc.* **117**, 93–103.
1976 The summer of 1976. *Weather, Lond.* **31**, 395–6.
1977 Sir Daniel Fleming's meteorological observations at Rydal 1689–1693. *Trans Cumb. Westm. Antiq. Archaeol Soc.* **77**, 121–6.
1977 A note on the summer of 1976 in Lancashire. *Mem. Proc. Manchr Lit. Phil Soc.* **119**, 96–9.
1977 1684: the coldest winter in the English instrumental record. *Marine Observer* **47**, 77–81.
1977 Annual rainfall in England since 1725: some comments. *Q. J. R. Met. Soc.* **103**, 820–22.
1978 Reflections on climatological research. A climatologist's view. In *Climate change and variability, a southern perspective*, A. B. Pittock, L. A. Frakes, D. Jenssen, J. A. Peterson and J. Zillman (eds), 360–3. Cambridge: Cambridge University Press.
1978 Meteorological observations on Royal Deeside. *Weather, Lond.* **33**, 457–9.
1978 Variation in the frequency of snowfall in east-central Scotland, 1708–1975. *Met. Mag., Lond.* **107**, 1–16.
1979 The climatic environment of the Outer Hebrides. *Proc. R. Soc. Edinb.* **77** B, 47–59.
1979 Temperature records on Fountains Fell, with some Pennine comparisons. *Field Studies* **5**, 85–92.
1980 The northern Pennines revisited: Moor House, 1932–1978. *Met. Mag., Lond.* **109**, 281–92.
1980 Cold winters at Oxford. *Weather, Lond.* **35**, 182–5.
1981 The use of archives and written records in meteorological research. *Archives* **15**(65), 3–10.

List of articles by Gordon Manley in *The Manchester Guardian*

PETER McNIVEN and MICHAEL J. TOOLEY

1954	26 August	p. 4, cols 6 & 7	The summer of 1954: not quite the worst
	9 September	p. 6, cols 4 & 5	Summer in England (letters to the Editor)
	1 December	p. 12, cols 5 & 6	Depressions off their courses upset November weather: on the way to a year of record wetness?
	31 December	p. 4, cols 6 & 7 p. 5, col. 6	The weather of 1954: a meteorological retrospect
1955	11 March	p. 6, cols 6 & 7 p. 7, col. 5	Arctic air over England: the lion in March
	26 May	p. 6, cols 6 & 7	Prospects for summer: a meteorological survey
	30 July	p. 1, cols 6 & 7	The warmest July for 21 years?
	24 August	p. 4, col. 6	Near the maximum hours of sunshine: present and previous summers compared
	1 September	p. 1, cols 4 & 5	The summer in statistics: possibility of 200 year record in NW
	17 December	p. 6, cols 6 & 7	The weather ahead: some puzzling questions
	21 December	p. 10, cols 5 & 6	Snow deceived forecasters: little changes had big effect
1956	2 January	p. 10, cols 5 & 6	The sunniest year of the century in the north-west? But 1955 was far from the warmest
	4 February	p. 6, cols 6 & 7	An Arctic anticyclone – our coldest weather
	29 February	p. 6, cols 6 & 7	The weather in February: fifth coldest in 250 years
	1 May	p. 6, cols 6 & 7	This year's dry spring: prospects of drought
	30 July	p. 12, cols 5 & 6	All on a summer's day . . . retreat of an anticyclone brings remarkable July weather

	4 August	p. 4, cols 6 & 7	Chances of a hot day and August floods
	1 September	p. 4, cols 6 & 7	End of a dismal August: faint hopes for September
	31 December	p. 1, col. 7	Perverse and cool: the weather in 1956
1957	9 February	p. 5, cols 1 & 2	Assessing the worth of a January spring: milder weather from the Atlantic
	19 March	p. 5, cols 1 & 2	Cautious optimism flowers in spring warmth: but short cold 'snaps' likely
	22 April	p. 1, col. 4 p. 2, cols 4 & 5	Weather in a pleasant mood: will 1921 experience be repeated this year?
	6 June	p. 5, cols 1 & 2	Best-season for a chance of sunshine: Whitsuntide's good record
	2 August	p. 1, col. 3	More settled in the North: week-end prospects
	10 October	p. 10, cols 3 & 5	The ideal indoor climate
	30 November	p. 6, cols 6 & 7	This curious autumn: prospect of a cold winter
1958	4 January	p. 4, cols 6 & 7	The weather in 1957: two notable months
	15 February	p. 4, cols 4, 5 & 6	Winds blowing hot and cold: the erratic British winter
	3 April	p. 5, cols 1 & 2	Meteorologist makes March journey: no escaping the weather
	26 May	p. 3, cols 1 & 2	Quest for good weather at Whitsuntide: England's favoured north-west
	13 September	p. 4, cols 6 & 7	Not so bad after all? A summer of ill repute
	13 December	p. 4, cols 6 & 7	Onward from the fog: cold winter in prospect?
	31 December	p. 4, cols 4 & 5	Wet summer, muddy autumn: mild end to a disappointing year
1959	21 March	p. 3, cols 1 & 2	More cold due before the summer: chance of a drier June
	25 April	p. 6, cols 6 & 7	An umbrella in reserve: guesses about the summer
	1 August	p. 4, cols 6 & 7	Bank Holiday weather: another vintage summer?
	29 September	p. 5, cols 1 & 2	Second, sixth or 18th best summer: measuring months in the sun
	10 October	p. 6, cols 4 & 5	The best summer ever known: 1959's place in weather history (Letters to the Editor)

	5 December	p. 4, cols 6 & 7	The prospects of fog: and steps to avoid it
1960	1 January	p. 16, cols 3 & 4	11 months warmer than average: stormy December ended splendid year
	2 April	p. 4, cols 6 & 7	The English spring: is it getting warmer?
	11 June	p. 6, cols 6 & 7	After the warm spring: an alpha-minus summer?
	1 August	p. 3, cols 3, 4 & 5	This English summer
	31 December	p. 1, col. 7 p. 2, cols 4 & 5	Rainy but warmer: 1960 maintained the trend
1961	3 March	p. 3, cols 1 & 2	Mildest February since 1869? Record-seekers count the points
	8 April	p. 3, cols 5 & 6	Catching the sun on the Celtic fringe: chance of brightness
	15 July	p. 1, col. 5	Under the sway of Atlantic depressions
	22 July	p. 6, cols 3, 4 & 5	St Swithin and the summer outlook
	26 August	p. 4, cols 3, 4 & 5	Well dressed for a windy August
	7 September	p. 8, col. 4	Warm and gusty winds (Letters to the Editor)
	17 December	p. 6, cols 3, 4 & 5	Will it be a cold winter?

Author index

Italic numerals refer to a page on which a figure, figure caption or table carries a name.

Subject and place index

Italic numerals refer to a page on which a figure, figure caption or table is indexed.

For Product Safety Concerns and Information please contact our EU
representative GPSR@taylorandfrancis.com
Taylor & Francis Verlag GmbH, Kaufingerstraße 24, 80331 München, Germany

www.ingramcontent.com/pod-product-compliance
Ingram Content Group UK Ltd.
Pitfield, Milton Keynes, MK11 3LW, UK
UKHW022217190926
475702UK00003B/399
* 9 7 8 0 3 6 7 3 6 6 4 8 3 *